Teacher Edition

SCIENCE Fusion

fusion [FYOO • zhuhn] a combination of two
or more things that releases energy

HOLT McDOUGAL

HOUGHTON MIFFLIN HARCOURT

Professional Development

Houghton Mifflin Harcourt and NSTA, the National Science Teacher's Association, have partnered to provide customized professional and development resources for teachers using *ScienceFusion*.

The Professional Development Resources in the NSTA Learning Center include:

—do-it-yourself resources, where you can study at your own pace.

—live and archived online seminars.

—journal articles, many of which include lesson plans.

—fee-based eBooks, eBook chapters, online short courses, symposia, and conferences.

Access to the NSTA Learning Center is provided in the *ScienceFusion* Online Resources.

Acknowledgments for Covers

Rice fields (bg) ©Keren Su/Corbis; *false color x-rays on hand* (l) ©Lester Lefkowitz/Getty Images; *primate* (cl) ©Bruno Morandi/The Image Bank/Getty Images; *red cells* (cr) ©Todd Davidson/Getty Images; *fossils* (r) ©Yoshihi Tanaka/amana Images/Getty Images.

Interior, digital screens: *giraffes* ©Corbis.

Printed in the U.S.A.

ISBN 978-0-547-59380-7

2 3 4 5 6 7 8 9 10 0914 20 19 18 17 16 15 14 13 12 11

4500309836   A B C D E F G

Contents in Brief

About the Program

Teaching Tools

Units at a Glance

Resources

Consulting Authors

Michael A. DiSpezio

Global Educator
North Falmouth, Massachusetts

Michael DiSpezio is a renaissance educator who moved from the research laboratory of a Nobel Prize winner to the K–12 science classroom. He has authored or coauthored numerous textbooks and written more than 25 trade books. For nearly a decade, he worked with the JASON Project under the auspices of the National Geographic Society, where he designed curriculum, wrote lessons, and hosted dozens of studio and location broadcasts.

Over the past two decades, he has developed supplementary material for organizations and shows that include PBS's *Scientific American Frontiers*, *Discover* magazine, and the Discovery Channel. He has extended his reach outside the United States and into topics of crucial importance today. To all his projects, he brings his extensive background in science and his expertise in classroom teaching at the elementary, middle, and high school levels.

Marjorie Frank

Science Writer and
Content-Area Reading Specialist
Brooklyn, New York

An educator and linguist by training, a writer and poet by nature, Marjorie Frank has authored and designed a generation of instructional materials in all subject areas, including past HMH Science programs. Her other credits include authoring science issues of an award-winning children's magazine; writing game-based digital assessments in math, reading, and language arts; and serving as instructional designer and coauthor of pioneering school-to-work software

for Classroom Inc., a nonprofit organization dedicated to improving reading and math skills for middle and high school learners. She wrote lyrics and music for *SCIENCE SONGS*, which was an American Library Association nominee for notable recording. In addition, she has served on the adjunct faculty of Hunter, Manhattan, and Brooklyn Colleges, teaching courses in science methods, literacy, and writing.

Michael R. Heithaus

Director, School of Environment and Society
Associate Professor, Department of Biological Sciences
Florida International University
North Miami, Florida

Mike Heithaus joined the Florida International University Biology Department in 2003. He has served as Director of the Marine Sciences Program and is now Director of the School of Environment and Society, which brings together the natural and social sciences and humanities to develop solutions to today's environmental challenges. While earning his doctorate, he began the research that grew into the Shark Bay Ecosystem Project in Western Australia, with which he still works. Back in the United States, he served as a Research Fellow with National Geographic, using remote imaging in his research and hosting a 13-part *Crittercam* television series on the National Geographic Channel. His current research centers on predator-prey interactions among vertebrates, such as tiger sharks, dolphins, dugongs, sea turtles, and cormorants.

Donna M. Ogle

Professor of Reading and Language
National-Louis University
Chicago, Illinois

Creator of the well-known KWL strategy, Donna Ogle has directed many staff development projects translating theory and research into school practice in middle and secondary schools throughout the United States. She is a past president of the International Reading Association and has served as a consultant on literacy projects worldwide. Her extensive international experience includes coordinating the Reading and Writing for Critical Thinking Project in Eastern Europe, developing an integrated curriculum for a USAID Afghan Education Project, and speaking and consulting on projects in several Latin American countries and in Asia. Her books include *Coming Together as Readers; Reading Comprehension: Strategies for Independent Learners; All Children Read;* and *Literacy for a Democratic Society.*

Program Reviewers

Content Reviewers

Paul D. Asimow, PhD
*Professor of Geology
and Geochemistry*
Division of Geological and Planetary Sciences
California Institute of Technology
Pasadena, CA

Laura K. Baumgartner, PhD
Postdoctoral Researcher
Molecular, Cellular, and Developmental Biology
University of Colorado
Boulder, CO

Eileen Cashman, PhD
Professor
Department of Environmental Resources Engineering
Humboldt State University
Arcata, CA

Hilary Clement Olson, PhD
Research Scientist Associate V
Institute for Geophysics, Jackson School of
Geosciences
The University of Texas at Austin
Austin, TX

Joe W. Crim, PhD
Professor Emeritus
Department of Cellular Biology
The University of Georgia
Athens, GA

Elizabeth A. De Stasio, PhD
*Raymond H. Herzog Professor
of Science*
Professor of Biology
Department of Biology
Lawrence University
Appleton, WI

Dan Franck, PhD
Botany Education Consultant
Chatham, NY

Julia R. Greer, PhD
*Assistant Professor of Materials Science and
Mechanics*
Division of Engineering and Applied Science
California Institute of Technology
Pasadena, CA

John E. Hoover, PhD
Professor
Department of Biology
Millersville University
Millersville, PA

William H. Ingham, PhD
Professor (Emeritus)
Department of Physics and Astronomy
James Madison University
Harrisonburg, VA

Charles W. Johnson, PhD
*Chairman, Division of Natural Sciences,
Mathematics, and Physical Education*
Associate Professor of Physics
South Georgia College
Douglas, GA

Tatiana A. Krivosheev, PhD
Associate Professor of Physics
Department of Natural Sciences
Clayton State University
Morrow, GA

Joseph A. McClure, PhD
Associate Professor Emeritus
Department of Physics
Georgetown University
Washington, DC

Mark Moldwin, PhD
Professor of Space Sciences
Atmospheric, Oceanic, and Space Sciences
University of Michigan
Ann Arbor, MI

Russell Patrick, PhD
Professor of Physics
Department of Biology, Chemistry, and Physics
Southern Polytechnic State University
Marietta, GA

Patricia M. Pauley, PhD
Meteorologist, Data Assimilation Group
Naval Research Laboratory
Monterey, CA

Stephen F. Pavkovic, PhD
Professor Emeritus
Department of Chemistry
Loyola University of Chicago
Chicago, IL

L. Jeanne Perry, PhD
Director (Retired)
Protein Expression Technology Center
Institute for Genomics and Proteomics
University of California, Los Angeles
Los Angeles, CA

Kenneth H. Rubin, PhD
Professor
Department of Geology and Geophysics
University of Hawaii
Honolulu, HI

Brandon E. Schwab, PhD
Associate Professor
Department of Geology
Humboldt State University
Arcata, CA

Marllin L. Simon, Ph.D.
Associate Professor
Department of Physics
Auburn University
Auburn, AL

Larry Stookey, PE
Upper Iowa University
Wausau, WI

Kim Withers, PhD
Associate Research Scientist
Center for Coastal Studies
Texas A&M University-Corpus Christi
Corpus Christi, TX

Matthew A. Wood, PhD
Professor
Department of Physics & Space Sciences
Florida Institute of Technology
Melbourne, FL

Adam D. Woods, PhD
Associate Professor
Department of Geological Sciences
California State University, Fullerton
Fullerton, CA

Natalie Zayas, MS, EdD
Lecturer
Division of Science and Environmental Policy
California State University, Monterey Bay
Seaside, CA

Teacher Reviewers

Ann Barrette, MST
Whitman Middle School
Wauwatosa, WI

Barbara Brege
Crestwood Middle School
Kentwood, MI

Katherine Eaton Campbell, M Ed
Chicago Public Schools-Area 2 Office
Chicago, IL

Karen Cavalluzzi, M Ed, NBCT
Sunny Vale Middle School
Blue Springs, MO

Katie Demorest, MA Ed Tech
Marshall Middle School
Marshall, MI

Jennifer Eddy, M Ed
Lindale Middle School
Linthicum, MD

Tully Fenner
George Fox Middle School
Pasadena, MD

Dave Grabski, MS Ed
PJ Jacobs Junior High School
Stevens Point, WI

Amelia C. Holm, M Ed
McKinley Middle School
Kenosha, WI

Ben Hondorp
Creekside Middle School
Zeeland, MI

George E. Hunkele, M Ed
Harborside Middle School
Milford, CT

Jude Kesl
Science Teaching Specialist 6–8
Milwaukee Public Schools
Milwaukee, WI

Joe Kubasta, M Ed
Rockwood Valley Middle School
St. Louis, MO

Mary Larsen
Science Instructional Coach
Helena Public Schools
Helena, MT

Angie Larson
Bernard Campbell Middle School
Lee's Summit, MO

Christy Leier
Horizon Middle School
Moorhead, MN

Helen Mihm, NBCT
Crofton Middle School
Crofton, MDL

Jeff Moravec, Sr., MS Ed
Teaching Specialist
Milwaukee Public Schools
Milwaukee, WI

Nancy Kawecki Nega, MST, NBCT, PAESMT
Churchville Middle School
Elmhurst, IL

Mark E. Poggensee, MS Ed
Elkhorn Middle School
Elkhorn, WI

Sherry Rich
Bernard Campbell Middle School
Lee's Summit, MO

Mike Szydlowski, M Ed
Science Coordinator
Columbia Public Schools
Columbia, MO

Nichole Trzasko, M Ed
Clarkston Junior High School
Clarkston, MI

Heather Wares, M Ed
Traverse City West Middle School
Traverse City, MI

Power up with

SCIENCE Fusion

Print

The **Write-in Student Edition** teaches science content through constant **interaction** with the text.

Labs and Activities

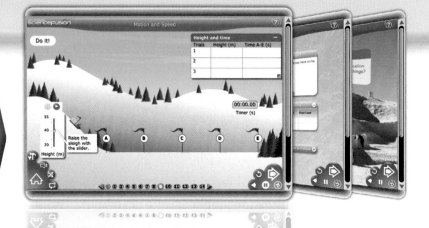

Digital

The parallel **Digital Curriculum** provides **e-learning digital lessons and virtual labs** for every print lesson of the program.

Energize your students through a multimodal blend of Print, Inquiry, and Digital experiences.

Unit Assessment

Formative Assessment
Strategies RTI
Throughout TE

Lesson Reviews SE

Unit PreTest

Summative Assessment
Alternative Assessment
(1 per lesson) RTI

Lesson Quizzes

Unit Tests A and B

Unit Review RTI
(with answer remediation)

Practice Tests
(end of module)

Project-Based Assessment
See the Assessment Guide for quizzes and tests.

Go Online to edit and create quizzes and tests.

See RTI teacher support materials.

The **Hands-on Labs** and **Virtual Labs**

provide meaningful and exciting inquiry experiences.

The **Write-in Student Edition** teaches science content through constant **interaction** with the text.

Write-in Student Edition

The *ScienceFusion* write-in student edition promotes a student-centered approach for

- learning and applying inquiry skills in the student edition
- building STEM and 21st Century skills
- keeping digital natives engaged and interactive

Research shows that an interactive text teaches students how to relate to content in a personal, meaningful way. They learn how to be attentive, energetic readers who reach a deep level of comprehension.

Big Ideas & Essential Questions

Each unit is designed to focus on a Big Idea and supporting lesson-level Essential Questions.

Connect Essential Questions

At the close of every unit, students build enduring understandings through synthesizing connections between different Essential Questions.

Active Reading

Annotation prompts and questions throughout the text teach students how to analyze and interact with content.

S.T.E.M.

STEM activities in every unit ask students to apply engineering and technology solutions in scenario-based learning situations.

Think Outside the Book

Students may wish to keep a Science Notebook to record illustrations and written work assignments. Blank pages at the end of each unit can also be used for this purpose.

Visualize It!

As concepts become more abstract, Visualize It! provides additional support for conceptual understanding.

Labs and Activities

The **Hands-on Labs** and **Virtual Labs** provide meaningful and exciting inquiry experiences.

360° of Inquiry

Labs and Activities

S.T.E.M. Engineering & Technology

STEM activities in every unit focus on

- **engineering and technology**
- **developing critical thinking and problem solving skills**
- **building inquiry, STEM, and 21st Century skills**

Scenario-Based STEM Activity

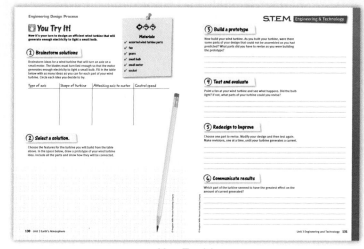

You Try It!

Hands-On and Virtual

Three levels—directed, guided, and independent—of labs and activities plus lesson level Virtual Labs give students wall-to-wall options for exploring science concepts and building inquiry skills.

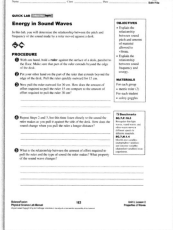

Hands-On Labs and Activities

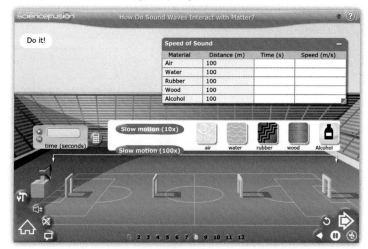

Virtual Lab

Digital

The parallel-to-print **Digital Curriculum** provides

e-learning digital lessons and virtual labs

for every print lesson of the program.

360° of Inquiry

Digital Lessons and Virtual Labs

Digital Lessons and Virtual Labs provide an e-Learning environment of interactivity, videos, simulations, animations, and assessment designed for the way digital natives learn. An online Student Edition provides students anytime access to their student book.

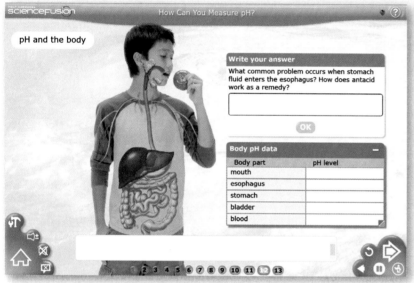

Digital Lessons

Online Student Edition

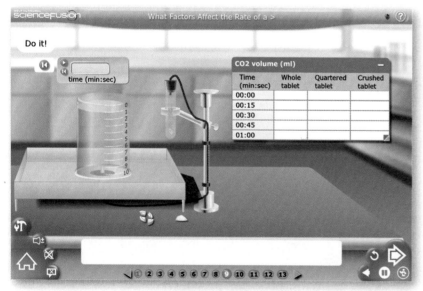

Virtual Labs

Video-Based Projects

Also available online:

- NSTA *SciLinks*
- Digital Lesson Progress Sheets
- Video-Based Projects
- Virtual Lab Datasheets
- People in Science Gallery
- Media Gallery
- Extra Support for Vocabulary and Concepts

Assessment

All paths lead to a full suite of print and online
Assessment Options right at your fingertips.

Classroom Management
Integrated Assessment Options

The *ScienceFusion* assessment options give you maximum flexibility in assessing what your students know and what they can do. Both the print and digital paths include formative and summative assessment. See the **Assessment Guide** for a comprehensive overview of your assessment options.

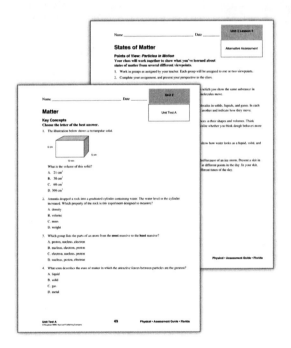

Teacher Online Management Center

Print Assessment

The print **Assessment Guide** includes

- Lesson Quizzes
- Unit Tests
- Unit Performance Assessments

Online Assessment

The **Digital Assessment** includes

- **assignable leveled assessments for individuals**
- **customizable lesson quizzes and unit tests**
- **individual and whole class reporting**

Customizing Assessment for Your Classroom

Editable quizzes and tests are available in ExamView and online at ⊙ **thinkcentral.com.** You can customize a quiz or test by adding or deleting items, revising difficulty levels, changing formats, revising sequence, and editing items. Students can also take quizzes and tests directly online.

Choose Your Options

with two powerful teaching tools— a comprehensive **Teacher Edition** and the **Teacher Online Management Center.**

Classroom Management Teacher Edition

Lesson level teaching support, includes activities, probing questions, misconception alerts, differentiated instruction, and interpreting visuals.

- Lessons organized around a 5E lesson format

- Comprehensive support—print, digital, or hands-on—to match all teaching styles.

- Extension strategies for every lesson give teacher more tools to review and reinforce.

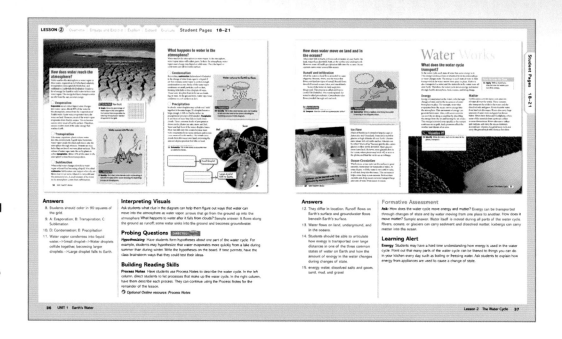

- Easy access to NSTA's e-professional development center, *The Learning Center*

- SciLinks provide students and teachers content-specific online support.

Additional support for STEM activities focuses on 21st century skills and helping students master the multi-dimensional abilities required of them in the 21st century.

  **Response to Intervention**

Response to Intervention is a process for identifying and supporting students who are not making expected progress toward essential learning goals.

Probing Questions

Lesson level questions and suggestions provide teachers with options for getting students to think more deeply and critically about a science concept.

 Professional Development

Unit and lesson level professional development focuses on supporting teachers and building educator capacity in key areas of academic achievement.

Learning Alert MISCONCEPTION

The Learning Alert section previews Inquiry Activities and Lessons to gather and manage the materials needed for each lesson.

xiv

Classroom Management
Online teaching and planning

ScienceFusion is a comprehensive, multimodal science program that provides all the digital tools teachers need to engage students in inquiry-based learning. *The Teacher Online Management Center,* at ⊘ **thinkcentral.com**, is designed to make it easier for teachers to access program resources to plan, teach, assess, and track.

▶ Program resources can be easily previewed in PDF format and downloaded for editing.

▶ Assign and schedule resources online, and they will appear in your students' inboxes.

▶ All quizzes and tests can be taken and automatically scored online.

▶ Easily monitor and track student progress.

Teaching with Technology Made Easy

ScienceFusion's 3,000+ animations, simulations, videos, & interactivities are organized to provide

▶ flexible options for delivering exciting and engaging digital lessons

▶ Teacher Resource Questions, for every lesson, to ensure that the important information is learned

▶ multimodal learning options that connect online learning to concepts learned from reading, writing, and hands-on inquiry

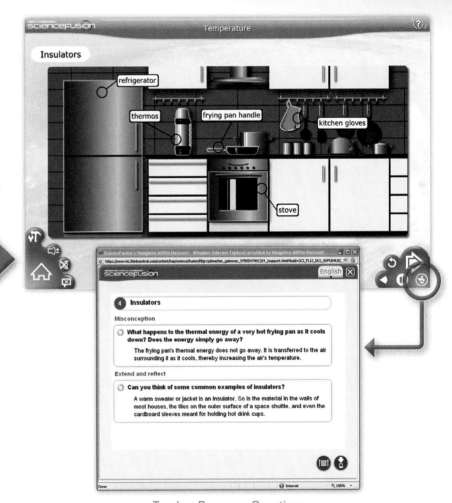

Teacher Resource Questions

Student Edition Contents

Talons are very useful in snatching fish right out of the water. To prey, the sharp talons of an eagle are deadly weapons!

Assignments:

_____
_____
_____
_____
_____
_____

Although the coral animal is tiny, some corals help build reefs that support millions of organisms. The Great Barrier Reef is so large that it can be seen from space.

Student Edition Contents

Careful management of renewable resources, such as trees and fish, will help maintain their populations for the future.

Protecting our resources helps us and all of the other organisms that rely on the same resources.

Assignments:

© Houghton Mifflin Harcourt Publishing Company • Image Credits: ©artpartner-images/Photographer's Choice/Getty Images; ©NASA Image by Marit Jentoft-Nilsen, based on data from NOAA GOES. Blue Marble imagery by NASA's Earth Observatory Team; ©Tyrone Turner/National Geographic/Getty Images

Program Scope and Sequence

ScienceFusion is organized by five major strands of science. Each strand includes Big Ideas that flow throughout all grade levels and build in rigor as students move to higher grades.

ScienceFusion Grade Levels and Units

	GRADE K	GRADE 1	GRADE 2	GRADE 3
Nature of Science	**Unit 1** Doing Science	**Unit 1** How Scientists Work	**Unit 1** Work Like a Scientist	**Unit 1** Investigating Questions
STEM		**Unit 2** Technology All Around Us	**Unit 2** Technology and Our World	**Unit 2** The Engineering Process
Life Science	**Unit 2** Animals **Unit 3** Plants **Unit 4** Habitats	**Unit 3** Animals **Unit 4** Plants **Unit 5** Environments	**Unit 3** All About Animals **Unit 4** All About Plants **Unit 5** Environments for Living Things	**Unit 3** Plants and Animals **Unit 4** Ecosystems and Interactions

GRADE 4	GRADE 5	GRADES 6-8

Unit 1 Studying Science	**Unit 1** How Scientists Work	**Module K** Introduction to Science and Technology
		   Unit 1 The Nature of Science
		   Unit 2 Measurement and Data

Unit 2 The Engineering Process	**Unit 2** The Engineering Process	**Module K** Introduction to Science and Technology **Unit 3** Engineering, Technology, and Society

Unit 3 Plants and Animals
Unit 4 Energy and Ecosystems
	Unit 3 Cells to Body Systems
	Unit 4 Living Things Grow and Reproduce
	Unit 5 Ecosystems
	Unit 6 Energy and Ecosystems
		Module A Cells and Heredity
		   Unit 1 Cells
		   Unit 2 Reproduction and Heredity
		Module B The Diversity of Living Things
		   Unit 1 Life over Time
		   Unit 2 Earth's Organisms
		Module C The Human Body
		   Unit 1 Human Body Systems
		   Unit 2 Human Health
		Module D Ecology and the Environment
		   Unit 1 Interactions of Living Things
		   Unit 2 Earth's Biomes and Ecosystems
		   Unit 3 Earth's Resources
		   Unit 4 Human Impact on the Environment

ScienceFusion Grade Levels and Units

GRADE 4	GRADE 5	GRADES 6-8

Unit 5 Weather
Unit 6 Earth and Space
	Unit 7 Natural Resources
	Unit 8 Changes to Earth's Surface
	Unit 9 The Rock Cycle
	Unit 10 Fossils
	Unit 11 Earth's Oceans
	Unit 12 The Solar System and the Universe
		Module E The Dynamic Earth
		  Unit 1 Earth's Surface
		  Unit 2 Earth's History
		  Unit 3 Minerals and Rocks
		  Unit 4 The Restless Earth
		Module F Earth's Water and Atmosphere
		  Unit 1 Earth's Water
		  Unit 2 Oceanography
		  Unit 3 Earth's Atmosphere
		  Unit 4 Weather and Climate
		Module G Space Science
		  Unit 1 The Universe
		  Unit 2 The Solar System
		  Unit 3 The Earth-Moon-Sun System
		  Unit 4 Exploring Space

Unit 7 Properties of Matter
Unit 8 Changes in Matter
Unit 9 Energy
Unit 10 Electricity
Unit 11 Motion
	Unit 13 Matter
	Unit 14 Light and Sound
	Unit 15 Forces and Motion
		Module H Matter and Energy
		  Unit 1 Matter
		  Unit 2 Energy
		  Unit 3 Atoms and the Periodic Table
		  Unit 4 Interactions of Matter
		  Unit 5 Solutions, Acids, and Bases
		Module I Motion, Forces, and Energy
		  Unit 1 Motion and Forces
		  Unit 2 Work, Energy, and Machines
		  Unit 3 Electricity and Magnetism
		Module J Sound and Light
		  Unit 1 Introduction to Waves
		  Unit 2 Sound
		  Unit 3 Light

ScienceFusion
Video-Based Projects

Available in Online Resources

This video series, hosted by program authors Michael Heithaus and Michael DiSpezio, develops science learning through real-world science and engineering challenges.

Ecology

Leave your lab coat at home! Not all science research takes place in a lab. Host Michael Heithaus takes you around the globe to see ecology field research, including tagging sharks and tracking sea turtles. Students research, graph, and analyze results to complete the project worksheets.

S.T.E.M. Science, Technology, Engineering, and Math

Host Michael DiSpezio poses a series of design problems that challenge students' ingenuity. Each video follows the engineering process. Worksheets guide students through the process and help them document their results.

Module	Video Title
A	Photosynthesis
B	Expedition Evolution Animal Behavior
D	A Trip Down Shark River The Producers of Florida Bay
E	Transforming Earth
I	Animals in Motion
J	Animals and Sound
K	Invaders in the Everglades Data from Space

Module	Video Title
A	An Inside View**
C	Prosthetics Robotic Assist**
D	Got Water?
E	Seismic Monitoring
F	When the Wind Blows Tornado Warning
G	Soft Landing
H	Just Add Heat
I	Take the Long Way

** In partnership with Children's Hospital Of Boston

Enduring Understandings

Big Ideas, Essential Questions

It goes without saying that a primary goal for your students is to develop understandings of science concepts that endure well past the next test. The question is, what is the best way to achieve that goal?

by Marjorie Frank

Research and learning experts suggest that students learn most effectively through a constructivist approach in which they build concepts through active involvement in their own learning. While constructivism may lead to superior learning on a lesson-by-lesson basis, the approach does not address how to organize lessons into a program of instruction. Schema theory, from cognitive science, suggests that knowledge is organized into units and that information is stored in these units, much as files are stored in a digital or paper folder. Informed by our understanding of schema theory, we set about organizing *ScienceFusion*. We began by identifying the Big Ideas of science.

Big Ideas are generalizations—broad, powerful concepts that connect facts and events that may otherwise seem unrelated. Big Ideas are implicit understandings that help the world make sense. Big Ideas define the "folders," or units, of *ScienceFusion*. Each is a statement that articulates the overarching teaching and learning goals of a unit.

Essential Questions define the "files," or information, in a unit. Each Essential Question identifies the conceptual focus of a lesson that contributes to your students' growing understanding of the associated Big Idea. As such, Essential Questions give your students a sense of direction and purpose.

With *ScienceFusion*, our goal is to provide you with a tool that helps you help your students develop Enduring Understandings in science. Our strategy for achieving that goal has been to provide lesson plans with 5E-based learning experiences organized in a framework informed by schema theory.

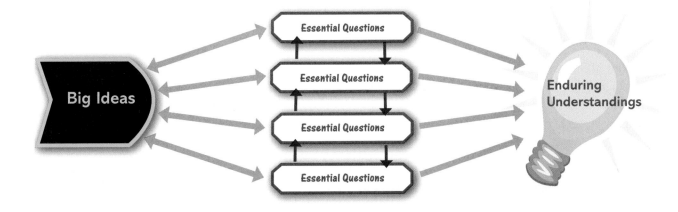

21st Century Skills/STEM

Skills Redefined

Our world has changed. Globalization and the digital revolution have redefined the skill set that is essential for student success in the classroom and beyond. Known collectively as 21st Century Skills, these areas of competence and aptitude go beyond the three Rs of reading, writing, and arithmetic. 21st Century Skills incorporate a battery of high-level thinking skills and technological capabilities.

by Michael A. DiSpezio

21st Century SKILLS A Sample List

Learning and Innovation Skills

- Creativity and Innovation
- Critical Thinking and Problem Solving
- Communication and Collaboration

Information, Media, and Technology Skills

- Information Literacy
- Media Literacy
- ICT (Information, Communications, and Technology) Literacy

Life and Career Skills

- Flexibility and Adaptability
- Initiative and Self-Direction
- Productivity and Accountability
- Leadership and Responsibility

S.T.E.M.

Curriculum that integrates Science, Technology, Engineering, and Mathematics

21st Century Skills are best taught in the context of the core subject areas. Science makes an ideal subject for integrating these important skills because it involves many skills, including inquiry, collaboration, and problem solving. An even deeper level of incorporating these skills can be found with Science, Technology, Engineering, and Mathematics (STEM) lessons and activities. Hands-on STEM lessons that provide students with engineering design challenges are ideal for developing Learning and Innovation Skills. Students develop creativity and innovation as they engineer novel solutions to posed problems. They communicate and collaborate as they engage higher-level thinking skills to help shape their inquiry experience. Students assume ownership of the learning. From this emerges increased self-motivation and personal accountability.

With STEM lessons and activities, related disciplines are seamlessly integrated into a rich experience that becomes far more than the sum of its parts. Students explore real-world scenarios using their understanding of core science concepts, ability for higher level analysis, technological know-how, and communication skills essential for collaboration. From this experience, the learner constructs not only a response to the STEM challenge, but the elements of 21st Century Skills.

ScienceFusion provides deep science content and STEM lessons, activities, and Video-Based Projects that incorporate and develop 21st Century Skills. This provides an effective learning landscape that will prepare students for success in the workplace—and in life.

Differentiated Instruction

Reaching All Learners

by Marjorie Frank

Your students learn in different ways, at different speeds, and through different means. Channeling the energy and richness of that diversity is part of the beauty of teaching. A classroom atmosphere that encourages academic risk-taking encourages learning. This is especially true in science, where learning involves making predictions (which could turn out to be inaccurate), offering explanations (which could turn out to be incomplete), and doing things (which could result in observable mistakes).

Like most people, students are more likely to take risks in a low-stress environment. Science, with its emphasis on exploring through hands-on activities and interactive reading, provides a natural vehicle for low-stress learning. Low stress, however, may mean different things to different people. For students with learning challenges, low stress may mean being encouraged to respond at the level they are able. Another factor in meeting the needs of diverse students is the instructional tools. Are they flexible? Inviting? *ScienceFusion* addresses the needs of diverse students at every step in the instructional process.

As You Plan

Select from these resources to meet individual needs.

- For each unit, the Differentiated Instruction page in the Teacher Edition identifies program resources specifically geared to diverse learners.

- Leveled activities in the Lesson Planning pages of the Teacher Edition provide additional learning opportunities for students with beginning, intermediate, or advanced proficiency.

- A bibliography contains notable trade books with in-depth information on content. Many of the books are recommendations of the National Science Teachers Association and the Children's Book Council.

- Online Resources: Alternative Assessment worksheets for each lesson provide varied strategies for learning content.

- Online Resources: Digital lessons, virtual labs, and video-based projects appeal to all students, especially struggling readers and visual learners.

- Student Edition with Audio is online as PDF files with audio readings for use with students who have vision impairments or learning difficulties.

- Student Edition reading strategies focus on vocabulary, concept development, and inquiry skills.

As You Teach

Take advantage of these point-of-use features.

- A mix of Directed Inquiry and Independent Inquiry prompts suitable for different kinds of learners

- Short-cut codes to specific interactive digital lessons

Take It Home

As you reach out to families, look for these school-home connections.

- Take It Home activities found at the beginning of many units in the Student Edition

- Additional Take It Home worksheets are available in the Online Resources

- School-Home Connection Letters for every unit, available online as files you can download and print as-is or customize

The 5E Model and Levels of Inquiry

How do students best learn science? Extensive research and data show that the most effective learning emerges from situations in which one builds understanding based upon personal experiences. Learning is not transmitted from instructor to passive receiver; instead, understanding is constructed through the experience.

by Michael A. DiSpezio

The 5E Model for Effective Science Lessons

In the 1960s, Robert Karplus and his colleagues developed a three-step instructional model that became known as the Learning Cycle. This model was expanded into what is today referred to as the 5E Model. To emulate the elements of how an actual scientist works, this model is broken down into five components for an effective lesson: Engage, Explore, Explain, Extend (or Elaborate), and Evaluate.

Engage—The engagement sets the scene for learning. It is a warm-up during which students are introduced to the learning experience. Prior knowledge is assessed and its analysis used to develop an effective plan to meet stated objectives. Typically, an essential question is then posed; the question leads the now motivated and engaged students into the exploration.

Explore—This is the stage where the students become actively involved in hands-on process. They communicate and collaborate to develop a strategy that addresses the posed problem. Emphasis is placed on inquiry and hands-on investigation. The hands-on experience may be highly prescribed or open-ended in nature.

Explain—Students answer the initial question by using their findings and information they may be reading about, discussing with classmates, or experiencing through digital media. Their experience and understanding of concepts, processes, and hands-on skills is strengthened at this point. New vocabulary may be introduced.

Extend (or Elaborate)—The explanation is now extended to other situations, questions, or problems. During this stage the learner more closely examines findings in terms of context and transferable application. In short, extension reveals the application and implication of the internalized explanation. Extension may involve connections to other curriculum areas.

Evaluate—Although evaluation is an ongoing process, this is the stage in which a final assessment is most often performed. The instructor evaluates lesson effectiveness by using a variety of formal and informal assessment tools to measure student performance.

The 5E lesson format is used in all the *ScienceFusion* Teacher Edition lessons.

Levels of Inquiry

It wasn't that long ago that science was taught mostly through demonstration and lecture. Today, however, most instructional strategies integrate an inquiry-based approach to learning science. This methodology is founded in higher-level thinking and facilitates the students' construction of understanding from experience. When offered opportunities to ask questions, design investigations, collect and analyze data, and communicate their findings, each student assumes the role of an active participant in shaping his or her own learning process.

The degree to which any activity engages the inquiry process is variable, from highly prescribed steps to a completely learner-generated design. Researchers have established three distinct levels of inquiry: directed (or structured) inquiry, guided inquiry, and independent (or open) inquiry. These levels are distinguished by the amount of guidance offered by the instructor.

DIRECTED inquiry

In this level of inquiry, the instructor poses a question or suggests an investigation, and students follow a prescribed set of instructions. The outcome may be unknown to the students, but it is known to the instructor. Students follow the structured outline to uncover an outcome that supports the construction of lesson concepts.

GUIDED inquiry

As in Directed Inquiry, the instructor poses to the students a question to investigate. While students are conducting the investigation, the instruction focuses on developing one or more inquiry skills. Focus may also be provided for students to learn to use methods or tools of science. In *ScienceFusion*, the Teacher Edition provides scaffolding for developing inquiry skills, science methods, or tools. Student pages accompany these lessons and provide prompts for writing hypotheses, recording data, and drawing conclusions.

INDEPENDENT inquiry

This is the most complex level of inquiry experience. A prompt is provided, but students must design their own investigation in response to the prompt. In some cases, students will write their own questions and then plan and perform scientific investigations that will answer those questions. This level of inquiry is often used for science fair projects. Independent Inquiry does not necessarily mean individual inquiry. Investigations can be conducted by individual students or by pairs or teams of students.

Response to Intervention

In a traditional model, assessment marks the end of an instructional cycle. Students work through a unit, take a test, and move on, regardless of their performance. However, current research suggests that assessment should be part of the instructional cycle, that it should be ongoing, and that it should be used to identify students needing intervention. This may sound like a tall order—who wants to give tests all the time?—but it may not be as difficult as it seems. In some ways, you are probably doing it already.

by Marjorie Frank

Assessment

Every student interaction has the potential to be an assessment. It all depends on how you perceive and use the interaction.

- Suppose you ask a question. You can just listen to your student's response, or you can assess it. Does the response indicate comprehension of the concept? If not, intervention may be needed.

- Suppose a student offers an explanation of a phenomenon depicted in a photo. You can assess the explanation. Does it show accurate factual knowledge? Does it reveal a misconception? If so, intervention may be needed.

- Suppose a student draws a diagram to illustrate a concept. You can assess the diagram. Is it accurate? If not, intervention may be needed.

As the examples indicate, assessing students' understandings can—and should—be an integral part of the instructional cycle and be used to make decisions about the next steps of instruction. For students making good progress, next steps might be exploring a related concept, a new lesson, or an additional challenge. For students who are not making adequate progress, intervention may be needed.

Assessment and intervention are tightly linked. Assessment leads to intervention—fresh approaches, different groupings, new materials—which, in turn, leads to assessment. Response to Intervention (RTI) gives shape and substance to this linkage.

Response to Intervention

Response to Intervention is a process for identifying and supporting students who are not making expected progress toward essential learning goals.

RTI is a three-tiered approach based on an ongoing cycle of superior instruction, frequent monitoring of students' learning (assessments), and appropriate interventions. Students who are found not to be making expected progress in one Tier move to the next higher Tier, where they receive more intense instruction.

- **Tier I:** Students receive whole-class, core instruction.
- **Tier II:** Students work in small groups that supplement and reinforce core instruction.
- **Tier III:** Students receive individualized instruction.

How RTI and *ScienceFusion* Work

ScienceFusion provides many opportunities to assess students' understanding and many components appropriate for students in all Tiers.

TIER III
Intensive
Intervention
Individualized instruction,
with options for auditory, visual,
and second language learners.
Special education is a possibility.

Differentiated Instruction Strategies

Online Student Edition

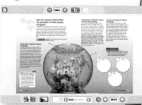

ScienceFusion Components

Online Student Edition lessons with audio recordings

Differentiated Instruction strategies in the Teacher Edition for every lesson

Appropriate for:
• Auditory learners

Appropriate for:
• Struggling readers
• Second-language learners

Students achieving at a lower level than their peers in Tier II

TIER II Strategic Intervention
Small Group Instruction in addition to core instruction

Leveled TE Activities

Alternative Assessment Worksheets

ScienceFusion Components

Leveled activities in the Lesson Planning pages of the Teacher Edition

Alternative Assessment Worksheets

Appropriate for:
• Struggling readers
• Visual learners
• Second-language learners
• Screening tools to assess students' responses to Tier II instruction

Students achieving at a lower level than their peers in Tier I

Teacher Edition

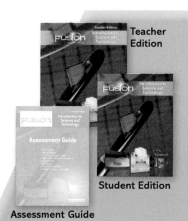

TIER I Core Classroom Instruction
With the help of extensive point-of-use strategies that support superior teaching, students receive whole-class instruction and engage productively in small-group work as appropriate.

ScienceFusion Components

Student Edition

Differentiated Instruction strategies in the TE for every lesson

Teacher Edition

Assessment Guide

Online Digital Curriculum

Appropriate for:
• Screening tools to assess students' responses to Tier I instruction
• Tier I intervention for students unable to complete the activity independently

Digital Curriculum

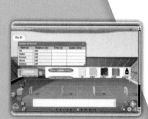

Student Edition

Assessment Guide

Active Reading

Reading is a complex process in which readers use their knowledge and experience to make meaning from text. Though rarely accompanied by obvious large-muscle movement, reading is very much an active endeavor.

by Marjorie Frank

Think back to your days as a college student when you pored over your textbooks to prepare for class or for an exam—or, more recently, concentrated on an article or book with information you wanted to remember.

▶ You probably paid close attention to the text.

▶ Perhaps you paused to ask yourself questions.

▶ You might have broken off temporarily to look up an important, but unfamiliar, word.

▶ You may have stopped to reread a challenging passage or to "catch up" if your mind wandered for a moment.

If you owned the reading material, you also may have used a pencil or marker to interact with the text right there on the page (or in a digital file).

In short, you were having a conversation with yourself about the text. You were engaged. You were thinking critically.

These are the characteristics of active readers. This is precisely the kind of reader you want your students to be, because research suggests that active reading enables readers to understand and remember more information.

Active Reading involves interacting with text cognitively, metacognitively, and quite literally. You can actually see active readers at work. They are not sitting quietly as they read; they're underlining, marking, boxing, bracketing, drawing arrows, numbering, and writing comments. Here is what they may be noting:

▶ key terms and main ideas

▶ connections between ideas

▶ questions they have, opinions, agreements, and disagreements

▶ important facts and details

▶ sequences of events

▶ words, such as *because, before,* and *but,* that signal connections between ideas

▶ problems/solutions

▶ definitions and examples

▶ characteristics

The very process of interacting actively with text helps keep readers focused, thinking, comprehending, and remembering. But interacting in this way means readers are marking up the text. This is exactly why *ScienceFusion* Student Editions are consumable. They are meant to be marked up.

Active Reading and *ScienceFusion*

ScienceFusion includes Active Reading prompts throughout the Student Editions. The prompts appear as part of the lesson opener and on most two-page spreads.

Students are often given an Active Reading prompt before reading a section or paragraph. These prompts ask students to underline certain words or number the steps in a process. Marking the text in this way is called *annotating*, and the students' marks are called *annotations*. Annotating the text can help students identify important concepts while reading. Other ways of annotating the text include placing an asterisk by vocabulary terms, marking unfamiliar or confusing terms and information with a question mark, and underlining main ideas. Students can even invent their own systems for annotating the text. An example of an annotation prompt is shown at right.

> **Active Reading** 5 **Identify** As you read, underline sources of energy for living things.

In addition, there are Active Reading questions throughout each lesson. These questions have write-on lines accompanying them, so students can answer right on the page. Students will be asked to **describe** what they've just read about, **apply** concepts, **compare** concepts, **summarize** processes, and **identify cause-and-effect** relationships. By answering these Active Reading questions while reading the text, students will be strengthening those and other critical thinking skills that are used so often in science.

> **Active Reading** 16 **Compare** What is the difference between the pulmonary and systemic circulations?

Students' Responses to Active Reading Prompts

Active Reading has benefits for you as well as for your students. You can use students' responses to Active Reading prompts and the other interactive prompts in *ScienceFusion* as ongoing assessments. A quick review of students' responses provides a great deal of information about their learning.

▶ Are students comprehending the text?
▶ How deeply do they understand the concepts developed?
▶ Did they get the main idea? the cause? the order in which things happen?
▶ Which part of a lesson needs more attention? for whom?

Answers to these questions are available in students' responses to Active Learning prompts throughout a lesson—long before you might see poor results on an end-of-lesson or end-of-unit assessment. If you are following Response to Intervention (RTI) protocols, these frequent and regular assessments, no matter how informal, are integral parts of an effective intervention program.

The Active Reading prompts in *ScienceFusion* help make everyone a winner.

Project-Based Learning

For a list of the *ScienceFusion* Video-Based Projects, see page xxiv.

by
Michael R. Heithaus

When asked why I decided to become a biologist, the answer is pretty simple. I was inspired by spending almost every day outdoors, exploring under every rock, getting muddy in creeks and streams, and fishing in farm ponds, rivers, and—when I was really lucky—the oceans. Combine that with the spectacular stories of amazing animals and adventure that I saw on TV and I was hooked. As I've progressed in my career as a biologist, that same excitement and curiosity that I had as a ten-year-old looking for a salamander is still driving me.

But today's kids live in a very different world. Cable and satellite TV, Twitter, MP3 players, cell phones, and video games all compete with the outdoors for kids' time and attention. Education budget cuts, legal issues, and the pressures of standardized testing have also limited the opportunities for students to explore outdoors with their teachers.

How do we overcome these challenges so as to inspire kids' curiosity, help them connect with the natural world, and get them to engage in science and math? This is a critical issue. Not only do we need to ensure our national competitiveness and the conservation of our natural resources by training the next generation of scientists, we also need to ensure that every kid grows up to understand how scientists work and why their work is important.

To overcome these challenges, there is no question that we need to grab students' attention and get them to actively engage in the learning process. Research shows that students who are active and engaged participants in their learning have greater gains in concept and skills development than students who are passive in the classroom.

Project-based learning is one way to engage students. And when the stimulus for the project is exciting video content, engaged and active learning is almost guaranteed. Nothing captures a student's attention faster than exciting video. I have noticed that when my university students have video to accompany a lesson, they learn and retain the material better. It's no different for younger students! Videos need to do more than just "talk at" students to have a real impact. Videos need to engage students and require participation.

Teachers and students who use *ScienceFusion* video-based projects have noticed the following:

- The videos use captivating imagery, dynamic scientists, and cool stories to inspire kids to be curious about the world around them.
- Students connect to the projects by having the videos present interesting problems for them to solve.
- The videos engage students with projects woven into the story of the video so students are doing the work of real scientists!

The start-to-finish nature of the video projects, where students do background research and develop their own hypotheses, should lead to students' personal investment in solving the challenges that are presented. By seeing real scientists who are excellent role models gather data that they have to graph and interpret, students will not only learn the science standards being addressed, they will see that they can apply the scientific method to their lives. One day, they too could be a scientist!

Based on my experiences teaching in the university classroom, leading field trips for middle school students, and taking the first project-based videos into the classroom, project-based learning has considerable benefits. The video-based projects generate enthusiasm and curiosity. They also help students develop a deeper understanding of science content as well as how to go about a scientific investigation. If we inspire students to ask questions and seek answers for themselves, we will go a long way toward closing achievement gaps in science and math and facilitate the development of the next generation of scientists and scientifically literate citizens.

(c) ©Adam Rosenblatt; (b) ©David Ponton/Design Pics/Corbis

Developing Visual Literacy

Science teachers can build the bridges between students' general literacy and their scientific literacy by focusing attention on the particular kinds of reading strategies students need to be successful. One such strategy is that of knowing how to read and interpret the various visual displays used in science.

by Donna M. Ogle

Many young readers receive little instruction in reading charts, tables, diagrams, photographs, or illustrations in their language arts/reading classes. Science is where these skills can and must be developed. Science provides a meaningful context where students can learn to read visually presented forms of information and to create their own visual representations. Research studies have shown that students take longer to read science materials containing combinations of visual displays and narrative texts than they do to read narrative text alone. The process of reading the combination materials is slower and more difficult because the reader must relate the visual displays to the narrative text and build a meaning that is based on information from both.

We also know that students benefit when teachers take time to explain how each visual form is constructed and to guide students in the thinking needed to make sense of these forms. Even the seemingly simple act of interpreting a photograph needs to be taught to most students. Here are some ways to help students develop the ability to think more critically about what they view:

▶ Model for students how to look carefully at a photograph and list what they notice.

▶ Divide the photograph into quadrants and have students think more deeply about what the photographer has used as the focus of the image and what context is provided.

▶ Have students use language such as *zoom, close-up, foreground, background,* or *panorama views* to describe photographs.

The ability to interpret a photograph is clearly a part of the scientific skill of engaging in careful observation. This skill helps students when they are using print materials, observing nature, and making their own photographs of aspects of their experiments.

Attention to the other forms of visual displays frequently used in science is also important to students' learning of scientific concepts and processes. For example, students in grades 4 through 8 need to learn to interpret and then construct each of the types of graphs, from circle graphs and bar graphs to more complex line graphs.

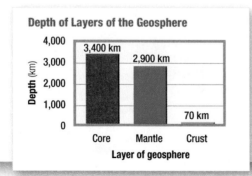

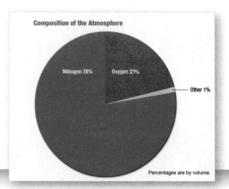

Students also need to be able to read diagrams and flow charts. Yet, in a recent study asking students to think aloud and point to how they visually scan tables and diagrams, we learned how inadequate many students were as readers of these visual forms. Because so much of the scientific information students will encounter is summarized in these visual formats, it is essential that students learn to interpret and construct visual displays.

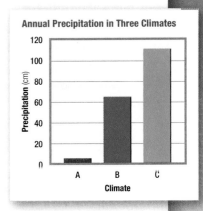

A second aspect of interpreting visual displays is connecting the information in the visual formats with the narrative text information. Some students misinterpret what they see in visuals when even a few words differ between the text and the illustration. For example, in the excerpt below from a middle school Student Edition, the text says, "the arm of a human, the front leg of a cat, and the wing of a bat do not look alike . . . but they are similar in structure."

The diagram labels (lower right) showing the bat wing and the cat's leg use *front limb*, not *wing* or *leg*. For students who struggle with English, the differing terms may cause confusion unless teachers show students how to use clues from later in the paragraph, where limb and wing/arm are connected, and how to connect this information to the two drawings. In some cases teachers have students draw lines showing where visual displays connect with the more extensive narrative text content. Developing students' awareness of how visual and narrative information support each other and yet provide different forms in which information can be shared is an important step in building scientific literacy.

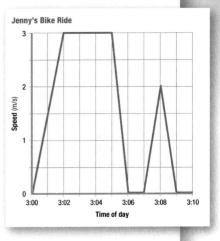

Reading science requires students to use specific reading strategies. The more carefully science teachers across grade levels assess what students already know about reading scientific materials, the more easily they can focus instruction to build the scaffolds students need to gain independence and confidence in their reading and learning of science. Time spent explaining, modeling, and guiding students will yield the rewards of heightened student enjoyment, confidence, and engagement in the exciting world of scientific inquiry.

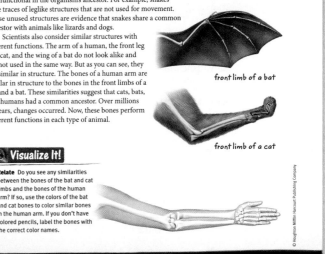

Common Structures

Scientists have found that related organisms share structural traits. Structures reduced in size or function may have been complete and functional in the organism's ancestor. For example, snakes have traces of leglike structures that are not used for movement. These unused structures are evidence that snakes share a common ancestor with animals like lizards and dogs.

Scientists also consider similar structures with different functions. The arm of a human, the front leg of a cat, and the wing of a bat do not look alike and are not used in the same way. But as you can see, they are similar in structure. The bones of a human arm are similar in structure to the bones in the front limbs of a cat and a bat. These similarities suggest that cats, bats, and humans had a common ancestor. Over millions of years, changes occurred. Now, these bones perform different functions in each type of animal.

front limb of a bat

front limb of a cat

Visualize It!

10 Relate Do you see any similarities between the bones of the bat and cat limbs and the bones of the human arm? If so, use the colors of the bat and cat bones to color similar bones in the human arm. If you don't have colored pencils, label the bones with the correct color names.

Science Notebooking

Science Notebooks are powerful classroom tools. They lead your students deep into the learning process, and they provide you with a window into that process as well as a means to communicate about it. Most middle-school students will have had some experience using a Science Notebook during their elementary years.

Notebook ▶ Why Use a Science Notebook?

A Science Notebook contains the writer's ideas, observations, and perceptions of events and endeavors. A Science Notebook also contains ideas and observations of scientific processes, data, conclusions, conjectures, and generalizations.

Inquiry Skills A Science Notebook is especially important when students do inquiry-based activities. It offers students a single place to record their observations, consider possibilities, and organize their thoughts. As such, it is a learner's version of the logs that professional scientists keep.

In their Science Notebooks, students can

▶ sketch their ideas and observations from experiments and field trips

▶ make predictions about what will happen in an experiment

▶ reflect on their work and the meaning they derived from experiments

▶ make inferences based on the data they have gathered

▶ propose additional experiments to test new hypotheses

▶ pose new questions based on the results of an activity or experiment

Process Skills A Science Notebook is an excellent extension of the textbook, allowing students to further practice and hone process skills. Students will not only apply these skills in relation to the specific science content they are learning, they will be gaining a deeper insight into scientific habits of mind.

In their Science Notebooks, students can

▶ record and analyze data

▶ create graphs and charts

▶ infer outcomes

▶ draw conclusions

▶ collect data from multiple experimental trials

▶ develop 21st Century organizational skills

A student's Science Notebook entry for a *ScienceFusion* Quick Lab
▼

> Quick Lab: Balancing Act
>
> Partner: Evan
>
> <u>Answers</u>
>
> 2. Me: 12 adjustments
>   Evan: 10 adjustments
>
> 3. No, I was not aware of my muscles making adjustments the first time. I think I didn't notice because I was concentrating more on just staying on one leg.
>
> 4. Yes, I was aware of my muscles making adjustments the second time. I think my muscles worked harder the second time because my leg was getting tired.
>
> 5. 12 times
>
> 6. Your body is always having to make adjustments to maintain a balanced internal environment. Most of these adjustments aren't even noticed by a person, just like I didn't notice my leg muscles adjusting during the first balancing test.

Science Notebooks and *ScienceFusion*

In many ways, the *ScienceFusion* worktexts are Science Notebooks in themselves. Students are encouraged to write answers directly in the text and to annotate the text for better understanding. However, a separate Science Notebook can still be an invaluable part of your student's learning experience with *ScienceFusion*. Student uses for a Science Notebook along with the worktext include:

▶ writing answers for the Unit Review

▶ writing responses to the Think Outside the Book features in each lesson

▶ planning for and writing answers to the Citizen Science feature in each unit

▶ working through answers before writing them in the worktext

▶ writing all answers if you choose not to have students work directly in the worktext

▶ taking notes on additional materials you present outside of the worktext

▶ making observations and recording data from Daily Demos and additional activities provided in the Teacher Edition

▶ collecting data and writing notes for labs performed from the Lab Manual

▶ making notes and writing answers for Digital Lessons and Virtual Labs

▶ collecting data and writing answers for the Project-Based Videos

The Benefits (for You and Your Students) of Science Notebooking

No doubt, it takes time and effort to help students set up and maintain Science Notebooks, not to mention the time it takes you to review them and provide meaningful feedback. The payoff is well worth it. Here's why:

Keeping a Science Notebook:

▶ leads each learner to engage with ideas

▶ engages students in writing—an active, thinking, analytical process

▶ causes students to organize their thinking

▶ provides students with multiple opportunities and modes to process new information

▶ makes learning experiences more personal

▶ provides students with a record of their own progress and accomplishments

▶ doubles as a study guide for formal assessments

▶ creates an additional vehicle for students to improve their reading and writing skills

As you and your students embrace Science Notebooking, you will surely find it to be an engaging, enriching, and very valuable endeavor.

Using the *ScienceFusion* Worktext

Research shows that an interactive text teaches students how to relate to content in a personal, meaningful way. They learn how to be attentive, energetic readers who reach a deep level of comprehension. Still, the worktext format may be new to you and your students. Below are some answers to questions—both pedagogical and practical—you may have about *ScienceFusion's* worktext format.

How does the worktext format help my students learn?

▶ In this format, your students will interact with the text and visuals on every page. This will teach them to read expertly, to think critically, and to communicate effectively—all skills that are crucial for success in the 21st century.

▶ The use of images and text on every page of the *ScienceFusion* worktext accommodates both visual and verbal learners. Students are engaged by the less formal, magazine-like presentation of the content.

▶ By the end of the school year, the worktexts become a record of the knowledge and skills your students learned in class. Students can use their books as a study guide to prepare for tests.

What are some features that make the *ScienceFusion* worktext different from a regular textbook?

Some of the special features of the *ScienceFusion* worktext include these prompts for writing directly in the worktext:

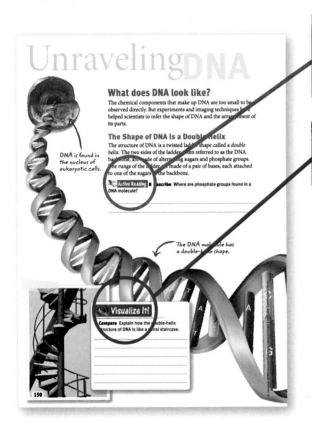

Active Reading
Annotation prompts and questions throughout the worktext teach students how to analyze and interact with content as they read.

Visualize It!
Questions and completion prompts that accompany images help develop visual literacy.

Engage Your Brain
Math problems, with on-page guidance, allow students to understand the relationships between math and science and to practice their math skills.

Do the Math
Interesting questions and activities on the lesson opener pages help prepare students for the lesson content.

Are my students really supposed to write directly in the book?

Yes! Write-on lines are provided for students to answer questions on-page, while the student is reading. Additional prompts are given for students to annotate the pages. You can even encourage your students to experiment with their own systems of annotation. More information can be found in "A How-To Manual for Active Reading" in the Look It Up! Section at the end of the Student Edition and Teacher Edition.

You might wish to encourage your students to write in the worktexts using pencils so that they can more easily revise their answers and notes as needed

We will have to use the same set of worktexts for several years. How can students use the worktexts if they can't write in them?

Though *ScienceFusion* is set up in a worktext format, the books can still be used in a more traditional fashion. Simply tell your students that they cannot write in the textbooks but should instead use their Science Notebooks for taking notes and answering questions. (See the article titled "Science Notebooking" for more information about using Notebooks with *ScienceFusion*.)

How do I grade my students' answers in the worktext?

The pages in the worktext are conveniently perforated so that your students can turn in their work. Or you may wish for your students to leave the pages in the book, but turn in the books to you on a daily or weekly basis for you to grade them.

The Lesson Reviews and Unit Reviews are designed so students can turn in the pages but still keep their annotated pages for reference when moving on to the next lesson or unit or for review before a lesson or unit test.

- Tour the classroom while students are writing in their worktexts. Address any issues you see immediately or make note of items that need to be addressed with students later.

- Have students do 'self checks' and 'partner checks.' Choose a question in the worktext, and have all students check their responses. Or, have students trade their worktext with a partner to check each other's responses.

- Once a week, have students copy five questions and their responses from the worktext onto a sheet of notebook paper. You can review student answers to ensure they're using the worktext correctly without having students turn in worktext pages or the books themselves.

- Use a document camera to show students correct worktext answers.

- Every two weeks, review and grade one class's worth of student worktext answers per day. Or, grade a class's worktexts while the students are taking a test.

Pacing Guide

You have options for covering the lesson materials: you may choose to follow the digital path, the print path, or a combination of the two. Customize your Pacing Guide to plan print, inquiry, digital, and assessment mini-blocks based on your teaching style and classroom needs.

Pressed for Time? Follow the faster-paced compressed schedule.

	Traditional 1 = 45 min	Block 1 = 90 min	Compressed (T/B)	Print Path	Inquiry Labs & Activities	Digital Path	Review & Assess
UNIT 1 Interactions of Living Things							
Unit Project	3	1.5	3 (1.5)				
Lesson 1 Introduction to Ecology	5	2.5	4 (2)				
Lesson 2 Roles in Energy Transfer	5	2.5	4 (2)				
Lesson 3 Population Dynamics	5	2.5	4 (2)				
Lesson 4 Interactions in Communities	4	2	3 (1.5)				
Unit Review	2	1	1 (0.5)				
Total Days for Unit 1	24	12	19 (9.5)				
UNIT 2 Earth's Biomes and Ecosystems							
Unit Project	3	1.5	3 (1.5)				
Lesson 1 Land Biomes	5	2.5	4 (2)				
Lesson 2 Aquatic Ecosystems	5	2.5	4 (2)				
Lesson 3 Energy and Matter in Ecosystems	5	2.5	4 (2)				
Lesson 4 Changes in Ecosystems	4	2	3 (1.5)				
Lesson 5 Human Activity and Ecosystems	5	2.5	4 (2)				
Unit Review	2	1	1 (0.5)				
Total Days for Unit 2	29	14.5	23 (11.5)				

Columns grouped under: **Total Days** (Traditional, Block, Compressed) and **Customize Your Pacing Guide** (Print Path, Inquiry Labs & Activities, Digital Path, Review & Assess)

	Total Days			Customize Your Pacing Guide			
	Traditional 1 = 45 min	Block 1 = 90 min	Compressed (T/B)	Print Path	Inquiry Labs & Activities	Digital Path	Review & Assess

UNIT 3 Earth's Resources

	Traditional	Block	Compressed				
Unit Project	3	1.5	3 (1.5)				
Lesson 1 Earth's Support of Life	4	2	3 (1.5)				
Lesson 2 Natural Resources	5	2.5	4 (2)				
Lesson 3 Nonrenewable Energy Resources	5	2.5	4 (2)				
Lesson 4 Renewable Energy Resources	5	2.5	4 (2)				
Lesson 5 Managing Resources	4	2	3 (1.5)				
Unit Review	2	1	1 (0.5)				
Total Days for Unit 3	28	14	22 (11)				

UNIT 4 Human Impact on the Environment

	Traditional	Block	Compressed				
Unit Project	3	1.5	3 (1.5)				
Lesson 1 Human Impact on Water	6	3	5 (2.5)				
Lesson 2 Human Impact on Land	4	2	3 (1.5)				
Lesson 3 Human Impact on the Atmosphere	5	2.5	4 (2)				
Lesson 4 Protecting Earth's Water, Land, and Air	6	3	5 (2.5)				
Unit Review	2	1	1 (0.5)				
Total Days for Unit 4	26	13	21 (10.5)				

Teacher Notes

UNIT 1 Interactions of Living Things

The Big Idea and Essential Questions

This Unit was designed to focus on this Big Idea and Essential Questions.

Big Idea Organisms interact with each other and with the nonliving parts of their environment.

Lesson	ESSENTIAL QUESTION	Student Mastery	PD Professional Development	Lesson Overview
LESSON 1 Introduction to Ecology	How are different parts of the environment connected?	To analyze the parts of an ecosystem	Content Refresher, TE p. 6	TE p. 12
LESSON 2 Roles in Energy Transfer	How does energy flow through an ecosystem?	To relate the roles of organisms to the transfer of energy in food chains and food webs	Content Refresher, TE p. 7	TE p. 28
LESSON 3 Population Dynamics	What determines a population's size?	To explain how population size changes in response to environmental factors and interactions between organisms	Content Refresher, TE p. 8	TE p. 42
LESSON 4 Interactions in Communities	How do organisms interact?	To predict the effects of different interactions in communities	Content Refresher, TE p. 9	TE p. 56

 **Professional Development** Science Background

Use the key words at right to access

- Professional Development from **The NSTA Learning Center**
- **SciLinks** for additional online content appropriate for students and teachers

Key words

communities   predator-prey
  ecology   relationships
populations

 National Science Teachers Association

 SCiLINKS. THE WORLD'S A CLICK AWAY

©Comstock/age Fotostock

Options for Instruction

Two parallel paths provide coverage of the Essential Questions, with a strong **Inquiry** strand woven into each. Follow the **Print Path,** the **Digital Path,** or your customized combination of print, digital, and inquiry.

	LESSON 1 Introduction to Ecology	**LESSON 2** Roles in Energy Transfer	**LESSON 3** Population Dynamics
Essential Questions	*How are different parts of an environment connected?*	*How does energy flow through an ecosystem?*	*What determines a population's size?*
Key Topics	• Ecology • Levels of Organization in an Environment • Biomes • Habitat and Niche	• Producers • Decomposers • Consumers • Food Chains and Webs	• Size of Populations • Populations and Limiting Factors • Interactions within Populations
Print Path	Teacher Edition pp. 12–25 Student Edition pp. 4–15	Teacher Edition pp. 28–41 Student Edition pp. 18–29	Teacher Edition pp. 42–55 Student Edition pp. 30–41
Inquiry Labs	Lab Manual **Field Lab** What's in an Ecosystem? **Quick Lab** Which Biome? Virtual Lab Classifying Biomes	Lab Manual **Field Lab** Food Webs **Quick Lab** Making Compost **Quick Lab** Energy Role Game	Lab Manual **Exploration Lab** How Do Populations Interact? **Quick Lab** Investigate an Abiotic Limiting Factor
Digital Path	Digital Path TS693092	Digital Path TS673330	Digital Path TS673352

LESSON 4
Interactions in Communities

How do organisms interact?

- Predation
- Symbiosis
- Competition

Teacher Edition
pp. 56–68

Student Edition
pp. 42–51

Lab Manual
Exploration Lab Modeling the Predator-Prey Cycle

Quick Lab Prey Coloration

 Virtual Lab Competing for Resources

Digital Path
TS673340

UNIT 1
Unit Projects

 Citizen Science Project
Sharing Spaces

Teacher Edition p. 11

Student Edition
pp. 2–3

A Trip Down Shark River

Unit Assessment
Formative Assessment
Strategies RTI
Throughout TE
Lesson Reviews SE
Unit PreTest
Summative Assessment
Alternative Assessment
(1 per lesson) RTI
Lesson Quizzes
Unit Tests A and B
Unit Review RTI
(with answer remediation)
Practice Tests
(end of module)
Project-Based Assessment
See the Assessment Guide for quizzes and tests.

Go Online to edit and create quizzes and tests.

Response to Intervention

See RTI teacher support materials on p. PD6.

Differentiated Instruction

Strategies for **English Language Learners (ELL)** are provided for each lesson, under the Explain tabs.

LESSON 1 *Ecological Terms,* TE p. 17

LESSON 2 *Tracing Energy Flow in Food Chains,* TE p. 33

LESSON 3 *Population Diagrams,* TE p. 47

LESSON 4 *Symbiotic Terms,* TE p. 61
Interaction Cartoons, TE p. 61

Vocabulary strategies provided for all students can also be a particular help for ELL. Use different strategies for each lesson or choose one or two to use throughout the unit. Vocabulary strategies can be found in the Explain tab for each lesson (TE pp. 17, 33, 47, and 61).

Inquiry labs, activities, probing questions, and daily demos provide a range of inquiry levels. Preview them under the Engage and Explore tabs starting on TE pp. 14, 30, 44, and 58.

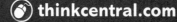

Levels of **Inquiry**	DIRECTED inquiry	GUIDED inquiry	INDEPENDENT inquiry
	introduces inquiry skills within a structured framework.	develops inquiry skills within a supportive environment.	deepens inquiry skills with student-driven questions or procedures.

Each long lab has two inquiry options:

LESSON 1 **Field Lab** *What's in an Ecosystem?*

LESSON 2 **Field Lab** *Food Webs*

LESSON 3 **Exploration Lab** *How Do Populations Interact?*

LESSON 4 **Exploration Lab** *Modeling the Predator-Prey Cycle*

 Go Digital! 🖱 **thinkcentral.com**

Digital Path

The Unit 1 Resource Gateway is your guide to all of the digital resources for this unit. To access the Gateway, visit thinkcentral.com.

Digital Interactive Lessons

Lesson 1 Introduction to Ecology TS693092

Lesson 2 Roles in Energy Transfer TS673330

Lesson 3 Population Dynamics TS673352

Lesson 4 Interactions in Communities TS673340

More Digital Resources

In addition to digital lessons, you will find the following digital resources for Unit 1:

Video-Based Project: A Trip Down Shark River (previewed on TE p. 10)

People in Science: Kenneth Krysko

Virtual Labs: Classifying Biomes (previewed on p. 15) Competing for Resources (previewed on p. 59)

RTI ▸ Response to Intervention

Response to Intervention (RTI) is a process for identifying and supporting students who are not making expected progress toward essential learning goals. The following *ScienceFusion* components can be used to provide strategic and intensive intervention.

Component	Location	Strategies and Benefits
STUDENT EDITION Active Reading prompts, Visualize It!, Think Outside the Book	**Throughout each lesson**	Student responses can be used as screening tools to assess whether intervention is needed.
TEACHER EDITION Formative Assessment, Probing Questions, Learning Alerts	**Throughout each lesson**	Opportunities are provided to assess and remediate student understanding of lesson concepts.
TEACHER EDITION Extend Science Concepts	**Reinforce and Review, TE pp. 18, 34, 48, 62** **Going Further, TE pp. 18, 34, 48, 62**	Additional activities allow students to reinforce and extend their understanding of lesson concepts.
TEACHER EDITION Evaluate Student Mastery	**Formative Assessment, TE pp. 19, 35, 49, 63** **Alternative Assessment, TE pp. 19, 35, 49, 63**	These assessments allow for greater flexibility in assessing students with differing physical, mental, and language abilities as well as varying learning and communication modes.
TEACHER EDITION Unit Review Remediation	**Unit Review, TE pp. 70–72**	Includes reference back to Lesson Planning pages for remediation activities and assignments.
INTERACTIVE DIGITAL LESSONS and VIRTUAL LABS	**thinkcentral.com** **Unit 1 Gateway** **Lesson 1 TS693092** **Lesson 2 TS673330** **Lesson 3 TS673352** **Lesson 4 TS673340**	Lessons and labs make content accessible through simulations, animations, videos, audio, and integrated assessment. Useful for review and reteaching of lesson concepts.

Content Refresher

Professional Development

Introduction to Ecology

ESSENTIAL QUESTION
How are different parts of the environment connected?

1. Ecology

Students will learn that ecology is the scientific study of the interactions among organisms and their environment.

A key unit of ecological study is the ecosystem. Within an ecosystem are biotic factors (the interactions between living organisms, such as competition, cooperation, and predation) and abiotic factors (water, air, soil, and so on). Each organism within an ecosystem interacts with and is affected by other organisms that share the ecosystem. For example, moles and earthworms make their homes in soil. The tunneling activity of these organisms helps aerate soil, which provides essential materials to other soil organisms and the roots of plants. Moles prey on earthworms. All organisms depend on abiotic factors for their survival. Organisms can be affected by changes in abiotic factors such as salinity, temperature, and amount of rainfall.

2. Levels of Organization in an Environment

Students will learn that the environment is organized into levels of varying complexity.

The levels of organization in an ecosystem contain different numbers of organisms and encompass different-sized areas. The most basic level is the individual, which is one living thing. Next is population, which includes all the members of the same species that live in the same area at the same time. A species consists of individuals that have the same characteristics that can mate to produce fertile offspring.

A community includes all populations of species that live in the same area at the same time. The interactions within a community may include competition, symbiosis, and feeding relationships.

An ecosystem includes all the organisms living in an area and the abiotic factors in that environment.

3. Biomes

Students will learn what biomes are and what factors characterize a biome.

A biome is a region of Earth that is characterized by certain climatic conditions (particularly temperature and precipitation) and the types of communities of living things that can be found there.

Biomes are large, and can contain many ecosystems. Ecosystems found across the globe within the same biome tend to have similar plant and animal species.

Biomes are terrestrial. Their aquatic counterparts are referred to as aquatic ecosystems. Aquatic ecosystems include freshwater ecosystems, marine ecosystems, and estuaries.

4. Habitat and Niche

Students will learn that two factors that help determine where a population lives are habitat and niche.

A habitat is the place where an organism lives. Organisms get everything they need to survive (air, water, living space, food) from their habitat. The size of an organism's habitat is determined by the needs of that organism.

The niche of a population is its role within its ecosystem. A population's niche includes its habitat and its interactions with other populations. Two populations cannot share exactly the same niche for a sustained period of time before one population drives the other from the ecosystem.

Teacher  Teacher

Matt Moller, M.Ed.
Carmel Middle School
Carmel, IN

Lesson 1 Introduction to Ecology If your school grounds are easily accessible, take your students outside. Have students list all living things they see, as well as any evidence of unseen organisms—spider webs, for example. Students should also note all nonliving parts of the ecosystem. Have students discuss their observations. Ask students to consider how your school's ecosystem might differ from that of another school in the area.

Lesson 2

Roles in Energy Transfer

ESSENTIAL QUESTION
How does energy flow through an ecosystem?

1. Producers, Decomposers, and Consumers

Organisms play roles in the movement of energy.

The sun is the primary energy source for most ecosystems on Earth. Plants, algae, and some bacteria use sunlight for photosynthesis, using light energy to make food from water and carbon dioxide. Some producers, such as bacteria living near deep-sea vents, use chemosynthesis to make food.

Decomposers feed on the wastes or remains of other organisms and return nutrients to the environment. Scavengers feed on the remains of dead organisms, which also aids the process of decomposition.

Consumers eat other organisms. Consumers can be classified by organisms they use as food, as follows:

• Herbivores, such as cows and grasshoppers, feed on plants.

• Carnivores, such as orcas and lions, feed on other animals.

• Omnivores, such as bears and rats, feed on plants and animals.

2. Food Chains and Food Webs

Food chains and food webs model the movement of energy through an ecosystem.

A food chain is a model that shows a single path of energy transfer from a producer through the different consumers in an ecosystem. Arrows in a food chain show the direction in which energy flows. In a typical food chain, this flow of energy moves from a producer to a consumer (an herbivore or omnivore) and then possibly to another consumer (a carnivore). The last consumer in the food chain is generally a top predator in the ecosystem, which is not usually eaten by other animals.

Most ecosystems have many overlapping food chains. The relationships among these overlapping food chains are shown in a food web, a model that shows energy transfer through the feeding relationships among the ecosystems's organisms. As in a food chain, the arrows in a food web represent energy flow from the organism that is consumed to the organism that is feeding.

Global food webs show feeding relationships that begin on land and move to water or vice versa. They are connected by organisms that live or spend time in both terrestrial and aquatic habitats, such as shore birds, amphibians, and insects that lay eggs in water.

 COMMON MISCONCEPTIONS  **RTI**

PRODUCERS, DECOMPOSERS, AND CONSUMERS Students sometimes think an omnivore is classified as an herbivore when it is actively feeding on plants and is a carnivore when it is eating another animals.

This is addressed in the Learning Alert on p. 37.

FOOD CHAINS AND FOOD WEBS Students often think of feeding relationships as linear. They may misunderstand the food chain model in several ways:

1. They think arrows represent who eats whom rather than flow of energy.

This misconception is addressed in the Activity on p. 30.

2. They see linear food chains as unconnected to a food web.

This misconception is addressed in the Activity on p. 30.

3. They think organisms high up in the food chain eat everything that is lower on the chain.

This is addressed in the Learning Alert on p. 39.

Content Refresher (continued)

Lesson 3

Population Dynamics

ESSENTIAL QUESTION

What determines a population's size?

1. Size of Populations

Students will learn how population size can change and what factors affect population growth and the carrying capacity of the environment.

Populations increase through the birth of new individuals or the arrival of new individuals from outside of the existing population. The latter can be particularly beneficial to the population because the new arrival can bring new genetic variation to the population.

Conversely, populations decrease when individuals move out of a population and into another population (emigration) and when individuals die.

These factors are evident when young bucks leave, or emigrate from, the population of deer into which they were born (thus decreasing that population). They may emigrate in search of resources such as mating partners. When the bucks join a new population, the size of that population has increased due to immigration.

The growth of the deer population will be affected by the amount of resources that are available, such as food, water, and shelter. If predators are scarce and resources are plentiful, the deer's survival and reproduction rates will be high. If resources are scarce or new threats to the population arise, survival and reproduction rates will drop. The number of members of a population an environment can support is its **carrying capacity**. Carrying capacity can change when the environment changes.

A population crash occurs when the carrying capacity for a population suddenly drops, making the environment unable to support the same number of organisms. Events that could result in a population crash include a drought, fire, or flood.

2. Populations and Limiting Factors

Students will learn that limiting factors prevent unbridled growth of populations.

Even when resources are plentiful, populations of living things do not grow unchecked. There are **limiting factors** present in the environment that will keep populations from growing too large. Limiting factors can be biotic (living) or abiotic (nonliving). Biotic limiting factors include food availability, predation, and disease. Abiotic limiting factors include water, light, nutrients, living space, unusual weather, and natural disasters. For example, when a population of mice grows due to an increased birth rate (because of plentiful food and water), a number of limiting factors may come into play regarding the offspring, such as the mother's ability to care for them (especially if the litter is large), disease, and the increased number of mice attracting the attention of predators.

3. Interactions within Populations

Students will learn that members of a population may interact with each other.

Students may think that organisms are always competing with each other for limited resources, such as food and water. It's true that **competition** occurs when individuals struggle for a limited resource. However, organisms can also cooperate to ensure their survival. For example, herd animals such as zebra and wildebeest live in large groups so there are many eyes to watch for predators—and there are many targets for predators to choose from. A remarkable example of **cooperation** can be seen among musk oxen. When confronted by predators, musk oxen form a defensive circle around the vulnerable young.

Populations of some species have a set social hierarchy. Members of a population may belong to different groups with distinct roles and responsibilities. Social insects, such as bees, include workers and guards. The workers gather food, and the guards protect the hive.

Interactions in Communities

ESSENTIAL QUESTION
How do organisms interact?

1. Predation

Predation is a key interaction between organisms of different species.

Predation is a feeding relationship in which one organism, the predator, captures and eats another organism, the prey. Because many organisms are consumers that must eat food, it is possible within a given food web for a single organism to serve first as a predator of one species and then as the prey of another.

Predation is important because it serves as a limiting factor to regulate population size. If a predator is removed from an ecosystem, the population of its prey animals may increase rapidly, to the point of doing harm to the ecosystem. At Yellowstone, the loss of wolves, major predators of elk, has allowed the elk population to grow quickly. This overpopulation of elk has stripped the forest of vegetation.

2. Symbiosis

Organisms of different species may interact in symbiotic relationships.

Symbiosis is a close relationship between two organisms of different species. Three types of symbiosis are mutualism, commensalism, and parasitism.

- Mutualism is a form of symbiosis in which both organisms derive benefit from the relationship.

- Commensalism is a symbiotic relationship that occurs when one species in the interaction derives benefit, while the other is unharmed or not affected.

- Parasitism is a form of symbiosis in which one species (the parasite) derives benefit at the expense of the other species (the host). In parasitism, the parasite lives on or within the cells or tissues of the host for the purpose of deriving nourishment. This interaction may sicken or weaken the host but usually does not bring about the host's death.

3. Competition

Organisms of the same or of different species may compete with each other for resources.

In all ecosystems, organisms vie with other organisms for resources. This is called competition and can occur between organisms of different species as well as among members of the same species. For example, organisms of different species may compete for food, water, and living space. Individuals of the same species may compete for mates. Competition serves as a limiting factor in ecosystems by restricting the sizes of the populations making up the community.

 COMMON MISCONCEPTIONS **RTI**

SYMBIOSIS VS. MUTUALISM Common use of the terms *symbiosis* and *symbiotic* may lead students to believe that the term means the same as *mutualism*. *Symbiosis* is the more general of the two terms; it describes any close relationship between organisms, regardless of whether the relationship benefits, harms, or has no effect on one of the organisms in the relationship. By contrast, *mutualism* is the term used to describe a form of symbiosis in which both organisms receive some benefit.

This misconception is addressed in the ELL Activity *Symbiotic Terms* on p. 61 and in the Learning Alert on p. 66.

Advance Planning

These activities may take extended time or special conditions.

Unit 1

Video-Based Project A Trip Down Shark River, p. 10
multiple activities spanning several lessons

Project Sharing Spaces, p. 11
class discussion and writing time

Graphic Organizers and Vocabulary pp. 17, 18, 33, 34, 47, 48, 61, 62
ongoing with reading

Lesson 1

Activity Living or Nonliving, p. 14
pictures of nature scenes

Daily Demo Identifying Biotic and Abiotic Factors, p. 15
established aquarium; live brine shrimp

Field Lab What's in an Ecosystem?, p. 15
requires two 45-min periods and outdoor observations

Lesson 2

Daily Demo Let It Rot!, p. 31
moldy bread in sealed plastic bag

Quick Lab Making Compost, p. 31
collect kitchen waste and yard waste in advance

Field Lab Food Webs, p. 31
requires multiple class periods; outdoor observations

Lesson 3

Quick Lab Investigate an Abiotic Limiting Factor, p. 45
students collect data after two weeks

Lesson 4

Daily Demo Observing a Predator in Action, p. 59
live predator (lizard, toad, salamander, nonpoisonous snake) and food for predator

What Do You Think?

Have students think about how living things depend on one another for survival. List ideas on the board.

Ask: How can you tell if an ecosystem is healthy? Sample answer: It will be diverse, with many plant and animal species coexisting.

Ask: What might happen if the population of one plant species in an ecosystem declines? Sample answer: Other plants may take its place. If an animal species depends largely on that plant for food or shelter, then the animal species might decline, too.

UNIT 1

Interactions of Living Things

Big Idea
Organisms interact with each other and with the nonliving parts of their environment.

Fish and sponges in a coral reef.

What do you think?
Ecosystems consist of living things that depend on each other to survive. How might these fish depend on a coral reef? How might this bird depend on a dragonfly population?

Eastern bluebirds feed on insects.

1

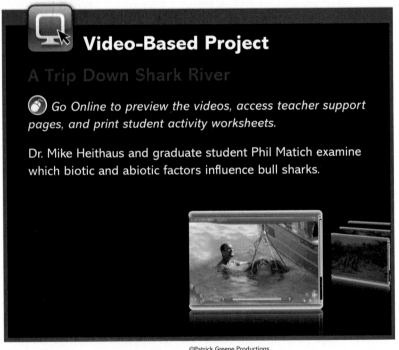

Video-Based Project

A Trip Down Shark River

Go Online to preview the videos, access teacher support pages, and print student activity worksheets.

Dr. Mike Heithaus and graduate student Phil Matich examine which biotic and abiotic factors influence bull sharks.

©Patrick Greene Productions

Unit 1
Interactions of Living Things

CITIZEN SCIENCE
Sharing Spaces

Wetlands provide living space for many kinds of birds. Ospreys are large birds of prey that eat mostly fish. They often nest on telephone poles and other man-made structures. Yellow-rumped warblers are small birds that live in trees and eat insects and berries.

① Ask A Question

How can organisms affect each other and a whole ecosystem?

An ecosystem is made up of all the living and nonliving things in an environment. Ospreys and yellow-rumped warblers are part of the same ecosystem. With your teacher and your classmates, brainstorm ways in which ospreys and yellow-rumped warblers might affect each other.

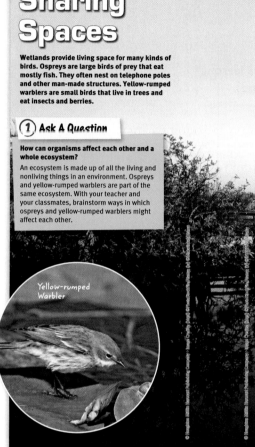

Yellow-rumped Warbler

② Think About It

A Look at the photos of the ospreys in their environment. List at least two resources they need to survive and explain how the ospreys get them.

_____

_____

B What are two ways nonliving things could affect yellow-rumped warblers?

_____

_____

③ Apply Your Knowledge

A List the ways in which yellow-rumped warblers and ospreys share resources.

_____

_____

B Yellow-rumped warblers have a diet that consists mainly of insects and berries. Make a list of other organisms you know that might compete with the warblers for these same food resources.

_____

_____

_____

C Describe a situation that could negatively affect both the osprey population and the yellow-rumped warbler population.

_____

_____

Osprey nest

Take It Home

Are ecologists looking for people to report observations in your community? Contact a university near your community to see if you can help gather information about plants, flowers, birds, or invasive species. Then, share your results with your class.

2 Unit 1 Interactions of Living Things

3

CITIZEN SCIENCE

Unit Project **Sharing Spaces**

1. Ask a Question

Encourage students to think broadly when brainstorming ways in which ospreys and yellow-rumped warblers might affect each other. List ideas on the board.

🖱 *Optional Online rubric: Class Discussion*

2. Think About It

- Sample answers: Some resources include fish for food, nesting materials, and high places on which to nest. Students should identify that fish come from the water, and nesting materials include sticks and leaves.

- Sample answers include habitat destruction through fire or flooding.

3. Apply Your Knowledge

A. Resources they may share include nesting materials and fresh water.

B. Organisms that might compete with the warblers for food include frogs, squirrels, and some other birds.

C. Habitat destruction through development could negatively affect both populations.

Take It Home

Encourage students to work with an adult as they contact ecologists and universities. When students present their results to the class, ask them to give detailed descriptions of their observations, and have them explain what type of study the observations might be used for.

🖱 *Optional Online rubric: Oral Presentations*

Introduction to Ecology

Essential Question How are different parts of the environment connected?

 Professional Development

For more detailed information about the topics in this lesson, refer to the Content Refresher in the Unit Opener pages.

Opening Your Lesson

Begin the lesson by assessing students' prerequisite and prior knowledge.

Prerequisite Knowledge

- Basic needs of organisms
- Distinctions between living and nonliving things

Accessing Prior Knowledge

Ask: What are the basic needs shared by almost all living things? food, water, shelter (living space), a temperature that allows the organism to survive

Ask: Where do living things get all of the things they need to survive? from the place where they live, from their surroundings, from the environment

Customize Your Opening

☐ **Accessing Prior Knowledge,** above

☐ **Print Path** Engage Your Brain, SE p. 5 #1–2

☐ **Print Path** Active Reading, SE p. 5 #3–4

☐ **Digital Path** Lesson Opener

Key Topics/Learning Goals	Supporting Concepts
Ecology 1 Describe the field of ecology. 2 Distinguish between abiotic and biotic factors.	• Ecology is the study of interactions of organisms with their environment. • The abiotic factors of an environment are the nonliving parts, such as water, rocks, light, and temperature. • The biotic factors of an environment include all of the interactions between living organisms, such as competition, cooperation, and predation.
Levels of Organization in an Environment 1 Describe the different levels of organization in an environment.	• The levels of organization in an environment are individual, population, community, ecosystem, and biome. • An individual is one organism. A population is the individuals of a species that live in the same area at the same time. A community is the populations in an area. An ecosystem is a community and its abiotic environment. A biome has a spe-cific climate and certain plants and animals.
Biomes 1 Describe the factors that characterize a biome. 2 Relate ecosystems to biomes. 3 Identify major land biomes. 4 Identify major aquatic ecosystems.	• A biome can contain many ecosystems, and ecosystems within the same biome tend to have similar plant and animal species. • Major land biomes include tropical and temperate rain forest and grassland, desert, temperate deciduous forest, taiga, and tundra. • Aquatic ecosystems include freshwater systems, estuaries, and marine systems.
Habitat and Niche 1 Tell where populations live. 2 Define *habitat* and *niche*.	• An organism lives where its needs are met. • A habitat is the place an organism lives. • A niche is the role of a species in its community.

Options for Instruction

Two parallel paths provide coverage of the Essential Questions, with a strong **Inquiry** strand woven into each. Follow the **Print Path,** the **Digital Path,** or your customized combination of print, digital, and inquiry.

 **Print Path**
Teaching support for the Print Path appears with the Student Pages.

 Inquiry Labs and Activities

 **Digital Path**
Digital Path shortcut: TS693092

The Web of Life, SE pp. 6–7
How are all living things connected?
- Through the Living Environment
- Through the Nonliving Environment

Activity
Living or Nonliving?
Recognizing Relationships

Quick Lab
Which Abiotic and Biotic Factors Are Found in an Ecosystem?

What Is Ecology?
Interactive Images

Stay Organized!, SE pp. 8–9
What are the levels of organization in the environment?
- Populations
- Communities
- Ecosystems

Activity
Making an Organizational Model

Activity
Making Connections

Hierarchy
Interactive Images

Ecosystem Organization
Interactive Images

Levels of Organization
Slideshow

Think Globally!, SE pp. 10–11
What is a biome?
What characteristics define a biome?
- Climate Conditions
- Communities of Living Things

Virtual Lab
Classifying Biomes

Quick Lab
Which Biome?

Earth's Biomes
Interactive Graphics

Home Sweet Home, SE p. 12
What determines where a population can live?
- Niche

Field Lab
What's in an Ecosystem?

Habitat and Niche
Interactive Graphics

Options for Assessment

See the Evaluate page for options, including Formative Assessment, Summative Assessment, and Unit Review.

Engage and Explore

Activities and Discussion

Activity *Living or Nonliving?*

 Engage

Introducing Key Topics

 small groups or whole class
🕐 20 min
Inquiry **GUIDED** inquiry

Provide students with pictures of nature scenes. Direct them to classify elements of the picture as living or nonliving things. Prompt students to identify examples from each group that cannot be seen in the picture (microorganisms, air). Challenge students to describe some of the ways living things on their list depend upon other living things and the nonliving parts of the environment.

Activity *Recognizing Relationships*

Ecology

👥 individuals, then pairs
🕐 15 min
Inquiry **GUIDED** inquiry

Think, Pair, Share Give students two minutes to write down as many examples as they can of biotic factors and abiotic factors common to the area where they live. Once the time is up, have students select six biotic and six abiotic factors from their list. Pairs of students should then work together to identify as many relationships and dependencies as possible between the biotic and abiotic factors they have selected. Call on pairs to share the relationships they selected.

Activity *Making an Organizational Model*

Levels of Organization in an Environment

👥 individuals
🕐 20 min

Have students cut sheets of paper into four shapes of their choice, with each shape smaller than the next. Explain that each of the shapes can be used to model a level of organization in the environment. Have students use what they've learned about the environment's levels of organization to label each shape with the level it represents. Encourage students to enhance their models by adding illustrations or writing captions that clarify what each shape represents. Then have students connect their finished shapes with string or glue.

Take It Home *Home and Work*

Habitat and Niche

👥 adult-student pairs
🕐 20–30 min
Inquiry **GUIDED** inquiry

Have students work with an adult to talk about living things they have observed in the past, perhaps during their travels or even on television. The pair should select two organisms and try to describe the habitat and niche of each within its ecosystem.

 Online resource: Student worksheet

Discussion *Hermit Crabs*

Habitat and Niche

👥 whole class
🕐 10 min

Hermit crabs are crustaceans. Unlike other crabs, hermit crabs lack a protective carapace, or hard outer shell, on their abdomens. To protect its vulnerable parts, a hermit crab will move into an abandoned shell, usually a snail shell. The crab wedges its abdomen and rear pairs of legs into the shell. It walks with two pairs of legs and uses the front pair as claws. It uses the large claw for defense and for tearing apart food and the smaller claw for feeding. As a hermit crab grows, it becomes too large for its acquired home. At that point, the crab finds a larger shell, sometimes evicting a smaller hermit crab in the process. A hermit crab outgrows its home many times during its life and spends much of its time looking for new shells. Have students discuss and describe the hermit crab's habitat and niche.

Customize Your Labs

 See the Lab Manual for lab datasheets.

 Go Online for editable lab datasheets.

Labs and Demos

Daily Demo *Identifying Biotic and Abiotic Factors*

Engage

Synthesizing Key Concepts

 whole class
 10 min
 Inquiry **GUIDED** inquiry

PURPOSE To recognize biotic and abiotic factors

MATERIALS

- established aquarium
- live brine shrimp
  CAUTION Do not allow students to handle live animals.

1 Drop some brine shrimp into the aquarium and have students observe the fish as they feed.

2 **Observing** What biotic factors and abiotic factors do you see?

3 **Applying** Tell what levels of organization can be observed in this environment.

Quick Lab *Which Abiotic and Biotic Factors Are Found in an Ecosystem?*

PURPOSE To analyze an ecosystem and describe the organisms that can be supported by an ecosystem

See the Lab Manual or go Online for planning information.

Quick Lab *Which Biome?*

PURPOSE To identify to which biome an animal is best adapted

See the Lab Manual or go Online for planning information.

Field Lab *What's in an Ecosystem?*

Engage

Synthesizing Key Concepts

 small group
 2 45 min periods
Inquiry **GUIDED** or **INDEPENDENT** inquiry

Students observe organisms and abiotic factors in progressively smaller sample areas and consider habitats and niches.

PURPOSE To observe organisms in their environments

MATERIALS

- hand lens
- tape measure or meterstick
- field guide
- colored markers
- posterboard

 Virtual Lab *Classifying Biomes*

Biomes

flexible
45 min
Inquiry **GUIDED** inquiry

Students investigate how to classify the world's 11 major biomes.

PURPOSE To understand that temperature and rainfall are major distinguishing characteristics of biomes

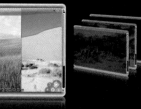

Activities and Discussion

- ☐ **Activity** Living or Nonliving?
- ☐ **Activity** Making an... Model
- ☐ **Activity** Recognizing Relationships
- ☐ **Discussion** Hermit Crabs
- ☐ **Take It Home** Home and Work

Labs and Demos

- ☐ **Daily Demo** Identifying... Factors
- ☐ **Quick Lab** Which... Ecosystem?
- ☐ **Quick Lab** Which Biome?
- ☐ **Field Lab** What's in an Ecosystem?
- ☐ **Virtual Lab** Classifying Biomes

Your Resources

_____

_____

_____

Explain Science Concepts

Key Topics	📖 Print Path	💻 Digital Path
Ecology	☐ **The Web of Life,** SE pp. 6–7 • Active Reading, #5 • Visualize It!, #6 • Visualize It!, #7 🔘 *Optional Online resource: KWL support*	☐ **What Is Ecology?** Learn about the study of ecology. ☐ **Hierarchy** Explore the different levels of organization in an environment, and learn about the difference between biotic and abiotic factors.
Levels of Organization in an Environment	☐ **Stay Organized!,** SE pp. 8–9 • Active Reading (Annotation strategy), #8 • Visualize It!, #9 • Visualize It!, #10	☐ **Levels of Organization** Explore levels of organization within an ecosystem.
Biomes	☐ **Think Globally!,** SE pp. 10–11 • Active Reading (Annotation strategy), #11 • Think Outside the Book, #12 • Visualize It!, #13	☐ **Earth's Biomes** Learn about the different biomes on Earth.
Habitat and Niche	☐ **Home Sweet Home,** SE p. 12 • Relate, #14 • Visualize It!, #15	☐ **Habitat and Niche** Learn about the differences between a habitat and a niche.

Differentiated Instruction

Basic *Visualizing Environmental Levels of Organization*

Levels of Organization in an Environment

 individuals
 varies

Posters Have students find a picture in a magazine or online of an ecosystem that includes multiple species. Direct students to use the image as the basis for a poster that identifies each level of organization in an environment.

Advanced *Investigating Biomes*

Biomes

 individuals
 varies

Displays Have students research major biomes. Students should choose one biome and prepare a display or PowerPoint presentation that identifies the biome's major features. Important features of the biome include its average temperature and precipitation, geographic location(s), and the plants and animals that typify the biome. Have students share their completed displays or presentations with the rest of the class.

ELL *Ecological Terms*

Ecology

individuals
15 min

Four Square EL learners may have difficulty with some of the vocabulary in the lesson. Help EL learners master the differences between biotic and abiotic factors by having them complete a four-square diagram for each term. Students write the vocabulary term in the center oval. Next, they fill in the boxes around the center by writing a definition of the term in one box, characteristics used to identify each factor in a second box, examples that illustrate the term in the third box, and nonexamples of the term in the fourth.

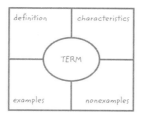

Lesson Vocabulary

ecology	biotic factor	abiotic factor
population	species	community
ecosystem	biome	habitat
niche		

Previewing Vocabulary

 whole class   15 min

Word Parts Share the following to help students remember terms.
• **Ecology** contains the word root *ecos*, which means "house." Ecology can be thought of as the study of where organisms live.
• **Biotic** contains the root *bio*, which means "living."
• **Abiotic** contains the prefix *a-*, which means "not" or "without" and the root *bio*, which means "living."

Reinforcing Vocabulary

individuals   ongoing

Frame Game To reinforce students' understanding of vocabulary introduced in the lesson, have them create a Frame Game graphic organizer for each term.

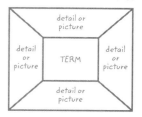

Customize Your Core Lesson

Core Instruction
☐ **Print Path** choices
☐ **Digital Path** choices

Vocabulary
☐ **Previewing Vocabulary** Word Parts
☐ **Reviewing Vocabulary** Frame Game

Your Resources

Differentiated Instruction
☐ **Basic** Visualizing Environmental Levels of Organization
☐ **Advanced** Investigating Biomes
☐ **ELL** Ecological Terms

Extend Science Concepts

Reinforce and Review

Activity *Making Connections*

Synthesizing Key Topics   small groups   ⏱ 20 min

Jigsaw Organize the class into 3, 6, 9, or 12 small groups. Assign each group a key topic from the lesson. Have members of each group work together to become experts on their topic as it relates to the Essential Question, "How are different parts of the environment connected?" Reassign students to new mixed groups that include experts for each topic. Have individuals in each mixed group share their expertise with other group members until all students are able to explain how each lesson topic relates to the essential question for the lesson.

Graphic Organizer

Synthesizing Key Topics   individuals   ⏱ 10 min

Cluster Diagram After students have studied the lesson, ask them to create a cluster diagram using the vocabulary terms.

⊘ *Optional Online resource: Cluster Diagram support*

Going Further

Social Studies Connection

Synthesizing Key Topics   small groups   ⏱ 20 min

Discussion In many places, new housing developments are being constructed as part of a planned community concept. Planned communities are often large, mixed-land-use areas that include homes as well as playgrounds, walking or bike trails, natural areas, or pools. Within such a community, each member has equal access to the amenities of the community. Have students use the planned community concept to create their own ecosystem. Have students brainstorm what populations to include in their community. Then have them identify the abiotic factors that their planned ecosystem will need to support the organisms they have included. Challenge students to explain how the biotic and abiotic factors of their ecosystem are dependent upon each other.

Earth Science Connection

Biomes   individuals or pairs   ⏱ varied

Research Project Climate is a major defining factor in a biome. *Climate* refers to the average weather conditions in an area over time. Temperature and precipitation are the main aspects used to describe climate. Have students research the climate conditions for the area in which they live. You may wish to have students find out how temperature and precipitation vary month to month. Have them summarize and analyze their findings in a table or PowerPoint presentation.

Customize Your Closing

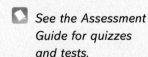 See the Assessment Guide for quizzes and tests.

⊘ Go Online to edit and create quizzes and tests.

Reinforce and Review

☐ **Activity** Making Connections

☐ **Graphic Organizer** Cluster Diagram

☐ **Print Path** Visual Summary, SE p. 14

☐ **Print Path** Lesson Review, SE p. 15

☐ **Digital Path** Lesson Closer

Evaluate Student Mastery

Formative Assessment

See the teacher support below the Student Pages for additional Formative Assessment questions.

Ask: How are the levels of organization in an ecosystem connected? Individual organisms of the same species make up a population; populations of various species make up a community; a community of organisms and the abiotic factors (water, air, rock, and so on) comprise an ecosystem. A number of different ecosystems can be found within a biome.

Reteach

Formative assessment may show that students need reinforcement for certain topics. The resources below are recommended for reteaching. If students were introduced to a topic through the Print Path, you can also use the Digital Path to reteach, and vice versa.
🎧 *Can be assigned to individual students.*

Ecology
Quick Lab Which Abiotic and Biotic Factors are Found in an Ecosystem?
Activity Recognizing Relationships 🎧

Levels of Organization in an Environment
Activity Making an Organizational Model 🎧

Biomes
Virtual Lab Classifying Biomes 🎧
Quick Lab Which Biome?

Habitat and Niche
Discussion Hermit Crabs
Field Lab What's in an Ecosystem?

Summative Assessment

Alternative Assessment
Ecology and Ecosystems

🌐 *Online resources: student worksheet, optional rubrics*

Introduction to Ecology

Choose Your Meal: *Ecology and Ecosystems*
Complete the activities to show what you've learned about ecology.

1. Work on your own, with a partner, or with a small group.
2. Choose one item from each section of the menu, with an optional dessert. Check your choices.
3. Have your teacher approve your plan.
4. Submit or present your results.

Appetizers

_____ **An Ecologist for a Day** Imagine you are an ecologist who is speaking to a group of students about your job. Present a monologue in which you talk about your job and the things you study.

_____ **Individual vs. Population** Make a Venn diagram that compares and contrasts an individual organism and its population. Choose a population and complete the diagram by including information about the similarities and differences between the population and the individual.

_____ **Finding a Niche** Find out about an animal or other organism that lives in or near your neighborhood. Determine the animal's niche in its ecosystem. Write a song or poem about it.

Main Dish

_____ **A Newsworthy Ecosystem** Imagine scientists have discovered a new ecosystem. Present a news report in which you describe the ecosystem. Describe at least two populations in the ecosystem and the ways they interact. List some abiotic factors in the ecosystem.

Side Dishes

_____ **Charting Organization** Design a chart that shows the organization in an ecosystem. First, invent an ecosystem. Then draw and label a community within the ecosystem, a population within the community, and an individual within the population.

_____ **Advertising Factors** Design a brochure that describes an environment. Identify and describe some of the abiotic and biotic factors in the environment. Include at least one image.

Desserts (optional)

_____ **Who Will Fit?** Imagine you are in charge of filling a niche in an ecosystem. First describe the niche to be filled. Then write a questionnaire to see how well other organisms will fit in with your ecosystem. Include questions about the organism's current habitat and niche.

_____ **Creating Competition** Write a story about an organism that competes with another organism for food or a resource in an ecosystem. Describe the ecosystem and the organisms' interactions.

Going Further
- ☐ Social Studies Connection
- ☐ Earth Science Connection
- ☐ **Print Path** Why It Matters, SE p. 13

Formative Assessment
- ☐ **Strategies** Throughout TE
- ☐ **Lesson Review** SE

Summative Assessment
- ☐ **Alternative Assessment** Ecology and Ecosystems
- ☐ Lesson Quiz
- ☐ Unit Tests A and B
- ☐ Unit Review SE End-of-Unit

Your Resources

_____   _____

_____   _____

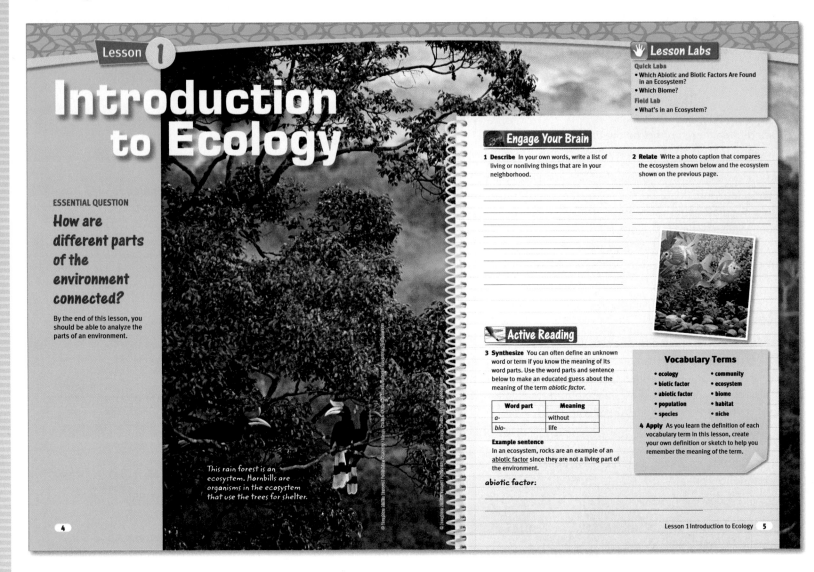

Answers

Answers to 1–3 should represent students' current thoughts, even if incorrect.

1. List should include reasonable factors in the students' neighborhoods.

2. Sample answer: The hornbills live in a rainforest ecosystem while the goldfish live in an aquatic ecosystem. Also, the rainforest ecosystem is natural, and the aquatic ecosystem is artificial.

3. Sample answer: An abiotic factor is nonliving.

4. Students should define or sketch each vocabulary term in the lesson.

Opening Your Lesson

Discuss student responses to the Engage Your Brain questions to assess students' knowledge and to estimate what they already know about the key topics.

Prerequisites Students should already know that organisms need food, water, air, living space, and a proper temperature for their survival and that these needs are obtained from the environment.

Building Reading Skills

KWL Direct students to make a KWL chart by folding a sheet of paper lengthwise to form three columns. Have students title the columns: What I Know, What I Want to Find Out, and What I Learned. Allow students time to complete the first two columns of the chart to help them answer the Essential Question. At the end of the lesson, students can return to the chart to complete the last column.

🌐 *Optional Online resource: KWL support*

The Web of Life

How are all living things connected?

Organisms need energy and matter to live. Interactions between organisms cause an exchange of energy and matter. This exchange creates a web of life in which all organisms are connected to each other and to their environment. **Ecology** is the study of how organisms interact with one another and with the environment.

Through the Living Environment

Each individual organism has a role to play in the flow of energy and matter. In this way, organisms are connected to all other organisms. Relationships among organisms affect each one's growth and survival. A **biotic factor** is an interaction between organisms in an area. Competition is one way that organisms interact. For example, different kinds of plants might compete for water in the desert.

Through the Nonliving Environment

All organisms rely on the nonliving environment for survival. An **abiotic factor** is a nonliving part of an environment, such as water, nutrients, soil, sunlight, rainfall, or temperature. Some of these are resources that organisms need to grow and survive. For example, plants use sunlight, water, and soil nutrients to make food. Similarly, some organisms rely on soil or rocks for shelter.

Abiotic factors influence where organisms can survive. In a terrestrial environment, temperature and rainfall are important abiotic factors. In aquatic environments, the water's temperature, salt, and oxygen content are important abiotic factors. Changes in these basic abiotic factors affect where organisms can live and how many individuals are able to survive in the environment.

Active Reading **5 Infer** How does the environment determine where an organism can survive? Explain your answer.

_____
_____
_____
_____
_____

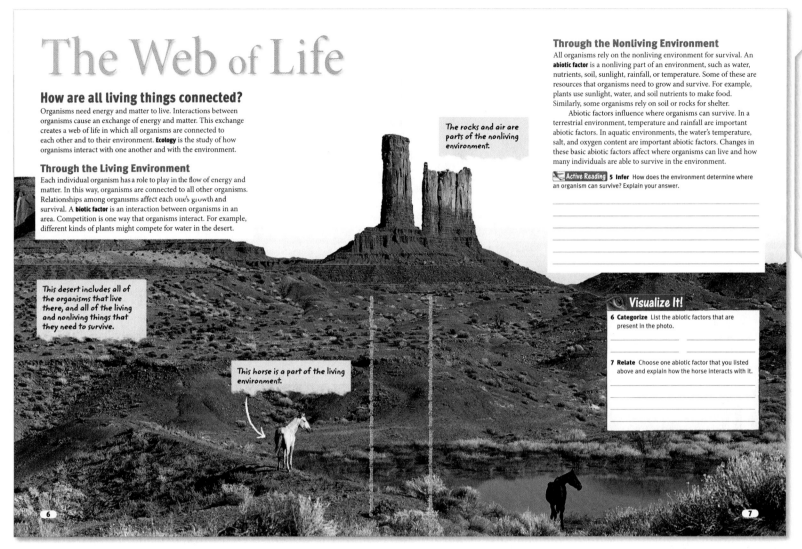

The rocks and air are parts of the nonliving environment.

This desert includes all of the organisms that live there, and all of the living and nonliving things that they need to survive.

This horse is a part of the living environment.

Visualize It!

6 Categorize List the abiotic factors that are present in the photo.

_____   _____
_____   _____

7 Relate Choose one abiotic factor that you listed above and explain how the horse interacts with it.

_____
_____
_____

Answers

5. Sample answer: An organism lives where it does because it can survive under the conditions in that environment.

6. Sample answers: water, dirt, rocks, air

7. Accept all reasonable answers that demonstrate an understanding of how the horse might interact with a nonliving factor in the environment.

Interpreting Visuals

Have students analyze the image of the ecosystem. **Ask:**

• What are some ways the biotic factors of this ecosystem interact with one another? Sample answers: Horses eat grass; Small animals use plants for shelter.

• What are some ways the biotic factors of this ecosystem interact with the abiotic factors? Sample answers: Horses drink the water; Insects fly in the air.

Probing Questions   GUIDED Inquiry

Synthesizing How do plants and animals differ in the ways they interact with biotic and abiotic factors to meet the basic need of food? Sample answer: Plants rely on abiotic factors for their food because plants make their food through photosynthesis, which requires sunlight, carbon dioxide, and water. Animals rely on biotic factors such as predation and other feeding relationships between living organisms for their food.

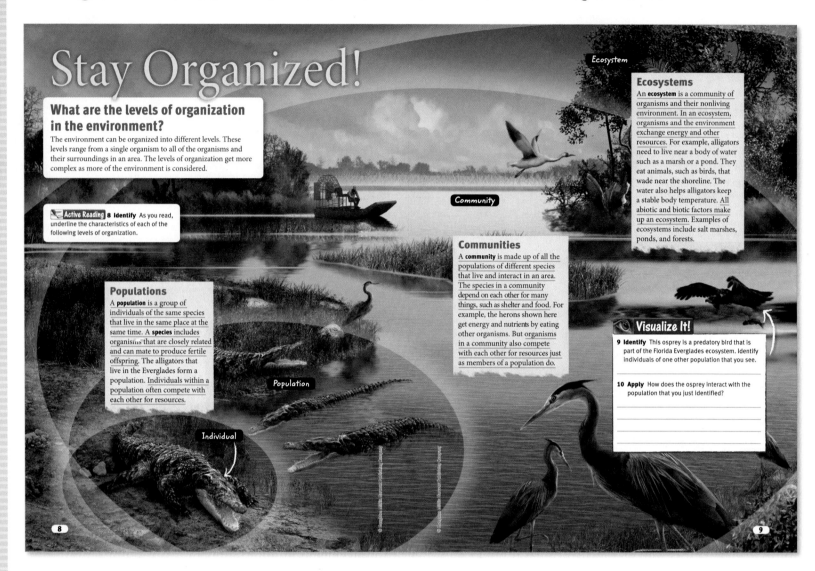

Stay Organized!

What are the levels of organization in the environment?

The environment can be organized into different levels. These levels range from a single organism to all of the organisms and their surroundings in an area. The levels of organization get more complex as more of the environment is considered.

Active Reading 8 Identify As you read, underline the characteristics of each of the following levels of organization.

Populations

A **population** is a group of individuals of the same species that live in the same place at the same time. A **species** includes organisms that are closely related and can mate to produce fertile offspring. The alligators that live in the Everglades form a population. Individuals within a population often compete with each other for resources.

Individual

Population

Community

Ecosystem

Communities

A **community** is made up of all the populations of different species that live and interact in an area. The species in a community depend on each other for many things, such as shelter and food. For example, the herons shown here get energy and nutrients by eating other organisms. But organisms in a community also compete with each other for resources just as members of a population do.

Ecosystems

An **ecosystem** is a community of organisms and their nonliving environment. In an ecosystem, organisms and the environment exchange energy and other resources. For example, alligators need to live near a body of water such as a marsh or a pond. They eat animals, such as birds, that wade near the shoreline. The water also helps alligators keep a stable body temperature. All abiotic and biotic factors make up an ecosystem. Examples of ecosystems include salt marshes, ponds, and forests.

Visualize It!

9 Identify This osprey is a predatory bird that is part of the Florida Everglades ecosystem. Identify individuals of one other population that you see.

10 Apply How does the osprey interact with the population that you just identified?

8

9

Answers

8. *See students' pages for annotations.*

9. Sample answer: herons

10. Sample answer: The osprey might interact with the herons by competing with them for food.

Formative Assessment

Ask: How does a species differ from a population? A species is a single kind of organism that can mate and produce offspring. A population is a group of organisms of the same species that exists within a certain place. **Ask:** What is the difference between a community and an ecosystem? A community is made up of all the living things that live in an area. An ecosystem includes the community of living things and the nonliving parts of their environment. **Ask:** Would a group of alligators that live at a particular wildlife refuge be considered a population or a community? a population **Ask:** What would you call all the animals that live at the refuge? a community

Interpreting Visuals

Visual Clues Point out the white circular shapes in the illustration. Note that each circle encompasses more organisms, moving outward from the left-hand page where the smallest circle, representing the most basic level of organization, surrounds the individual: a single alligator. **Ask:** What level of organization is represented by the largest circle? an ecosystem Invite students to brainstorm other ways this information could be presented graphically.

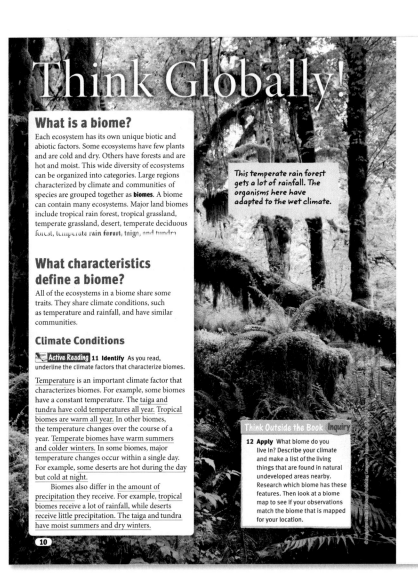

Think Globally!

What is a biome?

Each ecosystem has its own unique biotic and abiotic factors. Some ecosystems have few plants and are cold and dry. Others have forests and are hot and moist. This wide diversity of ecosystems can be organized into categories. Large regions characterized by climate and communities of species are grouped together as **biomes**. A biome can contain many ecosystems. Major land biomes include tropical rain forest, tropical grassland, temperate grassland, desert, temperate deciduous forest, temperate rain forest, taiga, and tundra.

What characteristics define a biome?

All of the ecosystems in a biome share some traits. They share climate conditions, such as temperature and rainfall, and have similar communities.

Climate Conditions

Active Reading **11 Identify** As you read, underline the climate factors that characterize biomes.

Temperature is an important climate factor that characterizes biomes. For example, some biomes have a constant temperature. The taiga and tundra have cold temperatures all year. Tropical biomes are warm all year. In other biomes, the temperature changes over the course of a year. Temperate biomes have warm summers and colder winters. In some biomes, major temperature changes occur within a single day. For example, some deserts are hot during the day but cold at night.

Biomes also differ in the amount of precipitation they receive. For example, tropical biomes receive a lot of rainfall, while deserts receive little precipitation. The taiga and tundra have moist summers and dry winters.

This temperate rain forest gets a lot of rainfall. The organisms here have adapted to the wet climate.

Think Outside the Book Inquiry

12 Apply What biome do you live in? Describe your climate and make a list of the living things that are found in natural undeveloped areas nearby. Research which biome has these features. Then look at a biome map to see if your observations match the biome that is mapped for your location.

10

Communities of Living Things

Biomes contain communities of living things that have adapted to the climate of the region. Thus, ecosystems within the same biome tend to have similar species across the globe. Monkeys, vines, and colorful birds live in hot and humid tropical rain forests. Grasses, large mammals, and predatory birds inhabit tropical grasslands on several continents.

Only certain types of plants and animals can live in extreme climate conditions. For example, caribou, polar bears, and small plants live in the tundra, but trees cannot grow there. Similarly, the plant and animal species that live in the desert are also unique. Cacti and certain animal species have adaptations that let them tolerate the dry desert climate.

World biomes

- Desert
- Tropical grassland
- Temperate grassland
- Tropical rain forest
- Temperate deciduous forest
- Temperate rain forest
- Taiga
- Tundra

Visualize It!

13 Compare The photos below show two different biomes. Use what you learned about the characteristics of biomes to compare these environments, and then explain why they are categorized as different biomes. Write your answers in the space provided.

Compare: _____

Explain: _____

Lesson 1 Introduction to Ecology 11

Answers

Note to teacher: The appendix includes a list of the characteristics of each biome, which may help students complete the exercises on this spread.

11. *See students' pages for annotations.*

12. Sample answer: My region is usually hot and dry. The plants in this area are cacti and low shrubs, and the animals include lizards, rodents, and birds. This matches a description of a desert biome. The biome map shows me that the area I live in is part of the desert biome.

13. Sample answers: Compare: The top photo has less plant diversity, but both photos show large mammals. Explain: The plant communities look quite different, which could help explain why they are categorized as different biomes.

Interpreting Visuals

Map Reading Have students take a closer look at the map. **Ask:** Which of the biomes shown on the map is the least common? temperate rain forests **Ask:** Which biomes are most common on the African continent? desert and tropical grassland **Ask:** What are some other conclusions you can draw from this map? Sample answers: The tundra and taiga biomes are located farther from the equator than other biomes. Deserts, tropical grasslands, and tropical rainforests are often found near the equator.

Building Reading Skills

Vocabulary: Context Clues Remind students that they can use context clues to help them understand the meanings of unfamiliar words. Have students underline some context clues that can help them understand the meanings of some of the terms on this page. Sample answers: biome: "ecosystems can be organized into categories," "Large regions characterized by climate and communities of species," "can contain many ecosystems," "land biomes include tropical rain forest, tropical grassland, temperate grassland..."; precipitation: "rainfall," "moist"; inhabit: "similarly... live"

Home Sweet Home

What determines where a population can live?

Ecologists study the specific needs of different kinds of organisms and the role each species plays in the environment. Organisms that live in the same area have different ways of getting the resources they need.

Niche

Each population in an ecosystem plays a specific role. A population's **niche** (NICH) is the role the population plays in the ecosystem, such as how it gets food and interacts with other populations. For example, one part of a shark population's niche is eating fish.

A **habitat** is the place where an organism usually lives and is part of an organism's niche. The habitat must provide all of the resources that an organism needs to grow and survive. Abiotic factors, such as temperature, often influence whether a species can live in a certain place. Biotic factors, such as the interactions with other organisms that live in the area, also play a role. For example, the habitat of a shark must include populations of fish it can eat.

Two populations cannot occupy exactly the same niche. Even small differences in habitats, roles, and adaptations can allow similar species to live together in the same ecosystem. For example, green and brown anoles sometimes live on the same trees, but they avoid competition by living in different parts of the trees.

14 Relate How is a habitat like a person's address? How is a niche like a person's job?

_____
_____
_____
_____
_____
_____

🔎 Visualize It!

15 Infer Describe the prairie dog's niche. How does it find shelter and impact the environment?

_____
_____
_____
_____
_____

Prairie dogs dig burrows in grassy plains. They eat plants and are hunted by predators such as owls and foxes.

Why It Matters

EYE ON THE ENVIRONMENT

Lizard Invasion

Green anole lizards (*Anolis carolinensis*) have been part of the South Florida ecosystem for a long time. Recently, a closely related lizard, the nonnative brown anole (*Anolis sagrei*), invaded the green anoles' habitat. How do they avoid competing with each other for resources?

Home Base
Green anoles live on perches throughout a tree. Brown anoles live mainly on branches that are close to the ground. If they have to share a tree, green anoles will move away from perches close to the ground. In this way, both kinds of anoles can live in the same tree while avoiding competition with each other.

Intrusive Neighbors
Although brown and green anoles can coexist by sharing their habitats, they do not live together peacefully. For example, brown anoles affect green anoles by eating their young.

Extend

16 Describe How do green and brown anoles avoid competition? Draw a picture of a tree showing both green and brown anoles living in it.

17 Research What are other examples of two species dividing up the parts of a habitat?

18 Relate Infer what would happen if the habitats of two species overlapped. Present your findings in a format such as a short story, a music video, or a play.

Inquiry

13

Answers

14. A habitat is where an organism lives, and a niche is the organism's role in the community.

15. Sample answer: The prairie dog digs a burrow in which to live, which affects the soil and limits the places where plants can grow.

16. Students' drawings should illustrate green anoles at the top of the tree and brown anoles near the bottom.

17. Answers should reflect an understanding of how two organisms divide up a niche or habitat.

18. The presentation should define the niche differences that are required for two species to live in the same habitat.

Probing Questions   GUIDED *Inquiry*

Synthesizing Why might an organism's habitat change at different stages of its life? Give an example to support your answer. Sample answer: An organism gets everything it needs to survive from its habitat. As an organism grows, its needs may change, requiring it to change its habitat. For example, the habitat for a mosquito in the larval stage is water. As an adult, a mosquito lives on land.

Why It Matters

Have students look closely at the images of the two types of lizards and consider the habitat of each. Challenge students to explain how the color of each lizard serves as an adaptation to its specific habitat within the tree. Sample answer: The brown anole lives primarily on branches near the ground. Its brown coloring helps it to blend in with the brown branches and soil, and avoid being easily seen by predators. The green anole lives higher up in the tree, where its green color helps it to blend in with the tree's leaves. Therefore, the coloring of the green anole helps it to blend in with its surroundings to avoid predators.

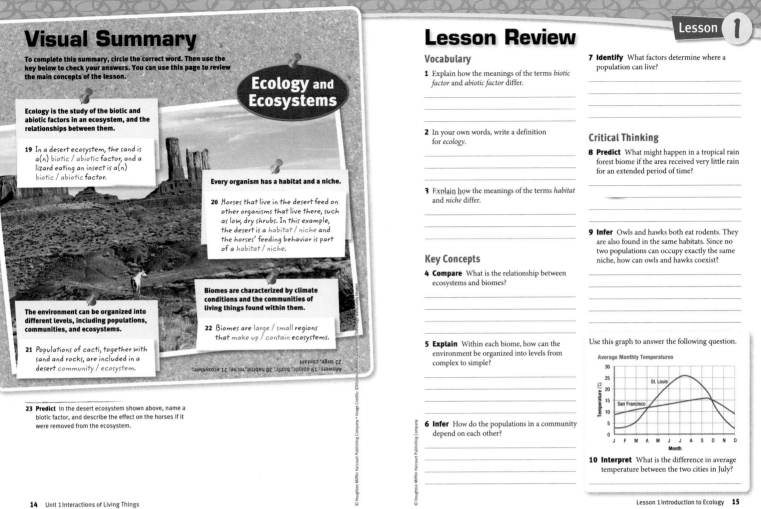

Visual Summary Answers

19. abiotic; biotic

20. habitat; niche

21. ecosystem

22. large; contain

23. Sample answer: An example of a biotic factor is the horses feeding on the shrubs. If the horses were not able to feed on shrubs because the shrubs were removed, the horses would need to find another food source.

Lesson Review Answers

1. A biotic factor is an interaction between living parts of the environment, and an abiotic factor is part of the nonliving environment.

2. Sample answer: Ecology is the study of interactions of organisms with one another and with their environment.

3. A habitat is an organism's living environment, and a niche is its role in the ecosystem.

4. Similar ecosystems are contained within larger regions called biomes.

5. ecosystem, community, population, organism (individual)

6. Populations depend on each other for food, for protection, or for shelter.

7. Biotic and abiotic factors determine whether a species can live in a certain place. The habitat needs to have adequate food, shelter, and water for a species to survive.

8. Organisms living there would have trouble surviving because they have adapted to lots of rainfall.

9. The owls and hawks need to hunt at different times of day. Owls hunt at night and hawks hunt in the daytime.

10. about 12 degrees Celsius

Kenneth Krysko

Purpose To learn about Kenneth Krysko and the work that ecologists do

Learning Goals
- Describe some different types of work ecologists do.
- Understand the impact of invasive species on native populations.

Informal Vocabulary
ecologist, herpetology, subtropical, invasive, molecular genetics, naturalist

Prerequisite Knowledge
- Basic understanding of ecology
- Levels of organization in an environment

Activity *Career Quiz*

 small groups   varied
                     GUIDED inquiry

Have students write on separate index cards the following phrases: *What You'll Do, Where You Might Work, Education,* and *Other Job Requirements.* Then have students use these phrases to quiz each other on what people in the professions described on these pages do. If students do not know the answer to a question, have them reread or conduct research to find the answer.

Variation Students can also make up questions based on job descriptions. For example: Which professional might study an endangered species of fish? Which professional might give a lecture about how a mountain formed?

Differentiated Instruction

Basic *Burmese Pythons*

👥 pairs   🕐 30 min

Have student pairs conduct research to find out about Burmese pythons in Asia. Encourage them to find out about the python's life cycle, the animals that prey on it in Asia, and what it eats in its native habitat. Then have students brainstorm ways that scientists might use this information to help control Florida's python population.

Advanced *Invasive Species*

👥 individuals or pairs   🕐 30 min

Oral Presentations Have students prepare an oral presentation about invasive species in Florida. Encourage students to include tables or charts with their presentations that list some invasive species, where they originated, and how they were introduced to Florida. Have students explain why invasive species are often difficult to eradicate and why they often proliferate.

🌐 *Optional Online rubric: Oral Presentations*

ELL *Snakes*

👥 small groups   🕐 30 min

Have small groups each create a poster about snakes in Florida. Help groups conduct basic research as needed. Tell groups to first give their posters a descriptive title. Beneath the title, have them include drawings or photographs of various snakes. Then direct them to write a brief description beside each type of snake.

🌐 *Optional Online rubric: Posters and Displays*

Customize Your Feature

- ☐ **Activity** Career Quiz
- ☐ **People in Science** Online
- ☐ **Basic** Burmese Pythons
- ☐ **Advanced** Invasive Species
- ☐ **ELL** Snakes
- ☐ **People in Science News**
- ☐ **Building Reading Skills**

People in Science

Kenneth Krysko

ECOLOGIST

Snakes have fascinated Dr. Kenneth Krysko since he was four years old. Now he is an ecologist specializing in herpetology—the study of snakes. You can often find him in the Florida Everglades looking for Burmese pythons. He tracks these pythons to help limit the effect they have on Florida ecosystems.

Burmese pythons can grow to be 6 meters long. They are native to southeast Asia and were illegally brought to Florida as pets. Many owners released them into the wild when the snakes grew too large. The snakes breed well in Florida's subtropical climate. And they eat just about any animal they can swallow, including many native species. Dr. Krysko tracks down these invasive pythons. Through wildlife management, molecular genetics, and other areas of study, he works with other scientists to search for ways to reduce the python population.

Dr. Krysko studies many other invasive species, that is, nonnative species that can do harm in Florida ecosystems. He shares what he learns, including ways to identify and deal with invasive species with other ecologists. Along with invasion ecology, he has done research in reproduction and conservation biology. Dr. Krysko also works as a collections manager in the herpetology division at the Florida Museum of Natural History.

Dr. Krysko works to get a handle on what to do about the invasive pythons.

16

JOB BOARD

Park Naturalist

What You'll Do: Teach visitors at state and national parks about the park's ecology, geology, and landscape. Lead field trips, prepare and deliver lectures with slides, and create educational programs for park visitors. You may participate in research projects and track organisms in the park.

Where You Might Work: State and national parks

Education: An advanced degree in science and teacher certification

Other Job Requirements: You need to be good at communicating and teaching. Having photography and writing skills helps you prepare interesting educational materials.

Conservation Warden

What You'll Do: Patrol an area to enforce rules, and work with communities and groups to help educate the public about conservation and ecology.

Where You Might Work: Indoors and outdoors in state and national parks and ecologically sensitive areas

Education: A two-year associate's degree or at least 60 fully accredited college-level credits

Other Job Requirements: To work in the wild, good wilderness skills, map-reading, hiking, and excellent hearing are useful.

PEOPLE IN SCIENCE NEWS

Phil McCRORY

Saved by a Hair!

Phil McCrory, a hairdresser in Huntsville, Alabama, asked a brilliant question when he saw an otter whose fur was drenched with oil from the Exxon Valdez oil spill. If the otter's fur soaked up oil, why wouldn't human hair do the same? McCrory gathered hair from the floor of his salon and performed his own experiments. He stuffed hair into a pair of pantyhose and tied the ankles together. McCrory floated this bundle in his son's wading pool and poured used motor oil into the center of the ring. When he pulled the ring closed, not a drop of oil remained in the water! McCrory's discovery was tested as an alternative method for cleaning up oil spills. Many people donated their hair to be used for cleanup efforts. Although the method worked well, the engineers conducting the research concluded that hair is not as useful as other oil-absorbing materials for cleaning up large-scale spills.

Unit 1 People in Science 17

© Houghton Mifflin Harcourt Publishing Company • Image Credits: (bkgd) ©Willard Clay/Taxi/Getty Images; (tr) ©Dorling Kindersley/Getty Images; (bl) ©Dr. Kenneth Krysko
© Houghton Mifflin Harcourt Publishing Company • Image Credits: (bkgd) ©Willard Clay/Taxi/Getty Images; (br) ©Terry Fincher.Photo Int/Alamy

People in Science News

Have students conduct research to learn more about an oil spill such as the Exxon *Valdez* oil spill or Gulf oil spill. Encourage them to discover when, where, and why the spill occurred; what damage it caused to the local environment; what methods were used to clean it up; and what the lasting effects of the spill are.

Building Reading Skills

Suffixes Ask: What is the meaning of the suffix *-ist*? one who specializes in **Ask:** Using what you know about the meaning of the suffix *-ist*, what do *ecologist, biologist,* and *naturalist* mean? Sample answers: one who specializes in ecology; one who specializes in biology; one who specializes in the natural world

Optional Online resource: Suffixes support

Roles in Energy Transfer

Essential Question How does energy flow through an ecosystem?

 Professional Development

For more detailed information about the topics in this lesson, refer to the Content Refresher in the Unit Opener pages.

Opening Your Lesson

Begin the lesson by assessing students' prerequisite and prior knowledge.

Prerequisite Knowledge

- Basic needs of organisms
- Definitions of *species, population,* and *ecosystem*

Accessing Prior Knowledge

Ask: How do organisms get the energy they need for growth and other activities? Sample answers: through respiration; organisms break down food to release energy

Ask: How do animals get the food they need to carry out respiration? by eating other organisms

Ask: Where do plants get their food? They make it through photosynthesis.

Customize Your Opening

☐ **Accessing Prior Knowledge,** above

☐ **Print Path** Engage Your Brain, SE p. 19 #1–2

☐ **Print Path** Active Reading, SE p. 19 #3–4

☐ **Digital Path** Lesson Opener

Key Topics/Learning Goals	Supporting Concepts
Producers 1 Name life's energy source. 2 Explain how producers get energy. 3 Give examples of producers. 4 Define *photosynthesis*.	• The sun powers most life on Earth. • Producers use light energy to make food. • Plants, algae, and some bacteria are producers. • Photosynthesis is the process of using light energy to make food from water and CO_2.
Decomposers 1 Explain how decomposers get energy. 2 Give examples. 3 Describe their importance.	• Decomposers get energy by breaking down the remains of plants and animals. • Fungi and some bacteria are decomposers. • Decomposers return nutrients from the bodies of dead organisms to the environment.
Consumers 1 Explain how consumers get energy. 2 Compare and contrast types of consumers, and identify examples of each.	• Consumers get energy by eating other organisms. • Herbivores eat only plants. Carnivores eat only animals. Omnivores eat plants and animals.
Food Chains and Webs 1 Define *food chain, food web*. 2 Explain energy flow in a web and identify organisms in it. 3 Infer the consequences of removing an organism from a food web.	• A food chain is the path of energy transfer. A food web is the feeding relationships among organisms in an ecosystem. • Energy flows from producers to consumers. • When an organism is removed, the population size of organisms that it eats may increase and the population size of organisms that eat it may decrease.

Options for Instruction

Two parallel paths provide coverage of the Essential Questions, with a strong **Inquiry** strand woven into each.
Follow the **Print Path,** the **Digital Path,** or your customized combination of print, digital, and inquiry.

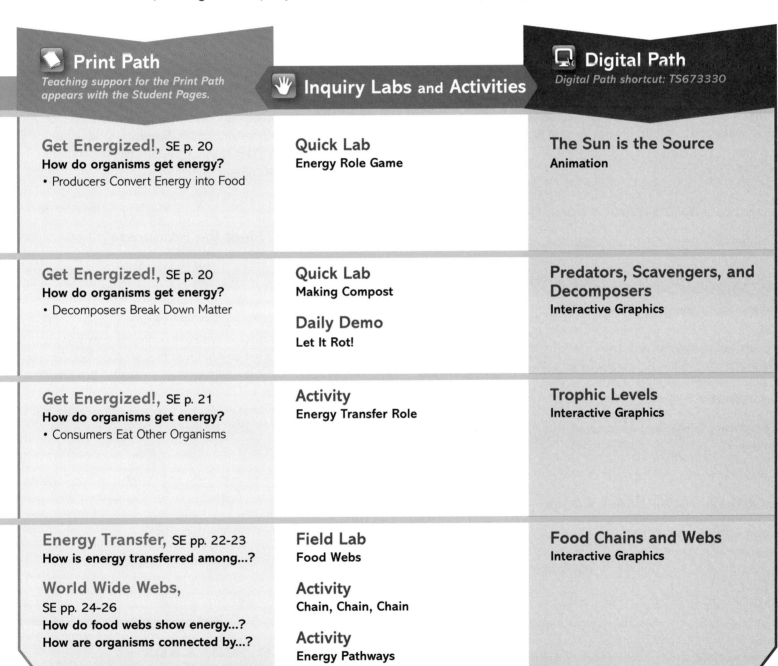

Print Path
Teaching support for the Print Path appears with the Student Pages.

Inquiry Labs and Activities

Digital Path
Digital Path shortcut: TS673330

Print Path	Inquiry Labs and Activities	Digital Path
Get Energized!, SE p. 20 **How do organisms get energy?** • Producers Convert Energy into Food	**Quick Lab** Energy Role Game	**The Sun is the Source** Animation
Get Energized!, SE p. 20 **How do organisms get energy?** • Decomposers Break Down Matter	**Quick Lab** Making Compost **Daily Demo** Let It Rot!	**Predators, Scavengers, and Decomposers** Interactive Graphics
Get Energized!, SE p. 21 **How do organisms get energy?** • Consumers Eat Other Organisms	**Activity** Energy Transfer Role	**Trophic Levels** Interactive Graphics
Energy Transfer, SE pp. 22-23 **How is energy transferred among...?** **World Wide Webs,** SE pp. 24-26 **How do food webs show energy...?** **How are organisms connected by...?**	**Field Lab** Food Webs **Activity** Chain, Chain, Chain **Activity** Energy Pathways	**Food Chains and Webs** Interactive Graphics

Options for Assessment

See the Evaluate page for options, including Formative Assessment, Summative Assessment, and Unit Review.

Engage and Explore

Activities and Discussion

Discussion *No Stomach, No Problem*

Decomposers

 whole class
🕐 15 min

Ask students where digestion occurs. In most organisms, digestion is internal. However, in fungi that act as decomposers, digestion takes place mostly externally when the fungi release enzymes that break down matter, then absorb nutrients through rootlike structures called *rhizoids*.

Take It Home *What's For Dinner?*

Consumers

 individuals
🕐 varies
 GUIDED inquiry

Students work with an adult to visit a pet shop or the homes of neighbors or relatives who have pets to find out what different kinds of pets eat; classify the pets as herbivore, carnivore, or omnivore. As an alternative, pairs can do Internet research or survey others for this information.

⊘ *Optional Online resource: student worksheet*

Activity *Chain, Chain, Chain*

Food Chains and Webs

 small groups
🕐 25–30 min
 GUIDED inquiry

Provide students with magazines or access to online resources that contain nature photos. Have students work in small groups to make two or three food chains using the pictures they find. They should label the feeding level of each organism as *producer, primary consumer, secondary consumer, tertiary consumer,* and *decomposer*. Advise students not to mix organisms from different ecosystems in their posters.

Activity *Energy Pathways*

Food Chains and Webs

 small groups
🕐 20–25 min
 DIRECTED inquiry

Divide the class into groups of five. Assign a role (producer, primary consumer, secondary consumer, tertiary consumer, or decomposer) to each group member. Give each group a ball, representing energy. Have students pass the ball around the group to model energy flow in a food chain. Discuss the path the energy takes.

Discussion *Meet the Producer*

Producers

 whole class
🕐 15 min

Display a potted plant and ask students how **the plant** gets food. it makes food by photosynthesis Point out to students that plants are called producers not only because they produce food for themselves, but also because they store the energy that feeds the whole food web.

Help students recall what plants need to carry out photosynthesis by writing a simple equation for photosynthesis on the board or an overhead transparency.

carbon dioxide + water + sunlight → glucose (food) + oxygen

©Getty Images

Customize Your Labs

 See the Lab Manual for lab datasheets.

 Go Online for editable lab datasheets.

Levels of **Inquiry**   **DIRECTED** inquiry   **GUIDED** inquiry   **INDEPENDENT** inquiry
introduces inquiry skills   develops inquiry skills   deepens inquiry skills
within a structured   within a supportive   with student-driven
framework.   environment.   questions or procedures.

Labs and Demos

Daily Demo *Let It Rot!*

Decomposers

👥 whole class
🕐 10 min
Inquiry **DIRECTED** inquiry

PURPOSE **To observe decomposers**

MATERIALS

• piece of moldy bread in sealed plastic bag

CAUTION **Do not allow students to open the sealed plastic bags.**

1 **Observing** Hold up the plastic bag containing the bread.
Ask: What do you see? mold growing on bread Explain to
students that the mold is an example of a fungus that acts
as a decomposer. Remind students that decomposers are
organisms that feed on the remains of other organisms and that
their activities return nutrients back to the environment in the
process. **Ask:** Why does the mold grow on the bread? Sample
answer: The bread provides the mold with food.

Quick Lab *Energy Role Game*

**Synthesizing Key
Topics**

👥 small groups
🕐 20 min
Inquiry **DIRECTED** inquiry

Students use clues to identify the energy roles and identities of
different organisms.

PURPOSE **To draw conclusions about how organisms obtain
energy from the environment**

MATERIALS

• descriptive clues (9)

• time

Field Lab *Food Webs*

**Food Chains
and Webs**

👥 small groups
🕐 one 20-min, two 45-min
periods
Inquiry **GUIDED** or **INDEPENDENT**
inquiry

Students conduct field research in a local natural area to identify local
food webs.

PURPOSE **To use observations to infer relationships among
producers, consumers, and decomposers**

MATERIALS

• binoculars

• camera

• field notebook

• local field guides

• magnifying lens

• markers, colored

• pencil (or pen)

• poster board

• protective gloves

• protective clothing

Quick Lab *Making Compost*

PURPOSE **To observe decomposition of organic waste**

See the Lab Manual or go Online for planning information.

Activities and Discussion

☐ **Discussion** No Stomach, No Problem

☐ **Take It Home** What's for Dinner?

☐ **Activity** Chain, Chain, Chain

☐ **Activity** Energy Pathways

☐ **Discussion** Meet the Producer

☐ **Labs and Demos**

☐ **Daily Demo** Let It Rot!

☐ **Quick Lab** Energy Role Game

☐ **Field Lab** Food Webs

☐ **Quick Lab** Making Compost

Your Resources

_____

_____

_____

Explain Science Concepts

<table>
<tr><th>Key Topics</th><th>📖 Print Path</th><th>🖥 Digital Path</th></tr>
<tr>
<td>Producers</td>
<td>

☐ **Get Energized!,** SE p. 20
- Think Outside the Book, #5
- Active Reading (Annotation strategy), #6

This plant is a producer. Producers make food using light energy from the sun.
</td>
<td>

☐ **The Sun is the Source**
Learn why the Sun is necessary for the survival of most organisms in an ecosystem.
</td>
</tr>
<tr>
<td>Decomposers</td>
<td>

☐ **Get Energized!,** SE p. 20
- Think Outside the Book, #5
- Active Reading (Annotation strategy), #6

These mushrooms are decomposers. They break down the remains of plants and animals.
</td>
<td>

☐ **Predators, Scavengers, and Decomposers**

Examine the role of predators, scavengers, and decomposers in an ecosystem.

</td>
</tr>
<tr>
<td>Consumers</td>
<td>

☐ **Get Energized!,** SE p. 21
- Visualize It!, #7
- Infer, #8

8 Infer Explain how carnivores might be affected if the main plant species in a community were to disappear.
</td>
<td>

☐ **Trophic Levels**
Explore the connection between producers and consumers (including primary, secondary, and tertiary consumers).

</td>
</tr>
<tr>
<td>Food Chains and Webs</td>
<td>

☐ **Energy Transfer,** SE pp. 22-23
- Active Reading, #9
- Visualize It!, #10–13

☐ **World Wide Webs,** SE pp. 24-26
- Active Reading (Annotation strategy), #14
- Visualize It!, #15
</td>
<td>

☐ **Food Chains and Webs**
Learn how food chains and food webs differ. Explore land and aquatic food webs and what can happen if a food web is disrupted.

</td>
</tr>
</table>

Differentiated Instruction

Basic *Classifying Organisms by Feeding Habits*

Producers, Decomposers, Consumers

 individuals or pairs

🕐 varied

Layered Book Have students make a Layered Book FoldNote that contains pictures or illustrations of organisms that represent producer, decomposer, herbivore, carnivore, and omnivore. Encourage students to provide captions for each illustration that indicate why each organism is classified as it is.

🌐 *Optional Online resource: Layered Book support*

Advanced *Predicting Impacts of Changing Food Webs*

Food Chains and Webs

 individuals

🕐 20 min

Have students study the food webs in this lesson. Assign the student one organism from each food web. Then ask the student to predict how removal of that organism from the ecosystem would affect other organisms in its food web.

ELL *Tracing Energy Flow in Food Chains*

Food Chains and Webs

 individuals

🕐 15 min

Sequence Diagram Encourage EL learners to make a sequence diagram to show how energy flows in an ecosystem via a food chain. Have students use these terms to complete their diagram: *producer, decomposer, primary consumer, secondary consumer.*

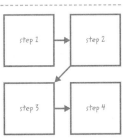

🌐 *Optional Online resource: Sequence Diagram support*

Lesson Vocabulary

energy	carnivore	decomposer
producer	omnivore	food chain
consumer		food web
herbivore		

Previewing Vocabulary

 whole class

🕐 10 min

Using Base Words Tell students that by understanding a word's base, they can better remember its meaning.
Consumer Discuss the base word *consume*, which means "to take in." Thus, a consumer is an organism that takes in its food.
Producer Underline the base word *produce*, and explain that it means "to make." A producer is an organism that makes food.

Reinforcing Vocabulary

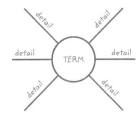 individuals

🕐 ongoing

Description Wheel Have students make Description Wheels for lesson terms.

🌐 *Optional Online resource: Description Wheel support*

Customize Your Core Lesson

Core Instruction
- ☐ **Print Path** choices
- ☐ **Digital Path** choices

Vocabulary
- ☐ **Previewing Vocabulary** Using Base Words
- ☐ **Reinforcing Vocabulary** Description Wheel

Your Resources

Differentiated Instruction
- ☐ **Basic** Classifying Organisms by Feeding Habits
- ☐ **Advanced** Predicting Impacts of Changing Food Webs
- ☐ **ELL** Tracing Energy Flow in Food Chains

Extend Science Concepts

Reinforce and Review

Activity *Energy Transfer Roles*

Synthesizing Key Topics

 whole class
🕐 30 min

Inside/Outside Circles

1 Give each student an index card with a question written on one side. Have them write an answer for the question on the back of the card.

2 Check student answers to make sure they are correct. Allow students time to adjust incorrect answers.

3 Have students pair up to form two circles, one inner and one outer. The circles face each other.

4 Have the student on the inside circle ask his or her partner the question and allow the partner to respond. If the answer is incorrect, have the student who asked the question teach his or her partner the correct answer. Repeat with the outside-circle students asking questions.

5 Have each student on the outside circle rotate one person to the right and then ask the new partner the question. Continue repeating steps 4 and 5 until all students on the outside circle have answered all the questions.

Graphic Organizer

Synthesizing Key Topics

 individuals
🕐 15 min

Cluster Diagram After students have read the lesson, ask them to make a cluster diagram that uses these terms: *producer, consumer, primary consumer, secondary consumer, herbivore, carnivore, omnivore, scavenger,* and *decomposer.*

main idea
key topic
key topic
detail
detail
detail
detail

⊘ *Optional Online resource: Cluster Diagram*

Going Further

Earth Science Connection

Synthesizing Key Topics

 whole class
🕐 15 min

Discussion Oil, coal, and natural gas are examples of fossil fuels. Fossil fuels have formed from the remains of plants and animals that were buried under sediments millions of years ago. The chemical energy stored in fossil fuels originated as light energy from the sun. Discuss with students how the sun's energy from millions of years ago provides the energy that is used today to heat homes and power cars.

Mathematics Connection

Synthesizing Key Topics

 whole class
🕐 15 min

Making Calculations Food energy in an ecosystem is measured in kilocalories. As energy moves from one feeding level to the next, only some of the energy that existed in the original organism is passed on. This occurs because organisms use some of the energy they take in or release it into the environment as heat. Scientists estimate that 90% of the energy is lost between one feeding level and the next. Have students calculate how much energy is available to primary consumers if the producers contain 12,000 kilocalories of energy. 1,200 kilocalories **Ask:** How much energy will be available to the secondary consumers? 120 kilocalories

Customize Your Closing

🗨 *See the Assessment Guide for quizzes and tests.*

⊘ *Go Online to edit and create quizzes and tests.*

Reinforce and Review

☐ **Activity** Energy Transfer Roles

☐ **Graphic Organizer** Cluster Diagram

☐ **Print Path** Visual Summary, SE p. 28

☐ **Digital Path** Lesson Closer

Evaluate Student Mastery

Formative Assessment

See the teacher support below the Student Pages for additional Formative Assessment questions.

Have students look back to the food chain and food web they have seen during the lesson. **Ask:** What is the relationship between food chains and food webs? Food chains show the transfer of energy from one organism to another in an ecosystem. Food webs show the transfer of energy through overlapping food chains within an ecosystem.

Reteach

Formative assessment may show that students need reinforcement for certain topics. The resources below are recommended for reteaching. If students were introduced to a topic through the Print Path, you can also use the Digital Path to reteach, and vice versa.
🎧 *Can be assigned to individual students.*

Producers
Discussion Meet the Producer

Basic Classifying Organisms by Feeding Habits 🎧

Decomposers
Discussion No Stomach, No Problem

Daily Demo Let It Rot! 🎧

Consumers
Take It Home What's for Dinner?

Food Chains and Webs
Activity Chain, Chain, Chain 🎧

Activity Energy Pathways

Summative Assessment

Alternative Assessment
Energy Transfer

🔘 *Online resources: student worksheet, optional rubrics*

Roles in Energy Transfer

Choose Your Meal: *Energy Transfer*
Complete the activities to show what you've learned about energy transfer.

1. Work on your own, with a partner, or with a small group.

2. Choose one item from each section of the menu, with an optional dessert. Check your choices.

3. Have your teacher approve your plan.

4. Submit or present your results.

Appetizers

_____ **Guess the Consumer** Play a game in which you identify types of consumers. On index cards, draw pictures of consumers. On the backs of the cards, list things the organisms eat. Ask classmates to identify each consumer. If your classmates need help, read the animal's diet from the card.

_____ **Local Food Webs** Think about one local area. Make a diagram of the food web in this area. Identify each of the organisms as a producer, consumer, or decomposer.

_____ **Promoting Producers** Make a commercial in which you promote producers. Explain how producers make their own food and get energy. Also explain why producers are vital to their ecosystems. Give three examples of producers.

Main Dish

_____ **A Link in the Chain** Choose one food that you eat, and draw a food chain that shows how you receive energy from that food.

Side Dishes

_____ **How Will It Change?** Find an image of a food web that includes an endangered species. Cross out the endangered species and consider how the food web would change without that organism.

_____ **Defending Decomposers** Imagine that you are a decomposer. You believe that decomposers do not get enough respect for what they do in ecosystems. Present a persuasive speech in which you describe decomposers' roles and the reasons that they are important in their ecosystems.

Desserts (optional)

_____ **Concentrating on Consumers** In a group, discuss the three types of consumers. Describe each animal's diet and how they get energy.

_____ **A Producer's Blog** You are a producer. Write a blog entry explaining how you make your own food and the role you play in food chains and webs.

Going Further
☐ Earth Science Connection
☐ Mathematics Connection
☐ **Print Path** Why It Matters, SE p. 27

Formative Assessment
☐ **Strategies** Throughout TE
☐ **Lesson Review** SE

Summative Assessment
☐ **Alternative Assessment** Energy Transfer
☐ **Lesson Quiz**
☐ **Unit Tests A and B**
☐ **Unit Review** SE End-of-Unit

Your Resources

_____   _____

_____   _____

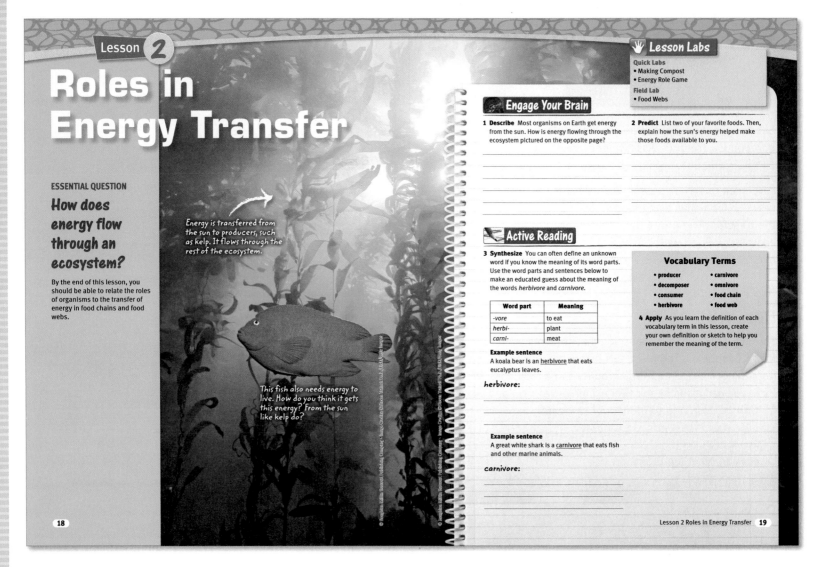

Answers

Answers for 1–3 should represent students' current thoughts, even if incorrect.

1. Energy flows from plants to the rest of the organisms in the ecosystem that eat the plants.

2. Answer should indicate that the sun provides energy for photosynthesis for a plant to make food, which either the student eats or some chain of animals eats and the student eats the last animal of the chain.

3. Students' sentences should indicate that herbivores eat plants and that carnivores eat meat.

4. Students should define or sketch each vocabulary term in the lesson.

Opening Your Lesson

Discuss student responses to the Engage Your Brain questions to assess students' prior knowledge about key topics.

Prerequisites Students should know that a species is defined as a group of organisms with similar characteristics that can mate and produce fertile offspring; a population consists of all the members of a species that live in the same place and time; and that an ecosystem consists of a community of organisms and their abiotic surroundings.

Learning Alert

Chemosynthesis Not all producers make food through photosynthesis. Scientists have discovered communities of organisms living deep in the ocean near hydrothermal vents. Bacteria that carry out chemosynthesis serve as the producers for this community. In the absence of sunlight, these bacteria use chemicals rising through the vent to provide the energy that drives the food-making process. As in other ecosystems, the energy contained in the food made by these bacteria is then passed through the food chain to other populations within the community.

Get Energized!

How do organisms get energy?

Energy is all around you. Chemical energy is stored in the bonds of molecules and holds molecules together. The energy from food is chemical energy in the bonds of food molecules. All living things need a source of chemical energy to survive.

Think Outside the Book

5 Apply Record what you eat at your next meal. Where do you think these items come from, before they reach the market?

Active Reading 6 Identify As you read, underline examples of producers, decomposers, and consumers.

Producers Convert Energy Into Food

A **producer**, also called an autotroph, uses energy to make food. Most producers use sunlight to make food in a process called photosynthesis. The sun powers most life on Earth. In photosynthesis, producers use light energy to make food from water, carbon dioxide, and nutrients found in water and soil. The food contains chemical energy and can be used immediately or stored for later use. All green plants, such as grasses and trees, are producers. Algae and some bacteria are also producers. The food that these producers make supplies the energy for other living things in an ecosystem.

This plant is a producer. Producers make food using light energy from the sun.

Decomposers Break Down Matter

An organism that gets energy and nutrients by breaking down the remains of other organisms is a **decomposer**. Fungi, such as the mushrooms on this log, and some bacteria are decomposers. Decomposers are nature's recyclers. By converting dead organisms and animal and plant waste into materials such as water and nutrients, decomposers help move matter through ecosystems. Decomposers make these simple materials available to other organisms.

These mushrooms are decomposers. They break down the remains of plants and animals.

Consumers Eat Other Organisms

A **consumer** is an organism that eats other organisms. Consumers use the energy and nutrients stored in other living organisms because they cannot make their own food. A consumer that eats only plants, such as a grasshopper or bison, is called an **herbivore**. A **carnivore**, such as a badger or this wolf, eats other animals. An **omnivore** eats both plants and animals. A *scavenger* is a specialized consumer that feeds on dead organisms. Scavengers, such as the turkey vulture, eat the leftovers of the meals of other animals or eat dead animals.

This wolf is a consumer. It eats other organisms to get energy.

Consumers

Visualize It!

7 List Beside each image, place a check mark next to the word that matches the type of consumer the animal is.

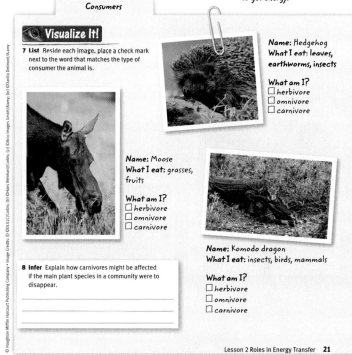

Name: Hedgehog
What I eat: leaves, earthworms, insects

What am I?
☐ herbivore
☐ omnivore
☐ carnivore

Name: Moose
What I eat: grasses, fruits

What am I?
☐ herbivore
☐ omnivore
☐ carnivore

Name: Komodo dragon
What I eat: insects, birds, mammals

What am I?
☐ herbivore
☐ omnivore
☐ carnivore

8 Infer Explain how carnivores might be affected if the main plant species in a community were to disappear.

_____

_____

_____

Answers

5. Students' answers should indicate that the food they eat comes from an animal or a farm, or another reasonable source.

6. See students' pages for annotations.

7. moose = herbivore; hedgehog = omnivore; komodo dragon = carnivore

8. If plant species disappeared, many of the consumers that eat the plants (herbivores and omnivores) would also disappear, and the carnivores would have less food to eat.

Building Reading Skills

Main Idea and Details Provide students with the main idea web graphic organizer. As they read, they can complete the organizer with details that support each main idea.

🔘 *Optional Online resource: Main Idea Web support*

Learning Alert ⚠ MISCONCEPTION ⚠

Omnivores Students often misclassify omnivores based on the type of food they eat at a given time. For example, students may think a bear is an herbivore when it eats berries and a carnivore when it feeds on animals such as rabbits, squirrels, and fish. Explain that a black bear is always an omnivore regardless of what type of food it is eating at any given time. Its classification does not change based upon its immediate feeding habits.

Probing Questions DIRECTED Inquiry

Contrasting Scavengers and decomposers both feed on dead animals. How do the two types of organisms differ? Scavengers get food and energy by eating other animals that are dead; decomposers get food and energy by breaking down the remains of other organisms.

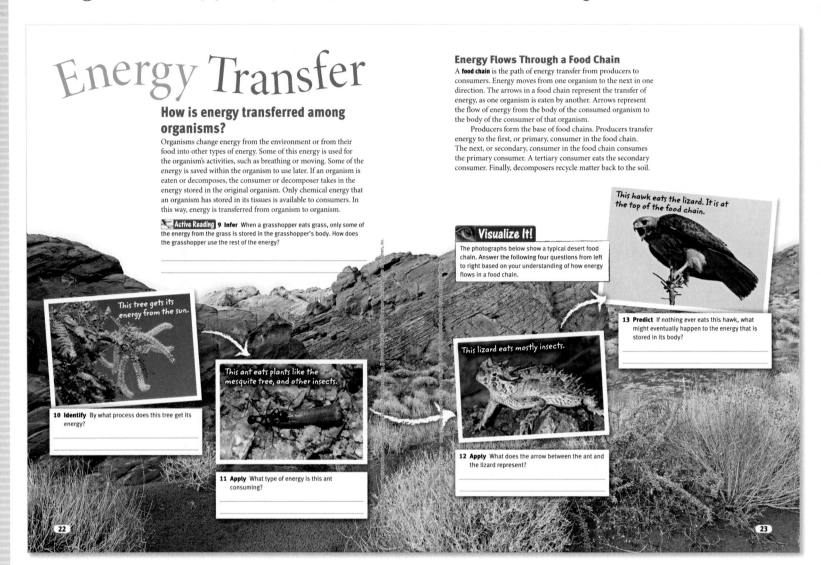

Energy Transfer

How is energy transferred among organisms?

Organisms change energy from the environment or from their food into other types of energy. Some of this energy is used for the organism's activities, such as breathing or moving. Some of the energy is saved within the organism to use later. If an organism is eaten or decomposes, the consumer or decomposer takes in the energy stored in the original organism. Only chemical energy that an organism has stored in its tissues is available to consumers. In this way, energy is transferred from organism to organism.

Active Reading 9 **Infer** When a grasshopper eats grass, only some of the energy from the grass is stored in the grasshopper's body. How does the grasshopper use the rest of the energy?

_____

_____

This tree gets its energy from the sun.

10 Identify By what process does this tree get its energy?

_____

This ant eats plants like the mesquite tree, and other insects.

11 Apply What type of energy is this ant consuming?

_____

_____

Energy Flows Through a Food Chain

A **food chain** is the path of energy transfer from producers to consumers. Energy moves from one organism to the next in one direction. The arrows in a food chain represent the transfer of energy, as one organism is eaten by another. Arrows represent the flow of energy from the body of the consumed organism to the body of the consumer of that organism.

Producers form the base of food chains. Producers transfer energy to the first, or primary, consumer in the food chain. The next, or secondary, consumer in the food chain consumes the primary consumer. A tertiary consumer eats the secondary consumer. Finally, decomposers recycle matter back to the soil.

Visualize It!

The photographs below show a typical desert food chain. Answer the following four questions from left to right based on your understanding of how energy flows in a food chain.

This hawk eats the lizard. It is at the top of the food chain.

13 Predict If nothing ever eats this hawk, what might eventually happen to the energy that is stored in its body?

_____

This lizard eats mostly insects.

12 Apply What does the arrow between the ant and the lizard represent?

_____

_____

22

23

Answers

9. The rest of the energy is used for activities, such as hopping.

10. photosynthesis

11. chemical energy

12. The arrow represents the flow of energy from the ant to the lizard.

13. The energy will get consumed by scavengers or get broken down by decomposers.

Learning Alert

Decomposers in Food Chains and Webs Decomposers are often not drawn in food chains and food webs. However, these vital organisms are present in all ecosystems; students should assume they are always part of the energy transfer and feeding relationships in an ecosystem.

Interpreting Visuals

Help students interpret the food chain by asking these questions. **Ask:**

• What do the arrows in the food chain show? movement of energy
• A primary consumer feeds on a producer. What are some other names for consumers that feed on plants? herbivore, omnivore
• What group of organisms is not shown in the food chain? decomposers

Probing Questions   DIRECTED (Inquiry)

Analyzing What is the lowest possible feeding level that can be occupied by a carnivore in a food chain? secondary consumer

World Wide Webs

How do food webs show energy connections?

Active Reading

14 Identify Underline the type of organism that typically forms the base of the food web.

Few organisms eat just one kind of food. So, the energy and nutrient connections in nature are more complicated than a simple food chain. A **food web** is the feeding relationships among organisms in an ecosystem. Food webs are made up of many food chains.

The next page shows a coastal food web. Most of the organisms in this food web live in the water. The web also includes some birds that live on land and eat fish. Tiny algae called phytoplankton form the base of this food web. Like plants on land, phytoplankton are producers. Tiny consumers called zooplankton eat phytoplankton. Larger animals, such as fish and squid, eat zooplankton. At the top of each chain are top predators, animals that eat other animals but are rarely eaten. In this food web, the killer whale is a top predator. Notice how many different energy paths lead from phytoplankton to the killer whale.

Visualize It!

15 Apply Complete the statements to the right with the correct organism names from the food web.

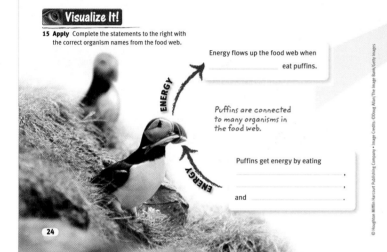

Energy flows up the food web when _____ eat puffins.

Puffins are connected to many organisms in the food web.

Puffins get energy by eating

_____ ,

_____ ,

and _____ .

ENERGY

24

Food Web

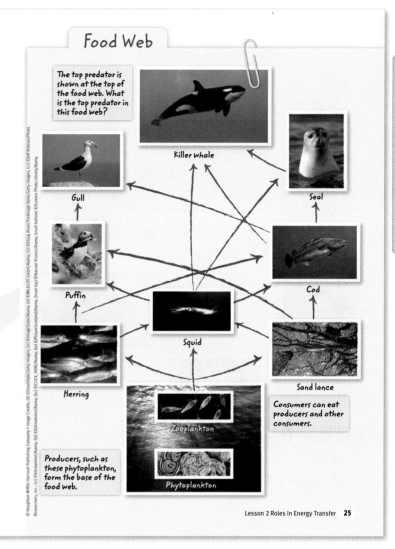

The top predator is shown at the top of the food web. What is the top predator in this food web?

Killer whale

Gull

Seal

Puffin

Cod

Squid

Herring

Sand lance

Consumers can eat producers and other consumers.

Zooplankton

Producers, such as these phytoplankton, form the base of the food web.

Phytoplankton

Answers

14. *See students' pages for annotations.*
15. gulls; herring, squid, sand lances

Learning Alert ⚠ MISCONCEPTION ⚠

Students sometimes think that organisms at higher feeding levels in a food web eat everything that is lower on the chain. Using an example from the food web shown, point out to students that each organism in a food web eats only certain kinds of organisms that feed at lower levels. For example, the gull shown, a black backed gull, does not eat herring. It does, however, eat cod, which do feed on herring.

Interpreting Visuals

To help students interpret the food web, ask:

- What organisms shown feed on squid? cod, puffin, seal, killer whale
- Why are there no arrows pointing away from the killer whale? There are no arrows because the killer whale is the top predator and does not serve as a food source for other organisms in this ecosystem.

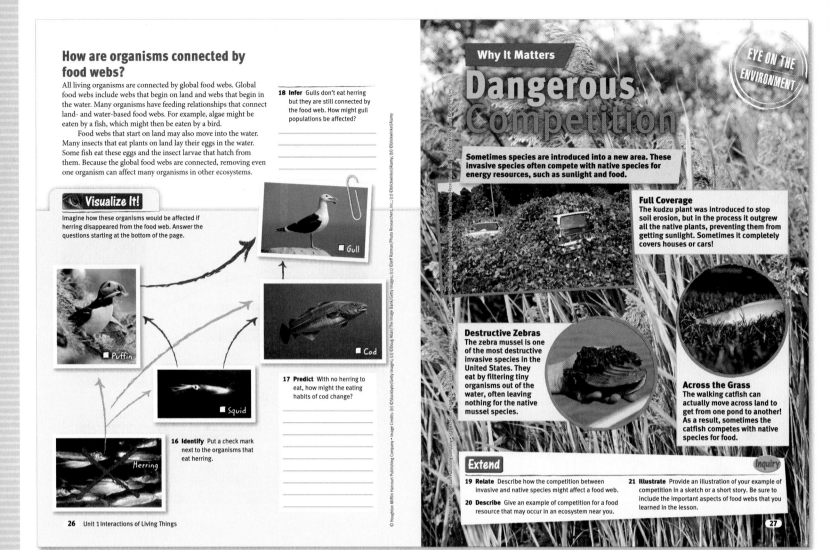

How are organisms connected by food webs?

All living organisms are connected by global food webs. Global food webs include webs that begin on land and webs that begin in the water. Many organisms have feeding relationships that connect land- and water-based food webs. For example, algae might be eaten by a fish, which might then be eaten by a bird.

Food webs that start on land may also move into the water. Many insects that eat plants on land lay their eggs in the water. Some fish eat these eggs and the insect larvae that hatch from them. Because the global food webs are connected, removing even one organism can affect many organisms in other ecosystems.

18 Infer Gulls don't eat herring but they are still connected by the food web. How might gull populations be affected?

Visualize It!

Imagine how these organisms would be affected if herring disappeared from the food web. Answer the questions starting at the bottom of the page.

☐ Gull

☐ Cod

☐ Squid

☐ Puffin

Herring

17 Predict With no herring to eat, how might the eating habits of cod change?

16 Identify Put a check mark next to the organisms that eat herring.

26 Unit 1 Interactions of Living Things

Why It Matters

Dangerous Competition

EYE ON THE ENVIRONMENT

Sometimes species are introduced into a new area. These invasive species often compete with native species for energy resources, such as sunlight and food.

Full Coverage
The kudzu plant was introduced to stop soil erosion, but in the process it outgrew all the native plants, preventing them from getting sunlight. Sometimes it completely covers houses or cars!

Destructive Zebras
The zebra mussel is one of the most destructive invasive species in the United States. They eat by filtering tiny organisms out of the water, often leaving nothing for the native mussel species.

Across the Grass
The walking catfish can actually move across land to get from one pond to another! As a result, sometimes the catfish competes with native species for food.

Extend

Inquiry

19 Relate Describe how the competition between invasive and native species might affect a food web.

20 Describe Give an example of competition for a food resource that may occur in an ecosystem near you.

21 Illustrate Provide an illustration of your example of competition in a sketch or a short story. Be sure to include the important aspects of food webs that you learned in the lesson.

27

Answers

16. Check marks should be next to images of puffins, squid, and cod.

17. Cod would have to find another food source. They would eat more squid.

18. Gulls eat puffins and cod, which feed on herring. Gull populations might decline because their food supply would be reduced.

19. Competition might affect a food web by eliminating the food resources of important parts of the food web.

20. Students' answers should reflect the definition of competition for food resources.

21. Students' drawings should include aspects of food webs described in the lesson.

Formative Assessment

Have students identify three food chains that are part of the food web shown. In each, have students label the organisms as producer; primary, secondary, or tertiary consumer; and as carnivores or omnivores.

Why It Matters

Introduced species, which are brought to an ecosystem by human activity, can disrupt feeding relationships because they may compete with native species for food, or they may prey on the native species themselves.

Visual Summary

To complete this summary, circle the correct word. Then use the key below to check your answers. You can use this page to review the main concepts of the lesson.

Energy Transfer
in Ecosystems

Organisms get energy in different ways.

• Producers make their own food.
• Consumers eat other living organisms.
• Decomposers break down dead organisms.

22 Herbivores, carnivores, and omnivores are three types of producers / consumers / decomposers.

Food chains and food webs describe the flow of energy in an ecosystem.

23 All food chains start with producers / consumers / decomposers.

Answers: 22 consumers, 23 producers

24 Predict Describe the effects on global food webs if the sun's energy could no longer reach Earth.

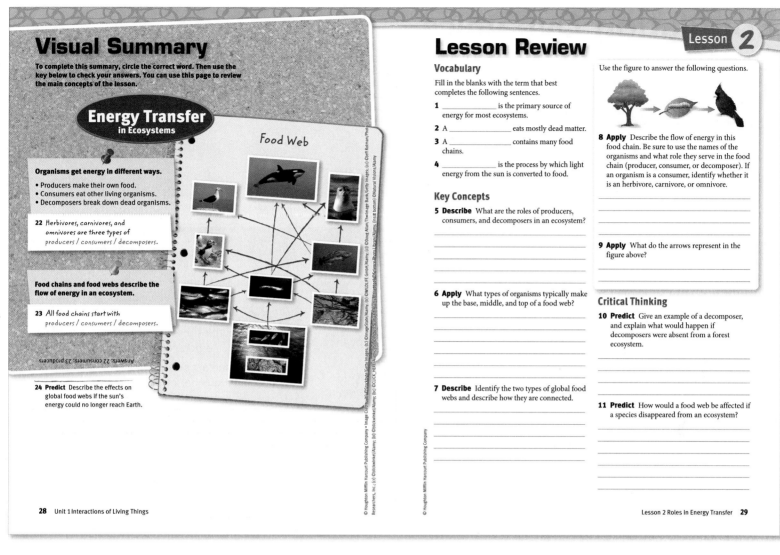

Food Web

© Houghton Mifflin Harcourt Publishing Company • Image Credits: (t) ©Stockbyte/Getty Images; (tc) ©ImageState/Alamy; (c) ©Jeff Rotman/Photo Researchers, Inc.; (cr) ©blickwinkel/Alamy; (bl) ©blickwinkel/Alamy; (br) ©Doug Allan/The Image Bank/Getty Images; (cl) ©WILDLIFE GmbH/Alamy; (insb) ©Chris Newbert/Minden Pictures; (insc) ©Brandon Cole Marine Photography/Alamy; (inst) ©Visual&Written SL/Alamy; (insd bottom) ©Natural Visions/Alamy

---

Lesson Review

Lesson 2

Vocabulary

Fill in the blanks with the term that best completes the following sentences.

1 _____ is the primary source of energy for most ecosystems.

2 A _____ eats mostly dead matter.

3 A _____ contains many food chains.

4 _____ is the process by which light energy from the sun is converted to food.

Key Concepts

5 Describe What are the roles of producers, consumers, and decomposers in an ecosystem?

6 Apply What types of organisms typically make up the base, middle, and top of a food web?

7 Describe Identify the two types of global food webs and describe how they are connected.

Use the figure to answer the following questions.

8 Apply Describe the flow of energy in this food chain. Be sure to use the names of the organisms and what role they serve in the food chain (producer, consumer, or decomposer). If an organism is a consumer, identify whether it is an herbivore, carnivore, or omnivore.

9 Apply What do the arrows represent in the figure above?

Critical Thinking

10 Predict Give an example of a decomposer, and explain what would happen if decomposers were absent from a forest ecosystem.

11 Predict How would a food web be affected if a species disappeared from an ecosystem?

© Houghton Mifflin Harcourt Publishing Company

Visual Summary Answers

22. consumers

23. producers

24. Producers would die, and the food web would break down.

Lesson Review Answers

1. The sun

2. decomposer or scavenger

3. food web

4. Photosynthesis

5. Producers make food from the sun. Consumers eat producers or other consumers. Decomposers break down dead material and recycle it so it can be used by producers to make food.

6. Producers form the base of food webs. Primary and secondary consumers make up the middle of food webs. Tertiary consumers (top predators) make up the top of food webs.

7. Global food webs include those that begin on land and those that begin in the water. They are connected by organisms that spend time in both land and water.

8. The energy from the sun is used to make food by producers. That energy is consumed by a consumer. Whatever energy is not used is consumed by another consumer. The energy that is not used by the end of the food chain is broken down by decomposers so it can be used, along with more solar energy, by producers to make food.

9. The arrows represent the flow of energy in the food chain.

10. Sample answer: fungi; Dead matter would not get recycled into needed nutrients for producers, and dead plant matter would pile up.

11. Sample answer: The food web might be changed greatly if a species disappeared from an ecosystem. The organisms that fed on that species would have to find new sources of energy.

Population Dynamics

Essential Question What determines a population's size?

 Professional Development

For more detailed information about the topics in this lesson, refer to the Content Refresher in the Unit Opener pages.

Opening Your Lesson

Begin the lesson by assessing students' prerequisite and prior knowledge.

Prerequisite Knowledge

- Definition of *population*
- Definition of *species*
- Understanding of biotic and abiotic factors

Accessing Prior Knowledge

Invite students to make a tri-fold FoldNote KWL chart about how plants and animals may depend on each other to survive in an environment. Have students put what they know in the first column, what they want to know in the second column. After they have finished the lesson, they can complete the third column with what they learned.

🌐 *Optional Online resource: KWL support*

Customize Your Opening

- ☐ **Accessing Prior Knowledge,** above
- ☐ **Print Path** Engage Your Brain, SE p. 31 #1–2
- ☐ **Print Path** Active Reading, SE p. 31 #3–4
- ☐ **Digital Path** Lesson Opener

Key Topics/Learning Goals

Size of Populations

1 Describe factors that increase or decrease population size.
2 Relate population growth to available resources.
3 Explain how the carrying capacity can change when the environment changes.
4 Provide examples of what can cause a population crash.

Populations and Limiting Factors

1 Explain how limiting factors limit the size of a population.
2 Provide examples of biotic and abiotic limiting factors.

Interactions within Populations

1 Describe how members of a population may interact with each other.
2 Explain how social hierarchy can influence a population.

Supporting Concepts

- Populations increase when individuals are born or move into it (immigrate) and decrease when they leave (emigrate) or die.
- The amount of resources available determines a population's growth rate.
- An environment's carrying capacity, or the maximum number of individuals of a given species it can support, can change.
- A dramatic decrease in population is called a crash. Harsh weather, lack of food or water, competition from exotic species, or a new predator can cause a population to crash.

- A limiting factor is an environmental factor that limits the growth of a population.
- Limiting factors can be biotic (living) or abiotic (nonliving).
- Biotic limiting factors include food availability, predation, and disease.
- Abiotic limiting factors include water, light, nutrients, living space, unusual weather, and natural disasters.

- Competition occurs when individuals attempt to obtain the same limited resource. It may occur within a species or between species.
- Cooperation occurs when individuals work in a way that benefits them all.
- Some populations, such as bees, have social hierarchies, which prescribe different roles.

Options for Instruction

Two parallel paths provide coverage of the Essential Questions, with a strong **Inquiry** strand woven into each. Follow the **Print Path,** the **Digital Path,** or your customized combination of print, digital, and inquiry.

 **Print Path**
Teaching support for the Print Path appears with the Student Pages.

 Inquiry Labs and Activities

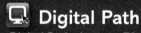 **Digital Path**
Digital Path shortcut: TS673352

Movin' Out,
SE pp. 32–33
How can a population grow or get smaller?
- By Immigration and Emigration
- By Birth and Death

Quick Lab
What Factors Influence a Population Change?

Resources Meet Needs
Video

Carrying Capacity
Graphic Sequence

Know Your Limits, SE pp. 34–35
What environmental factors influence population size?
- Resource Availability
- Changes in the Environment

Maximum Capacity, SE p. 36
What factors can limit population size?
- Abiotic Factors
- Biotic Factors

Daily Demo
When the Going Gets Tough

Quick Lab
Investigate an Abiotic Limiting Factor

Biotic Limiting Factors
Interactive Graphics

Abiotic Limiting Factors
Interactive Images

Teamwork, SE pp. 38–39
What interactions between organisms can influence population size?
- Competition
- Cooperation

Activity
Interaction Poster

Exploration Lab
How Do Populations Interact?

Competition
Slideshow

Cooperation
Interactive Graphics

Options for Assessment

See the Evaluate page for options, including Formative Assessment, Summative Assessment, and Unit Review.

Engage and Explore

Activities and Discussion

Probing Questions *The Local Population*

Engage

Introducing Key Topics

whole class
10 min
GUIDED inquiry

Ask: What populations of animals live in our area? Mice, mosquitoes, rabbits, deer, crows, and trout live in our area.

Ask: Would a population of rabbits increase or decrease if each adult female produced six young per year? increase

Ask: What if four of the six offspring died before reaching adulthood? Would the population increase or decrease? It would still increase, but more slowly.

Ask: What is an example of how a population might change, but at a slower rate? Sample answer: If an organism lives a very long life and reproduces slowly.

Discussion *Biotic or Abiotic?*

Populations and Limiting Factors

adult-student pairs
ongoing
GUIDED inquiry

Tell students that both living and nonliving things affect populations. Tell groups to choose an animal population that they know something about. Then have them list living things that affect the animals' ability to survive. food, predators, trees for shelter, and disease-carrying organisms Next, have them list nonliving things that affect the animals' ability to survive. availability of water, space, weather conditions, natural disasters, and so on When students are finished, have a volunteer from each group share the group's ideas.

Activity *Interaction Poster*

Interactions within Populations

individuals or pairs
ongoing
GUIDED inquiry

Have students work together to make a poster that shows how animals (or plants) can work together to help each other survive or how animals can compete with each other to survive. Students should include a title for their poster, and indicate how the organisms interact and who benefits from the interaction. When students are finished, display the posters and discuss students' ideas about the interactions of organisms.

Take It Home *Plants and Animals*

Populations and Limiting Factors

adult-student pairs
ongoing
GUIDED inquiry

Students and adults work together to list plants and animals that live near their home. Pairs can walk around outside and list all of the plants and animals they see. Then they can categorize organisms by whether they are plants or animals. They can also try to observe what each animal and plant needs to survive. For example, a squirrel might eat nuts, while grass and trees need sunlight and water, as well as room to grow.

Customize Your Labs

 See the Lab Manual for lab datasheets.

 Go Online for editable lab datasheets.

Levels of **Inquiry**   **DIRECTED** inquiry   **GUIDED** inquiry   **INDEPENDENT** inquiry

introduces inquiry skills   develops inquiry skills   deepens inquiry skills
within a structured   within a supportive   with student-driven
framework.   environment.   questions or procedures.

Labs and Demos

Daily Demo *When the Going Gets Tough*

Engage

Populations and Limiting Factors

 whole class
🕐 10 min
Inquiry GUIDED inquiry

You will need three egg cartons (18-, 12-, and 6-cup size) and 18 marshmallows or cotton balls. Display for students the 18-cup egg carton. Point out that each cup represents a resource, such as shelter. Place a marshmallow or cotton ball in each cup. Note that the population of organisms, which are modeled by the marshmallows or cotton balls, is fully utilizing the available shelter.

Next, display the 12-cup carton. Explain to students that a storm has blown through and destroyed a third of the available shelter. Move the marshmallows or cotton balls from the larger carton to this smaller one and ask what the result of the storm has been. Six organisms no longer have shelter. What do students think will happen to the displaced organisms? They will probably die or emigrate elsewhere.

Last, show a 6-cup carton. Explain that a flood came and destroyed half of the remaining shelter. Move the marshmallows or cotton balls into the smaller egg carton. What has happened to the original population due to the weather conditions and the natural disaster? It has been reduced by two-thirds.

Ask: What would happen if the marshmallows shared the cups? They would compete, perhaps even fight, and one would either die or be forced to leave.

©C. Lee/PhotoLink/Getty Images

Quick Lab *What Factors Influence a Population Change?*

Size of Populations

 small groups
🕐 15 min
Inquiry DIRECTED inquiry

Students investigate how a wolf population changes over 10 years.

Quick Lab *Investigate an Abiotic Limiting Factor*

Populations and Limiting Factors

 individuals
🕐 15 min
Inquiry INDEPENDENT inquiry

Students design an experiment to investigate a limiting factor.

Exploration Lab *How Do Populations Interact?*

Interactions within Populations

 small groups
🕐 45 min
Inquiry DIRECTED or GUIDED inquiry

Students explore ways populations interact.

See the Lab Manual or go Online for planning information.

Activities and Discussion

☐ **Probing Questions** The Local Population

☐ **Discussion** Biotic or Abiotic?

☐ **Activity** Interaction Poster

☐ **Take It Home** Plants and Animals

Labs and Demos

☐ **Daily Demo** When Going Gets Tough

☐ **Quick Lab** Factors... Pop. Change?

☐ **Quick Lab** Investigate... Factor

☐ **Exploration Lab** How Do Populations Interact?

Your Resources

_____

_____

Explain Science Concepts

Key Topics	 Print Path	🖥 Digital Path
Size of Populations	☐ **Movin' Out,** SE pp. 32–33 • Active Reading (Annotation strategy), #5 • Visualize It!, #6 • Visualize It!, #7 	☐ **Resources Meet Needs** Explore the effects of resource availability on a population. ☐ **Carrying Capacity** Investigate carrying capacity. 
Populations and Limiting Factors	☐ **Know Your Limits,** SE pp. 34–35 • Visualize It!, #8 • Active Reading, #9 • Think Outside the Book, #10 ☐ **Maximum Capacity,** SE p. 36 • Apply, #11 • Visualize It!, #12 	☐ **Biotic Limiting Factors** Identify three biotic limiting factors. ☐ **Abiotic Limiting Factors** Identify six abiotic limiting factors. 
Interactions Within Populations	☐ **Teamwork,** SE pp. 38–39 • Visualize It!, #16 • Active Reading (Annotation strategy), #17 • Compare, #18 	☐ **Competition** Explore the causes of competition. ☐ **Cooperation** Study cooperation. 

Differentiated Instruction

Basic *Modeling Populations*

Size of Populations

 pairs or small groups
🕐 10 min

Modeling Have student pairs use beans or counters to show increases or decreases to a population of animals over the four seasons. Invite them to show what happens when offspring are born, when animals die, when food is easy to find, and when it is hard to find. Invite students to explain to a partner why the population increases or decreases each season.

Advanced *Graphing Change in Populations*

Synthesizing Key Topics

 individuals or pairs
🕐 15 min

Invite students to make a graph showing how a population of animals or plants changes during the course of a year. Encourage students to think of as many factors affecting a population as they can (including births, deaths, immigration, emigration, carrying capacity, food availability, predation, disease, water, light, nutrients, living space, weather conditions, and natural disasters). Once students have considered how all of these factors affect the population at different times of the year, have them develop the graph. When they have finished, invite students to share their ideas with the class.

ELL *Population Diagrams*

Populations and Limiting Factors

 individuals or pairs
🕐 15 min

Direct students to draw a chart or diagram that shows how a population of animals is affected by factors such as food availability, predators, or climate. Encourage students to use labels, arrows, or numbers to clearly explain what happens to the population over time.

Lesson Vocabulary

carrying capacity   immigration   emigration
limiting factor   competition   cooperation

Previewing Vocabulary

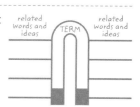 whole class   🕐 10 min

Suffixes Remind students that the suffix *-tion* means "the act of." When they encounter a word ending in *-tion*, they should ask themselves what the base word means.

- For example, **immigration** is formed from the base word *immigrate*. *Immigrate* means "to come in to a place," so *immigration* is "the act of coming to a place."
- **Emigration** refers to the act of exiting or leaving a place.
- **Competition** refers to the act of competing.
- **Cooperation** refers to the act of cooperating.

Reinforcing Vocabulary

individuals   🕐 ongoing

Magnet Word Have students create a Magnet Word for difficult or challenging vocabulary. After writing the term in a magnet, students write words and phrases that are associated with the term on the surrounding lines.

Customize Your Core Lesson

Core Instruction

☐ **Print Path** choices
☐ **Digital Path** choices

Vocabulary

☐ **Previewing Vocabulary** Suffixes
☐ **Reinforcing Vocabulary** Magnet Word

Your Resources

Differentiated Instruction

☐ **Basic** Modeling Populations
☐ **Advanced** Graphing Change in Populations
☐ **ELL** Population Diagrams

Extend Science Concepts

Reinforce and Review

Activity *Populations Review*

Synthesizing Key Topics | 👥 whole class
| 🕐 20 min

Carousel Review Help students review the material by following these steps:

1 Arrange chart paper in different parts of the room. On each paper, write a question to review the lesson content.

2 Divide students into small groups and assign each group a chart. Give each group a different colored marker.

3 Groups review their question, discuss the answer, and write a response.

4 After five to ten minutes, each group rotates to the next station. Groups put a check mark by each answer they agree with, comment on answers they don't agree with, and add their own answers. Continue until all groups have reviewed all charts.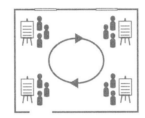

5 Invite each group to share information with the class.

Graphic Organizer

Size of Populations | 👥 individuals
| 🕐 10 min

Idea Wheel Have students draw a large circle with a small circle inside. Inside the small circle, students should write *Population Decreases*. Students then divide the outer ring into sections (as many as needed). Each outer section is labeled with characteristics or details that describe why populations might decrease. Invite students to share one of their details with the class. Write student details in an idea wheel on the board. Continue until all ideas are discussed.

Going Further

Real World Connection

Size of Populations | 👥 individuals
| 🕐 varied

Have interested students conduct research to find out what changes have taken place to one animal population in a certain region during the last century. Encourage students to describe any trends they notice, and explain what factors have caused any changes in the population.

Fine Arts Connection

Population and Limiting Factors | 👥 individual
| 🕐 20 min

Writing a Poem Invite interested students to write a poem or song about how a population of plants or animals increases and decreases over time due to limiting factors. Allow students time to share their poem or song with the class. Have students leave their poem or song in a class library.

Customize Your Closing

📝 *See the Assessment Guide for quizzes and tests.*

💍 *Go Online to edit and create quizzes and tests.*

Reinforce and Review

☐ **Activity** Populations Review

☐ **Graphic Organizer** Idea Wheel

☐ **Print Path** Visual Summary, SE p. 40

☐ **Digital Path** Lesson Closer

Evaluate Student Mastery

Formative Assessment

See the teacher support below the Student Pages for additional Formative Assessment questions.

Ask: What factors can increase or decrease the size of a population? births, deaths, immigration, emigration, food availability, temperature, predation, disease, availability of water, living space, natural disasters, and weather conditions.

Ask: What is competition? When resources are limited, organisms compete to get the resources they need to survive, such as sunlight, space, or food.

Reteach

Formative assessment may show that students need reinforcement for certain topics. The resources below are recommended for reteaching. If students were introduced to a topic through the Print Path, you can also use the Digital Path to reteach, or vice versa.

🎧 *Can be assigned to individual students*

Size of Populations

Quick Lab What Factors Influence Population Change?

Graphic Organizer Idea Wheel 🎧

Populations and Limiting Factors

ELL Population Diagrams 🎧

Quick Lab Investigate an Abiotic Limiting Factor 🎧

Interactions Within Populations

Activity Interaction Poster 🎧

Summative Assessment

Alternative Assessment
Population Ups and Downs

⊘ *Online resources: student worksheet, optional rubric*

Population Dynamics

Climb the Pyramid: *Population Ups and Downs*
Climb the pyramid to show how much you know about population dynamics.

1. Work on your own, with a partner, or with a small group.
2. Choose one item from each layer of the pyramid. Check your choices.
3. Have your teacher approve your plan.
4. Submit or present your results.

___ **Changing or Stable?**

Write three equations. One should show how a population can increase in a year (this would have a positive number as its answer). One should show how a population can decrease in a year (with a negative number as its answer), and one should show a stable population (with zero as its answer).

___ **High or Low?**

Make two pictures, either by drawing or making a collage, of two ecosystems. One should have a high carrying capacity, and the other should have a low carrying capacity. Explain why the carrying capacity is high or low in each case.

___ **Crash Course!**

Write a paragraph that describes why an ecosystem might have a high carrying capacity and why another might have a low carrying capacity. Explain how the resources in each might vary, and what might cause a population to crash.

___ **What's the Limit?**

Choose an ecosystem. Draw a bar graph that shows the amount of three abiotic and three biotic factors in the ecosystem. Indicate the limiting factor with an arrow and tell why it is the limiting factor.

___ **Cooperate or Compete?**

Draw two cartoons. One should show competition between individuals in a population. The other should show cooperation between individuals in a population. Write a caption for each that tells the effect of the competition or cooperation.

___ **Best Pest Solution**

Suppose you have a mosquito problem in your neighborhood. Research and list several abiotic and biotic factors that you could use to reduce the mosquito population. Which factor do you think would work best, and why?

Going Further

- ☐ Real World Connection
- ☐ Fine Arts Connection
- ☐ Print Path Why It Matters, SE p. 37

Formative Assessment

- ☐ Strategies Throughout TE
- ☐ Lesson Review SE

Summative Assessment

- ☐ Alternative Assessment Population Ups and Downs
- ☐ Lesson Quiz
- ☐ Unit Tests A and B
- ☐ Unit Review SE End-of-Unit

Your Resources

_____

_____

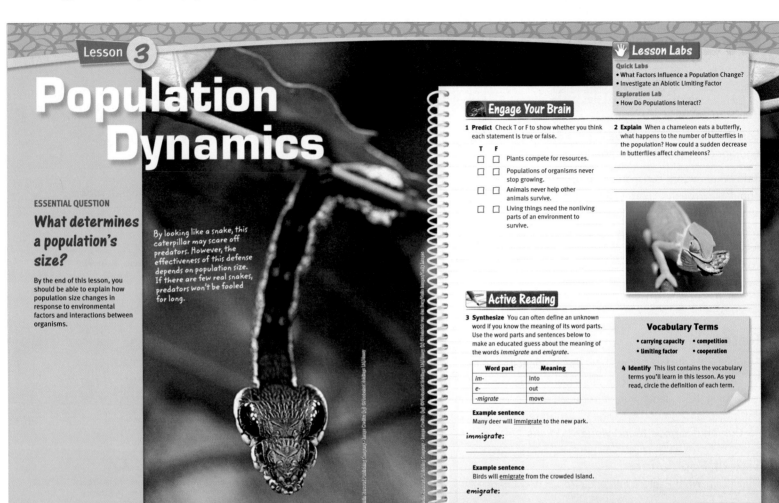

Answers

Answers for 1–3 should represent students' current thoughts, even if incorrect.

1. True; False; False; True

2. Sample answer: The butterfly population decreases. If butterflies are an important part of the chameleons' diet, then their population will decrease, too.

3. Students' answers should indicate that immigrate means to move into a place and emigrate means to move out of a place.

4. Students' annotations will vary.

Opening Your Lesson

Discuss students' answers to item 1 to assess their understanding of how populations change in response to environmental factors and interactions between organisms.

Prerequisites Students should already have some understanding of ecology, habitats, what plants and animals need to survive, where plants and animals live, how organisms get energy, how energy is transferred between organisms, food webs, and how these webs show energy connections.

Learning Alert

Difficult Concept Students may need to be reminded that resources are limited and that populations of organisms, therefore, cannot keep increasing forever. In fact, even if food, for example, is plentiful, a population of animals might not increase if water is scarce, there is not a safe place to live, or there are many predators. Invite students to suggest other things that might affect whether a population will increase. List ideas on the board, and add to the list as you work through the lesson.

Movin' Out

How can a population grow or get smaller?

Active Reading 5 **Identify** As you read, underline the processes that can cause a population to grow or to get smaller.

A population is a group of organisms of one species that lives in the same area at the same time. If new individuals are added to the population, it grows. The population gets smaller if individuals are removed from it. The population stays at about the same size if the number of individuals that are added is close to the number of individuals that are removed.

By Immigration and Emigration

Populations change in size when individuals move to new locations. *Immigration* occurs when individuals join a population. For example, fruit flies may travel on fruit to a new island. The population of fruit flies on the new island grows as fruit flies immigrate. *Emigration* occurs when individuals leave a population. The population of fruit flies on the original island decreases when fruit flies emigrate.

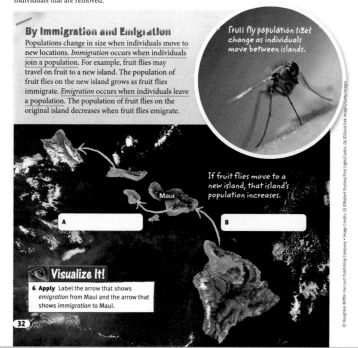

Fruit fly population sizes change as individuals move between islands.

If fruit flies move to a new island, that island's population increases.

Maui

A

B

Visualize It!

6 **Apply** Label the arrow that shows *emigration* from Maui and the arrow that shows *immigration* to Maui.

32

By Birth and Death

Populations increase as individuals are born. For example, consider a population of 100 deer in a forest. The population will increase if 20 fawns are born that year. But what if 12 deer are killed by predators or disease that year? Populations decrease as individuals die. If 20 deer are added and 12 are lost, the population will have an overall increase. At the end of the year, there will be 108 deer. The number of births compared to the number of deaths helps to determine if a population is increasing or decreasing.

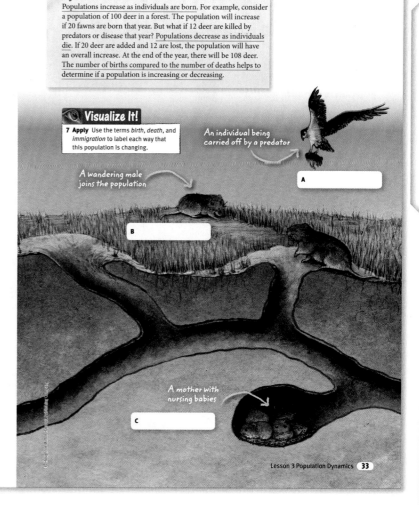

Visualize It!

7 **Apply** Use the terms *birth*, *death*, and *immigration* to label each way that this population is changing.

An individual being carried off by a predator

A wandering male joins the population

A

B

A mother with nursing babies

C

Lesson 3 Population Dynamics 33

Answers

5. *See students' pages for annotations.*
6. A. emigration; B. immigration
7. A. death; B. immigration; C. birth

Building Reading Skills

Supporting Main Ideas When discussing how populations increase and decrease, draw a two-column chart on the board. Label one column *Population Increases*. Label the other *Population Decreases*. Read the student text aloud. Whenever you read a factor that causes a population increase or decrease, invite student volunteers to write the factor in the correct column. When you are finished, have students discuss whether each factor is in the proper place and how they know.

Interpreting Visuals

Analyzing Invite students to examine the illustration showing the prairie vole community. **Ask:** What factors do you see that might cause the population of prairie voles to increase or decrease? Sample answers: A mother having babies will cause the population to increase. Predators will cause a population to decrease. Wandering male voles coming into the community will cause the population to increase. **Ask:** What other factors can you think of that might cause this population to increase or decrease? Sample answers: Availability of food, weather conditions, reaching the carrying capacity.

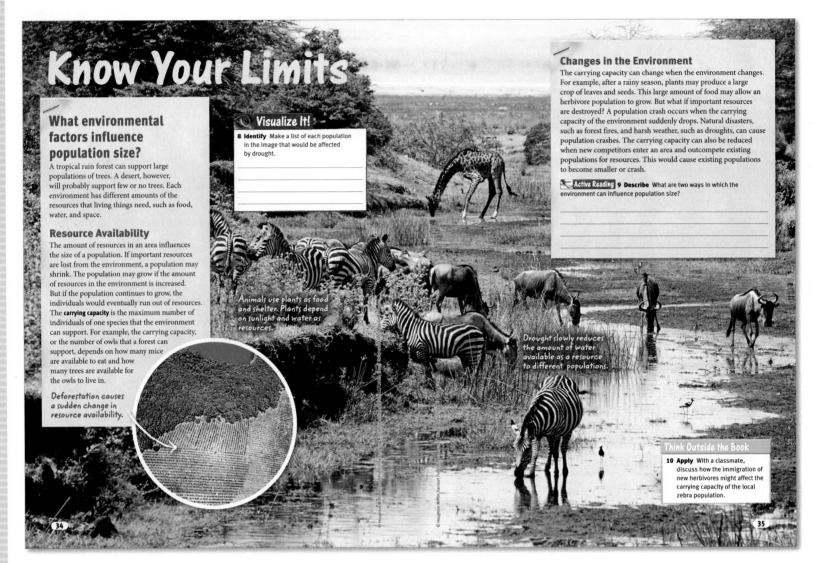

Know Your Limits

What environmental factors influence population size?

A tropical rain forest can support large populations of trees. A desert, however, will probably support few or no trees. Each environment has different amounts of the resources that living things need, such as food, water, and space.

Resource Availability

The amount of resources in an area influences the size of a population. If important resources are lost from the environment, a population may shrink. The population may grow if the amount of resources in the environment is increased. But if the population continues to grow, the individuals would eventually run out of resources. The **carrying capacity** is the maximum number of individuals of one species that the environment can support. For example, the carrying capacity, or the number of owls that a forest can support, depends on how many mice are available to eat and how many trees are available for the owls to live in.

Deforestation causes a sudden change in resource availability.

Visualize It!

8 Identify Make a list of each population in the image that would be affected by drought.

Animals use plants as food and shelter. Plants depend on sunlight and water as resources.

Drought slowly reduces the amount of water available as a resource to different populations.

Changes in the Environment

The carrying capacity can change when the environment changes. For example, after a rainy season, plants may produce a large crop of leaves and seeds. This large amount of food may allow an herbivore population to grow. But what if important resources are destroyed? A population crash occurs when the carrying capacity of the environment suddenly drops. Natural disasters, such as forest fires, and harsh weather, such as droughts, can cause population crashes. The carrying capacity can also be reduced when new competitors enter an area and outcompete existing populations for resources. This would cause existing populations to become smaller or crash.

Active Reading 9 Describe What are two ways in which the environment can influence population size?

Think Outside the Book

10 Apply With a classmate, discuss how the immigration of new herbivores might affect the carrying capacity of the local zebra population.

34   35

Answers

8. Sample answer: zebras, giraffes, wildebeests, grasses, trees, shrubs

9. Sample answer: Changes in the weather or natural disasters can influence resource availability. If a predator population increases or decreases, the prey population can decrease or increase, respectively.

10. Student discussion should demonstrate an understanding that if the new herbivores eat the same plants as the zebras, the environment's carrying capacity for zebras would be reduced.

Interpreting Visuals

Synthesizing Ask: What resources do the images show? Sample answers: There is water for the animals to drink and plants for them to eat; there is open land that provides them with living space; there is air that the animals can breathe.

Probing Questions

Identifying Do you think an arctic environment or a tropical environment can support a larger population of butterflies? Why? A tropical environment could because there are more resources, so more plants grow. Butterflies depend on plants for survival, so the region with more plants will have more butterflies.

Applying What conditions might affect the butterfly population? Sample answer: climate, predators, food, water, availability of shelter, droughts, flooding **Ask:** What might cause the butterfly population to crash? Sample answer: The population might crash if there were a forest fire, a drought, very hot or cold conditions, disease, a new predator, increased competition, and so on.

Maximum Capacity

What factors can limit population size?

A part of the environment that keeps a population's size at a level below its full potential is called a **limiting factor**. Limiting factors can be living or nonliving things in an environment.

Abiotic Factors

The nonliving parts of an environment are called *abiotic factors*. Abiotic factors include water, nutrients, soil, sunlight, temperature, and living space. Organisms need these resources to survive. For example, plants use sunlight, water, and carbon dioxide to make food. If there are few rocks in a desert, lizard populations that use rocks for shelter will not become very large.

Biotic Factors

Relationships among organisms affect each one's growth and survival. A *biotic factor* is an interaction between living things. For example, zebras interact with many organisms. Zebras eat grass, and they compete with antelope for this food. Lions prey on zebras. Each of these interactions is a biotic factor that affects the population of zebras.

Inquiry

11 Apply Think about how people limit the populations of pests such as insects and mice. List one abiotic factor and one biotic factor that humans use to limit these pest populations.

Abiotic _____

Biotic _____

Visualize It!

12 Identify Label each of the following factors that limits plant population growth as abiotic or biotic.

This plant has a disease.

A

This plant grows between the rocks.

B

Herbivores are eating this leaf.

C

36

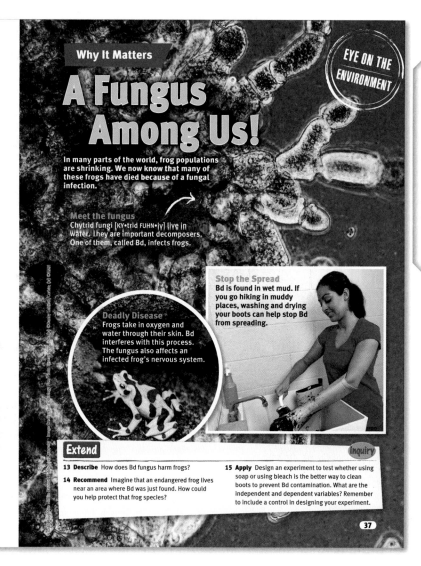

Why It Matters

EYE ON THE ENVIRONMENT

A Fungus Among Us!

In many parts of the world, frog populations are shrinking. We now know that many of these frogs have died because of a fungal infection.

Meet the fungus
Chytrid fungi [KY•trid FUHN•jy] live in water. They are important decomposers. One of them, called Bd, infects frogs.

Deadly Disease
Frogs take in oxygen and water through their skin. Bd interferes with this process. The fungus also affects an infected frog's nervous system.

Stop the Spread
Bd is found in wet mud. If you go hiking in muddy places, washing and drying your boots can help stop Bd from spreading.

Extend

13 Describe How does Bd fungus harm frogs?

14 Recommend Imagine that an endangered frog lives near an area where Bd was just found. How could you help protect that frog species?

15 Apply Design an experiment to test whether using soap or using bleach is the better way to clean boots to prevent Bd contamination. What are the independent and dependent variables? Remember to include a control in designing your experiment.

Inquiry

37

Answers

11. Sample answer: An example of an abiotic factor is using insecticides to control insect populations. An example of a biotic factor is using cat predation to control populations of mice.

12. A. biotic; B. abiotic; C. biotic

13. Bd prevents water and oxygen from penetrating a frog's skin. It also affects a frog's nervous system.

14. Sample answer: I could post signs telling hikers to wash the mud from their boots before and after entering each area.

15. Sample answer: I could wash some boots with soap and some with bleach, and keep some unwashed (as a control). Then I could test for Bd on each and compare. Independent variable: type of washing. Dependent variable: amount of Bd.

Why It Matters

Ask: Why are chytrid fungi important? Sample answer: They are important decomposers. **Ask:** Why are chytrid fungi harmful to frogs? Sample answer: They interfere with a frog's ability to take in oxygen and water through the skin. **Ask:** What abiotic and biotic factors might affect fungus growth? Sample answers: Abiotic: changes in temperature, humidity; Biotic: more predators, less food to decompose

Formative Assessment

Ask: Would the immigration or emigration of frogs cause the frog population size to increase? Why? immigration, because it occurs when new members enter a community, which would increase the population

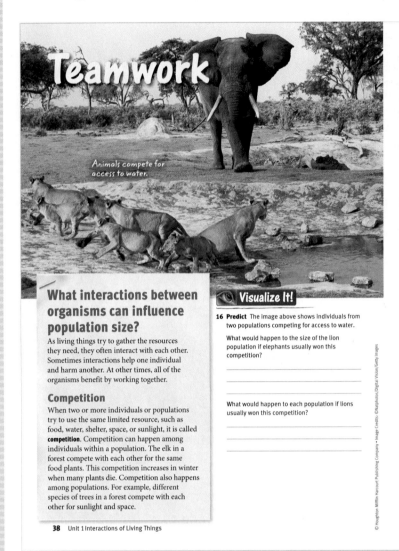

Teamwork

Animals compete for access to water.

What interactions between organisms can influence population size?

As living things try to gather the resources they need, they often interact with each other. Sometimes interactions help one individual and harm another. At other times, all of the organisms benefit by working together.

Competition

When two or more individuals or populations try to use the same limited resource, such as food, water, shelter, space, or sunlight, it is called **competition**. Competition can happen among individuals within a population. The elk in a forest compete with each other for the same food plants. This competition increases in winter when many plants die. Competition also happens among populations. For example, different species of trees in a forest compete with each other for sunlight and space.

38 Unit 1 Interactions of Living Things

Visualize It!

16 Predict The image above shows individuals from two populations competing for access to water.

What would happen to the size of the lion population if elephants usually won this competition?

_____

_____

What would happen to each population if lions usually won this competition?

_____

_____

Active Reading 17 Identify As you read, underline how cooperation can influence population dynamics.

Cooperation

Cooperation occurs when individuals work together. Some animals, such as killer whales, hunt in groups. Emperor penguins in Antarctica stay close together to stay warm. Some populations have a structured social order that determines how the individuals work with each other. For example, ants live in colonies in which the members have different jobs. Some ants find food, others defend the colony, and others take care of the young. Cooperation helps individuals get resources, which can make populations grow.

18 Compare Make an analogy between an ant colony and a sports team. How does each group work together to achieve a goal?

_____

_____

_____

_____

These ants cooperate to protect aphids that produce a substance that ants eat.

39

Answers

16. Sample answer: If elephants always won, the lion population might decrease. If lions always won, the lion population might increase, and the elephant population might decrease.

17. *See students' pages for annotations.*

18. Sample answer: Both ant colonies and sports teams are made up of individuals that work together to meet a common goal. In both cases, certain individuals are assigned specific roles.

Building Reading Skills

Venn Diagram To compare and contrast cooperation and competition, you may wish to have students make a Venn diagram. After they finish their diagrams, they can exchange them with a partner. Allow students to add ideas from their partner's diagram to their own.

🔘 *Online resource: Venn Diagram support*

Formative Assessment

Ask: What are some examples of limiting factors? Answer: If food is abundant but water is scarce, then water is the limiting factor. If an organism uses trees for shelter, but there aren't many trees, then trees would be a limiting factor. **Ask:** What is carrying capacity? Carrying capacity refers to how many plants or animals an environment can support. **Ask:** What can affect carrying capacity? natural disasters, harsh weather, availability of food, shelter, and water

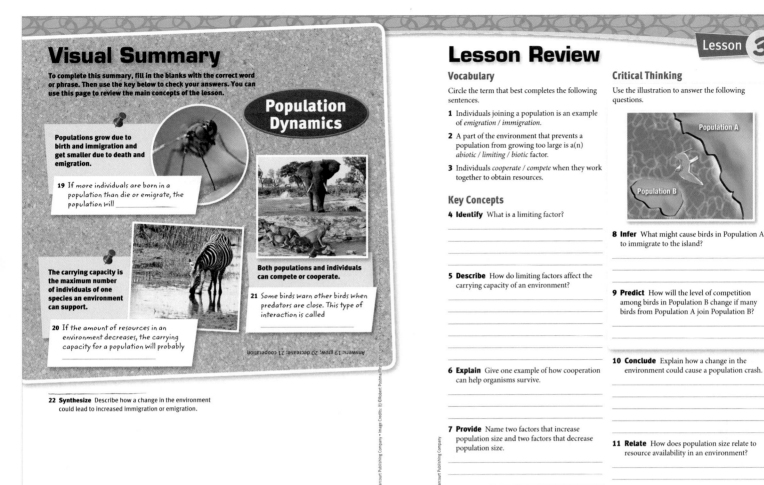

Visual Summary

To complete this summary, fill in the blanks with the correct word or phrase. Then use the key below to check your answers. You can use this page to review the main concepts of the lesson.

Population Dynamics

Populations grow due to birth and immigration and get smaller due to death and emigration.

19 If more individuals are born in a population than die or emigrate, the population will _____

The carrying capacity is the maximum number of individuals of one species an environment can support.

20 If the amount of resources in an environment decreases, the carrying capacity for a population will probably _____

Both populations and individuals can compete or cooperate.

21 Some birds warn other birds when predators are close. This type of interaction is called _____

Answers: 19 grow; 20 decrease; 21 cooperation

22 Synthesize Describe how a change in the environment could lead to increased immigration or emigration.

40 Unit 1 Interactions of Living Things

Lesson Review

Lesson 3

Vocabulary

Circle the term that best completes the following sentences.

1 Individuals joining a population is an example of *emigration / immigration*.

2 A part of the environment that prevents a population from growing too large is a(n) *abiotic / limiting / biotic* factor.

3 Individuals *cooperate / compete* when they work together to obtain resources.

Key Concepts

4 Identify What is a limiting factor?

5 Describe How do limiting factors affect the carrying capacity of an environment?

6 Explain Give one example of how cooperation can help organisms survive.

7 Provide Name two factors that increase population size and two factors that decrease population size.

Critical Thinking

Use the illustration to answer the following questions.

Population A

Population B

8 Infer What might cause birds in Population A to immigrate to the island?

9 Predict How will the level of competition among birds in Population B change if many birds from Population A join Population B?

10 Conclude Explain how a change in the environment could cause a population crash.

11 Relate How does population size relate to resource availability in an environment?

Lesson 3 Population Dynamics 41

Visual Summary Answers

19. grow
20. decrease
21. cooperation
22. Accept all reasonable answers. Sample answer: A change in the environment that reduces the resources available, such as a forest fire, could cause emigration. A change that decreases the risk of disturbance, such as turning a forest from a hunting area to a protected park, could cause immigration.

Lesson Review Answers

1. immigration
2. limiting
3. cooperate
4. A limiting factor is a living or nonliving part of the environment that prevents a population from becoming too large.
5. Increasing the amount of an available limiting factor increases the carrying capacity for the population.
6. Sample answer: Cooperation can help organisms get more food.
7. increase: birth and immigration; decrease: death and emigration

8. Sample answer: Birds from Population A might be searching for more nesting sites.
9. Competition will increase.
10. Sample answer: If water became too polluted for plants to grow in, the population of fish that eat those plants could decrease quickly.
11. Sample answer: Resource availability can determine the carrying capacity of a population.

Interactions in Communities

Essential Question How do organisms interact?

 Professional Development

For more detailed information about the topics in this lesson, refer to the Content Refresher in the Unit Opener pages.

Opening Your Lesson

Begin the lesson by assessing students' prerequisite and prior knowledge.

Prerequisite Knowledge

- Energy and nutrient needs of organisms
- Definitions of *resources, population*

Accessing Prior Knowledge

Ask: What are some ways that different animals interact with each other? Sample answers: fight with each other, eat each other, mate, hunt together, protect each other in a herd

Ask: What other interactions between organisms can you think of? Which of the organisms are helped by the interaction? Which are hurt by it? Sample answers: Bird eats an insect off a plant: helps bird and plant, hurts insect; Person keeps a dog as a pet: helps person and dog.

Customize Your Opening

☐ **Accessing Prior Knowledge,** above

☐ **Print Path** Engage Your Brain, SE p. 43, #1–2

☐ **Active Reading** SE p. 43, #3–4

☐ **Digital Path** Lesson Opener

Key Topics/Learning Goals	Supporting Concepts
Predation 1 Define *predator* and *prey*. 2 Explain how the abundance of a prey species affects the abundance of a predator species, and vice versa. 3 Identify adaptations that help predators and prey survive.	• Predators kill and eat prey animals for energy and nutrients. • Predator populations are affected by the abundance of prey. More prey may lead to more predators; less prey, fewer predators. • Too many predators may shrink the prey population, and few predators may cause prey population to increase. • Both are adapted to their roles.
Symbiosis 1 Explain symbiosis. 2 Distinguish among the three types of symbiosis.	• Symbiotic relationships are close relationships between different species. • In mutualism, both species benefit from the relationship. • In commensalism, one species benefits and the other species is unaffected. • In parasitism, one species (the parasite) benefits and the other (host) is harmed.
Competition 1 State the reason competition occurs. 2 List resources for which organisms compete. 3 Predict effects of competition for a resource.	• Competition occurs when multiple individuals or populations try to use the same limited resource, such as food, water, mates, or space. • Competition reduces the availability of a resource.

Options for Instruction

Two parallel paths provide coverage of the Essential Questions, with a strong **Inquiry** strand woven into each. Follow the **Print Path,** the **Digital Path,** or your customized combination of print, digital, and inquiry.

 **Print Path**
Teaching support for the Print Path appears with the Student Pages.

 Inquiry Labs and Activities

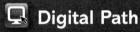 **Digital Path**
Digital Path shortcut: TS673340

Print Path	Inquiry Labs and Activities	Digital Path
Feeding Frenzy!, SE pp. 44–45 **How do predator and prey interact?** • Predators Eat Prey • Predator and Prey Populations are Connected	**Exploration Lab** Modeling the Predator-Prey Cycle **Quick Labs** Identifying Predators and Prey Prey Coloration **Daily Demo** Observing a Predator in Action	**Predator or Prey?** Interactive Graphics
Living Together, SE pp. 46–47 **What are the types of symbiotic relationships?** • Mutualism • Commensalism • Parasitism	**Activity** Who Does What?	**Symbiosis** Interactive Images
Let the Games Begin!, SE p. 48 **Why does competition occur in communities?**	**Activity** What Are You Fighting For? **Virtual Lab** Competing for Resources	**Competition** Interactive Graphics

Options for Assessment

See the Evaluate page for options, including Formative Assessment, Summative Assessment, and Unit Review.

Engage and Explore

Activities and Discussion

Activity *Who Does What?*

Introducing Key Topics

 small groups or whole class
🕐 20 min
Inquiry **GUIDED** inquiry

Have students find a picture of a nature scene and list or describe organisms they see or think would be in that environment. Prompt students to consider plants, animals, and tiny, hidden organisms. Then have students classify some ways these organisms might interact.

Take It Home *Identifying Interactions*

Introducing Key Topics

 adult-student pairs
🕐 10–30 min
Inquiry **GUIDED** inquiry

Students work with an adult to observe organisms seen during a neighborhood walk, through a window, or within a home. They might consider organisms that are too small to be visible. The pair should choose one organism and try to identify the ways it interacts with other organisms within its ecosystem.

🌐 *Optional Online resource: student worksheet*

Discussion *Brown-headed Cowbird*

Symbiosis

 whole class
🕐 20 min

Tell students that the brown-headed cowbird is a parasite. It lays its eggs in the nests of other birds, which incubate the cowbird's eggs and raise its chicks. **Ask:** What do you think happens to the host birds and their chicks? The host birds expend a lot of energy raising a chick that is not their own; their own chicks may starve because they cannot compete successfully with the cowbird chicks for food. **Ask:** How do you think the brown-headed cowbird should be dealt with—if at all? Have students discuss their viewpoints. Remind them that there is no "good" or "bad" in nature; all organisms, including parasites, are just trying to survive.

Activity *What Are You Fighting For?*

Competition

 individuals
🕐 20 min
Inquiry **GUIDED** inquiry

Think, Pair, Share Give students 3 minutes to write down as many examples as they can of competition in nature. Remind students to consider different types of resources that organisms might compete for, such as food, water, living space, and, within a species, mates. After the 3 minutes are up, have each student choose three examples from his or her list and discuss the examples with a partner. Each student should explain why he or she selected each example of competition and tell what resource the species in each example is competing for. Call on pairs to share an example with the class and discuss how and why they chose their examples.

⊙ 🔲 Exploration Lab *Modeling the Predator-Prey Cycle*

Predation

 pairs
🕐 45 min
Inquiry **GUIDED** or **INDEPENDENT** inquiry

PURPOSE To investigate how predator and prey populations vary to result in a predator-prey population cycle

MATERIALS

- cardboard squares, 5 cm × 5 cm (20)
- cardboard squares, 1 cm × 1 cm (100)
- paper, graphing
- table top, about 75 cm × 75 cm
- pencil

Customize Your Labs

 See the Lab Manual for lab datasheets.

🌐 *Go Online for editable lab datasheets.*

Levels of **Inquiry** **DIRECTED** inquiry introduces inquiry skills within a structured framework. **GUIDED** inquiry develops inquiry skills within a supportive environment. **INDEPENDENT** inquiry deepens inquiry skills with student-driven questions or procedures.

Labs and Demos

Daily Demo *Observing a Predator in Action*

Engage

Predation

whole class
15 min
Inquiry GUIDED inquiry

Use this short demo after you have introduced the topic of predator adaptations or discussed examples.

PURPOSE **To show a predator catching its prey**

MATERIALS

- live predator, such as a lizard, toad, salamander, or nonpoisonous snake
- food for the predator, such as live crickets

CAUTION **Do not allow students to handle the animal.**

1 Feed the animal and have students observe how it catches prey.

2 **Observing** What adaptations does this predator use to catch its prey? speed, camouflage, strength

Quick Lab *Identifying Predators and Prey*

Predation

pairs
20 min
Inquiry GUIDED inquiry

PURPOSE **To investigate characteristics of animals to identify adaptations that help them survive in their roles as predators or prey**

MATERIALS

- images of animals (from Online search)

Quick Lab *Prey Coloration*

Predation

pairs
30 min
Inquiry GUIDED inquiry

Students run an experiment to test the effectiveness of camouflage in helping prey animals avoid being caught by predators.

PURPOSE **To investigate how predator efficiency is affected by prey coloration**

MATERIALS

- 3 cups
- paper circles, black
- paper circles, white
- paper circles, newsprint
- paper, black, 8.5 × 11
- paper, white, 8.5 × 11
- paper, newsprint, 8.5 × 11
- stopwatch

Virtual Lab *Competing for Resources*

Competition

flexible
45 min
Inquiry GUIDED inquiry

Students manipulate population levels in an ecosystem and see how this affects competition

PURPOSE **To study competition**

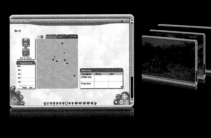

Activities and Discussion

- ☐ **Activity** Who Does What?
- ☐ **Take It Home** Identifying Interactions
- ☐ **Discussion** Brown-headed Cowbird
- ☐ **Activity** What Are You Fighting For?

Labs and Demos

- ☐ **Exploration Lab** Predator-Prey Cycle
- ☐ **Daily Demo** Observing a Predator
- ☐ **Quick Lab** Identifying Predators
- ☐ **Quick Lab** Prey Coloration
- ☐ **Virtual Lab** Competing for Resources

Your Resources

Explain Science Concepts

	📖 Print Path	🖥 Digital Path

Key Topics		
Predation	☐ **Feeding Frenzy!,** SE pp. 44–45 • Active Reading (Annotation strategy), #5 • Compare, #6 • Think Outside the Book, #7 • Visualize It!, #8 	☐ **Predator or Prey?** Determine which organism is a predator and which organism is its prey. 
Symbiosis	☐ **Living Together,** SE pp. 46–47 • Active Reading (Annotation strategy), #9 • Compare, #10 • Summarize, #11 • Think Outside the Book, #12 	☐ **Symbiosis** Learn about the three different types of symbiotic relationships. 
Competition	☐ **Let the Games Begin!,** SE p. 48 • Active Reading (Annotation strategy), #13 • Predict, #14 • Think Outside the Book, #15 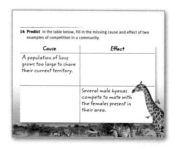	☐ **Competition** Explore how predators compete for prey within a community of organisms. 

Basic *Adaptations*

Predation

 individuals
🕐 varied

After students have learned about adaptations of predator and prey organisms, have them look for a photograph of an organism in its natural environment and analyze the image to list the organism's adaptations to the environment.

Advanced *Multiple Relationships*

Synthesizing Key Topics

 individuals
🕐 40 min

Quick Research The relationships between living things are complex. Some organisms that exhibit predator-prey relationships under certain circumstances will exhibit mutualistic relationships at other times. Encourage students to find out more about the relationships between two organisms that are sometimes one way and sometimes another. Have them share what they learn with the class through a multimedia or oral presentation.

ELL *Symbiotic Terms*

Symbiosis

 individuals
 20 min

Description Wheel Struggling or EL students may be unfamiliar with the words *benefit* and *mutual*. Define these words for students (*benefit*: have some need met, have some help; *mutual*: shared, equally taking part in). Then have students make a Description Wheel, in which *mutual* is the central word and *benefit* is one of the related words.

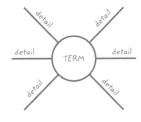

ELL *Interaction Cartoons*

Synthesizing Key Concepts

 pairs or small groups
🕐 20 min

Have students create a cartoon to show predation, parasitism, mutualism, commensalism, or competition. Gather finished cartoons into a booklet or display them on a bulletin board.

Lesson Vocabulary

predator	**prey**	**symbiosis**
mutualism	**parasitism**	**commensalism**
competition		

Previewing Vocabulary

 whole class   15 min

Word Origins Share the following to help students remember terms:
- **Symbiosis** comes from a Greek term that means "live together"; *bio-* in this term means "life," as in *biotic* or *biology*.
- **Parasite** comes from the Greek *parasitos*, meaning "one who eats at someone else's table."
- **Commensal** is from Latin and means "together at the same table."
- **Mutual** is from Latin and means "reciprocal, done in exchange."

Reinforcing Vocabulary

 individuals   ongoing

Four Square To help students remember the different terms in the lesson, provide them with the Four Square graphic organizer. Students place the term in the oval and then fill in the cells with definitions, characteristics, examples, and nonexamples.

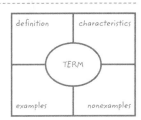

Customize Your Core Lesson

Core Instruction
- ☐ **Print Path** choices
- ☐ **Digital Path** choices

Vocabulary
- ☐ **Previewing Vocabulary** Word Origins
- ☐ **Reinforcing Vocabulary** Four Square

Your Resources

Differentiated Instruction
- ☐ **Basic** Adaptations
- ☐ **Advanced** Multiple Relationships
- ☐ **ELL** Symbiotic Terms
- ☐ **ELL** Interaction Cartoons

_____

_____

Extend Science Concepts

Reinforce and Review

Activity *Symbiosis Game*

Symbiosis　　　　　　 whole class
　　　　　　　　　　　　🕐 15 min

Four Corners Label each corner of the classroom as "Mutualism," "Commensalism," "Parasitism," or "None of These." Read the following relationships to students. After each one, ask the students to stand in the corner they think describes the relationship. Give each student in the correct corner 1 point. You can continue the game with additional examples provided by volunteers.

1　Acacia ants live on the bullhorn acacia tree, which provides the ants with food and shelter. The ants deter grazing animals from eating the tree by attacking and biting them. mutualism

2　Creosote bushes compete with other creosote bushes for the same water supply. The toxins produced by the roots of one bush prevent other bushes from growing. none of these; the competition is not interspecific

3　Barnacles grow on the shell of a scallop, a kind of bivalve mollusk. The barnacles get a solid place to live and the scallop is unharmed. commensalism

4　A tick attaches itself to a white-tailed deer. parasitism

5　The boxer crab carries a small sea anemone in each claw. When a threat approaches, the crab waves the anemones at it, making it back away. The anemones feed from the scraps the crab drops. mutualism

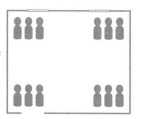

Graphic Organizer

Synthesizing Key Topics　　 individual
　　　　　　　　　　　　　　　🕐 ongoing

Cluster Diagram After students have studied the lesson, ask them to create a cluster diagram with the following terms: *competition, predator, symbiosis, commensalism, prey, parasitism, mutualism, interactions, parasite, host*

⊘ *Optional Online resource: Cluster Diagram support*

Going Further

Social Studies Connection

Competition　　　　　　 whole class
　　　　　　　　　　　　　🕐 15 min

Discussion Explain that competition in an ecosystem can be compared with competition in a free-enterprise economic system. In both, if the supply of a resource decreases or the need increases, competition increases. **Ask:** If businesses need more workers than there are available, what might happen? Employers may compete with one another by paying higher wages. **Ask:** If more workers are available than jobs, what might happen? Wages may fall as workers have to compete with one another for jobs. Students might discuss competition relevant to current or local issues, such as jobs, money, energy resources, water, or space.

Human Biology Connection

Synthesizing Key Concepts　　🧑 individual
　　　　　　　　　　　　　　　🕐 varies

Research Project Human bodies can host populations of other organisms, including bacteria, fungi, and protists. Some relationships are commensal, some are mutualistic, and some are parasitic. Have students research an example of one type of interaction and the specific organism involved and prepare a poster or a computer presentation to share with the class.

⊘ *Optional Online rubrics: Posters and Displays, Multimedia Presentations*

Customize Your Closing

📖 *See the Assessment Guide for quizzes and tests.*

⊘ *Go Online to edit and create quizzes and tests.*

Reinforce and Review

☐ **Activity** Symbiosis Game

☐ **Graphic Organizer** Cluster Diagram

☐ **Print Path** Visual Summary, SE p. 50

☐ **Digital Path** Lesson Closer

Evaluate Student Mastery

Formative Assessment

See the teacher support below the Student Pages for additional Formative Assessment questions.

Describe for students, or have them review, the example of the rhinoceros and tickbirds that appears at the beginning of the print lesson. **Ask·** How many different types of interactions can you find? Birds are predators to ticks; rhinoceros's horn and other characteristics of organisms may be adaptations related to predation; ticks are parasites to rhinoceros; birds and rhinoceros show mutualism; no clear example of commensalism; birds and ticks may compete within their species for food; no clear example of cross-species competition

Reteach

Formative assessment may show that students need reinforcement for certain topics. The resources below are recommended for reteaching. If students were introduced to a topic through the Print Path, you can also use the Digital Path to reteach, and vice versa.
🎧 *Can be assigned to individual students*

Predation
Daily Demo Observing a Predator in Action
Quick Lab Identifying Predators and Prey 🎧

Symbiosis
Activity Symbiosis Game
Discussion Brown-headed Cowbird

Competition
Activity What Are You Fighting For? 🎧
Virtual Lab Competing for Resources 🎧

Summative Assessment

Alternative Assessment
Symbiosis

🌐 *Online resources: student worksheet; optional rubrics*

Interactions in Communities

Points of View: *Symbiosis*
Your class will work together to show what you've learned about symbiosis from several different viewpoints.

1. Work in groups as assigned by your teacher. Each group will be assigned to one or two viewpoints.

2. Complete your assignment, and present your perspective to the class.

Symbiosis

 Vocabulary Describe the similarities and differences between *mutualism*, *commensalism*, and *parasitism*.

 Examples Present a news report in which you describe commensalism. List and compare examples of the three types of relationships.

 Analysis Imagine that you've been invited on a trip to the rain forest to confirm previous observations on symbiotic relationships. Your task is to confirm that the relationships you see are indeed symbiotic, and then classify them by the type of symbiotic relationship. Write your findings.

 Details Write about a symbiotic relationship that is an example of mutualism. Identify the way it uses symbiosis. Include details about the organisms' relationship and the benefits both organisms receive.

 Models Identify one symbiotic relationship that is an example of parasitism. Create a two-column chart that shows the benefits the parasite receives and the harm that comes to the host as a result of the relationship.

Going Further
☐ Social Studies Connection
☐ Human Biology Connection
☐ Print Path Why It Matters, SE p. 49

Formative Assessment
☐ **Strategies** Throughout TE
☐ **Lesson Review** SE

Summative Assessment
☐ **Alternative Assessment** Symbiosis
☐ **Lesson Quiz**
☐ **Unit Tests A and B**
☐ **Unit Review** SE End-of-Unit

Your Resources

_____   _____

_____   _____

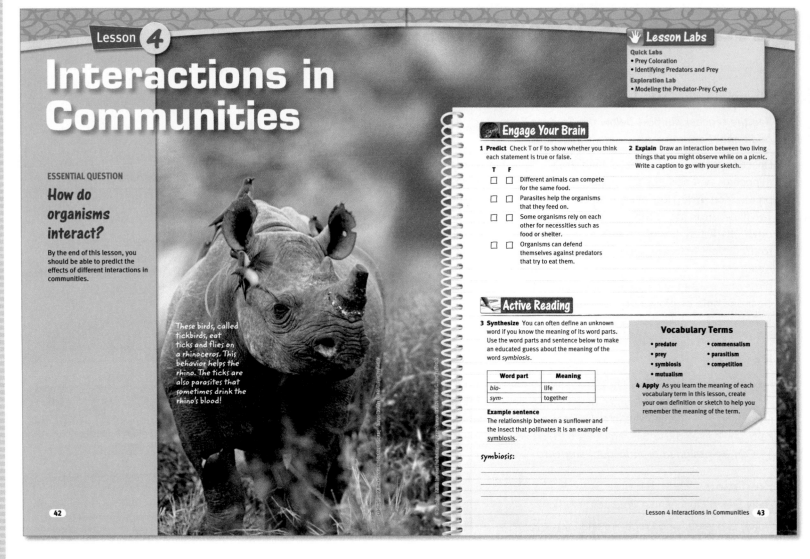

Lesson ④

Interactions in Communities

Lesson Labs

Quick Labs
• Prey Coloration
• Identifying Predators and Prey

Exploration Lab
• Modeling the Predator-Prey Cycle

ESSENTIAL QUESTION

How do organisms interact?

By the end of this lesson, you should be able to predict the effects of different interactions in communities.

These birds, called tickbirds, eat ticks and flies on a rhinoceros. This behavior helps the rhino. The ticks are also parasites that sometimes drink the rhino's blood!

Engage Your Brain

1 Predict Check T or F to show whether you think each statement is true or false.

T F

☐ ☐ Different animals can compete for the same food.

☐ ☐ Parasites help the organisms that they feed on.

☐ ☐ Some organisms rely on each other for necessities such as food or shelter.

☐ ☐ Organisms can defend themselves against predators that try to eat them.

2 Explain Draw an interaction between two living things that you might observe while on a picnic. Write a caption to go with your sketch.

Active Reading

3 Synthesize You can often define an unknown word if you know the meaning of its word parts. Use the word parts and sentence below to make an educated guess about the meaning of the word *symbiosis*.

Word part	Meaning
bio-	life
sym-	together

Example sentence
The relationship between a sunflower and the insect that pollinates it is an example of symbiosis.

symbiosis: _____

Vocabulary Terms

• predator   • commensalism
• prey   • parasitism
• symbiosis   • competition
• mutualism

4 Apply As you learn the meaning of each vocabulary term in this lesson, create your own definition or sketch to help you remember the meaning of the term.

42

Lesson 4 Interactions in Communities 43

Answers

Answers for 1–3 should represent students' current thoughts, even if incorrect.

1. T; F; T; T

2. Students should draw two organisms that are interacting in some way. The caption should describe the interaction.

3. Accept all reasonable answers that suggest two organisms coexisting.

4. Students should define or sketch each vocabulary term in the lesson.

Opening Your Lesson

Discuss student drawings in response to item 2 to assess their prerequisite knowledge and to estimate what they already know about the key topics.

Preconceptions Discuss everyday definitions of *predator* as someone bad, of *symbiosis* as a mutually beneficial relationship, and of *parasite* as a small insect or animal.

Prerequisites Students should already know how organisms obtain energy and nutrients; that organisms interact with one another and with the environment; that a population is the organisms of the same species living in the same area; and that resources help organisms meet their needs.

Learning Alert

Types of Interactions Not all interactions among organisms fall into the categories in this lesson. Many types of interactions can occur between organisms, depending on the circumstances. For example, students may think that sharks eat anything they can get near. However, in certain locations called *cleaning stations*, sharks put their predatory instincts on hold while cleaner shrimp or fish scour their hides, removing ectoparasites, and even enter the sharks' mouths to clean their teeth and tongues.

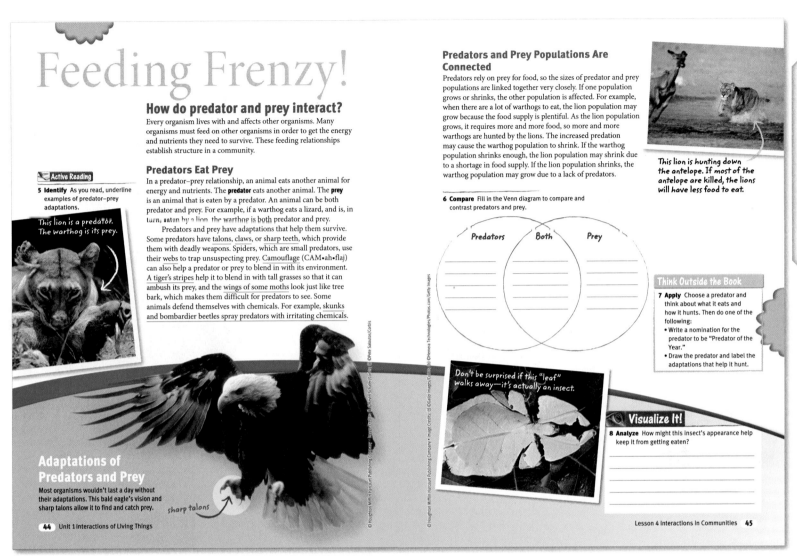

Feeding Frenzy!

How do predator and prey interact?

Every organism lives with and affects other organisms. Many organisms must feed on other organisms in order to get the energy and nutrients they need to survive. These feeding relationships establish structure in a community.

Active Reading

5 Identify As you read, underline examples of predator–prey adaptations.

This lion is a predator. The warthog is its prey.

Predators Eat Prey

In a predator–prey relationship, an animal eats another animal for energy and nutrients. The **predator** eats another animal. The **prey** is an animal that is eaten by a predator. An animal can be both predator and prey. For example, if a warthog eats a lizard, and is, in turn, eaten by a lion, the warthog is both predator and prey.

Predators and prey have adaptations that help them survive. Some predators have talons, claws, or sharp teeth, which provide them with deadly weapons. Spiders, which are small predators, use their webs to trap unsuspecting prey. Camouflage (CAM•ah•flaj) can also help a predator or prey to blend in with its environment. A tiger's stripes help it to blend in with tall grasses so that it can ambush its prey, and the wings of some moths look just like tree bark, which makes them difficult for predators to see. Some animals defend themselves with chemicals. For example, skunks and bombardier beetles spray predators with irritating chemicals.

Adaptations of Predators and Prey

Most organisms wouldn't last a day without their adaptations. This bald eagle's vision and sharp talons allow it to find and catch prey.

sharp talons

Unit 1 Interactions of Living Things   **44**

Predators and Prey Populations Are Connected

Predators rely on prey for food, so the sizes of predator and prey populations are linked together very closely. If one population grows or shrinks, the other population is affected. For example, when there are a lot of warthogs to eat, the lion population may grow because the food supply is plentiful. As the lion population grows, it requires more and more food, so more and more warthogs are hunted by the lions. The increased predation may cause the warthog population to shrink. If the warthog population shrinks enough, the lion population may shrink due to a shortage in food supply. If the lion population shrinks, the warthog population may grow due to a lack of predators.

This lion is hunting down the antelope. If most of the antelope are killed, the lions will have less food to eat.

6 Compare Fill in the Venn diagram to compare and contrast predators and prey.

Predators   Both   Prey

Think Outside the Book

7 Apply Choose a predator and think about what it eats and how it hunts. Then do one of the following:
- Write a nomination for the predator to be "Predator of the Year."
- Draw the predator and label the adaptations that help it hunt.

Don't be surprised if this "leaf" walks away—it's actually an insect.

Visualize It!

8 Analyze How might this insect's appearance help keep it from getting eaten?

Lesson 4 Interactions in Communities   **45**

Answers

5. *See students' page for annotations.*

6. Sample answer: [left] eat other animals; [both] have adaptations to survive; [right] are eaten by predators

7. Students' nomination or drawing should reflect an understanding of the predator, what it eats, and the adaptations that help it capture food.

8. Sample answer: The insect looks like a leaf, so a predator might not think that it is an insect.

Probing Questions GUIDED Inquiry

Identifying What predators can you think of that are also prey? Sample answers: salamander, frog, snake, lizard, weasel, armadillo

Applying Think about white-tail deer. Today they are so numerous some people consider them pests. How did this happen? Over the years, the predators that controlled the deer population, such as wolves and cougars, have been wiped out in many places. As a result, the deer reproduced unchecked, damaging forests and causing other problems.

Interpreting Visuals

Have students identify adaptations of predators and prey. Sample answers: Coloring serves as camouflage; hearing and vision helps catch prey or avoid predators.

Learning Alert

Predators and Prey Remind students that the relationship between predators and prey is not a constant game of chase. The prey animals get respites from the pressure of predation. These "time outs" may come in the form of a safe, predator-free location, or during the time when the local predators are digesting their most recent kill. Without such respites, the prey animals would be driven to extinction.

Living Together

What are the types of symbiotic relationships?

A close long-term relationship between different species in a community is called **symbiosis** (sim•bee•OH•sis). In symbiosis, the organisms in the relationship can benefit from, be unaffected by, or be harmed by the relationship. Often, one organism lives in or on the other organism. Symbiotic relationships are classified as mutualism, commensalism, or parasitism.

Active Reading **9 Identify** As you read, underline examples of symbiotic relationships.

Think Outside the Book (Inquiry)

12 Predict Observe and take notes about how the organisms in your area interact with one another. Imagine what would happen if one of these organisms disappeared. Write down three effects that you can think of.

Mutualism

A symbiotic relationship in which both organisms benefit is called **mutualism**. For example, when the bee in the photo drinks nectar from a flower, it gets pollen on its hind legs. When the bee visits another flower, it transfers pollen from the first flower to the second flower. In this interaction, the bee is fed and the second flower is pollinated for reproduction. So, both organisms benefit from the relationship. In this example, the mutualism benefits the bee and the two parent plants that are reproducing.

Bees pollinate flowers. This is an example of mutualism.

Commensalism

A symbiotic relationship in which one organism benefits while the other is unaffected is called **commensalism**. For example, orchids and other plants that often live in the branches of trees gain better access to sunlight without affecting the trees. In addition, the tree trunk shown here provides a living space for lichens, which do not affect the tree in any way. Some examples of commensalism involve protection. For example, certain shrimp live among the spines of the fire urchin. The fire urchin's spines are poisonous but not to the shrimp. By living among the urchin's spines, the shrimp are protected from predators. In this relationship, the shrimp benefits and the fire urchin is unaffected.

Lichens can live on tree bark.

10 Compare How does commensalism differ from mutualism?

Parasitism

A symbiotic relationship in which one organism benefits and another is harmed is called **parasitism** (PAR•uh•sih•tiz•uhm). The organism that benefits is the *parasite*. The organism that is harmed is the *host*. The parasite gets food from its host, which weakens the host. Some parasites, such as ticks, live on the host's surface and feed on its blood. These parasites can cause diseases such as Lyme disease. Other parasites, such as tapeworms, live within the host's body. They can weaken their host so much that the host dies.

parasite

host

11 Summarize Using the key, complete the table to show how organisms are affected by symbiotic relationships.

Symbiosis	Species 1	Species 2
Mutualism	+	
	+	0
Parasitism		

Key + organism benefits
0 organism not affected
− organism harmed

46 Unit 1 Interactions of Living Things

47

Answers

9. *See students' pages for annotations.*

10. Commensalism only helps one of the two species that are interacting. Mutualism helps both species.

11. +; commensalism; +; −, +

12. Students' answers should accurately describe interactions between organisms. The three effects they list should reflect an understanding of symbiotic relationships and the impact of an organism's removal on the other organisms.

Learning Alert ⚠ MISCONCEPTION ⚠

Symbiosis vs. Mutualism Students may think that symbiosis is exactly the same as mutualism, instead of recognizing that *symbiosis* is the more general term. Look for signs of confusion by describing examples of parasitism and asking whether it is symbiosis. If students confuse the terms, remind them that a term's scientific definition might not match its everyday use, and then brainstorm additional examples together.

Formative Assessment

Ask: Can a plant be a parasite of another plant? How? Sample answer: Yes, it might climb another plant and cut off its light or take nutrients from the other plant.

Let the Games Begin!

Why does competition occur in communities?

In a team game, two groups compete against each other with the same goal in mind—to win the game. In a biological community, organisms compete for resources. **Competition** occurs when organisms fight for the same limited resource. Organisms compete for resources such as food, water, sunlight, shelter, and mates. If an organism doesn't get all the resources it needs, it could die.

Sometimes competition happens among individuals of the same species. For example, different groups of lions compete with each other for living space. Males within these groups also compete with each other for mates.

Competition can also happen among individuals of different species. Lions mainly eat large animals, such as zebras. They compete for zebras with leopards and cheetahs. When zebras are scarce, competition increases among animals that eat zebras. As a result, lions may steal food or compete with other predators for smaller animals.

Active Reading

13 Identify Underline each example of competition.

14 Predict In the table below, fill in the missing cause and effect of two examples of competition in a community.

Cause	Effect
A population of lions grows too large to share their current territory.	
	Several male hyenas compete to mate with the females present in their area.

Many organisms rely on the same water source.

Think Outside the Book

15 Apply With a classmate, discuss how competition might affect the organisms in this photo.

48

Why It Matters

Strange Relationships

WEIRD SCIENCE

Glow worms? Blind salamanders? Even creepy crawlers in this extreme cave community interact in ways that help them meet their needs. How do these interactions differ from ones in your own community?

A Blind Hunter
Caves are very dark and, over generations, these salamanders have lost the use of their eyes for seeing. Instead of looking for food, they track prey by following water movements.

Guano Buffet
Cave swiftlets venture out of the cave daily to feed. The food they eat is recycled as bird dung, or guano, which piles up beneath the nests. The guano feeds many cave dwellers, such as insects. As a result, these insects never have to leave the cave!

Sticky Traps
Bioluminescent glow worms make lines of sticky beads to attract prey. Once a prey is stuck, the worm pulls in the line to feast.

Extend *Inquiry*

16 Identify Name the type of relationship illustrated in two of the examples shown above.

17 Research Name some organisms in your community and the interactions they have.

18 Create Illustrate two of the interactions you just described by doing one of the following:
• make a poster • write a play
• write a song • draw a graphic novel

49

Answers

13. *See students' page for annotations.*

14. Lions will compete for food and shelter.; There are more male hyenas in a population than female hyenas.

15. Sample answer: Competition for food, mates, land, or shelter could exist between members of the same species or different species.

16. Bioluminescent worms and salamanders have a predator-prey relationship with their prey.; Cave swiftlets have a commensalistic relationship with insects that feed on guano.

17. Students' answer should accurately describe how organisms interact.

18. Students' drawings should reflect the interactions they described.

Probing Questions GUIDED *Inquiry*

Applying What are some ways that you compete or cooperate with others? Sample answers: compete for grades, cooperate in doing class projects; compete in sports, cooperate on teams

Synthesizing How are animals interacting when they hunt in packs? They are cooperating by working together with others of their species, they are competing with other predators, and they are preying on another species.

Why It Matters

Have each student point to an organism in the feature *Strange Relationships*. Students should then challenge a partner to identify any relationship their organism has with other organisms in the cave community. **Reminder:** Not all relationships can be classified as predation, symbiosis, or competition. Glow worms may compete for space, mates, or prey and are predators for unspecified prey; salamanders may compete for space, mates, and prey; insects and other cave dwellers may compete for guano.

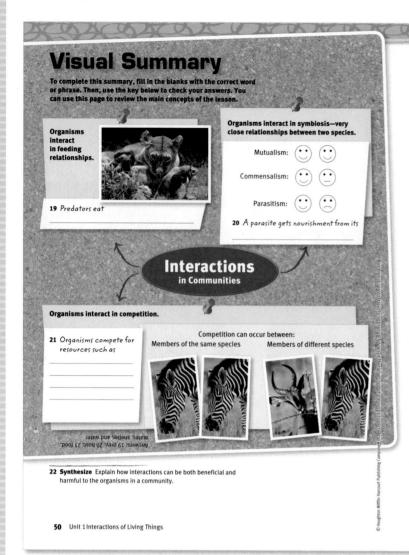

Visual Summary

To complete this summary, fill in the blanks with the correct word or phrase. Then, use the key below to check your answers. You can use this page to review the main concepts of the lesson.

Organisms interact in feeding relationships.

19 Predators eat _____

Organisms interact in symbiosis—very close relationships between two species.

Mutualism: ☺ ☺

Commensalism: ☺ 😐

Parasitism: ☺ ☹

20 A parasite gets nourishment from its _____

Interactions in Communities

Organisms interact in competition.

21 Organisms compete for resources such as _____

Competition can occur between:
Members of the same species   Members of different species

Answers: 19 prey, 20 host, 21 food, mates, shelter, and water.

22 Synthesize Explain how interactions can be both beneficial and harmful to the organisms in a community.

50   Unit 1 Interactions of Living Things

Lesson Review

Lesson ④

Vocabulary

Fill in the blank with the term that best completes the following sentences.

1 A _____ is an animal that kills and eats another animal, known as prey.

2 A long-term relationship between two different species within a community is called _____

3 _____ occurs when organisms fight for limited resources.

Key Concepts

Fill in the table below.

Example	Type of symbiosis
4 Identify Tiny organisms called mites live in human eyelashes and feed on dead skin, without harming humans.	
5 Identify Certain bacteria live in human intestines, where they get food and also help humans break down their food.	

6 Describe Think of an animal, and list two resources that it might compete for in its community. Then describe what adaptations the animal has to compete for these resources.

7 Explain What is the relationship between the size of a predator population and the size of a prey population?

Critical Thinking

Use this graph to answer the following question.

Predator and Prey Populations Over Time

8 Analyze At which point (A or B) on this graph would you expect competition within the predator population to be the highest?

9 Infer Think of a resource, and predict what happens to the resource when competition for it increases.

10 Apply Identify a community near where you live, such as a forest, a pond, or your own backyard. Think about the interactions of the organisms in this community. Describe an interaction and identify it as predation, mutualism, commensalism, parasitism, or competition.

Lesson 4 Interactions in Communities   **51**

Visual Summary Answers

19. prey

20. host

21. food; mates; shelter; water

22. Sample answer: One organism can have a beneficial interaction with one organism in the community and a harmful interaction with a different organism in the community.

Lesson Review Answers

1. predator

2. symbiosis

3. competition

4. commensalism

5. mutualism

6. Sample answer: A squirrel might compete for food and nesting sites. Squirrels have claws that help them dig for food that they have hidden. They are also able to climb up trees to find nesting sites.

7. As the predator population grows, the prey population gets smaller.

8. At point B because there are many predators and few prey.

9. Sample answer: If the resource is water, the availability of the water decreases when competition for water increases.

10. Sample answer: In a pond community, a heron eats fish, which is predation. Leeches may attach to turtles and feed from their blood, which is parasitism.

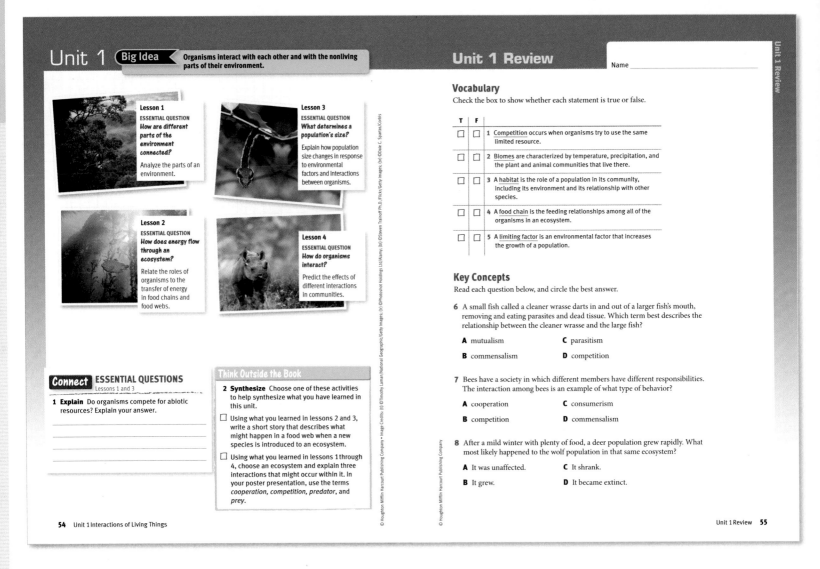

Unit Summary Answers

1. Yes, organisms do compete for abiotic resources. For example, they may compete for water and shelter.

2. Option 1: Students should explain that a new species may out-compete native species for resources such as food or space. Introduced species may also be predators of native species. When native species are depleted from an ecosystem, the entire food web may be affected, as their predators may no longer have a food source.

   Option 2: Poster presentations should include a reasonable example of competition (organisms fight over the same limited resource), cooperation (organisms work together in a way that benefits all), predator (an organism that eats another organism), and prey (the organism that is eaten by the predator).

Unit Review ▶ Response to Intervention

A Quick Grading Chart follows the Answers. See the Assessment Guide for more detail about correct and incorrect answer choices. Refer back to the Lesson Planning pages for activities and assignments that can be used as remediation for students who answer questions incorrectly.

Answers

1. True This statement is true because competition occurs between two or more individuals or groups over resources such as food, water, and space. (Lesson 4)

2. True This statement is true because biomes are characterized by climate conditions and their ecosystems. (Lesson 1)

3. False This statement is false because a niche is the role of a population in its community; a habitat is the place where an organism lives. (Lesson 1)

Unit 1 Review continued

9 The diagram below shows an aquatic ecosystem.

What is one abiotic factor shown in this diagram?

A the snails   **C** the crab

B the water   **D** the tree roots

10 Which of the following is an example of a biotic limiting factor for a population?

A water availability   **C** disease

B climate   **D** natural disasters

11 Which of the following is the most likely reason that a population might crash?

A The competition for the same resource suddenly drops.

B The number of prey suddenly increases.

C The number of predators suddenly decreases.

D The carrying capacity of the environment suddenly drops.

12 Grizzly bears are classified in the order Carnivora. Their diet consists of roots, tubers, berries, nuts, fungi, insects, rodents, and fish. What ecological role best describes grizzly bears?

A carnivores   **C** herbivores

B omnivores   **D** producers

13 The graph below shows the size of a squirrel population over 20 years.

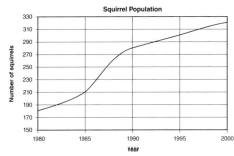

The trend displayed on the graph could be a result of what factor?

A emigration   **C** increased death rate

B immigration   **D** scarce resources

Critical Thinking
Answer the following questions in the space provided.

14 The diagram below shows how a manatee gets its energy.

Energy source   Sea grass   Manatee

What provides the energy for the sea grass, the manatee, and most life on Earth? _____.

What role does the sea grass play in this food chain? _____

According to this diagram, what type of consumer is the manatee? _____

Answers *(continued)*

4. False This statement is false because a food web illustrates the feeding relationships in an ecosystem. A food chain describes a single path of energy transfer from producers to consumers. (Lesson 2)

5. False This statement is false because a limiting factor limits the growth of a population. (Lesson 3)

6. Answer A is correct because the wrasse benefits by getting food, and the larger fish benefits by getting its mouth cleaned. (Lesson 4)

7. Answer A is correct because individual bees work together in their defined roles to benefit the entire population. (Lesson 3)

8. Answer B is correct because when prey are abundant, the predator population is more likely to grow because of the plentiful food source. (Lesson 4)

9. Answer B is correct because the water is a nonliving part of the environment. (Lesson 1)

10. Answer C is correct because the disease-causing agent could be living, and disease affects living organisms. (Lesson 3)

11. Answer D is correct because a sudden drop in what the environment can sustain will cause a population crash. (Lesson 3)

12. Answer B is correct because grizzly bears eat both plants and animals. (Lesson 2)

13. Answer B is correct because immigration is when individuals move into a population. (Lesson 3)

14. Key Elements:
    • Identifies that the sun powers most life on Earth
    • Identifies sea grass as a producer
    • Identifies manatee as an herbivore (Lesson 2)

15. Key Elements:
    • Identifies that individuals may starve
    • Identifies that populations may decrease or go extinct

Unit 1 Review continued

15 Use the diagram to help you answer the following question.

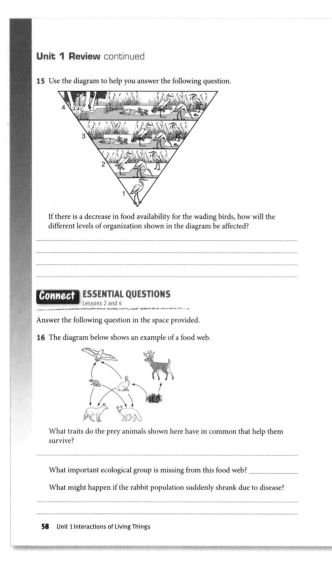

If there is a decrease in food availability for the wading birds, how will the different levels of organization shown in the diagram be affected?

_____

_____

_____

Connect **ESSENTIAL QUESTIONS**
Lessons 2 and 4

Answer the following question in the space provided.

16 The diagram below shows an example of a food web.

What traits do the prey animals shown here have in common that help them survive?

_____

What important ecological group is missing from this food web? _____

What might happen if the rabbit population suddenly shrank due to disease?

_____

_____

58   Unit 1 Interactions of Living Things

© Houghton Mifflin Harcourt Publishing Company

Quick Grading Chart

Use the chart below for quick test grading. The lesson correlations can help you target reteaching for missed items.

Item	Answer	Cognitive Complexity	Lesson
1.	—	Low	4
2.	—	Low	1
3.	—	Moderate	1
4.	—	Low	2
5.	—	Low	3
6.	A	High	4
7.	A	Moderate	3
8.	B	High	4
9.	B	Low	1
10.	C	Moderate	3
11.	D	Moderate	3
12.	B	High	2
13.	B	Low	3
14.	—	Moderate	2
15.	—	Moderate	1
16.	—	High	2, 4

Cognitive Complexity refers to the demand on thinking associated with an item, and may vary with the answer choices, the number of steps required to arrive at an answer, and other factors, but not the ability level of the student.

Answers *(continued)*

- Recognizes that communities and entire ecosystems may be affected as organisms interact through food webs; species that are prey or competitors of the wading birds may increase, and species that are predators of the wading birds may decrease. (Lesson 1)

16. Key Elements:

- Mice and rabbits are the prey in this diagram.
- Traits that help avoid predators include *quick reaction times/movements, relatively large ears, muscular hind legs, alert nature.*
- Decomposers are missing from the diagram.
- When one organism is removed from the food web, the populations of organisms that feed on it may decrease, and the changes in population sizes may affect other organisms. The rodent population might decrease as animals that preyed on rabbits ate more rodents. (Lessons 2, 4)

The Big Idea and Essential Questions

This Unit was designed to focus on this Big Idea and Essential Questions.

Big Idea Matter and energy together support life within an environment.

Lesson	ESSENTIAL QUESTION	Student Mastery	PD Professional Development	Lesson Overview
LESSON 1 Land Biomes	What are land biomes?	To describe the characteristics of different biomes that exist on land	Content Refresher, TE p. 78	TE p. 86
LESSON 2 Aquatic Ecosystems	What are aquatic ecosystems?	To describe the characteristics of marine, freshwater, and other aquatic ecosystems	Content Refresher, TE p. 79	TE p. 100
LESSON 3 Energy and Matter in Ecosystems	How do energy and matter move through ecosystems?	To explain the flow of energy and the cycles of matter in ecosystems	Content Refresher, TE p. 80	TE p. 116
LESSON 4 Changes in Ecosystems	How do ecosystems change?	To describe how natural processes change ecosystems and help them develop after a natural disturbance	Content Refresher, TE p. 81	TE p. 130
LESSON 5 Human Activity and Ecosystems	How do human activities affect ecosystems?	To describe the effects of human activities on ecosystems, and explain the role of conservation in protecting natural resources	Content Refresher, TE p. 82	TE p. 148

©L. Newman & A. Flowers/Photo Researchers, Inc.

Professional Development Science Background

Use the key words at right to access

- Professional Development from **The NSTA Learning Center**
- **SciLinks** for additional online content appropriate for students and teachers

Key words
biomes
ecosystems
food chains and food webs
living and nonliving things

NSTA National Science Teachers Association

SciLINKS
THE WORLD'S A CLICK AWAY

Options for Instruction

Two parallel paths provide coverage of the Essential Questions, with a strong **Inquiry** strand woven into each. Follow the **Print Path,** the **Digital Path,** or your customized combination of print, digital, and inquiry.

	LESSON 1 Land Biomes	**LESSON 2** Aquatic Ecosystems	**LESSON 3** Energy and Matter in Ecosystems
Essential Questions	*What are land biomes?*	*What are aquatic ecosystems?*	*How do energy and matter move through ecosystems?*
Key Topics	• Biomes • Tundra and Taiga • Desert and Grasslands • Temperate Forests and Tropical Rain Forest	• Aquatic Ecosystems • Freshwater Ecosystems • Estuaries • Marine Ecosystems	• Matter and Energy in Ecosystems • Energy Pyramids • Cycles of Matter
Print Path	**Teacher Edition** pp. 86–99 **Student Edition** pp. 62–73	**Teacher Edition** pp. 100–113 **Student Edition** pp. 74–85	**Teacher Edition** pp. 116–129 **Student Edition** pp. 88–99
Inquiry Labs	**Lab Manual** **Field Lab** Survey of a Biome's Biotic and Abiotic Factors **Quick Lab** Identify Your...Biome **Quick Lab** Climate Determines Plant Life	**Lab Manual** **Quick Lab** Life in Moving Water **Quick Lab** Light Penetration and Water Clarity	**Lab Manual** **Quick Lab** Pyramid of Energy **Quick Lab** Condensation and Evaporation ▢ Virtual Lab Investigating the Carbon Cycle
Digital Path	**Digital Path** TS661815	**Digital Path** TS661818	**Digital Path** TS693082

LESSON 4	LESSON 5	UNIT 2
Changes in Ecosystems	**Human Activity and Ecosystems**	**Unit Projects**

How do ecosystems change?	*How do human activities affect ecosystems?*	**Citizen Science Project** It's Alive! Teacher Edition p. 85 Student Edition pp. 60–61

• Changes in Ecosystems • Succession in Ecosystems • Ecosystems and Diversity	• Human Activities Affect Land Ecosystems • Human Activities Affect Aquatic Ecosystems • Ecosystem Conservation	**Video-Based Projects** The Producers of Florida Bay

Teacher Edition pp. 130–142	Teacher Edition pp. 148–161	**Unit Assessment**
Student Edition pp. 100–109	Student Edition pp. 114–125	**Formative Assessment** **Strategies** RTI Throughout TE **Lesson Reviews** SE **Unit PreTest**
		Summative Assessment **Alternative Assessment** (1 per lesson) RTI **Lesson Quizzes**
Lab Manual **Field Lab** ...Succession Follows a Human Disturbance **Quick Lab** Measuring...Diversity Virtual Lab Changes in Ecosystems	Lab Manual **Field Lab** Field Investigation of Plant Quantity and Diversity **Quick Lab** ...Acidity of Water **Quick Lab** Biodiversity All Around Us	**Unit Tests A and B** **Unit Review** RTI (with answer remediation) **Practice Tests** (end of module)
		Project-Based Assessment See the Assessment Guide for quizzes and tests. Go Online to edit and create quizzes and tests.
Digital Path TS673498 	Digital Path TS673869 	**Response to Intervention** See RTI teacher support materials on p. PD6.

Differentiated Instruction

English Language Proficiency

Strategies for **English Language Learners (ELL)** are provided for each lesson, under the Explain tabs.

LESSON 1 *Biotic and Abiotic Breakdown,* TE p. 91

LESSON 2 *Modeling Freshwater Ecosystems,* TE p. 105

LESSON 3 *Understanding Matter and Energy,* TE p. 121

LESSON 4 *Self-Stick Note Ecosystems,* TE p. 135

LESSON 5 *Diagramming Acid Rain Formation,* TE p. 153

Vocabulary strategies provided for all students can also be a particular help for ELL. Use different strategies for each lesson or choose one or two to use throughout the unit. Vocabulary strategies can be found in the Explain tab for each lesson (TE pp. 91, 105, 121, 135, and 153).

Leveled Inquiry

Inquiry labs, activities, probing questions, and daily demos provide a range of inquiry levels. Preview them under the Engage and Explore tabs starting on TE pp. 88, 102, 118, 132, and 150.

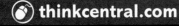

Levels of **Inquiry**	**DIRECTED** inquiry	**GUIDED** inquiry	**INDEPENDENT** inquiry
	introduces inquiry skills within a structured framework.	develops inquiry skills within a supportive environment.	deepens inquiry skills with student-driven questions or procedures.

Each long lab has two inquiry options:

LESSON 1 **Field Lab** *Survey of a Biome's Biotic and Abiotic Factors*

LESSON 4 **Field Lab** *Predicting How Succession Follows a Human Disturbance*

LESSON 5 **Field Lab** *Field Investigation of Plant Quantity and Diversity*

 Go Digital! 🔍 **thinkcentral.com**

Digital Path

The Unit 2 Resource Gateway is your guide to all of the digital resources for this unit. To access the Gateway, visit thinkcentral.com.

Digital Interactive Lessons

Lesson 1 Land Biomes TS661815

Lesson 2 Aquatic Ecosystems TS661818

Lesson 3 Energy and Matter in Ecosystems TS693082

Lesson 4 Changes in Ecosystems TS673498

Lesson 5 Human Activity and Ecosystems TS673869

More Digital Resources

In addition to digital lessons, you will find the following digital resources for Unit 2:

Video-Based Project: The Producers of Florida Bay (previewed on TE p. 84)

Virtual Labs: Investigating the Carbon Cycle (previewed on p. 119) Changes in Ecosystems (previewed on p. 133)

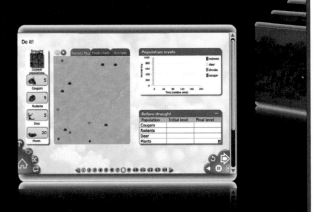

RTI ▶ Response to Intervention

Response to Intervention (RTI) is a process for identifying and supporting students who are not making expected progress toward essential learning goals. The following *ScienceFusion* components can be used to provide strategic and intensive intervention.

Component	Location	Strategies and Benefits
STUDENT EDITION Active Reading prompts, Visualize It!, Think Outside the Book	**Throughout each lesson**	Student responses can be used as screening tools to assess whether intervention is needed.
TEACHER EDITION Formative Assessment, Probing Questions, Learning Alerts	**Throughout each lesson**	Opportunities are provided to assess and remediate student understanding of lesson concepts.
TEACHER EDITION Extend Science Concepts	**Reinforce and Review, TE pp. 92, 106, 122, 136, 154** **Going Further, TE pp. 93, 107, 123, 137, 155**	Additional activities allow students to reinforce and extend their understanding of lesson concepts.
TEACHER EDITION Evaluate Student Mastery	**Formative Assessment, TE pp. 93, 107, 123, 137, 155** **Alternative Assessment, TE pp. 93, 107, 123, 137, 155**	These assessments allow for greater flexibility in assessing students with differing physical, mental, and language abilities as well as varying learning and communication modes.
TEACHER EDITION Unit Review Remediation	**Unit Review, TE pp. 162–164**	Includes reference back to Lesson Planning pages for remediation activities and assignments.
INTERACTIVE DIGITAL LESSONS and VIRTUAL LABS	**thinkcentral.com Unit 2 Gateway** **Lesson 1 TS661815** **Lesson 2 TS661818** **Lesson 3 TS693082** **Lesson 4 TS673498** **Lesson 5 TS673869**	Lessons and labs make content accessible through simulations, animations, videos, audio, and integrated assessment. Useful for review and reteaching of lesson concepts.

Content Refresher

Professional Development

Land Biomes

ESSENTIAL QUESTION
What are land biomes?

1. Biomes

Students will learn to identify the factors that distinguish land biomes.

A biome is a region of Earth that has a specific climate and community of plants and animals. Examples of biomes include deserts, grasslands, and temperate forests. In every biome, plants and animals have adaptations that help them survive.

A biome may have many ecosystems where organisms live together and interact. An ecosystem encompasses all the biotic and abiotic factors in a particular area. Biotic factors describe the interactions between organisms. Abiotic factors include climate, water, sunlight, wind, rocks, and soil.

Climate is the long-term average temperature and precipitation in a region. Climate, which characterizes a biome, is determined by latitude and continental position. Regions near the poles, for example, have cold climates.

The amount of sunlight an area receives directly affects the populations in an ecosystem within a biome. Other factors include soil type and water availability.

2. Tundra and Taiga

Students will learn to identify the characteristic climates and communities of the tundra and taiga biomes.

Tundra, the biome near the polar regions, has a cold climate with very little precipitation. Permafrost, a thick layer of permanently frozen soil beneath the surface of the ground, can only support plants with shallow roots. Many animals that live in the tundra migrate to warmer places during the winter. Other animals, such as musk oxen, can live in the tundra year-round because of thick layers of fur or fat.

Taiga [TY•guh], or boreal forest, has a cold climate but is wetter than tundra. Taiga is located in Canada and northern Europe and Asia. Coniferous trees, which have needlelike leaves, thrive in taiga. Animals that live in taiga include wolves, owls, and elk, which live there year-round, and migratory birds that leave for the winter.

3. Desert and Grasslands

Students will learn to identify the characteristic climates and communities of the desert and grassland biomes.

Desert has rocky or sandy soil and very little precipitation. Many deserts are hot during the day and cold at night. Desert plants and animals have adaptations to conserve water and to stay cool. Some desert animals, such as kangaroo rats, are active only at night. Many snakes and lizards seek out shady places during hot days.

Tropical grasslands, such as the African savanna, have warm or hot average temperatures and seasonal rainfall. Temperate grasslands, such as the North American prairie, have moderate precipitation, hot summers, and cold winters. Grazing animals, such as zebras, gazelles, or bison, feed on the abundant grasses. Predators, such as cheetahs and coyotes, hunt the grazers.

4. Temperate Forests and Tropical Rain Forest

Students will learn to identify the characteristic climates and communities of temperate and tropical forests.

Temperate deciduous forests have moderate precipitation, hot summers, and cold winters. This biome contains deciduous, or broadleaf, trees that drop their leaves as winter approaches. Fallen leaves decay and add humus to the soil, making it nutrient-rich. Animals that live in these forests include bears, squirrels, rabbits, and hawks.

Temperate rain forests have a long, wet, cool season and a relatively dry summer. This biome is home to many coniferous trees. Plants grow well here throughout the year. Animals that live in these forests include bobcats, minks, and salamanders.

Tropical rain forests are located near the equator, where the climate is warm and rainy. Although the soil is low in nutrients, this biome supports dense layers of diverse plants. Animals that live here include jaguars, monkeys, and butterflies.

Teacher to Teacher

Matt Moller, M.Ed.
Carmel Middle School
Carmel, IN

Lesson 5 Human Activity and Ecosystems   Design a "Current Events" bulletin board for which students bring in news clippings or online articles about local, state, and/or national environmental issues. Have students share a summary of each offering and describe whether the news is about a positive or negative impact of human activity on the environment.

Lesson 2

Aquatic Ecosystems
ESSENTIAL QUESTION
What are aquatic ecosystems?

1. Aquatic Ecosystems

Students will learn to describe the factors that characterize aquatic ecosystems.

Nearly three-fourths of Earth is covered with water. The different bodies of water are home to aquatic ecosystems. Like organisms on land, organisms that live in or near water are affected by environmental conditions. Abiotic (nonliving) factors that affect aquatic organisms include the water's temperature, depth, pH, light penetration, salt content (salinity), nutrient availability, and water flow rate. Salinity determines the three major types of aquatic ecosystems.

2. Freshwater Ecosystems

Students will learn to identify and describe freshwater ecosystems.

Freshwater ecosystems contain very little salt. Bodies of fresh water are limited in area and account for less than one percent of all water on Earth. Fresh water is susceptible to pollution from runoff and sewage from land.

Lakes and ponds are relatively still bodies of fresh water. Plankton and algae are typically the main producers in freshwater ecosystem food webs.

Wetlands, including bogs, marshes, and swamps, are areas that are saturated with water for at least part of the year. Wetlands are important because they filter polluted water and prevent flooding by absorbing and slowly releasing large amounts of water. Wetlands have a diverse community of organisms because they are often nutrient-rich.

Rivers and streams often originate inland and flow through several land ecosystems toward the ocean. Organisms have adaptations to help them survive in various water flow rates.

3. Estuaries

Students will learn to identify and describe estuaries.

An estuary is a partially enclosed body of water formed where a river meets the ocean. It contains a mixture of fresh and salt water. Estuaries are often referred to as the ocean's "nursery" because many ocean-dwelling fish, sea birds, and other animals lay eggs and raise young there. Estuaries also help protect coastal regions from erosion and flooding.

4. Marine Ecosystems

Students will learn to identify and describe marine ecosystems.

Marine ecosystems have high salinity. Marine ecosystems in and along coastal oceans are found in the intertidal and neritic zones. The intertidal zone is the area above water at low tide and underwater at high tide. Crustaceans, mollusks, algae, and other organisms are adapted to withstand changing conditions and battering ocean waves. The neritic zone, or coastal ocean, is the underwater zone between the coastline and the continental shelf. Here, the water supports abundant life because it is nutrient-rich and receives plenty of sunlight. Commercial fisheries are often found in the coastal ocean.

In the open ocean, phytoplankton live on the water's surface, where sunlight is able to penetrate. This is where the majority of photosynthesis on Earth takes place. The deep ocean receives little sunlight. Organisms there have adaptations that help them obtain energy without photosynthesis.

 COMMON MISCONCEPTIONS **RTI**

CORAL REEFS Students might not know that the primary structure of a coral reef is a living part of the ecosystem.

This misconception is addressed on p. 112.

Content Refresher (continued)

 Professional Development

Energy and Matter in Ecosystems

ESSENTIAL QUESTION
How do energy and matter move through ecosystems?

1. Matter and Energy in Ecosystems

Students will learn that living things are made of matter and are fueled by energy.

All matter is made of atoms held together by bonds. Energy can be either chemical energy from food, or light and heat energy from the sun.

Plants take in matter from their surroundings. They combine this matter with light energy from the sun to produce sugars during photosynthesis. It is for this reason that plants are called producers. These sugars store chemical energy. Consumers are animals that cannot produce their own food energy. They get food, or matter and energy, by eating producers and other consumers.

In a closed system, matter and energy are conserved. Although the total amount stays the same, matter changes form through chemical reactions. Chemical reactions involve the making, breaking, or rearranging of bonds between atoms. Likewise, energy also changes form. Organisms use energy for life processes such as moving, growing, and reproducing. Most of the remaining energy is released into the environment as heat, a waste product of these activities. Unlike closed systems, ecosystems are open systems through which matter and energy flow.

2. Energy Pyramids

Students will learn that an energy pyramid illustrates the energy flow within an ecosystem.

An energy pyramid is organized with producers on the bottom tier and consumers on higher tiers. Producers get their energy by converting energy from the sun into chemical energy. At each level, most energy is used by the organism or converted to heat. A small amount is stored. This stored energy is obtained by consumers when they eat an organism at a lower level. Therefore, the consumers at the top of the food chain have the least amount of energy available to them.

3. Cycles of Matter

Students will learn that water, nitrogen, and carbon cycle through ecosystems.

The continuous movement of water from one place and one form to another is known as the water cycle. The water cycle involves several processes. Evaporation is the change of water from liquid to vapor. Condensation is the change of water vapor to liquid. Precipitation is the water that falls from clouds.

Nitrogen also cycles in the environment. Lightning breaks apart nitrogen molecules, which are absorbed by soil when it rains. Bacteria change nitrogen into a usable form. Plants take in nitrogen compounds through their roots. Animals get nitrogen by eating plants or animals. Decomposers return nitrogen to the atmosphere and soil by breaking down dead organisms.

Carbon cycles between organisms and the nonliving environment through four main processes: photosynthesis, cellular respiration, decomposition, and combustion.

 COMMON MISCONCEPTIONS   RTI

CONSERVATION OF MATTER AND ENERGY Students struggle with the concept of matter and energy being conserved. They may misunderstand the concept in the following ways:

1. They think that when something burns, it disappears.

2. When energy is "used up," it is gone.

3. Students tend to think matter and energy are created and destroyed rather than undergoing form changes and transformations.

This misconception is addressed in the Activity on p. 118 and the Learning Alert on p. 125.

Changes in Ecosystems

ESSENTIAL QUESTION

How do ecosystems change?

1. Changes in Ecosystems

Students will learn about gradual and sudden changes to ecosystems.

Ecosystems may change slowly, as months and years pass, or quite suddenly if a storm hits or a volcano erupts. Natural eutrophication is one example of a gradual change that transforms a body of water, such as a lake or a pond, into a meadow. It occurs when a body of water receives enough nutrients to support large amounts of plant or algal growth. Human actions sometimes result in artificial eutrophication, such as when fertilizer washes into a lake from farms or lawns.

Sudden changes to ecosystems can occur due to natural events, such as severe storms, fires, and volcanic eruptions. For example, the eruption of Mount St. Helens buried the surrounding area in ash and debris, yet the ecosystem recovered relatively quickly. Burrowing animals, including moles, pocket gophers, and ants, survived underground. After the eruption these animals helped mix the soil and allow new plants to grow. Although these events may seem to have strictly negative effects, they can be an essential part of life; the cones of black spruce, in fact, release seeds only after a forest fire. Fires also clear out understory vegetation that blocks light and adds nitrogen-rich ash to the soil.

2. Succession in Ecosystems

Students will learn that one ecosystem can change into another.

Succession is the gradual development or replacement of one ecological community by another. In primary succession, a community develops where no life exists and there is no soil. Pioneer species, which are the first organisms to arrive, help break down rock and form soil. Producers, such as lichens, are the first pioneer species to arrive.

After the pioneer species come a succession of plants, including mosses, ferns, grasses and herbs, woody shrubs, and, finally, trees. Each type of plant helps form deeper and richer soil that will support the roots of a larger plant. The smaller plants eventually decline or die out as the larger plants take up space and block the light.

Secondary succession occurs in regions that have been disturbed but where soil still exists. Examples include the succession that occurs after a severe storm or natural disaster or on an abandoned farm. Typically, secondary succession occurs much faster than primary succession. Opportunistic species, such as dandelions and other plants often considered to be weeds, quickly colonize the soil in these places.

Over time, succession creates a *climax community*, such as a hardwood forest. A climax community does not last forever and will over time be replaced by a community of different species following another disturbance. Mature communities may actually be slightly less diverse than intermediate communities because climax species dominate.

3. Ecosystems and Diversity

Students will learn how succession leads to biodiversity.

An ecosystem begins with a few pioneer species, yet as soil forms and new plants and animals arrive, the ecosystem becomes able to support a wide variety of organisms. *Biodiversity* is a measure of the number and variety of species in an area.

Biodiversity helps an ecosystem withstand change, while low biodiversity can allow devastating changes to occur. For example, beginning in the 1930s, the fungus that causes Dutch Elm disease spread rapidly across North America because of the large numbers of elm trees growing in towns and cities. Millions of elm trees died, approximately half the entire population in the United States.

Content Refresher (continued)

Professional Development

Human Activity and Ecosystems

ESSENTIAL QUESTION
How do human activities affect ecosystems?

1. Human Activities Affect Land Ecosystems

Students will learn that human activities affect land ecosystems.

In only the last 200 years, Earth's human population has grown from 1 billion to more than 6 billion people. This growth has resulted in changes to Earth's natural land environments as humans increase their need for land and other resources and seek ways to dispose of their wastes.

The production of wastes and pollutants is one of the ways in which human activities adversely impact ecosystems. Pollution can be defined as any material or condition that harms the environment, or any deleterious change in the environment caused by the addition of harmful materials (chemical, biological, etc.) or the production of harmful conditions (sound, light, or heat). Pollution can be disruptive to land ecosystems by creating conditions that are harmful to Earth's organisms.

Students may think of pollution as being only trash or chemicals; however, light can be a pollutant too, as they can see on the lesson opener in the student book, which depicts a sea turtle. Sea turtles often hatch at night and determine where the ocean is by the reflection of moonlight on the water. However, coastal development has increased the amount of light near nesting beaches, and as a result turtle hatchlings may mistakenly turn toward land, rather than toward water.

2. Human Activities Affect Aquatic Ecosystems

Students will learn that human activities affect aquatic ecosystems, both marine and freshwater.

One of the main ways humans impact aquatic ecosystems is through the production and release of pollution and the improper disposal of wastes, such as sewage or garbage. Some of the pollution of aquatic ecosystems, such as the release of oil into the Gulf of Mexico following the explosion of an oil rig in the summer of 2010, is point-source pollution that can be traced to its point of origin. However, much of the pollution that affects aquatic ecosystems is nonpoint-source pollution that cannot be tracked to a single source. Such pollution often occurs when chemicals leaked onto land are washed into aquatic environments with runoff. Ocean pollution also includes garbage, particularly plastic waste. Some plastic products, such as the rings used to hold beverage containers together and plastic bags, pose a direct threat to ocean animals that become entangled in the plastic or ingest the material when they mistake it for food. In recent years, scientists have identified several "garbage patches," regions of the ocean where debris (largely plastics) collects in the Pacific and Atlantic Oceans.

3. Ecosystem Conservation

Students will learn how human activities such as stewardship and conservation can help to protect Earth's ecosystems.

The growing demand of humans on Earth's resources is responsible for much of the damage done to Earth's ecosystems. However, good stewardship and the implementation of conservation methods enable people to manage their resource use in a sustainable manner that does less harm to natural environments.

Because Earth is a global system, however, conservation efforts will require the cooperation of many people, not only within nations but also internationally, to be most effective.

Teacher Notes

Advance Planning

These activities may take extended time or special conditions.

Unit 2

Video-Based Project The Producers of Florida Bay, p. 84
    multiple activities spanning several lessons

Project It's Alive!, p. 85
    design, create, care for, and observe a classroom garden

Graphic Organizers and Vocabulary pp. 91, 92, 105, 106, 121, 122, 135, 136, 153, 154
    ongoing with reading

Lesson 1

Daily Demo What's the Difference?, p. 89
    collect leaves and small branches in advance

Field Lab Survey of a Biome's Biotic and Abiotic Factors, p. 89
    requires outdoor observations

Lesson 4

Daily Demo Disaster Strikes!, p. 133
    foam and cornstarch-based packing peanuts

Field Lab Predicting How Succession Follows Human Disturbance, p. 133
    requires two 45-min periods and outdoor observations

Lesson 5

Activity Hay, What's That?, p. 150
    requires observations over several days

Field Lab Field Investigation of Plant Quantity and Diversity, p. 151
    requires three 45-min periods and outdoor observations

Quick Lab Investigate Acidity of Water, p. 151
    rainwater and pond, lake, or stream water

What Do You Think?

Have students think about how organisms get and use matter and energy.

Ask: What is matter? anything that has mass and takes up space

Ask: What things in this ecosystem are made of matter? Sample answer: everything you can see: mangroves, water, roseate spoonbills, air

Ask: Where do mangroves get the energy they need to live and grow? They make food through photosynthesis. They get energy from the food they make.

Ask: What kinds of matter do mangroves take in during photosynthesis? carbon dioxide, water

UNIT 2
Earth's Biomes and Ecosystems

Big Idea
Matter and energy together support life within an environment.

Mangroves

What do you think?
Mangroves and Roseate Spoonbills are both found in Florida. How do organisms like these get and use matter and energy?

Roseate Spoonbill

59

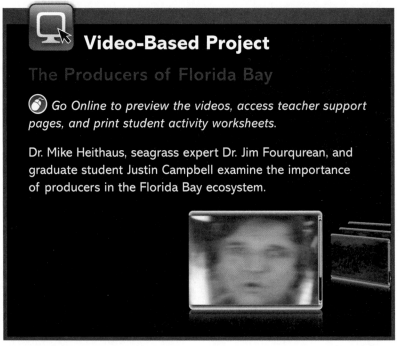

Video-Based Project
The Producers of Florida Bay

🖱 *Go Online to preview the videos, access teacher support pages, and print student activity worksheets.*

Dr. Mike Heithaus, seagrass expert Dr. Jim Fourqurean, and graduate student Justin Campbell examine the importance of producers in the Florida Bay ecosystem.

Unit 2
Earth's Biomes and Ecosystems

CITIZEN SCIENCE
It's Alive!

This garden is home to many vegetables and other plants.

(1) Think About It

What role do plants play in your life?

(2) Ask A Question

How do plants use matter and energy?
As a class, design a plan for a garden plot or window box garden in which the class can grow a variety of plants. Remember that plants have different growing periods and requirements.

Sketch It!
Draw your plan to show where each plant will be placed.

(3) Apply Your Knowledge

A What do your plants need in order to grow?

B Which of the things you listed above are examples of matter? Which are examples of energy?

C Create and care for your classroom garden and observe the plant growth.

Take It Home

Describe an area in your community that is used for growing food. If there is no such area, initiate a plan to plant in an area that you think could be used.

CITIZEN SCIENCE

Unit Project It's Alive!

1. Think About It

Students should explain that plants play an important role in their lives. Students should recognize that they eat plants (or animals that have eaten plants) to get energy and that they breathe oxygen produced by plants. Encourage students to think about the aesthetic value of plants and about the use of plants in clothing, building materials, medicines, fuels, and other products.

2. Ask a Question

Allow students to use library resources or the Internet to research plant species that interest them. Sketches should be clearly labeled and should indicate where each plant will be placed. Students might choose to group together plants with similar growing periods and requirements.

3. Apply Your Knowledge

Plants need air, water, nutrients (from soil), and light to grow. Air, water, and nutrients/soil are examples of matter; light is an example of energy.

Take It Home

Growing food in urban areas has become a popular trend in communities. By transforming formerly unused spaces such as rooftops into gardens and greenhouses, people are able to help and protect various ecosystems. Students' descriptions of such an area in their community should include information about where the area is located, what is grown there, how it is organized, and who is responsible for its care. If no such area exists, students' plans should include similar information, along with reasons for why the area they chose would be a good area for growing food.

Land Biomes

Essential Question What are land biomes?

 Professional Development

For more detailed information about the topics in this lesson, refer to the Content Refresher in the Unit Opener pages.

Opening Your Lesson

Begin the lesson by assessing students' prerequisite and prior knowledge.

Prerequisite Knowledge

- Basic principles of ecology
- Biotic and abiotic factors found in ecosystems

Accessing Prior Knowledge

Think, Pair, Share Direct students to make a two-column chart to list biotic and abiotic factors in an ecosystem. After they complete their charts individually, have them compare their lists with a partner. Then gather the whole class to create and display a master chart of biotic and abiotic factors.

◯ *Optional Online resource: Think, Pair, Share support*

Customize Your Opening

☐ **Accessing Prior Knowledge,** above
☐ **Print Path** Engage Your Brain, SE p. 63
☐ **Print Path** Active Reading, SE p. 63
☐ **Digital Path** Lesson Opener

Key Topics/Learning Goals	Supporting Concepts
Biomes 1 Explain what a biome is and provide examples of biomes. 2 Describe what differentiates one biome from another. 3 Describe the relationship between biomes and ecosystems.	• A biome is a major regional community of organisms, defined by climatic conditions and plant communities living there. • Plant and animal communities, climate, and other abiotic factors such as soil type, amount of sunlight, and water availability characterize a biome. • Biomes are large and contain several ecosystems.
Tundra and Taiga 1 Describe the tundra and taiga biomes. 2 Provide examples of plant and animal adaptations.	• Tundra is characterized by low average temperatures and little precipitation. • Taiga is characterized by low average temperatures similar to those in the tundra. • Animals that live in biomes that are cold all year often grow thick coats.
Desert and Grasslands 1 Describe the desert and grassland biomes. 2 Provide examples of plant and animal adaptations.	• Deserts are characterized by very dry climates and little precipitation. • Grasslands are characterized by moderate rainfall, warm summers, and cold winters. • Cacti are desert plants that have needle-like leaves that conserve water.
Temperate Forests and Tropical Rain Forest 1 Describe the temperate forest and tropical rain forest biomes. 2 Provide examples of plant and animal adaptations.	• Temperate deciduous forests are defined by moderate rainfall throughout the year, with hot summers and cold winters. • Tropical rain forests are found near the equator, are warm year-round, and receive the most rainfall of all of Earth's biomes. • Some plants grow on the branches of trees in order to receive sunlight.

Options for Instruction

Two parallel paths provide coverage of the Essential Questions, with a strong **Inquiry** strand woven into each. Follow the **Print Path,** the **Digital Path,** or your customized combination of print, digital, and inquiry.

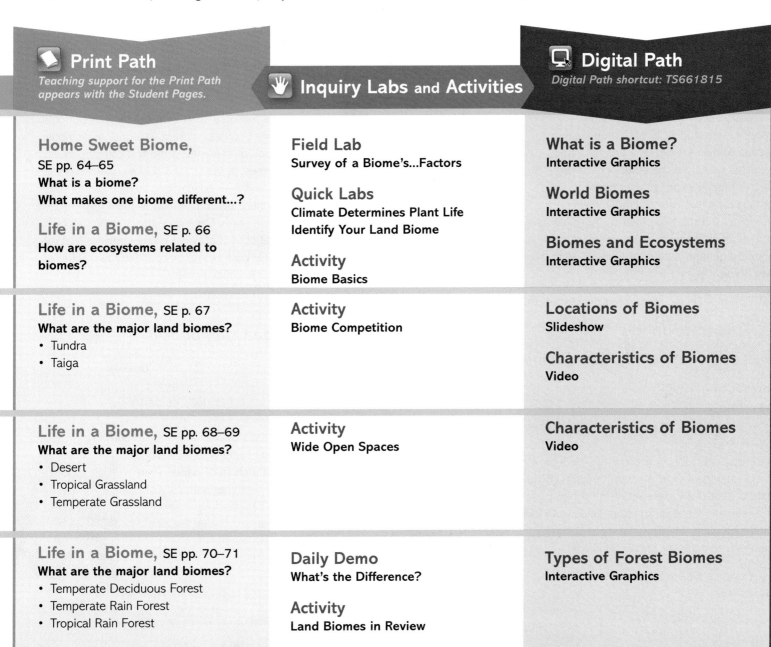

Print Path
Teaching support for the Print Path appears with the Student Pages.

Inquiry Labs and Activities

Digital Path
Digital Path shortcut: TS661815

Home Sweet Biome,
SE pp. 64–65
What is a biome?
What makes one biome different...?

Life in a Biome, SE p. 66
How are ecosystems related to biomes?

Field Lab
Survey of a Biome's...Factors

Quick Labs
Climate Determines Plant Life
Identify Your Land Biome

Activity
Biome Basics

What is a Biome?
Interactive Graphics

World Biomes
Interactive Graphics

Biomes and Ecosystems
Interactive Graphics

Life in a Biome, SE p. 67
What are the major land biomes?
• Tundra
• Taiga

Activity
Biome Competition

Locations of Biomes
Slideshow

Characteristics of Biomes
Video

Life in a Biome, SE pp. 68–69
What are the major land biomes?
• Desert
• Tropical Grassland
• Temperate Grassland

Activity
Wide Open Spaces

Characteristics of Biomes
Video

Life in a Biome, SE pp. 70–71
What are the major land biomes?
• Temperate Deciduous Forest
• Temperate Rain Forest
• Tropical Rain Forest

Daily Demo
What's the Difference?

Activity
Land Biomes in Review

Types of Forest Biomes
Interactive Graphics

Options for Assessment

See the Evaluate page for options, including Formative Assessment, Summative Assessment, and Unit Review.

Engage and Explore

Activities and Discussion

Activity *Biome Basics*

Biomes

👥 small groups
🕐 20 min
🔍 **GUIDED** inquiry

Jigsaw Divide the class into six groups and assign each group a major biome. Provide each student in each group with a picture of their biome. As a group, instruct students to discuss the biotic and abiotic factors that characterize their biome. Once groups think that every member of their group is an "expert" on their biome, direct students to intermingle with students from other groups. Then each student can describe the abiotic and biotic factors of their biome to the other members of their new group.

⊚ *Optional Online resource: Jigsaw support*

Take It Home *My Own Biome*

Introducing Key Topics

👥 Student-adult pairs
🕐 60 min
🔍 **GUIDED** inquiry

Have students identify and explore the biome in which they live. Encourage them to take a walk through a neighborhood, park, or local natural area and make a list of the ecosystems they see and the abiotic factors influencing their biome. Students should write a one-paragraph summary to complete this assignment.

⊚ *Optional Online resource: student worksheet*

Activity *Biome Competition*

Biomes, Tundra and Taiga, Desert and Grasslands, Temperate Forests and Tropical Rain Forest

👥 pairs
🕐 15 min
🔍 **GUIDED** inquiry

Competitive Game Set up a class competition with students working in pairs. Direct pairs to make a 2x6 grid, or distribute 2x6 grids to each pair of students. In the first column, list each of the six major biomes. In the second column, direct pairs to list as many organisms and their adaptations as they can for each biome. To enhance the class competition element of the activity, limit student response times. Determine the winning pair by counting up the total correct answers on the grid. Alternatively, determine winners for each biome by counting the number of correct answers for individual biomes.

Activity *Wide Open Spaces*

Grasslands

👥 pairs or small groups
🕐 varied
🔍 **GUIDED** inquiry

Direct students to research how a controlled burn in a grassland is accomplished. Ask students to list their sources on a separate sheet of paper. Then have each group write a brief summary of the process and its benefits to grassland survival. Students can share their findings with the class.

Customize Your Labs

🔲 *See the Lab Manual for lab datasheets.*

⊚ *Go Online for editable lab datasheets.*

Labs and Demos

Daily Demo *What's the Difference?*

Engage

Temperate Forests and Tropical Rain Forests

 whole class
 10 min
 DIRECTED inquiry

Use this short demo after discussing temperate deciduous and temperate rain forests.

PURPOSE **To demonstrate the difference between deciduous and coniferous trees**

MATERIALS

- leaves and small branches from deciduous trees
- needles and small branches from coniferous trees

1 Identify the deciduous and coniferous plant material for students.

2 Pass materials among students for them to touch and examine.

3 **Observing Ask:** What are the differences between the two leaf types? Deciduous leaves are flat and smooth. Coniferous leaves are dry, thin, and needle-shaped. **Ask:** How are these differences, or adaptations, appropriate for their corresponding biomes? Coniferous trees typically use stored reserves rather than rely on consistent inputs of solar energy and photosynthesis. Also, they do not waste energy re-growing leaves each spring. Deciduous trees have flat leaves to receive as much sunlight as possible for photosynthesis. When these leaves fall off, the leaves decay on the forest floor, replenishing the nutrients in the soil.

Quick Lab *Climate Determines Plant Life*

PURPOSE **To analyze the relationship between plant features and climate**

See the Lab Manual or go Online for planning information.

Field Lab *Survey of a Biome's Biotic and Abiotic Factors*

Biomes

 small groups
 45 min
GUIDED inquiry

Students will investigate biotic and abiotic factors in the biome in which they live and summarize those factors.

PURPOSE **To describe what characterizes the biome in which you live**

MATERIALS

- camera
- computer w/ Internet access
- light meter
- local field guides
- magnifying lens
- drawing paper
- colored pencils
- plastic bags
- garden shovel
- ruler

 Quick Lab *Identify Your Land Biome*

Biomes

small groups
30 min
GUIDED inquiry

Students will research and describe the climate and dominant plant community for the area in which they live.

PURPOSE **To describe abiotic and biotic factors that characterize your biome**

MATERIALS

- computer with Internet access
- field guide of local plants
- pencil

Activities and Discussion

- ☐ **Activity** Biome Basics
- ☐ **Take It Home** My Own Biome
- ☐ **Activity** Biome Competition
- ☐ **Activity** Wide Open Spaces

Labs and Demos

- ☐ **Daily Demo** What's the Difference?
- ☐ **Quick Lab** Climate...Plant Life
- ☐ **Field Lab** Survey of a Biome's Biotic and Abiotic Factors
- ☐ **Quick Lab** Identify Your Land Biome

Your Resources

_____

_____

_____

_____

Explain Science Concepts

Key Topics	📖 Print Path	💻 Digital Path
Biomes	☐ **Home Sweet Biome,** SE pp. 64–65 • Visualize It!, #5 • Active Reading (Annotation strategy), #6 • Visualize It!, #7 ☐ **Life in a Biome,** SE p. 66 • Visualize It!, #8	☐ **What is a Biome?** Define biome. ☐ **World Biomes** Locate Earth's biomes on a map. ☐ **Biomes and Ecosystems** Identify the differences between ecosystems and biomes.
Tundra and Taiga	☐ **Life in a Biome,** SE p. 67 • Active Reading (Annotation strategy), #9 • Visualize It!, #10 Active Reading 9 Identify Underline the abiotic features that characterize tundra and taiga biomes.	☐ **Locations of Biomes** Describe the characteristics of tundra and taiga biomes.
Desert and Grasslands	☐ **Life in a Biome,** SE pp. 68–69 • Active Reading (Annotation strategy), #11 • Visualize It!, #12 • Visualize It!, #13	☐ **Characteristics of Biomes** Compare and contrast the characteristics of a desert, tropical grassland, and temperate grassland.
Temperate Forests and Tropical Rain Forest	☐ **Life in a Biome,** SE pp. 70–71 • Visualize It!, #14 • Think Outside the Book, #15 • Visualize It!, #16	☐ **Types of Forest Biomes** Compare and contrast the characteristics of a temperate deciduous forest, temperate rain forest, and tropical rain forest.

Differentiated Instruction

Basic *Compare and Contrast*

Synthesizing Key Topics	👥 individuals
	🕐 15–20 min

Venn Diagram After students have learned about Earth's major biomes, direct them to create separate Venn diagrams to identify similarities and differences within the following pairs: tundra/taiga, desert/grassland, and temperate rain forest/ tropical rain forest.

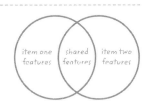

Variation The teacher could put information about biomes onto index cards. With partners, students could arrange cards on their desk and then make a Venn Diagram.

 Optional Online resource: Venn Diagram support

Advanced *Human-Biome Interaction*

Synthesizing Key Topics	👥 whole class
	🕐 10 min

Discussion Begin by telling students that humans alter ecosystems. Most scientists think that human activities are also affecting Earth's climate. Use the following questions to guide your class discussion. **Ask:** How can humans change ecosystems? Do you think humans can alter biomes? Is one more difficult to change than another? Why or why not? Insist that students support their opinions with logical arguments and reasons.

 Optional Online rubric: Class Discussion

ELL *Biotic and Abiotic Breakdown*

Biomes	👥 individuals or pairs
	🕐 10 min

Students may be unfamiliar with the words *biotic* and *abiotic*. Help students understand the meaning of these words by separating each into root, suffix, and prefix.

- *bio* means *life*
- *-ic* means *having to do with*
- *a-* means *not*

Direct students to write each word, then underneath each, have them arrange and write the meaning of the prefix, root, and suffix to create a definition for each word.

🌐 *Optional Online resources: Prefixes, Suffixes, Word Roots support*

Lesson Vocabulary

biome	grassland	desert
taiga	tundra	coniferous tree
deciduous tree		

Previewing Vocabulary

👥 whole class	🕐 15–20 min

Word Splash Before reading the lesson, complete a Word Splash activity for the following vocabulary words:

  biome-global region, determined by climate
  taiga-very cold, forest
  tundra-very cold, frozen ground
  coniferous-evergreen trees
  deciduous-broadleaf trees

Instruct students to write two or three sentences for each word to predict their definitions.

🌐 *Optional Online resource: Word Splash support*

Reinforcing Vocabulary

👥 individuals	🕐 30 min

Word Squares Direct students to develop Word Squares for each vocabulary word. Encourage students to create simple drawings based on the content learned in the lesson.

TERM translation	symbol or picture
my meaning dictionary definition	sentence

🌐 *Optional Online resource: Word Square support*

Customize Your Core Lesson

Core Instruction

- ☐ **Print Path** choices
- ☐ **Digital Path** choices

Vocabulary

- ☐ **Previewing Vocabulary** Word Splash
- ☐ **Reinforcing Vocabulary** Word Squares

Your Resources

Differentiated Instruction

- ☐ **Basic** Compare and Contrast
- ☐ **Advanced** Human-Biome Interaction
- ☐ **ELL** Biotic and Abiotic Breakdown

Extend Science Concepts

Reinforce and Review

Activity *Land Biomes in Review*

Synthesizing Key Topics
👥 whole class
🕐 20 min

Pictures and Captions Help students review the material by following these steps:

1   After students have read the material, direct them to combine the photos of different biomes they collected earlier in the lesson. As a class, choose one photo to represent each biome.

2   Display each photo one by one. Help students develop a list of characteristics for each biome as its corresponding photo is displayed. Direct students to write their responses on self-stick notes. Then post the photos around the room and allow students to place their self-stick notes near the corresponding biome.

3   Combine all correct student responses into a master chart describing the major biomes on Earth. Have students copy this chart into their notes, or make copies and distribute to the class.

Graphic Organizer

Summarizing Key Topics
👥 individuals
🕐 20 min

Layered Book Instruct students to create a Layered Book FoldNote. On the exposed bottom of each page, students should write the terms as follows: *biome, tundra* and *taiga, desert* and *grassland, temperate forest* and *tropical rain forest*. Then direct students to write a summary description of each biome on the corresponding page. For the *biome* page, students should write a detailed definition of a biome.

⦿ *Online resource: Layered Book support*

Going Further

Life Science Connection

Biomes
👥 individuals or pairs
🕐 varied

Poster Presentation Have students research one of the minor biomes, such as chaparral, semi-desert, tropical monsoon forest, or warm moist evergreen forest. After completing their research, students should create a poster to teach the class about their chosen minor biome. Remind students to include a list of resources with their presentation.

⦿ *Optional Online rubric: Posters and Displays*

Social Studies Connection

Desert and Grasslands
👥 individuals or pairs
🕐 varied

The Great Plains Explain that the Great Plains of the United States today include Iowa, Missouri, Oklahoma, Nebraska, parts of North and South Dakota, and parts of Minnesota. The clear western boundary of the Great Plains is the Rocky Mountains, but the eastern boundary is not as obvious. Direct students to research the Homestead Act of 1862 and learn how homesteaders lived and grew crops on the grasslands of the Great Plains. As students do their research, point out that the area eventually became known as the world's "bread basket." Have students prepare a poster or computer presentation to present their findings to the class. Remind students to include a list of resources with their presentation.

⦿ *Optional Online rubrics: Posters and Displays, Multimedia Presentations*

Customize Your Closing

🗂 *See the Assessment Guide for quizzes and tests.*

⦿ *Go Online to edit and create quizzes and tests.*

Reinforce and Review

☐ **Activity** Land Biomes in Review

☐ **Graphic Organizer** Layered Book

☐ **Print Path** Visual Summary, SE p. 72

☐ **Digital Path** Lesson Closer

Evaluate Student Mastery

Formative Assessment

See the teacher support below the Student Pages for additional Formative Assessment questions.

Ask students to review the characteristics of biomes and the relationship between a biome and an ecosystem. **Ask:** Explain the relationship between a biome and an ecosystem. A biome can contain many ecosystems; ecosystems are defined by a community of organisms and their abiotic environment. A biome is a regional or global community of organisms defined primarily by climate. Biomes are huge, and conditions within a single biome can be quite different. These differences can allow many ecosystems to thrive within a single biome.

Reteach

Formative assessment may show that students need reinforcement for certain topics. The resources below are recommended for reteaching. If students were introduced to a topic through the Print path, you can also use the Digital Path to reteach, or vice versa.
🎧 *Can be assigned to individual students*

Biomes
Activity Biome Basics 🎧

Tundra and Taiga
Activity Biome Competition

Desert and Grassland
Basic Venn Diagrams 🎧

Temperate Forest and Tropical Rain Forest
Graphic Organizer Layered Book 🎧

Summative Assessment

Alternative Assessment
Exploring Land Biomes

🌐 *Online resources: student worksheet, optional rubrics*

Land Biomes

Take Your Pick: *Exploring Land Biomes*
Show what you know about Earth's major land biomes.

1. Work on your own, with a partner, or with a small group.
2. Choose items below for a total of 10 points. Check your choices.
3. Have your teacher approve your plan.
4. Submit or present your results.

2 Points

_____ **Exit Cards** Develop a set of index cards to explain what you have learned about Earth's major biomes. Include the name of each biome type on one side, and a fact about that biome type on the other side. Develop a seventh card on the characteristics of biomes. Use these cards to quiz each other.

_____ **Map It!** Obtain a blank map of Earth from your teacher or from another resource. Research and draw Earth's six major biomes on the map. Choose a different color for each biome, and be sure to include a map key.

5 Points

_____ **Crossword Puzzle** Develop a crossword puzzle that includes all the vocabulary terms and key concepts from the lesson. Trade puzzles with a partner and see who can complete the puzzle correctly first.

_____ **Collage** Develop a collage from pictures of different biomes and characteristics of biomes. Make sure to include each of Earth's six major biomes. Be sure to include labels and description on your collage.

_____ **Quiz** Develop a quiz covering the key topics from the lesson. Your quiz can include multiple formats, such as matching, fill in the blank, short answer, and identification. Then administer your quiz to a group of classmates, grade the quizzes, and listen to feedback from quiz-takers on how to improve your quiz.

8 Points

_____ **Memo** Imagine you live on the edge of a protected grassland. Write a memo to convince or discourage local leaders to conduct a controlled burn of the grassland near your property. Make sure you support your choice by including facts about the advantages or disadvantages of grassland fires. Your memo should be approximately one page in length.

_____ **Web Page** Imagine you work for a company that teaches young children about nature. You have been asked to develop a web page explaining the characteristics of one of Earth's major biomes. Make sure your explanations of the biome's characteristics can be understood by children between the ages of 6–8. Include pictures, diagrams, and maps wherever possible on your web page.

Going Further
☐ Life Science Connection
☐ Social Studies Connection

Formative Assessment
☐ Strategies Throughout TE
☐ Lesson Review SE

Summative Assessment
☐ Alternative Assessment Exploring Land Biomes
☐ Lesson Quiz
☐ Unit Tests A and B
☐ Unit Review SE End-of-Unit

Your Resources

_____

_____

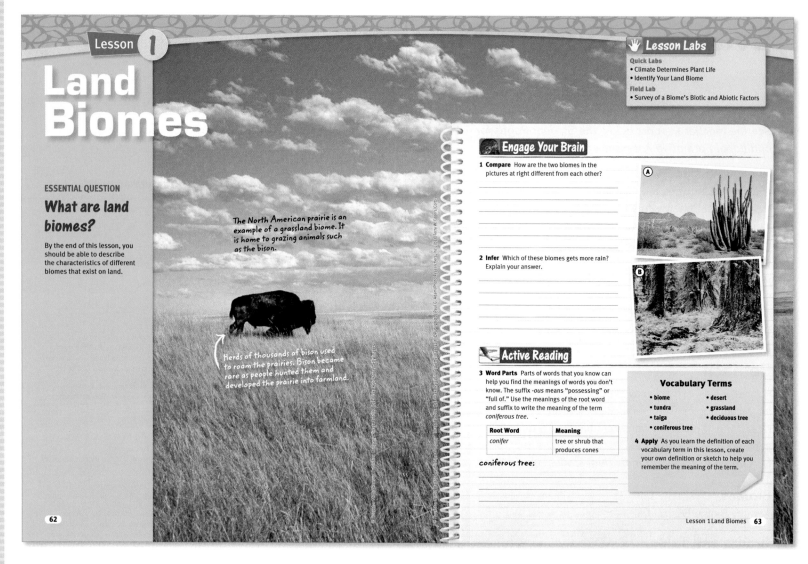

Lesson ①

Land Biomes

ESSENTIAL QUESTION

What are land biomes?

By the end of this lesson, you should be able to describe the characteristics of different biomes that exist on land.

The North American prairie is an example of a grassland biome. It is home to grazing animals such as the bison.

Herds of thousands of bison used to roam the prairies. Bison became rare as people hunted them and developed the prairie into farmland.

62

Lesson Labs

Quick Labs
- Climate Determines Plant Life
- Identify Your Land Biome

Field Lab
- Survey of a Biome's Biotic and Abiotic Factors

Engage Your Brain

1 Compare How are the two biomes in the pictures at right different from each other?

2 Infer Which of these biomes gets more rain? Explain your answer.

A

B

Active Reading

3 Word Parts Parts of words that you know can help you find the meanings of words you don't know. The suffix *-ous* means "possessing" or "full of." Use the meanings of the root word and suffix to write the meaning of the term *coniferous tree*.

Root Word	Meaning
conifer	tree or shrub that produces cones

coniferous tree:

Vocabulary Terms

- biome
- desert
- tundra
- grassland
- taiga
- deciduous tree
- coniferous tree

4 Apply As you learn the definition of each vocabulary term in this lesson, create your own definition or sketch to help you remember the meaning of the term.

Lesson 1 Land Biomes 63

Answers

Answers for 1–3 should represent students' current thoughts, even if incorrect.

1. Sample answer: Biome A has sandy or rocky soil and cactus plants. Biome B has large trees. Moss covers both the ground and trees in biome B.

2. Sample answer: Biome B looks like it gets more rain. The ground is mossy and there are a lot of plants growing. Biome A has soil that looks dry.

3. Sample answer: a type of tree that is full of cones

4. Students should define or sketch each vocabulary term in the lesson.

Opening Your Lesson

Discuss student responses to item 1 to assess students' prerequisite knowledge and to estimate what they already know about land biomes.

Preconceptions The desert always experiences hot temperatures. The tundra receives lots of snow.

Prerequisites Students should already know some of the characteristics of the land biome in which they live. The goal of this lesson is to understand the characteristics of different land biomes.

Interpreting Visuals

After students have compared the two photos of different biomes, **Ask:** What biome do you think each picture represents? a desert; a temperate forest **Ask:** What types of animals do you think live in each biome? Sample answer: desert: snakes, scorpions, lizards; forest: squirrels, rabbits, deer, bears

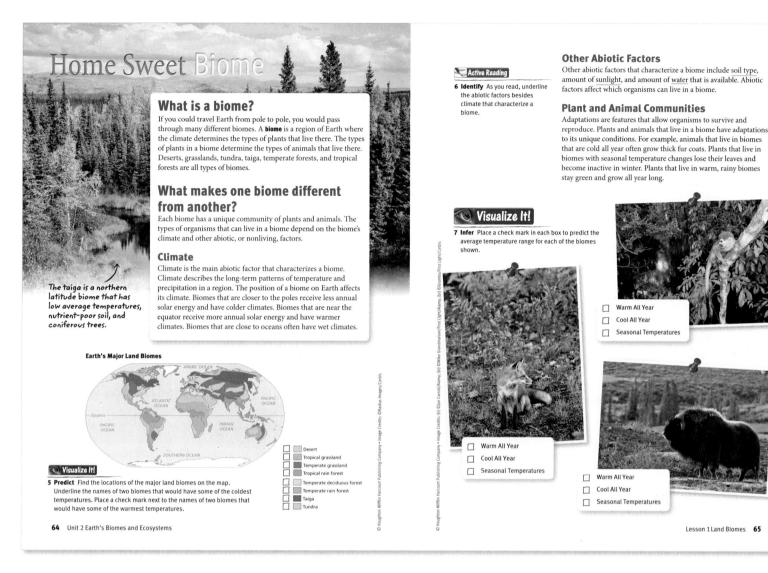

Home Sweet Biome

What is a biome?

If you could travel Earth from pole to pole, you would pass through many different biomes. A **biome** is a region of Earth where the climate determines the types of plants that live there. The types of plants in a biome determine the types of animals that live there. Deserts, grasslands, tundra, taiga, temperate forests, and tropical forests are all types of biomes.

What makes one biome different from another?

Each biome has a unique community of plants and animals. The types of organisms that can live in a biome depend on the biome's climate and other abiotic, or nonliving, factors.

Climate

Climate is the main abiotic factor that characterizes a biome. Climate describes the long-term patterns of temperature and precipitation in a region. The position of a biome on Earth affects its climate. Biomes that are closer to the poles receive less annual solar energy and have colder climates. Biomes that are near the equator receive more annual solar energy and have warmer climates. Biomes that are close to oceans often have wet climates.

The taiga is a northern latitude biome that has low average temperatures, nutrient-poor soil, and coniferous trees.

Earth's Major Land Biomes

Visualize It!

5 Predict Find the locations of the major land biomes on the map. Underline the names of two biomes that would have some of the coldest temperatures. Place a check mark next to the names of two biomes that would have some of the warmest temperatures.

- Desert
- Tropical grassland
- Temperate grassland
- Tropical rain forest
- Temperate deciduous forest
- Temperate rain forest
- Taiga
- Tundra

64 Unit 2 Earth's Biomes and Ecosystems

Active Reading

6 Identify As you read, underline the abiotic factors besides climate that characterize a biome.

Other Abiotic Factors

Other abiotic factors that characterize a biome include soil type, amount of sunlight, and amount of water that is available. Abiotic factors affect which organisms can live in a biome.

Plant and Animal Communities

Adaptations are features that allow organisms to survive and reproduce. Plants and animals that live in a biome have adaptations to its unique conditions. For example, animals that live in biomes that are cold all year often grow thick fur coats. Plants that live in biomes with seasonal temperature changes lose their leaves and become inactive in winter. Plants that live in warm, rainy biomes stay green and grow all year long.

Visualize It!

7 Infer Place a check mark in each box to predict the average temperature range for each of the biomes shown.

- ☐ Warm All Year
- ☐ Cool All Year
- ☐ Seasonal Temperatures

- ☐ Warm All Year
- ☐ Cool All Year
- ☐ Seasonal Temperatures

- ☐ Warm All Year
- ☐ Cool All Year
- ☐ Seasonal Temperatures

Lesson 1 Land Biomes 65

Answers

5. Students should underline tundra and taiga. Students should place a check mark next to two of the following: tropical rain forest, tropical grassland, or desert.

6. *See students' pages for annotations.*

7. *See students' pages for annotations.*

Building Reading Skills

Concept Map Have students work with a partner to develop a concept map about the characteristics of biomes. Once completed, discuss the maps as a class to ensure that partners included climate, abiotic factors, and organism communities.

Optional Online resource: Concept Map support

Interpreting Visuals

Direct students to the map of Earth's biomes. **Ask:** Do certain biomes tend to cluster together on the planet? For example, are two different biomes typically found next to each other on the map? Yes, taiga and tundra tend to share a border. Grasslands and forests also tend to share a border.

Building Math Skills

Climagraph A climagraph is a graph that shows the monthly precipitation and temperature conditions for a particular area. Direct students to a weather webpage, such as the National Weather Service, that has resources that would allow students to construct a climagraph for their ecosystem or biome. Students can compare their climagraphs to climagraphs of other areas in order to understand how climate affects communities.

Life in a Biome

How are ecosystems related to biomes?

Most biomes stretch across huge areas of land. Within each biome are smaller areas called ecosystems. Each *ecosystem* includes a specific community of organisms and their physical environment. A temperate forest biome can contain pond or river ecosystems. Each of these ecosystems has floating plants, fish, and other organisms that are adapted to living in or near water. A grassland biome can contain areas of small shrubs and trees. These ecosystems have woody plants, insects, and nesting birds.

Visualize It!

Three different ecosystems are shown in this temperate rain forest biome. Different organisms live in each of these ecosystems.

8 Identify List three organisms that you see in the picture that are part of each ecosystem within the biome.

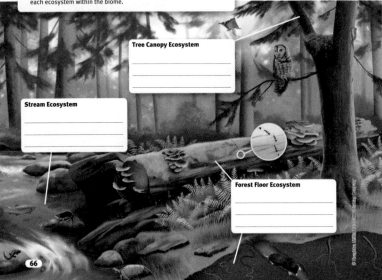

Tree Canopy Ecosystem

Stream Ecosystem

Forest Floor Ecosystem

66

What are the major land biomes?

There are six major land biomes. These include tundra, taiga, desert, grassland, temperate forest, and tropical forest.

Active Reading **9 Identify** Underline the abiotic features that characterize tundra and taiga biomes.

Tundra

Tundra has low average temperatures and very little precipitation. The ground contains permafrost, a thick layer of permanently frozen soil beneath the surface. Tundra is found in the Arctic and in high mountain regions. Tundra plants include mosses and woody shrubs. These plants have shallow roots, since they cannot grow into the permafrost. Tundra winters are dark, cold, and windy. Animals such as musk oxen have thick fur and fat deposits that protect them from the cold. Some animals, such as caribou, migrate to warmer areas before winter. Ground squirrels hibernate, or become dormant, underground.

Taiga

Taiga is also called the boreal forest. **Taiga** has low average temperatures like those in the tundra biome, but more precipitation. The soil layer in taiga is thin, acidic, and nutrient-poor. Taiga biomes are found in Canada and northern Europe and Asia. Taiga plants include **coniferous trees**, which are trees that have evergreen, needlelike leaves. These thin leaves let trees conserve water and produce food all year long. Migratory birds live in taiga in summer. Wolves, owls, and elk live in taiga year-round. Some animals, such as snowshoe hares, experience a change in fur color as the seasons change. Hares that match their surroundings are not seen by predators as easily.

Visualize It!

10 Describe Below each picture, describe how organisms that you see are adapted to the biome in which they live.

Tundra

Taiga

Answers

8. Tree Canopy Ecosystem: fir tree, moss, owl, flying squirrel, mouse

   Stream Ecosystem: fish, salamander, turtle, water shrew, moss

   Forest Floor Ecosystem: earthworm, moss, ferns, fungi (mushrooms), ants, mole

9. *See students' pages for annotations.*

10. Sample answers:

    Tundra: Animals like caribou migrate before winter; plants have shallow roots that grow above permafrost.

    Taiga: Animals like bears have thick coats and fat deposits to withstand cold; trees have needlelike leaves to conserve water and produce food all year.

Learning Alert

Difficult Concept Clarify the difference between an ecosystem and a biome by explaining that a biome is a region with a specific climate and community of organisms. An ecosystem is a particular community of organisms and their nonliving environment. Many ecosystems can exist within a single biome. Use the Visualize It! activity on the student page to assess students' understanding of biomes versus ecosystems.

Using Annotations

Mind Map Direct students to make a Mind Map summarizing the information they underlined in the text that relates to tundra and taiga. Remind students that it is important to identify and mark key phrases within the text, rather than each word in each paragraph.

🌐 *Optional Online resource: Mind Map support*

Probing Questions GUIDED Inquiry

Comparing Compare the characteristics of animals that remain in the tundra or taiga year-round with those that migrate to warmer biomes during the coldest months. Sample answer: Animals that live in the tundra or taiga year-round have thick fur. Animals that migrate from colder to warmer climates have wings and lightweight bodies.

Desert

11 Identify As you read, underline the characteristics of deserts.

Desert biomes are very dry. Some deserts receive less than 8 centimeters (3 inches) of precipitation each year. Desert soil is rocky or sandy. Many deserts are hot during the day and cold at night, although some have milder temperatures. Plants and animals in this biome have adaptations that let them conserve water and survive extreme temperatures. Members of the cactus family have needlelike leaves that conserve water. They also contain structures that store water. Many desert animals are active only at night. Some animals burrow underground or move into shade to stay cool during the day.

Visualize It!

12 Describe List the ways that each plant or animal in the picture is adapted to the desert biome.

Desert Tortoise
A tortoise can crawl into shade or retreat into its shell to avoid the heat. A tortoise has thick skin that prevents water loss.

Saguaro Cactus

Kangaroo Rat

Tropical Grassland

Temperate Grassland

Tropical Grassland

A **grassland** is a biome that has grasses and few trees. Tropical grasslands, such as the African savanna, have high average temperatures throughout the year. They also have wet and dry seasons. Thin soils support grasses and some trees in this biome. Grazing animals, such as antelope and zebras, feed on grasses. Predators such as lions hunt grazing animals. Animals in tropical grasslands migrate to find water during dry seasons. Plants in tropical grasslands are adapted to survive periodic fires.

Temperate Grassland

Temperate grasslands, such as the North American prairie, have moderate precipitation, hot summers, and cold winters. These grasslands have deep soils that are rich in nutrients. Grasses are the dominant plants in this biome. Bison, antelope, prairie dogs, and coyotes are common animals. Periodic fires sweep through temperate grasslands. These fires burn dead plant material and kill trees and shrubs. Grasses and other nonwoody plants are adapted to fire. Some of these plants regrow from their roots after a fire. Others grow from seeds that survived the fire.

Visualize It!

13 Describe Write captions to explain how fire shapes a temperate grassland biome.

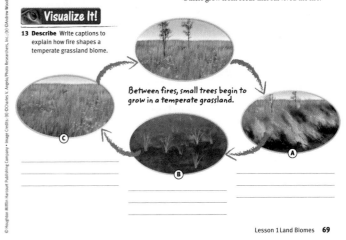

Between fires, small trees begin to grow in a temperate grassland.

Answers

11. *See students' pages for annotations.*

12. Sample answers:

    Saguaro Cactus: has needlelike leaves to conserve water; contains structures to store water

    Kangaroo Rat: active at night when it is cooler; stays in burrows to avoid heat of the day

13. Sample answers:

    A. Periodic fires sweep through temperate grasslands.

    B. Grasses and other nonwoody plants grow back soon after a fire.

    C. Grassland plants continue to grow. Dead plant material builds up.

Building Reading Skills

Venn Diagram Direct students to complete a Venn diagram to show the similarities and differences between temperate and tropical grassland. Review student answers as a class by displaying a copy of a blank Venn diagram and asking student volunteers to contribute their answers to complete the diagram. Add any missing information to accurately complete the graphic organizer.

🔵 *Optional Online resource: Venn Diagram support*

Formative Assessment

Ask: What abiotic and biotic factors characterize a desert? Sample answer: abiotic: little precipitation, dry rocky soil, hot temperatures during the day and cold temperatures at night; biotic: cacti, small rodents, reptiles **Ask:** Describe a plant and an animal adaptation that allows the organism to survive in the desert. Sample answer: Plants have needlelike leaves that help the plants conserve water. Some animals burrow during the day and are active only at night to avoid the heat.

Temperate Deciduous Forest

Temperate deciduous forests have moderate precipitation, hot summers, and cold winters. These forests are located in the northeastern United States, East Asia, and much of Europe. This biome has **deciduous trees**, which are broadleaf trees that drop their leaves as winter approaches. Fallen leaves decay and add organic matter to the soil, making it nutrient-rich. Songbirds nest in these forests during summer, but many migrate to warmer areas before winter. Animals such as chipmunks and black bears hibernate during winter. Deer and bobcats are active year-round.

👁 Visualize It!

14 Summarize Fill in the missing information on the cards to describe each of these temperate forest biomes.

Temperate Deciduous Forest

A. Climate: _____

B. Soil: _____

C. Plants: _____

D. Animals: _____

Temperate Rain Forest

Temperate rain forests have a long, cool wet season and a relatively dry summer. Temperate rain forests exist in the Pacific Northwest and on the western coast of South America. This biome is home to many coniferous trees, including Douglas fir and cedar. The forest floor is covered with mosses and ferns and contains nutrient-rich soil. Plants grow throughout the year in the temperate rain forest. Animals in this biome include spotted owls, shrews, elk, and cougars.

Temperate Rain Forest

A. Climate: _____

B. Soil: _____

C. Plants: _____

D. Animals: _____

Think Outside the Book Inquiry

15 Apply With a classmate, compare the adaptations of animals that migrate, hibernate, or stay active year-round in a temperate deciduous forest.

70 Unit 2 Earth's Biomes and Ecosystems

Tropical Rain Forest

Tropical rain forests are located near Earth's equator. This biome is warm throughout the year. It also receives more rain than any other biome on Earth. The soil in tropical rain forests is acidic and low in nutrients. Even with poor soil, tropical rain forests have some of the highest biological diversity on Earth. Dense layers of plants develop in a tropical rain forest. These layers block sunlight from reaching the forest floor. Some plants such as orchids grow on tree branches instead of on the dark forest floor. Birds, monkeys, and sloths live in the upper layers of the rain forest. Leaf-cutter ants, jaguars, snakes, and anteaters live in the lower layers.

👁 Visualize It!

16 Display Color in the band labeled *Light Level* next to the picture of the tropical rain forest. Make the band darkest at the level where the forest would receive the least light. Make the band lightest at the level where the forest would receive the most light.

Emergent Layer

Canopy

Understory

Forest Floor

Light Level

Lesson 1 Land Biomes 71

Answers

14. Temperate Deciduous Forest: Climate: moderate precipitation, hot summers, cold winters; Soil: nutrient-rich; Plants: deciduous trees; Animals: songbirds, chipmunks, black bears, deer, bobcats

    Temperate Rain Forest: Climate: long, cool wet season and dry summer; Soil: nutrient-rich; Plants: coniferous trees, mosses, ferns; Animals: spotted owls, shrews, elk, cougars

15. Accept all reasonable answers.

16. *See students' pages for annotations.*

Building Reading Skills

Text Structure: Main Idea/Details Direct students to identify the main idea and details for the sections on different types of forests. Ask them to mark up the text by making a box around the main idea in each paragraph and by underlining (or highlighting) the details that correspond to each main idea. Remind students not to highlight each word in each paragraph. Explain that identifying and marking key phrases within the text will make the details easier to see.

🔘 *Optional Online resource: Text Structure: Main Idea/Details support*

Learning Alert

Benefits of Burning The devastating fire in Yellowstone National Park in the late 1980s was a direct result of nearly a century of fire suppression practices. Fuel was allowed to build up in the understory because forest fires, human-made or natural, were put out. The build-up of fuel resulted in a "crown" fire, a fire that burns not just the understory and dead trees, but the crowns of mature trees. Crown fires are much hotter than normal forest fires and result in the actual burning of soils. Normal forest fires clear the understory, burn dead trees, open up the soil to light, and facilitate the germination of some seeds. The build-up of fuel and suppression of fire can result in devastating fires that cause loss of life and property, and that may be followed by mudslides if there is torrential rain.

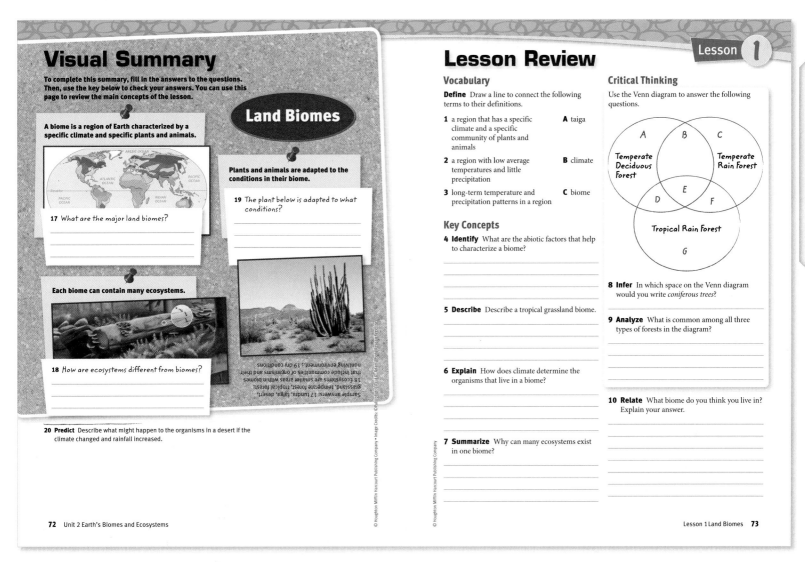

Visual Summary

To complete this summary, fill in the answers to the questions. Then, use the key below to check your answers. You can use this page to review the main concepts of the lesson.

Land Biomes

A biome is a region of Earth characterized by a specific climate and specific plants and animals.

17 What are the major land biomes?

Plants and animals are adapted to the conditions in their biome.

19 The plant below is adapted to what conditions?

Each biome can contain many ecosystems.

18 How are ecosystems different from biomes?

Sample answers: 17 tundra, taiga, desert, grassland, temperate forest, tropical forest. 18 Ecosystems are smaller areas within biomes that include communities of organisms and their nonliving environment. 19 dry conditions

20 Predict Describe what might happen to the organisms in a desert if the climate changed and rainfall increased.

72 Unit 2 Earth's Biomes and Ecosystems

Lesson Review

Vocabulary

Define Draw a line to connect the following terms to their definitions.

1 a region that has a specific climate and a specific community of plants and animals — **A** taiga

2 a region with low average temperatures and little precipitation — **B** climate

3 long-term temperature and precipitation patterns in a region — **C** biome

Key Concepts

4 Identify What are the abiotic factors that help to characterize a biome?

5 Describe Describe a tropical grassland biome.

6 Explain How does climate determine the organisms that live in a biome?

7 Summarize Why can many ecosystems exist in one biome?

Critical Thinking

Use the Venn diagram to answer the following questions.

Temperate Deciduous Forest (A), Temperate Rain Forest (C), Tropical Rain Forest (regions A B C D E F G)

8 Infer In which space on the Venn diagram would you write *coniferous trees*?

9 Analyze What is common among all three types of forests in the diagram?

10 Relate What biome do you think you live in? Explain your answer.

Lesson 1 Land Biomes 73

Visual Summary Answers

17. tundra, taiga, desert, grassland, temperate forest, tropical forest

18. Ecosystems are smaller areas within biomes that include communities of organisms and their nonliving environment.

19. dry conditions

20. Sample answer: Desert animals might migrate to somewhere drier. Plants that need more water could grow in the area and out-compete desert plants. Animals that need more water could move into the area. The shift in climate, plant, and animal communities could cause the area to change to a different biome.

Lesson Review Answers

1. C
2. A
3. B
4. temperature range, annual precipitation, soil type, sunlight, and water availability
5. Sample answer: A tropical grassland biome is warm all year and has wet and dry seasons. It has grasses, grazing animals, and predators that eat those grazing animals.
6. The plants and animals that live in a biome must be able to live and reproduce within the climate conditions of that biome.
7. A biome can be very large, so conditions in local areas of the biome can be different from each other.
8. *Coniferous trees* would be in space C, the part of the Venn diagram that describes only temperate rain forest.
9. All three types of forests have trees and moderate to heavy precipitation.
10. Answers may vary. Students should use the information in the lesson to choose the appropriate biome.

Lesson 1 Land Biomes 99

Aquatic Ecosystems

Essential Question What are aquatic ecosystems?

 Professional Development

For more detailed information about the topics in this lesson, refer to the Content Refresher in the Unit Opener pages.

Opening Your Lesson

Begin the lesson by assessing students' prerequisite and prior knowledge.

Prerequisite Knowledge

- Ecosystems support life.
- Biotic (living) and abiotic (nonliving) factors interact in an ecosystem.
- Different ecosystems support different communities of organisms.

Accessing Prior Knowledge

Tri-Fold Invite students to make a Tri-Fold FoldNote. Tell students to write where aquatic ecosystems are found in column 1, the type of water (freshwater or saltwater) in each ecosystem in column 2, and a list of organisms in each ecosystem in column 3. Use this information to discuss what they already know about aquatic ecosystems.

🌐 *Online resource: Tri-Fold support*

Customize Your Opening

- ☐ **Accessing Prior Knowledge,** above
- ☐ **Print Path** Engage Your Brain, SE p. 75
- ☐ **Print Path** Active Reading, SE p. 75
- ☐ **Digital Path** Lesson Opener

Key Topics/Learning Goals	Supporting Concepts
Aquatic Ecosystems 1 Describe the three major types of aquatic ecosystems. 2 List abiotic factors that affect aquatic ecosystems.	• Aquatic ecosystems can be divided into three main categories: freshwater ecosystems, estuaries, and marine, or saltwater, ecosystems. • Abiotic factors include water temperature, water depth/light penetration, oxygen levels, water pH, salinity, and water flow rate.
Freshwater Ecosystems 1 Describe freshwater ecosystems.	• Lakes and ponds are both bodies of fresh water. • A wetland is an area of land that is saturated by ground or surface water for at least part of the year. • Rivers and streams are characterized by moving water.
Estuaries 1 Describe the characteristics of an estuary.	• An estuary is a partially enclosed body of water formed where a river flows into an ocean. Therefore, estuaries are a mixture of fresh water and salt water.
Marine Ecosystems 1 Describe marine ecosystems.	• Coastal ocean ecosystems include beaches, tidal pools, coral reefs, and kelp forests. • Open ocean ecosystems, which are characterized by little sun and cold water temperatures, contain most of the sea life. • The deep ocean is the coldest and darkest marine ecosystem. Organisms have unique adaptations to survive here.

Options for Instruction

Two parallel paths provide coverage of the Essential Questions, with a strong **Inquiry** strand woven into each.
Follow the **Print Path,** the **Digital Path,** or your customized combination of print, digital, and inquiry.

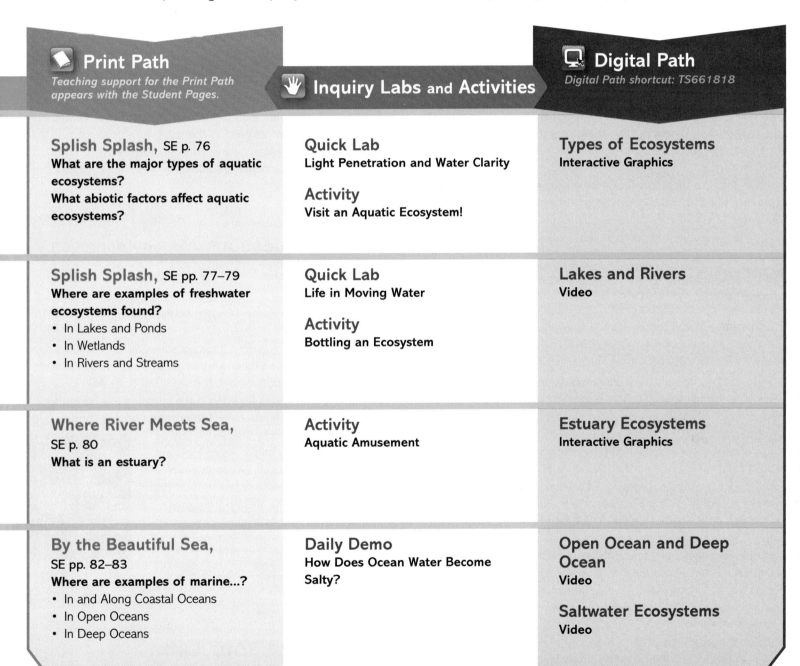

Print Path
Teaching support for the Print Path appears with the Student Pages.

Inquiry Labs and Activities

Digital Path
Digital Path shortcut: TS661818

Splish Splash, SE p. 76
What are the major types of aquatic ecosystems?
What abiotic factors affect aquatic ecosystems?

Quick Lab
Light Penetration and Water Clarity

Activity
Visit an Aquatic Ecosystem!

Types of Ecosystems
Interactive Graphics

Splish Splash, SE pp. 77–79
Where are examples of freshwater ecosystems found?
• In Lakes and Ponds
• In Wetlands
• In Rivers and Streams

Quick Lab
Life in Moving Water

Activity
Bottling an Ecosystem

Lakes and Rivers
Video

Where River Meets Sea,
SE p. 80
What is an estuary?

Activity
Aquatic Amusement

Estuary Ecosystems
Interactive Graphics

By the Beautiful Sea,
SE pp. 82–83
Where are examples of marine...?
• In and Along Coastal Oceans
• In Open Oceans
• In Deep Oceans

Daily Demo
How Does Ocean Water Become Salty?

Open Ocean and Deep Ocean
Video

Saltwater Ecosystems
Video

Options for Assessment

See the Evaluate page for options, including Formative Assessment, Summative Assessment, and Unit Review.

Engage and Explore

Activities and Discussion

Activity *Visit an Aquatic Ecosystem!*

Aquatic Ecosystems

 individuals or pairs
 varied
Inquiry DIRECTED inquiry

Travel Brochure Tell students to make a travel brochure for an aquatic animal. First have students select an aquatic animal and find out which type of ecosystem it lives in. Have students find out about the specific abiotic and biotic factors of this ecosystem. Then students can design a brochure that tells the animal why this ecosystem is the best place for it to live. Encourage students to use words and pictures in their brochure.

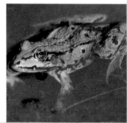

Activity *Bottling an Ecosystem*

Engage

Freshwater Ecosystems

 small groups
 varied
Inquiry GUIDED inquiry

Provide each group with a 2-L plastic bottle (in which the top has been cut off at the shoulder), water, sand, a sprig of *Elodea* (or other freshwater plant), and a few small freshwater snails. Help students assemble their own freshwater ecosystems by first adding sand, water, and the *Elodea* to the bottle. After the bottle has sat overnight, have students measure the pH of the water. Then allow students to add the snails to their ecosystems. **Ask:** What are the biotic factors in their ecosystem? Sample answer: snails, *Elodea*, microorganisms on the *Elodea* **Ask:** What are the abiotic factors in their ecosystem? Sample answer: sand, water temperature, dissolved oxygen content, sunlight, water pH Cover the bottles with plastic wrap that has been scored with holes and secure with an elastic band. Then place the bottles near a window. **Ask:** Why is it important to place the bottles near the window? Sample answer: to expose the *Elodea* to sunlight For the next week or more, encourage students to make observations of their freshwater ecosystems. They may note population changes, as well as changes to the condition of the water, including pH, temperature, and cloudiness. Students can examine samples of water from their ecosystem for microscopic life using a microscope. Use their observations to develop a discussion about the relationships between biotic and abiotic factors in a freshwater ecosystem.

Probing Question *Aquatic "Problems"*

Freshwater Ecosystems

 whole class
 10 min
 Inquiry DIRECTED and GUIDED inquiry

Calculating Ask students to solve the following word problem: Sunlight can penetrate a certain lake to a depth of 15 meters. The lake is 5.5 times as deep as the depth to which light can penetrate. In meters, how deep is the lake? 15 m x 5.5 = 82.5 m Encourage interested students to write similar types of word problems.

Probing Questions *Marine Adaptation*

Marine Ecosystems

 whole class
 10 min
Inquiry GUIDED inquiry

Inferring Explain to students that sea stars have structures on their undersides called tube feet that act similarly to suction cups when water is pumped through the sea star's body. **Ask:** How are tube feet an adaptation for living in the coastal ocean? Sample answer: They enable the animal to remain attached to rocky shores in the changing tide. **Ask:** How do you think a sea star might use its tube feet to eat? Sample answer: Sea stars wrap their legs around mussels, clams, and other bivalves and use the suction from their tube feet to pull the shells of their prey apart.

Customize Your Labs

 See the Lab Manual for lab datasheets.

 Go Online for editable lab datasheets.

 Levels of **Inquiry**   **DIRECTED** inquiry   **GUIDED** inquiry   **INDEPENDENT** inquiry

introduces inquiry skills within a structured framework.   develops inquiry skills within a supportive environment.   deepens inquiry skills with student-driven questions or procedures.

Labs and Demos

Daily Demo *How Does Ocean Water Become Salty?*

Engage

Marine Ecosystems

 whole class

 10 min

 Inquiry **GUIDED** inquiry

Use this short demo after discussing marine ecosystems.

PURPOSE **To model how ocean water becomes salty**

MATERIALS

- **aluminum pan**
- **cup**
- **food coloring**
- **salt**
- **soil**
- **water in a clear cup**

1 In a cup, mix several teaspoons of salt with food coloring. Next, put two cups of soil into a pan. Add the colored salt to the soil and mix together. Move the soil mixture so it is on one side of the pan.

2 **Predicting** Show students a cup of clear water. **Ask:** What will happen to the color of this water if it is poured onto the soil mixture? The color of the water should resemble the color of the dyed salt.

3 **Observing** Tell students to observe what happens to the color of the water when it reaches the other side of the pan. Slowly and carefully pour the water onto the soil mixture. Guide students to understand how this demonstration models runoff carrying salts from the land into the ocean.

Quick Lab *Life in Moving Water*

Freshwater Ecosystems

 individuals

20 min

Inquiry **DIRECTED** inquiry

Students will research a specific freshwater niche and develop a model of an organism that is suited to live in the environment.

PURPOSE **To explore adaptations useful for life in moving water**

MATERIALS

- bowl
- cup
- pan, rectangular
- small suction cups
- substrates to be used as ground material
- water

Quick Lab *Light Penetration and Water Clarity*

Aquatic Ecosystems

pairs

20 min

Inquiry **GUIDED** inquiry

Students will predict how the clarity of water will affect the penetration of light into water.

PURPOSE **To investigate how abiotic factors affect aquatic ecosystems**

MATERIALS

- 2 beakers, large
- 2 shiny coins
- mini flashlight
- flour
- dark sheet of paper
- stirring stick
- water

Activities and Discussion

☐ **Activity** Visit an Aquatic Ecosystem!

☐ **Activity** Bottling an Ecosystem

☐ **Probing Question** Aquatic "Problems"

☐ **Probing Questions** Marine Adaptation

Labs and Demos

☐ **Daily Demo** How Does Ocean Water Become Salty?

☐ **Quick Lab** Life in Moving Water

☐ **Quick Lab** Light Penetration and Water Clarity

Your Resources

_____

_____

_____

Explain Science Concepts

Key Topics	📖 Print Path	🖥 Digital Path
Aquatic Ecosystems	☐ **Splish Splash,** SE p. 76 • Visualize It!, #5 • Compare, #6 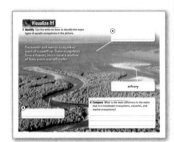	☐ **Types of Ecosystems** Describe the general characteristics of aquatic ecosystems, and the three major types of aquatic ecosystems. 
Freshwater Ecosystems	☐ **Splish Splash,** SE pp. 77–79 • Active Reading (Annotation strategy), #7 • Visualize It!, #8 • Think Outside the Book, #9 • Visualize It!, #10 • Visualize It!, #11 • Inquiry, #12 	☐ **Lakes and Rivers** Describe ecosystems found in lakes, ponds, wetlands, rivers, and streams. 
Estuaries	☐ **Where River Meets Sea,** SE p. 80 • Visualize It!, #13 	☐ **Estuary Ecosystems** Describe estuaries and the adaptations of species that live in these ecosystems.
Marine Ecosystems	☐ **By the Beautiful Sea,** SE pp. 82–83 • Visualize It!, #17 • Active Reading, #18 	☐ **Open Ocean and Deep Ocean** Describe ecosystems found in and along the coastal ocean, open ocean, and deep ocean. 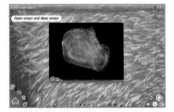

Differentiated Instruction

Basic *Animal Stories*

Estuaries   individuals
 varied

Short Story Ask each student to write a short story about (an) animal(s) in an estuary. Encourage students to be creative, but remind them to make the story realistic. Students should also include facts about the ecosystem in which their animal lives.

 Optional Online rubric: Written Pieces

Advanced *Mapping Aquatic Ecosystems*

Aquatic Ecosystems   individuals or pairs
 15–20 min

Using a Map Show students a large road map of your state. Have students determine where aquatic ecosystems can be found in your state, such as in rivers, lakes, and wetlands. Then, guide students to find the most common type of aquatic ecosystem, the largest body of water, and the closest ocean. Students should present a summary of their information orally to the class, showing the location of where the aquatic ecosystems are found on the map.

 Optional Online rubric: Presentations

ELL *Modeling Freshwater Ecosystems*

Freshwater Ecosystems   individuals or pairs
  varied

Model English language learners may gain a better understanding of ecosystems in rivers or streams by creating a visual display. Tell students to research a stream or river ecosystem and construct a poster or three-dimensional model (such as a diorama) representing that ecosystem. Encourage students to include a variety of producer and consumer organisms in their model. Display their posters or models for other students to see.

 Optional Online rubric: Posters and Displays

Lesson Vocabulary

wetland   estuary

Previewing Vocabulary

 whole class   5 min

Word Origins Share the following to help students remember terms:
wetland The word *wetland* comes from the word *wet* (adjective) and the word *land* (noun). Tell students that a wetland is land that is saturated with water.
estuary The word *estuary* comes from the Latin word *aestuarium*, which means tidal marsh.

Reinforcing Vocabulary

 individuals   15–20 min

Four Square To help students remember the vocabulary terms in the lesson, have them make Four Square graphic organizers for important terms in the lesson. After students draw the four squares, guide them to write the term in the center. Write notes or responses in the squares for *definition*, *characteristics*, and *examples* (or *nonexamples*, if they apply).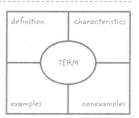

 Optional Online resource: Four Square support

Customize Your Core Lesson

Core Instruction
☐ **Print Path** choices
☐ **Digital Path** choices

Vocabulary
☐ **Previewing Vocabulary** Word Origins
☐ **Reinforcing** Four Square

Differentiated Instruction
☐ **Basic** Animal Stories
☐ **Advanced** Mapping Aquatic Ecosystems
☐ **ELL** Modeling Freshwater Ecosystems

Your Resources

_____

_____

Extend Science Concepts

Reinforce and Review

Activity *Aquatic Amusement*

Synthesizing Key Topics | 👥 small groups
🕐 15 min

Carousel Review Attach pieces of chart paper to the walls at different locations throughout the room. There should be one chart for freshwater ecosystems, one for estuaries, and one for marine ecosystems. Include the following questions on each chart: What are some of the biotic and abiotic factors of this ecosystem? What are some of the adaptations that organisms need to have to survive in this ecosystem? If an extra chart is needed for the review, include a general chart for the abiotic factors that affect aquatic ecosystems.

1 Divide the class into small groups and assign each group a chart. Provide each group with a different colored marker.

2 Have groups review their question, discuss their answer, and write a response.

3 After five minutes, tell each group to rotate to the next station. Groups place a check beside each answer they agree with, comment on answers they do not agree with, and add their own answers.

4 Repeat steps 2 and 3 until all groups have reviewed all charts.

5 Conclude the activity by reviewing the responses. Invite each group to share information about its responses with the class. Address any misconceptions or errors that arise.

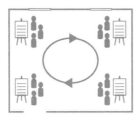

Graphic Organizer

Synthesizing Key Topics | 👥 individuals
🕐 15 min

Concept Map After students have studied the lesson, ask them to create a Concept Map graphic organizer with "Aquatic Ecosystems" as the key term. Help students use the key topics to guide them in identifying the details and linking words they include in their map.

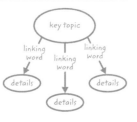

 Optional Online resource: Concept Map support

Going Further

Chemistry Connection

Marine Ecosystems | 👥 individuals or pairs
🕐 varied

Discussion Tell students that salinity is an abiotic factor that can have an effect on the organisms living in a marine ecosystem. For example, organisms living in coastal ocean ecosystems such as tidal pools must be able to adjust to changing concentrations of salt. Explain that salinity varies with ocean depth, especially near land. Have interested students use the Internet or library resources to learn more about varying levels of salinity in the ocean.

Social Studies Connection

Marine Ecosystems | 👥 individuals or pairs
🕐 varied

Cooking with Seaweed People in Japan and Korea use brown seaweed to make kombu soup. A red alga called nori is dried in sheets and wrapped around rice to make sushi. Seaweed provides iodine and other nutrients, but it is often used for the flavor and texture that it adds to food. Ask interested students to research foods made with algae. Give students the option of working with an adult to prepare or purchase dishes, such as dried nori.

Customize Your Closing

📖 *See the Assessment Guide for quizzes and tests.*

⏱ *Go Online to edit and create quizzes and tests.*

Reinforce and Review

☐ **Activity** Aquatic Amusement

☐ **Graphic Organizer** Concept Map

☐ **Print Path** Visual Summary, SE p. 84

☐ **Digital Path** Lesson Closer

Evaluate Student Mastery

See the teacher support below the Student Pages for additional Formative Assessment questions.

Ask the following questions to assess student mastery of the material. **Ask:** Where are examples of freshwater ecosystems found? Sample answer: lakes, ponds, rivers, streams, wetlands **Ask:** Where are examples of marine ecosystems found? the coastal ocean, open ocean, and deep ocean **Ask:** How is an estuary different from a freshwater ecosystem and a marine ecosystem? Estuaries are a mixture of fresh water and salt water. **Ask:** Pick one aquatic species and explain how it is adapted to its environment. Sample answer: Female anglerfish, which live in the deep ocean, use bioluminescent "bait" to attract prey.

Reteach

Formative assessment may show that students need reinforcement for certain topics. The resources below are recommended for reteaching. If students were introduced to a topic through the Print Path, you can also use the Digital Path to reteach, or vice versa.
🎧 *Can be assigned to individual students*

Aquatic Ecosystems
Graphic Organizer Concept Map 🎧

Freshwater Ecosystems
Quick Lab Life in Moving Water

Estuaries
Activity Aquatic Amusement

Marine Ecosystems
Daily Demo How Does Ocean Water Become Salty?

Summative Assessment

Alternative Assessment
Restoring an Aquatic Ecosystem

💿 *Online resources: student worksheet, optional rubrics*

Aquatic Ecosystems

Tic-Tac-Toe: *Restoring an Aquatic Ecosystem*
You are on a committee that is deciding to restore a threatened aquatic ecosystem.

1. Work on your own, with a partner, or with a small group.
2. Choose three activities from the game. Check the boxes you plan to complete. They must form a straight line in any direction.
3. Have your teacher approve your plan.
4. Do each activity, and turn in your results.

__ Local Research	__ Aquatic Adaptations	__ What Would You Do?
Observe an aquatic ecosystem near your home. It can be as small as a pond or stream, or as big as a lake or ocean. List the organisms that live there. Describe the type of water found in the ecosystem.	Pick one type of freshwater ecosystem. Describe two plants and two animals that live in this ecosystem. Write about the adaptations that help each organism survive in this ecosystem. Include pictures with your writing.	A planning committee is trying to decide if a road should be built through the local pond. Building the road will help the economy. It also means that the pond must be drained and filled. Write a persuasive paragraph that states your position.
__ Restoration Journal	__ Ocean Designer	__ Tiny Marine Ecosystem
Research how the Chesapeake Bay is being restored. Write a journal entry describing some ways people are protecting this aquatic environment.	Design and sketch the three major marine ecosystems. Label each ecosystem or zone. Include one organism that survives in each and describe how this organism is adapted to survive in a marine ecosystem.	Research salt water aquariums. Which organisms would it contain? What do you need to do to keep this ecosystem healthy?
__ Changing Tides	__ Estuary Advertisement	__ What's For Lunch?
Write a skit describing how several organisms such as barnacles and sea stars are adapted to survive in the intertidal zone, which has changing water depths and salinity.	Estuaries are unique aquatic ecosystems because they contain a mix of fresh and salt water. Write an advertisement, using words and visuals, to convince people why estuaries should be protected.	Write a poem describing how at least one organism in the deep ocean obtains energy, such as a bioluminescent fish or microbes that live near hydrothermal vents.

Going Further
- ☐ Chemistry Connection
- ☐ Social Studies Connection
- ☐ Print Path Why It Matters, SE p. 81

Formative Assessment
- ☐ **Strategies** Throughout TE
- ☐ **Lesson Review** SE

Summative Assessment
- ☐ **Alternative Assessment** Restoring an Aquatic Ecosystem
- ☐ **Lesson Quiz**
- ☐ **Unit Tests A and B**
- ☐ **Unit Review** SE End-of-Unit

Your Resources

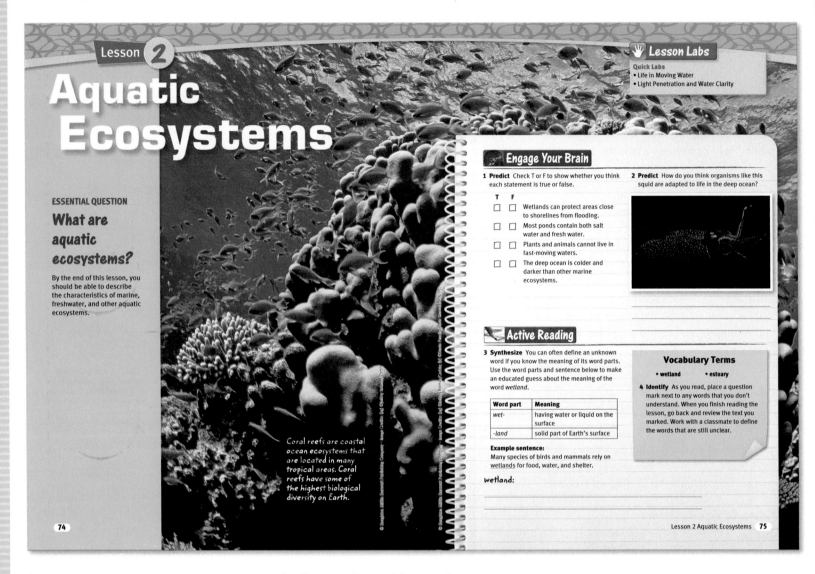

Lesson ②

Aquatic Ecosystems

Lesson Labs

Quick Labs
• Life in Moving Water
• Light Penetration and Water Clarity

ESSENTIAL QUESTION

What are aquatic ecosystems?

By the end of this lesson, you should be able to describe the characteristics of marine, freshwater, and other aquatic ecosystems.

Coral reefs are coastal ocean ecosystems that are located in many tropical areas. Coral reefs have some of the highest biological diversity on Earth.

Engage Your Brain

1 Predict Check T or F to show whether you think each statement is true or false.

T	F	
☐	☐	Wetlands can protect areas close to shorelines from flooding.
☐	☐	Most ponds contain both salt water and fresh water.
☐	☐	Plants and animals cannot live in fast-moving waters.
☐	☐	The deep ocean is colder and darker than other marine ecosystems.

2 Predict How do you think organisms like this squid are adapted to life in the deep ocean?

Active Reading

3 Synthesize You can often define an unknown word if you know the meaning of its word parts. Use the word parts and sentence below to make an educated guess about the meaning of the word *wetland*.

Word part	Meaning
wet-	having water or liquid on the surface
-land	solid part of Earth's surface

Example sentence:
Many species of birds and mammals rely on wetlands for food, water, and shelter.

wetland:

Vocabulary Terms
• wetland   • estuary

4 Identify As you read, place a question mark next to any words that you don't understand. When you finish reading the lesson, go back and review the text you marked. Work with a classmate to define the words that are still unclear.

74   Lesson 2 Aquatic Ecosystems   75

Answers

Answers for 1–3 should represent students' current thoughts, even if incorrect.

1. true, false, false, true

2. Sample answer: The squid would have to have adaptations that allow it to survive in cold, dark water. It looks as if it has "lights" that might allow it to attract prey.

3. Sample answer: A wetland is an area of land that has water on its surface.

4. Answers may vary.

Opening Your Lesson

Discuss student responses to item 1 to assess students' prerequisite knowledge and to estimate what they already know about aquatic ecosystems.

Prerequisites Students should already know that ecosystems are made up of biotic (living) and abiotic (nonliving) factors. Light and temperature are important abiotic factors. Different ecosystems have different plant and animal communities because the plants and animals have adaptations that allow them to successfully survive and reproduce in each ecosystem. In this lesson, students will apply this understanding to aquatic ecosystems.

Learning Alert

Roles in Aquatic Ecosystems Students may think that similar aquatic ecosystems around the world are filled with the same species of animals and plants. Tell students that different species play similar ecological roles in widely separated ecosystems. For example, in the Mississippi River Basin in the United States, alligators are common predators. In Egypt's Nile River, crocodiles play a predatory role. Have students research the plant and animal communities of different aquatic ecosystems around the world to see which species play similar ecological roles.

Splish Splash

What are the major types of aquatic ecosystems?

Have you ever gone swimming in the ocean, or fishing on a lake? Oceans and lakes support many of the aquatic ecosystems on Earth. An *aquatic ecosystem* includes any water environment and the community of organisms that live there.

The three main types of aquatic ecosystems are freshwater ecosystems, estuaries, and marine ecosystems. Freshwater ecosystems can be found in rivers, lakes, and wetlands. Marine ecosystems are found in oceans. Rivers and oceans form estuaries where they meet at a coastline.

What abiotic factors affect aquatic ecosystems?

Abiotic factors are the nonliving things in an environment. The major abiotic factors that affect aquatic ecosystems include water temperature, water depth, amount of light, oxygen level, water pH, salinity (salt level), and the rate of water flow. An aquatic ecosystem may be influenced by some of these factors but not others. For example, a river would be influenced by rate of water flow but not salinity.

Visualize It!

5 Identify Use the write-on lines to identify the major types of aquatic ecosystems in the picture.

Freshwater and marine ecosystems meet at a coastline. These ecosystems form estuaries, which have a mixture of fresh water and salt water.

A

estuary

B

6 Compare What is the main difference in the water that is in freshwater ecosystems, estuaries, and marine ecosystems?

76

Where are examples of freshwater ecosystems found?

Freshwater ecosystems contain water that has very little salt in it. Freshwater ecosystems are found in lakes, ponds, wetlands, rivers, and streams. Although freshwater ecosystems seem common, they actually contain less than one percent of all the water on Earth.

In Lakes and Ponds

Lakes and ponds are bodies of water surrounded by land. Lakes are larger than ponds. Some plants grow at the edges of these water bodies. Others live underwater or grow leaves that float on the surface. Protists such as algae and amoebas float in the water. Frogs and some insects lay eggs in the water, and their young develop there. Clams, bacteria, and worms live on the bottom of lakes and ponds and break down dead materials for food. Frogs, turtles, fish, and ducks have adaptations that let them swim in water.

Active Reading

7 Identify As you read, underline the names of organisms that live in or near lakes and ponds.

Visualize It!

8 Describe Pick a plant and animal in the picture. Describe how each is adapted to a pond.

Plant
_____
_____
_____

Animal
_____
_____
_____

Lesson 2 Aquatic Ecosystems **77**

Answers

5. A. marine ecosystem; B. freshwater ecosystem

6. The water in these ecosystems has different levels of salt in it. Marine ecosystems have the highest levels of salt, estuaries have a mixture of salt water and fresh water, and freshwater ecosystems have the lowest levels of salt.

7. *See students' pages for annotations.*

8. Sample answer: Plant: The plant the frog is sitting on is adapted to take root at the bottom of a pond and grow leaves that float on the surface to gather sunlight. Animal: Frogs lay eggs and develop in water. They are adapted to swim in water.

Interpreting Visuals

Abiotic and Biotic Factors Ask: How are aquatic ecosystems alike? Sample answer: All contain abiotic factors that determine the types of organisms that can survive in each ecosystem. **Ask:** Which abiotic factors do you think are the most important in a river ecosystem? Sample answer: oxygen levels, rate of water flow **Ask:** Which abiotic factors do you think are the most important in an estuary? Sample answer: salinity, amount of light **Ask:** Which abiotic factors do you think are the most important in ocean ecosystems? Sample answer: water temperature, water depth

Probing Questions DIRECTED (Inquiry)

Analyzing Why do you think most plants live near the edge of the pond or float on its surface? Here plants can get the water and sunlight they need to carry out photosynthesis.

Synthesizing Choose two abiotic factors and describe how they affect plants in a freshwater ecosystem. Sample answer: Water depth can determine the amount of sunlight a plant receives. If the water is too deep, a plant may not get enough sunlight for photosynthesis.

In Wetlands

A **wetland** is an area of land that is saturated, or soaked, with water for at least part of the year. Bogs, marshes, and swamps are types of wetlands. Bogs contain living and decomposing mosses. Many grasslike plants grow in marshes. Swamps have trees and vines. Plants that live in wetlands are adapted to living in wet soil.

Wetlands have high species diversity. Common wetland plants include cattails, duckweed, sphagnum moss, sedges, orchids, willows, tamarack, and black ash trees. Animals found in wetlands include ducks, frogs, shrews, herons, and alligators. Water collects and slowly filters through a wetland. In this way, some pollutants are removed from the water. Since wetlands can hold water, they also protect nearby land and shore from floods and erosion.

Think Outside the Book Inquiry

9 Apply Use library and Internet resources to put together an identification guide to common wetland plants.

Visualize It!

Wetland | Development That Replaced Wetland

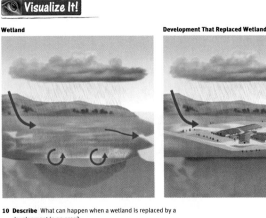

10 Describe What can happen when a wetland is replaced by a development in an area?

_____
_____
_____
_____
_____

In Rivers and Streams

Water moves in one direction in a stream. As water moves, it interacts with air and oxygen is added to the water. A large stream is called a river. Rivers and streams are home to many organisms, including fish, aquatic insects, and mosses. Freshwater ecosystems in streams can have areas of fast-moving and slow-moving water. Some organisms that live in fast-moving water have adaptations that let them resist being washed away. Immature black flies can attach themselves to rocks in a fast-moving stream. Rootlike rhizoids let mosses stick to rocks. In slow-moving waters of a stream, water striders are adapted to live on the water's surface.

The slope of a river's channel and the river's depth determine how quickly water moves.

Visualize It!

11 Match Match the correct captions to the pictures showing areas of fast-moving and slow-moving water.

A Water striders move across the surface of a pool of water in a river.

B Rocks form small waterfalls in areas of some streams.

C Aquatic plants can live below the surface of a river.

D Mosses can grow on the surface of rocks even in fast-moving water.

 Inquiry

12 Infer Why might stream water have more oxygen in it than pond water does?

_____
_____
_____
_____

Answers

9. Student guides should include drawings and accurate descriptions of wetland plants.

10. Development in a wetland can increase polluted runoff and flooding in the area.

11. D, B, A, C

12. The flowing water in a stream has more movement and greater interaction with air, which adds more oxygen to stream water.

Formative Assessment

Ask: How are bogs, marshes, and swamps alike? Sample answer: They are all areas of land that are saturated with water for at least part of the year. **Ask:** How are they different? Sample answer: Bogs contain decomposing vegetation; marshes contain grass-like plants; swamps contain trees and vines.

Probing Questions   DIRECTED Inquiry

Adapting What types of adaptations might plants and animals have living in a steep, rocky stream? Sample answer: Animals might have suction-like structures on their bodies, and plants might have long roots. What might happen to organisms without these adaptations? Organisms that do not have these adaptations will be washed downstream.

Learning Alert

Decomposers Let students know that decomposers play an important role in aquatic ecosystems. For example, bacteria decompose large amounts of organic material (dead plants and animals) that build up in wetlands. Hagfish feed on the decomposing bodies of whales and other large mammals that have died and fallen onto the ocean floor. Encourage students to think of other decomposers and how they may affect aquatic ecosystems.

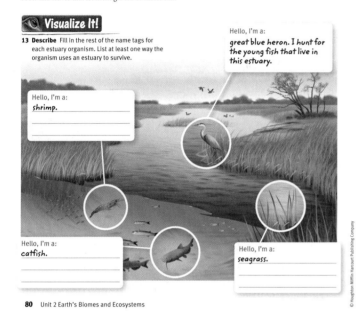

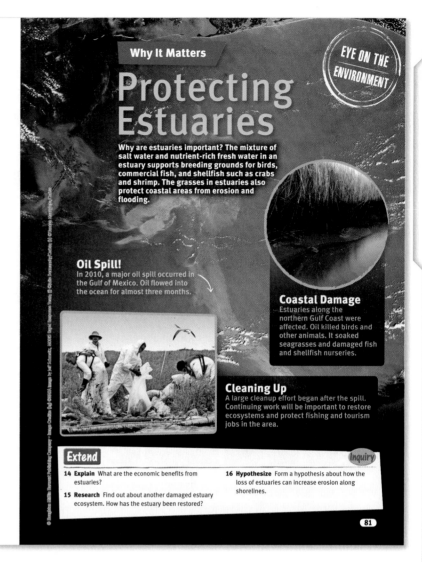

Where River Meets Sea

What is an estuary?

An **estuary** is a partially enclosed body of water formed where a river flows into an ocean. Because estuaries have a mixture of fresh water and salt water, they support ecosystems that have a unique and diverse community of organisms. Seagrasses, mangrove trees, fish, oysters, mussels, and water birds all live in estuaries. Fish and shrimp lay eggs in the calm waters of an estuary. Their young mature here before moving out into the ocean. Many birds feed on the young shrimp and fish in an estuary.

Organisms in estuaries must be able to survive in constantly changing salt levels due to the rise and fall of tides. Some estuary grasses, such as smooth cordgrass, have special structures in their roots and leaves that let them get rid of excess salt.

Visualize It!

13 Describe Fill in the rest of the name tags for each estuary organism. List at least one way the organism uses an estuary to survive.

Hello, I'm a:
shrimp.

Hello, I'm a:
catfish.

Hello, I'm a:
great blue heron. I hunt for the young fish that live in this estuary.

Hello, I'm a:
seagrass.

80 Unit 2 Earth's Biomes and Ecosystems

© Houghton Mifflin Harcourt Publishing Company

Why It Matters

EYE ON THE ENVIRONMENT

Protecting Estuaries

Why are estuaries important? The mixture of salt water and nutrient-rich fresh water in an estuary supports breeding grounds for birds, commercial fish, and shellfish such as crabs and shrimp. The grasses in estuaries also protect coastal areas from erosion and flooding.

Oil Spill!
In 2010, a major oil spill occurred in the Gulf of Mexico. Oil flowed into the ocean for almost three months.

Coastal Damage
Estuaries along the northern Gulf Coast were affected. Oil killed birds and other animals. It soaked seagrasses and damaged fish and shellfish nurseries.

Cleaning Up
A large cleanup effort began after the spill. Continuing work will be important to restore ecosystems and protect fishing and tourism jobs in the area.

Extend   Inquiry

14 Explain What are the economic benefits from estuaries?

15 Research Find out about another damaged estuary ecosystem. How has the estuary been restored?

16 Hypothesize Form a hypothesis about how the loss of estuaries can increase erosion along shorelines.

81

Answers

13. Sample answers: shrimp: I matured in the calm waters of the estuary. catfish: I lay eggs in the estuary. seagrass: I have structures that let me get rid of excess salt.

14. The wildlife supported by estuaries is important for jobs and tourism.

15. Student answers should demonstrate knowledge of the damage and repair made in an estuary ecosystem that is different from the one discussed in this feature.

16. Student answers should demonstrate knowledge of the importance of plants in preventing erosion along shorelines.

Building Reading Skills

Main Ideas/Details An important reading strategy is being able to identify the main idea and the supporting details of a passage. Instruct students to draw a Main Idea Web graphic organizer using the question at the top of the page (What is an estuary?). Have them read the question aloud. **Ask:** What will these pages be about? the characteristics of an estuary Then ask students to read the page. **Ask:** What is unique about an estuary? It contains a mixture of fresh water and salt water. Direct students to add the main idea and the details that relate to estuaries to their Main Idea Webs.

🌐 *Optional Online resources: Main Ideas/Details, Main Idea Web support*

Why It Matters

Encourage students to research another damaged aquatic ecosystem, perhaps one in their own state. Then, in groups, tell students to write and produce a public service announcement (PSA) about the ecosystem. PSAs should identify threats to the ecosystem such as invasive species, habitat loss, or changes in water flow due to development. PSAs should also explain why this aquatic ecosystem is important. Finally, students should conclude their PSAs with what people are doing to restore and protect this ecosystem.

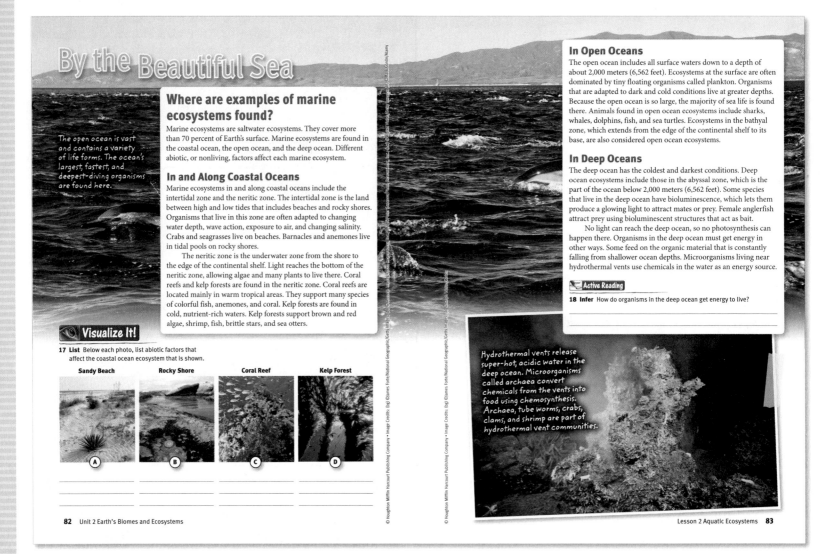

By the Beautiful Sea

The open ocean is vast and contains a variety of life forms. The ocean's largest, fastest, and deepest-diving organisms are found here.

Where are examples of marine ecosystems found?

Marine ecosystems are saltwater ecosystems. They cover more than 70 percent of Earth's surface. Marine ecosystems are found in the coastal ocean, the open ocean, and the deep ocean. Different abiotic, or nonliving, factors affect each marine ecosystem.

In and Along Coastal Oceans

Marine ecosystems in and along coastal oceans include the intertidal zone and the neritic zone. The intertidal zone is the land between high and low tides that includes beaches and rocky shores. Organisms that live in this zone are often adapted to changing water depth, wave action, exposure to air, and changing salinity. Crabs and seagrasses live on beaches. Barnacles and anemones live in tidal pools on rocky shores.

The neritic zone is the underwater zone from the shore to the edge of the continental shelf. Light reaches the bottom of the neritic zone, allowing algae and many plants to live there. Coral reefs and kelp forests are found in the neritic zone. Coral reefs are located mainly in warm tropical areas. They support many species of colorful fish, anemones, and coral. Kelp forests are found in cold, nutrient-rich waters. Kelp forests support brown and red algae, shrimp, fish, brittle stars, and sea otters.

Visualize It!

17 List Below each photo, list abiotic factors that affect the coastal ocean ecosystem that is shown.

Sandy Beach (A) **Rocky Shore** (B) **Coral Reef** (C) **Kelp Forest** (D)

In Open Oceans

The open ocean includes all surface waters down to a depth of about 2,000 meters (6,562 feet). Ecosystems at the surface are often dominated by tiny floating organisms called plankton. Organisms that are adapted to dark and cold conditions live at greater depths. Because the open ocean is so large, the majority of sea life is found there. Animals found in open ocean ecosystems include sharks, whales, dolphins, fish, and sea turtles. Ecosystems in the bathyal zone, which extends from the edge of the continental shelf to its base, are also considered open ocean ecosystems.

In Deep Oceans

The deep ocean has the coldest and darkest conditions. Deep ocean ecosystems include those in the abyssal zone, which is the part of the ocean below 2,000 meters (6,562 feet). Some species that live in the deep ocean have bioluminescence, which lets them produce a glowing light to attract mates or prey. Female anglerfish attract prey using bioluminescent structures that act as bait.

No light can reach the deep ocean, so no photosynthesis can happen there. Organisms in the deep ocean must get energy in other ways. Some feed on the organic material that is constantly falling from shallower ocean depths. Microorganisms living near hydrothermal vents use chemicals in the water as an energy source.

Active Reading

18 Infer How do organisms in the deep ocean get energy to live?

Hydrothermal vents release super-hot, acidic water in the deep ocean. Microorganisms called archaea convert chemicals from the vents into food using chemosynthesis. Archaea, tube worms, crabs, clams, and shrimp are part of hydrothermal vent communities.

Answers

17. A: water depth, wave action; B: water depth, wave action, salinity levels; C: water temperature, light levels; D: water temperature, light levels

18. Some organisms eat organic material that falls from shallow ocean depths. Microorganisms near a hydrothermal vent can use chemicals as an energy source.

Formative Assessment

Ask: Describe where marine ecosystems are found. Sample answer: Marine ecosystems are found in and along coastal oceans. This includes the intertidal zone and the neritic zone. The intertidal zone is the strip of land between high and low tides, which is exposed to air for part of the day. The neritic zone is the underwater zone from the coastline to the continental shelf. Marine ecosystems are also found in the open ocean, which starts where the sea floor drops sharply. Finally, marine ecosystems are found in the deep ocean, including the abyssal plain.

Learning Alert ⟍⟍ MISCONCEPTION ⟍⟍

Living Coral Reefs Show students a large photograph of a coral reef. Based on the appearance of the coral reef, students may think that the primary reef structure is not a living part of the ecosystem. Clarify this misconception by pointing out to students that coral reefs are made up of living coral (animals that live in colonies), coral skeletons, and calcium carbonate deposits from algae, mollusks, and protozoans. Coral reefs grow upward from the sea floor as corals secrete calcium carbonate to cement themselves to the reef structure below. Reefs provide homes for many organisms, including algae, sponges, jellyfish, turtles, fishes, crustaceans, and mollusks. Allow interested students to research the types and locations of different reefs, as well as why coral reefs are in danger.

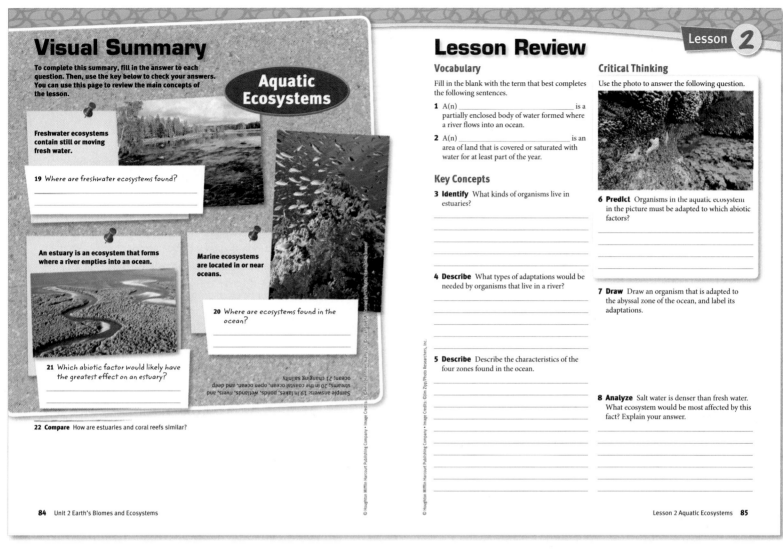

Visual Summary

To complete this summary, fill in the answer to each question. Then, use the key below to check your answers. You can use this page to review the main concepts of the lesson.

Aquatic Ecosystems

Freshwater ecosystems contain still or moving fresh water.

19 Where are freshwater ecosystems found?

An estuary is an ecosystem that forms where a river empties into an ocean.

Marine ecosystems are located in or near oceans.

20 Where are ecosystems found in the ocean?

21 Which abiotic factor would likely have the greatest effect on an estuary?

Sample answers: 19 in lakes, ponds, wetlands, rivers, and streams; 20 in the coastal ocean, open ocean, and deep ocean; 21 changing salinity

22 Compare How are estuaries and coral reefs similar?

84 Unit 2 Earth's Biomes and Ecosystems

© Houghton Mifflin Harcourt Publishing Company • Image Credits:

Lesson Review

Lesson **2**

Vocabulary

Fill in the blank with the term that best completes the following sentences.

1 A(n) _____ is a partially enclosed body of water formed where a river flows into an ocean.

2 A(n) _____ is an area of land that is covered or saturated with water for at least part of the year.

Key Concepts

3 Identify What kinds of organisms live in estuaries?

4 Describe What types of adaptations would be needed by organisms that live in a river?

5 Describe Describe the characteristics of the four zones found in the ocean.

Critical Thinking

Use the photo to answer the following question.

6 Predict Organisms in the aquatic ecosystem in the picture must be adapted to which abiotic factors?

7 Draw Draw an organism that is adapted to the abyssal zone of the ocean, and label its adaptations.

8 Analyze Salt water is denser than fresh water. What ecosystem would be most affected by this fact? Explain your answer.

Lesson 2 Aquatic Ecosystems 85

Visual Summary Answers

19. in lakes, ponds, wetlands, rivers, and streams

20. in the coastal ocean, open ocean, and deep ocean

21. changing salinity

22. Sample answer: They both have high biological diversity. They are both in relatively shallow areas that have lots of light.

Lesson Review Answers

1. estuary

2. wetland

3. seagrasses, mangrove trees, plankton, fish, crustaceans, and sea birds

4. Organisms that live in a river would need to be able to survive in fresh water. They might have to be able to avoid being swept away by moving water.

5. Sample answer: The intertidal zone is a shoreline ecosystem that is exposed to air. The neritic zone is an underwater ecosystem that has lots of sunlight. The bathyal zone has dark, cold water and is deeper than the neritic zone. The abyssal zone is the deepest, darkest, and coldest ocean zone.

6. Sample answer: This photo shows an example of a coastal ocean ecosystem. Organisms living here must be adapted to intense light, strong wave action, changing salt concentrations, exposure to air, and changing temperatures.

7. Student drawings should demonstrate knowledge of adaptations needed for dealing with darkness, cold temperature, and no direct energy from sunlight.

8. An estuary would be affected, because it is a mixture of salt water and fresh water. Organisms in an estuary would have to cope with water layers that have different salt concentrations.

 **Think Science**

Interpreting Circle Graphs

Purpose To learn about how to interpret circle graphs and make calculations based on the data contained in circle graphs

Learning Goals

- Construct and analyze circle graphs.
- Organize information to show understanding of relationships among facts, ideas, and events.

Informal Vocabulary

circle graph, sector, percentage, ratio, fraction

Prerequisite Knowledge

- Basic understanding of matter in ecosystems

Discussion *Graphing*

 whole class   10 min

 Inquiry GUIDED inquiry

Have the class think about what they already know about graphs. **Ask:** What type of graphs do you know? Sample answers: bar graph, line graph, circle graph Have students describe each type of graph, and sketch an example of each on the board. **Ask:** Why might you want to display data in a graph instead of in a table? Sample answers: A graph can make it easier to read the data. A graph can help you compare the data or find patterns.

For greater depth, provide students with a set of data and walk them through the process of making it into a graph.

🌐 *Optional Online rubric: Class Discussion*

Differentiated Instruction

Basic *Atmosphere Graph*

 pairs   🕐 20 min

Provide students with a circle graph that gives the quantities of gases in the atmosphere in values, such as parts per million. Help them interpret the data in the graph, using the tutorial as a guide. Tell them to calculate percentages for each entry in the graph. Then have them answer questions such as the following: What are the three most abundant gases in the atmosphere? What percentage of the total atmosphere is made of these gases?

Advanced *Class Polls*

 small groups   🕐 45 min

Displays Direct each group to choose a topic to poll the class on. For example, one group's poll could ask students what their favorite fruit is. After they conduct their polls, direct the groups to make circle graphs to represent the data. As part of their displays, they should also include a brief summary of their data that interprets their findings. In the fruit example the summary would probably name the fruit that got the most votes and indicate the percentage or ratio of votes it received out of the whole.

🌐 *Optional Online resources: Circle Graph, Analyzing Data support*

ELL *Mathematical Language*

 pairs   🕐 20 min

Two-Column Chart Have pairs make a Two-Column Chart to help them differentiate among the related mathematical words presented, such as *value, percentage, ratio,* and *fraction*. In one column, they should write the math word and a brief definition. In the second column, they should provide examples for each word.

Customize Your Feature

- ☐ **Discussion** Graphing
- ☐ **Basic** Atmosphere Graph
- ☐ **Advanced** Class Polls
- ☐ **ELL** Mathematical Language
- ☐ **Building Math Skills**

Think Science

Interpreting Circle Graphs

Scientists display data in tables and graphs in order to organize it and show relationships. A *circle graph*, also called a *pie graph*, is used to show and compare the pieces of a whole.

Tutorial

In a circle graph, the entire circle represents the whole, and each piece is called a *sector*. Follow the instructions below to learn how to interpret a circle graph.

1 Evaluating Data Data on circle graphs may be given in one of two ways: as values (such as dollars, days, or numbers of items) or as percentages of the whole.

2 Changing Percentage to Value The word *percent* means "per hundred," so 25% means 25 per 100, or 25/100. To find the total volume represented by a sector, such as the volume of fresh water in surface water, multiply the whole value by the percent of the sector, and then divide by 100.

$$35,030,000 \text{ km}^3 \times \frac{0.3}{100} = 105,090 \text{ km}^3 \text{ of Earth's fresh water is in surface water.}$$

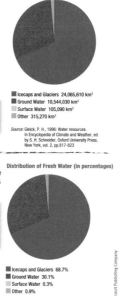

Distribution of Fresh Water (in values)

■ Icecaps and Glaciers 24,065,610 km³
■ Ground Water 10,544,030 km³
■ Surface Water 105,090 km³
■ Other 315,270 km³

Source: Gleick, P. H., 1996: Water resources. In Encyclopedia of Climate and Weather, ed. by S. H. Schneider, Oxford University Press, New York, vol. 2, pp.817-823

3 Changing Value to Ratio The sum of the sectors, 35,030,000 km³, is the whole, or total value. Divide the value of a sector, such as the icecaps and glaciers sector, by the value of the whole. Simplify this fraction to express it as a ratio.

$$\frac{24,065,610 \text{ km}^3}{35,030,000 \text{ km}^3} \approx \frac{25}{35} = \frac{5}{7}$$

About $\frac{5}{7}$ of Earth's fresh water is in icecaps and glaciers.

This ratio can be expressed as $\frac{5}{7}$, 5:7, or 5 to 7.

4 Changing Value to Percentage The whole circle graph is 100%. To find the percentage of a sector, such as the world's fresh water that is found as groundwater, divide the value of the sector by the value of the whole, and then multiply by 100%.

$$\frac{10,544,030 \text{ km}^3}{35,030,000 \text{ km}^3} \times 100\% = 30.1\% \text{ of Earth's fresh water is groundwater.}$$

Distribution of Fresh Water (in percentages)

■ Icecaps and Glaciers 68.7%
■ Ground Water 30.1%
■ Surface Water 0.3%
■ Other 0.9%

Source: Gleick, P. H., 1996: Water resources. In Encyclopedia of Climate and Weather, ed. by S. H. Schneider, Oxford University Press, New York, vol. 2, pp.817-823

You Try It!

Use the circle graphs below to answer the following questions.

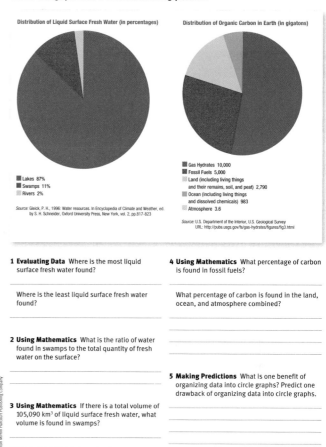

Distribution of Liquid Surface Fresh Water (in percentages)

■ Lakes 87%
■ Swamps 11%
■ Rivers 2%

Source: Gleick, P. H., 1996: Water resources. In Encyclopedia of Climate and Weather, ed. by S. H. Schneider, Oxford University Press, New York, vol. 2, pp.817-823

Distribution of Organic Carbon in Earth (in gigatons)

■ Gas Hydrates 10,000
■ Fossil Fuels 5,000
■ Land (including living things and their remains, soil, and peat) 2,790
■ Ocean (including living things and dissolved chemicals) 983
■ Atmosphere 3.6

Source: U.S. Department of the Interior, U.S. Geological Survey URL: http://pubs.usgs.gov/fs/gas-hydrates/figures/fig3.html

1 Evaluating Data Where is the most liquid surface fresh water found?

Where is the least liquid surface fresh water found?

2 Using Mathematics What is the ratio of water found in swamps to the total quantity of fresh water on the surface?

3 Using Mathematics If there is a total volume of 105,090 km³ of liquid surface fresh water, what volume is found in swamps?

4 Using Mathematics What percentage of carbon is found in fossil fuels?

What percentage of carbon is found in the land, ocean, and atmosphere combined?

5 Making Predictions What is one benefit of organizing data into circle graphs? Predict one drawback of organizing data into circle graphs.

Answers

You Try It!

1. In lakes; in rivers

2. 11:100 (can be rounded to 1:10)

3. 11,559.9 km³

4. 26.6%; 20.12%

5. A benefit is that it allows the viewer to see information in terms of parts of a whole and easily make comparisons. A drawback is that very small parts of a whole may be difficult to see.

Building Math Skills

Ratios and Simplifying Fractions Provide students with simple sets of values from which to calculate ratios. Emphasize that to express a fraction as a ratio, it must be simplified to its lowest terms. Remind students that to simplify a fraction, they must determine the greatest common factor (GCF)—the largest number that divides two or more numbers evenly—of the numerator and denominator, and then divide both the numerator and the denominator by that number. Provide examples such as the following: 6/18. The factors of 6 are 1, 2, 3, and 6. The factors of 18 are 1, 2, 3, 6, 9, and 18. The GCF is 6. Dividing the numerator and denominator by 6 yields the simplified fraction 1/3.

Have students look at example 3 in the Tutorial section of the Think Science activity. Use a calculator to demonstrate that if the numerator and the denominator are both divided by 1,000,000 the quotients are 24.07 and 35.03. Students can use these quotients to approximate that a ratio of $^{24.07}/_{35.03}$ is close to $^{25}/_{35}$.

Energy and Matter in Ecosystems

Essential Question How do energy and matter move through ecosystems?

 Professional Development

For more detailed information about the topics in this lesson, refer to the Content Refresher in the Unit Opener pages.

Opening Your Lesson

Begin the lesson by assessing students' prerequisite and prior knowledge.

Prerequisite Knowledge

- Energy roles of organisms in food chains and food webs
- Photosynthesis and cellular respiration

Accessing Prior Knowledge

Ask: How does energy flow from the sun through a food web? Plants convert light energy from the sun into chemical energy (food) through photosynthesis. Some animals eat plants to get energy. Other animals eat animals that eat the plants to get energy.

Customize Your Opening

- ☐ **Accessing Prior Knowledge,** above
- ☐ **Print Path** Engage Your Brain, SE p. 89
- ☐ **Print Path** Active Reading, SE p. 89
- ☐ **Digital Path** Lesson Opener

Key Topics/Learning Goals	Supporting Concepts
Matter and Energy in Ecosystems 1 Explain how ecosystems function as open systems. 2 State the laws of conservation of energy and mass. 3 Explain how organisms get energy and building materials.	• Ecosystems lack clear boundaries. Matter and energy are exchanged with the environment beyond the ecosystem. • The laws of conservation of energy and mass state that neither energy nor mass can be created or destroyed. • Producers get energy from the sun, consumers get energy from the organisms they eat. Decomposers get energy by breaking down the remains of other organisms. All three get building materials from their environments.
Energy Pyramids 1 Describe how some energy obtained by an organism is used immediately and some is stored. 2 Interpret an energy pyramid.	• An organism uses most of the energy it obtains. Only a small amount of energy is stored in the organism for later use. This stored energy is the only energy that can be transferred to the next group of feeders. • An energy pyramid shows the flow of energy in a food chain. It shows that at each level, less energy is available for the next level.
Cycles of Matter 1 Describe the water cycle. 2 Describe the nitrogen cycle. 3 Describe the carbon cycle.	• The water cycle is the pathway of water on Earth from the atmosphere, to the surface, below ground, and back again. • The nitrogen cycle is the path of nitrogen from the air, to soil, to plants and animals, to decomposers, and back to the air. • The carbon cycle is the transfer of carbon-containing molecules among organisms and between organisms and the environment. Respiration, photosynthesis, combustion, and decomposition are parts of the carbon cycle.

Options for Instruction

Two parallel paths provide coverage of the Essential Questions, with a strong **Inquiry** strand woven into each. Follow the **Print Path,** the **Digital Path,** or your customized combination of print, digital, and inquiry.

 Print Path
Teaching support for the Print Path appears with the Student Pages.

 Inquiry Labs and Activities

 **Digital Path**
Digital Path shortcut: TS693082

Print Path	Inquiry Labs and Activities	Digital Path
Soak Up the Sun, SE pp. 90–91 **How do organisms get energy and matter?** • From the Sun • From Other Organisms **What happens to energy and matter in ecosystems?** • Energy and Matter Are Conserved • Energy and Matter Leave Ecosystems	**Activity** It Matters in the Real World **Activity** Interconnection Challenge	**Energy From the Sun** Slideshow
Cycle and Flow, SE p. 92 **How does energy move through an ecosystem?**	**Quick Lab** Pyramid of Energy **Activity** Modeling an Energy Pyramid	**Energy Pyramids** Interactive Graphics
Cycle and Flow, SE pp. 93–97 **How does matter move through an ecosystem?** **What is the water cycle?** **What is the nitrogen cycle?** **What is the carbon cycle?**	**Quick Lab** Model the Carbon Cycle Condensation and Evaporation **Activity** Carbon In and Out **Virtual Lab** Investigating the Carbon Cycle	**Cycling Matter** Interactive Graphics **The Carbon Cycle** Interactive Image

Options for Assessment

See the Evaluate page for options, including Formative Assessment, Summative Assessment, and Unit Review.

Engage and Explore

Activities and Discussion

Activity *It Matters in the Real World*

Matter and Energy in Ecosystems

 flexible
 15 min
Inquiry **GUIDED** inquiry

Direct each group to write a list of real-world scenarios about the matter, energy, and cycling that would relate to a student's personal life. Sample answer: Matter: Oxygen is inhaled and carbon dioxide is exhaled. The food the student ate is used for growth, repair, daily activities, and other functions. Energy: Chemical energy from the food is used to allow the student's brain and eyes to work together to read. Ask students how this example illustrates the laws of conservation of mass and energy. Matter and energy are transformed for use but not used up.

Activity *Modeling an Energy Pyramid*

Engage

Energy Pyramids

whole class
20 min
Inquiry **DIRECTED** inquiry

Take 80 index cards and write the word *energy* on each card. On construction paper, make four signs: "Energy source," "Producers," "Primary consumers," and "Secondary consumers." Choose one student to be the "sun" or "energy source." Next, choose four students to be producers, two to be primary consumers, and one to be a secondary consumer. To make an energy pyramid, have the producers line up in the first row, with the primary consumers in the next row, and the secondary consumer in the last row. Place the sun close to the producers. Give the energy cards to the sun. Have the producers take 20 cards each. The producers throw 15 cards to the ground as heat and then pass five cards up to the primary consumers. (Really only 10% is passed to the next energy level but that would require many more cards!) Each primary consumer should now have ten cards total. The primary consumers throw eight cards to the ground as heat and then pass two cards up to the secondary consumer. Point out how energy moves in only one direction and that there are fewer individuals on higher levels of the pyramid because less energy is available to them.

For greater depth, have students figure out what percentage of the energy the plants received was used by the secondary consumers.

Activity *Carbon In and Out*

Cycles of Matter

whole class
15 min
Inquiry **DIRECTED** inquiry

Think Fast Write out a list of situations involving photosynthesis, cellular respiration, decomposition, and combustion. After reading the examples below, instruct students to identify the process involved and use the phrases *carbon into* or *carbon out*. After each answer, fully explain the details.

1 A rose plant growing new leaves: Photosynthesis; "carbon into" the plant as it uses carbon dioxide to make new leaves; "carbon out" from the atmosphere as the plant uses the carbon dioxide

2 A jaguar running fast: Cellular respiration; "carbon out" of the jaguar as it uses energy; "carbon into" the atmosphere as the jaguar exhales carbon dioxide

3 Mold growing on a dead log: Decomposition; "carbon out" of the log and "carbon into" the mold as it decomposes the log (also cellular respiration as the mold uses energy to decompose the log)

4 A forest fire: Combustion; "carbon out" of the burning plants (stored carbon molecules released) and "carbon into" the atmosphere

Customize Your Labs

 See the Lab Manual for lab datasheets.

Go Online for editable lab datasheets.

Levels of **Inquiry**   **DIRECTED** inquiry   **GUIDED** inquiry   **INDEPENDENT** inquiry

introduces inquiry skills within a structured framework.   develops inquiry skills within a supportive environment.   deepens inquiry skills with student-driven questions or procedures.

Labs and Demos

Quick Lab *Pyramid of Energy*

Energy Pyramids

👥 individuals
🕐 10 min
Inquiry DIRECTED inquiry

Students will study how energy moves through an ecosystem.

PURPOSE **To create a personal energy pyramid and to describe the relationship between consumers and producers**

MATERIALS

• colored pencils, red, blue, and green

Quick Lab *Condensation and Evaporation*

Cycles of Matter

👥 individuals
🕐 20 min
Inquiry DIRECTED inquiry

Students will observe the processes of condensation and evaporation and make connections to open and closed systems.

PURPOSE **To describe the processes of condensation and evaporation and to describe the difference between open and closed systems**

MATERIALS

• jars, clear
• measuring cup
• plastic wrap
• rubber band
• water

Quick Lab *Model the Carbon Cycle*

Cycles of Matter

👥 small groups
🕐 25 min
Inquiry INDEPENDENT inquiry

Students will model the movement of carbon from one reservoir to another in the carbon cycle.

PURPOSE **To construct a model to show how matter moves continuously in the carbon cycle**

MATERIALS

• paper
• pencils
• other materials as requested by students (e.g., cardboard, construction paper, glue, marbles, plastic cups, glitter)

Virtual Lab *Investigating the Carbon Cycle*

Cycles of Matter

👥 flexible
🕐 45 min
Inquiry GUIDED inquiry

Students investigate how carbon flows through ecosystems.

PURPOSE **To understand how the carbon cycle works**

Activities and Discussion

☐ **Activity** It Matters in the Real World
☐ **Activity** Modeling an Energy Pyramid
☐ **Activity** Carbon In and Out

Labs and Demos

☐ **Quick Lab** Pyramid of Energy
☐ **Quick Lab** Condensation and Evaporation
☐ **Quick Lab** Model the Carbon Cycle
☐ **Virtual Lab** Investigating the Carbon Cycle

Your Resources

_____

_____

_____

_____

Explain Science Concepts

	Print Path	Digital Path
Key Topics		

Matter and Energy in Ecosystems

Print Path

☐ **Soak Up the Sun,** SE pp. 90–91
- Active Reading (Annotation strategy), #5
- Infer, #6
- Visualize It!, #7
- Venn Diagram, #8

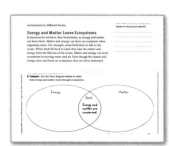

Digital Path

☐ **Energy From the Sun**
Learn how plants and animals get energy.

Energy Pyramids

Print Path

☐ **Cycle and Flow,** SE p. 92
- Visualize It!, #9

Digital Path

☐ **Energy Pyramids**
Learn how an energy pyramid is used to describe the amount of energy in an ecosystem.

Cycles of Matter

Print Path

☐ **Cycle and Flow,** SE pp. 93–97
- Active Reading, #10
- Visualize It!, #11
- Active Reading, #12
- Visualize It!, #13
- Visualize It!, #14
- Active Reading, #15
- Visualize It!, #16
- Think Outside the Book, #17

Digital Path

☐ **Cycling Matter**
Learn about how matter is cycled in an ecosystem.

☐ **The Carbon Cycle**
Explore how carbon is cycled through an ecosystem.

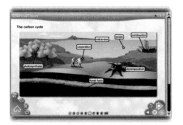

Differentiated Instruction

Basic *Ode to Matter*

Synthesizing Key Topics	individuals
	🕐 20 min

Creative Writing Carbon, nitrogen, and water are integral parts of all life on Earth, including humans. Students can combine recognition of this fact with the concepts they have learned in the lesson by writing a poem of recognition to one of the three substances. Require them to include the lesson concepts.

🌐 *Optional Online rubric: Written Pieces*

Advanced *Where Does It Go?*

Synthesizing Key Topics	small groups, individuals
	🕐 30 min

Jigsaw Even though matter and energy are both conserved, they are not conserved within a single ecosystem. Divide the class into small groups and assign each group a nature scene. Give each person in the group a photo of their group's nature scene and have students write out all the movement and storage of matter and energy in and out of the ecosystem shown. Once each member of the group is an "expert" about the nature scene, direct students to intermingle with other groups, and teach them about energy flow in their picture.

🌐 *Optional Online resource: Jigsaw support*

ELL *Understanding Matter and Energy*

Matter and Energy in Ecosystems	individuals
	🕐 15 min

Description Wheel Struggling readers or English language learners may have a hard time understanding just what is considered matter and what is considered energy. Have them make a Description Wheel for matter and a second Description Wheel for energy. Include examples as the details on the wheel.

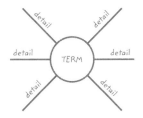

🌐 *Optional Online resource: Description Wheel support*

Lesson Vocabulary

energy	matter	energy pyramid
carbon cycle	water cycle	nitrogen cycle
law of conservation of mass		law of conservation of energy

Previewing Vocabulary

individuals	🕐 10 min

Key-Term FoldNote Direct students to make a Key-Term FoldNote for the vocabulary words in the lesson.

🌐 *Online resource: Key-Term FoldNote support*

Reinforcing Vocabulary

individuals	🕐 15 min

Word Relationships All the words in this lesson connect with one another in many ways. Instruct students to write sentences with pairs of vocabulary words that show a relationship between them.

For greater depth, incorporate the use of the following words: *ecosystem, food chain, food web, producer, consumer,* and *decomposer.*

Customize Your Core Lesson

Core Instruction
- [ ] **Print Path** choices
- [ ] **Digital Path** choices

Vocabulary
- [ ] **Previewing Vocabulary** Key-Term FoldNote
- [ ] **Reinforcing Vocabulary** Word Relationships

Your Resources

Differentiated Instruction
- [ ] **Basic** Ode to Matter
- [ ] **Advanced** Where Does It Go?
- [ ] **ELL** Understanding Matter and Energy

Extend Science Concepts

Reinforce and Review

Activity *Interconnection Challenge*

Synthesizing Key Topics

 small groups, then whole class

 20 min

Class Challenge Divide the class into four or six groups (must be an even number). Give each of them a picture from a magazine, newspaper, or Internet site showing any scene involving living things, including complete wilderness, urban settings, and ocean images. Be sure there are at least three living things in the photos. Instruct each group to write out the flow pathways for both matter and energy. Remind them that the flow can be in more than one direction and can happen in more than one path. Require them to explain each point of flow and the process that is involved. Then, bring two groups together and challenge them to connect their pathways. Give them no more than 10 minutes to accomplish this task. After writing down the links, join each set of groups together. The goal is to get a linear pathway for both matter and energy through all groups.

FoldNote

Energy Pyramids

 individuals

 30–45 min

Pyramid Direct students to bring in a magazine or Internet picture showing several organisms in the same ecosystem. (You may also provide the pictures to save time.) Instruct students to construct a Pyramid FoldNote. Then have them design an energy pyramid based on the organisms in the picture and explain each choice. They should complete their Pyramid FoldNote as follows: side 1: images of the organisms; side 2: names of organisms; side 3: identification of organisms as producers, primary, or secondary consumers; and side 4: define producers, primary or secondary consumers.

 Optional Online resource: Pyramid support

Going Further

Environmental Science Connection

Synthesizing Key Topics

 whole class

10–15 min

Discussion Carbon dioxide is a natural molecule that enters the atmosphere from cellular respiration. Humans are pumping enormous amounts of carbon dioxide from burning fossil fuels into the atmosphere. At the same time, the amount of oxygen is decreasing. Forests that produce oxygen are being cleared. The phytoplankton in the ocean, which produce half of the oxygen on the planet, are at risk from human pollution and changes in the climate. Pose open-ended questions to the students and ask them to discuss or write about how understanding this lesson can help a person understand issues facing the planet. **To extend the activity,** have students write an article for the school paper.

Engineering Connection

Matter and Energy in Ecosystems

 whole class, then individuals

15 min

Engineering Ideas Take a few minutes to discuss green technology advancements and our interest in developing these technologies. Solar panels, windmills, and energy efficiency are a few examples. As facilitator, help them see these ideas were once only dreams but today are realities. Then, have students identify an area in their lives where they are wasting or using too much energy. Instruct them to come up with an invention that will help them use less energy. Encourage them to be as creative as they can. Then have them share ideas with the class.

Customize Your Closing

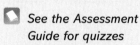 *See the Assessment Guide for quizzes and tests.*

Go Online to edit and create quizzes and tests.

Reinforce and Review

- ☐ **Activity** Interconnection Challenge
- ☐ **FoldNote** Energy Pyramids
- ☐ **Print Path** Visual Summary, SE p. 98
- ☐ **Print Path** Lesson Review, SE p. 99
- ☐ **Digital Path** Lesson Closer

Evaluate Student Mastery

See the teacher support below the Student Pages for additional Formative Assessment questions.

Ask: If energy is conserved, why do ecosystems need sunlight every day as a source of energy? The amount of energy remains the same, but it changes form and travels. Producers, which utilize light energy from the sun, transform solar energy into the form of energy (chemical) that ecosystems need. **Ask:** How are photosynthesis and cellular respiration linked? Sample answer: Photosynthesis releases oxygen, which is used in cellular respiration. Cellular respiration releases carbon dioxide, which is used in photosynthesis.

Reteach

Formative assessment may show that students need reinforcement for certain topics. The resources below are recommended for reteaching. If students were introduced to a topic through the Print Path, you can also use the Digital Path to reteach, or vice versa.
🎧 *Can be assigned to individual students*

Matter and Energy in Ecosystems
Activity It Matters in the Real World 🎧

Energy Pyramids
Quick Lab Pyramid of Energy 🎧

Cycles of Matter
Activity Carbon In and Out

Virtual Lab Investigating the Carbon Cycle 🎧

Summative Assessment

Alternative Assessment
Energy and Matter Add Up

🕭 *Online resources: student worksheet, optional rubrics*

Energy and Matter in Ecosystems

Take Your Pick: *Energy and Matter Add Up*
Take your pick from these activities to show what you have learned about the flow of matter and energy in ecosystems.

1. Work on your own, with a partner, or with a small group.
2. Choose items below for a total of 10 points. Check your choices.
3. Have your teacher approve your plan.
4. Submit or present your results.

Write About It: 2 Points

_____ **Poem of Flow** Pick one ecosystem or situation involving living things and write a poem that describes the flow of matter and energy through the ecosystem.

_____ **Quiz** Write a quiz on the concepts that relate to the cycles of matter. Be sure to include questions on the water cycle, the nitrogen cycle, and the carbon cycle. Use a variety of question formats, such as multiple choice, fill-ins, matching, short answers, etc.

_____ **Carbon Cycle Brochure** Write a brochure that describes how carbon cycles through both living and nonliving things. Be sure to include all four main processes (photosynthesis, cellular respiration, combustion, and decomposition).

Draw About It: 5 Points

_____ **Conservation Comic Strip** Design a comic strip about the conservation of matter and energy. The characters might be the sun, carbon atom, oxygen atom, and any plants and animals you'd like to include. The basic message of the comic should focus on how matter or energy is always conserved.

_____ **Pyramid Poster** Choose an organism found somewhere on Earth and construct an energy pyramid that includes it. Present your energy pyramid on a poster.

_____ **Water Cycle Diagram** Draw a diagram using colored arrows and labels to show how water cycles through an ecosystem. Include precipitation, evaporation, transpiration, and condensation in your diagram.

Speak About It: 8 Points

_____ **Flash News Report** Write out and present a news report on an ecosystem that needs more matter and/or energy. Be sure to explain why the ecosystem is short on matter and/or energy, what is happening now, and what will happen if it does not get it.

_____ **Matter and Energy Skit** Plan and perform a mini skit of how energy from the sun ends up as energy in an animal (insects, birds, reptiles, fish, humans, etc.) that is doing something.

Going Further
☐ Environmental Science Connection
☐ Engineering Connection

Formative Assessment
☐ Strategies Throughout TE
☐ Lesson Review SE

Summative Assessment
☐ Alternative Assessment Energy and Matter Add Up
☐ Lesson Quiz
☐ Unit Tests A and B
☐ Unit Review SE End-of-Unit

Your Resources

_____

_____

Answers

Answers for 1–3 should represent students' current thoughts, even if incorrect.

1. Students should underline lizard, salamander, turtle, butterfly, mountain lion, and bluebird.

2. Students should draw a diagram that indicates that the sun is the source of all energy, producers such as plants use the sun's energy to make food, and consumers such as animals eat producers or other consumers.

3. Sample answer: Energy is excitement. Energy is the ability to do everyday things. Energy is imagination.

4. Students should define or sketch each vocabulary term in the lesson.

Opening Your Lesson

Discuss student diagrams (item 2) to assess students' prerequisite knowledge and to estimate what they already know about key topics.

Prerequisites Students should already know the function of photosynthesis and cellular respiration; that photosynthesis produces sugar molecules that store chemical energy; and that cellular respiration converts the energy in food molecules into a form that cells can use. They should also have some basic knowledge of food chains and food webs.

Learning Alert

Forms of Energy Students are easily confused when trying to keep track of energy since there is no physical form to describe it. As organisms use light energy (from the sun) and chemical energy (from food), it is transformed into heat. It may be hard for students to understand that heat is no longer usable, rather than "used up." An example to use for explaining this concept is a car. A car burns gasoline, some of which is converted to kinetic energy so the car can move, but the hood also gets hot because most of the energy is converted to heat. The energy in the gasoline is transformed to kinetic energy and heat, but it is not used up.

Soak Up the Sun

How do organisms get energy and matter?

To live, grow, and reproduce, all organisms need matter and energy. **Matter** is anything that has mass and takes up space. Organisms use matter in chemical processes, such as digestion and breathing. For these processes to occur, organisms need energy. **Energy** is the ability to do work and enables organisms to use matter in life processes. Organisms have different ways of getting matter and energy from their environment.

Active Reading

5 Identify As you read, underline the characteristics of producers and consumers.

From the Sun

Organisms called *producers* use energy from their surroundings to make their own food. In most ecosystems, the sun is the original source of energy. Producers, like most plants and algae, use sunlight to convert water and carbon dioxide into sugars. In a few ecosystems, producers use chemical energy instead of light energy to make food. Producers take in matter, such as carbon dioxide, nitrogen, and water from air and soil.

From Other Organisms

Consumers are organisms that get energy by eating producers or other consumers. They get materials such as carbon, nitrogen, and phosphorus from the organisms they eat. So, consumers take in both energy and matter when they eat other organisms.

Roots help trees get matter, such as water and nutrients, from the soil.

6 Infer Use this table to identify where producers and consumers get energy and matter.

Type of organism	How it gets energy	How it gets matter
Producer		
Consumer		

90

What happens to energy and matter in ecosystems?

Energy and matter are constantly moving through ecosystems. Organisms need energy and matter for many functions, such as moving, growing, and reproducing. Some producers use carbon dioxide and water to make sugars, from which they get energy. They also collect materials from their environment for their life processes. Consumers get energy and matter for their life processes by eating other organisms. During every process, some energy is lost as heat. And, matter is returned to the physical environment as wastes or when organisms die.

Energy and Matter Are Conserved

The **law of conservation of energy** states that energy cannot be created or destroyed. Energy changes forms. Some producers change light energy from the sun to chemical energy in sugars. When sugars are used, some energy is given off as heat. Much of the energy in sugars is changed to another form of chemical energy that cells can use for life functions. The **law of conservation of mass** states that mass cannot be created or destroyed. Instead, matter moves through the environment in different forms.

Energy and Matter Leave Ecosystems

Ecosystems do not have clear boundaries, so energy and matter can leave them. Matter and energy can leave an ecosystem when organisms move. For example, some birds feed on fish in the ocean. When birds fly back to land, they take the matter and energy from the fish out of the ocean. Matter and energy can leave ecosystems in moving water and air. Even though the matter and energy enter and leave an ecosystem, they are never destroyed.

Visualize It!

7 Analyze How might energy and matter leave the ecosystem shown in the picture above?

_____

_____

_____

_____

8 Compare Use the Venn diagram below to relate how energy and matter move through ecosystems.

Energy — Both: Energy and matter are conserved. — Matter

Lesson 3 Energy and Matter in Ecosystems 91

Answers

5. *See students' pages for annotations.*

6. Producers: get energy from the sun and matter from their surroundings; consumers: get energy and matter by eating other organisms.

7. Sample answer: Matter and energy might leave when a consumer eats a plant and then moves to a new environment.

8. Sample answer: Energy: Producers convert light energy to chemical energy; Matter: Producers get matter from the air, soil, and water. The matter in producers is used by consumers when they eat producers or other consumers.

Formative Assessment

Ask: What are two things food provides to an organism? energy and building materials

Ask: Are producers making new matter and energy? No, according to the laws of conservation, no new energy and matter can be created. Producers are capturing existing matter and energy and transforming them into different forms.

Learning Alert ⚠ MISCONCEPTION ⚠

Conservation of Matter and Energy To help students understand that matter and energy are conserved, compare the laws to how students move in and out of classrooms throughout the school day. The total number of students in the building does not change, but the number and arrangement of students in the classrooms do.

Building Reading Skills

Text Structure: Main Idea/Details Instruct students to make a Supporting Main Ideas graphic organizer using the main idea *Energy and matter are constantly moving through ecosystems.* Encourage students to use the headings to identify supporting details.

🌐 *Online resources: Text Structure: Main Idea/Details, Supporting Main Ideas*

Cycle and Flow

How does energy move through an ecosystem?

Energy enters most ecosystems as sunlight, which some producers use to make food. Primary consumers, such as herbivores, get energy by consuming producers. Secondary consumers, such as carnivores, get energy by eating primary consumers, and so on up the food chain. An organism uses most of the energy it takes in for life processes. However, some energy is lost to the environment as heat. A small amount of energy is stored within an organism. Only this stored energy can be used by a consumer that eats the organism.

An **energy pyramid** is a tool that can be used to trace the flow of energy through an ecosystem. The pyramid's shape shows that there is less energy and fewer organisms at each level. At each step in the food chain, energy is lost to the environment. Because less energy is available, fewer organisms can be supported at higher levels. The bottom level—the producers—has the largest population and the most energy. The other levels are consumers. At the highest level, consumers will have the smallest population because of the limited amount of energy available to them.

Visualize It!

9 Analyze Describe how energy flows through each level in this energy pyramid. Is all the matter and energy from one level transferred to the next level?

_____
_____
_____
_____
_____
_____
_____

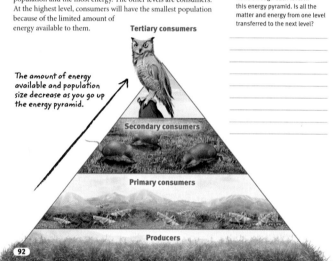

The amount of energy available and population size decrease as you go up the energy pyramid.

Tertiary consumers

Secondary consumers

Primary consumers

Producers

92

© Houghton Mifflin Harcourt Publishing Company

How does matter move through an ecosystem?

Matter cycles through an ecosystem. For example, water evaporates from Earth's surface into the atmosphere and condenses to form clouds. After forming clouds, water falls back to Earth's surface, completing a cycle.

Carbon and nitrogen also cycle through an ecosystem. Producers take in compounds made of carbon and nitrogen from the physical environment. They use these compounds for life processes. Primary consumers get matter by consuming producers.

Secondary consumers eat primary consumers. The matter in primary consumers is used in chemical processes by secondary consumers. In this way, carbon and nitrogen flow from producers through all levels of consumers.

Consumers do not use all of the matter that they take in. Some of the matter is turned into waste products. Decomposers, such as bacteria and fungi, break down solid waste products and dead organisms, returning matter to the physical environment. Producers can then reuse this matter for life processes, starting the cycles of matter again.

All of these cycles can take place over large areas. Matter leaves some ecosystems and enters other ecosystems. For example, water that evaporates from a lake in the middle of a continent can later fall into an ocean. Because matter can enter and leave an ecosystem, it is called an *open system.*

Active Reading **10 Identify** What is the role of decomposers in cycling matter?

_____
_____

Visualize It!

11 Analyze Describe how water is moving through the ecosystem on this page.

_____
_____
_____
_____
_____

93

Answers

9. Sample answer: Producers capture light energy and make food. Primary consumers eat the producers. Secondary consumers eat the insects. Tertiary consumers eat the rodents. Only the energy stored in an organism is transferred. There is less energy available at higher levels, so populations are smaller.

10. Sample answer: Decomposers break down wastes and dead organisms, returning matter to the environment.

11. Sample answer: Liquid water becomes water vapor as it evaporates into the atmosphere, then condenses back into liquid water to form clouds. Rain falls from the clouds back to the ocean.

Interpreting Visuals

Top consumers such as lions and sharks have a reputation for being the most powerful and dominant, so students often assume that predators and larger animals have the most energy in the ecosystem. **Ask:** Using the energy pyramid to explain, how are top consumers affected by changes in ecosystems? Top consumers have the least amount of energy available to them. If the food chain changes or if any of the levels below decline, top consumers would be at risk for not having the energy they need to survive.

Learning Alert

Matter and Energy in Ecosystems Students may struggle with why energy changes into heat as organisms use it. To explain, use examples they can understand such as when they feel warm (from thermal energy) after exercising. If the class lists all the things an organism needs to do to survive, it may help them see just why so much energy is converted into heat.

Plant Respiration Students may incorrectly think that because plants use photosynthesis to make food, they do not use cellular respiration. Remind students that just as cellular respiration allows them to use the energy stored in the food they eat, cellular respiration allows plants to use the energy stored in food they made from the sun.

What is the water cycle?

The movement of water between the oceans, atmosphere, land, and living things is known as the **water cycle**. Three ways water can enter the atmosphere are evaporation, transpiration, and respiration. During *evaporation*, the sun's heat causes water to change from liquid to vapor. Plants release water vapor from their leaves in *transpiration*. Organisms release water as waste during *respiration*.

In *condensation*, the water vapor cools and returns to liquid. The water that falls from the atmosphere to the land and oceans is *precipitation*. Rain, snow, sleet, and hail are forms of precipitation. Most precipitation falls into the ocean. The precipitation that falls on land and flows into streams and rivers is called *runoff*. Some precipitation seeps into the ground and is stored underground in spaces between or within rocks. This water, called *groundwater*, will slowly flow back into the soil, streams, rivers, and oceans.

Active Reading

12 Explain How does water from the atmosphere return to Earth's surface?

_____
_____
_____
_____
_____

Visualize It!

13 Label Use the terms *evaporation*, *transpiration*, and *respiration* to correctly complete the diagram. Be sure the arrow for each term leads from the proper source.

Condensation

Precipitation

Water vapor in air

Runoff

A

B

C

Groundwater

The water cycle describes how water travels from Earth's surface to the atmosphere and back.

© Houghton Mifflin Harcourt Publishing Company

94   Unit 2 Earth's Biomes and Ecosystems

What is the nitrogen cycle?

Organisms need nitrogen to build proteins and DNA for new cells. The movement of nitrogen between the environment and living things is called the **nitrogen cycle**. Most of Earth's atmosphere is nitrogen gas. But most organisms cannot use nitrogen gas directly. However, bacteria in the soil are able to change nitrogen gas into forms that plants can use. This process is called *nitrogen fixation*. Lightning can also fix nitrogen into usable compounds. Plants take in and use fixed nitrogen. Consumers can then get the nitrogen they need by eating plants or other organisms.

When organisms die, decomposers break down their remains. Decomposition releases a form of nitrogen into the soil that plants can use. Finally, certain types of bacteria in the soil can convert nitrogen into a gas, which is returned to the atmosphere.

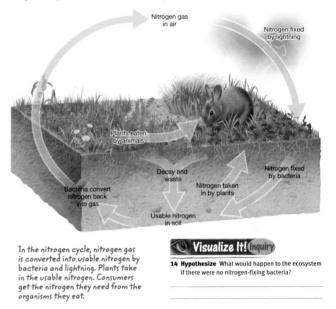

Nitrogen gas in air

Nitrogen fixed by lightning

Plants eaten by animals

Decay and waste

Nitrogen fixed by bacteria

Bacteria convert nitrogen back into gas

Nitrogen taken in by plants

Usable nitrogen in soil

In the nitrogen cycle, nitrogen gas is converted into usable nitrogen by bacteria and lightning. Plants take in the usable nitrogen. Consumers get the nitrogen they need from the organisms they eat.

Visualize It! Inquiry

14 Hypothesize What would happen to the ecosystem if there were no nitrogen-fixing bacteria?

_____
_____
_____
_____

© Houghton Mifflin Harcourt Publishing Company

Lesson 3 Energy and Matter in Ecosystems   95

Answers

12. Water from the atmosphere condenses and then falls back to Earth's surface in the form of precipitation, such as rain, snow, or hail.

13. A. Respiration; B. Transpiration; C. Evaporation.

14. Plants, animals, and other living things would not have the usable form of nitrogen they need to sustain life processes, such as making proteins.

Building Reading Skills

Text Structure: Main Idea/Details An important reading skill in science is being able to identify the main idea and supporting details of a passage. Instruct students to make two Mind Maps based on what they read: one for the water cycle and one for the nitrogen cycle. Students can use the definitions of each cycle as main ideas and the processes that contribute to each as the details.

🌐 *Online resources: Text Structure: Main Idea/Details, Mind Map*

Probing Questions   GUIDED Inquiry

Applying After discussing the processes that contribute to the water cycle, direct students' attention to the illustration of the water cycle. Explain that eutrophication is an overgrowth of algae that depletes the water's dissolved oxygen content causing marine life to essentially suffocate. Fertilizers used on farms and on lawns can cause eutrophication. **Ask:** Based on what you know about the water cycle, how do fertilizers, which are used on land, cause pollution in bodies of water? Sample answer: The precipitation that falls on land flows back to a body of water as runoff. This runoff can also carry soil and other materials.

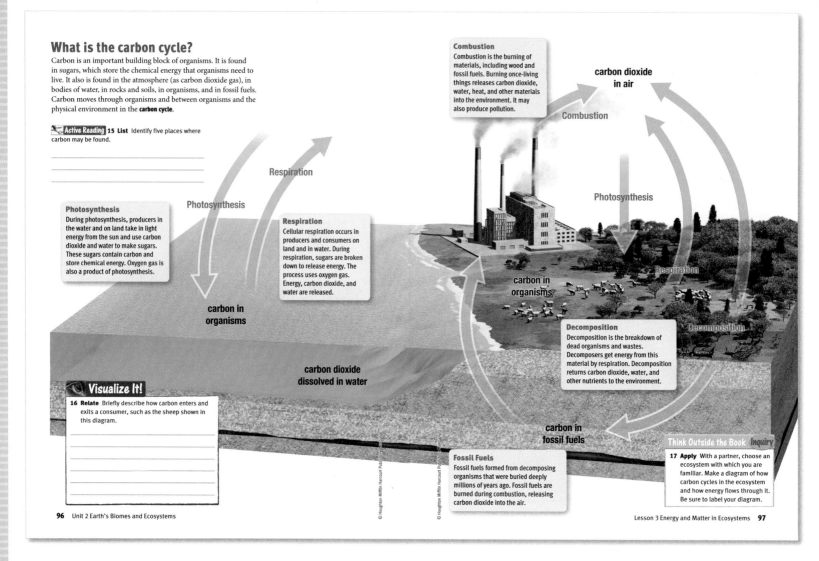

What is the carbon cycle?

Carbon is an important building block of organisms. It is found in sugars, which store the chemical energy that organisms need to live. It also is found in the atmosphere (as carbon dioxide gas), in bodies of water, in rocks and soils, in organisms, and in fossil fuels. Carbon moves through organisms and between organisms and the physical environment in the **carbon cycle**.

Active Reading 15 List Identify five places where carbon may be found.

_____

_____

_____

Photosynthesis
During photosynthesis, producers in the water and on land take in light energy from the sun and use carbon dioxide and water to make sugars. These sugars contain carbon and store chemical energy. Oxygen gas is also a product of photosynthesis.

Respiration
Cellular respiration occurs in producers and consumers on land and in water. During respiration, sugars are broken down to release energy. The process uses oxygen gas. Energy, carbon dioxide, and water are released.

Combustion
Combustion is the burning of materials, including wood and fossil fuels. Burning once-living things releases carbon dioxide, water, heat, and other materials into the environment. It may also produce pollution.

Decomposition
Decomposition is the breakdown of dead organisms and wastes. Decomposers get energy from this material by respiration. Decomposition returns carbon dioxide, water, and other nutrients to the environment.

Fossil Fuels
Fossil fuels formed from decomposing organisms that were buried deeply millions of years ago. Fossil fuels are burned during combustion, releasing carbon dioxide into the air.

carbon dioxide in air

Combustion

Photosynthesis

Respiration

Decomposition

carbon in organisms

Respiration

Photosynthesis

carbon in organisms

carbon dioxide dissolved in water

carbon in fossil fuels

Visualize It!

16 Relate Briefly describe how carbon enters and exits a consumer, such as the sheep shown in this diagram.

_____

_____

_____

_____

_____

_____

Think Outside the Book Inquiry

17 Apply With a partner, choose an ecosystem with which you are familiar. Make a diagram of how carbon cycles in the ecosystem and how energy flows through it. Be sure to label your diagram.

96 Unit 2 Earth's Biomes and Ecosystems

Lesson 3 Energy and Matter in Ecosystems 97

© Houghton Mifflin Harcourt Publishing Company

© Houghton Mifflin Harcourt Publishing Company

Answers

15. Sample answer: Carbon is found in living things, in the atmosphere (as carbon dioxide), in water, in rocks and soils, and in fossil fuels.

16. Sample answer: Carbon from sugars enters a sheep when the sheep eats grass. Carbon exits the sheep as carbon dioxide when it breathes. Carbon also exits as wastes or when the sheep dies. The dead sheep and wastes are broken down by decomposers, releasing carbon dioxide into the air.

17. Students should demonstrate an understanding of the carbon cycle and the roles of producers, consumers, and decomposers within the cycle. They should also describe the flow of energy in the ecosystem.

Building Reading Skills

Relationships Instruct students to classify each process in the carbon cycle as moving carbon into or out of the atmosphere. out of the atmosphere: photosynthesis; into the atmosphere: combustion, respiration, decomposition

Formative Assessment

Ask: Why are photosynthesis and respiration considered complementary processes? Photosynthesis uses carbon dioxide and produces oxygen as a byproduct; respiration uses oxygen and produces carbon dioxide as a byproduct. **Ask:** What is the relationship between decomposition and fossil fuels? Fossil fuels are formed from the bodies of mostly decomposed organisms.

Probing Questions GUIDED Inquiry

Synthesizing How are humans involved in the carbon cycle? Humans use cellular respiration to break down sugars (carbon molecules) and release carbon dioxide. Humans also significantly increase the amount of combustion because we burn so many fossil fuels.

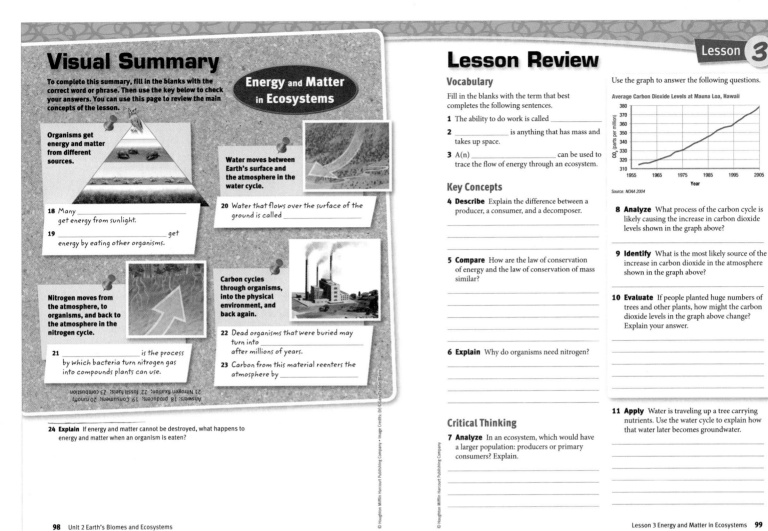

Visual Summary Answers

18. producers

19. Consumers

20. runoff

21. Nitrogen fixation

22. fossil fuels

23. combustion

24. When an organism eats another organism, some of the matter and energy are transferred to the consumer. Some of the matter and energy help the new organism live and grow. Some of the matter becomes waste. Some of the energy is released as heat to the environment.

Lesson Review Answers

1. energy

2. Matter

3. energy pyramid

4. A producer uses energy from the sun to make food. A consumer eats other organisms to get its energy. A decomposer gets its energy and nutrients by breaking down the remains of other organisms.

5. Sample answer: Both laws state that something can neither be created nor destroyed.

6. Organisms use nitrogen to make proteins and DNA.

7. The producer population would be larger because energy is lost as heat to the environment or used between each level in an energy pyramid. So, there is less energy available to the primary consumers.

8. combustion

9. fossil fuels

10. Sample answer: The carbon dioxide levels may decrease. Trees and other plants are producers, so they take in carbon dioxide to make sugars. The carbon would be stored in the bodies of the plants.

11. The water enters the atmosphere though transpiration. It condenses in clouds. It precipitates to Earth's surface. It seeps down between rocks underground and is stored as groundwater.

Changes in Ecosystems

Essential Question How do ecosystems change?

 Professional Development

For more detailed information about the topics in this lesson, refer to the Content Refresher in the Unit Opener pages.

Opening Your Lesson

Begin the lesson by assessing students' prerequisite and prior knowledge.

Prerequisite Knowledge

- A general understanding of biotic and abiotic factors in ecosystems
- A general understanding of how living things interact in communities

Accessing Prior Knowledge

Ask: What are some abiotic factors in ecosystems? Sample answers: temperature, amount of water, type of soil

Ask: How might a change in an abiotic factor in an ecosystem affect the living things there? Sample answer: A change in temperature might cause some of the living things in an area to leave or die, while other living things might move in due to the temperature change.

Customize Your Opening

☐ **Accessing Prior Knowledge,** above
☐ **Print Path** Engage Your Brain, SE p. 101
☐ **Print Path** Active Reading, SE p. 101
☐ **Digital Path** Lesson Opener

Key Topics/Learning Goals	Supporting Concepts
Changes in Ecosystems 1 Recognize that ecosystems change over time. 2 Explain eutrophication.	• Ecosystems are constantly changing. Over time, one ecosystem may change into another. This change may result from succession, long-term climate changes, human disturbances, or a catastrophic event. • Eutrophication, an example of ecosystem change, occurs when nutrients build up in a body of water. The body of water may fill in with organic matter and become a meadow.
Succession in Ecosystems 1 Describe succession. 2 Differentiate primary succession from secondary succession. 3 Explain the role a pioneer species plays in succession.	• Succession is the gradual replacement of one biological community by another. • Primary succession is the establishment of an ecosystem in an area where none had existed, such as after glacial retreat or a volcanic eruption. Secondary succession is the reestablishment of a damaged ecosystem in an area where the soil was left intact, such as after a fire or flood. • In primary succession, pioneer species, such as mosses and lichens, enter an area and break down rock into soil, which helps establish plant communities.
Ecosystems and Diversity 1 Explain how mature ecological communities support biodiversity. 2 Describe how biodiversity contributes to the sustainability of an ecosystem.	• In the early stages of succession, few species are present. As the ecosystem matures, more species establish populations, and diverse communities form. • Biodiversity is the number and variety of organisms in a given area during a specific period of time. Higher biodiversity increases the possibility that some species will survive an environmental change.

Options for Instruction

Two parallel paths provide coverage of the Essential Questions, with a strong **Inquiry** strand woven into each. Follow the **Print Path,** the **Digital Path,** or your customized combination of print, digital, and inquiry.

 Print Path
Teaching support for the Print Path appears with the Student Pages.

 Inquiry Labs and Activities

 Digital Path
Digital Path Shortcut TS673498

Nothing Stays the Same,
SE p. 102
How quickly do ecosystems change?
- Ecosystems May Change Slowly
- Ecosystems May Change Suddenly

Activity
All Kinds of Changes

Virtual Lab
Changes in Ecosystems

Rapid and Slow Changes
Interactive Graphics

The Speed of Change
Interactive Graphics

Nothing Stays the Same,
SE pp. 104–105
What are the two types of ecological succession?
- Primary Succession
- Secondary Succession

Quick Lab
Investigate Evidence of Succession

Field Lab
Predicting How Succession Follows a Human Disturbance

Activity
Modeling Succession

Eutrophication
Video

Succession
Slideshow

Primary Succession
Interactive Graphics

Secondary Succession
Interactive Graphics

It's a Balancing Act,
SE pp. 106–107
What are two signs of a mature ecosystem?
- Climax Species
- Biodiversity

Daily Demo
Disaster Strikes!

Quick Lab
Measuring Species Diversity

Biodiversity
Interactive Graphics

Options for Assessment

See the Evaluate page for options, including Formative Assessment, Summative Assessment, and Unit Review.

Engage and Explore

Activities and Discussion

Activity *All Kinds of Changes*

Engage

Introducing Key Topics

 individuals, then pairs
10 min
GUIDED inquiry

Think, Pair, Share Give students three minutes to write down as many examples as they can of changes that occur in ecosystems. Tell students to consider daily, seasonal, and long-term changes when they make their lists. After time is up, have each student choose three examples from his or her list, and discuss those examples with a partner. Have each pair of students choose two examples to share with the class. Pairs of students should explain why they chose their examples.

Probing Question *Should Changes Be Prevented?*

Changes in Ecosystems

 pairs or small groups
20 min
DIRECTED inquiry

Evaluating Human actions are the cause of many ecosystem changes. Human actions also prevent many ecosystem changes. For example, people often extinguish naturally occurring forest fires and dam rivers to prevent flooding. Even the application of herbicides in gardens prevents changes from occurring. Ask students to consider the following questions: In what circumstances should humans prevent naturally occurring ecosystem changes? What might be some consequences of preventing these changes? Encourage students to express a variety of viewpoints, but remind them to support their opinions with facts.

Activity *Modeling Succession*

Succession in Ecosystems

 whole class
15 minutes
GUIDED inquiry

Simulation Beforehand, prepare index cards with the following terms: *bare rock*, *lichen*, *moss*, *insect*, *fern*, *grass*, *wildflower*, *shrub*, *small tree*. Prepare enough cards for the class. Distribute the cards at random. Then, explain that the front of the room is an ecosystem that has just undergone a volcanic eruption. Have students model primary succession by moving into the "ecosystem" in the correct order. Note that pioneer species must be producers, fixing their own organic carbon for the consumers that follow.

Discussion *Preserving Biodiversity*

Ecosystems and Biodiversity

 whole class
10 minutes
DIRECTED inquiry

Discuss with students the relationship between ecosystem stability and biodiversity. Tell students that loss of species and the associated decrease in biodiversity has many ramifications. One way that scientists have sought to address threats to global biodiversity is by identifying "biodiversity hot spots," areas where a great number of species are challenged by rapidly changing ecosystems (usually due to human actions). By focusing on these hot spots, scientists hope to be able to most effectively help the greatest number of species.

©Digital Vision/Getty Images

Customize Your Labs

 See the Lab Manual for lab datasheets.

 Go Online for editable lab datasheets.

Levels of  **Inquiry**

DIRECTED inquiry	**GUIDED** inquiry	**INDEPENDENT** inquiry
introduces inquiry skills within a structured framework.	develops inquiry skills within a supportive environment.	deepens inquiry skills with student-driven questions or procedures.

Labs and Demos

Daily Demo *Disaster Strikes!*

Ecosystems and Diversity

 whole class
 15 min
 DIRECTED inquiry

PURPOSE To show students that a biologically diverse ecosystem has a better chance of survival than a uniform one

MATERIALS

- marshmallows, small
- packing peanuts, foam
- packing peanuts, cornstarch-based
- shallow pie pans
- hot water
- sugar cubes

1 Tell students that as biodiversity increases, so does the likelihood that some species of plants or animals will survive following a natural disaster or other environmental change.

2 Place a dozen sugar cubes into each pie pan. To the second pie pan, add several small marshmallows and packing peanuts of both types.

3 Explain that the pie pans are models of ecosystems. One ecosystem, the pan containing only sugar cubes, has very low biodiversity. It is home to only one species, *Cubus sugarus*.

4 Point out that *Cubus sugarus* is also found in the other ecosystem, along with populations of *Mallow marshii, Peanutus foamae,* and *Peanutus cornstarchus.*

5 Add hot water to the first pan. Ask students to describe what happens. All the Cubus sugarus have been wiped out, and nothing living is left in the ecosystem.

6 Add hot water to the second pan. Ask students to describe what happens. Some of the organisms are still alive, despite the flood, although all the *Cubus sugarus* are gone.

7 Discuss which ecosystem would recover more quickly from the flood. The second, which has greater biodiversity.

Field Lab *Predicting How Succession Follows a Human Disturbance*

See the Lab Manual or go Online for planning information.

Quick Lab *Investigate Evidence of Succession*

See the Lab Manual or go Online for planning information.

Quick Lab *Measuring Species Diversity*

See the Lab Manual or go Online for planning information.

Virtual Lab *Changes in Ecosystems*

Food Chains and Webs

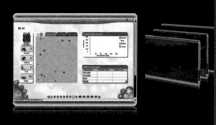 whole class
varies

Students analyze how a drastic change affects a food chain within an ecosystem.

PURPOSE To examine how a change in an ecosystem might affect its inhabitants

---

Activities and Discussion

- ☐ **Activity** All Kinds of Changes
- ☐ **Probing Question** Should Changes Be Prevented?
- ☐ **Activity** Modeling Succession
- ☐ **Discussion** Preserving Biodiversity

Labs and Demos

- ☐ **Daily Demo** Disaster Strikes!
- ☐ **Field Lab** Predicting... Disturbance
- ☐ **Quick Lab** Evidence of Succession
- ☐ **Quick Lab** Modeling Succession
- ☐ **Virtual Lab** Changes in Ecosystems

Your Resources

_____

_____

_____

Explain Science Concepts

	Print Path	Digital Path
Key Topics		
Changes in Ecosystems	☐ **Nothing Stays the Same,** SE p. 102 • Active Reading, #5 • Visualize It!, #6 Active Reading 5 Describe As you read, underline one example of a slow change and one example of a sudden change in an ecosystem.	☐ **Rapid and Slow Changes** Investigate rapid and gradual change ☐ **The Speed of Change** Learn about the speed of change in an ecosystem over time
Succession in Ecosystems	☐ **Nothing Stays the Same,** SE pp. 104–105 • Visualize It!, #10 • Identify, #11 • Think Outside the Book, #12 **Think Outside the Book** **12 Describe** Find an example of secondary succession in your community, and make a poster that describes each stage.	☐ **Eutrophication** Explore eutrophication ☐ **Succession** Investigate succession and compare primary and secondary succession
Ecosystems and Diversity	☐ **It's a Balancing Act,** SE pp. 106–107 • Active Reading, #13 • Venn Diagram, #14 🔘 *Optional Online Resource: Venn Diagram support* Active Reading 13 Summarize How is biodiversity beneficial to an ecosystem?	☐ **Biodiversity** Learn how biodiversity contributes to the sustainability of an ecosystem

Differentiated Instruction

Basic *Classifying Changes*

Changes in Ecosystems

 pairs

 10 min

Write the following terms on the board: *primary succession, forest fire, hurricane, eutrophication, volcanic eruption, secondary succession*. Tell each pair of students to sort these terms into two categories: slow changes and sudden changes. Students can use written lists or tables to organize their results.

Advanced *Researching Pioneer Species*

Succession in Ecosystems

 small groups

25 min

Research Project Have groups of students work together to research a specific pioneer species. Tell students to make sure that they find out how the pioneer species breaks down rock and how the pioneer species meets its needs in an ecosystem with no soil, as well as more specific information about the species they have chosen to research. Encourage students to share what they learn by preparing a slide presentation.

ELL *Self-Stick Note Ecosystems*

Ecosystems and Diversity

pairs

10 min

Model Have students fold a piece of paper in half and then unfold it. Give pairs of students self-stick notes in a variety of colors and sizes (alternative materials include scraps of paper or hole punches in various colors), making sure that students have a substantial number of at least one of the colors/sizes of notes. Tell students that the different sizes and colors of self-stick notes represent different species. Ask students to create a self-stick note ecosystem with high biodiversity on one side of the paper, and a self-stick note ecosystem with low biodiversity on the other side of the paper.

Lesson Vocabulary

eutrophication   succession   pioneer species
biodiversity

Previewing Vocabulary

 individuals   15 min

Word Splash Have students preview the lesson vocabulary by providing to each student a Word Splash graphic organizer, which has been prepared with the phrase *Ecosystem Change* in the center, surrounded by the lesson vocabulary terms *eutrophication, succession, pioneer species,* and *biodiversity*. Have students choose three of the vocabulary terms, and for each, have them write a sentence that predicts how each of the words relates to the phrase *Ecosystem Change*. As students read the lesson, have them note the accuracy of their predictions.

Reinforcing Vocabulary

whole class   15 min

Description Wheel Have students make a description wheel for each vocabulary term.

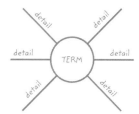

Customize Your Core Lesson

Core Instruction

☐ **Print Path** choices

☐ **Digital Path** choices

Vocabulary

☐ **Previewing Vocabulary** Word Splash

☐ **Reinforcing Vocabulary** Description Wheel

Your Resources

Differentiated Instruction

☐ **Basic** Classifying Changes

☐ **Advanced** Researching Pioneer Species

☐ **ELL** Self-Stick Note Ecosystems

Extend Science Concepts

Reinforce and Review

Activity *Ecosystem Changes*

Synthesizing Key Topics small groups
🕐 20 min

Carousel Review Help students review the material by following these steps:

1. After students have read the lesson, prepare four pieces of chart paper with the following questions: "Imagine an area in which a volcanic eruption occurs, followed by primary succession. Describe the changes that occur and compare the length of time each takes to occur." "Could primary succession occur without pioneer species? Explain why or why not." "Why is the phrase *balancing act* used to describe the interactions in a climax ecosystem?" "Define the term *biodiversity* and explain how it is related to ecosystem stability."

2. Divide students into small groups and assign each group a chart. Give each group a different colored marker.

3. Have the groups review their question, discuss their answer, and write a response.

4. After five minutes, each group should rotate to the next chart. Groups should put a check by each answer they agree with, comment on answers they don't agree with, and add their own answers. Continue until all groups have reviewed all charts.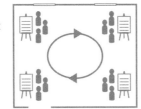

5. Invite each group to share information with the class.

Graphic Organizer

Succession in Ecosystems pairs
🕐 10 min

Process Chart Have one student in each pair make a process chart showing the steps of primary succession, and the other student in the pair make a process chart showing the steps of secondary succession. When they are finished, have students trade charts for additional review.

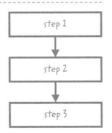

Going Further

Health Connection

Synthesizing Key Concepts small groups
🕐 20 min

Research Ecosystem changes can have direct and indirect effects on human health. For example, volcanic eruptions and forest fires can result in air pollution, which can affect human respiratory health. Have students work in small groups to research one example of an ecosystem change that impacts human health. Students should prepare a short oral presentation to share their information with the class.

Language Arts Connection

Changes in Ecosystems individuals
🕐 20 min

Descriptive Writing Have students write a descriptive paragraph about a specific type of ecosystem change. Point out that descriptive writing uses sensory language and vivid details. A well-written descriptive paragraph should allow readers to experience the sights, sounds, or smells associated with a particular type of ecosystem change. When students have finished, provide time for them to share their paragraphs with the class.

Customize Your Closing

🖼 *See the Assessment Guide for quizzes and tests.*

🌐 *Go Online to edit and create quizzes and tests.*

Reinforce and Review

☐ **Activity** Ecosystem Changes

☐ **Graphic Organizer** Process Chart

☐ **Print Path** Visual Summary, SE p. 108

☐ **Digital Path** Lesson Closer

Evaluate Student Mastery

Formative Assessment

See the teacher support below the Student Pages for additional Formative Assessment questions.

Ask the following questions to assess student mastery of the material. **Ask:** Describe an example of a slow change that occurs in ecosystems. Answer: Eutrophication is a change that occurs as a pond slowly fills in with debris and becomes a meadow. **Ask:** How does the biodiversity in an ecosystem change as the ecosystem undergoes primary succession? Answer: As primary succession proceeds, biodiversity increases. **Ask:** Describe a type of change that would be unlikely to occur in an undisturbed climax ecosystem. Sample answer: A type of change that would be unlikely to occur in a climax ecosystem is one type of species being replaced by another.

Reteach

Formative assessment may show that students need reinforcement for certain topics. The resources below are recommended for reteaching. If students were introduced to a topic through the Print path, you can also use the Digital Path to reteach, or vice versa.
🎧 *Can be assigned to individual students*

Changes in Ecosystems
Activity All Kinds of Changes

Succession in Ecosystems
Quick Lab Modeling Primary and Secondary Succession

ELL Venn Diagram 🎧

Ecosystems and Diversity
Daily Demo Disaster Strikes! 🎧

Summative Assessment

Alternative Assessment
Changes in Ecosystems

🌐 *Online resources: student worksheet; optional rubrics*

Changes in Ecosystems

Points of View: *Changes in Ecosystems*
Your class will work together to show what you've learned about changes in ecosystems from several different viewpoints.

1. Work in groups as assigned by your teacher. Each group will be assigned to one or two viewpoints.

2. Complete your assignment, and present your perspective to the class.

Vocabulary Choose two terms from the following list: *succession, pioneer species, eutrophication,* and *biodiversity.* Include the two terms you choose in a single rap, poem, or short song. Within the rap, poem, or short song, you must clearly state a definition for each term, and specifically state the relationship between the two terms you have chosen. Share your rap, poem, or song with the class.

Examples Research to identify one specific example of primary succession and one specific example of secondary succession that have occurred in the past or are currently occurring. Examples can be from anywhere. For each example, write a paragraph describing the changes.

Illustrations Make a collage that shows images associated with ecosystem change. The images you choose must include examples of both slow and sudden ecosystem changes. Present your collage to the class. For each image you include, describe the change in detail, including information about changes in both abiotic and biotic factors.

Analysis Some ecosystem changes occur over hundreds of years. Imagine that you are a part of a team of scientists who have been assigned to develop a database about world ecosystems. This information will be stored so that future scientists will have accurate information about ecosystems of the past. What categories of information about ecosystems would you store? What keywords would you use so that future scientists could access this information? Write a thorough description of your database.

Observations Identify a part of the schoolyard, an area near your home, or a part of your neighborhood. Set up a grid that outlines an area approximately one square meter in size. Carefully observe the living things that you find in your study area. Document your observations using written descriptions, sketches, photographs, or video. Present your observations to the class.

Details Write a short story from the point of view of a pioneer species. Describe your role in succession, and what you experience as the ecosystem changes around you. Include a description of your interactions with living and nonliving parts of the ecosystem. Be creative, but include accurate scientific details. Share your story with other students in your class.

Going Further
- ☐ **Health Connection** Research
- ☐ **Language Arts Connection** Descriptive Writing
- ☐ **Print Path** Why It Matters, SE p. 103

Your Resources

Formative Assessment
- ☐ **Strategies** Throughout TE
- ☐ **Lesson Review** SE

Summative Assessment
- ☐ **Alternative Assessment** Changes in Ecosystems
- ☐ **Lesson Quiz**
- ☐ **Unit Tests A and B**
- ☐ **Unit Review** SE End-of-Unit

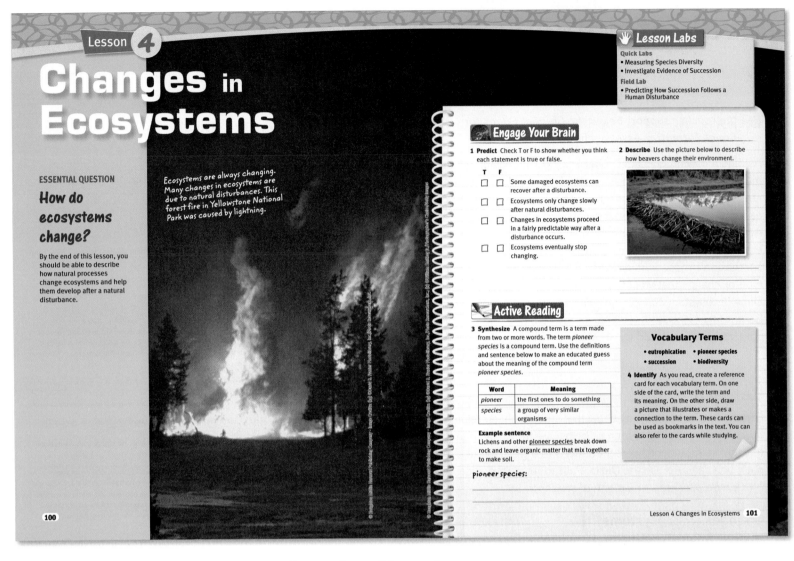

Lesson ④

Changes in Ecosystems

ESSENTIAL QUESTION

How do ecosystems change?

By the end of this lesson, you should be able to describe how natural processes change ecosystems and help them develop after a natural disturbance.

Ecosystems are always changing. Many changes in ecosystems are due to natural disturbances. This forest fire in Yellowstone National Park was caused by lightning.

Lesson Labs

Quick Labs
• Measuring Species Diversity
• Investigate Evidence of Succession

Field Lab
• Predicting How Succession Follows a Human Disturbance

Engage Your Brain

1 Predict Check T or F to show whether you think each statement is true or false.

T	F	
☐	☐	Some damaged ecosystems can recover after a disturbance.
☐	☐	Ecosystems only change slowly after natural disturbances.
☐	☐	Changes in ecosystems proceed in a fairly predictable way after a disturbance occurs.
☐	☐	Ecosystems eventually stop changing.

2 Describe Use the picture below to describe how beavers change their environment.

Active Reading

3 Synthesize A compound term is a term made from two or more words. The term *pioneer species* is a compound term. Use the definitions and sentence below to make an educated guess about the meaning of the compound term *pioneer species*.

Word	Meaning
pioneer	the first ones to do something
species	a group of very similar organisms

Example sentence
Lichens and other pioneer species break down rock and leave organic matter that mix together to make soil.

pioneer species:

Vocabulary Terms

• eutrophication • pioneer species
• succession • biodiversity

4 Identify As you read, create a reference card for each vocabulary term. On one side of the card, write the term and its meaning. On the other side, draw a picture that illustrates or makes a connection to the term. These cards can be used as bookmarks in the text. You can also refer to the cards while studying.

100

Lesson 4 Changes in Ecosystems 101

Answers

Answers for 1–3 should represent students' current thoughts, even if incorrect.

1. True; False; True; False

2. Beavers cut down trees to build dams that change rivers into ponds.

3. a group of organisms that are the first ones to live in an area

4. Students should define and sketch each vocabulary term in the lesson.

Opening Your Lesson

Discuss students' answers to item 1 above to assess their understanding of how ecosystems change over time.

Preconceptions Students believe that ecosystems do not naturally change unless something disastrous happens. However, even climax communities, to which students are introduced in this lesson, continually change. Some changes, such as volcanic eruptions, are rare and dramatic, which may lead to students to believe that changes in ecosystems occur rarely. Throughout the lesson, remind students that ecosystems continually undergo change.

Prerequisites Students should already have some knowledge of interactions in communities, and interactions between abiotic and biotic components of ecosystems. In this lesson, students will extend this information as they learn how changes in one or more factors in an ecosystem bring about changes in other factors.

Learning Alert

Preconceptions Students may believe that all ecosystem change is harmful or negative, because they may associate ecosystem change exclusively with events such as volcanic eruptions, floods, or fires.

Nothing Stays the Same

How quickly do ecosystems change?

Ecosystems and organisms are constantly changing and responding to daily, seasonal, and long-term changes in the environment. Most ecosystem changes are gradual. Some are sudden and irregular.

 **Active Reading** 5 **Describe** As you read, underline one example of a slow change and one example of a sudden change in an ecosystem.

Ecosystems May Change Slowly

Some changes happen slowly. Over time, a pond can develop into a meadow. **Eutrophication** (yoo•trohf•ih•KAY• shuhn) is the process in which organic matter and nutrients slowly build up in a body of water. The nutrients increase the growth of plants and microorganisms. When these organisms die, decaying matter sinks to the bottom of the pond. This organic matter can eventually fill the pond and become soil that grasses and other meadow plants can grow in.

Ecosystem changes can also be caused by seasonal or long-term changes in climate.

Ecosystems May Change Suddenly

Ecosystems can suddenly change due to catastrophic natural disturbances. A hurricane's strong winds can blow down trees and destroy vegetation in a few hours. Lightning can start a forest fire that rapidly clears away plants and alters animal habitats. A volcano, such as Washington's Mount St. Helens, can erupt and cause massive destruction to an ecosystem. But destruction is not the end of the story. Recovery brings new changes to an ecosystem and the populations that live in it.

Visualize It! Inquiry

6 Hypothesize What natural ecological change might happen to the meadow that forms where the pond was?

_____

_____

The organic matter growing in a pond dies and falls to the bottom. The pond gets shallower as the matter piles up.

Eventually, the pond fills in, and land plants grow there. The pond becomes a level meadow.

102 Unit 2 Earth's Biomes and Ecosystems

Why It Matters

A CHANGING WORLD

Ruin and Recovery

Ecosystems can change very fast. The volcanic eruption of Mount St. Helens in southern Washington devastated the mountain on May 18, 1980, killing 57 people. The hot gas and debris also killed native plant and animal species and damaged 596 square kilometers (230 square miles) of forest.

1979

Today

A Changed Landscape
The eruption changed the ecosystem dramatically. Trees fell and forests burned. Much of the ice and snow melted. The water mixed with ash and dirt that covered the ground. Thick mud formed and slid down the mountain. Flowing mud removed more trees and changed the shape of the landscape.

Road to Recovery
How did the ecosystem recover? Snow patches and ice protected some species. Some small mammals were sheltered in burrows. With the trees gone, more sunlight reached the ground. Seeds sprouted, and the recovery began.

Extend Inquiry

7 Explain How do sudden catastrophes such as the eruption of Mount St. Helens change the landscape of ecosystems?

8 Research Find out about how natural catastrophic events, such as volcanic eruptions, can affect the climate on Earth.

9 Hypothesize Form a hypothesis based on your research in question 8 about how changes in climate can lead to changes in ecosystems.

103

Answers

5. *See students' pages for annotations.*

6. Sample answer: The meadow may become a forest.

7. Natural sudden disturbances can destroy habitats, such as forestland. In recovery, new habitats such as meadows form.

8. Students may discuss volcanic eruptions releasing dust and gas into the atmosphere that can block sunlight and cause climate cooling.

9. Climate cooling due to volcanic eruptions may change plant communities, followed by changes in the animals that feed upon those plants.

Interpreting Visuals

Have students examine the image. **Ask:** What specific type of change has occurred in the pictures? eutrophication **Ask:** Is this change a slow change or a sudden change? slow change **Ask:** How have the living things and the abiotic factors in this ecosystem changed? Sample answer: The living things in this ecosystem were originally aquatic plants, fish, and other aquatic organisms. Now the living things consist of land plants and animals. The ecosystem has changed from a water environment to a land environment, so abiotic factors such as air temperature and wind speed have replaced abiotic factors such as water temperature.

Why It Matters

Point out that the volcanic eruption of Mount St. Helens provides an example of a sudden change in an ecosystem. The recovery of the surrounding area is an example of a slow change in an ecosystem.

What are the two types of ecological succession?

Ecosystems can develop from bare rock or cleared land. This development is the result of slow and constructive gradual changes. The slow development or replacement of an ecological community by another ecological community over time is called **succession**.

Primary Succession

A community may start to grow in an area that has no soil. This process is called primary succession. The first organisms to live in an uninhabited area are called **pioneer species**. Pioneer species, such as lichens, grow on rock and help to form soil in which plants can grow.

🔍 **Visualize It!**

10 Label Write a title for each step of primary succession.

A A slowly retreating glacier exposes bare rock where nothing lives, and primary succession begins.

B Acids from lichens break down the rock into particles. These particles mix with the remains of dead lichens to make soil.

C After many years, there is enough soil for mosses to grow. The mosses replace the lichens. Insects and other small organisms begin to live there, enriching the soil.

D As the soil deepens, mosses are replaced by ferns. The ferns may slowly be replaced by grasses and wildflowers. If there is enough soil, shrubs and small trees may grow.

E After hundreds or even thousands of years, the soil may be deep and fertile enough to support a forest.

Secondary Succession

Succession also happens to areas that have been disturbed but that still have soil. Sometimes an existing ecosystem is damaged by a natural disaster, such as a fire or a flood. Sometimes farmland is cleared but is left unmanaged. In either case, if soil is left intact, the original community may regrow through a series of stages called secondary succession.

11 Identify Underline one or two distinctive features of each stage of secondary succession.

A The first year after a farmer stops growing crops or the first year after some other major disturbance, wild plants start to grow. In farmland, crabgrass often grows first.

B By the second year, new wild plants appear. Their seeds may have been blown into the field by the wind, or they may have been carried by insects or birds. Horseweed is common during the second year.

C In 5 to 15 years, small conifer trees may start growing among the weeds. The trees continue to grow, and after about 100 years, a forest may form.

D As older conifers die, they may be replaced by hardwoods, such as oak or maple trees, if the climate can support them.

Think Outside the Book

12 Describe Find an example of secondary succession in your community, and make a poster that describes each stage.

104 / 105

Answers

10. Sample Answers: A: Bare Rock; B: Lichens Form Soil; C: Mosses and Insects Move In; D: Larger Plants Grow; E: A Forest Grows

11. *See students' pages for annotations.*

12. Students' answers will vary, but examples may include succession in abandoned farmland, vacant lots, unlandscaped back yards, delayed construction projects, or cleared land next to roads.

Formative Assessment

Ask: How are primary succession and secondary succession similar? Sample answer: Both are a series of changes in an ecosystem. **Ask:** Which type of succession could successfully occur without pioneer species? Explain. Secondary succession could occur without pioneer species, because pioneer species contribute to soil formation. In secondary succession, soil formation is not required.

Learning Alert

Oh, Pioneers Note that because a disturbed area may offer few or no nutrients, the first organisms to colonize the area must be autotrophic. Later organisms can be consumers, but these first pioneers must be able to make their own food.

Using Annotations

Text Structure: Main Idea/Details As students write titles for each of the steps of primary succession, have them focus on the main idea presented in each caption, and then summarize that main idea to create a title for each stage. Remind students that they are looking for details that *distinguish* one stage from another.

⊘ *Text Structure: Main Ideas/Details support*

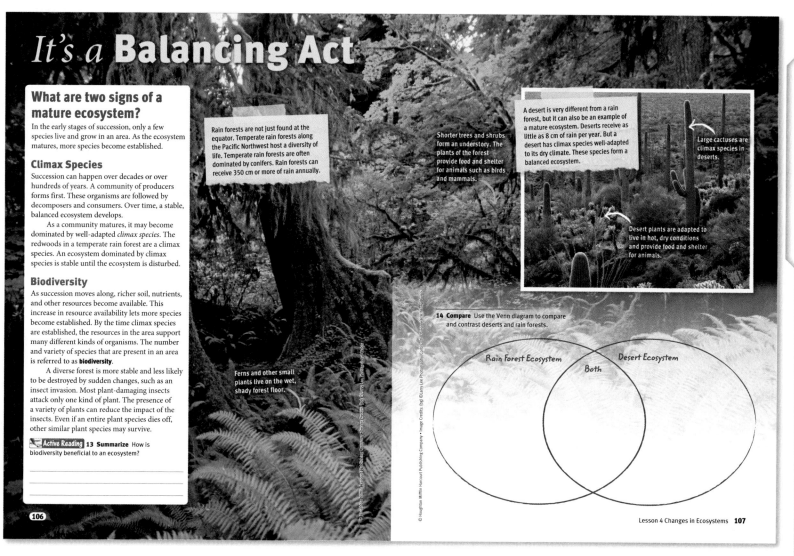

It's a Balancing Act

What are two signs of a mature ecosystem?

In the early stages of succession, only a few species live and grow in an area. As the ecosystem matures, more species become established.

Climax Species

Succession can happen over decades or over hundreds of years. A community of producers forms first. These organisms are followed by decomposers and consumers. Over time, a stable, balanced ecosystem develops.

As a community matures, it may become dominated by well-adapted *climax species*. The redwoods in a temperate rain forest are a climax species. An ecosystem dominated by climax species is stable until the ecosystem is disturbed.

Biodiversity

As succession moves along, richer soil, nutrients, and other resources become available. This increase in resource availability lets more species become established. By the time climax species are established, the resources in the area support many different kinds of organisms. The number and variety of species that are present in an area is referred to as **biodiversity**.

A diverse forest is more stable and less likely to be destroyed by sudden changes, such as an insect invasion. Most plant-damaging insects attack only one kind of plant. The presence of a variety of plants can reduce the impact of the insects. Even if an entire plant species dies off, other similar plant species may survive.

Active Reading 13 **Summarize** How is biodiversity beneficial to an ecosystem?

Rain forests are not just found at the equator. Temperate rain forests along the Pacific Northwest host a diversity of life. Temperate rain forests are often dominated by conifers. Rain forests can receive 350 cm or more of rain annually.

Shorter trees and shrubs form an understory. The plants of the forest provide food and shelter for animals such as birds and mammals.

Ferns and other small plants live on the wet, shady forest floor.

A desert is very different from a rain forest, but it can also be an example of a mature ecosystem. Deserts receive as little as 8 cm of rain per year. But a desert has climax species well-adapted to its dry climate. These species form a balanced ecosystem.

Large cactuses are climax species in deserts.

Desert plants are adapted to live in hot, dry conditions and provide food and shelter for animals.

14 **Compare** Use the Venn diagram to compare and contrast deserts and rain forests.

Rain Forest Ecosystem — Both — Desert Ecosystem

106

Answers

13. Biodiversity helps communities remain stable. If one species dies off, other similar species may survive.

14. Rain forest ecosystem: over 350 cm of rain; tall conifers and ferns

    Desert ecosystem: gets as little as 8 cm of rain per year; cactuses and hardy flowering plants

    Both: composed of climax species that are well adapted to the conditions; plants that provide food and habitat for animals

Interpreting Visuals

Have students identify living things and abiotic factors in the rain forest ecosystem picture. Sample answers: trees, warm temperatures Then, have students identify living things and abiotic factors in the desert ecosystem picture. Sample answers: cacti, sandy soil

Learning Alert

Change in Climax Ecosystems Students may think that a climax community is described as stable because it does not change in any way. Point out that changes occur in all ecosystems. Then, have students work with a partner to identify a type of change that might occur within a climax community and a type of change that probably would not occur in a climax community. Have each pair share their ideas with the class.

Probing Question DIRECTED Inquiry

Evaluate Explain that people often apply herbicides (substances that kill certain plants) to gardens and farm fields to prevent the growth of plant species that are considered weeds. **Ask:** How does this action impact the biodiversity and stability of these small ecosystems? Applying herbicides to landscape gardens and farm fields decreases biodiversity in these ecosystems, and in turn, decreases stability in these ecosystems.

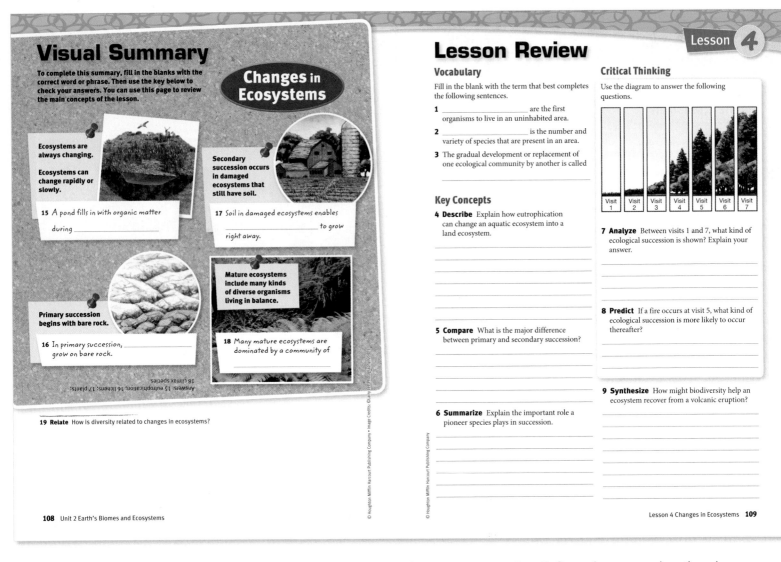

Lesson 4

Visual Summary

To complete this summary, fill in the blanks with the correct word or phrase. Then use the key below to check your answers. You can use this page to review the main concepts of the lesson.

Changes in Ecosystems

Ecosystems are always changing.

Ecosystems can change rapidly or slowly.

15 A pond fills in with organic matter during _____

Secondary succession occurs in damaged ecosystems that still have soil.

17 Soil in damaged ecosystems enables _____ to grow right away.

Mature ecosystems include many kinds of diverse organisms living in balance.

Primary succession begins with bare rock.

16 In primary succession, _____ grow on bare rock.

18 Many mature ecosystems are dominated by a community of _____

Answers: 15 eutrophication; 16 lichens; 17 plants; 18 climax species

19 Relate How is diversity related to changes in ecosystems?

Lesson Review

Vocabulary

Fill in the blank with the term that best completes the following sentences.

1 _____ are the first organisms to live in an uninhabited area.

2 _____ is the number and variety of species that are present in an area.

3 The gradual development or replacement of one ecological community by another is called _____

Key Concepts

4 Describe Explain how eutrophication can change an aquatic ecosystem into a land ecosystem.

5 Compare What is the major difference between primary and secondary succession?

6 Summarize Explain the important role a pioneer species plays in succession.

Critical Thinking

Use the diagram to answer the following questions.

Visit 1 | Visit 2 | Visit 3 | Visit 4 | Visit 5 | Visit 6 | Visit 7

7 Analyze Between visits 1 and 7, what kind of ecological succession is shown? Explain your answer.

8 Predict If a fire occurs at visit 5, what kind of ecological succession is more likely to occur thereafter?

9 Synthesize How might biodiversity help an ecosystem recover from a volcanic eruption?

Visual Summary Answers

15. eutrophication

16. lichens

17. plants

18. climax species

19. Sample answer: Ecosystems become more diverse as they move through succession to maturity. A diverse ecosystem may be more resilient to changes that happen in ecosystems.

Lesson Review Answers

1. Pioneer species

2. Biodiversity

3. succession

4. Eutrophication is the increase in nutrients in a pond or lake. This increases plant growth. As plants die, they fill in the pond. Over time, the pond can fill in completely.

5. Primary succession takes place on exposed surfaces with no soil, where nothing has lived before; secondary succession takes place where soil and some plant life still exist.

6. Pioneer species are the first organisms that can live in a previously uninhabited area. These species make soil.

7. Secondary succession; there is some grass and soil present at Visit 1.

8. Secondary succession; a forest fire would leave the soil intact.

9. Diverse organisms have different adaptations for survival. A variety of different adaptations would help ensure some species survive to regrow.

Teacher Notes

Design an Ecosystem

Purpose To design and analyze a closed ecosystem

Learning Goals
• Estimate the quantity of plants needed to support a food web.
• Research, design, build, and evaluate an ecosystem.

Vocabulary
ecosystem, population, producer, photosynthesis, consumer, herbivore, carnivore, omnivore, decomposer, biomass

Prerequisite Knowledge
• Basic understanding of ecosystems, including the roles of producers, consumers, and decomposers
• Understanding of energy and matter in ecosystems
• Familiarity with changes in ecosystems

Materials
1-gallon glass jar or plastic container, with lid

fresh water, preferably from natural source

gravel

aquatic plants and animals

light source

decorative aquarium objects (optional)

Teacher Note If possible, collect pond water for students to use in their ecosystems. Explain that pond water typically contains dissolved nutrients, algae, bacteria, and other microscopic organisms. If possible, allow students to observe a sample of pond water under a microscope.

Caution! Students should wash their hands with soap and water after handling plants and animals. Do not allow students to open their containers once they are sealed.

Content Refresher

Professional Development

Ecosystems An ecosystem is a community of different species that interact with each other and with the environment. An ecosystem is made up of all of the organisms in an area and their interactions with both biotic and abiotic factors. Abiotic (non-living) factors include water, soil, weather, temperature, humidity, and so on. Biotic (living) parts of an ecosystem can be classified according to their roles:

• Producers are plants and other organisms that make their own food. They take in carbon dioxide, and they add oxygen to the system.

• Consumers are organisms that feed on plants or other living things. Consumers contribute carbon dioxide and waste to an ecosystem.

• Decomposers recycle waste products. Examples of decomposers in an aquatic system include bacteria, snails, and ghost shrimp.

Producers, consumers, and decomposers must all be in balance for an ecosystem to thrive. For example, if there are not enough plants or other producers in an aquatic ecosystem, the animals will starve or suffocate from lack of oxygen.

In a closed aquatic ecosystem, dissolved oxygen is needed for aquatic organisms to survive. Oxygen from the air dissolves in water. Water plants also produce oxygen during photosynthesis. Bacteria remove oxygen from water as they decompose organic materials.

21st Century SKILLS   Theme: Environmental Literacy

Activities focusing on 21st Century Skills are included for this feature and can be found on the following pages.

These activities focus on the following skills:

• **Critical Thinking and Problem Solving**

• **Media Literacy**

• **Productivity and Accountability**

You can learn more about the 21st Century Skills in the front matter of this Teacher's Edition.

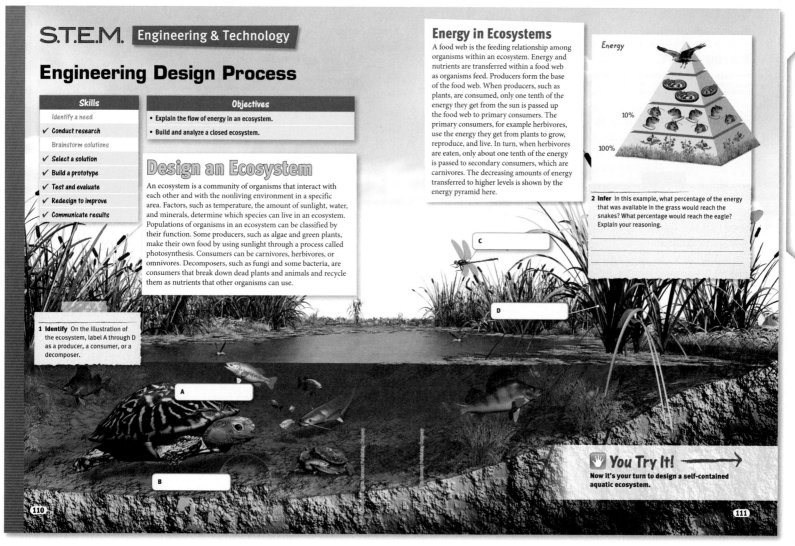

S.T.E.M. Engineering & Technology

Engineering Design Process

Skills
Identify a need
✓ Conduct research
Brainstorm solutions
✓ Select a solution
✓ Build a prototype
✓ Test and evaluate
✓ Redesign to improve
✓ Communicate results

Objectives
• Explain the flow of energy in an ecosystem.
• Build and analyze a closed ecosystem.

Design an Ecosystem

An ecosystem is a community of organisms that interact with each other and with the nonliving environment in a specific area. Factors, such as temperature, the amount of sunlight, water, and minerals, determine which species can live in an ecosystem. Populations of organisms in an ecosystem can be classified by their function. Some producers, such as algae and green plants, make their own food by using sunlight through a process called photosynthesis. Consumers can be carnivores, herbivores, or omnivores. Decomposers, such as fungi and some bacteria, are consumers that break down dead plants and animals and recycle them as nutrients that other organisms can use.

1 Identify On the illustration of the ecosystem, label A through D as a producer, a consumer, or a decomposer.

Energy in Ecosystems

A food web is the feeding relationship among organisms within an ecosystem. Energy and nutrients are transferred within a food web as organisms feed. Producers form the base of the food web. When producers, such as plants, are consumed, only one tenth of the energy they get from the sun is passed up the food web to primary consumers. The primary consumers, for example herbivores, use the energy they get from plants to grow, reproduce, and live. In turn, when herbivores are eaten, only about one tenth of the energy is passed to secondary consumers, which are carnivores. The decreasing amounts of energy transferred to higher levels is shown by the energy pyramid here.

2 Infer In this example, what percentage of the energy that was available in the grass would reach the snakes? What percentage would reach the eagle? Explain your reasoning.

_____

_____

_____

✋ **You Try It!** ⟶

Now it's your turn to design a self-contained aquatic ecosystem.

110

111

Answers

1. Students should label plants as producers, fish and turtle and insects as consumers, and bacteria as decomposers.

2. Sample answer: The snakes would get one-tenth of the energy from the mice; $0.1 \times 0.1 = 0.01 = 1\%$ (1/100) of the energy from the grass in the ecosystem. The eagle would get one tenth of the energy from the snakes; $0.1 \times 0.01 = 0.001 = 0.1\%$ (1/1000) of the energy from the grass in the ecosystem.

Engineering Design Process

✋ You Try It!

Now it's your turn to design and analyze a self-contained aquatic ecosystem. Your ecosystem should allow the occupants to survive just from the light provided.

① Conduct Research

Write down the plants and animals that you want to put into your ecosystem. Use fast-growing plants to provide oxygen and food for the animals. Also, write down how decomposers get into the system.

_____

_____

_____

② Select a Solution

Based on the flow of energy and biomass in an ecosystem, determine the rough proportion of producers and consumers needed in the ecosystem you are designing. Write down how many plants to animals you think that you will need. Explain your reasoning.

_____

_____

_____

_____

③ Build a Prototype

Follow these steps to build a prototype of your system.

- Clean your container, and record its mass.
- Put enough gravel in to cover the bottom.
- Fill the container with water, and add decorative items.
- Let the water and decorative items settle for at least 24 hours to allow the chemicals in the water to evaporate and the water to come to room temperature.
- Add your plants, and wait 24 hours.

- Before releasing the animals into the tank, float the containers holding the animals in the water in the tank for a few hours. This allows the animals to adjust to the temperature of the water in the tank.
- Close the lid tightly to prevent evaporation, and then record the mass of your ecosystem.
- Store your ecosystem where it will receive indirect sunlight.

You Will Need

- ✔ one-gallon glass jar with tight-fitting lid or sealable clear plastic container
- ✔ fresh water; can use tap water, but water from natural source is preferable
- ✔ gravel
- ✔ aquatic plants and animals to be selected by students
- ✔ light source if needed
- ✔ decorative aquarium items (optional)

S.T.E.M. Engineering & Technology

④ Test and Evaluate

List five things that you think would be important to record before you close your system completely. Keep a journal in which you record daily observations of your ecosystem for several weeks.

_____

_____

_____

_____

⑤ Redesign to Improve

After observing your system and keeping a journal for several weeks, what would you change about your system?

_____

_____

_____

_____

⑥ Communicate Results

Summarize the observations you made in your journal. Consider these questions: What things do you think made your ecosystem successful or unsuccessful? What things, if any, would you change to improve your ecosystem even more? Finally, make a report of your ecosystem to present to the class.

_____

_____

_____

_____

_____

_____

Answers

1. Sample answer: I think decomposers, such as bacteria, will already be in the water that I put into my ecosystem. I have to put in plants first and then introduce animals carefully. Plants I can use include Elodea, Anacharis, Egeria, or duckweed, which all grow fast. Fish, frogs, snails, shrimps, or crabs can be used as animals.

2. Sample answer: I will use Elodea as plants and snails and mosquito fish as animals. For the plants and animals, I know that the primary consumers will only get one tenth of the energy the producers have, so I will start with many more plants than animals.

4. Sample answer: I think it would be important to record the water temperature, how clear the water is, how many fish are alive, how many snails are alive, and the mass of the whole ecosystem (including the container) to make sure that no mass is being exchanged with the outside.

5. Sample answer: The water became cloudy, so I added more plants. The sides of the container became greenish with algae, so I added another snail.

6. Sample answer: I did not have enough plants at first. Almost all my fish died, but there were still a few snails. After adding more plants, the fish that were left stayed alive. The plants grew very well, and eventually the container got crowded with plants. To improve my ecosystem even more, I would put more plants in at the beginning.

21st Century SKILLS

Learning and Innovation Skills

 individuals or small groups   ⏱ ongoing

Critical Thinking and Problem Solving Based on what they have observed in their model ecosystem, have students design an experiment that simulates a real-world problem that affects aquatic ecosystems. For example, what happens when fertilizer runoff enters a lake or pond? How does acid rain affect an aquatic ecosystem? Support students as they gather materials and conduct their experiment. Invite students to share the design of their experiment and their results with the class.

🌐 *Optional Online resource: Design Your Own Investigations: Experiments*

Information, Media, and Technology Skills

 small groups   ⏱ ongoing

Media Literacy Invite small groups of students to create a documentary about how to build an aquatic ecosystem, what problems are likely to be encountered during the process, and how to solve the problems. Students could take a daily video during the development of their ecosystem and then make a time-lapse video of the process. Encourage students to share their documentaries with the class.

Life and Career Skills

 small groups   20 min

Productivity and Accountability Invite small groups of students to choose a plant or animal from their aquatic ecosystem and find out more about its natural history. Ask students to build a portfolio about the organism that includes images and information about its life cycle and interactions with other organisms in an ecosystem. Students may want to assign topics for each member of the group to research, or they may divide up the work in any other way that seems fair. Invite students to share their portfolio with the class, and explain what each person contributed to the entire presentation.

Differentiated Instruction

Basic *Create an Energy Pyramid*

 individuals   ⏱ 20 min

Provide students with information about a specific food chain in another ecosystem (for example, a coral reef or rainforest ecosystem). Have students identify the producer, primary consumer, and secondary consumer in the food chain and draw an energy pyramid like the one shown on the student page. Help students compare the biomass at each energy level.

Advanced *Cleaning Polluted Ecosystems*

individuals or pairs   ⏱ ongoing

Invite interested students to research the role of microbes in cleaning polluted aquatic ecosystems. Have students use the Internet or library resources to do their research and then report on what they learn. If interested, students can design an experiment to see how decomposers can clean polluted waters.

ELL *Food Webs in Ecosystems*

individuals or pairs   ⏱ 10 min

Have students draw a food web based on what they observe in their ecosystem. Have students label the plants and animals in the food web. Invite students to explain the food web to a partner or to a small group.

Customize Your Feature

- ☐ **21st Century Skills** Learning and Innovation Skills
- ☐ **21st Century Skills** Information, Media, and Technology Skills
- ☐ **21st Century Skills** Life and Career Skills
- ☐ **Basic** Create an Energy Pyramid
- ☐ **Advanced** Cleaning Polluted Ecosystems
- ☐ **ELL** Food Webs in Ecosystems

Human Activity and Ecosystems

Essential Question How do human activities affect ecosystems?

Professional Development

For more detailed information about the topics in this lesson, refer to the Content Refresher in the Unit Opener pages.

Opening Your Lesson

Begin the lesson by assessing students' prerequisite and prior knowledge.

Prerequisite Knowledge

- Basic principles of ecology
- Definition of *ecosystem* and knowledge of interactions in ecosystems
- Population dynamics including limiting resources and population size
- Cycles of matter

Accessing Prior Knowledge

Ask: What is an ecosystem? all the living and nonliving things in an environment along with their interactions

Ask: What are some resources that are recycled through living things and the environment by natural processes? water, oxygen, carbon dioxide, nitrogen

Customize Your Opening

- ☐ **Accessing Prior Knowledge,** above
- ☐ **Print Path** Engage Your Brain, SE, p. 115
- ☐ **Print Path** Active Reading, SE p. 115
- ☐ **Digital Path** Lesson Opener

Key Topics/Learning Goals

Human Activities Affect Land Ecosystems

1. Explain how human activities affect ecosystems on land.
2. Tell how human population growth affects ecosystems.
3. Define urbanization.
4. Define exotic species.

Human Activities Affect Aquatic Ecosystems

1. Explain how human activities impact water quality and quantity.
2. Define water pollution, eutrophication, and acid rain.
3. Explain how human activities and pollutants affect ocean ecosystems.

Ecosystem Conservation

1. Explain what conservation is.
2. Explain how stewardship can help protect Earth's ecosystems.
3. Describe how maintaining biodiversity enhances a species' chance of survival.
4. List five strategies that can help protect the environment.

Supporting Concepts

- Pollution and development affect land ecosystems.
- Urbanization, an increase in the density of people living in urban areas, often leads to the destruction of natural habitats.
- An exotic species is a species that is not native to a particular region. Invasive exotic species can outcompete native species for resources.

- Water quality may decline due to chemical contaminants, raw sewage, etc. Quantity may decline through overuse, waste, and dams.
- Eutrophication is an increase in the amount of nutrients in a water ecosystem.
- Acid rain is precipitation that forms when air pollutants enter the water cycle and cause the pH of rain to drop below normal levels.
- Human activities that affect oceans include pollution, overfishing, and development.

- Conservation is the protection and wise use of natural resources.
- Stewardship, the careful and responsible management of a resource, can prevent ecosystem damage.
- Maintaining biodiversity, the number and variety of organisms in a given area during a period of time, enhances species survival.
- Strategies for protecting the environment include reducing pollution and pesticide use, protecting habitats, and developing alternative energy sources.

Options for Instruction

Two parallel paths provide coverage of the Essential Questions, with a strong **Inquiry** strand woven into each. Follow the **Print Path**, the **Digital Path,** or your customized combination of print, digital, and inquiry.

 **Print Path**
Teaching support for the Print Path appears with the Student Pages.

 Inquiry Labs and Activities

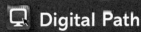 **Digital Path**
Digital Path shortcut: TS673869

Growing Pains, SE pp. 116–117
How do humans harm ecosystems?
- By Depleting Resources
- By Destroying Habitats

Field Lab
Field Investigation of Plant Quantity and Diversity

Activity
Modeling Pollution Uptake in Plants

Evidence of Human Impact
Interactive Images

A Growing Population
Animation

Humans and Land Ecosystems
Video

Water, Water, Everywhere?,
SE pp. 118–120
How do humans impact oceans?
- Through Fishing and Overfishing
- Through Coastal Development
How do humans affect freshwater ecosystems?

Daily Demo
Eggs and Oil Don't Mix

Quick Lab
Investigate Acidity of Water

Humans and Aquatic Ecosystems
Interactive Images

Humans and Ocean Ecosystems
Graphic Sequence

Save It!, SE pp. 122–123
How do humans protect ecosystems?
- Maintain Biodiversity
- Conserve Natural Resources

Quick Lab
Biodiversity All Around Us

Activity
Reusing Trash

Conservation and Stewardship
Slideshow

Biodiversity
Interactive Images

Options for Assessment

See the Evaluate page for options, including Formative Assessment, Summative Assessment, and Unit Review.

Engage and Explore

Activities and Discussion

Activity *Hay, What's That?*

**Ecosystem
Conservation**

 individuals or pairs
🕐 10 min/day for a week
GUIDED inquiry

Provide students with glass jars, grass clippings or hay, and water (if you use tap water, allow it to sit overnight so the chlorine can dissipate). Have them add the plant material and water to the jar and cover the jar loosely. Have them look at a sample of the water under the microscope and record their observations. After four and seven days, observe another water sample. Discuss the increase in organisms students observe, and what the organisms are.

Activity *Modeling Pollution Uptake in Plants*

**Human Activities Affect
Land Ecosystems**

 small groups
🕐 10 min day 1; 10 min day 2
DIRECTED inquiry

Provide each group with a stalk of celery, a plastic knife, a clear plastic cup, and water that contains food coloring. Have students fill half the cup with colored water. Ask students to observe the celery and record a description of its color and appearance. Then have one student use the knife to cut a small piece off the bottom of the celery stalk. Have them stand the celery in the cup of water and allow the celery to remain in the cup overnight. Allow students a few minutes to observe the celery the next day. **Ask:** What changes do you observe in the celery stalk and leaves? Some parts of the celery have taken on the color of the water **Ask:** What do your observations suggest about plants growing in polluted soil or near polluted water? Plants growing in or near polluted land or water will take in some of the pollution from their surroundings. Relate student observations to what they have learned about how pollutants can be harmful to organisms.

Take It Home *Identifying Conservation Opportunities*

**Ecosystem
Conservation**

 adult-student pairs
🕐 10–30 min
GUIDED inquiry

Students work with an adult to identify the types of materials people discard as litter during a neighborhood walk. Students will classify the litter according to the type of material it is made of and identify items suitable for recycling.

Activity *Reusing Trash*

**Ecosystem
Conservation**

 small groups
🕐 varies
DIRECTED inquiry

Organize students into groups of four. Provide each group with plastic grocery bags or other materials that might otherwise be discarded, such as gallon-sized water bottles or cardboard boxes. Challenge students to use their materials to make something that would not only reuse what might otherwise be trash, but also that is beneficial to the environment (for example, make a water bottle bird feeder). Display student projects.

©PhotoDisc/Getty Images; ©Jonathan Kantor/Getty Images

Customize Your Labs

 See the Lab Manual for lab datasheets.

 Go Online for editable lab datasheets.

Levels of  **Inquiry**

DIRECTED inquiry
introduces inquiry skills
within a structured
framework.

GUIDED inquiry
develops inquiry skills
within a supportive
environment.

INDEPENDENT inquiry
deepens inquiry skills
with student-driven
questions or procedures.

Labs and Demos

Daily Demo *Eggs and Oil Don't Mix*

**Human Activities Affect
Aquatic Ecosystems**

 whole class
 25 min
DIRECTED inquiry

PURPOSE **To demonstrate how oil spills affect marine birds**

MATERIALS

- bowl containing 250 mL vegetable oil colored with oil-soluble red food coloring
- 5 hard-boiled eggs
- protective gloves
- wall clock or timer

1 Prepare the colored vegetable oil prior to class by mixing powdered food coloring in the oil. Place the colored oil in a large glass bowl. Explain to students that the bowl represents oil spilled into ocean water.

2 Peel one egg and have students record what they observe about the egg's appearance. Then, carefully place each of the remaining hard-boiled eggs into the bowl containing the oil. **Ask:** What effect, if any, do you think the oil will have on the eggs? The oil will coat the outside of the egg; some oil will penetrate the shell and enter the egg.

3 **Observing** After five minutes remove one egg from the oil. Peel the egg and allow students to observe its appearance. Have students record their observations.

4 **Draw Conclusions** Repeat step 3 every five minutes for the remaining eggs. Have students record their observations and note how much time passes before a shelled egg shows red coloring. **Ask:** What does red coloring on the shelled egg indicate? Some of the oil has penetrated the shell. **Ask:** How might an oil spill affect unborn sea birds and sea-bird populations? The oil might kill developing birds or interfere with their development in a way that makes them less likely to survive. If many eggs are affected, the survival of the sea birds may be threatened.

Field Lab *Field Investigation of Plant Quantity and Diversity*

**Human Activities Affect
Land Ecosystems**

 small groups
 three 45-min periods
 GUIDED inquiry

PURPOSE **To observe the impact of human activity on plants**

See the Lab manual or go Online for planning information.

Quick Lab *Biodiversity All Around Us*

**Ecosystem
Conservation**

 small groups
 40 min
DIRECTED inquiry

PURPOSE **To explore the variety of living things**

See the Lab manual or go Online for planning information.

Quick Lab *Investigate Acidity of Water*

**Human Activities Affect
Aquatic Ecosystems**

 pairs
 20 min
DIRECTED inquiry

PURPOSE **To learn more about the acidity of water**

See the Lab manual or go Online for planning information.

Activities and Discussion

- ☐ **Activity** Hay, What's That?
- ☐ **Activity** Modeling Pollution... Plants
- ☐ **Take It Home** Identifying Conservation Opportunities
- ☐ **Activity** Reusing Trash

Labs and Demos

- ☐ **Daily Demo** Eggs and Oil Don't Mix
- ☐ **Field Lab** Field investigation of Plant Quantity and Diversity
- ☐ **Quick Lab** Biodiversity All Around Us
- ☐ **Quick Lab** Investigate Acidity of Water

Your Resources

_____

_____

_____

_____

Explain Science Concepts

	📖 Print Path	💻 Digital Path

Key Topics		
Human Activities Affect Land Ecosystems	☐ **Growing Pains,** SE pp. 116–117 • Relate, #5 • Active Reading, #6 • Think Outside the Book, #7 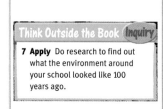 **Think Outside the Book** Inquiry **7 Apply** Do research to find out what the environment around your school looked like 100 years ago.	☐ **Evidence of Human Impact** Find out how humans have changed Earth. ☐ **Humans and Land Ecosystems** Discover how human activities, including introducing non-native species, affect ecosystems. 
Human Activities Affect Aquatic Ecosystems	☐ **Water, Water Everywhere?** SE pp. 118–120 • Active Reading (annotation strategy), #8 • Visualize It!, #9 • List, #10 • Active Reading, #11 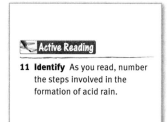 **Active Reading** **11 Identify** As you read, number the steps involved in the formation of acid rain.	☐ **Humans and Aquatic Ecosystems** See how human activities affect water quality and quantity. ☐ **Humans and Ocean Ecosystems** Investigate how humans affect the ocean. 
Ecosystem Conservation	☐ **Save It!,** SE pp. 122–123 • Active Reading (annotation strategy), #15 • State, #16 • Synthesize, #17 **Active Reading** **15 Identify** As you read, underline the definition of stewardship.	☐ **Conservation and Stewardship** Investigate conservation and stewardship. ☐ **Biodiversity** Explore how maintaining biodiversity enhances a species' chances of survival.

Differentiated Instruction

Basic *Environmental Problems*

Synthesizing Key Topics

 small groups
🕐 20 min

Have students work in groups of four or five to develop a list of environmental problems caused by humans. Have groups pick from the list the four problems that they feel are most important, and share with the class why they think these problems are important.

Advanced *Environmental Protection*

Synthesizing Key Topics

 individuals
🕐 ongoing

Quick Research Have students research environmental legislation such as the Superfund Act (CERCLA), the Clean Water Act, or the Endangered Species Act. Have students find out when and why the law was passed, if it has been changed, and what it does to protect the environment. Have them share what they learn with the class through a multimedia or oral presentation.

Advanced *Modeling Habitat Change through Urbanization*

Human Activities Affect Land Ecosystems

 individuals
🕐 ongoing

Have students develop maps, models, or cartoon panels that illustrate how urbanization and development can divide or destroy natural habitats. Students may wish to focus on one aspect of development, such as construction of a new roadway or housing development. Encourage students to be creative in their approach and share their completed models with the class.

ELL *Diagramming Acid Rain Formation*

Human Activities Affect Aquatic Ecosystems

 individuals
🕐 25 min

Have students use the text descriptions of acid rain to make an easy-to-understand diagram of acid rain formation. For example, students can outline the steps of acid rain formation and draw arrows between each step in the process. Allow students to display their diagrams.

Lesson Vocabulary

urbanization   eutrophication   conservation
biodiversity   stewardship

Previewing Vocabulary

 whole class
🕐 25 min

Prefixes Use the prefixes of the words to help students understand the word meanings. To teach this skill, use the transparency available online. Then, explain the meanings of the prefixes *bio-* and *urban-* to help students understand the meanings of the terms biodiversity and urbanization.

🌐 *Online resource: Prefixes*

Reinforcing Vocabulary

 individuals, then pairs
🕐 30 min

Word Triangles Have students create Word Triangles for each vocabulary term. Have them share their completed Word Triangles with a partner.

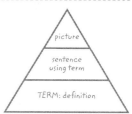

Customize Your Core Lesson

Core Instruction
☐ **Print Path** choices
☐ **Digital Path** choices

Vocabulary
☐ **Previewing Vocabulary** Prefixes
☐ **Reinforcing Vocabulary** Word Triangles

Differentiated Instruction
☐ **Basic** Environmental Problems
☐ **Advanced** Environmental Protection
☐ **Advanced** Modeling Habitat Change through Urbanization
☐ **ELL** Diagramming Acid Rain Formation

Your Resources

Extend Science Concepts

Reinforce and Review

Activity *Carousel Review*

Synthesizing Key Topics   small groups · 25 min

1 Arrange chart paper in different parts of the room. On each paper, write a question to review content.

2 Divide students into small groups and assign each group a chart. Give each group a different colored marker.

3 Groups discuss their question, discuss their answer, and write a response.

4 After 5 to 10 minutes, each group rotates to the next station. Groups put a check by each answer they agree with, comment on answers they don't agree with, and add their own answers. Continue until all groups have reviewed all charts.

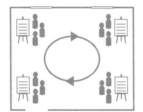

5 Invite each group to share information with the class.

Graphic Organizer

Ecosystem Conservation   individual · 20 min

Description Wheel Have students write the term biodiversity at the center of a description wheel diagram. On the spokes of the wheel have them write terms or phrases that help them better understand and remember the concept of biodiversity and its importance.

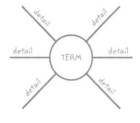

⊘ *Optional Online Resource: Description Wheel support*

Going Further

Art Connection

Ecosystem Conservation   whole class · varies

Logo Design Ask students if they are familiar with the three-arrow symbol that is used to identify materials that are made from recycled materials or that can be recycled. Explain that this logo was developed by architecture student Gary Anderson in 1970. Anderson developed the symbol as an entry for a contest sponsored by the Container Corporation of American (CCA), a company that makes paperboard products. Challenge students to develop their own logos that can be used to identify and encourage other environmentally friendly practices such as conserving water, protecting wildlife habitat, or discouraging littering. Have students share their designs with the class.

Real World Connection

Human Activities Affect Land Ecosystems   individual · varies

Under Construction Many people enjoy watching birds. To attract birds to their yards, many people put up birdhouses and bird feeders. These structures do not only benefit people, but also birds that may have difficulty finding food as their habitat disappears as a result of urbanization. Have students research, design, and build a simple birdhouse or bird feeder appropriate for a native or migrating species. Encourage students to reuse scrap lumber or other items that would otherwise be discarded as they develop their designs.

Customize Your Closing

◆ See the Assessment Guide for quizzes and tests.

⊘ Go Online to edit and create quizzes and tests.

Reinforce and Review

☐ **Activity** Carousel Review

☐ **Graphic Organizer** Description Wheel

☐ **Print Path** Visual Summary, SE p. 124

☐ **Print Path** Lesson Review, SE p. 125

☐ **Digital Path** Lesson Closer

Evaluate Student Mastery

See the teacher support below the Student Pages for additional Formative Assessment questions.

Describe for students or have them review the different ways in which human population growth impacts ecosystems. **Ask:** How does rapid human population growth impact the availability of natural resources? Sample answer: As the human population grows, its demand for resources also grows. Too much of a demand can lead to depletion of resources. **Ask:** How does urbanization harm ecosystems? Sample answer: Urbanization can lead to destruction of habitat, which in turn may lead to a decrease in the biodiversity in an area.

Reteach

Formative assessment may show that students need reinforcement for certain topics. The resources below are recommended for reteaching. If students were introduced to the topic through the Print Path, you can also use the Digital Path to reteach, and vice versa.

🎧 *Can be assigned to individual students*

Human Activities Affect Land Ecosystems
Activity Modeling Pollution Uptake in Plants 🎧

Human Activities Affect Aquatic Ecosystems
Daily Demo Eggs and Oil Don't Mix 🎧

Ecosystem Conservation
Activity Reusing Trash 🎧

Quick Lab Biodiversity All Around Us 🎧

Alternative Assessment
Human Impact on Ecosystems

🌐 *Online resources: student worksheet; optional rubrics*

Human Activity and Ecosystems

Choose Your Meal: *Human Impact on Ecosystems*
Complete the activities to show what you've learned about how human activities change ecosystems.

1. Work on your own, with a partner, or with a small group.
2. Choose one item from each section of the menu, with an optional dessert. Check your choices.
3. Have your teacher approve your plan.
4. Submit or present your results.

Appetizers

_____ **A Changing Landscape** Design an illustrated pamphlet that describes at least three ways that human activities affect land ecosystems.

_____ **Concept Map** Develop a concept map that identifies and compares the types of human activities that pose a threat to ocean ecosystems. Display your completed concept map in the classroom.

_____ **Make a Model** Develop a model that can be used to illustrate how materials that are spilled or discarded on land make their way into water ecosystems. Share your model with the class.

Main Dish

_____ **Conservation PSA** Write a public service announcement that encourages people to protect ecosystems by maintaining biodiversity and conserving natural resources.

_____ **Breaking News** Develop a news video that highlights a local environmental problem related to human activity; include the problem's cause and effect.

Side Dishes

_____ **Post It!** Create an illustrated poster that encourages people to make use of the "three R's" to conserve resources. Include specific examples of how each method of conservation might be used.

_____ **Wanted!** Do research to identify an exotic species that poses a threat to a natural ecosystem in your state. Make a Wanted poster about the species and the problems it poses in your state.

Desserts (optional)

_____ **Environmental Cleanup** Organize an environmental cleanup day for your community. Prepare flyers that identify an area such as a vacant lot, roadside, or stream, in which you want volunteers to work to help pick up discarded materials.

_____ **Species Awareness Presentation** Prepare a multimedia presentation about a species in your state that is threatened or endangered. Include why it is threatened and what efforts are being made to protect it.

Going Further
- ☐ Art Connection
- ☐ Real World Connection
- ☐ **Print Path** Why it Matters, SE p. 121

Formative Assessment
- ☐ **Strategies** Throughout TE
- ☐ **Lesson Review** SE

Summative Assessment
- ☐ Alternative Assessment Human Impact on Ecosystems
- ☐ Lesson Quiz
- ☐ Unit Tests A and B
- ☐ Unit Review SE End-of-Unit

Your Resources

_____

_____

Answers

Answers for 1–3 should represent students' current thoughts, even if incorrect.

1. litter; I think litter makes everything ugly. I would put more trash cans on the sidewalks.

2. Sample answer: Picking up trash and recycling plastic helps prevent harm to wildlife.

3. Sample answers: Urbanization means the effect that people have on the environment because of increasing city sizes. Biodiversity means the amount of variety among living things.

4. Students' annotations will vary.

Opening Your Lesson

Have students share the ideas in their captions (item 2) to assess their prior knowledge about Key Topics.

Prerequisites Students should already know that ecology is the branch of science that deals with the study of how organisms interact with their environments; that an ecosystem is composed of the organisms that live in an area and their interactions with the living and nonliving parts of their environment; that living things rely upon resources in their environment to meet their life needs; that population size can be affected by resource availability; and that matter and energy are continuously recycled through the environment.

Accessing Prior Knowledge Develop an Anticipation Guide to preview the content of the lesson and to assess students' prior knowledge about human activities that harm the environment. The key to the guide is to choose some statements that seem plausible but that students will discover to be untrue after they read the material. Have students revisit the statements at the end of the lesson to allow them to evaluate the accuracy of their initial responses.

⊘ *Optional Online resource: Anticipation Guide support*

Growing Pains

How do humans negatively affect ecosystems?

Human activities can change and even harm ecosystems. An *ecosystem* is all of the living and nonliving things within a given area. Changing one thing in an ecosystem can affect many other things, because everything in an ecosystem is connected.

Humans can affect ecosystems through pollution. *Pollution* is caused by any material or condition that harms the environment. For example, factories and automobiles burn fossil fuels. This releases harmful chemicals into the environment. Farms that produce our food may also burn fossil fuels and release chemicals, such as pesticides or fertilizers, into the environment.

Even simple actions can harm ecosystems. For example, the trash we throw out may end up in a landfill. Landfills take up space and may contain harmful materials like batteries. Toxic metals in batteries can leak into soil or groundwater, with drastic consequences for organisms and ecosystems.

5 Relate Identify a form of pollution that you observe in your community.

_____

_____

▶ Tons of garbage are put into landfills every day.

▶ As cities and suburbs expand closer to natural areas, wildlife may wander into our backyards and onto our streets.

116

By Depleting Resources

The number of people on Earth has increased from 1 billion to more than 6 billion people in the last 200 years. The growing human population has created a greater need for natural resources. This need has created problems for ecosystems. When we cut down trees, we remove a resource that many organisms need for food and shelter. The loss of many trees in an area can affect shade and local temperatures. These changes can disturb ecosystems.

The overuse of resources causes them to be depleted, or used up. *Resource depletion* occurs when a large fraction of a resource has been used up. Fresh water was once a renewable resource. But in some areas, humans use fresh water faster than it can be replenished by the water cycle.

By Destroying Habitats

Human population growth in and around cities is called **urbanization** (er•buh•nih•ZAY•shuhn). Urban growth within ecosystems often destroys natural habitats. Roads can divide habitats and prevent animals from safely roaming their territory. If animals cannot interact with each other and their surroundings, the ecosystem will not thrive.

An ecosystem may be converted into housing and shopping areas that further shrink habitats. This can bring humans and wildlife into contact. Deer, raccoons, and even coyotes have become common sights in some suburban areas.

Every habitat has its own number and variety of organisms, or **biodiversity**. If a habitat is damaged or destroyed, biodiversity is lost. Because living things are connected with each other and with their environment, loss of biodiversity affects the entire ecosystem.

Active Reading 6 Provide Give one example of how urbanization affects natural ecosystems.

_____

_____

An open-pit mine like this one is one way that humans remove minerals from the ground. Minerals are nonrenewable resources.

▶ Cutting down forests destroys habitats and affects the physical features of the ecosystem.

Think Outside the Book Inquiry

7 Apply Do research to find out what the environment around your school looked like 100 years ago.

117

Answers

5. Sample answer: Some people throw litter out of their car windows.

6. Sample answer: Cutting down wooded areas to build shopping centers destroys natural habitats.

7. Student output should include a detailed description of the area around your school, noting the type of ecosystem (e.g., forest, prairie, desert) and the types of plants and animals that might have lived there.

Interpreting Visuals

Have students use the visuals to relate how the increased use of resources by a growing human population is related to resource depletion, habitat destruction, and decreased biodiversity. **Ask:** How might open-pit mining activities cause habitat destruction? Open-pit mining requires large areas of land to be dug up and moved to create access to minerals. This destroys the habitat of the organisms that live on or in the land. **Ask:** How does cutting down forests lead to resource depletion? decreased biodiversity? Resource depletion occurs when the trees in a forest are removed from an area faster than they can grow back. This leads to decreased biodiversity as the number and variety of trees is decreased along with an overall decrease in biodiversity as populations that live in or around the trees lose their habitat.

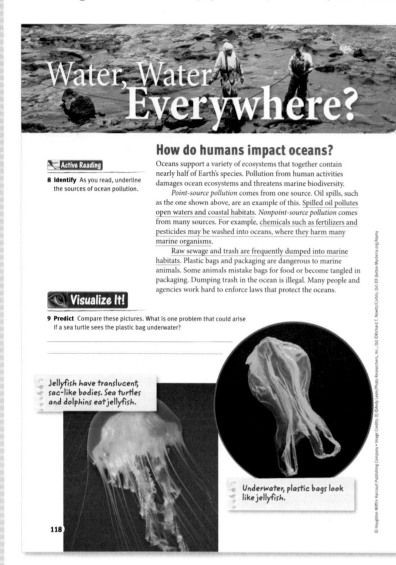

Water, Water Everywhere?

Active Reading

8 Identify As you read, underline the sources of ocean pollution.

How do humans impact oceans?

Oceans support a variety of ecosystems that together contain nearly half of Earth's species. Pollution from human activities damages ocean ecosystems and threatens marine biodiversity.

Point-source pollution comes from one source. Oil spills, such as the one shown above, are an example of this. Spilled oil pollutes open waters and coastal habitats. *Nonpoint-source pollution* comes from many sources. For example, chemicals such as fertilizers and pesticides may be washed into oceans, where they harm many marine organisms.

Raw sewage and trash are frequently dumped into marine habitats. Plastic bags and packaging are dangerous to marine animals. Some animals mistake bags for food or become tangled in packaging. Dumping trash in the ocean is illegal. Many people and agencies work hard to enforce laws that protect the oceans.

Visualize It!

9 Predict Compare these pictures. What is one problem that could arise if a sea turtle sees the plastic bag underwater?

_____

_____

Jellyfish have translucent, sac-like bodies. Sea turtles and dolphins eat jellyfish.

Underwater, plastic bags look like jellyfish.

118

Through Fishing and Overfishing

A greater demand for seafood from the growing human population has led to *overfishing* of some ocean species. Many fish species cannot reproduce fast enough to replace individuals that are harvested for food. When large numbers of a single fish population are caught, the remaining population may be too small to successfully reproduce. If the population cannot replace itself, it can become locally extinct. The local loss of a species can disturb ocean food webs and threaten ecosystem stability.

Through Coastal Development

The growing human population also has led to increased coastal development. That means building homes and businesses on and near beaches and wetlands. Sadly, this can destroy the very coastlines we want to be near. Roads and shopping centers divide habitats. Increased human activity increases pollution both on shore and in coastal waters.

In some places, development has almost completely replaced natural coastlines. For example, construction of new homes and businesses is rapidly destroying mangrove forests. Mangroves are unique trees found only in certain coastal regions. Mangrove forests play a key role in maintaining coastlines. The thick roots stabilize the sandy soil and prevent erosion. The trees are home to a wide range of species.

Human activity has also damaged coral reefs, but people and scientists are working to correct this damage. Coral reefs are vital ecosystems because so many species live in or around them. To replace this lost habitat, scientists have created artificial reefs. First, different fish species will find safety in the structures. Next, algae and soft corals begin to grow. Over time, hard corals grow and other sea life can be seen. Artificial reefs preserve the reef food web and stabilize the ecosystem.

Overfishing means that the rate at which fish are caught exceeds the rate at which the species can reproduce.

10 List What are three ways that human activities impact ocean ecosystems?

_____

_____

_____

Artificial reefs, such as sunken ships or other human-made objects, are being used to make up for the loss of natural coral reefs.

119

Answers

8. *See students' pages for annotations.*

9. Sample answer: The turtle may accidentally eat the plastic bag.

10. Students should list any three of the following: pollution, oil spills, overfishing, coastal development, seawall construction.

Building Reading Skills

Combination Notes Three ways in which human activities impact oceans are discussed in the text. Encourage students to use Combination Notes to help them identify the main ideas relating to each activity. Have them title their notes "Human Activities that Affect Oceans." On the left side of a sheet of paper, students can list each of the activities discussed along with a description of the activity and how it impacts oceans. On the right side, they can make drawings to illustrate each activity.

🔘 *Optional Online Resource: Combination Notes support*

Formative Assessment

Ask: What is the difference between point-source pollution and nonpoint-source pollution? Give an example of each. Point-source pollution is pollution that can be traced to a single source, such as a leak from an oil tanker. Nonpoint-source pollution is pollution that may be generated by several different sources, such as oil that leaks from cars on a road and then washes off the roadway into soil or water. **Ask:** Why are mangrove forests important? The roots of the mangrove tree stabilize soil and prevent erosion. The trees themselves are home to many species. Marine species find shelter in the roots while birds and other species live in the branches.

How do humans affect freshwater ecosystems?

11 Identify As you read, number the steps involved in the formation of acid rain.

Human activities have decreased the amount of water, or *water quantity*, in many river ecosystems. Dams and river channelization are two examples of this. Dams block the flow of river water. That means there is less water downstream of the dam. Channelization is used to straighten rivers to improve travel and other activities. However, changing the natural course of a river also changes the amount of water in it. Differences in water levels can change water temperature and chemistry. These changes can affect the reproduction and survival of many river species.

Human activities can also decrease *water quality*, or change how clean or polluted the water is, in ecosystems. Pollution disturbs water quality. Animal waste and fertilizer from farms contain nutrients that can enter ponds and lakes as runoff. An increase in the amount of nutrients, such as nitrates, in an aquatic ecosystem is called **eutrophication** (yoo•trohf•ih•KAY•shuhn). The extra nutrients cause overgrowth of algae. The excess algae die and decompose, using up the pond's dissolved oxygen. As dissolved oxygen levels decrease, fish begin to die. If eutrophication continues, the pond ecosystem will not recover.

Water quality is also affected by air pollution. For example, some freshwater ecosystems are affected by acid rain. Burning fossil fuels releases chemicals into the air. Some of these combine with rain to form acids. Small amounts of acid in rain cause its pH to fall below its normal value of 5.6. Acid rain can damage both aquatic and land ecosystems.

Eutrophication causes overgrowth of algae and can disrupt pond ecosystems.

120

Why It Matters

Exotic Species

An organism that makes a home for itself in a new place outside its native home is an *exotic species*. Exotic species often thrive in new places because they are free from the predators found in their native homes. Exotic species that outcompete native species for resources, such as food or space, are known as *invasive exotic species*.

European rabbits were introduced into Australia in 1859 for sport hunting. With plenty of space and food—and no predators—Australia's rabbit population exploded.

The rabbits threatened the survival of many native Australian animals and plants. Many efforts were made to control the rabbit population. Their dens were poisoned. Rabbit-proof fences were built. Rabbits were even "herded" by cowboys.

So far, all efforts to remove rabbits have failed. There are still more than 200 million rabbits in Australia.

Extend

Inquiry

12 Explain How do exotic species contribute to habitat destruction?

13 Hypothesize Form a hypothesis about a method that might be effective in controlling an invasive exotic species.

14 Research Identify a non-native plant species that has been introduced into the United States. Explain where the species came from, how or why it was brought to the United States, and how it has affected the ecosystem.

121

Answers

11. *See students' pages for annotations.*

12. Sample answer: Exotic species often do not have natural predators. This allows their populations to expand and use up resources faster than they can be naturally renewed.

13–14. Student output should demonstrate an understanding of invasive exotic species and offer reasonable ideas for dealing with them.

Probing Questions GUIDED Inquiry

Apply Eutrophication results from an excess of nutrients in a body of water. All organisms need nutrients to survive. Why then are the nutrients that lead to eutrophication considered a form of pollution? **Prompt:** Think about the definition of pollution. Pollution is any material or condition that harms the environment. The nutrients that cause eutrophication initially benefit algae, but in time change the ecosystem in a way that makes it unfit for other organisms.

Why It Matters

Point out that not all exotic species enter ecosystems via human activities. For example, cattle egrets, which are indigenous to Africa and Asia, are believed to have been introduced to the Americas by a hurricane in the 19th century. These egrets compete with native species for resources and thus have the same potential to adversely affect native populations as species introduced by humans. When an exotic species outcompetes native species and has few natural predators in their new habitat, the species is called an *invasive* exotic species. These conditions allow the invasive exotic species to thrive, reproduce, and consume resources to such an extent that native species may become extinct.

Save It!

Active Reading

15 Identify As you read, underline the definition of stewardship.

How do humans protect ecosystems?

There are many ways that humans can protect ecosystems. One way is by using Earth's resources in a careful manner. The careful and responsible management of a resource is called **stewardship**. The resources of an ecosystem include all of its living and nonliving parts.

By Maintaining Biodiversity

The organisms in an ecosystem depend on each other and interact with each other in a vast interconnected food web. Each species has a place in this web and a role to play. The loss of a species or introduction of an exotic species creates gaps in the web. This can disrupt species interactions. Protecting habitats and helping species survive protects the biodiversity in an ecosystem. The greater the biodiversity, the healthier the ecosystem.

16 State What are two ways that humans can help maintain biodiversity in ecosystems?

By Conserving Natural Resources

Humans can protect ecosystems through conservation. **Conservation** is the protection and wise use of natural resources. Practicing conservation means using fewer natural resources and reducing waste. It also helps prevent habitat destruction.

The "three Rs" are three ways to conserve resources.

- *Reduce* what you buy and use—this is the first goal of conservation.
- *Reuse* what you already have. For example, carry water in a reusable bottle and lunch in a reusable lunch bag.
- *Recycle* by recovering materials from waste and by always choosing to use recycling bins.

You can practice conservation every day by making wise choices. Even small changes make a difference!

17 Synthesize Suppose you wanted to stop eating fast food to cut down on excess fat and sodium. How might this benefit the environment as well?

You can help prevent water shortages by turning off the water as you brush your teeth.

You can reduce pollution by participating in a local cleanup project.

You can protect habitats by staying on marked trails when visiting national parks and forests.

You can reduce pesticide use by supporting responsible agriculture.

You can reduce the use of fossil fuels by turning off lights and supporting alternative energy sources.

Answers

15. *See students' pages for annotations.*

16. Sample answer: We can maintain biodiversity by protecting species and protecting habitats.

17. Sample answer: Fast food creates a lot of trash. Each item is wrapped. Items all come in a bag with paper napkins. Cutting out fast food would reduce garbage.

Building Reading Skills

Problem-Solution Notes Specific ways in which humans can work to protect ecosystems are discussed in the text. Encourage students to use Problem-Solution Notes to help them identify the human activities that harm the environment and how each problem might be addressed. Students should list the problem in the column on the left side of a sheet of paper. On the right side, they can describe actions that can be taken to lessen the impact of each problem.

Optional Online Resource: Problem-Solution Notes support.

Probing Questions GUIDED *Inquiry*

Comparing Help students to recognize that stewardship is actually a part of the conservation process. **Ask:** How are stewardship and conservation related? Both stewardship and conservation involve the responsible and wise use of resources.

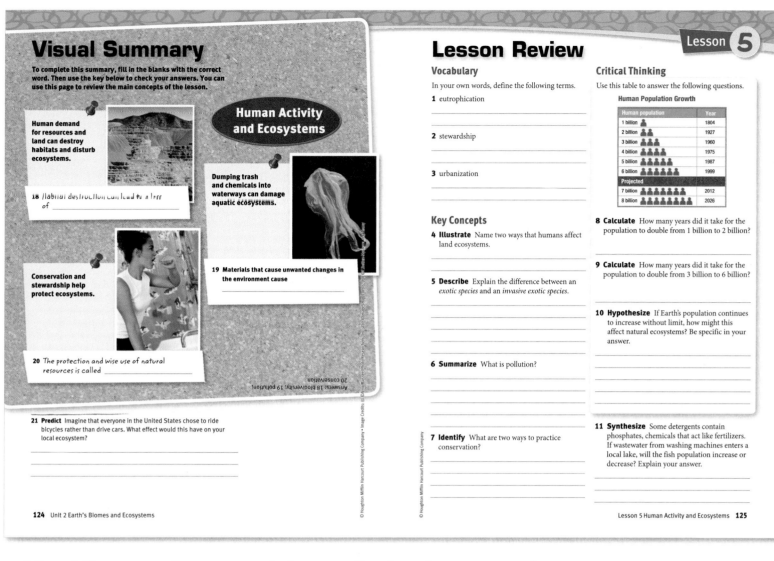

Visual Summary

To complete this summary, fill in the blanks with the correct word. Then use the key below to check your answers. You can use this page to review the main concepts of the lesson.

Human demand for resources and land can destroy habitats and disturb ecosystems.

18 *Habitat destruction can lead to a loss of* _____

Human Activity and Ecosystems

Dumping trash and chemicals into waterways can damage aquatic ecosystems.

19 **Materials that cause unwanted changes in the environment cause** _____

Conservation and stewardship help protect ecosystems.

20 *The protection and wise use of natural resources is called* _____

Answers: 18 biodiversity; 19 pollution; 20 conservation.

21 **Predict** Imagine that everyone in the United States chose to ride bicycles rather than drive cars. What effect would this have on your local ecosystem?

_____
_____
_____

124   Unit 2 Earth's Biomes and Ecosystems

Lesson Review

Lesson 5

Vocabulary

In your own words, define the following terms.

1 eutrophication

_____

2 stewardship

_____

3 urbanization

_____

Key Concepts

4 **Illustrate** Name two ways that humans affect land ecosystems.

_____

5 **Describe** Explain the difference between an *exotic species* and an *invasive exotic species*.

_____
_____
_____
_____

6 **Summarize** What is pollution?

_____
_____
_____
_____
_____

7 **Identify** What are two ways to practice conservation?

_____
_____

Critical Thinking

Use this table to answer the following questions.

Human Population Growth

Human population	Year
1 billion	1804
2 billion	1927
3 billion	1960
4 billion	1975
5 billion	1987
6 billion	1999
Projected	
7 billion	2012
8 billion	2026

8 **Calculate** How many years did it take for the population to double from 1 billion to 2 billion?

9 **Calculate** How many years did it take for the population to double from 3 billion to 6 billion?

10 **Hypothesize** If Earth's population continues to increase without limit, how might this affect natural ecosystems? Be specific in your answer.

_____
_____

11 **Synthesize** Some detergents contain phosphates, chemicals that act like fertilizers. If wastewater from washing machines enters a local lake, will the fish population increase or decrease? Explain your answer.

_____
_____

Lesson 5 Human Activity and Ecosystems   125

Visual Summary Answers

18. biodiversity

19. pollution

20. conservation

21. Sample answer: It would reduce use of fossil fuels, which would decrease air pollution.

Lesson Review Answers

1. overgrowth of plants caused by addition of excessive nutrients into a body of water

2. responsible care of Earth and its resources

3. effect of more and more people living in cities, causing urban sprawl

4. resource depletion; habitat destruction

5. Sample answer: An exotic species is a species that is not native to a particular region. An invasive exotic species can outcompete native species for resources.

6. Sample answer: Pollution is an unwanted change in the environment caused by substances or forms of energy.

7. Sample answer: use fewer natural resources and reduce waste

8. 1927 − 1804 = 123 years

9. 1999 − 1960 = 39 years

10. Sample answer: As the human population expands, land will need to be developed to build houses. This will destroy natural habitats.

11. Sample answer: Decrease. Wastewater runoff will increase algae growth. As the algae die and decompose, dissolved oxygen levels will decrease and the fish will die.

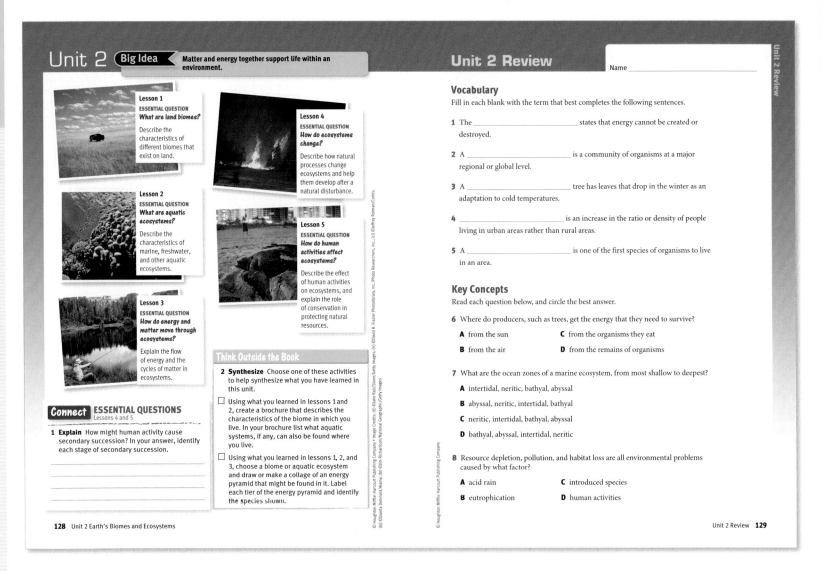

Unit 2 Big Idea ▸ Matter and energy together support life within an environment.

Lesson 1
ESSENTIAL QUESTION
What are land biomes?
Describe the characteristics of different biomes that exist on land.

Lesson 2
ESSENTIAL QUESTION
What are aquatic ecosystems?
Describe the characteristics of marine, freshwater, and other aquatic ecosystems.

Lesson 3
ESSENTIAL QUESTION
How do energy and matter move through ecosystems?
Explain the flow of energy and the cycles of matter in ecosystems.

Lesson 4
ESSENTIAL QUESTION
How do ecosystems change?
Describe how natural processes change ecosystems and help them develop after a natural disturbance.

Lesson 5
ESSENTIAL QUESTION
How do human activities affect ecosystems?
Describe the effect of human activities on ecosystems, and explain the role of conservation in protecting natural resources.

Connect ESSENTIAL QUESTIONS
Lessons 4 and 5

1 **Explain** How might human activity cause secondary succession? In your answer, identify each stage of secondary succession.

Think Outside the Book

2 **Synthesize** Choose one of these activities to help synthesize what you have learned in this unit.

☐ Using what you learned in lessons 1 and 2, create a brochure that describes the characteristics of the biome in which you live. In your brochure list what aquatic systems, if any, can also be found where you live.

☐ Using what you learned in lessons 1, 2, and 3, choose a biome or aquatic ecosystem and draw or make a collage of an energy pyramid that might be found in it. Label each tier of the energy pyramid and identify the species shown.

128 Unit 2 Earth's Biomes and Ecosystems

Unit 2 Review Name _____

Vocabulary
Fill in each blank with the term that best completes the following sentences.

1 The _____ states that energy cannot be created or destroyed.

2 A _____ is a community of organisms at a major regional or global level.

3 A _____ tree has leaves that drop in the winter as an adaptation to cold temperatures.

4 _____ is an increase in the ratio or density of people living in urban areas rather than rural areas.

5 A _____ is one of the first species of organisms to live in an area.

Key Concepts
Read each question below, and circle the best answer.

6 Where do producers, such as trees, get the energy that they need to survive?

A from the sun   C from the organisms they eat

B from the air   D from the remains of organisms

7 What are the ocean zones of a marine ecosystem, from most shallow to deepest?

A intertidal, neritic, bathyal, abyssal

B abyssal, neritic, intertidal, bathyal

C neritic, intertidal, bathyal, abyssal

D bathyal, abyssal, intertidal, neritic

8 Resource depletion, pollution, and habitat loss are all environmental problems caused by what factor?

A acid rain   C introduced species

B eutrophication   D human activities

Unit 2 Review **129**

Unit Summary Answers

1. Sample answer: A fire caused by human activity could burn down a forest and lead to secondary succession as the ecosystem recovers. In secondary succession, the soil remains intact in an ecosystem. First, plants sprout from seeds or preexisting stems and roots. Then shrubs begin to grow, followed by trees. Trees continue to grow into a mature forest.

2. Option 1: Brochures should correctly identify the land biome in which students live and the characteristics of that biome. Brochures should also correctly identify any aquatic ecosystems in the area.

   Option 2: Energy pyramid illustrations should include reasonable species from the chosen biome or aquatic ecosystem. The bottom tier should show producers (plant species), the second tier should show primary consumers (herbivores), the third tier should show secondary consumers (carnivores), and the top tier should show tertiary consumers.

Unit Review Response to Intervention

A Quick Grading Chart follows the Answers. See the Assessment Guide for more detail about correct and incorrect answer choices. Refer back to the Lesson Planning pages for activities and assignments that can be used as remediation for students who answer questions incorrectly.

Answers

1. law of conservation of energy The law of conservation of energy states energy can only change forms. (Lesson 3)

2. biome Biomes are usually characterized by their climate conditions and the plant communities that thrive there. (Lesson 1)

3. deciduous Deciduous trees are broadleaf trees and make up temperate deciduous forests. (Lesson 1)

Unit 2 Review continued

Name _____

9 Below is an energy pyramid diagram.

Energy Pyramid

Why is the level at 4 so much smaller than the level at 1?

A Organisms gain energy as the food chain moves down the pyramid.

B Fewer organisms are supported as you move down the pyramid.

C Only the energy that is used is available to organisms at a higher level.

D Only the energy that is stored is available to organisms at a higher level.

10 What element can be changed by lightning into a form that plants can use?

A oxygen   **C** phosphorous

B carbon   **D** nitrogen

11 Below is a diagram of the carbon cycle.

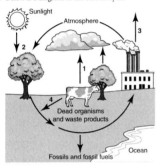

Which number corresponds to combustion and the release of CO_2, water, and the loss of energy as heat into the environment?

A 1   **C** 3

B 2   **D** 4

130   Unit 2 Earth's Biomes and Ecosystems

12 What is an adaptation that allows some animals to survive in the tundra?

A living underground   **C** being active at night only

B having thick layers of fur   **D** living within the upper branches of trees

13 Some grass species need fire in order for their seeds to germinate. Why might this adaptation be useful for grasses?

A Fire allows trees to grow and provide shade for the grasses.

B The hot temperature of the fire helps the grasses grow faster.

C Seeds can germinate in an area that has been cleared by a fire.

D Fire discourages grazing by large animals so grass can grow higher.

Critical Thinking

Answer the following questions in the space provided.

14 Draw a diagram of the water cycle and label it with the terms given below.

In the space provided, identify what each term means.

Precipitation: _____

Evaporation: _____

Transpiration: _____

Condensation: _____

Unit 2 Review   **131**

Answers *(continued)*

4. **Urbanization** Higher concentrations of people living in one area put greater pressure on the natural resources in that area. As urban growth continues, natural habitats are often destroyed to accommodate the urban sprawl. (Lesson 5)

5. **pioneer species** Pioneer species are able to break down rock into soil, which helps to establish plant communities. (Lesson 4)

6. Answer A is correct because these kinds of producers photosynthesize. (Lesson 3)

7. Answer A is correct because the intertidal zone is the most shallow, followed by neritic, bathyal, and abyssal. (Lesson 2)

8. Answer D is correct because human activities can lead to resource depletion, pollution, and habitat loss. (Lesson 5)

9. Answer D is correct because only the small amount of energy that is stored by an organism is available to higher-level consumers. (Lesson 3)

10. Answer D is correct because lightning breaks apart nitrogen molecules and converts them into a form that plants can use. (Lesson 3)

11. Answer C is correct because 3 shows organic materials are being burned (undergoing combustion). (Lesson 3)

12. Answer B is correct because the tundra has a cold climate, and thick layers of fur protect the native animals. (Lesson 1)

13. Answer C is correct because seeds that require fire to germinate will establish quickly after a fire because there would be little competition from other plants in the scorched area. (Lesson 4)

14. Key Elements:

   • Draws circular pathway from atmosphere to ground surface to below ground and back to atmosphere.

   • Labels *precipitation* and defines as *rain or snow that falls to the ground;* labels *evaporation* and defines as *water that reenters the atmosphere.*

Unit 2 Review continued

15 The picture below shows a land ecosystem that experiences annual flooding.

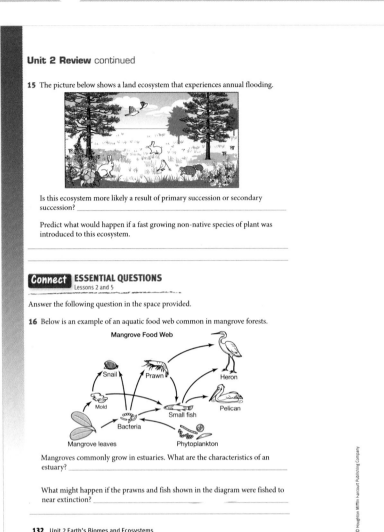

Is this ecosystem more likely a result of primary succession or secondary succession? _____

Predict what would happen if a fast growing non-native species of plant was introduced to this ecosystem.

_____

_____

Connect ESSENTIAL QUESTIONS
Lessons 2 and 5

Answer the following question in the space provided.

16 Below is an example of an aquatic food web common in mangrove forests.

Mangrove Food Web

Snail · Prawn · Heron · Mold · Small fish · Pelican · Bacteria · Mangrove leaves · Phytoplankton

Mangroves commonly grow in estuaries. What are the characteristics of an estuary? _____

What might happen if the prawns and fish shown in the diagram were fished to near extinction? _____

_____

© Houghton Mifflin Harcourt Publishing Company

Quick Grading Chart

Use the chart below for quick test grading. The lesson correlations can help you target reteaching for missed items.

Item	Answer	Cognitive Complexity	Lesson
1.	—	Low	3
2.	—	Low	1
3.	—	Low	1
4.	—	Low	5
5.	—	Low	4
6.	A	Low	3
7.	A	Moderate	2
8.	D	Moderate	5
9.	D	Moderate	3
10.	D	Moderate	3
11.	C	Moderate	3
12.	B	Moderate	1
13.	C	High	4
14.	—	High	3
15.	—	High	4
16.	—	High	5

Cognitive Complexity refers to the demand on thinking associated with an item, and may vary with the answer choices, the number of steps required to arrive at an answer, and other factors, but not the ability level of the student.

Answers (continued)

- Labels *transpiration* and defines as *some water is released to the atmosphere by plants;* labels *condensation* and defines as *water vapor in the atmosphere forms clouds.* (Lesson 3)

15. Key Elements:

- Identifies that picture better represents secondary succession.

- Indicates that the ecosystem would probably survive with few changes because it is already a mature ecosystem with diverse vegetation and organisms. (Lesson 4)

16. Key Elements:

- Identifies an estuary as being a partially enclosed mix of fresh and salt water, formed where rivers meet the ocean.

- The removal of fish and prawns could reduce heron, pelican, and phytoplankton populations, and increase bacteria and mold populations. Mangrove leaves may also have more disease due to increased bacteria and mold populations. (Lesson 5)

The Big Idea and Essential Questions

This Unit was designed to focus on this Big Idea and Essential Questions.

Big Idea — Humans depend on natural resources for materials and for energy.

Lesson	ESSENTIAL QUESTION	Student Mastery	🍎 PD Professional Development	Lesson Overview
LESSON 1 Earth's Support of Life	How can Earth support life?	To explain how the unique properties of Earth make it possible for life to exist	Content Refresher, TE p. 170	TE p. 178
LESSON 2 Natural Resources	What are Earth's natural resources?	To understand the types and uses of Earth's natural resources	Content Refresher, TE p. 171	TE p. 192
LESSON 3 Nonrenewable Energy Resources	How do we use nonrenewable energy resources?	To describe how humans use energy resources and the role of nonrenewable energy resources in society	Content Refresher, TE p. 172	TE p. 206
LESSON 4 Renewable Energy Resources	How do humans use renewable energy resources?	To describe how humans use energy resources and the role of renewable energy resources in society	Content Refresher, TE p. 173	TE p. 220
LESSON 5 Managing Resources	Why should natural resources be managed?	To explain the consequences of society's use of natural resources and the importance of managing these resources wisely	Content Refresher, TE p. 174	TE p. 238

Professional Development — Science Background

Use the keywords at right to access

- Professional Development from **The NSTA Learning Center**
- **SciLinks** for additional online content appropriate for students and teachers

Keywords

conservation   natural resources

energy resources

National Science Teachers Association

SCiLINKS.
THE WORLD'S A CLICK AWAY

©Philip Quirk/Alamy Images

Options for Instruction

Two parallel paths provide coverage of the Essential Questions, with a strong **Inquiry** strand woven into each. Follow the **Print Path,** the **Digital Path,** or your customized combination of print, digital, and inquiry.

	LESSON 1 Earth's Support of Life	LESSON 2 Natural Resources	LESSON 3 Nonrenewable Energy Resources
Essential Questions	*How can Earth support life?*	*What are Earth's natural resources?*	*How do we use nonrenewable energy resources?*
Key Topics	• The Sun • Water • The Atmosphere	• Natural Resources • Renewable and Nonrenewable Resources • Material Resources • Energy Resources	• Energy Resources • Fossil Fuels • Nuclear Energy
Print Path	Teacher Edition pp. 178–190 Student Edition pp. 136–145	Teacher Edition pp. 192–205 Student Edition pp. 146–157	Teacher Edition pp. 206–219 Student Edition pp. 158–169
Inquiry Labs	Lab Manual **Exploration Lab** Modeling the Greenhouse Effect **Quick Lab** Temperature Variations on Earth **Quick Lab** How Water Forms...	Lab Manual **Field Lab** Natural Resources Used at Lunch **Quick Lab** Renewable or Not? **Quick Lab** Production Impacts	Lab Manual **Quick Lab** Modeling Nonrenewable Resources Virtual Lab How Can We Measure the Impact of Nonrenewable Energy?
Digital Path	Digital Path TS672338 	Digital Path TS691073 	Digital Path TS661724

LESSON 4	LESSON 5	UNIT 3
Renewable Energy Resources	Managing Resources	Unit Projects

LESSON 4
Renewable Energy Resources

How do humans use renewable energy resources?

- Energy Resources
- Energy from the Sun
- Energy from Earth

Teacher Edition
pp. 220–233

Student Edition
pp. 170–181

Lab Manual
S.T.E.M. Lab Modeling Geothermal Power

 Virtual Lab
How Can We Use Renewable Energy Resources?

Digital Path
TS661734

LESSON 5
Managing Resources

Why should natural resources be managed?

- Resources
- Managing Resources
- Advantages and Disadvantages of Managing Resources

Teacher Edition
pp. 238–250

Student Edition
pp. 186–195

Lab Manual
Quick Lab Managing a Resource

Quick Lab The Impact of Resource Extraction

Digital Path
TS661728

UNIT 3
Unit Projects

 Citizen Science Project
Energy Sources

Teacher's Edition p. 177

Student Edition
pp. 134–135

 Video-Based Projects
Got Water?

Unit Assessment
Formative Assessment
Strategies (RTI)
Throughout TE
Lesson Reviews SE
Unit PreTest
Summative Assessment
Alternative Assessment
(1 per lesson) (RTI)
Lesson Quizzes
Unit Tests A and B
Unit Review (RTI)
(with answer remediation)
Practice Tests
(end of module)
Project-Based Assessment
See the Assessment Guide for quizzes and tests.
Go Online to edit and create quizzes and tests.

Response to Intervention
See RTI teacher support materials on p. PD6.

Differentiated Instruction

English Language Proficiency

Strategies for **English Language Learners (ELL)** are provided for each lesson, under the Explain tabs.

LESSON 1 *Earth Vocabulary,* TE p. 183

LESSON 2 *Resourceful Word Squares,* TE p. 197

LESSON 3 *Picture Dictionary,* TE p. 211

LESSON 4 *Act It Out,* TE p. 225

LESSON 5 *Think Globally,* TE p. 243

Vocabulary strategies provided for all students can also be a particular help for ELL. Use different strategies for each lesson or choose one or two to use throughout the unit. Vocabulary strategies can be found in the Explain tab for each lesson (TE pp. 183, 197, 211, 225, and 243).

Leveled Inquiry

Inquiry labs, activities, probing questions, and daily demos provide a range of inquiry levels. Preview them under the Engage and Explore tabs starting on TE pp. 180, 194, 208, 222, and 240.

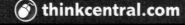

Levels of Inquiry	DIRECTED inquiry	GUIDED inquiry	INDEPENDENT inquiry
	introduces inquiry skills within a structured framework.	develops inquiry skills within a supportive environment.	deepens inquiry skills with student-driven questions or procedures.

Each long lab has two inquiry options:

LESSON 1 **Exploration Lab** *Modeling the Greenhouse Effect*

LESSON 2 **Field Lab** *Natural Resources Used at Lunch*

LESSON 4 **S.T.E.M. Lab** *Modeling Geothermal Power*

 Go Digital! ⊚ **thinkcentral.com**

Digital Path

The Unit 3 Resource Gateway is your guide to all of the digital resources for this unit. To access the Gateway, visit thinkcentral.com.

Digital Interactive Lessons

Lesson 1 Earth's Support of Life TS672338

Lesson 2 Natural Resources TS691073

Lesson 3 Nonrenewable Energy Resources TS661724

Lesson 4 Renewable Energy Resources TS661734

Lesson 5 Managing Resources TS661728

More Digital Resources

In addition to digital lessons, you will find the following digital resources for Unit 3:

Video-Based Project: Got Water? (previewed on TE p. 176)

Virtual Labs: How Can We Measure the Impact of Nonrenewable Energy? (previewed on p. 209) How Can We Use Renewable Energy Resources? (previewed on p. 223)

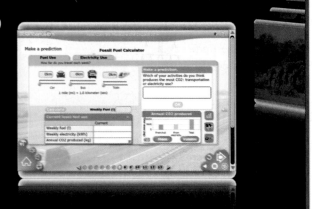

RTI ▶ Response to Intervention

Response to Intervention (RTI) is a process for identifying and supporting students who are not making expected progress toward essential learning goals. The following *ScienceFusion* components can be used to provide strategic and intensive intervention.

Component	Location	Strategies and Benefits
STUDENT EDITION Active Reading prompts, Visualize It!, Think Outside the Book	**Throughout each lesson**	Student responses can be used as screening tools to assess whether intervention is needed.
TEACHER EDITION Formative Assessment, Probing Questions, Learning Alerts	**Throughout each lesson**	Opportunities are provided to assess and remediate student understanding of lesson concepts.
TEACHER EDITION Extend Science Concepts	**Reinforce and Review, TE pp. 184, 198, 212, 226, 244** **Going Further, TE pp. 185, 199, 213, 227, 245**	Additional activities allow students to reinforce and extend their understanding of lesson concepts.
TEACHER EDITION Evaluate Student Mastery	**Formative Assessment, TE pp. 185, 199, 213, 227, 245** **Alternative Assessment, TE pp. 185, 199, 213, 227, 245**	These assessments allow for greater flexibility in assessing students with differing physical, mental, and language abilities as well as varying learning and communication modes.
TEACHER EDITION Unit Review Remediation	**Unit Review, TE pp. 252–254**	Includes reference back to Lesson Planning pages for remediation activities and assignments.
INTERACTIVE DIGITAL LESSONS and VIRTUAL LABS	**thinkcentral.com** **Unit 3 Gateway** **Lesson 1 TS672338** **Lesson 2 TS691073** **Lesson 3 TS661724** **Lesson 4 TS661734** **Lesson 5 TS661728**	Lessons and labs make content accessible through simulations, animations, videos, audio, and integrated assessment. Useful for review and reteaching of lesson concepts.

Content Refresher

Professional Development

Earth's Support of Life

ESSENTIAL QUESTION

How can Earth support life?

1. The Sun

Students will learn how the sun affects life on Earth.

Although there are many different types of living things on Earth, all living things have a set of basic needs: a source of energy, water, gas exchange (in most cases, air), a habitat to live in, and a way to dispose of wastes. Life can exist on Earth because its conditions allow living things to meet these needs.

Earth's distance from the sun means that Earth receives just the right amount of solar energy to support life. Earth is said to exist in the "Goldilocks Zone" in the solar system. In other words, it is in a position relative to the sun that keeps it "just right" (not too cold and not too hot) for supporting life. Other planets are not as hospitable. Venus, for example, is so close to the sun that the surface of the planet is too hot to support life. Mars, on the other hand, is so far from the sun that the planet is too cold to support life. In addition to being different distances from the sun, the presence or absence of an atmosphere plays a key role the differences in temperatures among the inner planets.

Earth's rotation on its axis also plays an important part in maintaining a range of temperatures on Earth that are compatible with life. Earth rotates once every 24 hours. Therefore, there are no extreme hot or cold patches on Earth. Earth's rotation also means that plants on most of Earth's surface receive sunlight on a regular basis. Plants convert the sun's energy into food (in the form of the sugar glucose) during photosynthesis. Plant life on Earth forms the foundation for many food chains.

2. Earth's Water

Students will learn how Earth's water helps support life.

Liquid water is essential for life as we know it. Living things are largely composed of water and require water for almost every bodily process. Earth is the only planet in the solar system that has a large supply of liquid water on its surface—71 percent of Earth's surface is covered with liquid water.

During Earth's formation, several processes contributed to the supply of liquid water on Earth. When Earth's core cooled, it released steam, which formed clouds. Eventually water fell as rain and formed Earth's oceans. A large amount of the water in Earth's oceans also came from ice meteors. These meteors melted after they entered Earth's atmosphere. Earth's gravity is essential for holding Earth's water on its surface.

Today, water is found on Earth in three states: solid, liquid, and gas. Water moves between the living and nonliving parts of the Earth system in a set of processes called the water cycle. Without water, life as we know it could not exist on Earth.

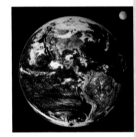

3. Earth's Atmosphere

Students will learn how Earth's atmosphere helps support life.

An atmosphere is a mixture of gases that surrounds a celestial body. Some of the planets in our solar system have an atmosphere, others do not. Atmospheres of different planets have differing compositions. For example, Earth's current atmosphere is made up mostly of nitrogen and oxygen, with a very small percentage of carbon dioxide. Venus and Mars have atmospheres comprised largely of carbon dioxide. Many forms of life on Earth need the oxygen and carbon dioxide in the atmosphere, but some bacteria, viruses, and archaea can live and reproduce in environments without oxygen.

The ozone layer is a gas layer in Earth's atmosphere. Ozone is a molecule made of three oxygen atoms (oxygen molecules in the atmosphere consist of two oxygen atoms). The ozone layer and other gases in the atmosphere insulate Earth by trapping the sun's heat near the surface of the planet, keeping the temperature within a range in which life is possible. Human activities have affected the ozone layer in two ways. First, burning fossil fuels has added ozone to the lower atmosphere, where it is a pollutant. Second, the use of certain chemicals has decreased the amount of ozone in the upper atmosphere, where it benefits life by reflecting back into space much of the harmful ultraviolet radiation from the sun.

©NASA/Corbis

Teacher  Teacher

Angie Larson
Bernard Campbell Middle School
Lee's Summit, MO

Lesson 5 Managing Resources   Have your students brainstorm ideas for conserving energy at school and at home. Take your discussions one step further by having students create and implement plans for conservation. At the end of the school year, work together to estimate how much energy your entire class has saved. Students will feel great about the difference they're making!

Lesson 2

Natural Resources

ESSENTIAL QUESTION
What are Earth's natural resources?

1. Natural Resources

Students will learn what a natural resource is.

A natural resource is any natural material that is used by humans to help them survive and improve their lives. Natural resources can come from Earth's atmosphere, crust, water sources, and from other living things. Some natural resources are air, soil, water, oil, rocks, minerals, plants, and wildlife.

2. Renewable and Nonrenewable Resources

Students will learn the difference between renewable and nonrenewable resources.

Renewable resources are those that can be replaced at the same (or nearly the same) rate at which the resource is used. For example, water is continuously replenished through the water cycle. Trees are considered a renewable resource because cut trees can be replaced with seedlings. Some renewable resources are considered inexhaustible because they cannot be used up. Solar energy and wind energy are considered inexhaustible resources.

A nonrenewable resource is a natural resource that forms much more slowly than the rate it is used. These resources may take thousands or millions of years to form. Coal, oil, copper, and bauxite (aluminum ore) are nonrenewable resources.

The sustainability of a resource is a function of how quickly the resource is replaced versus how quickly it is consumed. For example, forests are renewable resources because trees can be replaced, but the rate of harvest has a great impact on the sustainability of the resource. The same is true for groundwater and wildlife.

3. Material Resources

Students will learn what a material resource is.

Natural resources are used in many ways. Natural resources can be categorized as material resources based on how they are used. A material resource can be used as food or drink, or to make objects. For example, iron is used to make steel. Wheat is harvested and processed into food. As with all natural resources, material resources are also classified as renewable or nonrenewable.

Trees are a material resource when they are used to make products, such as this guitar.

4. Energy Resources

Students will learn what an energy resource is.

Energy is the ability to do work. An energy resource is any natural resource that humans use to generate energy. Energy cannot be created or destroyed, but it can be converted from one form to another. For example, when coal is burned in a power plant, the chemical energy in the coal is converted to heat, which forms steam that drives turbines. Energy can also be transferred from one object to another, such as the conversion of electrical energy to light energy, sound energy, and mechanical energy. Similar to material resources, energy resources are classified as renewable or nonrenewable.

 **COMMON MISCONCEPTIONS** 🟦 **RTI**

RENEWABLE AND NONRENEWABLE RESOURCES Students may think renewable resources can never be used up. Some renewable resources may be inexhaustible, such as solar resources. Others that are generally renewable can be used up, such as clean water

and trees, if not used wisely.

This misconception is addressed in the Daily Demo on p. 195 and p. 201.

Content Refresher (continued)

Professional Development

Nonrenewable Energy Resources

ESSENTIAL QUESTION

How do we use nonrenewable energy resources?

1. Energy Resources

Students will learn to distinguish nonrenewable energy resources from renewable energy resources.

An energy resource is a natural resource that humans use to generate energy. Natural processes can replace renewable energy resources at least as quickly as they are used up. Nonrenewable energy resources are used up faster than they can be replaced.

Fossil fuels and nuclear fuel are the two main types of nonrenewable energy resources. They provide most of the energy in the United States and other developed countries. Fossil fuels form from the remains of ancient organisms. Nuclear energy is the energy released when the atoms of nuclei are split or combined by fission or fusion, respectively.

2. Fossil Fuels

Students will learn to identify the characteristics of fossil fuels, how they are formed and used, and the advantages and disadvantages of using fossil fuels.

All living things contain carbon. Fossil fuels form from the remains of organisms that lived millions of years ago. Most of the carbon in fossil fuels is in the form of hydrocarbons (compounds of carbon and hydrogen).

Petroleum is a fossil fuel made up of a mixture of crude oil and natural gas. Crude oil is a liquid that is refined, or separated, into useful products such as fuels and plastics. Natural gas is a mixture of methane and other gaseous hydrocarbons. Natural gas is used for heating and cooking, and to power some vehicles. Coal is a solid fossil fuel. Coal once was used for heating homes and buildings and to power locomotives. Today it provides fuel for generating electricity.

Fossil fuels form below Earth's surface. Over many millions of years, heat from Earth's interior and pressure from overlying rocks convert organic remains into hydrocarbons. Petroleum forms from the remains of microscopic sea organisms. Coal forms from the remains of swamp plants. Over time, as the decayed sediment is buried and temperature and pressure increase, a material called *peat* forms. Eventually the peat may be changed to lignite, bituminous coal, and finally, anthracite.

Fossil fuels are relatively inexpensive and are convenient to use. However, byproducts from burning fossil fuels in cars and power plants increase smog and can contribute to acid rain. Coal mining can disturb or pollute habitats, and oil spills can damage ocean environments for many years.

3. Nuclear Energy

Students will learn how nuclear energy is generated, how electricity is produced from nuclear fuel, and the advantages and disadvantages of nuclear energy.

Nuclear fuels, such as uranium-235, produce energy through a process called fission during which the nuclei of radioactive atoms split into smaller fragments. This process releases energy as heat and radiation. At a nuclear power plant, the heat is used to generate steam. The steam is used to generate electricity, similar to coal-fired power plants.

Nuclear energy can be used to generate electricity without air pollution, and uranium can be mined with less damage to the environment than coal mining. However, the radioactive waste from nuclear power plants is dangerous, and must be stored safely for thousands of years.

COMMON MISCONCEPTIONS ⬛ **RTI**

ENERGY ON EARTH Students might think that all energy on Earth comes from the sun.

This misconception is addressed in the Quick Lab Modeling Nuclear Fission on p. 209 and on p. 215.

Renewable Energy Resources

ESSENTIAL QUESTION

How do humans use renewable energy resources?

1. Energy Resources

Students will learn that renewable energy resources are replaced at least at the same rate as they are used.

Natural energy resources are used by humans to generate different forms of energy, such as electrical energy needed to power technology. Renewable energy resources, such as solar energy, wind energy, and hydroelectric energy, are those that are replenished at least as quickly as they are used. Renewable resources are not instantly renewable however; instead they are renewed in a reasonable time period (years to decades). There are two sources of renewable energy resources: the sun and energy from within Earth.

Some renewable resources can become poorly managed if they are used at a faster rate than they can be replaced. For example, if forests are cut and cleared faster than they can grow, the forest resource is poorly managed and cannot be sustained.

2. Energy from the Sun

Students will learn that many renewable energy resources are powered by the sun, such as solar energy, wind energy, hydroelectric energy, and biomass.

Nuclear fusion, the process by which two or more atomic nuclei join together, occurs in the sun, producing large amounts of energy released in the form of radiation and heat. Solar energy is the source of much of Earth's energy resources, both renewable and nonrenewable. Fossil fuels are nonrenewable energy resources formed from the remains of ancient plants and animals that relied on the sun for energy. Renewable energy resources, such as solar energy, wind energy, hydroelectric energy, and biomass energy, are also powered by the sun.

When heat from the sun reaches Earth, it warms the air, ground, and water. Winds form as the sun's radiation warms Earth's air masses unevenly. Pressure changes caused by this uneven warming of air masses generate wind. Solar energy also drives the water cycle. Moving wind and water can be harnessed to spin turbines, which can generate electricity.

Solar energy can be used to warm buildings directly or it can be collected by solar panels and converted into electricity. Photovoltaic cells capture, store, and convert light energy to electricity.

Most life on Earth relies on organisms that use sunlight to make food. Undigested food matter that is eliminated from organisms can be burned as fuel. Biomass is the energy obtained from plant material, manure, or any other organic material. Biomass can be burned or used to produce ethanol, a biofuel used in cars.

3. Energy from Earth

Students will learn that geothermal energy results from Earth's composition.

Geothermal energy is energy in the form of heat from Earth's interior. The energy comes from two sources: the decay of radioactive isotopes in Earth's mantle and crust caused by fission, the splitting of nuclei of radioactive atoms; and energy stored during Earth's formation. Geothermal energy can be used to warm water, which is then circulated through buildings. It can also be used to warm water to produce steam, which can then turn turbines that generate electricity.

Content Refresher (continued)

Professional Development

Managing Resources

ESSENTIAL QUESTION
Why should natural resources be managed?

1. Resources

Students will learn about the two categories of natural resources and the effects of using, extracting, and disposing of them.

A natural resource is any natural material that is used by humans. For example, people need space to build and live, which uses land resources. They make metal tools and equipment, which requires mining for minerals. They need soil, plants, livestock, fish, and water for food and drink, all of which are natural resources.

Natural resources can be categorized as renewable or nonrenewable. Renewable resources can be replaced at least at the same rate at which they are used. Renewable resources include plants, animals, and if managed carefully, water. Nonrenewable resources are used at a faster rate than they can be replaced. Nonrenewable resources include minerals, and fossil fuels such as natural gas, oil, and coal. Often, extracting and/or using natural resources can pollute or damage the environment and other natural resources (such as air, land, and water).

2. Managing Resources

Students will learn about management practices that can help conserve renewable and nonrenewable resources.

As the human population grows, the demands on natural resources also grow. People can ensure that resources are available and usable for a longer time through stewardship and conservation. Stewardship is the careful and responsible management of resources. Conservation is the wise use of and preservation of natural resources, which is an important part of stewardship.

For renewable resources, conservation practices focus on reducing pollution and erosion to maintain clean water, land, and air. Other tools of stewardship for renewable resources include limiting how much of the resource can be used in a certain period of time and replacing resources as they are used.

For nonrenewable resources, management focuses on increasing the efficiency with which resources are used. This helps to increase the sustainability of that resource because the resources are used more slowly. For example, improving the efficiency of gasoline-powered equipment would mean that oil reserves could last longer.

Reducing, reusing, and recycling resources not only help increase the efficiency with which the resources are used, but also result in less pollution. Agreements between nations can help manage resources internationally. For example, a global ban on whaling has been important in the recovery of some whale species. Many U.S. national conservation policies promote the sustainable use of resources. They also promote recycling and invest in finding alternative materials and new technologies that can use resources more efficiently. Individuals can help manage resources by reducing, reusing, and recycling goods, by changing their buying habits, and by making lifestyle changes at home, school, work, and play.

3. Advantages and Disadvantages of Managing Resources

Students will learn about the advantages and disadvantages of managing resources.

Wise use of resources reduces waste, landfill space, and pollution. Recycling reduces the amount of energy needed to extract new resources to make new consumer goods. However, managing resources does have disadvantages, the greatest relating to cost. Recycling used materials, designing and building more efficient equipment, and finding alternative materials that use fewer resources are expensive undertakings. Managing resources can also be inconvenient. For example, it is easier to throw out food than it is to compost it.

Teacher Notes

Advance Planning

These activities may take extended time or special conditions.

Unit 3

Video-Based Project Got Water?, p. 176
    multiple activities spanning several lessons

Project Energy Sources, p. 177
    research and plan

Graphic Organizers and Vocabulary pp. 183, 184, 197, 198, 211, 212, 225, 226, 243, 244
    ongoing with reading

Lesson 1

Activity Measuring the Sun's Heat, p. 180
    requires outdoor observations

Lesson 2

Field Lab Natural Resources Used at Lunch, p. 195
    students collect lunch waste in advance of lesson

Activity Visualizing Natural Resources, p. 198
    students bring in magazines from home

Lesson 5

Daily Demo Non-Biodegradable Peanuts?, p. 241
    starch-based and polystyrene packing peanuts

Quick Lab The Impact of Resource Extraction, p. 241
    prepare gelatin in advance of lesson

What Do You Think?

Encourage students to consider how humans depend on natural resources.

Ask: Think about the objects that you use every day. What natural resources are these things made from? Sample answers: wood, metal, rubber, cotton, stone, fossil fuels

Ask: Why is it important to manage or conserve the resources that we depend on? Sample answer: If they are not conserved, we could run out of those resources.

Ask: Another way that we use resources is by producing energy. What are some of the things we use energy for? Sample answers: heat, air conditioning, lighting, hot water, cars, computers, televisions, refrigerators, airplanes

UNIT 3

Earth's Resources

Big Idea
Humans depend on natural resources for materials and for energy.

Common building materials such as lumber, bricks, and glass are all made from natural resources.

Wood for buildings comes from forests that have to be managed wisely.

What do you think?
The resources that humans need to live are found on Earth or come from the sun. What would happen if one or more of these resources were used up?

133

Video-Based Project

Got Water?

Go Online to preview the videos, access teacher support pages, and print student activity worksheets.

Students design a water filter system and test its ability to remove debris from a sample of contaminated water.

©Patrick Greene Productions

134 Unit 3 Earth's Resources

CITIZEN SCIENCE

Energy Sources

The world is filled with valuable resources. How we use, reuse, or use up those resources is important to this and future generations.

1 Think About It

Every time you walk into school on a normal school day, the lights are on, the rooms are comfortable, and there are material resources available for teacher and student use. Where does your school get its energy? Is it from a renewable or nonrenewable resource? Could the energy be used more efficiently?

2 Ask a Question

What is the energy source for your school's heating and cooling system?
With a partner or as a class, learn more about the source of energy for your school's heating and cooling system and the energy efficiency of your school building. As you talk about it, consider the items below.

Things to Consider
- ☐ Does your school have more than one energy source?
- ☐ Is your school building energy efficient?

3 Make a Plan

Once you have learned about your school building's energy efficiency, develop a proposal for your principal. Propose an alternative energy source for the heating and cooling system and ways to improve the building's energy efficiency.

A Describe the current energy source for your school's heating and cooling system.

B Describe one alternative energy source your school could use.

C List any noted energy inefficiencies and suggestions for improvements.

Many older schools have been modified with new windows, doors, and insulation. These changes were made to save on heating and cooling costs and to provide a more comfortable learning environment.

The type of lighting as well as the quality of doors and windows can make a difference in a building's energy costs and efficiency.

Ideas for saving resources can help schools save money.

Take It Home
What energy sources supply your home? With an adult, talk about possible ways to improve energy efficiency where you live.

135

CITIZEN SCIENCE

Unit Project Energy Sources

1. Think About It

Encourage students to think about where the school's energy may come from. Possible sources include power plants that burn coal or natural gas, nuclear power plants, hydroelectric plants, and other renewable sources such as wind or solar. Discuss the difference between renewable and nonrenewable energy sources.

2. Ask a Question

Prior to beginning the project, research the energy resources used for the school's electricity and heating/cooling. You can share this information with students. Alternatively, you could invite the school's facility manager to speak to the class and answer student questions.

3. Make a Plan

When recommending alternative energy sources, students should focus on cleaner or renewable resources. Students should also describe how the school could use energy more efficiently. Energy-efficiency improvements might include installing new windows and doors, adding insulation, or replacing systems (such as a furnace or boiler) with a more efficient technology.

Take It Home

Ask students to provide a note from an adult confirming that the student discussed the topic with him or her. Ask students to share with the class some of the ideas that resulted from brainstorming with adults.

🌐 *Optional Online rubric: Class Discussion*

Earth's Support of Life

Essential Question How can Earth support life?

Professional Development

For more detailed information about the topics in this lesson, refer to the Content Refresher in the Unit Opener pages.

Opening Your Lesson

Begin the lesson by assessing students' prerequisite and prior knowledge.

Prerequisite Knowledge

- A general understanding of ecology
- A solid understanding of energy, matter, and changes in ecosystems

Accessing Prior Knowledge

To gauge what students already know about how Earth supports life, invite students to explain what is needed for life on Earth to survive. Write student ideas on the board. Return to these ideas again after you have completed the lesson.

Customize Your Opening

☐ **Accessing Prior Knowledge,** above
☐ **Print Path** Engage Your Brain, SE p. 137
☐ **Print Path** Active Reading, SE p. 137
☐ **Digital Path** Lesson Opener

Key Topics/Learning Goals	Supporting Concepts
The Sun 1 Name what is required by all living things on Earth. 2 State how Earth's proximity to the sun produces a unique surface temperature range. 3 Explain how Earth's rotation allows efficient energy use. 4 See how plants on Earth use solar energy to make food.	• Living things need energy, water, and air to survive, and a place to live. • Earth's distance from the sun allows it to receive an amount of energy appropriate to support life. • Because Earth spins on its axis, each side of the planet receives sunlight regularly. • Plant life on Earth is the foundation for many food chains. Plants make their own food through photosynthesis.
Earth's Water 1 Compare the supply of water on Earth to the supply of water on other planets in our solar system. 2 Understand how water accumulated on Earth's surface. 3 Explain how water supports the existence of life on Earth.	• Earth is the only planet that has a large supply of liquid water on its surface. • The cooling of Earth's core caused the release of steam, which formed clouds that eventually fell as rain and formed oceans. • A large amount of the water in Earth's oceans also came from ice meteors that melted when they landed on Earth's surface. • Water can be found on Earth as solid, liquid, and gas due to Earth's temperature range.
Earth's Atmosphere 1 Compare the composition of Earth's atmosphere to those of other planets in the solar system. 2 Describe both the composition of and the formation of the atmosphere. 3 Understand how the atmosphere supports life.	• An atmosphere is a mixture of gases that surrounds a celestial body. • Gravity keeps Earth's atmosphere in place. • Earth's current atmosphere is made of mostly nitrogen and oxygen; many life forms depend on oxygen and carbon dioxide. • The ozone layer and other gases in the atmosphere insulate the Earth. The ozone layer reflects much of the potentially harmful ultraviolet radiation from the sun.

Options for Instruction

Two parallel paths provide coverage of the Essential Questions, with a strong **Inquiry** strand woven into each. Follow the **Print Path,** the **Digital Path,** or your customized combination of print, digital, and inquiry.

 Print Path
Teaching support for the Print Path appears with the Student Pages.

 Inquiry Labs and Activities

Digital Path
Digital Path Shortcut: TS672338

Living It Up, SE pp. 138–139
What do living things need to survive?
How do Earth and the sun interact to support life on Earth?
• Earth's Rotation Distributes the Sun's Energy
• Earth Has a Unique Temperature Range

Activity
Measuring the Sun's Heat

Quick Lab
Temperature Variations on Earth

Living It Up
Video

Earth is Close to the Sun
Interactive Images

Water, Water, Everywhere,
SE pp. 140
What is unique about Earth's water?
• Only Earth Has Liquid Water to Support Life

Quick Lab
How Water Forms on Earth's Surface

Activity
Why We Need Water

Atmosphere and Water
Interactive Graphics

Protective Covering, SE pp. 142–143
How does Earth's atmosphere support life?
• Gases Fuel Life Processes
• Gases Insulate Earth
• The Ozone Layer Protects Earth from Radiation

Exploration Lab
Modeling the Greenhouse Effect

Daily Demo
Whip It Up!

Activity
Modeling the Atmosphere

Earth's Atmosphere
Video

Options for Assessment

See the Evaluate page for options, including Formative Assessment, Summative Assessment, and Unit Review.

Engage and Explore

Activities and Discussion

Discussion *Why Is There Life on Earth?*

Engage

Introducing Key Topics

   whole class
10 min
GUIDED inquiry

Use the following questions to generate a class discussion of the factors that make it possible for life to exist on Earth. **Ask:** What do you know about life on Earth? Sample answer: Life on Earth is varied. There are plants and animals—large and small. **Ask:** Is there life on other planets? Sample answers: Not that we know of. Perhaps there are microorganisms on some. Scientists haven't found any multicellular life forms. **Ask:** Why is it hard for life to exist on other planets like Mars? Sample answers: Other planets are too hot or too cold. There is no water. The atmosphere is not breathable. **Ask:** Which temperatures do they think would be most conducive to life? Sample answer: temperatures that are similar to Earth's **Ask:** What other things beside temperature would affect whether life can exist? Sample answers: amount of water, air quality

Activity *Measuring the Sun's Heat*

Engage

The Sun

   whole class
10 min
GUIDED inquiry

Go outside on a sunny day. Encourage students to make predictions about which places in the school yard are warmest and coolest. Choose several areas, both sunny and shaded, and have students use thermometers to collect temperature data. **Ask:** How do the temperatures of concrete, grass, dirt, and asphalt differ? Sample answers: Asphalt is the warmest; grass the coolest. **Ask:** Is the temperature different in the sunlight and the shade? Sample answer: Yes. It is warmer in the sun, cooler in the shade. **Ask:** What accounts for these temperature differences? Sample answers: The sun doesn't shine directly on surfaces in the shade. Dark colors absorb more heat; light colors reflect more heat.

Activity *Why We Need Water*

Engage

Water

   adult-student pairs
ongoing
INDEPENDENT inquiry

Write Fast Use the following activity to introduce the concept that water is essential for life on Earth. Give students two minutes to write as many ways as they can think of that humans and other living things on Earth use water. At the conclusion of the two minutes, have students share what they have written with the class.

Activity *Modeling the Atmosphere*

The Atmosphere

   pairs or small groups
15 min
GUIDED inquiry

Give pairs or small groups beans of three distinct colors or shapes. Have students count out 78 beans of one kind to represent the 78 percent of the atmosphere that is nitrogen. Have students count out 21 beans of another kind to represent the 21 percent of the atmosphere that is oxygen. Have students add one bean of another color to represent the 1 percent of the atmosphere that is argon. Explain to students that greenhouse gases, such as ozone and carbon dioxide, are present in very small amounts (about one-hundredth of one percent, or 0.01%).

Customize Your Labs

 See the Lab Manual for lab datasheets.

 Go Online for editable lab datasheets.

Labs and Demos

Daily Demo *Whip It Up!*

The Atmosphere

👥 whole class
🕐 15 min
ⓘ **DIRECTED** inquiry

Show students that the "ozone hole" is not a static entity, but actually leads to worldwide decrease in protective ozone.

PURPOSE **To model the effect of ozone depletion**

MATERIALS

- whipped topping tinted pink with red food coloring
- uncolored whipped topping
- 2 pie pans
- whisk
- spoon

1 Put the pink whipped topping on the pie pan. Explain that the topping is a model of the atmosphere, and the pink tint represents the protective ozone in the atmosphere.

2 Remove a scoop of pink topping from one pie pan and replace it with white, uncolored topping. Mix the topping thoroughly. **Ask:** What has happened to the "ozone"? The topping is a lighter pink, so that must mean there's less ozone.

3 Repeat several times. Explain that the ozone hole is not an actual hole, but rather a thinning over Antarctica. However, the movement of the atmosphere causes mixing, and as a result, there is less protective ozone all over the planet, not just near the location of the hole.

Quick Lab *Temperature Variations on Earth*

See the Lab Manual or go Online for planning information.

Exploration Lab *Modeling the Greenhouse Effect*

The Atmosphere

👥 pairs or small groups
🕐 45 min
ⓘ **GUIDED/INDEPENDENT** inquiry

Students will build a model of the greenhouse effect on Earth.

MATERIALS

- 2 cardboard boxes
- plastic wrap
- potting soil
- lamp
- tape
- 2 thermometers

See the Lab Manual or go Online for planning information.

Quick Lab *How Water Forms on Earth's Surface*

Water

👥 small groups
🕐 20 min
ⓘ **DIRECTED** inquiry

Students will explore how bodies of water formed on Earth.

MATERIALS

- glass bottle, 400 mL
- funnel
- ice
- metal lid
- hot water
- spoon

See the Lab Manual or go Online for planning information.

Activities and Discussion

☐ **Discussion** Why Is There Life on Earth?
☐ **Activity** Why We Need Water
☐ **Activity** Measuring the Sun's Heat
☐ **Activity** Modeling the Atmosphere

Labs and Demos

☐ **Daily Demo** Whip It Up!
☐ **Exploration Lab** Modeling the Greenhouse Effect
☐ **Quick Lab** Water...on Earth's Surface
☐ **Quick Lab** Temperature...on Earth

Your Resources

_____

_____

_____

_____

Explain Science Concepts

Key Topics	🗐 Print Path	🖵 Digital Path
The Sun	☐ **Living It Up,** SE pp. 138–139 • Visualize It!, #5 • Identify, #6 • Think Outside the Book, #7 • Visualize It!, #8 **Think Outside the Book** Inquiry **7 Apply** Write a news story about what would happen to life on Earth if Earth stopped rotating.	☐ **Living It Up** Learn what life needs to exist. ☐ **Earth is Close to the Sun** Find out how the position of Earth in relation to the sun led to conditions appropriate for life.
Earth's Water	☐ **Water, Water, Everywhere,** SE pp. 140 • Active Reading (Annotation strategy), #9 • Visualize It!, #10 **Active Reading** **9 Infer** As you read, underline the reason that liquid water is essential to life.	☐ **Atmosphere and Water** Investigate how Earth's waters came to be.
Earth's Atmosphere	☐ **Protective Covering,** SE pp. 142–143 • Infer, #15 • Visualize It!, #16 **15 Infer** If Venus has an atmosphere, why doesn't it support the kind of life that is now found on Earth?	☐ **Earth's Atmosphere** Explore the atmosphere.

Differentiated Instruction

Basic *How Earth Supports Life*

Synthesizing Key Topics

 individuals or pairs

🕐 10 min

Have students draw a picture of Earth, labeling the atmosphere, water, and sunlight. Underneath the picture of Earth, encourage students to describe ways that Earth's atmosphere and water, as well as the sun, support life on Earth. Invite students to explain their drawings to a partner or to the class.

Advanced *What's Most Important?*

Synthesizing Key Topics

 individuals

🕐 15 min

Invite students to rank the importance to life of Earth's sun, water, and atmosphere. Students should write reasons to justify their rankings. Encourage students to think about the following questions when developing their rankings: If it changed a little, could life on Earth still exist? What if it changed a lot? Invite students to share and defend their rankings with classmates or the entire class. Emphasize that there are no correct or incorrect responses to this activity, but students should offer a well-reasoned response.

ELL *Earth Vocabulary*

Synthesizing Key Topics

 individuals or pairs

🕐 10 min

Word Squares Have students use word squares to help them remember difficult vocabulary from the lesson. Have them write one of the lesson vocabulary terms in one square and draw an image that helps them remember the term's meaning in another square. Beneath these squares, encourage them to write a definition of the term, and in the last square, have them use the term in a sentence. Invite students to explain their word squares to a partner.

TERM translation	symbol or picture
my meaning dictionary definition	sentence

Lesson Vocabulary

photosynthesis   atmosphere   ultraviolet radiation

ozone

Previewing Vocabulary

 whole class

🕐 10 min

Word Origins Explain that thinking and talking about word origins helps you remember the words better. For example, the word *ozone* comes from a Greek word that means "to smell." Explain that ozone has a strong, irritating odor; it is the smell we detect after thunderstorms. **Ask:** Why might ozone have been given its name? Sample answer: because it has a strong odor

Reinforcing Vocabulary

 individuals

🕐 ongoing

Frame Game To help students remember the meaning of each vocabulary term, have students use frames. Encourage students to write a term in the center of each frame. Then they can decide which information to frame the term with. They can use examples, a definition, descriptions, sentences that use the term, pictures, or other words that help them remember the term.

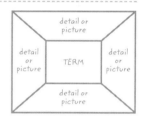

Customize Your Core Lesson

Core Instruction

- [ ] **Print Path** choices
- [ ] **Digital Path** choices

Vocabulary

- [ ] **Previewing Vocabulary** Word Origins
- [ ] **Reinforcing Vocabulary** Frame Game

Your Resources

Differentiated Instruction

- [ ] **Basic** How Earth Supports Life
- [ ] **Advanced** What's Most Important?
- [ ] **ELL** Earth Vocabulary

Extend Science Concepts

Reinforce and Review

Activity *Inside/Outside Circles*

Synthesizing Key Topics whole class
🕐 15 min

1 After students have read the lesson, give each an index card with a question from the text. Have students write their answer on the back of the index card. Check to make sure the answers are correct. Have students adjust incorrect answers.

2 Have students pair up and form two circles. One partner is in an inside circle; the other is in an outside circle. The students in the inside circle face out, and the students in the outside circle face in.

3 Each student in the inside circle asks his or her partner the question on the index card. The partner answers. If the answer is incorrect, the student in the inside circle teaches the other student the correct answer. Repeat this step with the outside-circle students asking the questions.

4 Have each student on the outside circle rotate one person to the right. He or she faces a new partner and repeats the process. Students rotate after each pair of questions. Vary the rotation, if desired, by moving more than one person, moving to the left, and so on, but make sure that partners are always new.

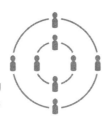

FoldNote

Synthesizing Key Topics individuals
🕐 10 min

Tri-Fold FoldNote Have students make a tri-fold FoldNote to organize ideas about how Earth supports life. In the first column, have them list ways that the sun is important in supporting life. In the second column, have students list ways that water on Earth is important for supporting life. Finally, in the third column, have students list ways that the atmosphere is important for supporting life.

Going Further

Music Connection

Synthesizing Key Topics individuals
🕐 varied

Invite interested students to write and perform a song or poem about how Earth supports life. Encourage students to be creative and think about effects that the sun, water, and atmosphere have on living organisms. When their songs are complete, invite students to perform their work for the class.

Real World Connection

Synthesizing Key Topics individuals
🕐 ongoing

Encourage interested students to make an enclosed terrarium that supports life. What do they think they will need to make oxygen in the terrarium? How will they remove wastes? How will plants make food? Invite interested students to draw sketches of their terrariums. Then have students conduct research to see if they have left out any important details. Finally, invite students to build their terrariums.

Customize Your Closing

🔷 *See the Assessment Guide for quizzes and tests.*

💿 *Go Online to edit and create quizzes and tests.*

Reinforce and Review

☐ **Activity** Inside/Outside Circles

☐ **FoldNote** Trifold FoldNote

☐ **Print Path** Visual Summary, SE p. 144

☐ **Print Path** Lesson Review, SE p. 145

☐ **Digital Path** Lesson Closer

Evaluate Student Mastery

See the teacher support below the Student Pages for additional Formative Assessment questions.

Ask the following questions to assess student mastery of the material. **Ask:** What are some ways that the sun supports life on Earth? Sample answers: Plants use the sun's energy to make food through photosynthesis. Earth's distance from the sun makes Earth's temperature one that can support life. **Ask:** What are some ways Earth's water supports life? Earth has liquid water, which is needed to support life. **Ask:** What are some ways Earth's atmosphere supports life? Earth's atmosphere is composed mostly of nitrogen and oxygen. Most organisms on Earth need oxygen to survive. The atmosphere also keeps Earth's temperature within a range that supports life. The ozone layer protects Earth from ultraviolet radiation.

Reteach

Formative assessment may show that students need reinforcement for certain topics. The resources below are recommended for reteaching. If students were introduced to a topic through the Print Path, you can also use the Digital Path to reteach, and vice versa.
🎧 *Can be assigned to individual students*

The Sun
Activity Measuring the Sun's Heat

Water
Quick Lab How Water Forms on Earth's Surface
ELL Earth Vocabulary 🎧

The Atmosphere
Activity Modeling the Atmosphere 🎧

Summative Assessment

Alternative Assessment
That's Life!

🔘 *Online resources: student worksheet; optional rubrics*

Earth's Support of Life

Climb the Pyramid: *That's Life!*
Complete the activities below to show what you have learned about the properties that allow Earth to support life.

1. Work on your own, with a partner, or with a small group.
2. Choose one item from each layer of the pyramid. Check your choices.
3. Have your teacher approve your plan.
4. Submit or present your results.

__ **Sequence Diagram**
Draw a timeline, sequence diagram, or flow chart that shows how Earth got so much liquid water. Include illustrations.

__ **I Am the Sun**
Write a paragraph that explains how interactions of the sun and Earth allow life to exist on Earth.

__ **Solar Effects**
Draw a diagram or illustration that shows how the Earth's rotation, distance from the sun, and sun's energy affect life on Earth.

__ **This Place Has No Atmosphere**
Make a booklet that explains why some celestial bodies have an atmosphere and some do not, and gives examples of each.

__ **Acting Out!**
Write a skit that explains the importance of the atmosphere in supporting life on Earth. Perform your skit for the class.

__ **Protecting Earth**
Make a model that shows how the ozone layer protects Earth from radiation and how gases insulate Earth. Share your model with the class, and use it to explain the importance of the ozone layer to living things on Earth.

Going Further
☐ Music Connection Life on Earth Song
☐ Real World Connection Terrarium Life
☐ Print Path Why It Matters, SE p. 141

Your Resources
_____

Formative Assessment
☐ Strategies Throughout TE
☐ Lesson Review SE

Summative Assessment
☐ Alternative Assessment That's Life!
☐ Lesson Quiz
☐ Unit Tests A and B
☐ Unit Review SE End-of-Unit

_____

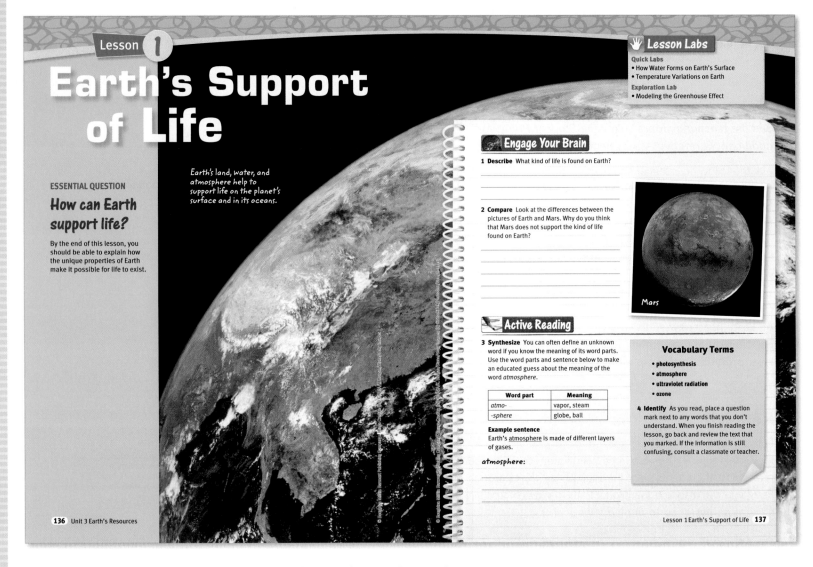

Lesson ①

Earth's Support of Life

ESSENTIAL QUESTION

How can Earth support life?

By the end of this lesson, you should be able to explain how the unique properties of Earth make it possible for life to exist.

Earth's land, water, and atmosphere help to support life on the planet's surface and in its oceans.

🖐 Lesson Labs

Quick Labs
• How Water Forms on Earth's Surface
• Temperature Variations on Earth

Exploration Lab
• Modeling the Greenhouse Effect

🧠 Engage Your Brain

1 Describe What kind of life is found on Earth?

2 Compare Look at the differences between the pictures of Earth and Mars. Why do you think that Mars does not support the kind of life found on Earth?

Mars

📖 Active Reading

3 Synthesize You can often define an unknown word if you know the meaning of its word parts. Use the word parts and sentence below to make an educated guess about the meaning of the word *atmosphere*.

Word part	Meaning
atmo-	vapor, steam
-sphere	globe, ball

Example sentence
Earth's <u>atmosphere</u> is made of different layers of gases.

atmosphere:

Vocabulary Terms

• photosynthesis
• atmosphere
• ultraviolet radiation
• ozone

4 Identify As you read, place a question mark next to any words that you don't understand. When you finish reading the lesson, go back and review the text that you marked. If the information is still confusing, consult a classmate or teacher.

136 Unit 3 Earth's Resources

Lesson 1 Earth's Support of Life **137**

Answers

Answers for 1–3 should represent students' current thoughts, even if incorrect.

1. Sample answer: Earth supports plants, animals, fungi, and microorganisms.

2. Sample answer: Mars does not appear to have any water; Mars does not look like it has any air.

3. An atmosphere contains gases that surround a planet.

4. Students' annotations will vary.

Opening Your Lesson

Discuss student answers to questions 1 and 2 to assess their prerequisite knowledge and to estimate what they already know about properties that are essential for life to exist on Earth.

Accessing Prior Knowledge Read aloud the title of the lesson. Invite students to describe about what they already know about conditions on Earth that make life possible. Invite them to also explain the needs of different forms of life, such as plants, animals, and microorganisms.

Prerequisites Students should already have some understanding of energy and matter in ecosystems, energy transfer from the sun, photosynthesis, and the history of life on Earth.

Learning Alert

Difficult Concepts Students may think that all organisms need oxygen to survive. Explain that some viruses, bacteria, and archaea do not need oxygen. Recently, in fact, scientists have found the first multicellular organisms that do not need oxygen. These organisms live in sediment under the Mediterranean Sea.

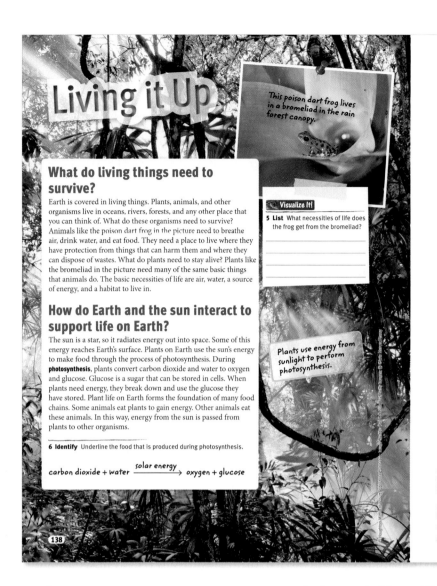

Living it Up

This poison dart frog lives in a bromeliad in the rain forest canopy.

What do living things need to survive?

Earth is covered in living things. Plants, animals, and other organisms live in oceans, rivers, forests, and any other place that you can think of. What do these organisms need to survive? Animals like the poison dart frog in the picture need to breathe air, drink water, and eat food. They need a place to live where they have protection from things that can harm them and where they can dispose of wastes. What do plants need to stay alive? Plants like the bromeliad in the picture need many of the same basic things that animals do. The basic necessities of life are air, water, a source of energy, and a habitat to live in.

Visualize It!

5 List What necessities of life does the frog get from the bromeliad?

How do Earth and the sun interact to support life on Earth?

The sun is a star, so it radiates energy out into space. Some of this energy reaches Earth's surface. Plants on Earth use the sun's energy to make food through the process of photosynthesis. During **photosynthesis**, plants convert carbon dioxide and water to oxygen and glucose. Glucose is a sugar that can be stored in cells. When plants need energy, they break down and use the glucose they have stored. Plant life on Earth forms the foundation of many food chains. Some animals eat plants to gain energy. Other animals eat these animals. In this way, energy from the sun is passed from plants to other organisms.

Plants use energy from sunlight to perform photosynthesis.

6 Identify Underline the food that is produced during photosynthesis.

$$\text{carbon dioxide} + \text{water} \xrightarrow{\text{solar energy}} \text{oxygen} + \text{glucose}$$

138

Earth's Rotation Distributes Solar Energy

Earth rotates continuously on its axis, spinning around completely every 24 hours. Earth's rotation allows most regions of Earth to receive sunlight regularly. Regular sunlight allows plants to grow in almost all places on Earth. Earth's rotation also protects areas on Earth from temperature extremes. Imagine how hot it would be if your town always faced the sun. And imagine how cold it would be if your town never faced the sun!

Earth Has a Unique Temperature Range

Earth's distance from the sun also protects it from temperature extremes. If Earth were closer to the sun, it might be like Venus. Venus has extremely high temperatures because it is closer to the sun, and because it has a very thick atmosphere. These factors make it is too hot to support life. If Earth were farther away from the sun, it might be like Mars. Mars has extremely low temperatures, so it is too cold to support life as we know it. Earth has an average temperature of 15 °C (59 °F). Regions of Earth range from freezing temperatures below 0 °C (32 °F) to hot temperatures above 38 °C (100 °F). This temperature range allows life to survive in even the coldest and hottest places on Earth.

axis

Earth's rotation allows all parts of Earth to receive energy from the sun.

Think Outside the Book Inquiry

7 Apply Write a news story about what would happen to life on Earth if Earth stopped rotating.

Visualize It!

8 Identify Write whether each planet in the drawing is too hot, too cold, or just right to support life.

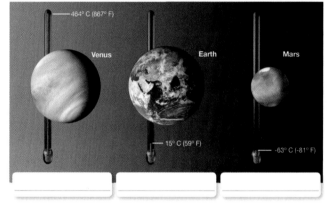

464° C (867° F)
Venus
Earth
15° C (59° F)
Mars
-63° C (-81° F)

Lesson 1 Earth's Support of Life **139**

Answers

5. Sample answer: The frog can drink water that collects inside the bromeliad. It can also use the bromeliad for shelter.

6. Students should underline the term "glucose."

7. Answers will vary.

8. Venus: too hot; Earth: just right; Mars: too cold

Annotation Strategy

To complete the annotation strategy for question 6, have students locate and circle the word in the text that identifies the food produced during photosynthesis (glucose). Then, extend the activity by having students write a short paragraph that correctly uses the following words and phrases: *glucose, photosynthesis, food chains,* and *life on Earth.* Have several students share their completed paragraphs with the class.

Interpreting Visuals

Invite students to examine the image that compares the temperature ranges of Venus, Earth, and Mars. **Ask:** What temperature range is tolerable for humans? Sample answer: about 7 °C to 38 °C **Ask:** Which planet has temperatures within this range? Answer: Earth **Ask:** Do you think life can exist on planets that are much hotter or colder than Earth? Sample answers: Yes, but the life forms would be much different than forms on Earth. No, the temperatures are too extreme to support life as we know it.

Water, Water Everywhere

What is unique about Earth's water?

When you look at a picture of Earth, you see lots and lots of water. How did Earth get so much water? Early Earth formed from molten materials, such as iron, nickel, and silica. These materials separated into layers and began to cool. As Earth cooled, it released steam and other gases into the air around its surface. The steam formed clouds, and water fell to Earth as rain. This was the beginning of Earth's oceans. A large amount of the water that is now on Earth came from outer space. Icy comets and meteors impacted Earth and added water to Earth's oceans.

Only Earth Has Liquid Water to Support Life

Earth is unique in the solar system because it contains water in three states: solid, liquid, and gas. Most of Earth's water is in liquid form. In fact, Earth is the only known planet with a large supply of liquid water on its surface. About 71% of Earth's surface is now covered with water. Liquid water is essential to life because cells need liquid water in order to perform life processes. Water remains a liquid on Earth because surface temperatures generally stay above the freezing point of water. Temperatures also stay far below water's boiling point.

Active Reading

9 Infer As you read, underline the reason that liquid water is essential to life.

Visualize It!

10 Summarize The pictures below show how Earth's oceans formed. Write a caption for the last two pictures in your own words.

Earth's Formation **Objects from Space** **Modern Earth**

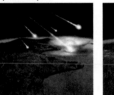 

As Earth cooled, it released steam. The steam cooled to form clouds. Rain fell and began to form oceans.

_____

140 Unit 3 Earth's Resources

Why It Matters

Extremophiles

WEIRD SCIENCE

Extremophiles are organisms that live in extreme environments. Most extremophiles are unicellular, but some are multicellular. Extremophiles live in some of the coldest, hottest, driest, and saltiest places on Earth.

Living in the Cold
The Antarctic is home to ice-covered lakes and cold, dry valleys. Surprisingly, life can still be found in these harsh conditions.

Extreme Adaptations
A type of worm called a nematode survives in the cold by producing antifreeze in its cells. The nematode can also dry itself out when groundwater is not available. The nematode can then become active when water flows again underground.

Life on Other Planets?
The cold, dry Antarctic has some similarities to the cold, dry surface of Mars. The presence of organisms in extreme environments on Earth makes it seem more possible that some kind of life could exist in the extreme conditions on other planets.

Extend
Inquiry

11 Explain What is an extremophile?

12 Describe What are some adaptations that an extremophile might have in order to survive in a very salty environment?

13 Extend How could a greater knowledge of extremophiles help scientists to search for life on other planets?

141

© Houghton Mifflin Harcourt Publishing Company

Answers

9. *See students' pages for annotations.*

10. Sample answers: Objects from Space: Icy comets and meteors added water to Earth's surface; Modern Earth: 71% of Earth's surface is now covered with liquid water.

11. Sample answer: An extremophile is an organism that lives in an environment that has extreme conditions, such as very cold or very hot temperatures.

12. Sample answer: The extremophile might be adapted to get rid of salt as a waste product.

13. Student output should demonstrate knowledge of the similarities between conditions in extreme Earth environments and conditions on other planets.

Formative Assessment

Ask: Why does Earth look blue when seen from space? Sample answer: Almost three-fourths of Earth's surface is covered by water. **Ask:** Why isn't there liquid water on other planets? Other planets are too hot or too cold. **Ask:** If a planet were very hot, what would happen to the water? It would boil and form steam. **Ask:** If a planet were very cold, what would happen to the water? Sample answer: It would freeze.

Annotation Strategy

Text Structure: Main Ideas/Details For question 9, have students underline the ways in which liquid water supports life. Point out that these are details that support the main idea "Only Earth has liquid water to support life." Encourage students to review their underlined statements for review at the end of the lesson.

🌐 *Optional Online resource: Text Structure: Main Ideas/Details support*

Why It Matters

To help students understand the importance of studying extremophiles, **Ask:** What can humans learn by studying extremophiles? Sample answers: Humans might learn how life on other planets could exist. They could learn how humans could survive in space or on other planets. They might learn how to raise crops in extreme places on Earth.

Security Blanket

How does Earth's atmosphere support life?

Take a deep breath. The air you are breathing is part of Earth's atmosphere. An **atmosphere** is a mixture of gases that surround a planet, moon, or other space object.

Some space objects have atmospheres, and some do not. It often depends on the object's gravity. Earth and Venus have atmospheres because their gravity is strong enough to hold gases in place. Mercury and the Moon each have weaker gravity, so they do not have atmospheres.

Gases Fuel Life Processes

Earth's atmosphere is composed mainly of nitrogen and oxygen. It also has traces of other gases like carbon dioxide. Carbon dioxide and oxygen support most forms of life. Plants and some single-celled organisms use carbon dioxide for photosynthesis. Plants, animals, and most other organisms use oxygen to perform cell processes. Anaerobic bacteria are some forms of life that do not need oxygen to survive.

Earth's atmosphere has not always contained nitrogen, oxygen, and carbon dioxide. It was originally just hydrogen and helium. These gases were too light for Earth's gravity to hold, so they escaped into space. Volcanoes released water vapor, carbon dioxide, and ammonia into Earth's early atmosphere. Solar energy broke ammonia apart to add nitrogen and hydrogen to the atmosphere. Hydrogen escaped into space, but the nitrogen stayed in the atmosphere. Bacteria used carbon dioxide to perform photosynthesis, which released oxygen into the atmosphere.

Planet	% Gravity Compared to Earth
Mercury	38%
Venus	91%
Earth	100%

14 Infer Why doesn't Mercury have an atmosphere?

Major Atmospheric Gases on Earth and Venus

Bar chart: Percentage (%) vs Atmospheric gases (Nitrogen, Oxygen, Carbon Dioxide) comparing Earth and Venus.

15 Infer If Venus has an atmosphere, why doesn't it support the kind of life that is now found on Earth?

Gases Insulate Earth

The gases in Earth's atmosphere support life in other ways. As radiation from the sun reaches Earth's atmosphere, some of it is reflected back into space. Some is absorbed by water vapor, carbon dioxide, and other gases in the atmosphere. Some solar radiation passes through the atmosphere and is absorbed by Earth's surface. Radiation from Earth's surface then moves into the atmosphere. This energy is absorbed and re-radiated by atmospheric gases, through a process called the greenhouse effect. The greenhouse effect keeps Earth warmer than it would be if Earth had no atmosphere.

The Ozone Layer Protects Earth

One type of solar radiation that can harm life is **ultraviolet radiation**. Ultraviolet radiation is harmful because it can damage the genetic material in organisms. Earth has a protective ozone layer that blocks most ultraviolet radiation before it reaches Earth's surface. The ozone layer contains ozone gas in addition to the other atmospheric gases. **Ozone** is a molecule that is made up of three oxygen atoms. Some human-made chemicals have damaged the ozone layer by breaking apart ozone molecules. International laws have banned the use of these ozone-destroying chemicals.

Solar Radiation

Visible Light and Infrared Radiation

Ultraviolet Radiation

Earth's ozone layer blocks most ultraviolet radiation.

Ozone Layer

Atmospheric gases absorb and re-radiate energy through a process called the greenhouse effect.

Infrared Radiation

Visualize It!

16 Explain How does the ozone layer protect life on Earth?

142 | 143

Answers

14. Sample answer: Mercury's gravity is too weak to hold an atmosphere.

15. Sample answer: Venus's atmosphere does not contain oxygen, which is necessary for photosynthesis.

16. Sample answer: The ozone layer blocks ultraviolet radiation, which can damage organisms.

Interpreting Visuals

Ask: Based on the chart, which planets have a strong enough gravitational pull to hold gases in an atmosphere in place? Earth and Venus have similar gravitational pulls. **Ask:** What are the atmospheres of Earth and Venus composed of? Earth's atmosphere is mostly nitrogen and oxygen. Venus's atmosphere is mostly carbon dioxide. **Ask:** Why do you think Venus does not have life as we know it? Sample answers: Its atmosphere would not support many of the organisms we know. Because it is closer to the sun than Earth is, it is too hot for life as we know it. Venus's atmosphere does not have an ozone layer to block ultraviolet radiation, which is harmful to life.

Formative Assessment

Ask: How does the sun support life on Earth? Sample answers: It provides energy that plants can convert to food energy. It heats the planet to a temperature that can support life. **Ask:** How does water support life on Earth? Sample answer: Liquid water is necessary to support life, and Earth has a large amount of liquid water. **Ask:** How does the atmosphere support life on Earth? Sample answer: Earth's atmosphere is mostly nitrogen and oxygen. Oxygen is needed for most life on Earth. The atmosphere also insulates Earth to keep it warm, and the ozone layer blocks and absorbs harmful ultraviolet radiation.

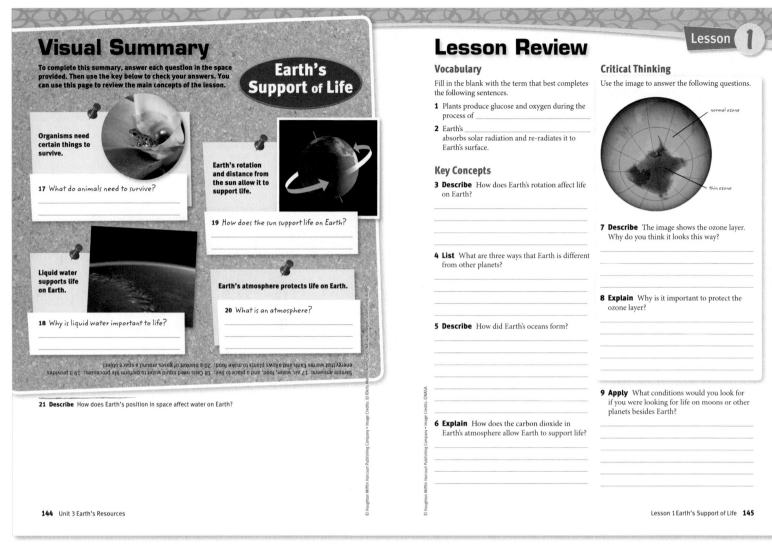

Visual Summary Answers

17. air, water, food, and a place to live

18. Cells need liquid water to perform life processes.

19. It provides energy that warms Earth and allows plants to make food.

20. a blanket of gases around a space object

21. Sample answer: Earth's distance from the sun causes a temperature range on Earth that allows water to be in a liquid form. Liquid water is needed to support life.

Lesson Review Answers

1. photosynthesis

2. atmosphere

3. Sample answer: Earth's rotation allows all parts of Earth to receive energy from the sun. This allows organisms to exist in all parts of Earth.

4. Sample answer: Earth has moderate temperatures, an atmosphere that contains oxygen, and liquid water.

5. Sample answer: Water vapor from volcanoes formed clouds that produced rain that fell to Earth. Icy comets and meteors also added water to Earth's surface.

6. Carbon dioxide traps radiation from the sun to warm Earth and is used by plants during photosynthesis.

7. Sample answer: There are thin spots in the layer because ozone has been destroyed by human-made chemicals.

8. Sample answer: The ozone layer protects life from damaging ultraviolet radiation.

9. Student output should demonstrate knowledge of the necessities of life, but it can also discuss extremophiles and the conditions that they might need.

Natural Resources

Essential Question What are Earth's natural resources?

Professional Development

For more detailed information about the topics in this lesson, refer to the Content Refresher in the Unit Opener pages.

Opening Your Lesson

Begin the lesson by assessing students' prerequisite and prior knowledge.

Prerequisite Knowledge

- Humans depend on Earth's land, water, and atmosphere to live and for many different materials.

Accessing Prior Knowledge

KWL Invite students to make a Trifold FoldNote KWL chart about what they know about Earth's natural resources. Have students put what they Know in the first column, and what they Want to know in the second column. After they finish the lesson, they can complete the third column with what they Learned.

🌐 *Optional Online resources: KWL, Trifold support*

Customize Your Opening

- ☐ **Accessing Prior Knowledge,** above
- ☐ **Print Path** Engage Your Brain, SE p. 147
- ☐ **Print Path** Active Reading, SE p. 147
- ☐ **Digital Path** Lesson Opener

Key Topics/Learning Goals	Supporting Concepts
Natural Resources 1 Recognize a natural resource. 2 List examples of natural resources.	• A natural resource is any natural material that is used by people to survive and improve their lives. • Some natural resources are air, soil, fresh water, oil, minerals, forests, and wildlife.
Renewable and Nonrenewable Resources 1 Compare renewable resources and nonrenewable resources. 2 Explain how some resources can be considered both renewable and nonrenewable.	• A renewable resource can be replaced at the same rate at which it is used. A nonrenewable resource is replaced at a slower rate than the rate at which it is used. • Inexhaustible resources, like solar energy, are so plentiful that they cannot be used up. • Renewable resources can be considered nonrenewable if they are used up faster than they can be replaced.
Material Resources 1 Explain how material resources are used. 2 Recognize that material resources can be renewable or nonrenewable.	• Material resources are used to make objects or to make food or drink. • Material resources can come from Earth's atmosphere, crust, waters and oceans, and from organisms that live on Earth. They can be renewable or nonrenewable.
Energy Resources 1 Explain how energy resources are used. 2 Recognize that energy can be converted from one form into another. 3 Describe how the conversion between potential and kinetic energy provides energy that is useful to people.	• An energy resource is any natural resource that humans use to generate energy. Energy resources are used by converting the energy of the resource into a form of energy that is useful to people. • Energy is found in many different forms, but cannot be created or destroyed. • Much of the energy we get from natural resources comes from the conversion of potential energy into kinetic energy.

Options for Instruction

Two parallel paths provide coverage of the Essential Questions, with a strong **Inquiry** strand woven into each. Follow the **Print Path**, the **Digital Path**, or your customized combination of print, digital, and inquiry.

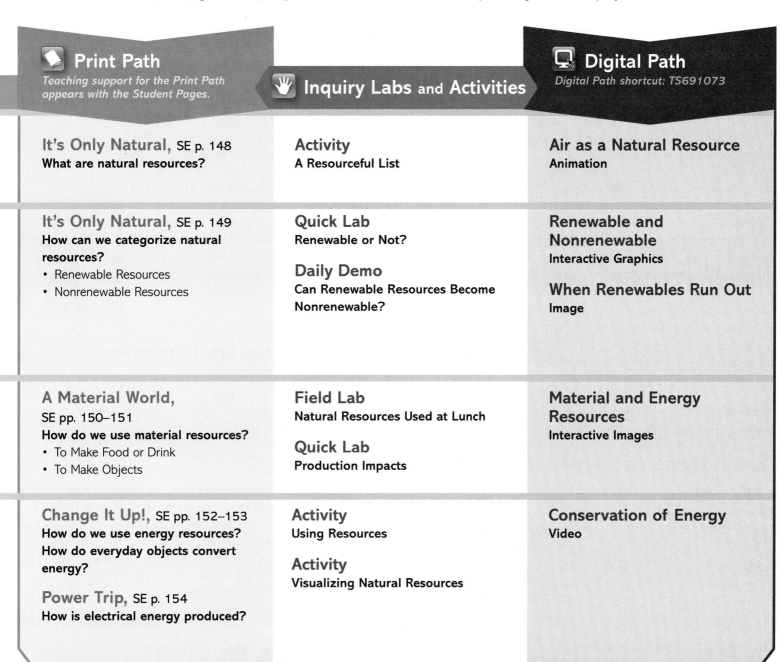

Print Path *Teaching support for the Print Path appears with the Student Pages.*	**Inquiry Labs and Activities**	**Digital Path** *Digital Path shortcut: TS691073*
It's Only Natural, SE p. 148 **What are natural resources?**	**Activity** A Resourceful List	**Air as a Natural Resource** Animation
It's Only Natural, SE p. 149 **How can we categorize natural resources?** • Renewable Resources • Nonrenewable Resources	**Quick Lab** Renewable or Not? **Daily Demo** Can Renewable Resources Become Nonrenewable?	**Renewable and Nonrenewable** Interactive Graphics **When Renewables Run Out** Image
A Material World, SE pp. 150–151 **How do we use material resources?** • To Make Food or Drink • To Make Objects	**Field Lab** Natural Resources Used at Lunch **Quick Lab** Production Impacts	**Material and Energy Resources** Interactive Images
Change It Up!, SE pp. 152–153 **How do we use energy resources?** **How do everyday objects convert energy?** **Power Trip,** SE p. 154 **How is electrical energy produced?**	**Activity** Using Resources **Activity** Visualizing Natural Resources	**Conservation of Energy** Video

Options for Assessment

See the Evaluate page for options, including Formative Assessment, Summative Assessment, and Unit Review.

Engage and Explore

Activities and Discussion

Activity *Using Resources*

Material Resources
Energy Resources

 individuals or pairs
10–15 min
DIRECTED inquiry

Three-Panel Flip Chart Invite students to make a Three-Panel Flip Chart FoldNote. Have them label the first panel Object, the second panel Food/Drink, and the third panel Energy. Explain that natural resources can be turned into objects, food, or drink, or can be used to generate energy. Have students list examples of natural resources that can be used for each of these purposes on the inside of each panel. Challenge students to identify resources that fit into all three categories. Sample answers: Objects: Trees can be used for lumber to build furniture or homes or to make paper or pencils. Minerals can be used to make objects such as aluminum cans and construction materials. Food/Drink: Some trees and plants are sources of food, such as nuts or maple syrup. Corn and oranges become cereal and juice; water is used for drinking. Energy: Trees can be burned for warmth. Oil can be made into gasoline to provide energy for cars.

🌐 *Online resource: Three Panel Flip Chart support*

Take It Home *Natural Resources at Home*

Natural Resources
Material Resources
Energy Resources

 adult-student pairs
15–30 min
GUIDED inquiry

Students work with an adult to list objects in their home and yard that are made using different natural resources. Some objects may be made from more than one natural resource.

🌐 *Optional Online resource: student worksheet*

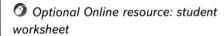

Activity *A Resourceful List*

Introducing Key Topics

 individuals, then whole class
ongoing
DIRECTED inquiry

Write Fast Have students divide a sheet of paper into two columns. Then, in 3 minutes or less, have them list all of the natural resources they can think of in the first column. Sample answer: plants, petroleum, fresh water, animals In the second column, have them list how these natural resources are used. Sample answers: clothing, fuel, plastics, drink, food Allow students to share their answers. List ideas on the board, and leave the list in place as a reference to students as they continue reading this lesson. Encourage students to add to the list during the lesson.

Probing Question *Renewable or Nonrenewable?*

Introducing Key Topics

 whole class
10 min
DIRECTED inquiry

Categorizing Ask students to look at the list of resources on the board from the previous activity before reading the lesson. Explain that renewable resources are those that can be replaced through natural processes at a rate that equals or exceeds the rate at which they are used. **Ask:** Identify whether each natural resource listed on the board is renewable or nonrenewable. If students are unsure, place a question mark beside the resource and revisit it at the end of the lesson.

Customize Your Labs

 See the Lab Manual for lab datasheets.

 Go Online for editable lab datasheets.

Levels of  **DIRECTED** inquiry   **GUIDED** inquiry   **INDEPENDENT** inquiry

introduces inquiry skills within a structured framework.   develops inquiry skills within a supportive environment.   deepens inquiry skills with student-driven questions or procedures.

Labs and Demos

Daily Demo *Can Renewable Resources Become Nonrenewable?*

Engage

Renewable and Nonrenewable Resources

 whole class
 10–15 min
 DIRECTED inquiry

PURPOSE **To model how a renewable resource can be used up**

MATERIALS

- bottle filled with water
- bucket
- 3 clear plastic containers of equal size: one with 1 hole in the bottom, one with 6 holes, one with 12 or more holes

1 Ask a student to hold the container with 1 hole over the bucket. Explain that water collected in the bottle represents rainfall. The water flowing out represents water used by people.

2 **Observing** Slowly pour the water into the container with 1 hole. **Ask:** What do you observe? The container fills with water even though some of the water is being used.

3 **Comparing** Repeat Step 2 using the container with 6 holes. **Ask:** How does the rate at which the container fills now compare to the rate earlier? It does not fill as quickly as the first did.

4 **Comparing** Repeat Step 3 using the container with 12 holes. **Ask:** How does the rate at which the container fills now compare to the rates earlier? The water is flowing out of the container as quickly as it is being poured in. Emphasize that although water is a renewable resource, it can be used more quickly than nature can renew it.

Variation Provide three piles of things such as erasers, pencils, or paper clips that the students pick up by row. Continue to replenish the items in pile 1, replenish the items slower in pile 2, and replenish the items in pile 3 so there isn't enough for all students.

Field Lab *Natural Resources Used at Lunch*

Material Resources

 small groups
   45 min
   DIRECTED/GUIDED inquiry

Students will analyze the trash they generated during their lunch period in order to determine what natural resources were consumed.

PURPOSE **To help students understand how their product consumption impacts the environment**

MATERIALS

- balance or scale
- calculator
- gloves
- lunch waste
- mask, disposable filter
- paper towels

Quick Lab *Production Impacts*

Material Resources

   small groups
   15 min
   DIRECTED inquiry

Students will research the origins of raw materials and the ways in which these materials are processed to create a finished product.

PURPOSE **To show how the production of items impacts Earth**

MATERIALS

- finished product
- raw material

Quick Lab *Renewable or Not?*

PURPOSE **To identify the origins of product raw materials**

See the Lab Manual or go Online for planning information.

Activities and Discussion

☐ **Activity** Using Resources
☐ **Take It Home** Natural Resources...
☐ **Activity** A Resourceful List
☐ **Probing Question** Renewable or Nonrenewable?

Labs and Demos

☐ **Daily Demo** Can Renewable Resources Become Nonrenewable?
☐ **Field Lab** Natural Resources Used...
☐ **Quick Lab** Production Impacts
☐ **Quick Lab** Renewable or Not?

Your Resources

_____
_____
_____
_____

Explain Science Concepts

	Print Path	Digital Path

Key Topics		
Natural Resources	☐ **It's Only Natural,** SE p. 148 • Active Reading, #5 • Visualize It!, #6 	☐ **Air as a Natural Resource** Use air to explore the idea of natural resources.
Renewable or Nonre-newable Resources	☐ **It's Only Natural,** SE p. 149 • Think Outside the Book, #7 • Compare, #8 	☐ **Renewable and Nonrenewable** Learn about resources and how renewable each one is. ☐ **When Renewables Run Out** Find out how resources can be used quickly to be renewed.
Material Resources	☐ **A Material World,** SE pp. 150–151 • Active Reading (Annotation strategy), #9 • Visualize It!, #10 • Visualize It!, #11 	☐ **Material and Energy Resources** Learn about resources involved in everyday objects.
Energy Resources	☐ **Change It Up!,** SE pp. 152–153 • Active Reading (Annotation strategy), #12 • List, #13 • Visualize It!, #14–16 ☐ **Power Trip,** SE p. 154 • Active Reading (Annotation strategy), #17 • Visualize It!, #18 	☐ **Conservation of Energy** Recognize how energy can be converted from one form to another, and how energy resources are used.

Differentiated Instruction

Basic *How Much Water?*

Synthesizing Key Topics

 whole class

🕐 10 min

Direct a student to place a plastic gallon water jug under a tap and time how long it takes to fill the jug with water. Next, ask the class to estimate how long it takes to brush their teeth. **Ask:** If you leave the water running while you brush, how much water do you use? Sample answer: 45 s to fill the jug and 2.5 min for teeth brushing; change 2.5 min to 150 s and divide by 45 = 3.3 gal of water To avoid wasting the water, use it to water plants, wash the board, or clean glassware and equipment. **For greater depth,** calculate how much water is used when showering.

Advanced *Calculating Gallons of Rain*

Synthesizing Key Topics

 individuals, pairs, whole class

🕐 varied

Provide students with this rainfall data:
• If it rains 1 in. over a 10 × 10 ft plot, the plot receives 62 gal.
• If it rains 1 in. over 1 acre, the acre receives 27,154 gal.
• If it rains 1 in. over 1 mi², the area receives 17,378,560 gal.
Have students use maps and weather reports to calculate how much rain fell in local areas during recent storms. **For greater depth,** have students calculate how much rain fell locally in 1 year and compare the total to the amount of water needed for all students in the class to brush their teeth twice each day for 1 year.

ELL *Resourceful Word Squares*

Synthesizing Key Topics

individuals or pairs

🕐 15 min

Word Square To help English language learners make the distinction between renewable and nonrenewable resources, instruct them to make word squares for each term. In the first box students write the term and a translation of the term in their native language. In the second box they write the textbook definition in English and in their own language. In the third box they draw images of examples of each term. In the fourth box, students write a sentence in English that uses the word.

TERM translation	symbol or picture
my meaning dictionary definition	sentence

🌐 *Optional Online resource: Word Square support*

Lesson Vocabulary

natural resource	renewable resource	nonrenewable resource
fossil fuel	material resource	energy resource

Previewing Vocabulary

 whole class

🕐 5 min

Word Parts Share the following to help students remember terms:
• **Natural resource** combines the words *natural*, meaning "from nature" and *resource*, which means "something that can be used."
• *Renew* means "to make new again."
• The prefix *non-* means "not."

Reinforcing Vocabulary

individuals

🕐 20 min

Word Triangles Direct students to make a word triangle for these terms: natural resource, renewable resource, nonrenewable resource, material resource, and energy resource. Students should write the term and its definition in the bottom layer, use the word in a sentence in the second layer, and a picture or symbol of the term in the top layer.

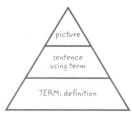

🌐 *Optional Online resource: Word Triangle support*

Customize Your Core Lesson

Core Instruction
☐ **Print Path** choices
☐ **Digital Path** choices

Vocabulary
☐ **Previewing Vocabulary** Word Parts
☐ **Reinforcing** Word Triangles

Differentiated Instruction
☐ **Basic** How Much Water?
☐ **Advanced** Calculating Gallons of Rain
☐ **ELL** Resourceful Word Squares

Your Resources

Extend Science Concepts

Reinforce and Review

Activity *Visualizing Natural Resources*

Synthesizing Key Topics   individuals or pairs 🕐 varied

Collage Ask students to use magazines from home and find images relating to natural resources. Allow students to use images to make a display. Displays should have descriptions of how the images relate to natural resources and whether they are renewable or nonrenewable. Invite students to share their finished work with the class.

Variation Students can also choose an object and research what natural resources are used to make it. For their display they can draw images of the natural resources or use images from the Internet.

🌐 *Optional Online resources: Writing for Displays: Labels, Captions, Summaries, Posters and Displays rubric*

Fold Note

Synthesizing Key Topics   individuals or pairs 🕐 15 min

Four-Corner Fold Help students make a Four-Corner Fold FoldNote to synthesize details learned in the lesson. At the top of each panel, students write renewable resource, nonrenewable resource, material resource, or energy resource. Then students list objects that fit each category. Encourage students to use examples not mentioned in the lesson.

🌐 *Online resource: Four-Corner Fold support*

Graphic Organizer

Synthesizing Key Topics   individuals or pairs 🕐 15–20 min

Cluster Diagram Have students make a cluster diagram using the terms: natural resources, renewable resources, nonrenewable resources, material resources, and energy resources. Ask students to include examples for each category.

Going Further

Earth Science Connection

Synthesizing Key Topics   individuals 🕐 10 min

Discussion Encourage students to examine the clothing they are wearing. Then ask them to list the natural resources that were likely used to make each article of clothing. Encourage them to consider resources used in the making of embellishments or closure devices (buttons, zippers, clasps) as well as the main materials in the articles. Sample answers: cotton; wool; oil; copper; iron; cattle Then have them discuss whether they think using a nonrenewable resource, such as oil or metals, to make clothing is a good idea. **Ask:** Is clothing the best use of a nonrenewable resource? Encourage them to share their ideas about the pros and cons of using each resource in the making of clothing.

Real World Connection

Synthesizing Key Topics   Individuals, pairs, whole class 🕐 10–15 min

Think, Pair, Share Ask individuals to think of ideas for how to protect or conserve a renewable resource that is threatened with overuse, such as fish or fresh water. Then have pairs of students talk about their ideas and decide which would be most effective for conserving a specific resource. Allow pairs to share their ideas with the class.

🌐 *Optional Online resource: Think, Pair, Share support*

Customize Your Closing

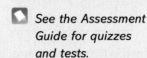 See the Assessment Guide for quizzes and tests.

🌐 Go Online to edit and create quizzes and tests.

Reinforce and Review

☐ **Activity** Visualizing Natural Resources

☐ **Fold Note** Four-Corner Fold

☐ **Graphic Organizer** Cluster Diagram

☐ **Print Path** Visual Summary, SE p. 156

☐ **Digital Path** Lesson Closer

Evaluate Student Mastery

Formative Assessment

See the teacher support below the Student Pages for additional Formative Assessment questions.

Ask: Identify two examples of resources that fit each category, and give an example of how they are used:

1 renewable, material resources Sample answers: crops—food; trees—paper; cotton and wool—clothing

2 renewable, energy resources Sample answers: the sun—solar power; water—drinking, cooking, and cleaning

3 nonrenewable, material resources Sample answers: granite—countertops; bauxite—aluminum beverage cans

4 nonrenewable, energy resources Sample answer: oil and coal—to move cars or run power plants

Reteach

Formative assessment may show that students need reinforcement for certain topics. The resources below are recommended for reteaching. If students were introduced to a topic through the Print Path, you can also use the Digital Path to reteach, or vice versa.
🎧 *Can be assigned to individual students*

Natural Resources
Activity A Resourceful List 🎧

Renewable and Nonrenewable Resources
Quick Lab Renewable or Not?

Material Resources
Field Lab Natural Resources Used at Lunch

Energy Resources
Fold Note Four-Corner Fold 🎧

Summative Assessment

Alternative Assessment
A Menu of Natural Resource Activities

🌐 *Online resources: student worksheet, optional rubrics*

Natural Resources

Choose Your Meal: *A Menu of Natural Resource Activities*
Show what you know about natural resources.

1. Work on your own, with a partner, or with a small group.
2. Choose one item from each section of the menu, with an optional dessert. Check your choices.
3. Have your teacher approve your plan.
4. Submit or present your results.

Appetizers

_____ **Resourceful Interview** Imagine you interview a scientist. You ask him to explain how renewable resources can become nonrenewable. Write the interview questions and answers.

_____ **Resourceful Flowchart** Make a flowchart that explains how natural resources are used to make objects, to make food or drink, or to generate energy.

Main Dish

_____ **Resourceful Report** Choose one resource. Make a podcast or news report that explains whether it is renewable or not, and how you know. Explain whether it is a material or energy resource, and what the resource is used for.

_____ **Resourceful Model** Choose one resource. Make a diagram or model that shows how a resource gets from the ground to a final product. Explain whether the resource is renewable or not, and whether it is a material or energy resource.

Side Dishes

_____ **Resourceful Poster** Make a poster that shows the different types of resources: renewable, nonrenewable, material, and energy resources. Include labels on your poster.

_____ **Resourceful Exhibit** Make a museum exhibit that shows the different types of resources: renewable, nonrenewable, material, and energy resources. Include descriptions for each item in your exhibit.

Desserts (optional)

_____ **Resourceful Acting** With several classmates, put on a skit that describes the relationship between items in your classroom and natural resources. Each student can play the role of one item, and explain where they started and how they ended up in the classroom.

Going Further
- ☐ Earth Science Connection
- ☐ Real World Connection
- ☐ **Print Path** Why It Matters, SE p. 155

Formative Assessment
- ☐ **Strategies** Throughout TE
- ☐ **Lesson Review** SE

Summative Assessment
- ☐ **Alternative Assessment** A Menu of Natural Resource Activities
- ☐ **Lesson Quiz**
- ☐ **Unit Tests A and B**
- ☐ **Unit Review** SE End-of-Unit

Your Resources

_____   _____

_____   _____

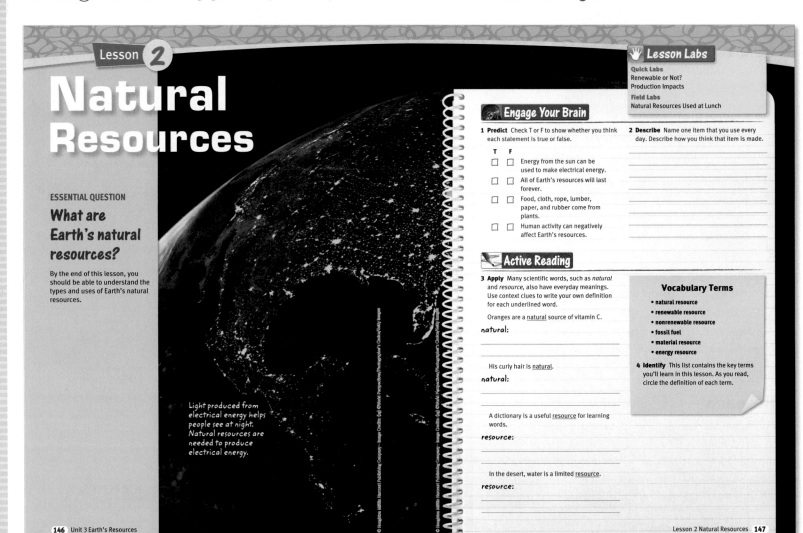

Answers

Answers for 1–3 should represent students' current thoughts, even if incorrect.

1. T; F; T; T

2. Answers will vary.

3. Sample answers: Natural: something that is produced by natural processes; something that is not changed by humans. Resource: something that contains useful information; something that can be used.

4. *See students' pages for annotations.*

Opening Your Lesson

Discuss student responses to items 1 and 2 to assess students' prerequisite knowledge and to estimate what they already know about natural resources.

Prerequisites Students should have some general knowledge of how people use resources to live and make products, such as plants and animals for clothing and food.

Interpreting Visuals

Tell students to examine the night scene of Earth from space. **Ask:** Can you identify this part of the world? The image shows part of the United States, Mexico, and Central America. **Ask:** What do you notice about the concentration of light in the different areas? Sample answer: The amount of light is different or more concentrated in certain areas.

Probing Question DIRECTED Inquiry

Comparing How might life be different for people living in parts of the world that do not have electricity? Sample answers: They probably do most tasks during the day. They might use fires to provide some light at night. They do not use electrical devices, such as television or computers, for entertainment. They rely on sources of energy other than electricity for warmth and cooking.

It's Only Natural

What are natural resources?

What do the water you drink, the paper you write on, the gasoline used in cars, and the air you breathe all have in common? They all come from Earth's natural resources. A **natural resource** is any natural material that is used by humans. Natural resources include air, soil, minerals, water, oil, plants, and animals.

Earth's natural resources provide everything needed for life. The atmosphere contains the air we breathe and produces rain as part of the water cycle. Rainfall from the atmosphere renews the water in oceans, rivers, lakes, streams, and underground. In turn, these water sources provide water for drinking, cleaning, and other uses. Earth's soil provides nutrients and a place for plants to grow. Plants provide food for some animals and humans. Animals provide food as well. Many of Earth's resources, such as oil and wind, provide energy for human use. The energy in these resources comes from the sun's energy. Earth's resources are also used to make products that make people's lives more convenient.

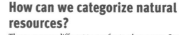
Active Reading

5 Identify List four examples of natural resources.

_____

_____

_____

Visualize It!

6 Illustrate Draw or label the missing natural resources.

Bauxite is a rock that is used to make aluminum.

A

How can we categorize natural resources?

There are many different types of natural resources. Some can be replaced more quickly than others. A natural resource may be categorized as a renewable resource or a nonrenewable resource.

Think Outside the Book Inquiry

7 Debate Research why water or soil can be a renewable or nonrenewable resource. Discuss your points with a classmate.

Renewable Resources

Some natural resources can be replaced in a relatively short time. A natural resource that can be replaced at the same rate at which it is consumed is a **renewable resource**. Solar energy, water, and air are all renewable resources. Some renewable resources are considered to be *inexhaustible resources* [in•ig•ZAW•stuh•buhl REE•sohrs•iz] because the resources can never be used up. Solar energy and wind energy, which is powered by the sun, are examples of inexhaustible resources. Other renewable resources are not inexhaustible. Trees and crops that are used for food must be replanted and regrown. Water must be managed so that it does not become scarce.

Nonrenewable Resources

A resource that forms much more slowly than it is consumed is a **nonrenewable resource**. Some natural resources, such as minerals, form very slowly. Iron ore and copper are important minerals. A **fossil fuel** is a nonrenewable resource formed from the buried remains of plants and animals that lived long ago. Coal, oil, and natural gas are examples of fossil fuels. Coal and oil take millions of years to form. Once these resources are used up, humans will have to find other resources to use instead. Some renewable resources, such as water and wood, may become nonrenewable if they are not used wisely.

8 Compare List some examples of renewable and nonrenewable resources.

Renewable resources	Nonrenewable resources

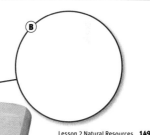
Natural fibers from cotton plants are processed to make fabric.

B

Answers

5. Students should list four of the following: air, soil, minerals, water, oil, plants, animals.

6. A: Students should describe and draw lettuce growing in a field; B: Students should describe and draw water in a natural setting.

7. Answers will vary. Students should understand that renewable resources, such as water, can become nonrenewable if they are used too quickly.

8. Sample answers: Renewable resources: cotton, water, wind, food, plants; Nonrenewable resources: oil, minerals, coal, natural gas

Learning Alert ⚠ MISCONCEPTION ⚠

Renewable Resources Find out what students think about renewable resources. **Ask:** Do renewable resources ever run out? If students answer that renewable resources never run out, they may hold the misconception that a renewable resource is unlimited. Explain that resources are replaced at a specific rate. When this rate exceeds or remains consistent with the rate at which a resource is used, the resource is considered renewable. However, if resources are used more quickly than they can be replaced, the supply of a renewable resource can be significantly reduced and could potentially become nonrenewable.

Learning Alert

Natural or Manufactured? Have students look at items in the classroom. Explain that some items thought to be made from renewable resources may actually be made from nonrenewable resources. For example, a wool jacket is made out of a renewable resource—wool, which is hair from sheep. By contrast, a fleece fabric jacket is made from polyester, which is made from petroleum—a nonrenewable resource. Fleece fabric can also be made from plastic bottles, another product made from petroleum. In this case, although fleece products are made from a nonrenewable resource, they conserve nonrenewable resources through reuse by keeping some plastic bottles out of landfills.

A Material World

How do we use material resources?

Look around your classroom. The walls, windows, desks, pencils, books, and even the clothing you see are made of material resources. Natural resources that are used to make objects, food, or drink are called **material resources**. Material resources can be either renewable or nonrenewable. The cotton used in T-shirts is an example of a renewable resource. The metal used in your desk is an example of a nonrenewable resource.

To Make Food or Drink

Active Reading

9 Identify As you read, underline examples of material resources.

Material resources come from Earth's atmosphere, crust, and waters. They also come from organisms that live on Earth. Think about what you eat and drink every day. All foods and beverages are made from material resources. Some foods come from plants, such as the wheat in bread or the corn in tortillas. These resources are renewable, since farmers can grow more. Other foods, such as milk, cheese, eggs, and meat, come from animals. Juices, sodas, and sport drinks contain water, which is a renewable resource.

Visualize It!

10 List List two types of food or drink that are made from the material resources in each picture.

To Make Objects

Any object you see is made from material resources. For example, cars are made of steel, plastic, rubber, glass, and leather. Steel comes from iron, which is mined from rock. Plastic is made from oil, which must be drilled from areas underground. Natural rubber comes from tropical trees. Glass is made from minerals found in sand. Leather comes from the hides of animals.

Iron, oil, and sand are nonrenewable. If these materials are used too quickly, they can run out. Rubber, leather, and wood are renewable resources. The plants and animals that produce these resources can be managed so that these resources do not run out.

Visualize It!

11 Label Write the name of each material resource that is used to make objects in this house.

A house is made from many material resources.

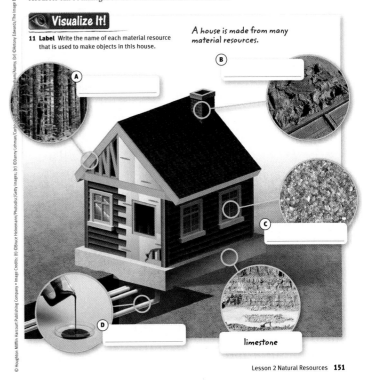

limestone

Answers

9. *See students' pages for annotations.*

10. Sample answers: A: corn flakes and tortillas; B: hamburger and steak; C: juice and soda

11. A: wood; B: clay; C: sand; D: oil

Building Reading Skills

Main Idea and Detail Notes Distinguishing between broad concepts and supporting details in note-taking is an important skill for students to learn. Tell students that headings can often help make the distinction. Invite students to make a concept map using the headings as a guide. A good strategy is to use nouns from these concepts in the ovals and to use the verb or verbs on the lines.

🌐 *Optional Online resources: Main Idea & Detail Notes, Concept Map support*

Formative Assessment

Ask: What material resources were used in producing your desk? Were they renewable or nonrenewable? Sample answer: Trees, a renewable resource, and metal ore, a nonrenewable resource, were used in making the desk. **Ask:** What material resources are used in your lunch? Are they renewable or nonrenewable? Sample answer: Plants, a renewable resource, produced the grain that was used to make bread. Animals, a renewable resource, were the meat in my sandwich. Cows, a renewable resource, produced the milk used to make my yogurt. Petroleum, a nonrenewable resource, was used to make the plastic bag that stored my sandwich.

Change It Up!

Active Reading

12 Identify As you read, underline the different forms of energy.

How do we use energy resources?

Many objects need energy in order to be useful. For example, a bus needs energy so that it can move people around. Natural resources used to generate energy are called **energy resources**.

Energy is often stored in objects or substances. Stored energy is called *potential energy*. Food and products made from oil have potential energy that is stored in their chemical bonds. For this energy to be useful, it must be converted to *kinetic energy*, which is the energy of movement. Body cells perform chemical reactions that convert the potential energy in food to the kinetic energy that moves your body. Gasoline engines break the bonds in gasoline to convert potential energy to the kinetic energy that moves a car.

An object can have potential energy because of its position. An object that is high above the ground has more potential energy than an object that is close to the ground. Potential energy is converted to kinetic energy when the object falls, such as when water falls over a dam to produce electricity in a power plant.

The gasoline being pumped into this car has potential energy in its chemical bonds.

This car's engine burns gasoline, converting the potential energy in the fuel into the kinetic energy of the moving car.

13 List Look at the examples in the table. Write down three more situations in which potential energy changes to kinetic energy.

When Does Potential Energy Change to Kinetic Energy?
when coal burns to produce electrical energy in a power plant
when your body digests food to give you energy to move

152 Unit 3 Earth's Resources

How do everyday objects convert energy?

Energy cannot be created or destroyed, and energy must be converted to be useful. Energy conversions happen around us every day. Think about the appliances in your home. An electric oven warms food by converting electrical energy to energy as heat. A television converts electrical energy to light energy and sound energy, which is a type of kinetic energy. A fan moves by converting electrical energy to kinetic energy. Your body converts the chemical energy in food to kinetic energy as well as thermal energy. When you talk on the phone, the sound energy from your voice is converted to electrical energy. The phone on the other end of the conversation changes the electrical energy back to sound.

Visualize It!

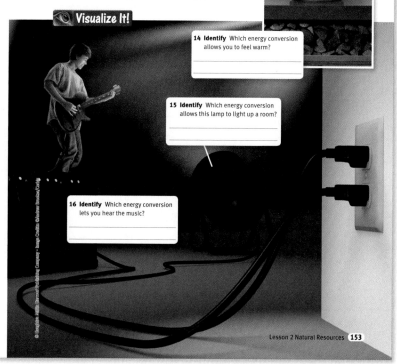

14 Identify Which energy conversion allows you to feel warm?

15 Identify Which energy conversion allows this lamp to light up a room?

16 Identify Which energy conversion lets you hear the music?

Lesson 2 Natural Resources 153

Answers

12. *See students' pages for annotations.*
13. Sample answers: when water falls over a dam to power a generator that produces electrical energy in a power plant; when natural gas causes water to boil in a pan on a stovetop; when a roller coaster speeds down a hill after stopping at the top of the hill
14. chemical energy to energy as heat
15. electrical energy to light energy
16. electrical energy to sound energy

Building Reading Skills

Context Clues: Comparison or Contrast Students often find concepts that relate to energy difficult to understand, particularly when they relate to energy changing forms. To help students make sense of *potential energy* and *kinetic energy*, show students how to use context clues that compare and contrast them. For example, use their contrasting definitions to introduce the terms. Then ask students to apply their definitions to each of the examples in the text.

⊙ *Optional Online resource: Context Clues: Comparison or Contrast support*

Probing Question DIRECTED (Inquiry)

Classifying Material resources and energy resources are not mutually exclusive. It is possible for an energy resource to serve as a material resource. **Ask:** What examples of resources can you give that can be classified as both material resources and energy resources? Sample answers: Trees can be harvested to provide paper or wood used in construction; they can also be harvested for wood that can be burned to provide warmth. Petroleum can be used to make plastic products; it can also be used to generate energy in homes and businesses.

Power Trip

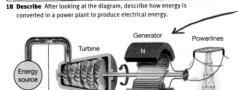**Active Reading**

17 Identify As you read, underline the resources that can provide energy for a power plant.

How is electrical energy produced?

Computers and appliances need electrical energy to work. Electrical energy is available from outlets, but how does this energy get to the outlets?

In most electrical power plants, an energy source converts potential energy to kinetic energy, causing wheels in a turbine to spin. The spinning wheels cause coils of wire to spin inside a magnet in a generator. The generator converts kinetic energy to electrical energy, which travels through wires to your school. Different energy resources can provide the energy for a power plant. Moving wind or water can turn wheels in a turbine. Burning coal or biofuels made from crop plants can warm water, producing steam that moves the turbine.

Fuel cells and batteries are other sources of electrical energy. A battery has chemicals inside that convert chemical energy to electrical energy. Fuel cells convert chemical energy from hydrogen to produce electrical energy.

Visualize It!

18 Describe After looking at the diagram, describe how energy is converted in a power plant to produce electrical energy.

Electrical energy is generated when coils of wire are turned inside a large magnet. This magnet might look different from bar magnets you have seen, but it still has north and south poles.

Turbine | Generator | Powerlines
Energy source
Steam

154 Unit 3 Earth's Resources

Why It Matters

Clean Machines

NEW FRONTIERS

Many car companies are introducing vehicles with hydrogen fuel cells. Hydrogen fuel cells use chemical reactions to produce electrical energy. These reactions produce no pollutants. If hydrogen fuel is made using renewable energy sources, these cars could truly be clean machines.

Fuel Cell

Hydrogen | Anode | Electrolyte | Cathode | Oxygen

H_2O

Excess Hydrogen (for reuse) H_2 | Electric Power | Water H_2O

Cell Technology
The fuel cell removes electrons from hydrogen atoms. Electron movement generates electrical energy. Hydrogen then combines with oxygen to form water. Water and excess hydrogen are the products of this reaction. No carbon dioxide or other pollutants are produced.

Small Packages
The hydrogen fuel cell in a car is about the size of a microwave oven.

Extend | Inquiry

19 Explain What kind of energy conversion happens in a hydrogen fuel cell?

20 Compare How is the process of energy conversion different between a fuel-cell vehicle and a gasoline vehicle?

21 Infer Hydrogen fuel must be produced by splitting water into hydrogen and oxygen. This process requires energy. Does it matter if nonrenewable energy is used to produce hydrogen fuel? Support your answer.

Lesson 2 Natural Resources 155

Answers

17. *See students' pages for annotations.*

18. An energy source converts potential energy to kinetic energy, which makes the turbine spin. As the turbine spins, it turns the coils of wire inside a magnet within a generator. The generator converts kinetic energy to electrical energy.

19. A hydrogen fuel cell converts chemical energy to electrical energy.

20. Fuel-cell vehicles don't burn fuel to convert chemical energy to electrical energy like gasoline vehicles do.

21. Sample answer: If nonrenewable energy were used to make hydrogen fuel, then pollutants would be produced when the fuel was made. This would make hydrogen fuel cell vehicles less "clean."

Using Annotations

Supporting Main Ideas To help students organize the different resources that provide energy for the power plant that they underlined, direct them to make a supporting main ideas graphic organizer. They can write "Energy Resources that Generate Electricity" as the main idea and list the resources used to generate electricity as the supporting details.

Context Clues: Examples Encourage a class discussion in which students use context clues in the text to help them define the different forms of energy.

⊙ *Optional Online resources: Supporting Main Ideas, Context Clues: Examples support*

Why It Matters

In addition to hydrogen fuel cells, scientists and engineers have been developing other alternative technologies to power vehicles. These include biodiesel (made from vegetable oils and animal fats), ethanol (an alcohol-based fuel made from starchy crops such as corn), propane (a liquefied petroleum gas that burns cleaner than fossil fuels used in typical internal combustion engines), and natural gas. Discuss whether each of these alternative fuels is renewable or nonrenewable. Then assign interested groups of students one of these five technologies, and ask them to research the advantages and disadvantages associated with each alternative fuel. Students can present their findings to the class.

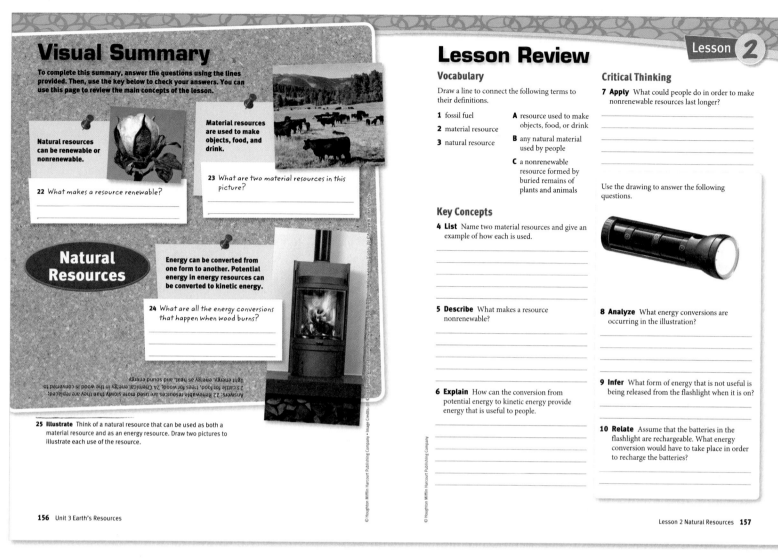

Visual Summary

To complete this summary, answer the questions using the lines provided. Then, use the key below to check your answers. You can use this page to review the main concepts of the lesson.

Natural resources can be renewable or nonrenewable.

22 What makes a resource renewable?

Material resources are used to make objects, food, and drink.

23 What are two material resources in this picture?

Natural Resources

Energy can be converted from one form to another. Potential energy in energy resources can be converted to kinetic energy.

24 What are all the energy conversions that happen when wood burns?

Answers: 22 Renewable resources are used more slowly than they are replaced; 23 cattle for food, trees for wood; 24 Chemical energy in the wood is converted to light energy, energy as heat, and sound energy

25 Illustrate Think of a natural resource that can be used as both a material resource and as an energy resource. Draw two pictures to illustrate each use of the resource.

Lesson Review

Lesson 2

Vocabulary

Draw a line to connect the following terms to their definitions.

1 fossil fuel

2 material resource

3 natural resource

A resource used to make objects, food, or drink

B any natural material used by people

C a nonrenewable resource formed by buried remains of plants and animals

Key Concepts

4 List Name two material resources and give an example of how each is used.

5 Describe What makes a resource nonrenewable?

6 Explain How can the conversion from potential energy to kinetic energy provide energy that is useful to people.

Critical Thinking

7 Apply What could people do in order to make nonrenewable resources last longer?

Use the drawing to answer the following questions.

8 Analyze What energy conversions are occurring in the illustration?

9 Infer What form of energy that is not useful is being released from the flashlight when it is on?

10 Relate Assume that the batteries in the flashlight are rechargeable. What energy conversion would have to take place in order to recharge the batteries?

Visual Summary Answers

22. Renewable resources are used more slowly than they are replaced.

23. cattle for food, trees for wood

24. Chemical energy in the wood is converted to light energy, energy as heat, and sound energy.

25. Students should show the same resource being used in two ways: one as a material resource and another as an energy resource. For example, wood can be used to build a tree house, and it can be burned for warmth.

Lesson Review Answers

1. C

2. A

3. B

4. Sample answers: Iron is used to make steel for cars; apple trees provide fruit for eating.

5. A resource is nonrenewable if it cannot be regrown or reformed as quickly as it is used.

6. Potential energy can move people or objects when it is converted to kinetic energy.

7. Sample answer: People could recycle and reuse nonrenewable resources, or rely more on renewable resources.

8. This illustration shows chemical energy from the battery being converted to electrical energy, which is being converted to light energy.

9. Energy as heat is also being released.

10. electrical energy to chemical energy

Nonrenewable Energy Resources

Essential Question How do we use nonrenewable energy resources?

 **Professional Development**

For more detailed information about the topics in this lesson, refer to the Content Refresher in the Unit Opener pages.

Opening Your Lesson

Begin the lesson by assessing students' prerequisite and prior knowledge.

Prerequisite Knowledge

- Natural resources are important to living things.
- Energy changes forms.

Accessing Prior Knowledge

Anticipation Guide Anticipation Guides help students review what they already know about a topic before reading the lesson. Invite students to make an Anticipation Guide about nonrenewable energy resources. Provide statements that are true and other statements that sound plausible but are untrue. Then have students write whether they agree or disagree before and after reading the lesson.

🌐 *Optional Online resource: Anticipation Guide support*

Customize Your Opening

☐ **Accessing Prior Knowledge,** above

☐ **Print Path** Engage Your Brain, SE p. 159

☐ **Print Path** Active Reading, SE p. 159

☐ **Digital Path** Lesson Opener

Key Topics/Learning Goals	Supporting Concepts
Energy Resources 1 Describe how humans use energy resources. 2 Distinguish between renewable and nonrenewable resources. 3 Identify the two main types of nonrenewable energy resources.	• Humans use energy resources to do work and to power technology. • Energy resources are natural resources that humans use to generate energy. Renewable energy resources are replaced at least at the same rate as they are used. Nonrenewable energy resources are used up at a faster rate than they can be replaced. • The two main types of nonrenewable energy resources are fossil fuels and nuclear fuel.
Fossil Fuels 1 Describe the characteristics of fossil fuels. 2 Explain how fossil fuels are used. 3 List the advantages and disadvantages of using fossil fuels.	• Fossil fuels, including natural gas, petroleum, and coal, form from the buried remains of plants and animals that lived long ago. • Fossil fuels are used for heating, cooking, and generating electricity. They are also used to make fuels to power vehicles and to make products such as plastics. • Fossil fuels are relatively easy to obtain and transport. The extraction and use of fossil fuels have an environmental impact.
Nuclear Energy 1 Explain how nuclear energy is generated. 2 Describe how nuclear energy is used to generate electricity. 3 List the advantages and disadvantages of using nuclear energy.	• Nuclear energy is energy released during atomic fission and fusion. • During atomic fission, the nuclei of radioactive elements, such as uranium, are split, releasing large amounts of energy. This energy is used to generate electricity. • Nuclear energy does not cause air pollution from burning. However, uranium ore must be mined. Also, nuclear power plants produce dangerous radioactive waste that must be safely stored for long periods of time.

Options for Instruction

Two parallel paths provide coverage of the Essential Questions, with a strong **Inquiry** strand woven into each.
Follow the **Print Path**, the **Digital Path**, or your customized combination of print, digital, and inquiry.

 **Print Path**
Teaching support for the Print Path appears with the Student Pages.

 Inquiry Labs and Activities

🖵 **Digital Path**
Digital Path shortcut: TS661724

Be Resourceful!, SE p. 160
What are the two main types of nonrenewable energy resources?
- Fossil Fuels
- Nuclear Fuel

🖵 **Virtual Lab**
How Can We Measure the Impact of Nonrenewable Energy?

Quick Lab
Modeling Nonrenewable Resources

Activity
Energy, Energy, Everywhere

Be Resourceful!
Video

Fossil Fuels and Nuclear Energy
Interactive Graphics

Be Resourceful!,
SE pp. 161–163
What are the three main types...?
How do fossil fuels form?

Power Trip, SE p. 164
How are fossil fuels used...?

The Pros and Cons, SE p. 167
How can we evaluate...?

Daily Demo
Acid Rain

Activity
Energy in Review

Petroleum and Natural Gas
Interactive Graphics

How We Use Fossil Fuels
Graphic Sequence

Power Trip
Interactive Graphics

Power Trip, SE p. 165
How is energy produced from nuclear fuels?

The Pros and Cons, SE p. 166
How can we evaluate nonrenewable energy resources?
- The Pros and Cons of Nuclear Fuel

Quick Lab
Modeling Nuclear Fission

Activity
Chain Reaction

How We Use Nuclear Energy
Interactive Graphics

Options for Assessment

See the Evaluate page for options, including Formative Assessment, Summative Assessment, and Unit Review.

Engage and Explore

Activities and Discussion

Activity *Energy, Energy, Everywhere*

Introducing Key Topics

 individuals or pairs
🕐 ongoing
GUIDED inquiry

Introduce the lesson by asking students to think about the first thing they do in the morning. Do they turn off an alarm? Turn on a light? Wash their faces with warm water? Point out that all these activities use energy resources. Direct students to list the ways they use energy resources throughout the day. Give them an example to help illustrate the amount of energy resources used for an everyday task. For example, tell students that you ate scrambled eggs this morning. Energy was used to package and transport the eggs from the farm to the store, and then to your home. Energy was used to refrigerate the eggs at the store and at your home, and then to cook the eggs. Energy was used to clean your plate afterwards in a dishwasher.

Give students time throughout the lesson to update their lists. At the end of the lesson, have them compare lists with a partner. Allow students to revise their lists. Use the opportunity to discuss the importance of energy resources in people's lives.

Probing Questions *Looking Ahead*

Energy Resources

 whole class
🕐 10 min
DIRECTED inquiry

Applying How would your life change if nonrenewable energy resources ran out? Sample answers: I could not do many activities that require nonrenewable energy resources, such as flying in a plane to see my grandparents or watching television. How do you think future generations will meet their demands for energy? Sample answer: They will probably rely more on renewable resources to meet their energy needs. They may also use less energy than we currently do.

Activity *Chain Reaction*

Engage

Nuclear Energy

 small groups
🕐 15 min
GUIDED inquiry

Model Place students in small groups. Give each group a set of dominoes. Direct students to set up the dominoes so that they will all fall once the first domino is knocked over. Relate the activity to the chain reaction that occurs during nuclear fission. Challenge students to come up with a way to control the reaction. For example, students can leave a gap among the dominoes so that the "reaction" stops.

Discussion *Is It Safe?*

Nuclear Energy

 whole class
🕐 20 min
GUIDED inquiry

Class Debate Tell students to imagine that a nuclear power plant is proposed for their area. **Ask:** What are some things that should be considered before the plant is built? Sample answers: Will the proposed plant be close to homes? How will radioactive waste be handled? Are there alternative energy sources available? Have the class take sides and debate the safety of the power plant. Encourage them to use scientific facts to back up their opinions.

 Optional Online rubric: Class Discussion

Customize Your Labs

 See the Lab Manual for lab datasheets.

Go Online for editable lab datasheets.

Levels of **Inquiry**   **DIRECTED** inquiry   **GUIDED** inquiry   **INDEPENDENT** inquiry

introduces inquiry skills   develops inquiry skills   deepens inquiry skills
within a structured   within a supportive   with student-driven
framework.   environment.   questions or procedures.

Labs and Demos

Daily Demo *Acid Rain*

Engage

Fossil Fuels

 whole class
 10 min
 DIRECTED inquiry

PURPOSE To show that acid rain from burning fossil fuels can harm buildings

MATERIALS

- 2 pieces of chalk
- jar of vinegar with lid
- jar of water with lid

1 Hold up a piece of chalk. Explain that many buildings and structures are made of limestone, a rock with a similar composition to chalk. Then hold up the water and vinegar. Tell students that the water represents normal rainfall. The vinegar represents acidic rainfall.

2 Drop a piece of chalk in each jar and put on the lids. Have students gather round to observe the jars for five minutes.

3 **Observing Ask:** What happened to the chalk and the liquid in each jar? Sample answer: The chalk in the water did not change. The water did not change. The chalk in the vinegar began to dissolve. The vinegar bubbled.

4 **Applying Ask:** What might happen if acid rain fell on a building that was made of limestone? Sample answer: The acid rain would damage the building.

Quick Lab *Modeling Nuclear Fission*

PURPOSE To model how energy is released in nuclear fission

See Lab Manual or go Online for planning information.

Quick Lab *Modeling Nonrenewable Resources*

Energy Resources

 pairs
 15 min
 GUIDED inquiry

Students will sort buttons that represent the energy consumption in the United States that is renewable and nonrenewable.

PURPOSE To show that nonrenewable resources are finite

MATERIALS

- bag, paper lunch
- buttons, 7 one color and 93 of another color

Virtual Lab *How Can We Measure the Impact of Nonrenewable Energy?*

Energy Resources

 flexible
45 min
GUIDED inquiry

Students will determine the amount of carbon dioxide they produce each year.

PURPOSE To investigate the impact of using fossil fuels for everyday activities

Activities and Discussion

☐ **Activity** Energy, Energy, Everywhere
☐ **Probing Questions** Looking Ahead
☐ **Activity** Chain Reaction
☐ **Discussion** Is It Safe?

Labs and Demos

☐ **Daily Demo** Acid Rain
☐ **Quick Lab** Modeling Nuclear Fission
☐ **Quick Lab** Modeling Nonrenewable Resources
☐ **Virtual Lab** How Can We Measure...?

Your Resources

_____
_____
_____
_____

Explain Science Concepts

	💎 Print Path	🖥 Digital Path
Key Topics		
Energy Resources	☐ **Be Resourceful!,** SE p. 160 • Do the Math, #5 • Compare, #6 🌐 *Optional Online Resource: Venn Diagram support* 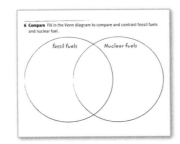	☐ **Be Resourceful!** Compare and contrast renewable and nonrenewable energy resources. ☐ **Fossil Fuels and Nuclear Energy** Identify fossil fuels and nuclear energy. 
Fossil Fuels	☐ **Be Resourceful!,** SE pp. 161–163 • Active Reading (Annotation strategy), #7 • Think Outside the Book, #8 • Active Reading (Annotation strategy), #9 • Visualize It!, #10 ☐ **Power Trip,** SE pp. 164–165 • Active Reading, #11 • Visualize It!, #12 ☐ **The Pros and Cons,** SE p. 167 • Evaluate, #15	☐ **Petroleum and Natural Gas** Explain how petroleum and natural gas form. ☐ **How We Use Fossil Fuels** Explain how coal forms. ☐ **Power Trip** Describe uses of fossil fuels. Identify the advantages and disadvantages of fossil fuels.
Nuclear Energy	☐ **Power Trip,** SE p. 165 • Visualize It!, #12 ☐ **The Pros and Cons,** SE pp. 166–167 • Active Reading (Annotation strategy), #13 • Visualize It!, #14 • Evaluate, #15	☐ **How We Use Nuclear Energy** Explain how nuclear energy can be generated, how it is used to produce electricity, and identify the advantages and disadvantages of nuclear energy. 

Basic *What Happened First?*

Fossil Fuels

👥 individuals or pairs
🕐 15 min

Make copies of the diagram that shows the four stages in the formation of petroleum and natural gas. Cut up each diagram into four separate stages. Mix up the stages. Distribute the stages to students. Ask them to sequence the stages in proper order and glue them to a separate piece of paper. Students can then add descriptions and labels to the sequence. For additional reinforcement, repeat the activity with the diagram of the formation of coal.

Advanced *Comparing Energy Sources*

Energy Resources

👥 pairs or small groups
🕐 varied

Graphing Ask students to choose an area of the world other than the United States and research the energy resources used by that area. Suggest that they use computer graphics applications to compile their data into circle graphs. The graphs should show the percentage of each energy resource used by their area. Students should then compare their area's energy resources to those used in the United States. Ask them to look for trends in the data and to infer reasons for those trends. For example, factors such as wind speed, proximity to large bodies of water, and high rates of tectonic activity often determine the type of energy resource used most widely in an area. Social, economic, and political factors also play important roles.

 Optional Online resource: Circle Graph support

ELL *Picture Dictionary*

Energy Resources

👥 individuals or pairs
🕐 15–20 min

Booklet Encourage students to make picture dictionaries of important terms in the lesson using a Booklet FoldNote. Brainstorm a list of important words with the students. Then, encourage students to use the illustrations in the book to define or describe the terms. Students should write each term on a separate page of the booklet. More advanced students can add labels and captions to their picture dictionaries.

 Online resource: Booklet support

energy resource	fossil fuel
nuclear energy	fission

Previewing Vocabulary

👥 whole class, individuals
🕐 ongoing

Word Splash Use a Word Splash to help students anticipate the meanings of key vocabulary terms and other important terms. Write the vocabulary term *energy resource* in the center of the board. Write the remaining vocabulary terms around the central term. Ask students to write three sentences that predict how each of the surrounding terms relates to the central term. After students have read the text, have them revise their predictions, if necessary.

 Optional Online resource: Word Splash support

Reinforcing Vocabulary

👥 individuals
🕐 15 min

Sort Cards Have students write the vocabulary terms and other important terms on index cards. Ask them to sort some or all of the cards into categories based on relationships among the terms. Afterwards, ask students to describe the criteria they used to classify the cards. For example, students may classify the cards according to the type of nonrenewable energy resource.

 Optional Online resource: Sort Cards support

Customize Your Core Lesson

Core Instruction
☐ **Print Path** choices
☐ **Digital Path** choices

Vocabulary
☐ **Previewing Vocabulary** Word Splash
☐ **Reinforcing Vocabulary** Sort Cards

Your Resources

Differentiated Instruction
☐ Basic What Happened First?
☐ Advanced Comparing Energy Sources
☐ ELL Picture Dictionary

_____

_____

Extend Science Concepts

Reinforce and Review

Activity *Energy in Review*

Synthesizing Key Topics whole class
🕐 15 min

Write Fast Help students review the material by following these steps:

1 Pose questions that require quick student written responses. Place a timer on your desk. Ask a question aloud, and then set the timer for approximately one minute, depending on the students in your class. Repeat the activity with brief pauses between each question.

2 Examples of questions for students include: What is the definition of an energy resource? What are the characteristics of a nonrenewable resource? What are some examples of nonrenewable energy resources? What are some disadvantages associated with using nonrenewable energy resources?

3 Afterwards, review the answers as a class. Identify which concepts, if any, need further reinforcement for students.

Graphic Organizer

Fossil Fuels individuals
 15 min

Process Chart Have each student draw a box. Inside the box, students should write the first step in the process of coal formation. Direct them to draw a second box below the first box with an arrow between the boxes. Students should write the next step in the process of coal formation in the second box. Tell them to continue adding boxes in a vertical row until each step of the process is written within a box. Students can make a second process chart for the formation of natural gas and petroleum. Encourage students to use their graphic organizers as study aids.

```
┌─────────┐
│ step 1  │
└─────────┘
     │
     ▼
┌─────────┐
│ step 2  │
└─────────┘
     │
     ▼
┌─────────┐
│ step 3  │
└─────────┘
```

Going Further

Health Connection

Fossil Fuels individuals, whole class
🕐 varied

Determine Air Quality Remind students that burning fossil fuels can cause smog and other types of air pollution. Explain that data about air quality can be found each day in a chart called an Air Quality Index (AQI). Have students look in local newspapers or on Internet weather sites for the AQI for their area. As a class, compare data the following day. Use the data to discuss the potential impact of air pollution on human health. Then help students brainstorm how they and their families can reduce air pollution.

Physical Science Connection

Nuclear Energy pairs
🕐 10–15 min

Model Nuclear Fusion Remind students that in addition to fission, nuclear energy is released during the process of fusion. Fusion takes place in the cores of stars. It happens when the nuclei of two lighter elements fuse together to form the nucleus of a heavier element. In the process, a great deal of energy is released. Have students use foam balls of different sizes to model nuclear fusion. Although the process of fusion would provide a large amount of energy, the technology for fusion power does not exist yet.

Customize Your Closing

🗨 *See the Assessment Guide for quizzes and tests.*

⏱ *Go Online to edit and create quizzes and tests.*

Reinforce and Review

☐ **Activity** Energy in Review

☐ **Graphic Organizer** Process Chart

☐ **Print Path** Visual Summary, SE p. 168

☐ **Digital Path** Lesson Closer

Evaluate Student Mastery

Formative Assessment

See the teacher support below the Student Pages for additional Formative Assessment questions.

Ask: A friend says that nonrenewable energy resources are no longer being formed by natural processes. Is this true? Explain. No, it is not true. The formation of nonrenewable energy resources like fossil fuels is an ongoing process, which takes millions of years. **Ask:** What do you think is the most important fossil fuel? Explain. Sample answer: Coal is the most important because the United States gets at least half of its electricity from burning coal. **Ask:** What is your greatest concern about the use of nonrenewable energy resources? Sample answers: running out of these resources before they are replaced; pollution **Ask:** How can we reduce pollution from fossil fuels? Sample answer: Use public transportation when possible.

Reteach

Formative assessment may show that students need reinforcement for certain topics. The resources below are recommended for reteaching. If students were introduced to a topic through the Print Path, you can also use the Digital Path to reteach, and vice versa.
🎧 *Can be assigned to individual students*

Energy Resources
Activity Energy, Energy, Everywhere 🎧

Fossil Fuels
Virtual Lab How Can We Measure the Impact of Nonrenewable Energy? 🎧

Nuclear Energy
Quick Lab Modeling Nuclear Fission

Summative Assessment

Alternative Assessment
Effects of Using Nonrenewable Energy

🔄 *Online resources: student worksheet, optional rubrics*

Nonrenewable Energy Resources

Mix and Match: *Effects of Using Nonrenewable Energy*
Mix and match ideas to show what you've learned about the effects of using nonrenewable energy resources.

1. Work on your own, with a partner, or with a small group.
2. Choose two information sources from Column A, one topic from Column B, and three options from Column C. You may add your own idea for an information source in Column A. You may also add your own idea of a way to communicate your analysis in Column C. Check your choices in all three columns.
3. Have your teacher approve your plan.
4. Submit or present your results.

A. Choose Two Information Sources	B. Choose One Thing to Analyze	C. Choose Three Ways to Communicate Analysis
___ government websites (such as the Department of Energy) that describe nonrenewable energy resources	___ effect of mines on habitats and water quality	___ diagram, chart, or map
___ photographs of mines, oil wells, and natural gas wells	___ effects of burning fossil fuels on air quality	___ model, such as a drawing or a diorama
___ diagrams of mines, wells, and power plants	___ potential effects of radiation leaks in nuclear power plants	___ booklet, such as a regulations guide
___ video that shows air, water, or land pollution caused by a nonrenewable energy resource	___ issues regarding storage of nuclear wastes	___ mathematical depictions, such as graphs or statistics
___ print articles that discuss the effects of using nonrenewable resources	___ regulations that reduce the potential for negative impacts on the environment	___ newspaper article or newscast
___ an Internet source about mining and drilling regulations		___ skit with supporting details
		___ multimedia presentation
_____		_____
_____		_____

Going Further
☐ Health Connection
☐ Physical Science Connection

Formative Assessment
☐ **Strategies** Throughout TE
☐ **Lesson Review** SE

Summative Assessment
☐ **Alternative Assessment** Effects of Using Nonrenewable Energy
☐ **Lesson Quiz**
☐ **Unit Tests**
☐ **Unit Review** SE End-of-Unit

Your Resources

_____   _____

_____   _____

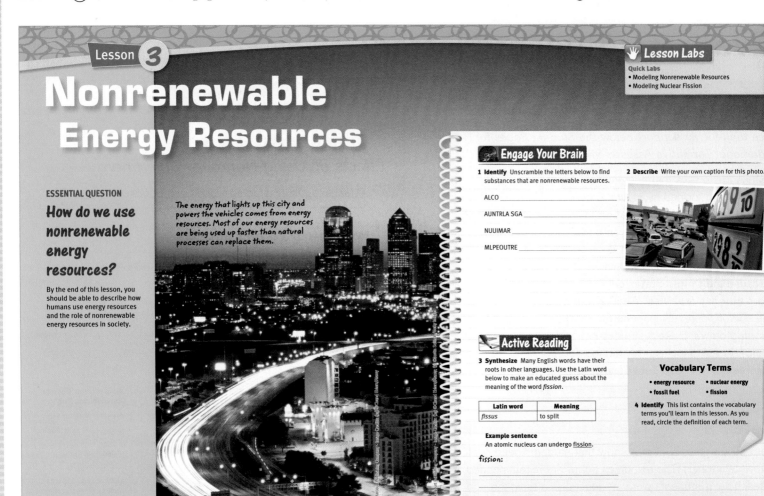

Lesson **3**

Nonrenewable
Energy Resources

Lesson Labs

ESSENTIAL QUESTION

How do we use nonrenewable energy resources?

By the end of this lesson, you should be able to describe how humans use energy resources and the role of nonrenewable energy resources in society.

The energy that lights up this city and powers the vehicles comes from energy resources. Most of our energy resources are being used up faster than natural processes can replace them.

Engage Your Brain

1 Identify Unscramble the letters below to find substances that are nonrenewable resources.

ALCO _____

AUNTRLA SGA _____

NUUIMAR _____

MLPEOUTRE _____

2 Describe Write your own caption for this photo.

_____

_____

_____

Active Reading

3 Synthesize Many English words have their roots in other languages. Use the Latin word below to make an educated guess about the meaning of the word *fission*.

Latin word	Meaning
fissus	to split

Example sentence
An atomic nucleus can undergo <u>fission</u>.

fission: _____

_____

_____

Vocabulary Terms

• energy resource   • nuclear energy
• fossil fuel   • fission

4 Identify This list contains the vocabulary terms you'll learn in this lesson. As you read, circle the definition of each term.

Answers

Answers for 1–3 should represent students' current thoughts, even if incorrect.

1. coal

   natural gas

   uranium

   petroleum

2. Sample answer: Some places are experiencing shortages of gasoline, a nonrenewable energy resource.

3. Sample answer: to split atomic nuclei

4. *See students' pages for annotations.*

Opening Your Lesson

Discuss student responses to item 2 to assess students' prerequisite knowledge and to estimate what they already know about the availability of natural resources.

Prerequisites Students may already know that Earth has limited resources, and that these resources provide people with energy and a wide variety of products. They may also realize that the use of certain resources can negatively impact the environment, resulting in habitat loss and the pollution of air, water, and land.

Learning Alert

Prefixes Point to the title of the lesson and explain that the prefix *non-* means "not." Ask students to infer the meaning of *nonrenewable*. They should realize that a nonrenewable energy resource is not renewable. Have students brainstorm other words that begin with *non-*, such as *nonfiction*, *nonbinding*, and *nonstop*.

⊙ *Optional Online resource: Prefixes support*

Be Resourceful!

What are the two main types of nonrenewable energy resources?

An **energy resource** is a natural resource that humans use to generate energy and can be renewable or nonrenewable. *Renewable resources* are replaced by natural processes at least as quickly as they are used. *Nonrenewable resources* are used up faster than they can be replaced. Most of the energy used in the United States comes from nonrenewable resources.

Fossil Fuels

A **fossil fuel** is a nonrenewable energy resource that forms from the remains of organisms that lived long ago. Fossil fuels release energy when they are burned. This energy can be converted to electricity or used to power engines. Fossil fuels are the most commonly used energy resource because they are relatively inexpensive to locate and process.

Nuclear Fuel

The energy released when the nuclei of atoms are split or combined is called **nuclear energy**. This energy can be obtained by two kinds of nuclear reactions—fusion and fission. Today's nuclear power plants use fission, because the technology for fusion power plants does not currently exist. The most common nuclear fuel is uranium. Uranium is obtained by mining and processing uranium ore, which is a nonrenewable resource.

6 Compare Fill in the Venn diagram to compare and contrast fossil fuels and nuclear fuel.

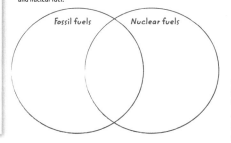

Fossil fuels | Nuclear fuels

Do the Math

You Try It

Nonrenewable Energy Resources Consumed in the U.S. in 2009

[pie chart]
- ■ Fossil Fuels 90.37%
- ■ Nuclear Fuel 9.63%

5 Calculate In 2009, 86.8 quadrillion BTUs of the energy used in the United States was produced from nonrenewable energy resources. Using the graph above, calculate how much of this energy was produced from nuclear fuel.

What are the three main types of fossil fuels?

All living things contain the element carbon. Fossil fuels form from the remains of living things, so they also contain carbon. Most of this carbon is in the form of hydrocarbons, which are compounds made of hydrogen and carbon. Fossil fuels can be liquids, gases, or solids. Fossil fuels include petroleum, natural gas, and coal.

Active Reading 7 Identify As you read, underline the state of matter for each fossil fuel.

Petroleum

Petroleum, or *crude oil*, is a liquid mixture of complex hydrocarbon compounds. Crude oil is extracted from the ground by drilling then processed for use. This process, called *refining*, separates the crude oil into different products such as gasoline, kerosene, and diesel fuel. More than 35 percent of the world's energy comes from crude oil products. Crude oil is also used to make products such as ink, bubble gum, and plastics.

This crude oil will be refined into gasoline, diesel fuel, heating oil, kerosene, and other products.

Natural Gas

Natural gas is a mixture of gaseous hydrocarbons. Most natural gas is used for heating and cooking, but some is used to generate electricity. Also, some vehicles use natural gas as fuel.

Methane is the main component of natural gas. Butane and propane can also be separated from natural gas. Butane and propane are used as fuel for camp stoves and outdoor grills. Some rural homes also use propane as a heating fuel.

Natural gas is a popular fuel for cooking because it is inexpensive.

Coal

The fossil fuel most widely used for generating electrical power is a solid called coal. Coal was once used to heat homes and for transportation. In fact, many trains in the 1800s and early 1900s were pulled by coal-burning steam locomotives. Now, most people use gasoline for transportation fuel. But more than half of our nation's electricity comes from coal-burning power plants.

Coal is a fossil fuel often used to generate electricity.

Answers

5. 86.8 × 0.0963 = 8.36 quadrillion BTUs

6. Students should note that both fuels are nonrenewable. Fossil fuels come from the remains of ancient organisms. Nuclear fuel includes uranium, an ore used during the process of fission.

7. *See students' pages for annotations.*

Learning Alert ⚠ MISCONCEPTION ⚠

Energy on Earth Many students think that all energy on Earth comes from the sun. Most energy sources can be traced directly or indirectly to the sun, including solar energy, wind energy, moving water, biomass, and fossil fuels. However, energy from nuclear fission and energy within Earth, or geothermal energy, do not come from the sun. Assess students' understanding of this concept by asking them to identify sources of energy on Earth. If students name only the sun, have a volunteer read aloud the paragraph about nuclear fuel. Point out that the energy released during fission is not related to the sun.

Do the Math

BTUs Explain that a BTU is a measure of heat energy. It stands for British Thermal Unit. Specifically, a BTU is the amount of heat needed to increase the temperature of one pound of water by 1°F. Tell students to imagine that they poured 16 ounces of water into a pot and placed the pot on a stove. The initial temperature of the water was 70°F. **Ask:** How many BTUs would it take to increase the temperature of the water to 75°F? 5 BTUs

How do fossil fuels form?

How might a sunny day 200 million years ago relate to your life today? If you traveled to school by bus or car, you likely used energy from sunlight that warmed Earth that long ago.

Fossil fuels form over millions of years from the buried remains of ancient organisms. Fossil fuels differ in the kinds of organisms from which they form and in how they form. This process is continuing, too. The fossil fuels forming today will be available for use in a few million years!

Petroleum and Natural Gas Form from Marine Organisms

Petroleum and natural gas form mainly from the remains of microscopic sea organisms. When these organisms die, their remains sink and settle on the ocean floor. There, the dead organisms are gradually buried by sediment. The sediment is compacted by more layers of dead organisms and sediment. Over time the sediment layers become layers of rock.

Over millions of years, heat and pressure turn the remains of the organisms into petroleum and natural gas. The petroleum and natural gas, along with groundwater, flow into pores in the rock. A rock with pores is a *permeable rock*. Permeable rocks become reservoirs where the petroleum and natural gas are trapped and concentrated over time. Humans can extract the fuels from these reservoirs.

Think Outside the Book Inquiry

8 Apply With a classmate, discuss how the process of petroleum formation might affect oil availability in the future.

Petroleum and Natural Gas Formation

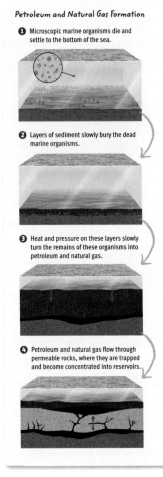

❶ Microscopic marine organisms die and settle to the bottom of the sea.

❷ Layers of sediment slowly bury the dead marine organisms.

❸ Heat and pressure on these layers slowly turn the remains of these organisms into petroleum and natural gas.

❹ Petroleum and natural gas flow through permeable rocks, where they are trapped and become concentrated into reservoirs.

Coal Formation

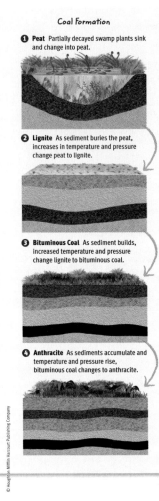

❶ **Peat** Partially decayed swamp plants sink and change into peat.

❷ **Lignite** As sediment buries the peat, increases in temperature and pressure change peat to lignite.

❸ **Bituminous Coal** As sediment builds, increased temperature and pressure change lignite to bituminous coal.

❹ **Anthracite** As sediments accumulate and temperature and pressure rise, bituminous coal changes to anthracite.

Coal Forms from Plant Remains

Active Reading **9 Identify** As you read, underline the factors that convert the buried plants into coal.

Coal is formed over millions of years from the remains of swamp plants. When the plants die, they sink to the swamp floor. Low oxygen levels in the water keep many plants from decaying and allow the process of coal formation to begin. Today's swamp plants may eventually turn into coal millions of years from now.

The first step of coal formation is plant matter changing into peat. Peat is made mostly of plant material and water. Peat is not coal. In some parts of the world, peat is dried and burned for warmth or used as fuel. Peat that is buried by layers of sediment can turn into coal after millions of years.

Over time, pressure and high temperature force water and gases out of the peat. The peat gradually becomes harder, and its carbon content increases. The amount of heat and pressure determines the type of coal that forms. Lignite forms first, followed by bituminous coal and, finally, anthracite. Anthracite is highly valued because it has the highest carbon content and gives off the most energy as heat when burned.

Today, all three types of coal are mined around the world. When burned, coal releases energy as heat and pollutes the air. The greater the carbon content of the coal, the fewer pollutants are released and the cleaner the coal burns.

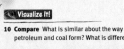

Visualize It!

10 Compare What is similar about the way petroleum and coal form? What is different?

_____
_____
_____
_____
_____

Answers

8. Students should understand that it takes millions of years to form petroleum, so at present rates of usage, oil availability will decrease in the future.

9. *See students' pages for annotations.*

10. Physical and chemical changes to the remains of ancient organisms over millions of years form fossil fuels. Petroleum forms from marine organisms, and coal forms from plant remains.

Building Reading Skills

Text Structure: Sequence Note that a sequence of events shows the order in which things occur. Words such as *first, followed by*, and *then* are clues that indicate the order of events. Captions, labels, arrows, and other elements in diagrams can offer additional clues. Have students work in pairs to make a sequence diagram summarizing the events in the formation of the fossil fuel of their choice.

🔘 *Optional Online resources: Text Structure: Sequence, Sequence Diagram support*

Formative Assessment

Ask: If fossil fuels are still forming, why are they considered a nonrenewable resource? They are being used up faster than they can form. **Ask:** What role do permeable rocks have in the formation of petroleum and natural gas? Permeable rocks have pores. Petroleum and natural gas flow into these pores so that the permeable rocks then become reservoirs that hold these fossil fuels. **Ask:** Which type of coal would you expect to cost the most? Explain. Anthracite probably costs the most because it has the highest carbon content so it gives off the most heat when burned and burns cleaner than other types of coal.

Power Trip

How are fossil fuels used as energy sources?

Active Reading

11 Identify As you read, underline the uses of fossil fuels.

In the United States, petroleum fuels are mainly used for transportation and heating. Airplanes, trains, boats, and cars all use petroleum for energy. Some people also use petroleum as a heating fuel. There are some oil-fired power plants in the United States, but most are found in other parts of the world.

Natural gas can be used as transportation fuel but is mainly used for heating and cooking. The use of natural gas as a source of electrical power is increasing. The U.S. Department of Energy projects that most power plants in the near future will use natural gas. Today, coal is mainly used in the U.S. to generate electricity, which we use for lighting and to power appliances and technology.

Visualize It!

Burning coal heats water to produce steam. The steam turns the turbines to generate electricity. Scrubbers and filters in the smokestack help reduce air pollution.

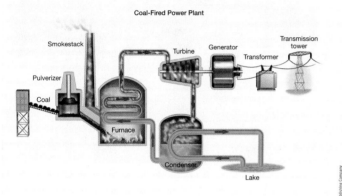

Coal-Fired Power Plant

How is energy produced from nuclear fuels?

During **fission**, the nuclei of radioactive atoms are split into two or more fragments. A small particle called a neutron hits and splits an atom. This process releases large amounts of energy as heat and radiation. Fission also releases more neutrons that bombard other atoms. The process repeats as a chain reaction. Fission takes place inside a reactor core. Fuel rods containing uranium, shown in green below, provide the material for the chain reaction. Control rods that absorb neutrons are used to regulate the chain reaction. The energy is released, which is used to generate electrical power. A closed reactor system contains the radioactivity. Nuclear wastes are contained separately for disposal.

During nuclear reactions, energy in the form of heat is released, which turns water into steam. Steam turns the turbines to generate electricity.

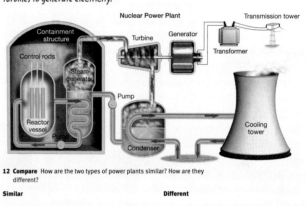

Nuclear Power Plant

12 Compare How are the two types of power plants similar? How are they different?

Similar	Different
_____	_____
_____	_____
_____	_____
_____	_____

Answers

11. *See students' pages for annotations.*

12. Both power plants use steam generated by nonrenewable resources to turn turbines that drive generators to make electricity. Coal-fired power plants use coal as fuel, and nuclear power plants use uranium as fuel.

Learning Alert

Conservation of Energy Remind students that energy cannot be created or destroyed, but it can change form. **Ask:** What energy conversions take place in a coal-fired power plant? Sample answer: Energy from heat produced by burning the coal is used to boil water to make steam. The steam turns turbines. The mechanical energy of the turbines powers a generator, producing electricity.

Interpreting Visuals

Direct students' attention to the diagram of a nuclear power plant. **Ask:** In which part of the plant does fission occur? inside the reactor vessel **Ask:** What fuel is used in this process and where is the fuel placed? Uranium is the fuel; it is placed in fuel rods inside the reactor. **Ask:** Why do you think is it necessary to place the reactor and fuel rods inside a containment structure? to prevent harmful radiation leaks **Ask:** Which part of the plant produces electricity? the generator

The Pros and Cons

How can we evaluate nonrenewable energy resources?

There are advantages and disadvantages to using nonrenewable energy resources. Nonrenewable resources provide much of the energy that humans need to power transportation, warm homes, and produce electricity relatively cheaply. But the methods of obtaining and using these resources can have negative effects on the environment.

Active Reading

13 Identify As you read, underline the effects that nuclear power plants have on their surroundings.

The Pros and Cons of Nuclear Fuel

Nuclear fission produces a large amount of energy and does not cause air pollution because no fuel is burned. Mining uranium also does not usually result in massive strip mines or large loss of habitats.

However, nuclear power does have drawbacks. Nuclear power plants produce dangerous wastes that remain radioactive for thousands of years. So the waste must be specially stored to prevent harm to anyone. Harmful radiation may also be released into the environment accidentally. Hot water released from the power plant can also be a problem. This heated water can disrupt aquatic ecosystems. So the hot water must be cooled before it is released into local bodies of water.

Visualize It!

14 Infer Why do you think nuclear fuel rods are usually transported by train instead of by trucks?

Used nuclear fuel rods must be transported in specially built steel containers.

166

The Pros and Cons of Fossil Fuels

Fossil fuels are relatively inexpensive to obtain and use. However, there are problems associated with their use. Burning coal can release sulfur dioxide, which combines with moisture in the air to form acid rain. Acid rain causes damage to structures and the environment. Coal mining also disturbs habitats, lowers water tables, and pollutes water.

Environmental problems are also associated with using oil. In 2010, a blown oil well spilled an estimated 200 million gallons of crude oil in the Gulf of Mexico for 86 days. The environmental costs may continue for years.

Burning fossil fuels can cause smog, especially in cities with millions of vehicles. Smog is a brownish haze that can cause respiratory problems and contribute to acid rain. Burning fossil fuels also releases carbon dioxide into the atmosphere. Increases in atmospheric carbon dioxide can lead to global warming.

Some coal is mined by removing the tops of mountains to expose the coal. This damages habitats and can cause water pollution as well.

15 Evaluate In the chart below, list the advantages and disadvantages of using nuclear fuel and fossil fuels.

Type of fuel	Pros	Cons
nuclear fuel		
fossil fuels		

Lesson 3 Nonrenewable Energy Resources **167**

Answers

13. *See students' pages for annotations.*
14. The fuel rods and their containers are extremely large and heavy. The containers would need oversize trucks and trailers. Trains also allow the nuclear fuel to travel away from areas with high populations.
15. Nuclear Fuel: advantages: produces a large amount of energy, does not cause air pollution, mining uranium does not disrupt habitats; disadvantages: difficult to safely store waste, potential for radiation leaks and the disruption of ecosystems from release of excess heat, waste must be stored for thousands of years; advantages of fossil fuels: relatively inexpensive to obtain and use; disadvantages of fossil fuels: coal mining and oil spills disrupt habitats, coal mining can lower water quality and the water table, burning fossil fuels can cause acid rain and smog and contribute to global warming

Learning Alert

Clarifying Concepts Point out that petroleum and natural gas are accessed by drilled wells rather than mines. **Ask:** Why can't these fossil fuels be mined like coal? They are a liquid and a gas, and cannot be mined like solid coal.

Probing Questions GUIDED *Inquiry*

Deciding Tell students that Europe has substantially higher gasoline prices than the United States, largely due to higher government taxes on fossil fuels. **Ask:** Do you think higher gas prices would encourage conservation and the use of public transportation in the United States and abroad? Why or why not? Sample answers: Yes, some people might change their driving habits or carpool more. No, many people such as truck drivers and fisherman rely on gasoline to work. Many people do not live in areas that have extensive public transportation systems. **Ask:** Which nonrenewable energy resource do you feel is safest to use in terms of environmental and health issues? Sample answer: Natural gas does not cause as much pollution as coal or petroleum, and it doesn't have the storage and health risks associated with nuclear energy.

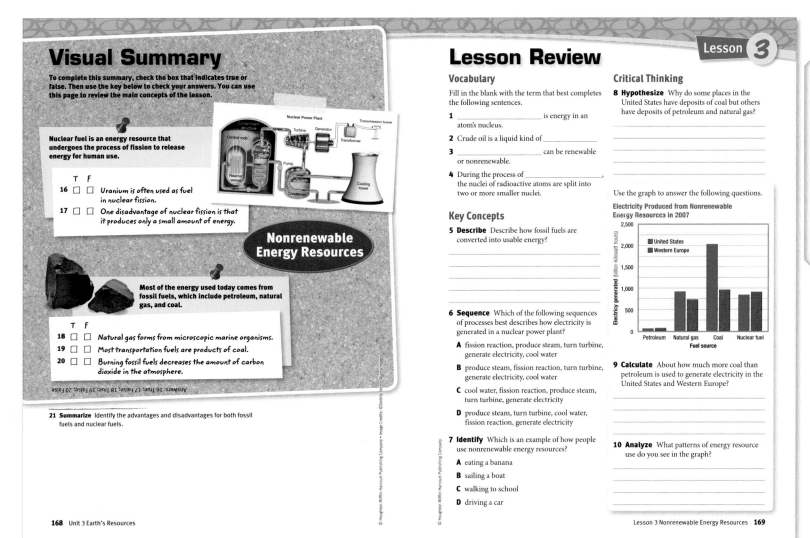

Visual Summary

To complete this summary, check the box that indicates true or false. Then use the key below to check your answers. You can use this page to review the main concepts of the lesson.

Nuclear fuel is an energy resource that undergoes the process of fission to release energy for human use.

T F
16 ☐ ☐ Uranium is often used as fuel in nuclear fission.
17 ☐ ☐ One disadvantage of nuclear fission is that it produces only a small amount of energy.

Nonrenewable Energy Resources

Most of the energy used today comes from fossil fuels, which include petroleum, natural gas, and coal.

T F
18 ☐ ☐ Natural gas forms from microscopic marine organisms.
19 ☐ ☐ Most transportation fuels are products of coal.
20 ☐ ☐ Burning fossil fuels decreases the amount of carbon dioxide in the atmosphere.

Answers: 16 True; 17 False; 18 True; 19 False; 20 False

21 Summarize Identify the advantages and disadvantages for both fossil fuels and nuclear fuels.

Lesson Review

Lesson 3

Vocabulary

Fill in the blank with the term that best completes the following sentences.

1 _____ is energy in an atom's nucleus.

2 Crude oil is a liquid kind of _____

3 _____ can be renewable or nonrenewable.

4 During the process of _____, the nuclei of radioactive atoms are split into two or more smaller nuclei.

Key Concepts

5 Describe Describe how fossil fuels are converted into usable energy?

_____
_____
_____

6 Sequence Which of the following sequences of processes best describes how electricity is generated in a nuclear power plant?

A fission reaction, produce steam, turn turbine, generate electricity, cool water

B produce steam, fission reaction, turn turbine, generate electricity, cool water

C cool water, fission reaction, produce steam, turn turbine, generate electricity

D produce steam, turn turbine, cool water, fission reaction, generate electricity

7 Identify Which is an example of how people use nonrenewable energy resources?

A eating a banana

B sailing a boat

C walking to school

D driving a car

Critical Thinking

8 Hypothesize Why do some places in the United States have deposits of coal but others have deposits of petroleum and natural gas?

_____
_____
_____

Use the graph to answer the following questions.

9 Calculate About how much more coal than petroleum is used to generate electricity in the United States and Western Europe?

_____

10 Analyze What patterns of energy resource use do you see in the graph?

_____
_____

Visual Summary Answers

16. T
17. F
18. T
19. F
20. F
21. Fossil Fuels: advantages: relatively cheap to obtain and use; disadvantages: coal mining and oil spills disrupt habitats, burning fossil fuels can cause acid rain and smog; Nuclear Fuel: advantages: produces a large amount of energy, does not cause air pollution, mining uranium does not disrupt habitats; disadvantages: difficult to safely store waste potential for radiation leaks and hot water leaks, waste must be stored for thousands of years

Lesson Review Answers

1. Nuclear energy
2. fossil fuel
3. Energy resources
4. fission
5. Fossil fuels are burned to generate energy as heat, which can be used directly or to generate electricity. Petroleum products are used to power vehicles.
6. A
7. D
8. Places with coal deposits were covered by ancient swamps, and places with petroleum and natural gas deposits were covered by ancient seas.

9. The United States and Western Europe combined use about 3000 billion kilowatt hours of electricity produced from coal and about 135 billion kilowatt hours of electricity produced from petroleum; $3000 \div 135 = 22.2$ times more.

10. Both regions use about the same amount of petroleum, natural gas, and nuclear power to generate electricity. The United States depends much more heavily on coal for energy production than does Western Europe.

Renewable Energy Resources

Essential Question How do humans use renewable energy resources?

 Professional Development

For more detailed information about the topics in this lesson, refer to the Content Refresher in the Unit Opener pages.

Opening Your Lesson

Begin the lesson by assessing students' prerequisite and prior knowledge.

Prerequisite Knowledge

- Earth's natural resources are used by people.
- Fossil fuels are nonrenewable resources.

Accessing Prior Knowledge

KWL Invite students to make a Trifold FoldNote KWL chart about what they know about renewable energy resources. Have students put what they **K**now in the first column, and what they **W**ant to know in the second column. After they finish the lesson, they can complete the third column with what they **L**earned.

🌐 *Optional Online resources: KWL, TriFold support*

Customize Your Opening

- ☐ **Accessing Prior Knowledge,** above
- ☐ **Print Path** Engage Your Brain, SE p. 171
- ☐ **Print Path** Active Reading, SE p. 171
- ☐ **Digital Path** Lesson Opener

Key Topics/Learning Goals

Energy Resources

1 Describe how humans use energy resources.
2 Explain the difference between renewable and nonrenewable energy resources.
3 Identify the two main kinds of renewable energy resources.

Energy from the Sun

1 Describe solar energy and how it is harnessed and used.
2 Explain why wind and flowing water occur and how their energy is harnessed and used.
3 Describe how biomass and alcohol form and how their energy is harnessed and used.

Energy from Earth

1 Describe what geothermal energy is and how it is used.

Supporting Concepts

- Humans use energy resources to power technology.
- Nonrenewable energy resources are used faster than they can be replenished.
- Renewable energy resources are used no faster than they can be replenished.
- Two main kinds of renewable energy resources are those powered by the sun (solar, wind, hydroelectric, biomass) and those by energy within Earth (geothermal).

- Solar energy is the energy received by Earth from the sun in the form of radiation. It can be used to heat buildings directly or converted into electricity by solar cells.
- Wind is formed by the uneven heating of air masses by the sun. Wind energy is used to do work or generate electricity by a windmill or a wind turbine.
- Hydroelectric energy is electrical energy produced by flowing water as it turns turbines. Energy from the sun drives the water cycle, thus replenishing Earth's water.
- Biomass energy is the energy obtained from plant material, manure, or any other organic matter. Biomass can be burned to cook food and warm homes.

- Geothermal energy is energy in the form of heat that is found inside Earth.
- Geothermal energy is transferred to rock formations deep within Earth, which heats nearby ground water. The hot water is then used to warm buildings and generate electricity.

Options for Instruction

Two parallel paths provide coverage of the Essential Questions, with a strong **Inquiry** strand woven into each.
Follow the **Print Path,** the **Digital Path,** or your customized combination of print, digital, and inquiry.

 Print Path
Teaching support for the Print Path appears with the Student Pages.

 Inquiry Labs and Activities

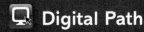 **Digital Path**
Digital Path shortcut: TS661734

Print Path	Inquiry Labs and Activities	Digital Path
Energy Déjà Vu, SE pp. 172–173 **What are the two main sources of renewable energy?** • The Sun • Earth **How might a renewable energy resource become nonrenewable?**	**Virtual Lab** How Can We Use Renewable Energy Resources? **Daily Demo** Pick Your Resources **Activity** New Again	**Which Show a Renewable Energy Source?** Interactive Graphics **Renewable Energy** Interactive Graphics
Turn, Turn, Turn, SE pp. 174–175 **How do humans use wind energy?** **How do humans get energy from moving water?** **Let the Sunshine In,** SE pp. 176–178 **How do humans use solar energy?** • To Provide Energy as Heat • To Produce Electricity **How do humans get energy from living things?** • By Burning Biomass • By Burning Alcohol	**Quick Lab** Design a Turbine **Quick Lab** Understanding Solar Panels **Activity** How It Works **Activity** Renewable Review	**Solar Energy** Interactive Graphics **Biomass Energy** Slideshow
Let the Sunshine In, SE p. 179 **How do humans use geothermal energy?** • To Provide Energy as Heat • To Produce Electricity	**S.T.E.M. Lab** Modeling Geothermal Power **Activity** The Future of Renewables	**Identify Types of Energy** Interactive Graphics

Options for Assessment

*See the Evaluate page for options, including Formative Assessment,
Summative Assessment, and Unit Review.*

Engage and Explore

Activities and Discussion

Activity *New Again*

Energy Resources

 individuals
 10 min
Inquiry **DIRECTED** inquiry

Venn Diagram Instruct students to complete a Venn diagram to compare and contrast nonrenewable and renewable energy resources. Then **Ask:** How does a renewable resource become nonrenewable?

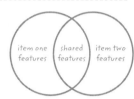

🌐 *Optional Online resource: Venn Diagram support*

Activity *How It Works*

Energy from the Sun
Energy from Earth

 individuals or pairs
 varied
Inquiry **GUIDED** inquiry

Display Using a variety of materials, instruct students to make a poster, diorama, or model showing how one renewable energy resource is produced, harnessed, and used. For example, students modeling wind energy would diagram how the sun causes wind, how wind is harnessed by turbines to produce electricity, and how the electricity is stored and distributed. **To extend the activity,** have students show energy transformations.

🌐 *Optional Online rubrics: Posters and Displays*

Activity *The Future of Renewables*

Energy from the Sun
Energy from Earth

 small groups
 30 min
Inquiry **DIRECTED** inquiry

Jigsaw Have each group become an expert on one renewable energy resource discussed in the lesson. Groups should know its advantages and disadvantages, as well as its feasibility as a future source of energy in the United States. Then, have students jigsaw into new groups with mixed experts. Groups will act as a scientific panel advising government policy on: In what type of renewable energy resources should the United States invest most heavily in the future? Why?

🌐 *Optional Online resource: Jigsaw support*

Labs and Demos

🌐 📄 S.T.E.M. Lab *Modeling Geothermal Power*

Energy from Earth

 small groups
 45 min
Inquiry **DIRECTED/GUIDED** inquiry

Students will build a model turbine using a variety of materials.

PURPOSE **To model how geothermal energy works**

MATERIALS

- beaker
- 5–6 books
- modeling clay
- hole punch
- hot plate
- permanent marker
- pencil
- 2 pipe cleaners
- posterboard
- ruler
- scissors
- shoebox
- stopwatch
- transparent tape
- thumbtack

🌐 📄 Quick Lab *Design a Turbine*

PURPOSE **To build a simple water turbine and explore some of the advantages and disadvantages of using hydropower as a source of energy**

See the Lab Manual or go Online for planning information.

Customize Your Labs

📄 *See the Lab Manual for lab datasheets.*

🌐 *Go Online for editable lab datasheets.*

Levels of

DIRECTED inquiry
introduces inquiry skills within a structured framework.

GUIDED inquiry
develops inquiry skills within a supportive environment.

INDEPENDENT inquiry
deepens inquiry skills with student-driven questions or procedures.

Daily Demo *Pick Your Resources*

Engage

Energy Resources

 whole class
 15 min
 GUIDED inquiry

PURPOSE **To demonstrate the difference between renewable and nonrenewable energy resources**

MATERIALS

• shoebox
• paper clips, buttons, pebbles, or other small objects

1 In the box, place equal quantities of two different types of small objects, such as paper clips and buttons.

2 *Round 1:* Pass the box around the classroom. Tell each student to take as many paper clips and buttons as they want.

3 Record the number of each object in the box and the number of students with objects. Return all items to the box.

4 *Round 2:* Repeat Step 2. This time replace all of the paper clips as students remove them. Do not replace buttons. Record results.

5 *Round 3:* Tell students that the buttons and paper clips represent nonrenewable and renewable resources. Repeat Step 4.

6 **Comparing Ask:** How did the number of energy resources that were left after each round compare? Sample answer: More renewable resources remained. **Ask** How are nonrenewable resources different from renewable resources? Unlike renewable resources, nonrenewable resources cannot be replaced as quickly as they are used up.

7 **Drawing Conclusions Ask:** In Round 3, how did knowledge about the choices you were making change your decisions? Sample answer: It made me choose to conserve nonrenewable resources more.

To extend the activity, suggest additional rounds to make the activity more realistic, such as assigning dollar value to resources.

Quick Lab *Understanding Solar Panels*

Energy from the Sun

 small groups
20 min
DIRECTED inquiry

Students will conduct simple tests to understand the function and design of solar panels.

PURPOSE **To explore how solar panels work**

MATERIALS

• modeling clay (red or orange)
• white cloth
• black cloth
• aluminum foil
• colored glass (green or blue)
• image of a solar panel
• gooseneck lamp

• stopwatch
• thermometer, alcohol

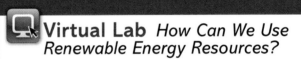 Virtual Lab *How Can We Use Renewable Energy Resources?*

Energy from the Sun

 flexible
 45 min
GUIDED inquiry

Students will investigate how location and total area of solar panels affect the amount of energy provided by solar panels.

PURPOSE **To explore factors that affect solar energy production**

Activities and Discussion

☐ **Activity** New Again
☐ **Activity** How It Works
☐ **Activity** The Future of Renewables

Labs and Demos

☐ **S.T.E.M. Lab** Modeling Geothermal...
☐ **Quick Lab** Design a Turbine
☐ **Daily Demo** Pick Your Resources
☐ **Quick Lab** Understanding Solar Panels
☐ **Virtual Lab** How Can We Use...?

Your Resources

_____
_____
_____
_____

Explain Science Concepts

	📖 **Print Path**	🖥 **Digital Path**
Key Topics		
Energy Resources	☐ **Energy Déjà Vu,** SE pp. 172–173 • Contrast, #5 • Apply, #6 • Distinguish, #7 • Think Outside the Book, #8	☐ **Which Show a Renewable Energy Source?** Identify the two main sources of renewable energy resources. ☐ **Renewable Energy** Discuss how renewable energy resources may become nonrenewable.
Energy from the Sun	☐ **Turn, Turn, Turn,** SE pp. 174–175 • Infer, #9 • Active Reading (Annotation strategy), #10 • Visualize It!, #11 ☐ **Let the Sunshine In,** SE pp. 176–178 • Infer, #12 • Active Reading (Annotation strategy), #13 • Visualize It!, #14 • Active Reading (Annotation strategy), #15 • List, #16	☐ **Solar Energy** Describe solar energy. ☐ **Biomass Energy** Describe how biomass and alcohol form, how they are harvested and used, and the advantages and disadvantages of using them.
Energy from Earth	☐ **Let the Sunshine In,** SE p. 179 • List, #17 	☐ **Identify Types of Energy** Describe how wind, hydroelectric, and geothermal energy are harnessed and used. 

Basic *Renewable Resources by Design*

Synthesizing Key Topics

 individuals or pairs

🕐 15–20 min

Graphic Tees Instruct students to design and draw a graphic logo, which might appear on a tee-shirt or business card, for an alternative energy company. Designs might feature wind turbines, solar cells, or another technology related to renewable resources.

Advanced *Evaluating Renewables*

Synthesizing Key Topics

 individuals, pairs, whole class

🕐 15 min

Think Pair Share First, students think about the answer to a question individually. Then they discuss their ideas with a partner. Finally, pairs share their ideas with the class. Possible questions include: How are nonrenewable energy resources different from renewable resources? What are the advantages and disadvantages of renewable resources? Do you think you will see a shift to the use of more renewable resources in your lifetime? Explain. What type of renewable resource would be most practical where you live? Sample answer: solar energy, because it's sunny most days of the year where I live How are solar energy, wind energy, and hydroelectric energy related? All of these resources result from energy from the sun. Compare and contrast fossil fuels and biomass. Both come from organic materials. Biomass is from today's plants and animal wastes, while fossil fuels are millions of years old.

ELL *Act It Out*

Synthesizing Key Topics

 whole class

🕐 15–20 min

Simulation Have English language learners act out the steps involved in harnessing and using renewable energy resources. Start with the source, the sun or Earth, and simulate the processes involved through use by humans. Using wind energy as an example, students might include nuclear fusion in the sun, light and heat radiating to Earth, uneven heating and movement of air masses forming wind, wind as moving air, wind turning turbines, blades driving a generator, and the electricity produced being stored, converted, and transferred for use. Encourage students to have a narrator during their simulation.

energy resource	wind energy	solar energy
hydroelectric energy	biomass	geothermal energy

Previewing Vocabulary

 individuals   🕐 15 min

Word Triangle Instruct students to complete word triangles for each vocabulary word. Each triangle has space for students to write the term, its definition, a sentence using the term, and a picture.

🌐 *Optional Online resource: Word Triangle support*

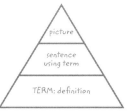

Reinforcing Vocabulary

 individuals   🕐 15 min

Cluster Diagram Use a cluster diagram to organize terms and show relationships between them. For example, students should recognize that wind energy, solar energy, hydroelectric energy, biomass, and geothermal energy are all energy resources. A different branch can be used to distinguish geothermal energy, which is from Earth.

🌐 *Optional Online resource: Cluster Diagram support*

Customize Your Core Lesson

Core Instruction

☐ **Print Path** choices

☐ **Digital Path** choices

Vocabulary

☐ **Previewing Vocabulary** Word Triangle

☐ **Reinforcing Vocabulary** Cluster Diagram

Your Resources

Differentiated Instruction

☐ **Basic** Renewable Resources by Design

☐ **Advanced** Evaluating Renewables

☐ **ELL** Act It Out

Extend Science Concepts

Reinforce and Review

Activity *Renewable Review*

Synthesizing Key Topics small groups · 20 min

Carousel Review

1 Arrange five stations with chart paper in different parts of the room. Title the stations: solar energy, wind energy, hydroelectric energy, biomass energy, and geothermal energy.

2 Divide the class into small groups and assign each group a chart. Give each group a different colored marker.

3 Groups review the topic and write key questions for other groups on the chart.

4 After five minutes, each group rotates to the next station. Groups discuss and answer the questions left by the previous group.

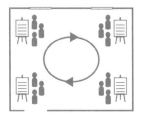

5 On subsequent rotations, groups can comment on answers they disagree with and add their own answers. Continue until all groups have reviewed all charts.

FoldNote

Synthesizing Key Topics individuals, then small groups · 25 min

Pyramid Assign one renewable energy resource to each student, evenly distributing them throughout the class. For their assigned resource, have students make a Pyramid FoldNote. On one side, have students describe the energy resource. On the second side, students should explain how the resource is harnessed and used. On the third side, ask students to list the advantages and the disadvantages of their resource. Then, arrange small groups so that each group has one Pyramid for every energy resource. Groups should use the pyramids to compare and contrast nonrenewable energy resources. On the bottom, students write a sentence stating how the resource is interesting or unique.

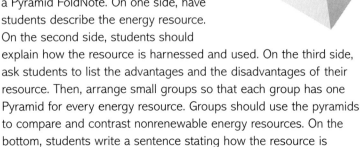

⊘ *Online resource: Pyramid support*

Going Further

Life Science Connection

Energy from the Sun individuals or pairs · varied

Multimedia Presentation How is wildlife impacted by wind farms or solar energy power plants? Allow interested students to conduct research on the advantages and disadvantages of these renewable energy sources for wildlife. Then, compare this to the impact of nonrenewable energy resources on wildlife. Have students create a short multimedia presentation that can be combined with other student multimedia presentations for one class presentation.

⊘ *Optional Online rubric: Multimedia Presentation*

Social Studies Connection

Synthesizing Key Topics individuals or pairs · varied

Quick Research Ask students if they have heard the phrase "reduce our dependence on foreign oil" used by the media, their teachers, family, or neighbors. Instruct students to bring in one news article, fact, or statistic that relates in some way to this idea. In class, share and use the information to draw ideas and conclusions about energy policies in the United States.

Customize Your Closing

🗂 *See the Assessment Guide for quizzes and tests.*

⊘ *Go Online to edit and create quizzes and tests.*

Reinforce and Review

☐ **Activity** Renewable Review

☐ **FoldNote** Pyramid

☐ **Print Path** Visual Summary, SE p. 180

☐ **Digital Path** Lesson Closer

Evaluate Student Mastery

Formative Assessment

See the teacher support below the Student Pages for additional Formative Assessment questions.

Provide students with the following **prompt:** Which type of renewable energy resource is most reasonable in the area in which you live? Explain how your choice would be harnessed and used, and include two reasons explaining your answer. Students should select a renewable energy resource, including solar energy, wind energy, hydroelectric energy, biomass energy, or geothermal energy. They should describe the technology used to harness and use the resource, such as photovoltaic cells for solar energy or wind turbines for wind energy. Reasons should take into account the local climate or geographic features and show knowledge of the advantages and limitations of the resource.

Reteach

Formative assessment may show that students need reinforcement for certain topics. The resources below are recommended for reteaching. If students were introduced to a topic through the Print Path, you can also use the Digital Path to reteach, and vice versa.
🎧 *Can be assigned to individual students*

Energy Resources
Virtual Lab How Can We Use Renewable Energy Resources? 🎧

Energy from the Sun
FoldNote Pyramid 🎧

Energy from Earth
S.T.E.M. Lab Modeling Geothermal Power

Summative Assessment

Alternative Assessment
Make a Renewable Energy Plan

🕐 *Online resources: student worksheet, optional rubrics*

Renewable Energy Resources

Tic-Tac-Toe: *Make a Renewable Energy Plan*
You are on an energy committee for your community. Your task is to explore, evaluate, and propose a plan for using a renewable energy resource in your city or town.

1. Work on your own, with a partner, or with a small group.
2. Choose three quick activities from the game. Check the boxes you plan to complete. They must form a straight line in any direction.
3. Have your teacher approve your plan.
4. Do each activity, and turn in your results.

__ Research	__ Sketch	__ Press Conference
How much electricity is used by an average household in your community? How many households could be supplied by renewable energy resources? Find out!	Make a quick sketch showing how one renewable energy resource could be put to use in your community.	Act out a press conference or community television broadcast in which your committee members address public questions and concerns.
__ FAQ	__ Put It to a Vote	__ Postcard
What are the most "Frequently Asked Questions" about renewable energy resources? Ask and answer five key questions about one renewable energy resource, as it might appear on an informational web site.	Present your best idea for using renewable energy resources in your community and ask the class to vote on it. In your presentation, you may use visuals, data, and information created for other activity boxes on this page.	Make a simple postcard that could be mailed to citizens in your community detailing the advantages and disadvantages of a specific renewable energy resource.
__ Survey	__ Infographics	__ Cartoon
What do different people think about renewable energy resources? Develop three specific questions that will help you find out. Take a quick public opinion poll by surveying at least ten people. Summarize what you learn.	How do renewable energy resources compare to nonrenewable energy resources? Make an infographic, a visual representation of data or information, comparing information about energy resources. Graphs, charts, and graphic organizers are all examples of infographics.	Draw a cartoon that expresses one point of view about renewable energy resources. Remember that cartoons make a political statement or use humor to get a point across.

Going Further
- ☐ Life Science Connection
- ☐ Social Studies Connection

Formative Assessment
- ☐ **Strategies** Throughout TE
- ☐ **Lesson Review** SE

Summative Assessment
- ☐ **Alternative Assessment** Make a Renewable Energy Plan
- ☐ **Lesson Quiz**
- ☐ **Unit Tests A and B**
- ☐ **Unit Review** SE End-of-Unit

Your Resources

_____

_____

_____

_____

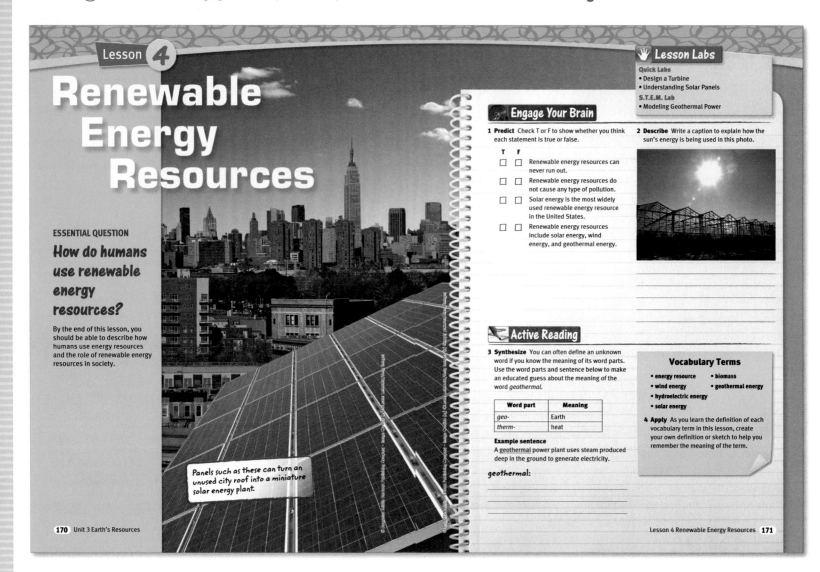

Answers

Answers for 1–3 should represent students' current thoughts, even if incorrect.

1. F; F; F; T

2. Sample answer: The greenhouse traps warmth from the sun. This helps protect the plants inside the greenhouse from cold winter temperatures.

3. of or relating to heat inside Earth

4. Students should define or sketch each vocabulary term in the lesson.

Opening Your Lesson

Discuss student responses to items 1 and 2 to assess students' prerequisite knowledge and to estimate what they already know about renewable energy resources.

Preconceptions "Renewable energy resources can never run out and do not cause any pollution at all." If students identify this statement as true, make sure to revisit this statement after the lesson to discuss it is not always true.

Prerequisites Students should already know that fossil fuels, including coal, oil, and natural gas, are nonrenewable resources. They should have an understanding that fossil fuels form over millions of years and cannot be replenished as quickly as they are being used by humans.

Learning Alert

Word Parts Discuss the meaning of other word parts found in the vocabulary terms. For example, students may know that *bio-* refers to "life," and *hydro-* is used to mean "water." Students may also be familiar with *solar lights* or *solar panels,* as shown. They can use their knowledge to understand that *solar* refers to something that uses the sun's energy to operate.

Energy *Déjà Vu*

What are the two main sources of renewable energy?

An **energy resource** is a natural resource used to generate electricity and other forms of energy. Most of the energy used by humans comes from *nonrenewable resources*. These resources are used more quickly than they can be replaced. But *renewable resources* can be replaced almost as quickly as they are used. Most renewable energy resources come from the sun and some from Earth itself.

The Sun

The sun's energy is a result of nuclear fusion. Fusion is the process by which two or more nuclei fuse together to form a larger nucleus. Fusion produces a large amount of energy, which is released into space as light and heat.

Solar energy warms Earth, causing the movement of air masses. Moving air masses form winds and some ocean currents. Solar energy also fuels plant growth. Animals get energy by eating plants. Humans can harness energy from wind, moving water, plant and animal materials, and directly from the light and heat that comes from the sun.

Earth

Energy from within Earth comes from two sources. One source is the decay of radioactive elements in Earth's mantle and crust, caused by nuclear fission. Fission is the splitting of the nuclei of radioactive atoms. The second source of energy within Earth is energy stored during Earth's formation. The heat produced from these sources radiates outward toward Earth's surface. Humans can harness this heat to use as an energy source.

5 Contrast Explain how energy production in the sun differs from energy production in Earth's interior.

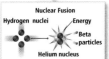

Not to scale.

Nuclear Fusion

Hydrogen nuclei → Energy
Beta particles
Helium nucleus

When atomic nuclei fuse, energy is released.

Not to scale.

Core

Earth's internal energy comes from the process of nuclear fission and the events that formed Earth.

172 Unit 3 Earth's Resources

How might a renewable energy resource become nonrenewable?

All of the energy resources you will learn about in this lesson are renewable. That doesn't mean that they can't become nonrenewable resources. Trees, for example, are a renewable resource. Some people burn wood from trees to heat their homes and cook food. However, some forests are being cut down but are not being replanted in a timely manner. Others are being cut down and replaced with buildings. If this process continues, eventually these forests will no longer be considered renewable resources.

6 Apply Read the caption below, then describe what might happen if the community uses too much of the water in the reservoir.

7 Distinguish What is the difference between nonrenewable and renewable energy resources?

Think Outside the Book

8 Apply Write an interview with a renewable resource that is afraid it might become nonrenewable. Be sure to include questions and answers.

A community uses this reservoir for water. The dam at the end of the reservoir uses moving water to produce electricity for the community.

173

Answers

5. Energy is produced in the sun when atomic nuclei are fused together. In Earth, energy is produced when nuclei split, or decay.

6. If the community uses too much water in the reservoir, there may not be enough water left to produce electricity for the community.

7. Sample answer: Renewable resources can be replaced at the same rate they are used, while nonrenewable resources take much longer to be replaced.

8. Student output should demonstrate an understanding of why the resource is considered to be renewable, and what conditions would render the resource nonrenewable.

Learning Alert

Difficult Concepts Heat, light, chemical, electrical, nuclear, and kinetic (motion) are some of the forms of energy. Natural energy resources result from the transformation of energy from one form to another. For example, nuclear fusion in the sun produces energy released as heat and light into space. These forms of energy are transformed into kinetic energy, such as moving wind and water on Earth, which can be harnessed to generate electrical energy. Emphasize that energy can be transformed from one form to another.

Interpreting Visuals

Ask: How does a visual model help you understand nuclear fusion in the sun? Sample answer: It provides a way to visualize a process that is too small to see with your eyes.

Building Reading Skills

Two-Column Chart Use a Two-Column Chart to compare the two main sources of renewable energy. In each column, have students list definitions and examples, as well as any advantages and disadvantages of these two types of energy resources that they can think of.

🔘 *Optional Online resource: Two-Column Chart support*

Turn, Turn, Turn

How do humans use wind energy?

Wind is created by the sun's uneven heating of air masses in Earth's atmosphere. **Wind energy** uses the force of moving air to drive an electric generator or do other work. Wind energy is renewable because the wind will blow as long as the sun warms Earth. Wind energy is harnessed by machines called wind turbines. Electricity is generated when moving air turns turbine blades that drive an electric generator. Clusters of wind turbines, called wind farms, generate large amounts of electricity.

Although wind energy is a renewable energy resource, it has several disadvantages. Wind farms can be placed only in areas that receive large amounts of wind. The equipment required to collect and convert wind energy is also expensive to produce and maintain. And the production and maintenance of this equipment produces a small amount of pollution. The turbine blades can also be hazardous to birds.

Windmills such as these have been used for centuries to grind grain and pump surface water for irrigation.

A wind-powered water pump can pull water from deep underground when electricity is not available.

9 Infer What is the main benefit of placing these turbines in open water?

Wind farms are a form of clean energy, because they do not generate air pollution as they generate electricity.

174

How do humans get energy from moving water?

Active Reading

10 Identify Underline the kind of energy that is found in moving water.

Like wind, moving water has kinetic energy. People have harnessed the energy of falling or flowing water to power machines since ancient times. Some grain and saw mills still use water to power their equipment. Electrical energy produced by moving water is called **hydroelectric energy**. Hydroelectric energy is renewable because the water cycle is driven by the sun. Water that evaporates from oceans and lakes falls on higher elevations and flows downhill in streams, rivers, and waterfalls. The energy in flowing water is converted to electrical energy when it spins turbines connected to electric generators inside the dam.

Hydroelectric energy is a good source of energy only in locations where there are large, reliable amounts of flowing water. Another disadvantage of hydroelectric energy is that hydroelectric dams and their technology are expensive to build. The dams also can block the movement of fish between the sea and their spawning grounds. Special fish ladders must be built to allow fish to swim around the dam.

Visualize It!

11 Explain What is the purpose of the lake that is located behind the dam of a hydroelectric plant?

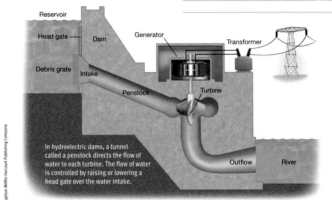

In hydroelectric dams, a tunnel called a penstock directs the flow of water to each turbine. The flow of water is controlled by raising or lowering a head gate over the water intake.

Lesson 4 Renewable Energy Resources **175**

Answers

9. There is a steady supply of wind to turn the turbines.

10. *See students' pages for annotations.*

11. The lake stores water for the dam and ensures that there will be an adequate flow of water.

Building Reading Skills

Three-Column Chart Use a Three-Column Chart to help students infer why turbines might be placed in open water. Title the columns "What I Read," "What I Know," and "What I Can Infer." Ask students to work with a partner to analyze the text and visual, and then share their inferences with the class. Have students use the chart to infer on the following pages as well.

🌐 *Optional Online resource: Three-Column Chart support*

Learning Alert

Cape Wind Explain that a project to put wind turbines off the coast of Cape Cod, MA has been met with opposition from some who say it could harm the marine environment and will spoil the view of the ocean. Discuss the issue using the visual for support.

Interpreting Visuals

Have students trace the flow of water through the hydroelectric dam with their pencils. **Ask:** What happens at the turbines? The energy in flowing water spins the turbines, which generate electrical energy. **Ask:** What would happen if it didn't rain for a long time? Sample answer: The water level would drop, decreasing the flow of water and thus the amount of electricity that can be generated.

Let the Sunshine In

How do humans use solar energy?

Most forms of energy come from the sun—even fossil fuels begin with the sun as an energy resource. **Solar energy** is the energy received by Earth from the sun in the form of radiation. Solar energy can be used to warm buildings directly. Solar energy can also be converted into electricity by solar cells.

To Provide Energy as Heat

We can use liquids warmed by the sun to warm water and buildings. Some liquids, such as water, have a high capacity for absorbing and holding heat. When the heat is absorbed by the liquid in a solar collector, it can be transferred to water that circulates through a building. The hot water can be used for bathing or other household uses, or to warm the building. The only pollution generated by solar heating systems comes from the manufacture and maintenance of their equipment. Solar heating systems work best in areas with large amounts of sunlight.

Solar collectors absorb energy from the sun in the form of heat. The heat is transferred to water that circulates through the house.

Solar collector

Energy from the sun heats a fluid inside the solar collector

Hot water for household use

Cold water from the water supply is heated by hot fluid inside the pipes coming from the solar collector

Pump

Backup water heater

12 Infer Not all solar collectors use water to absorb energy from the sun. Why might a solar heating system use a liquid other than water?

Active Reading 13 Identify As you read, underline the characteristics of a photovoltaic cell.

To Produce Electricity

Solar collectors can also be used to generate electricity. First, heated fluid is used to produce steam. Then, the steam turns a turbine connected to an electric generator.

Electricity can also be generated when sunlight is absorbed by a photovoltaic cell. A single photovoltaic cell produces a small amount of electricity. The electricity from joined photovoltaic cells can power anything from calculators to entire communities. Many cells must be joined together to form each solar panel, as shown in the solar power plant below. Solar power plants must be built in places with adequate space and abundant sunshine year-round. These requirements increase the costs of solar power.

This calculator is powered by solar cells instead of a battery.

Visualize It! Inquiry

14 Infer Based on this image and your reading, what might be a disadvantage to using solar energy to supply electricity to a large community?

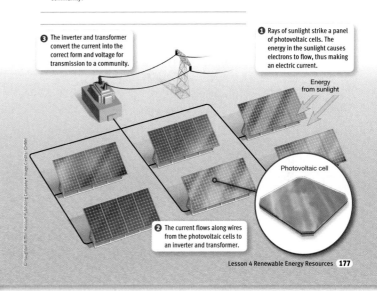

❸ The inverter and transformer convert the current into the correct form and voltage for transmission to a community.

❶ Rays of sunlight strike a panel of photovoltaic cells. The energy in the sunlight causes electrons to flow, thus making an electric current.

Energy from sunlight

❷ The current flows along wires from the photovoltaic cells to an inverter and transformer.

Photovoltaic cell

Answers

12. Sample answer: Water freezes at 0 °C, so it might not be wise to use it in a climate where winter temperatures are often below 0 °C.

13. *See students' pages for annotations.*

14. Sample answer: The solar panels may not generate enough electricity if there are several days of cloudy weather. Also, a large community would require many solar panels, which would need a lot of space.

Using Annotations

Text Structure: Main Idea/Details When students complete this annotation, instruct them to use the visuals for support so they do not miss any important characteristics.
To extend the activity, have students compare the structure and function of photovoltaic cells to the leaves on a plant. Ask: How are they alike? Sample answer: Both have a large surface area to collect energy from sunlight.

🌐 *Optional Online resource: Text Structure: Main Idea/Details support*

Formative Assessment

Ask: How are wind energy, hydroelectric energy, and solar energy related? Sample answer: The sun is the source of all of these energy resources. The sun warms air masses in Earth's atmosphere unevenly, causing changes in air pressure, which generates wind. The sun drives the water cycle, resulting in precipitation and the downward flow of water.

Probing Question DIRECTED Inquiry

Applying How could you use solar energy to warm water or cook food? Sample answer: I might use dark materials to absorb warmth from the sun. I could also use reflective materials to concentrate the sun's energy in one area, as in a solar cooker.

How do humans get energy from living things?

Plants absorb light energy from the sun and convert it to chemical energy through *photosynthesis*. This energy is stored in leaves, stems, and roots. Chemical energy is also present in the dung of animals. These sources of energy make up biomass.

By Burning Biomass

Biomass is organic matter from plants and from animal waste that contains chemical energy. Biomass can be burned to release energy. This energy can be used to cook food, provide warmth, or power an engine. Biomass sources include trees, crops, animal waste, and peat.

Biomass is inexpensive and can usually be replaced relatively quickly, so it is considered to be a renewable resource. Some types of biomass renew more slowly than others. Peat renews so slowly in areas where it is used heavily that it is treated as a nonrenewable resource. Like fossil fuels, biomass produces pollutants when it burns.

These peat pellets will be used to generate steam in the power plant in the background. The steam will generate electricity by turning turbines.

Active Reading 15 **Identify** As you read, number the steps that occur during the production of ethanol.

By Burning Alcohol

Biomass material can be used to produce a liquid fuel called ethanol, which is an alcohol. The sugars or cellulose in the plants are eaten by microbes. The microbes then give off carbon dioxide and ethanol. Over 1,000 L of ethanol can be made from 1 acre of corn. The ethanol is collected and burned as a fuel. Ethanol can also be mixed with gasoline to make a fuel called gasohol. The ethanol produced from about 40% of one corn harvest in the United States would provide only 10% of the fuel used in our cars!

16 **List** What are three examples of how biomass can be used for energy?

_____

_____

_____

These wagons are loaded with sugar cane wastes from sugar production. The cellulose from these plant materials will be processed to produce ethanol.

178 Unit 3 Earth's Resources

How do humans use geothermal energy?

The water in the geyser at right is heated by geothermal energy. **Geothermal energy** is energy produced by heat from Earth's interior. Geothermal energy heats rock formations deep within the ground. Groundwater absorbs this heat and forms hot springs and geysers where the water reaches Earth's surface. Geothermal energy is used to produce energy as heat and electricity.

To Provide Energy as Heat

Geothermal energy can be used to warm and cool buildings. A closed loop system of pipes runs from underground into the heating system of a home or building. Water pumped through these pipes absorbs heat from the ground and is used to warm the building. Hot groundwater can also be pumped in and used in a similar way. In warmer months, the ground is cooler than the air, so this system can also be used for cooling.

To Produce Electricity

Geothermal energy is also used to produce electricity. Wells are drilled into areas of superheated groundwater, allowing steam and hot water to escape. Geothermal power plants pump the steam or hot water from underground to spin turbines that generate electricity, as shown at right. A disadvantage of geothermal energy is pollution that occurs during production of the technology needed to capture it. The technology is also expensive to make and maintain.

Because Earth's core will be very hot for billions of years, geothermal energy will be available for a long time.

Geothermal Plant
Transformer
Turbine
Generator
Cooling system
Heated water
Hot rock

17 **List** What are some advantages and disadvantages to using geothermal energy?

Advantages	Disadvantages

Lesson 4 Renewable Energy Resources 179

Answers

15. *See students' pages for annotations.*

16. Sample answer: Biomass can be burned to cook food, heat a house, or produce fuel for vehicles.

17. Sample answers: Advantages: renewable, adds few pollutants to air and land; Disadvantages: cannot be used everywhere, pollution from production of the needed technology, technology expensive to produce and maintain

Learning Alert

Deforestation In many nations, wood from trees is a major source of fuel for cooking and heating homes. When trees are harvested too quickly, deforestation can occur. By growing and using fast-growing trees and grasses instead, biomass resources can be managed in a way that keeps them renewable.

Formative Assessment

Ask: How does geothermal energy differ from the other renewable energy resources in this lesson? The source of geothermal energy is heat produced within Earth's interior, not the sun.

Probing Questions GUIDED *Inquiry*

Analyzing How does where you live dictate the renewable energy resource that might be used by your community? Sample answer: Different areas in the U.S. have easier access to renewable resources such as wind energy (coastal or desert areas) or solar energy (desert areas). Ask students to find maps that show the state rankings for electricity production from renewable energy resources. Governmental organizations, such as the U.S. Energy Information Association, publish data by energy resources and by state.

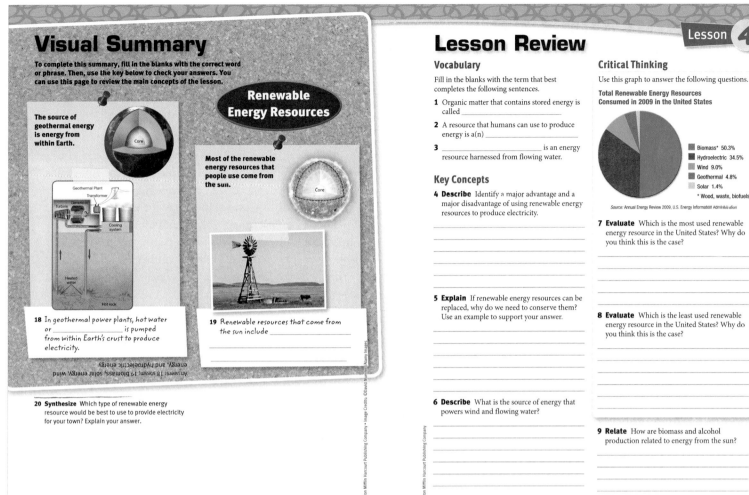

Visual Summary

To complete this summary, fill in the blanks with the correct word or phrase. Then, use the key below to check your answers. You can use this page to review the main concepts of the lesson.

Renewable Energy Resources

The source of geothermal energy is energy from within Earth.

Most of the renewable energy resources that people use come from the sun.

Geothermal Plant
Transformer
Generator
Turbine
Cooling system
Heated water
Hot rock

18 In geothermal power plants, hot water or _____ is pumped from within Earth's crust to produce electricity.

19 Renewable resources that come from the sun include _____

Answers: 18 steam, 19 biomass, solar energy, wind energy, and hydroelectric energy

20 Synthesize Which type of renewable energy resource would be best to use to provide electricity for your town? Explain your answer.

180 Unit 3 Earth's Resources

© Houghton Mifflin Harcourt Publishing Company • Image Credits: ©David Munoz/Alamy Images

Lesson Review

Vocabulary

Fill in the blanks with the term that best completes the following sentences.

1 Organic matter that contains stored energy is called _____

2 A resource that humans can use to produce energy is a(n) _____

3 _____ is an energy resource harnessed from flowing water.

Key Concepts

4 Describe Identify a major advantage and a major disadvantage of using renewable energy resources to produce electricity.

5 Explain If renewable energy resources can be replaced, why do we need to conserve them? Use an example to support your answer.

6 Describe What is the source of energy that powers wind and flowing water?

Critical Thinking

Use this graph to answer the following questions.

Total Renewable Energy Resources Consumed in 2009 in the United States

- Biomass* 50.3%
- Hydroelectric 34.5%
- Wind 9.0%
- Geothermal 4.8%
- Solar 1.4%

* Wood, waste, biofuels

Source: Annual Energy Review 2009, U.S. Energy Information Administration

7 Evaluate Which is the most used renewable energy resource in the United States? Why do you think this is the case?

8 Evaluate Which is the least used renewable energy resource in the United States? Why do you think this is the case?

9 Relate How are biomass and alcohol production related to energy from the sun?

© Houghton Mifflin Harcourt Publishing Company

Lesson 4 Renewable Energy Resources 181

Visual Summary Answers

18. steam
19. biomass, solar energy, wind energy, and hydroelectric energy
20. Answers will vary. Students should choose the energy resource based on local environmental conditions. For example, if a town is located in a rainy location, solar energy would not be an ideal choice. However, a hydroelectric dam may be well-suited to the area because of the large amount of water flowing through the region.

Lesson Review Answers

1. biomass
2. energy resource
3. Hydroelectric energy
4. A major advantage of using renewable energy resources is that most do not produce pollution during use. A major disadvantage is that their technology is expensive to produce and maintain.
5. It is possible for a renewable energy resource to be used up so quickly that it could be considered a nonrenewable energy resource. For example, peat is renewable, but in areas where it is heavily used, it is treated as a nonrenewable resource.
6. Wind occurs because the sun heats Earth's air masses unevenly. Flowing water occurs because the sun's heat causes water to evaporate. The evaporated water condenses and falls to Earth. The water flows from higher elevations to lower elevations.
7. Biomass is the most common renewable energy resource, probably because it is cheap, easy to use, and can power engines as well as produce electricity.
8. Solar energy is the least common renewable energy resource, probably because solar collectors and cells are expensive to make and maintain, and a large surface area is needed to produce adequate amounts of energy.
9. The energy in biomass is solar energy that was converted to chemical energy during photosynthesis. Alcohol is a form of chemical energy that is produced from biomass.

S.T.E.M. Engineering & Technology

Analyzing the Life Cycle of a Paper Cup

Purpose To analyze the impact a paper cup makes on Earth's resources over its life cycle

Learning Goals
- Estimate the carbon dioxide that could be saved by making paper cups out of recycled paper.
- Propose improvements for the life cycle of a paper cup.

Informal Vocabulary
life cycle, raw material, carbon dioxide, pulp, chlorine

Prerequisite Knowledge
- Basic understanding of natural resources
- Understanding the difference between renewable and nonrenewable resources

21st Century SKILLS
Theme: Environmental Literacy

Activities focusing on 21st Century Skills are included for this feature and can be found on the following pages.

These activities focus on the following skills:
- **Creativity and Innovation**
- **ICT (Information, Communications, and Technology) Literacy**
- **Social and Cross-Cultural Skills**

You can learn more about the 21st Century Skills in the front matter of this Teacher's Edition.

Content Refresher

 Professional Development

Environmental Impacts of Paper Cups Each year, Americans use 14 billion disposable coffee cups, which amount to about 900 million pounds of waste and occupy more than 1 million cubic meters of landfill space. This is enough waste to bury Manhattan one meter deep. In landfills, paper cups release methane when they degrade. Methane causes about 20 times more global-warming damage than an equal amount of carbon dioxide.

Federal regulations limit recycled fiber in disposable cups to 10 percent, so most of the materials in paper cups are raw materials. It takes about one square foot of natural habitat to make a single 16-ounce paper cup. To make one ton of paper using recycled fiber saves:

- 17 trees
- 3.3 cubic yards of landfill space
- 360 gallons of water
- 100 gallons of gasoline
- 60 pounds of air pollutants
- 10,401 kilowatts of electricity

In the past, most pulp mills in the United States bleached the wood pulp in paper products using elemental chlorine gas, a process that released significant amounts of carcinogenic chemicals called dioxins. Today, most pulp mills whiten paper using chlorine dioxide. Although this process produces far fewer toxins than the older method of bleaching with elemental chlorine gas, some dioxins are still produced. Alternative bleaching methods exist that are chlorine-free and do not release toxins, but these methods aren't widely used in the United States.

S.T.E.M. Engineering & Technology

Analyzing Technology

Skills
Identify risks
✓ Identify benefits
✓ Evaluate cost of technology
✓ Evaluate environmental impact
✓ Propose improvements
Propose risk reduction
Plan for technology failures
Compare technology
✓ Communicate results

Objectives
• Describe the effects of making paper cups on Earth's resources.
• Estimate the carbon dioxide saved by recycling paper cups.
• Propose improvements for the life cycle of a paper cup.

Analyzing the Life Cycle of a Paper Cup

A product's life cycle includes all of the phases in its "life," from getting raw materials to disposing of it once it has served its purpose. Most steps in the life cycle of a paper product affects the environment in some way.

Impact of a Paper Cup

A life cycle analysis of a paper cup shows that making it requires trees, water, ink, and plastic for a waterproof lining. The process also uses several different kinds of fuel, such as natural gas and diesel truck fuel for energy to make and transport the cups. The whole process releases about 110 grams (about ¼ pound) of carbon dioxide (KAR•buhn dy•AHK•syd) per cup into the atmosphere. This amount is 3 to 4 times the weight of a cup itself. And because of the plastic lining, paper cups are difficult to recycle.

1 Estimate Assume that a recycled paper cup is made up of only paper, and that paper could be recycled 5 times. About how much carbon dioxide would this prevent from being released into the atmosphere?

Newspapers awaiting recycling

These paper cups probably will not be recycled.

Recycling Paper Products

Many paper products are more easily recycled than paper cups are. Over 70% of newspaper is recycled to make various products such as cereal boxes, egg cartons, and tissue paper. Many paper products can be recycled 5 to 7 times, after which the paper fibers are too short and no longer stick together well enough to make paper. Recycling paper products not only saves trees but also saves a lot of water, electricity, and gas and reduces air pollution.

The life of a paper product starts with trees. Loggers cut the tree, and a paper mill grinds it into pulp.

Most newspapers are recycled, saving trees and energy used in logging.

The mill mixes the pulp with water and other chemicals to make paper, which is used to make paper products such as paper cups.

Most paper cups end up in a landfill.

These products are used by all of us and then either recycled, incinerated, or buried in a landfill.

2 Infer Most newspaper is recycled. Most paper cups are not. What is one difference in environmental impact between burial and incineration for used paper products?

You Try It!
Now it's your turn to analyze the life cycle of a paper cup.

Answers

1. If making one cup releases about 110 grams of carbon dioxide, then we would save about 550 grams of carbon dioxide from being released into the atmosphere.

2. Sample answer: Incineration releases many chemicals into the air. Burial takes up space in a landfill and could pollute the soil and/or groundwater.

Analyzing Technology

👋 You Try It!

Now it's your turn to analyze the life cycle of a paper cup. You'll consider things such as the benefits of paper cups and their cost in both money and environmental impact. Then you can suggest some ways to improve the cycle.

① Identify Benefits

With your class, research the benefits of making and using paper cups. List those benefits below.

Benefits
_____

② Evaluate Cost of Technology

A A paper mill uses about 16,000 gallons of water and about 400 kWh of electricity to produce one ton of paper cups. Using the information shown here, what is the cost of the water and electricity that are used to make one ton of paper cups?

_____
_____

B A modern paper mill costs around $1 billion to build. How many cups would a company need to sell to pay for the cost of the plant, the water, and the electricity?

_____
_____
_____

- Water costs about $0.0007 per gallon.
- Electricity costs about $0.072/kWh.
- 33,000 cups weighs about a ton.
- One ton of cups sells for $2,000.

③ Evaluate Environmental Impact

With a partner, discuss possible impacts of the life cycle of a paper cup on the environment. Consider things such as the harvesting of trees, the use of chlorine-based chemicals to bleach the pulp, the energy required by the paper mill, problems associated with disposal of paper cups after their use, etc.

_____
_____
_____
_____
_____

④ Propose Improvements

With a partner, propose some improvements to the process of making or disposing of paper cups that might help make the life cycle of paper cups more environmentally friendly.

_____
_____
_____
_____
_____

⑤ Communicate Results

With your partner, tell the class the most important thing you have learned about the life cycle of a paper cup, and explain why you think it is important.

_____
_____
_____
_____
_____

Answers

1. Sample answer: Benefits include convenience and hygiene.

2. 16,000 gallons × $0.0007/gallon ≈ $10; 400 kWh × $0.072/kWh ≈ $30; $2000 − $10 − $30 = $1960 after selling 1 ton of cups and paying for water and electricity. To pay for the $1 billion plant, you need to sell 33,000 × $1 billion/$1960 ≈ 17 billion cups.

3. Sample answer: Cutting down trees damages the environment by reducing habitat and biodiversity. It also lets a lot more soil wash into the rivers when it rains. Another bad thing is that roads are made into the wilderness to get the trees. The chlorine chemicals cause water pollution, which makes us sicker. The energy used causes more greenhouse gases to be released. Paper mills also make a lot of noise, so I wouldn't want to live nearby.

4. Sample answer: We can stop using so many paper cups. Scientists can research ways to make cups that let us recycle them more. We could put better pollution control on factory smokestacks and water pipes to keep chemicals from getting into the air and water. We could build factories in a way that prevents erosion of the soil.

5. Sample answer: I had no idea paper cups had such a big impact on the environment. I will try to use fewer paper cups, and I think I will tell my parents to use reusable cups for their coffee and tea.

21st Century SKILLS

Learning and Innovation Skills

 individuals or small groups   🕐 30 min

Creativity and Innovation Based on the results of the life cycle analysis, have students design a paper cup that is more environmentally friendly. Encourage them to think about what a cup could be made of to make it recyclable, how much recycled fiber is in the cup, the manufacturing process, and so on. Invite students to share their ideas with the class.

Information, Media, and Technology Skills

👥 pairs or small groups   🕐 45 min

ICT (Information, Communications, and Technology) Literacy Many types of plant materials can be used to make paper, but current technology uses wood. Invite small groups of students to research the obstacles involved with changing manufacturing processes so that mills could use plant materials (other than trees or wood pulp) to make paper. Ask students to assess whether such a change would benefit or harm the global environment. For example, would using other plant materials encourage the cutting down of forests in order to grow the new plants, or would it preserve forests? Encourage students to share their findings with the class.

Life and Career Skills

 pairs or small groups   🕐 ongoing

Social and Cross-Cultural Skills Challenge students to develop and implement a survey that will assess how the United States compares to other parts of the world in terms of paper cup usage. The survey should explore questions such as: Do people in other parts of the world use paper coffee cups? If so, how common are they? If not, what materials are used for cups? And how common are fast-food establishments in other parts of the world? Encourage students to survey people who have lived in other parts of the world, preferably people from several different continents or nations. What can we learn from these other nations? Encourage students to share their findings with the class.

Differentiated Instruction

Basic *The Impact of a Paper Cup*

👥 individuals   🕐 30 min

Invite students to make a poster that explains the impact of a paper cup on the environment. Posters can employ text, images, labels, graphs, and other elements, and should take a stand for or against the use of paper cups. Have students display their posters in the class or school.

Advanced *Comparing Coffee Cups*

👥 individuals or pairs   🕐 ongoing

Invite interested students to compare different types of coffee cups—foam, paper, ceramic, metal—including both reusable and disposable cups. What are the pros and cons of each type of cup? Which type of cup do students think is best for the environment, and why? Invite students to outline a campaign to convince people to use the most environmentally-friendly cups.

ELL *Life Cycles of Paper Products*

👥 individuals or pairs   🕐 10 min

Have students draw sketches that show the life cycle of a paper cup and the life cycle of a newspaper. Beneath the sketches have students explain in their own words why these two paper products have such different life cycles. Encourage students to explain their sketches to a partner.

Customize Your Feature

- ☐ **21st Century Skills** Learning and Innovation Skills
- ☐ **21st Century Skills** Information, Media, and Technology Skills
- ☐ **21st Century Skills** Life and Career Skills
- ☐ **Basic** The Impact of a Paper Cup
- ☐ **Advanced** Comparing Coffee Cups
- ☐ **ELL** Life Cycles of Paper Products

Managing Resources

Essential Question Why should natural resources be managed?

Professional Development

For more detailed information about the topics in this lesson, refer to the Content Refresher in the Unit Opener pages.

Opening Your Lesson

Begin the lesson by assessing students' prerequisite and prior knowledge.

Prerequisite Knowledge

- Earth supports life.
- Humans use natural resources that need to be managed carefully.

Accessing Prior Knowledge

Anticipation Guide Anticipation Guides help students review what they know about a topic before reading the lesson. Invite students to make one for natural resource management. Provide students with some statements that are true and some that sound plausible but are untrue. Then have students write whether they agree or disagree before and after reading the lesson.

🌐 *Optional Online resource: Anticipation Guide support*

Customize Your Opening

☐ **Accessing Prior Knowledge,** above
☐ **Print Path** Engage Your Brain, SE p. 187
☐ **Print Path** Active Reading, SE p. 187
☐ **Digital Path** Lesson Opener

Key Topics/Learning Goals	Supporting Concepts
Resources 1 Describe what a natural resource is. 2 Describe the two main kinds of resources. 3 Identify the impacts of resource extraction, resource use, and resource disposal.	• A natural resource is anything that can be used to take care of a need. • Renewable resources can be replaced at least at the same rate at which they are used. Nonrenewable resources are used at a faster rate than they can be replaced. • Resource extraction, resource use, and resource disposal can damage the environment and livelihoods.
Managing Resources 1 Explain the need for managing resources. 2 Identify how stewardship and conservation are related to resource management. 3 Describe the management practices for renewable and nonrenewable resources. 4 List ways to manage resources globally, nationally, and individually.	• As the human population continues to grow, demands on natural resources increase. • Humans can ensure that resources are available through stewardship and conservation. • Reducing pollution and erosion, limiting how much of a resource can be used, and implementing replacement programs help maintain the quality of renewable resources. • Nonrenewable resource management focuses on increasing the efficiency with which resources are used. • Managing natural resources takes place on global, national, local, and individual levels.
Advantages and Disadvantages of Managing Resources 1 Discuss the advantages of managing resources. 2 Discuss the disadvantages of managing resources.	• The advantages of resource management include producing less waste and pollution, using less landfill space and energy, and needing fewer new resources. • The disadvantages of resource management include the costs as well as the changes in convenient lifestyles.

Options for Instruction

Two parallel paths provide coverage of the Essential Questions, with a strong **Inquiry** strand woven into each. Follow the **Print Path,** the **Digital Path,** or your customized combination of print, digital, and inquiry.

 Print Path
Teaching support for the Print Path appears with the Student Pages.

 Inquiry Labs and Activities

Digital Path
Digital Path shortcut: TS661728

Print Path	Inquiry Labs and Activities	Digital Path
Useful Stuff, SE pp. 188–189 **What are the two main types of resources?** • Renewable Resources • Nonrenewable Resources **What can happen when we use resources?**	**Quick Lab** The Impact of Resource Extraction **Activity** Reviewing Your Resources	**Renewable and Nonrenewable Resources** Interactive Images **Impacts of Resource Use** Interactive Images
Best Practices, SE pp. 190–191 **What are some effective ways to manage resources?** • Conserving Renewable Resources • Reducing the Use of Nonrenewable Resources	**Quick Lab** Managing a Resource **Activity** How Resourceful Are You?	**Need for Management** Slideshow **Conserving Resources** Interactive Images **Multilevel Policies** Graphic Sequence
Pluses and Minuses, SE pp. 192–193 **What are the disadvantages and advantages of managing resources?** **What kinds of changes can we make to manage resources?**	**Daily Demo** Non-Biodegradable Peanuts?	**Nonrenewable Resources** Interactive Images **Recycling Resources** Interactive Images **Managing Resources** Interactive Images

Options for Assessment

See the Evaluate page for options, including Formative Assessment, Summative Assessment, and Unit Review.

Engage and Explore

Activities and Discussion

Probing Questions *Renewable or Not?*

Managing Resources

 whole class
 10 min
(Inquiry) **DIRECTED** inquiry

Categorizing Coal and oil are formed from the remains of plant and marine organisms. If plants are renewable resources, why are coal and oil nonrenewable resources? Forming coal and oil occurs over a long period of time and requires special geological circumstances. If water is a renewable resource, why is it important to practice water stewardship and conservation? Sample answer: Fresh water may become less available if it is wasted, polluted, or managed poorly.

Discussion *Making Changes*

Advantages and Disadvantages of Managing Resources

 whole class
 10 min
(Inquiry) **DIRECTED** inquiry

Use the following questions to spark a discussion about the advantages and disadvantages of managing resources. What changes can we make ourselves or in our communities to help manage resources? What changes can we make nationally to help manage resources? What changes can we make internationally to help manage resources? Which changes might be easiest? Why? Which changes might be the most difficult? Why?

©Ariel Skelley/Blend Images/Getty Images

Activity *How Resourceful Are You?*

Managing Resources

 individuals, pairs, whole class
 10 min
(Inquiry) **GUIDED** inquiry

Think, Pair, Share Invite students, individually, to brainstorm realistic ways they can participate in the conservation and stewardship of natural resources in their daily lives. Sample answers: reducing waste by using a lunch box or canvas grocery bag; recycling at home and/or returning bottles and cans for redemption; conserving energy by lowering heat and air-conditioner use; reducing air pollution by walking or biking Then direct students to work with a partner to trade ideas and perhaps think of new ones. Finally, have pairs share their best ideas with the entire class. Write ideas on the board. Add new ideas as students work through the lesson.

Variation To reinforce the differences between renewable and nonrenewable resources, encourage students to make a T-chart with "renewable resources" and "nonrenewable resources" as the headings. As they brainstorm ideas for conserving natural resources, they can categorize them as conserving renewable or nonrenewable resources.

🌐 *Optional Online resource: Think, Pair, Share support*

Take It Home *Changing Habits*

Managing Resources

 adult-student pairs
 varied
(Inquiry) **GUIDED** inquiry

Students will work with an adult to list items in their home that have some relationship to a natural resource. The items can be made from a natural resource or require the use of a natural resource. Students will identify whether the items relate to a renewable or nonrenewable resource and describe the relationship. Finally, students will think about ways to manage or conserve the resources at home or in their own lives.

🌐 *Optional Online resource: student worksheet*

(l) ©Digital Vision/Getty Images

Customize Your Labs

📄 *See the Lab Manual for lab datasheets.*

🌐 *Go Online for editable lab datasheets.*

Levels of  **Inquiry**   **DIRECTED** inquiry   **GUIDED** inquiry   **INDEPENDENT** inquiry

introduces inquiry skills within a structured framework.   develops inquiry skills within a supportive environment.   deepens inquiry skills with student-driven questions or procedures.

Labs and Demos

Daily Demo *Non-Biodegradable Peanuts?*

Engage

Introducing Key Topics

 whole class
 10 min
 DIRECTED inquiry

PURPOSE **To compare biodegradable and non-biodegradable products**

MATERIALS

- polystyrene packing peanuts
- starch-based packing peanuts that dissolve in water
- bowl of water

1 **Ask:** What will happen if I dip the polystyrene peanut in water? Nothing with happen. It will get wet. Dip the peanut in water to confirm student predictions. Allow students to examine it.

2 Do the experiment again, using a peanut that dissolves in water. **Ask:** What will happen if I dip this in water? Sample answer: Nothing with happen. It will get wet. Dip the peanut in water. Allow students to examine that the peanut is dissolving.

3 Explain that the first peanut was made out of polystyrene, a plastic made from petroleum products, and the second peanut was made from starch that dissolves in water.

4 **Evaluating** Invite students to think about the advantages and disadvantages of starch-based and polystyrene packing peanuts. Sample answers: Advantages: Starch-based peanuts are made of a renewable plant resource. They are biodegradable and will reduce the amount of landfill waste. Polystyrene peanuts are cheaper and sturdier than starch-based peanuts. Disadvantages: Polystyrene peanuts are made from a nonrenewable resource. Starch-based peanuts are more expensive to produce.

5 **Applying** Ask students to brainstorm other applications of starch-based products and their advantages and disadvantages.

Variation Demo can also be done as a student activity.

Quick Lab *Managing a Resource*

Managing Resources

 small groups
 25 min
 DIRECTED inquiry

Students will model the management of fresh water as a resource.

PURPOSE **To model the management of a resource**

MATERIALS

- buret, 50 mL
- buret stand (or clamp and ring stand)
- graduated cylinder, 100 mL
- index cards, each with scenarios (10–12)
- water

Quick Lab *The Impact of Resource Extraction*

Resources

 small groups
 20 min
 INDEPENDENT inquiry

Students will work with a model of an underground resource that they must extract.

PURPOSE **To model the impact of resource extraction**

MATERIALS

- pan of gelatin containing raisins
- plastic knives
- plastic spoons
- stop watch
- straws
- toothpicks

Activities and Discussion

☐ **Probing Questions** Renewable or Not?

☐ **Activity** How Resourceful Are You?

☐ **Discussion** Making Changes

☐ **Take It Home** Changing Habits

Labs and Demos

☐ **Daily Demo** Non-Biodegradable Peanuts?

☐ **Quick Lab** Managing a Resource

☐ **Quick Lab** The Impact of Resource Extraction

Your Resources

_____

_____

_____

Explain Science Concepts

Key Topics	📖 Print Path	🖥 Digital Path
Resources	☐ **Useful Stuff,** SE pp. 188–189 • Compare, #5 • Visualize It!, #6 • Active Reading (Annotation strategy), #7 • Visualize It!, #8–10 **5 Compare** How is a renewable resource different from a nonrenewable resource? _____ _____ _____ _____ _____ _____	☐ **Renewable and Nonrenewable Resources** Distinguish between renewable and nonrenewable resources. ☐ **Impacts of Resource Use** Identify the impacts of resource use and disposal.
Managing Resources	☐ **Best Practices,** SE pp. 190–191 • Active Reading (Annotation strategy), #11 • Visualize It!, #12 • Apply, #13 **13 Apply** How can you reduce the use of nonrenewable resources? Write your ideas in the table below. 	Resource	Is used to...	Ways to reduce
oil	Make plastic objects. Provide energy.	Use reusable containers. Recycle plastics. Drive less.
coal		
metal				☐ **Need for Management** Explain the need for managing natural resources. ☐ **Conserving Resources** List and describe some considerations in the management of renewable resources. ☐ **Multilevel Policies** List methods of managing resources at global, national, and individual levels.
Advantages and Disadvantages of Managing Resources	☐ **Pluses and Minuses,** SE pp. 192–193 • Active Reading (Annotation strategy), #14 • Visualize It!, #15 • Think Outside the Book, #16 • Visualize It!, #17	☐ **Nonrenewable Resources** List and describe some considerations in the management of nonrenewable resources. ☐ **Recycling Resources** Describe the importance and practice of recycling in the management of both renewable and nonrenewable material resources. ☐ **Managing Resources** Discuss the advantages and disadvantages of managing natural resources.

Basic *A Picture Is Worth 1,000 Words*

Synthesizing Key Topics

 individuals or pairs

🕐 varied

Designing a Logo In 1970, Container Corporation of America (CCA) sponsored a nationwide contest for students to create a design that would symbolize the paper recycling process. At that time CCA, a paperboard company, was the largest user of recycled fiber in the United States, and it wanted a symbol to identify packages made from recycled materials. Gary Anderson, an architecture student, designed the three-arrow symbol we see today, and won the contest. Ask students to design a poster with a logo for a new natural resource management strategy.

🌐 *Optional Online rubric: Posters and Displays*

Advanced *Resourceful Cartoon*

Synthesizing Key Topics

 individuals or pairs

🕐 varied

Instruct students to create political cartoons relating to natural resource management. Students can focus on renewable resources, nonrenewable resources, or a particular natural resource. Cartoons should provide insight into what happens when we use resources and/or effective ways to manage resources. To help inspire ideas, provide students with examples of political cartoons from newspapers or the Internet.

ELL *Think Globally*

Synthesizing Key Topics

 individuals or pairs

 varied

Class Discussion Encourage English language learners to share what they know about environmental issues that relate to natural resources in their native countries. Encourage them to discuss any local or community conservation efforts.

Variation ELL students can also research issues that relate to natural resource use and any conservation efforts in their native countries and create a brief multimedia presentation to show the class.

🌐 *Optional Online rubric: Multimedia Presentation*

Lesson Vocabulary

natural resource	**renewable resource**
nonrenewable resource	**conservation** **stewardship**

Previewing Vocabulary

👥 whole class   🕐 5 min

Root Words Share the following roots or bases with the class.
- natural resource (*source*): **Ask:** What does *source* mean? supply **Ask:** What does *resource* mean? to supply again
- renewable and nonrenewable resource (*renew*): **Ask:** What does *renew* mean? to make new again **Ask:** What does *nonrenew* mean? unable to make new again **Ask:** What does *nonrenewable* mean? the process of being unable to make new again

Reinforcing Vocabulary

👥 individuals   🕐 15–20 min

Four Square To help students remember the vocabulary terms in the lesson, direct them to use four square graphic organizers. Let students write each term in the center. In the four squares around each term, tell students to write a definition, characteristics, examples, and nonexamples.

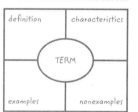

🌐 *Optional Online resource: Four Square support*

Customize Your Core Lesson

Core Instruction
☐ **Print Path** choices
☐ **Digital Path** choices

Vocabulary
☐ **Previewing Vocabulary** Root Words
☐ **Reinforcing Vocabulary** Four Square

Your Resources

Differentiated Instruction
☐ **Basic** A Picture is Worth 1,000 Words
☐ **Advanced** Resourceful Cartoon
☐ **ELL** Think Globally

Extend Science Concepts

Reinforce and Review

Activity *Reviewing Your Resources*

Synthesizing Key Topics   👥 whole class, small groups
            🕐 15–20 min

Carousel Review Help students review the material by following these steps:

1 Arrange chart paper in different parts of the room. (This strategy can be done on the board or on notebook paper if necessary.) On each paper, write a question to review the lesson content.

2 Divide students into small groups and assign each group a chart. Give each group a different colored marker.

3 Groups review their question, discuss the answer, and write a response.

4 After five minutes, each group rotates to the next station. Groups put a check by each answer they agree with, comment on answers they don't agree with, and add their own answers. Continue until all groups have reviewed all charts.

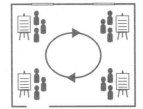

5 Invite each group to share information with the class.

Graphic Organizer

Synthesizing Key Topics   👥 Individuals or pairs
            🕐 15 min

Magnet Word After students have studied the lesson, ask them to complete Magnet Word graphic organizers to summarize key information. The first graphic organizer should focus on the term "Natural Resources" and include definitions, examples, and basic information about their use. The second graphic organizer should focus on the phrase "Natural Resource Management." Students can include information relating to why and how natural resources should be managed wisely.

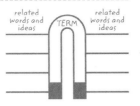

🌐 *Optional Online Resource: Magnet Word support*

Going Further

Math Connection

Managing Resources   👥 individuals, whole class
            🕐 varied

Solid Waste Statistics Invite interested students to conduct research on how much garbage each individual in the United States throws away each year. Provide students with information relating to the current U.S. population. Then as a class, ask students to calculate how much waste the entire nation produces each year. Students can also try to calculate how much land area this waste would occupy using a conversion (most likely from weight to volume).

Earth Science Connection

Resources   👥 individuals
            🕐 varied

Fossil Fuel Formation Timeline Fossil fuels are formed from remains of living things 50 to 350 million years ago. Coal was formed in great swamps, where plant remains first formed peat, which was later covered by sand and mud. Oil began as sediment formed from the remains of microscopic organisms living in oceans and seas. Over thousands of centuries, heat and pressure cause chemical changes that form both coal and petroleum. Encourage interested students to make a process chart or timeline that shows how coal or oil is formed.

Customize Your Closing

🗂 *See the Assessment Guide for quizzes and tests.*

🌐 *Go Online to edit and create quizzes and tests.*

Reinforce and Review

☐ **Activity** Carousel Review

☐ **Graphic Organizer** Magnet Word

☐ **Print Path** Visual Summary, SE p. 194

☐ **Digital Path** Lesson Closer

Evaluate Student Mastery

Formative Assessment

See the teacher support below the Student Pages for additional Formative Assessment questions.

Ask: How are renewable and nonrenewable resources different? Renewable resources can be replaced at the same rate or quicker than they are used. Nonrenewable resources cannot be replaced as quickly as they are used and may become unavailable. **Ask:** How can we conserve renewable resources? Sample answers: by placing limits on how much can be harvested; replanting or restocking **Ask:** How can we conserve nonrenewable resources? Sample answers: by using them efficiently; by reducing, reusing, and recycling **Ask:** What are advantages and disadvantages of managing resources? Sample answer: Advantages: We use less of the resource; it reduces waste, and causes less pollution. Disadvantages: Developing new technologies is expensive. Changing habits can be difficult.

Reteach

Formative assessment may show that students need reinforcement for certain topics. The resources below are recommended for reteaching. If students were introduced to a topic through the Print Path, you can also use the Digital Path to reteach, or vice versa.
🎧 *Can be assigned to individual students*

Resources
Quick Lab The Impact of Resource Extraction

Managing Resources
Graphic Organizer Magnet Word 🎧

Advantages and Disadvantages...
Discussion Making Changes

Summative Assessment

Alternative Assessment
Manage a Resource Wisely!

🌐 *Online resources: student worksheet, optional rubrics*

Managing Resources

Mix and Match: *Manage a Resource Wisely!*
Mix and match ideas to show what you've learned about managing resources.

1. Work on your own, with a partner, or with a small group.

2. Choose one resource from Column A, four methods from Column B, and one option from Column C. Check your choices.

3. Have your teacher approve your plan.

4. Submit or present your results.

A. Choose One Resource	B. Choose Four Ways to Manage the Resource	C. Choose One Way to Communicate Your Analysis
___ trees	___ limiting the amount that can be taken or used	___ diagram or illustration
___ fish		___ poster or brochure
___ iron ore	___ replacing what is used	___ 3-D model or computer-aided model
___ oil	___ reducing the use of chemicals to produce it	
___ clean water		___ booklet
___ fresh air	___ reducing the amount of energy needed to harvest or extract it	___ game
___ food (plant or animal product)		___ story, song, or poem, with supporting details
	___ using it more efficiently	___ skit, chant, or dance, with supporting details
___ cotton	___ recycling old products instead of harvesting or extracting new resources	___ multimedia presentation
___ coal		
_____	_____	___ mathematical explanation using statistics
		_____

Going Further
☐ Math Connection
☐ Earth Science Connection

Formative Assessment
☐ **Strategies** Throughout TE
☐ **Lesson Review** SE

Summative Assessment
☐ **Alternative Assessment** Manage a Resource Wisely!
☐ **Lesson Quiz**
☐ **Unit Tests A and B**
☐ **Unit Review** SE End-of-Unit

Your Resources

_____

_____

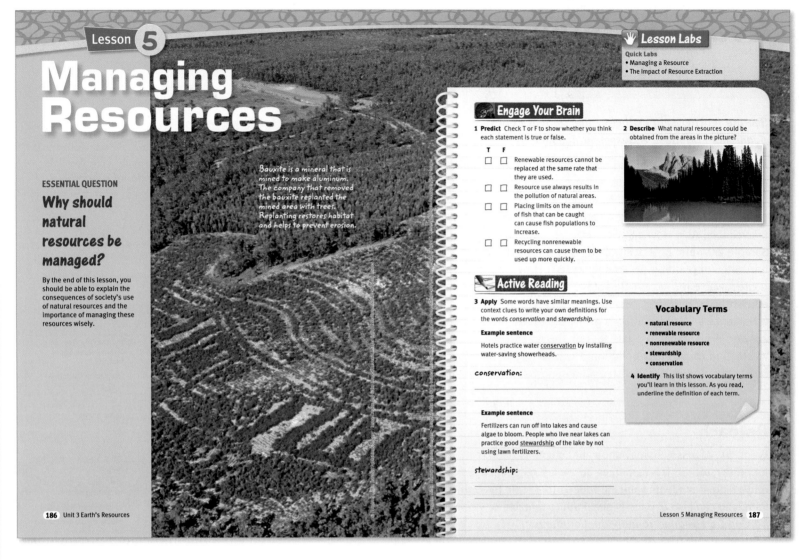

Answers

Answers for 1–3 should represent students' current thoughts, even if incorrect.

1. F; F; T; F

2. Natural resources include minerals from the mountain, wood from trees, and water from the lake.

3. Sample answers: Conservation is the wise use of resources so they will not run out; stewardship is being responsible for natural areas.

4. *See students' pages for annotations.*

Opening Your Lesson

Discuss student responses to items 1 and 2 to assess students' prerequisite knowledge and to estimate what they already know about managing natural resources.

Prerequisites Students should know that humans use energy to live and work, that natural resources can be categorized as renewable and nonrenewable resources, and that Earth's water, land, and air need to be protected.

Learning Alert

Difficult Concept Students may have difficulty understanding why renewable resources need to be managed. To help students understand why it is important to manage renewable resources, tell students that trees are a renewable resource because they can be replanted; however, if forests are cut down and used at a faster rate than they are replanted, the forest can become a nonrenewable resource. Invite students to think of other renewable resources that could be used at a faster rate than they are replaced. Sample answers: fish, clean water, plants and animals, unpolluted land

Useful Stuff

What are the two main types of resources?

Any natural material that is used by people is a **natural resource**. Water, trees, minerals, air, and oil are just a few examples of Earth's resources. Resources can be divided into renewable and nonrenewable resources.

Renewable Resources

A natural resource that can be replaced as quickly as the resource is used is a **renewable resource**. Water, trees, and fish are examples of renewable resources. Renewable resources can become nonrenewable resources if they are used too quickly. For example, trees in a forest can become nonrenewable if they are cut down faster than new trees can grow to replace them.

Nonrenewable Resources

A natural resource that is used much faster than it can be replaced is a **nonrenewable resource**. Coal is an example of a nonrenewable resource. It takes millions of years for coal to form. Once coal is used up, it is no longer available. Minerals, oil, and natural gas are other examples of nonrenewable resources.

5 Compare How is a renewable resource different from a nonrenewable resource?

_____
_____
_____
_____
_____

Visualize It!

6 Identify Label each picture as a renewable resource or nonrenewable resource.

Ⓐ

Ⓑ salt mine

Ⓒ

_____ _____ _____

What can happen when we use resources?

Natural resources can make people's lives easier. Natural resources allow us to heat and cool buildings, produce and use electricity, transport people and goods, and make products.

While natural resources are helpful, the way they are used can cause harm. Mining and oil spills can damage ecosystems. Oil spills can also harm local fishing or tourism industries. Burning coal or other fossil fuels can cause air and water pollution. Used products can fill landfills or litter beaches and other natural areas. Overuse of resources can make them hard to find. When resources are hard to find, they become more expensive.

Active Reading

7 Identify As you read, underline the possible effects of resource use by people.

Visualize It!

8 List What are three ways that natural resources are making life easier for this family?

_____
_____
_____
_____

9 Explain How can the extraction of natural resources damage the environment?

_____
_____
_____
_____

10 Describe How can human use of natural resources pollute the environment?

_____
_____
_____
_____

Answers

5. A renewable resource can be replaced as quickly as it is used. A nonrenewable resource is used much faster than it can be replaced.

6. A: renewable resource; B: nonrenewable resource; C: renewable resource

7. *See students' pages for annotations.*

8. Sample answer: Energy resources allow the family to cook food and stay warm. Other resources provided materials to make the appliances.

9. Sample answer: Accidents resulting in oil spills can damage beaches and kill wildlife.

10. Sample answer: Resources that are not properly disposed of can wash up onto beaches or cause pollution.

Building Reading Skills

Venn Diagram Invite students to compare renewable and nonrenewable resources using a Venn diagram.

🌐 *Optional Online resource: Venn Diagram support*

Interpreting Visuals

Direct students to examine the images that show renewable and nonrenewable resources. **Ask:** How can you determine whether or not a resource is renewable or nonrenewable? Sample answer: You have to figure out whether or not the resource can be replaced at a faster rate than it is used. **Ask:** Why are minerals such as salt considered nonrenewable? Sample answer: It takes a long time to form minerals, and they can be used at a faster rate than they are produced or extracted in nature.

Formative Assessment

Ask: What is a natural resource? any material that is used by people
Ask: What are some examples of natural resources? Sample answers: water, oil, gas, air, coal, trees **Ask:** How do natural resources make your life easier? Sample answers: They give us shelter; they help us store and cook food; they provide clothing and food.

Best Practices

What are some effective ways to manage resources?

As human populations continue to grow, we will need more and more resources in order to survive. People can make sure that resources continue to be available by practicing stewardship and conservation. **Stewardship** is the careful and responsible management of resources. **Conservation** is the protection and wise use of natural resources.

Conserving Renewable Resources

Stewardship of renewable resources involves a variety of conservation practices. Limits on fishing or logging can increase fish populations and protect forest ecosystems. Fish can be restocked in lakes and rivers. Logged areas can be replanted with trees. Water conservation can reduce the amount of water used in an area, so that rain can renew the water supply. Reducing the use of chemicals and energy resources can reduce the amount of pollution in air and water, and on land.

Active Reading

11 Identify As you read, underline the ways that resources can be managed effectively.

Visualize It!

12 Identify Describe the ways that each activity in the picture shows stewardship of natural resources.

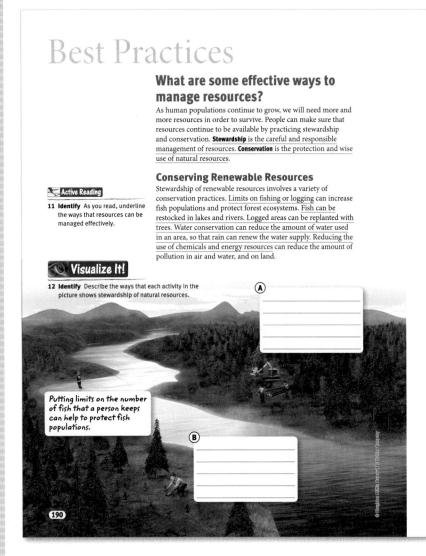

Putting limits on the number of fish that a person keeps can help to protect fish populations.

Ⓐ

Ⓑ

190

Reducing the Use of Nonrenewable Resources

Nonrenewable resources last longer if they are used efficiently. For example, compact fluorescent light bulbs, or CFLs, use much less energy to produce the same amount of light as incandescent light bulbs do. By using less electrical energy, fewer resources like coal are needed to produce electricity. Reducing, reusing, and recycling also reduce the amount of natural resources that must be obtained from Earth. Although recycling materials requires energy, it takes much less energy to recycle an aluminum can than it does to make a new one!

You can reuse a plastic water bottle instead of buying bottled water. Reusing conserves water and oil.

13 Apply How can you reduce the use of nonrenewable resources? Write your ideas in the table below.

Resource	Is used to...	Ways to reduce
oil	Make plastic objects. Provide energy.	Use reusable containers. Recycle plastics. Drive less.
coal		
metal		

Compact fluorescent bulbs last longer than incandescent bulbs and use a lot less energy.

Cans, wires, and other objects made of metal can be collected and recycled into new objects.

Lesson 5 Managing Resources **191**

Answers

11. *See students' pages for annotations.*

12. Sample answers: A: Harvesting individual trees instead of cutting whole forests can protect habitat for forest animals; B: Replanting logged areas can decrease erosion and increase forest habitat.

13. Sample answers: Coal is used to produce electricity. Turn off lights to conserve electricity. Metal is used to make objects. Recycle metal cans. Reuse metal objects like bolts and nails.

Learning Alert

President Theodore Roosevelt is depicted on Mount Rushmore because he was a strong advocate for conservation and stewardship. Because of him, Congress created the Forest Service in 1905 to manage federal forests. He set aside about 200 million acres as public lands, protecting them from commercial exploitation. He designated 150 national forests, the first 51 federal bird reservations, and five national parks. He pushed for the Reclamation Act of 1902, which established irrigation and other services for western lands. In 1911, the Reclamation Service completed Roosevelt Dam near Phoenix, Arizona.

Interpreting Visuals

Ask: How does using a refillable metal or plastic water bottle help reduce the use of resources? Sample answer: You don't need to buy disposable bottled water that you use once. Less plastic has to be manufactured, and less oil is used. **Ask:** Why is it more efficient to use a compact fluorescent bulb than a regular bulb? Sample answer: The CFL uses less energy, but gives the same amount of light over a longer time, so it saves on resources needed to make the bulb and saves electricity. **Ask:** How does recycling reduce our need to extract new resources, such as metal ores or oil? Sample answer: When we make new products out of old products, we don't have to extract more iron ore or oil to make the product.

Pluses and Minuses

What are the disadvantages and advantages of managing resources?

Active Reading

14 Identify As you read, underline the advantages of managing resources.

Managing resources has disadvantages. Developing new technologies that use fewer resources is expensive. Changing how people use resources can be difficult, because some people have a hard time breaking old habits. Recycling resources can sometimes be expensive and inconvenient.

Managing resources also has many advantages. Management can reduce the loss of a valuable resource. It can also reduce waste. Less waste means less space is needed for landfills. Many resources produce pollution as they are gathered or used, so resource management can lead to less pollution.

Visualize It!

15 Place a (–) next to each property of the hybrid electric car that is a disadvantage. Place a (+) next to each property of the car that is an advantage.

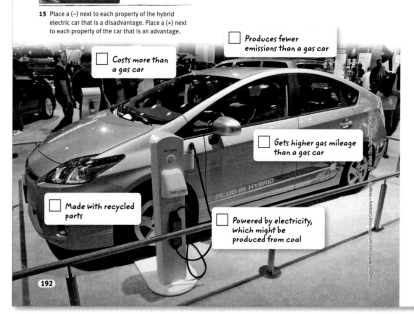

☐ Costs more than a gas car

☐ Produces fewer emissions than a gas car

☐ Gets higher gas mileage than a gas car

☐ Made with recycled parts

☐ Powered by electricity, which might be produced from coal

192

What kinds of changes can we make to manage resources?

Managing natural resources takes place on global, national, state, local, and individual levels. On the global level, countries make agreements to help manage international resources. For example, countries agreed to stop using chemicals called CFCs after scientists discovered that CFCs were causing damage to the ozone layer. The ozone layer is a resource that protects Earth from harmful radiation. Eliminating the use of CFCs has slowed the breakdown of the ozone layer.

Change Laws

On the national level, countries pass laws to manage resources. Many nations have laws that determine where, when, and how many trees can be harvested for timber. Laws also govern how materials must be disposed of to prevent and reduce harm to land and water. Governments spend money to promote recycling programs. In addition, government funding allows scientists to develop technologies for using resources more efficiently.

Change Habits

Think about all the things you do every day. Changing some of your habits can help to conserve resources. You can conserve water by taking shorter showers and turning off the faucet while brushing your teeth. You can use reusable lunch containers and water bottles. You can recycle disposable materials, such as plastic bottles or newspaper, instead of throwing them away. You can bike or walk instead of riding in a car. You can save energy by turning off lights or TV sets when they are not being used. Families can buy energy-efficient appliances to save even more energy.

16 Apply With a partner, suggest laws that could be enacted in your community to protect resources.

17 List What are some of the ways these students are conserving resources in their school lunchroom?

_____

_____

_____

_____

_____

_____

You can conserve resources in your school lunchroom.

ALUMINUM   MILK CARTONS   PLASTIC

Lesson 5 Managing Resources   193

Answers

14. *See students' pages for annotations.*

15. Pluses (+) should be next to: Made with recycled parts; Produces fewer emissions; Gets better gas mileage. Minuses (–) should be next to: Costs more than a gas car; Powered by electricity, which might be produced from coal.

16. Answers will vary.

17. Sample answer: Students are using reusable lunch containers, utensils, and water bottles. They are also recycling.

Probing Questions GUIDED Inquiry

Judging How do you determine whether the advantages of a conservation strategy outweigh the disadvantages? Sample answer: If it uses fewer resources and isn't too expensive, then it may be worth doing. Who decides if the costs are worth the savings in resources? Sample answers: Consumers decide if they are willing to change their habits. Governments can decide by enacting laws that make conservation a priority.

Evaluating How do you balance the conservation of the environment, on which it is hard to place a monetary value, against maintaining low prices for the resources extracted from that environment? Sample answer: Consider: Are there other alternatives? How important is the resource to our society? What are the long-term effects?

Using Annotations

Text Structure: Main Idea/Details To help students organize the information they underlined, instruct them to make a main idea web graphic organizer. Students can use "There are advantages and disadvantages to managing resources" as the main idea in the center and include the detail and examples that support the main idea around it.

Optional Online resources: Text Structure: Main Idea/Details, Main Idea Web support

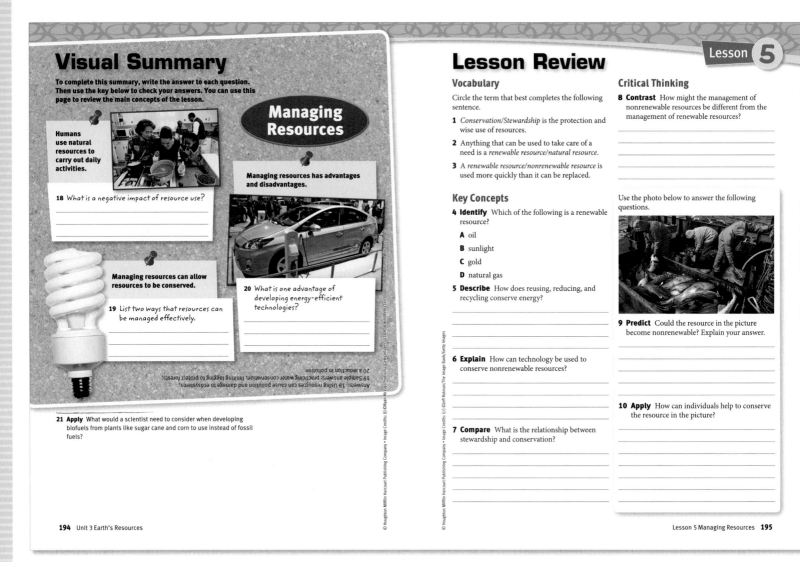

Visual Summary Answers

18. Using resources can cause pollution and damage to ecosystems.

19. Sample answers: practicing water conservation; limiting logging to protect forests.

20. a reduction in pollution

21. Sample answer: A scientist would need to consider whether the biofuel would be accepted by the public and whether it could be used by current technologies. The scientist would also have to determine whether the cost of developing the biofuel would outweigh the cost of extracting fossil fuels and cleaning up pollution caused by fossil fuels.

Lesson Review Answers

1. Conservation

2. natural resource

3. nonrenewable resource

4. B

5. When you reuse, reduce, or recycle, you use less energy than if you extract resources and make a new object.

6. Technology can be used to make appliances and vehicles more efficient to reduce the use of nonrenewable resources.

7. Sample answer: Stewardship of resources can be accomplished through the use of conservation practices.

8. Management of nonrenewable resources might focus on reducing the use of or reusing the resource; management of renewable resources might focus on controlling the amounts that are harvested and replacing the resource.

9. If the fish were harvested at a faster rate than they could reproduce, fish could become a nonrenewable resource.

10. Sample answer: Individuals could catch and release fish instead of keeping them. They could eat only certain kinds of fish that are plentiful. People who fish commercially could limit the amount of fish that they keep.

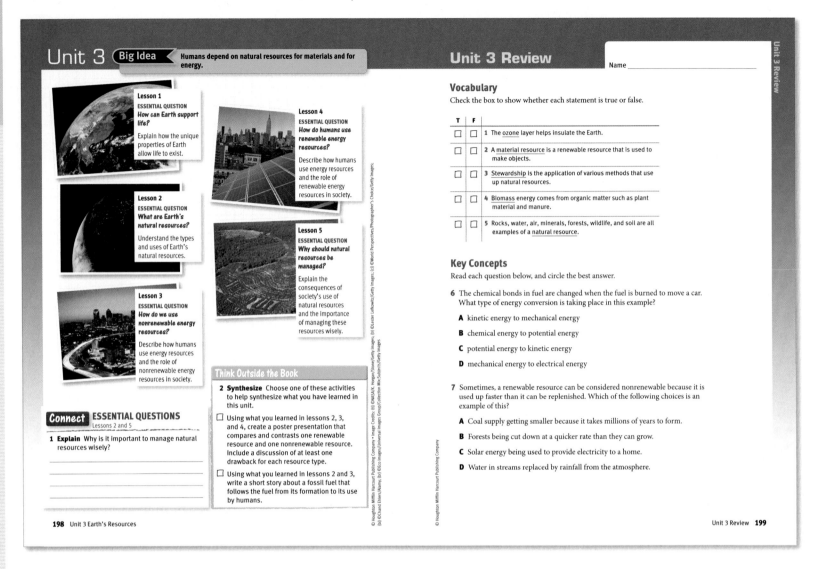

Unit Summary Answers

1. It is important to manage natural resources wisely because as the human population grows, so too does the demand for natural resources. By using resources wisely, humans can ensure that they are available for future generations.

2. Option 1: Sample answer: Natural gas is a gaseous fossil fuel that is a nonrenewable resource. Natural gas forms from the remains of tiny marine organisms. This fossil fuel is used for cooking, generating electricity, and warming buildings. A drawback is that its use contributes to air pollution. Wind energy is a renewable resource. Wind energy is used to do work or generate electricity. A benefit is that its use does not generate pollution, though the technology used to harness energy does generate some pollution. A drawback is that wind energy is practical only in areas that receive high amounts of wind.

   Option 2: Short stories should include an explanation of how the fossil fuel forms, how it is processed, if applicable, and how it is used by humans.

Unit Review Response to Intervention

A Quick Grading Chart follows the Answers. See the Assessment Guide for more detail about correct and incorrect answer choices. Refer back to the Lesson Planning pages for activities and assignments that can be used as remediation for students who answer questions incorrectly.

Answers

1. True This statement is correct because the ozone layer traps the sun's heat close to the surface, keeping the temperature range on Earth livable. (Lesson 1)

2. False This statement is incorrect because a material resource can be renewable or nonrenewable resources used to make objects, food, or drink. (Lesson 2)

3. False This statement is incorrect because stewardship is the management of resources, and not methods for using up resources. (Lesson 5)

Unit 3 Review continued

8 The diagram below shows the process of photosynthesis.

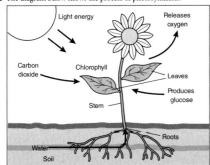

How is photosynthesis best summarized?

A The process by which oxygen enters a leaf and is converted into carbon dioxide.

B The process by which plants use the sun's energy to make chlorophyll.

C The process by which plants convert the sun's energy into energy stored as glucose.

D The process by which water enters through the roots and glucose is produced.

9 Which of the following is a disadvantage of managing resources?

A less of the natural resource is wasted

B reduction in pollution due to less manufacturing

C expense of recycling materials

D more resources extracted from Earth

10 What is a major reason solar energy is not used everywhere on a large scale?

A It is too difficult to purchase and install solar panels.

B Solar energy is not very effective at producing electricity.

C The manufacture of solar panels produces too much pollution.

D Solar panels are most efficient in places that receive lots of sunlight.

11 The chemicals released by burning petroleum in car engines contribute to what local and global effects?

A smog and global warming   **C** acid rain and fusion

B fog and radioactivity   **D** sulfur dioxide decrease and ozone buildup

12 What gas molecule found in Earth's atmosphere is made up of three oxygen atoms?

A ozone   **C** sulfur dioxide

B nitrogen   **D** carbon dioxide

13 Nuclear energy is best described as what type of energy resource?

A renewable   **C** renewable and inexhaustible

B nonrenewable   **D** nonrenewable because it is used up so rapidly

Critical Thinking

Answer the following questions in the space provided.

14 Below is an example of a technology used for alternative energy.

What type of energy does the equipment in the picture harness? _____

Is the type of energy harnessed by this equipment renewable or nonrenewable? Explain your answer. _____

_____

Name one advantage and one disadvantage of using this type of energy.

_____

_____

Answers *(continued)*

4. True Biomass energy is the energy obtained from plant material, manure, or any other organic matter. (Lesson 4)

5. True This statement is true because a natural resource is any natural material that is used by people. (Lesson 2)

6. Answer C is correct because the potential energy that is stored in the chemical bonds is being converted to kinetic energy when the engine runs. (Lesson 2)

7. Answer B is correct because trees are a renewable resource but could be cut down faster than they are replaced. (Lesson 2)

8. Answer C is correct because the sun's energy is required for the plant to make food, or glucose. (Lesson 1)

9. Answer C is correct because the cost of setting up recycling centers and equipment for people is expensive. (Lesson 5)

10. Answer D is correct because solar energy can be used only in areas that receive large amounts of sunshine. (Lesson 4)

11. Answer A is correct because the release of chemicals by burning petroleum products can cause smog, and the release of carbon dioxide contributes to climate change. (Lesson 3)

12. Answer A is correct because ozone is made of three oxygen atoms, and it forms a layer with other gases to insulate Earth. (Lesson 1)

13. Answer B is correct because uranium ore is a nonrenewable resource and the most widely used radioactive material from which nuclear energy is released. (Lesson 3)

14. Key Elements:

  • Identifies that wind energy is harnessed by a windmill or wind turbine; expresses understanding that wind energy is renewable energy because it originates from the sun

  • States a reasonable advantage and disadvantage of using wind energy (e.g., *Advantage: It generates only a small amount of pollution. Disadvantage: It can be used only where there is a fair amount of wind.*) (Lesson 4)

Unit 3 Review continued

15 The unique properties of Earth make life possible. What are the five basic necessities that all living things need to survive on Earth?

_____

_____

Why is the distance from Earth to the sun important for life on Earth?

_____

_____

Why is the rotation of Earth important to conditions on Earth?

_____

_____

Connect **ESSENTIAL QUESTIONS**
Lessons 3 and 5

Answer the following question in the space provided.

16 Below is a graph of the production and use of petroleum in the United States in the past, present, and likely usage in the future.

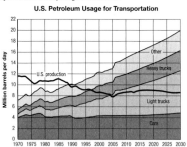

U.S. Petroleum Usage for Transportation

Summarize how current production and usage of petroleum compare.

_____

_____

Name two risks linked to offshore drilling and transporting petroleum.

_____

_____

202 Unit 3 Earth's Resources

© Houghton Mifflin Harcourt Publishing Company

Quick Grading Chart

Use the chart below for quick test grading. The lesson correlations can help you target reteaching for missed items.

Item	Answer	Cognitive Complexity	Lesson
1.	—	Low	1
2.	—	Low	2
3.	—	Moderate	5
4.	—	Low	4
5.	—	Low	2
6.	C	Moderate	2
7.	B	Moderate	2
8.	C	High	1
9.	C	Moderate	5
10.	D	Moderate	4
11.	A	Moderate	3
12.	A	Low	1
13.	B	Moderate	3
14.	—	Moderate	4
15.	—	High	1
16.	—	Moderate	3, 5

Cognitive Complexity refers to the demand on thinking associated with an item, and may vary with the answer choices, the number of steps required to arrive at an answer, and other factors, but not the ability level of the student.

Answers _(continued)_

15. Key Elements:

- Lists source of energy (e.g., food), water, air, habitat, and waste disposal as basic necessities for life to exist on Earth
- Expresses that Earth's distance from the sun allows for an appropriate amount of energy to support life on Earth and keep Earth's temperatures within a habitable range
- Recognizes that Earth's rotation allows for each side of Earth to receive sunlight regularly (Lesson 1)

16. Key Elements:

- Identifies that usage of petroleum is much greater than production
- Gives at least two examples of harm to the environment through spills (e.g., loss of income for the tourism and fishing industries, loss of habitat for wildlife, loss of life for wildlife) (Lessons 3, 5)

The Big Idea and Essential Questions

This Unit was designed to focus on this Big Idea and Essential Questions.

Big Idea Humans and human population growth affect the environment.

Lesson	ESSENTIAL QUESTION	Student Mastery	PD Professional Development	Lesson Overview
LESSON 1 Human Impact on Water	*What impact can human activities have on water resources?*	To explain the impact that humans can have on the quality and supply of fresh water	Content Refresher, TE p. 260	TE p. 266
LESSON 2 Human Impact on Land	*What impact can human activities have on land resources?*	To identify the impact that human activity has on Earth's land	Content Refresher, TE p. 261	TE p. 284
LESSON 3 Human Impact on the Atmosphere	*How do humans impact Earth's atmosphere?*	To identify the impact that humans have had on Earth's atmosphere	Content Refresher, TE p. 262	TE p. 298
LESSON 4 Protecting Earth's Water, Land, and Air	*How can Earth's resources be used wisely?*	To summarize the value of conserving Earth's resources and the effect that wise stewardship has on land, water, and air resources	Content Refresher, TE p. 263	TE p. 312

©Cameron Davidson/Photographer's Choice RF/Getty Images

 **Professional Development** Science Background

Use the keywords at right to access

- Professional Development from **The NSTA Learning Center**
- **SciLinks** for additional online content appropriate for students and teachers

Keywords

conservation   natural resources

humans and the environment

 National Science Teachers Association

 SCiLINKS.
THE WORLD'S A CLICK AWAY

Options for Instruction

Two parallel paths provide coverage of the Essential Questions, with a strong **Inquiry** strand woven into each. Follow the **Print Path,** the **Digital Path,** or your customized combination of print, digital, and inquiry.

	LESSON 1 Human Impact on Water	LESSON 2 Human Impact on Land	LESSON 3 Human Impact on the Atmosphere
Essential Questions	*What impact can human activities have on water quality?*	*What impact can human activities have on land resources?*	*How do humans impact Earth's atmosphere?*
Key Topics	• Water as a Resource • Water Pollution • Water Quality • Water Supply and Flow	• How Humans Use Land • Land Degradation	• Air and Air Pollution • Effects of Human Activities on Atmosphere • Air Quality and Health • Air Pollution and Earth
Print Path	Teacher Edition pp. 266–280 Student Edition pp. 206–219	Teacher Edition pp. 284–296 Student Edition pp. 222–231	Teacher Edition pp. 298–311 Student Edition pp. 232–243
Inquiry Labs	Lab Manual **Field Lab** Investigating Water Quality **Quick Lab** Ocean Pollution... **Quick Lab** Turbidity and Water Temperature	Lab Manual **Quick Lab** Investigating Human Impact on the Land **Quick Lab** Roots and Erosion	Lab Manual **Quick Lab** Collecting Air-Pollution Particles **Quick Lab** ... Indoor...Pollution ▣ Virtual Lab Air Pollution
Digital Path	Digital Path TS671350 	Digital Path TS671370 	Digital Path TS671340

LESSON 4
Protecting Earth's Water, Land, and Air

How can Earth's resources be used wisely?

- Conservation and Stewardship
- Preservation and Conservation of Water
- Land Management and Conservation
- Reducing Air Pollution

Teacher Edition
pp. 312–326

Student Edition
pp. 244–257

Lab Manual
Exploration Lab Filtering Water

Quick Lab Soil Erosion

 Virtual Lab
Human Impact

Digital Path
TS671371

UNIT 4
Unit Projects

Citizen Science Project
Investigating Water Resources

Teacher Edition p. 265

Student Edition
pp. 204–205

Unit Assessment
Formative Assessment
Strategies RTI
Throughout TE
Lesson Reviews SE
Unit PreTest
Summative Assessment
Alternative Assessment
(1 per lesson) RTI
Lesson Quizzes
Unit Tests A and B
Unit Review RTI
(with answer remediation)
Practice Tests
(end of module)
Project-Based Assessment
See the Assessment Guide for quizzes and tests.

Go Online to edit and create quizzes and tests.

Response to Intervention
See RTI teacher support materials on p. PD6.

Teacher Notes

Differentiated Instruction

English Language Proficiency

Strategies for **English Language Learners (ELL)** are provided for each lesson, under the Explain tabs.

LESSON 1 *Illustrated Dictionary*, TE p. 271
Diagramming Water Flow, TE p. 271

LESSON 2 *Vocabulary Cards*, TE p. 289

LESSON 3 *Illustrated Dictionary*, TE p. 303
Going with the (Air) Flow, TE p. 303

LESSON 4 *Role-Playing to Show Conservation*, TE p. 317

Vocabulary strategies provided for all students can also be a particular help for ELL. Use different strategies for each lesson or choose one or two to use throughout the unit. Vocabulary strategies can be found in the Explain tab for each lesson (TE pp. 271, 289, 303, and 317).

Leveled Inquiry

Inquiry labs, activities, probing questions, and daily demos provide a range of inquiry levels. Preview them under the Engage and Explore tabs starting on TE pp. 268, 286, 300, and 314.

Levels of **Inquiry**

DIRECTED inquiry	GUIDED inquiry	INDEPENDENT inquiry
introduces inquiry skills within a structured framework.	develops inquiry skills within a supportive environment.	deepens inquiry skills with student-driven questions or procedures.

Each long lab has two inquiry options:

LESSON 1 **Field Lab** *Investigating Water Quality*

LESSON 4 **Exploration Lab** *Filtering Water*

Go Digital! 🌐 thinkcentral.com

Digital Path

The Unit 4 Resource Gateway is your guide to all of the digital resources for this unit. To access the Gateway, visit thinkcentral.com.

Digital Interactive Lessons

Lesson 1 Human Impact on Water TS671350

Lesson 2 Human Impact on Land TS671370

Lesson 3 Human Impact on the Atmosphere TS671340

Lesson 4 Protecting Earth's Water, Land, and Air TS671371

More Digital Resources

In addition to digital lessons, you will find the following digital resources for Unit 4:

People in Science: Angel Montoya

Virtual Labs: Air Pollution Footprints (previewed on p. 301) Human Impact (previewed on p. 315)

RTI ▸ Response to Intervention

Response to Intervention (RTI) is a process for identifying and supporting students who are not making expected progress toward essential learning goals. The following *ScienceFusion* components can be used to provide strategic and intensive intervention.

Component	Location	Strategies and Benefits
STUDENT EDITION Active Reading prompts, Visualize It!, Think Outside the Book	**Throughout each lesson**	Student responses can be used as screening tools to assess whether intervention is needed.
TEACHER EDITION Formative Assessment, Probing Questions, Learning Alerts	**Throughout each lesson**	Opportunities are provided to assess and remediate student understanding of lesson concepts.
TEACHER EDITION Extend Science Concepts	**Reinforce and Review, TE pp. 272, 290, 304, 318** **Going Further, TE pp. 272, 290, 304, 318**	Additional activities allow students to reinforce and extend their understanding of lesson concepts.
TEACHER EDITION Evaluate Student Mastery	**Formative Assessment, TE pp. 273, 291, 305, and 319** **Alternative Assessment, TE pp. 273, 291, 305, and 319**	These assessments allow for greater flexibility in assessing students with differing physical, mental, and language abilities as well as varying learning and communication modes.
TEACHER EDITION Unit Review Remediation	**Unit Review, TE pp. 328–330**	Includes reference back to Lesson Planning pages for remediation activities and assignments.
INTERACTIVE DIGITAL LESSONS and VIRTUAL LABS	**thinkcentral.com** **Unit 4 Gateway** **Lesson 1 TS671350** **Lesson 2 TS671370** **Lesson 3 TS671340** **Lesson 4 TS671371**	Lessons and labs make content accessible through simulations, animations, videos, audio, and integrated assessment. Useful for review and reteaching of lesson concepts.

Content Refresher

Professional Development

Human Impact on Water

ESSENTIAL QUESTION
What impact can human activities have on water quality?

1. Water as a Resource

Fresh water is not so abundant as once believed.

Earth, it has been suggested, is misnamed; the planet should actually have been called "Water," because nearly three-fourths of Earth's surface is covered with water. However, the vast majority of that water is salty—useful for swimming in, but not so good for supporting life. Fresh water is essential to life on the planet, and there is increasing pressure on this limited resource.

As the human population increases, more water is demanded for drinking, bathing, cooking, growing food, and even playing. But humans are using the fresh water available more quickly than natural processes can replenish it. Once considered a renewable resource, water is being looked at differently—as nonrenewable.

2. Water Pollution

Natural and human sources cause water pollution.

Among the human causes are:

- chemical pollution, which occurs when fertilizers, pesticides, and other chemicals are improperly disposed of and enter water systems;

- thermal pollution, which occurs when water that has been warmed at a power plant is returned to streams without adequate cooling, affecting temperature and oxygen levels; and

- biological pollution, which occurs when living or dead organisms end up in water supplies.

Eutrophication occurs naturally in aging ponds and lakes, but artificial eutrophication occurs when humans increase the nutrients in a body of water, such as through fertilizer runoff, so that algae growth increases dramatically; when the algae die, their decomposition uses up oxygen in the water, making less oxygen available to aquatic life.

3. Water Quality

Water quality is a measure of water's cleanliness.

Some measures of water quality include temperature, pH level, dissolved oxygen level, and turbidity (cloudiness).

In large systems, such as those that supply water to cities, the fresh water undergoes a cleaning process that includes adding chemicals (such as chlorine, which kills microorganisms, and fluoride, which helps protect teeth from decay) and removing particles by filtering and settling. Used water enters the sewer or wastewater system to be treated before being returned to the environment.

4. Water Supply and Flow

To get fresh water where they need it, humans alter its natural flow.

They may reroute rivers to carry water to fields, or build canals to carry the water instead. In some areas, so much water is diverted that the lower parts of a river are dry at certain times of the year. Humans also build dams across rivers, which change the surrounding land greatly. Below the dam, the speed and volume of water flow change, resulting in a new ecosystem. Behind the dam, water may collect and form a lake (or a reservoir) in what had once been a valley, drowning what had been there.

Concerned citizens are working on ways to reduce water use and to make better use of the water we have. Students are probably familiar with low-flow toilets and showers, which use less water than old models. Researchers are developing "gray water" systems that use the water from household showers, tubs, sinks, and dishwashers to wash cars and flush toilets.

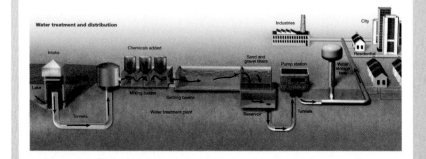

Lesson 4 Protecting Earth's Water, Land, and Air   Assign small groups of students to choose a specific strategy for protecting Earth's water, land, or atmosphere. Have each group write a one-minute skit in the format of a public service announcement. In the skits, students should clearly identify the problem and the strategy for solving it. Encourage students to be creative in writing and presenting their skits to the rest of the class.

Lesson 2

Human Impact on Land

Essential Question
What impact can human activities have on land resources?

1. How Humans Use Land

Humans use land in five major ways: for residential use, agricultural use, commercial/industrial use, transportation, and recreational use.

Agricultural use occurs mostly in rural areas, which contain few people and have large areas of open space. Rural areas or natural (wild) areas that have been altered very little by people are most likely to be sites for recreation.

Urban land is largely covered for the most part by buildings and roads. As cities and towns grow, rural and natural areas are changed, or urbanized. Urban sprawl occurs when natural or rural areas that lie near cities or towns are developed to create roads or housing in response to the expansion of the human population in the urban area. Sprawl is a cause for concern, and urbanization is one of the main causes of land degradation.

2. Land Degradation

Land degradation is the process by which human activity and natural processes damage land to the point that it can no longer support the local ecosystem. In addition to urbanization, deforestation and poor farming methods can cause land degradation.

Deforestation is the removal of trees and other plants, which leads to accelerated soil erosion. Surface mining techniques, in which vegetation is removed from the land, may have similar effects.

Poor farming methods also leave the soil vulnerable to erosion and land degradation. When cattle or other livestock are kept in one area for too long, they can eat too much of the vegetation, or overgraze, an area; as plants and their roots are removed from the soil, erosion increases. Another poor practice involves planting the same crops in the same place year after year, which causes some soil nutrients to be used up. Crop rotation can relieve this pressure on the soil, and contour plowing, no-till farming, and terracing on steep hillsides can help prevent soil erosion and land degradation.

When cities expand, natural vegetation is removed and land areas are paved; both of these actions change the rate of erosion and deposition and reduce the amount of available farmland. Impervious cover, such as concrete and asphalt, prevents the infiltration of water into aquifers (recharge zones), and may lead to flooding and runoff that causes erosion.

All three of these factors can lead to the desertification of an area. Desertification is the process by which land becomes more desertlike and unable to support living systems.

COMMON MISCONCEPTIONS RTI

LIVING THINGS AND SOIL Some students may hold the misconception that living things only live on top of the soil but not in it. They may not realize that many organisms—from earthworms and insects to bacteria and fungi—actually find a home within it.

This misconception is addressed in the Activity *Collect and Examine Soil* on p. 286, as well as on p. 294.

Content Refresher (continued)

Professional Development

Human Impact on Atmosphere

ESSENTIAL QUESTION

How do humans impact Earth's atmosphere?

1. Air and Air Pollution

Just about everything on Earth needs air to survive. As a result, air is an important resource. The gases in the atmosphere help regulate Earth's temperature and protect organisms from harmful radiation. However, there is not a lot of air; the thickness of the atmosphere around Earth can be compared to an eggshell around an egg.

Air pollution is the contamination of the atmosphere by pollutants from human and natural sources. Air pollution also refers to the contaminants in the atmosphere.

Pollutants may be put directly into the air, such as vehicle exhaust and volcanic ash. These pollutants are called primary pollutants. When a primary pollutant reacts with something else, secondary pollutants may form. For example, ground-level ozone forms when vehicle exhaust reacts with sunlight and air. Smog forms when vehicle exhaust and ozone react with sunlight. Particulates are tiny particles of solids or liquids in the air.

2. Air Quality and Health

Air quality is a measure of how clean or polluted the air is. It is commonly assessed by measuring the amount of ozone, other gaseous pollutants, and particulate matter, as well as rain pH, in the atmosphere in a specific location. Today, air quality reports are often part of the weather report on the evening news or in the newspaper; these forecasts allow people who are adversely affected by poor air quality to take steps to protect their health.

Prolonged exposure to air pollutants can cause serious health problems in humans, including asthma, allergies, lung problems, and heart problems. Short-term effects include headaches, difficulty breathing, and coughing. Long-term effects include asthma, lung cancer, and emphysema.

Even inside our homes and businesses, we face air pollution. Indoor air pollution includes smoke, dust, pet dander, chemicals from cleaners and paints, and even air fresheners! Because indoor air pollutants are contained in a small area, they can cause or increase respiratory disorders and other illnesses.

3. Air Pollution and Earth

Urbanization involves changing rural areas or open country into urban areas. As cities grow, more industry and increased vehicle traffic creates air pollution.

When burned, fossil fuels release pollutants that combine with the water in the air to form acid precipitation, which can damage trees, soils, and water. Damage to Earth's protective ozone layer remains a concern.

 COMMON MISCONCEPTIONS   RTI

THE OZONE HOLE Students may not understand what the ozone hole is. Because ozone is a gas, there cannot really be a hole in the ozone layer. When people talk about the "hole" in the ozone layer, they are referring to a region of the ozone layer that is thinner than it is in other places.

This misconception is addressed in the Probing Question on p. 300 and p. 310.

Protecting Earth's Water, Land, and Air

ESSENTIAL QUESTION

How can Earth's resources be used wisely?

1. Conservation and Stewardship

Conservation is the responsible use of natural resources.

Conservation involves using resources sustainably to ensure that their supplies will not be exhausted or unfit for use by future generations (e.g., through pollution). Conservation also includes obtaining and using resources in a manner that prevents harm to natural environments and organisms. Stewardship is an aspect of conservation. It is an ethic that involves taking responsibility for how resources are used and preserved. Good stewardship involves individuals, commerce (industry, agriculture, mining), and governments. Governments set guidelines and pass laws to help protect resources, including air, water, and land. By abiding by these rules and laws, commerce and individuals act as good stewards.

2. Preservation and Conservation of Water

Only a small amount of Earth's water is freshwater.

Freshwater needs to be used in a manner that maintains its quality and ensures it is not used more quickly than it can be cleaned for reuse or replaced by nature. Maintaining water quality is also vital to both humans and ecosystems. Reducing water pollution is one key to protecting water quality. Laws, such as the Clean Water Act and the Safe Drinking Water Act, exist to reduce and control water pollution.

3. Land Management and Conservation

Land can be protected through conservation and management.

Problems affecting land resources include, overuse, erosion, and pollution. Overuse depletes soil of nutrients vital to plants. Erosion carries away soil, depositing it in new locations. Soil conservation methods, such as contour plowing, strip cropping, terracing, no-till farming, and crop rotation, can reduce soil erosion and help maintain soil quality. Other means of preventing or repairing land degradation include reforestation (planting new trees to reestablish forests), reclamation (returning land to its original condition), preservation (protection), vertical development (mixed-used high-rise buildings), and recycling.

4. Reducing Air Pollution

Clean air is essential for healthy organisms.

Government agencies and international panels monitor the environment and pass laws, such as the Clean Air Act and the Kyoto Protocol, to reduce toxic emissions. Scientists have developed technologies to make burning fossil fuels more efficient (e.g., hybrid cars) and to reduce the amount of pollutants released into the atmosphere (e.g., scrubbers). Energy conservation efforts commonly focus on how to reduce air pollution by decreasing the amount of fossil fuels burned to generate electricity. Developing alternative energy sources, such as solar, wind, and geothermal energy, may reduce pollution by lessening our use of fossil fuels.

 COMMON MISCONCEPTIONS **RTI**

CONSERVATION OF MATTER Students may hold the misconception that when pollutants are removed from the environment (air, water, soil) they simply disappear. Point out that this idea contradicts the law of conservation of matter which states that matter cannot be created or destroyed.

This misconception is addressed in the Learning Alert on p. 322.

Advance Planning

These activities may take extended time or special conditions.

Unit 4

Project Investigating Water Resources, p. 265
research and writing time

Graphic Organizers and Vocabulary pp. 271, 272, 289, 290, 303, 304, 317, 318
ongoing with reading

Lesson 1

Field Lab Investigating Water Quality, p. 269
requires two 45-min periods and outdoor sampling

Lesson 2

Activity Collect and Examine Soil, p. 286
requires outdoor observations

Daily Demo Reducing Rainy Runoff, p. 287
prepare soda bottles prior to class

Quick Lab Investigating Human Impact on the Land, p. 287
identify online sources for news articles in advance

Lesson 3

Quick Lab Identifying Sources of Indoor Air Pollution, p. 301
digital camera for each student group

Lesson 4

Exploration Lab Filtering Water, p. 315
prepare lab materials in advance

Quick Lab Soil Erosion, p. 315
bottle caps, sod, and potting soil

What Do You Think?

Have students use the photographs and captions as clues to ways in which human activities affect the environment. For example, construction of roads and structures requires land to be altered and potentially affects the habitats of organisms. Use these questions to relate student ideas to the concept on the next page.

Ask: Where does the water we use every day come from? Sample answers: from a lake, a reservoir, or an underground aquifer

Ask: How did the water get into the lake, reservoir, or aquifer? Sample answer: Rain filled the lake or reservoir.

UNIT 4

Human Impact on the Environment

Big Idea
Humans and human population growth affect the environment.

Human actions, such as cutting down trees to build large housing developments, affect the surrounding ecosystem.

Factories cause pollution.

What do you think?
Human activities can affect Earth's air, water, and land resources in a variety of ways. What are some specific ways in which human activities affect the environment?

203

Interpreting Visuals

Have students compare the forest in the background of the photo with the homes and streets in the foreground.

Ask: How do you think the building of these homes impacted the forest ecosystem that had previously existed there? The construction of homes and streets may have destroyed habitats and forced animals to move. Construction debris may have polluted water that organisms depended on. Have students look at the photo of the factory. **Ask:** How can factories cause pollution? Factories can release smoke and other forms of pollution into the atmosphere. They can also release toxins into the water and land.

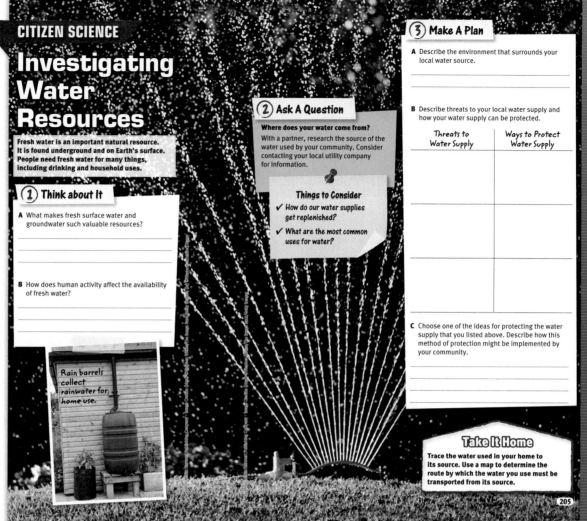

Unit 4
Human Impact on the Environment

CITIZEN SCIENCE
Investigating Water Resources

Fresh water is an important natural resource. It is found underground and on Earth's surface. People need fresh water for many things, including drinking and household uses.

1 Think about It

A What makes fresh surface water and groundwater such valuable resources?

B How does human activity affect the availability of fresh water?

Rain barrels collect rainwater for home use.

204 Unit 4 Human Impact on the Environment

2 Ask A Question

Where does your water come from?
With a partner, research the source of the water used by your community. Consider contacting your local utility company for information.

Things to Consider

✔ How do our water supplies get replenished?

✔ What are the most common uses for water?

3 Make A Plan

A Describe the environment that surrounds your local water source.

B Describe threats to your local water supply and how your water supply can be protected.

Threats to Water Supply	Ways to Protect Water Supply

C Choose one of the ideas for protecting the water supply that you listed above. Describe how this method of protection might be implemented by your community.

Take It Home
Trace the water used in your home to its source. Use a map to determine the route by which the water you use must be transported from its source.

205

CITIZEN SCIENCE

Unit Project Investigating Water Resources

1. Think About It

A. Clean, fresh water is in limited supply, but humans, animals, and plants all require water to live.

B. Human activity can pollute the fresh water that is available. We also change the course of rivers and modify the availability of fresh water for other organisms.

2. Ask a Question

Students should be able to get in touch with their local utility company to learn the source of fresh water in the community.

3. Make a Plan

A. Students should identify the local water source and describe whether it is surrounded by trees, residential developments, or industry, as well as any other features of the environment.

B. Threats may include industrial pollution, pollution from waste water, and agricultural runoff. Ideas for protecting a water supply may include enclosing it, restricting land use, or filtration.

C. Students should describe a specific action the community could take to protect the water supply. For example, students might describe specific land-use restrictions that could be implemented.

Take It Home

Students should assume that the water takes the most direct route, and they should plot a likely course. As a class, discuss the most likely route the water takes.

🌐 *Optional Online rubric: Class Discussion*

Human Impact on Water

Essential Question What impact can human activities have on water resources?

Professional Development

For more detailed information about the topics in this lesson,
refer to the Content Refresher in the Unit Opener pages.

Opening Your Lesson

*Begin the lesson by assessing students'
prerequisite and prior knowledge.*

Prerequisite Knowledge

- How the water cycle works
- Definition of *natural resources*

Accessing Prior Knowledge

Ask: Why do people need water? Sample
answers: to drink; to wash; to raise plants
and animals

Ask: Is water renewable or nonrenewable?
Water is renewable if people don't use
it up faster than the water cycle can
replenish it.

Customize Your Opening

☐ **Accessing Prior Knowledge,** above

☐ **Print Path** Engage Your Brain,
SE p. 207, #1–2

☐ **Print Path** Active Reading,
SE p. 207, #3–4

☐ **Digital Path** Lesson Opener

Key Topics/Learning Goals

Water as a Resource

1 Tell why humans need water.
2 Tell why fresh water is a
limited resource.
3 Explain the importance of
water quality.
4 Compare supply and quality.

Water Pollution

1 Define *water pollution,
point-source pollution,* and
non-point- source pollution.
2 Explain how humans can
cause water pollution.
3 Define *eutrophication* and
acid rain.

Water Quality

1 Discuss water quality
measures and monitoring.
2 Explain how water quality is
maintained in the U.S.
3 Tell how urbanization can
affect water quality.

Water Supply and Flow

1 Define *reservoir* and
urbanization.
2 Tell how humans affect the
fresh water flow and supply.

Supporting Concepts

- Humans need water to live.
- A fixed amount of water is available on
Earth. More and more people are using the
same amount of water.
- Water was once considered a renewable
resource. Now some consider it a
nonrenewable resource.

- Water circulation carries pollution to many
places.
- Humans can cause chemical, thermal, or
biological pollution of water.
- Artificial eutrophication occurs when humans
increase nutrients in a body of water.
- Acid rain can harm organisms in the water
or on land.

- Water quality measures include temperature,
pH, dissolved oxygen levels, and turbidity.
- Drinking water in large systems is cleaned
before people drink it.
- The Environmental Protection Agency (EPA)
sets standards for safe drinking water.
- Growing urban populations negatively affect
water quality.

- A reservoir is an artificial body of water,
usually behind a dam. Dams change the
landscape, river shape, and water flow.
- Humans require more and water. Aquifers
and groundwater are being overused.

Options for Instruction

Two parallel paths provide coverage of the Essential Questions, with a strong **Inquiry** strand woven into each. Follow the **Print Path,** the **Digital Path,** or your customized combination of print, digital, and inquiry.

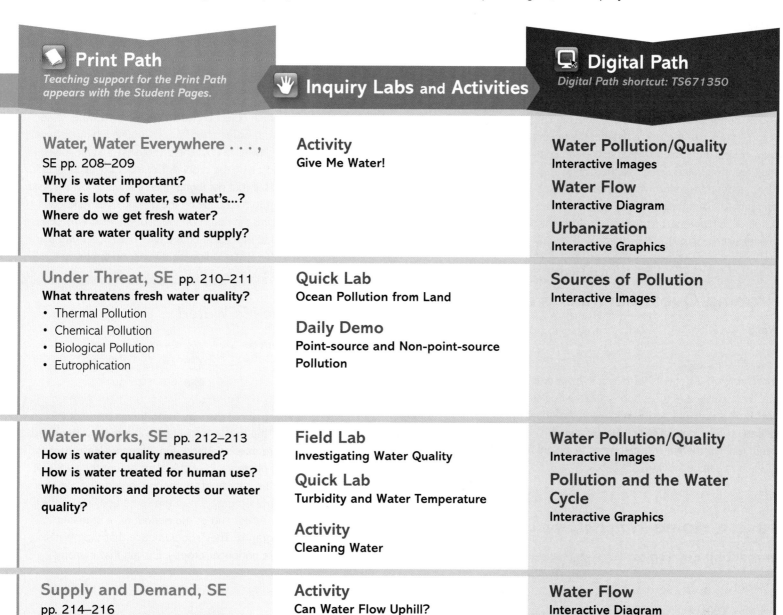

Print Path
Teaching support for the Print Path appears with the Student Pages.

Inquiry Labs and Activities

Digital Path
Digital Path shortcut: TS671350

Water, Water Everywhere . . . ,
SE pp. 208–209
Why is water important?
There is lots of water, so what's...?
Where do we get fresh water?
What are water quality and supply?

Activity
Give Me Water!

Water Pollution/Quality
Interactive Images

Water Flow
Interactive Diagram

Urbanization
Interactive Graphics

Under Threat, SE pp. 210–211
What threatens fresh water quality?
• Thermal Pollution
• Chemical Pollution
• Biological Pollution
• Eutrophication

Quick Lab
Ocean Pollution from Land

Daily Demo
Point-source and Non-point-source Pollution

Sources of Pollution
Interactive Images

Water Works, SE pp. 212–213
How is water quality measured?
How is water treated for human use?
Who monitors and protects our water quality?

Field Lab
Investigating Water Quality

Quick Lab
Turbidity and Water Temperature

Activity
Cleaning Water

Water Pollution/Quality
Interactive Images

Pollution and the Water Cycle
Interactive Graphics

Supply and Demand, SE
pp. 214–216
How does water get to the faucet?
What threatens our water supply?
How do efforts to supply water to...

Activity
Can Water Flow Uphill?

Water Flow
Interactive Diagram

Urbanization
Interactive Graphics

Options for Assessment

See the Evaluate page for options, including Formative Assessment, Summative Assessment, and Unit Review.

Engage and Explore

Activities and Discussion

Activity *Cleaning Water*

Engage

Water Quality

 individuals or pairs

 15 min

Inquiry **GUIDED** inquiry

Make some water dirty by mixing in a variety of substances such as soil, pepper, ketchup, and vegetable oil. Let students pour some of the dirty water through a strainer containing sand and gravel. Let them collect the strained water in a clean container. Have students compare the strained water to the dirty water and some tap water. Have students describe what happened to the strained water. Invite students to make their own polluted water using varying quantities of water, oil, dirt, pepper, and so on. Have them describe how hard it is to filter each pollutant out of the water.

Probing Question *Water in the Community*

Water Quality

 whole class

 10 min

Analyzing Ask students to think about water in their community. Are there ponds, lakes, streams, or rivers? If so, what do they look like? Are they safe to swim or boat in? What kind of things might run into the water from homes in the area? Are fish threatened locally? If so, how?

Take It Home *Water at Home*

Introducing Key Topics

 adult-student pairs

30 min each day

Have students work with an adult to list all the ways that they use water daily at home. They should estimate how much water is used for a variety of purposes such as showering, flushing the toilet, watering plants, and cooking. Invite students to share their findings with the class and compare calculations.

⏻ *Optional Online resource: student worksheet*

Activity *Can Water Flow Uphill?*

Water Supply and Flow

 pairs or small groups

 20 min

 GUIDED inquiry

Invite students to model how water gets to homes. Have them put a container up on a high object outside. This will be a water tower that supplies a city with water. Then have them use tubing or hoses to connect the water tower to containers (houses) that are lower. One container should be on the ground. The other container should be set up on a small hill (but not higher than the water tower). **Ask:** Can water flow down to the house on the ground? yes **Ask:** Can water flow up the hill to the house on the hill? yes **Ask:** Why does the water flow uphill to the house on the hill? The hill is lower than the water tower, so the water is flowing down from the tower.

Activity *Give Me Water!*

Water as a Resource

 small groups

 45 min

 GUIDED inquiry

Get students thinking about the way living things use water. At the beginning of the period, provide small groups with potted house plants that are due for a thorough watering. Have each group take a digital photograph of the plant before they water it. Every 10 min over the course of the period, one group member should take another photograph from the same position as the first one was taken. At the end of the period, have students compare the photographs. They should notice that the plant's leaves and stems are no longer droopy. Explain that in many plants, water pressure helps support the plant.

Customize Your Labs

 See the Lab Manual for lab datasheets.

 Go Online for editable lab datasheets.

Labs and Demos

Daily Demo *Point-source and Non-point-source Pollution*

Engage

Water Pollution

  whole class
  10 min
  GUIDED inquiry

PURPOSE **To show the difference between point-source pollution and non-point-source pollution**

MATERIALS

- food coloring
- sheet of chart paper
- sheet of white paper
- spray bottle filled with water
- water-soluble marker

1 Draw dots with a marker on a sheet of white paper.

2 Put the chart paper on the floor and have a student hold the paper above the chart paper while you spray it with water until water drips onto the chart paper.

3 **Explaining** Tell the students that this models non-point-source pollution because the pollution source consists of many places (the dots).

4 Then drip a spot of food coloring onto the chart paper.

5 **Explaining** Tell the students that this is point-source pollution because all of the pollution comes from one place.

Quick Lab *Ocean Pollution from Land*

PURPOSE **To build a model that shows how the water cycle helps land pollution enter bodies of water**

See the Lab Manual or go Online for planning purposes.

Quick Lab *Turbidity and Water Temperature*

Water Quality

  small groups
  30 min
  DIRECTED inquiry

Students measure temperature changes in water samples that have different levels of turbidity.

PURPOSE **To investigate how turbidity affects water temperature**

MATERIALS

- clear plastic cups (3)
- dirt or potting soil (about 3 tablespoons)
- marker
- spoon
- thermometer
- water (2 cups)

Field Lab *Investigating Water Quality*

Water Quality

  pairs
  two 45-min periods
  GUIDED or **INDEPENDENT** inquiry

Students compare the properties of water samples from various locations. Then students add garden fertilizer to each sample and observe changes.

PURPOSE **To understand that water from different sources varies in quality and chemistry**

MATERIALS

- bottles, 1 L (4)
- cups, clear plastic
- garden fertilizer
- marker
- pH meter or pH paper
- measuring spoons
- water samples

Activities and Discussion

☐ **Activity** Cleaning Water

☐ **Probing Question** Water in the Community

☐ **Activity** Can Water Flow Uphill?

☐ **Activity** Give Me Water!

Labs and Demos

☐ **Daily Demo** Point/Nonpoint

☐ **Quick Lab** Ocean Pollution from Land

☐ **Quick Lab** Turbidity and Temperature

☐ **Field Lab** Investigating Water Quality

Your Resources

_____

_____

_____

Explain Science Concepts

Key Topics	📖 Print Path	💻 Digital Path
Water as a Resource	☐ **Water, Water Everywhere . . . ,** SE pp. 208–209 • Visualize It!, #5 • Active Reading, #6 • Think Outside the Book, #7 **Active Reading** **6 List** What are the different sources of fresh water?	☐ **Water Pollution/Quality** Explore issues of water quality. ☐ **Water Flow** Learn about fresh water above and below ground. ☐ **Urbanization** Explore how development can affect the water supply.
Water Pollution	☐ **Under Threat,** SE pp. 210–211 • Active Reading (annotation strategy), #8 • Visualize It!, #9–10 **Active Reading** **8 Identify** As you read, underline the sources of water pollution.	☐ **Sources of Water Pollution** Explore issues of water quality. 
Water Quality	☐ **Water Works,** SE pp. 212–213 • Predict, #11 • Active Reading (annotation strategy), #12 • Active Reading, #13 **11 Predict** Why might increased turbidity increase the chance of something harmful being in the water?	☐ **Water Pollution/Quality** Explore issues of water quality. ☐ **Pollution and the Water Cycle** Learn how the water cycle can affect pollution.
Water Supply and Flow	☐ **Supply and Demand,** SE pp. 214–216 • Active Reading (annotation strategy), #14 • Infer, #15 • Visualize It!, #16 • Active Reading, #17 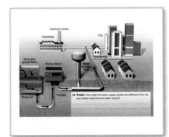	☐ **Water Flow** Learn about fresh water above and below ground. ☐ **Urbanization** Explore how development can affect the water supply.

Differentiated Instruction

Basic *Where Do We Get Water?*

Water as a Resource

👥 individuals
🕐 20 min

Have students use a concept map to list all of the places fresh water can be found. In the center, have them write *fresh water,* and list sources in surrounding circles. Sample answers: rivers, lakes, streams, reservoirs, aquifers, wells, rain, ice, snow

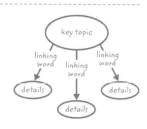

🌐 *Optional Online resource: Concept Map support*

Advanced *Calculating Demand*

Synthesizing Key Topics

👥 individuals
🕐 20 min

Provide students with these data: The typical person uses 80 to 100 gal of water per day. Based on these data, have students calculate how much water the people in their school and community use per week. **Answer: Students should multiply the number of people by the number of gallons by 7 days per week.** You may wish to have students convert gallons to liters.

ELL *Illustrated Dictionary*

Water Pollution

👥 pairs
🕐 20 min

Have students write each of these terms at the top of a separate sheet of paper or index card: *thermal pollution, chemical pollution, biological pollution,* and *eutrophication.* Under each term, have students draw examples that help them remember what each type of pollution is.

ELL *Diagramming Water Flow*

Water Supply and Flow

👥 individuals or pairs
🕐 20 min

Have students draw a diagram showing how water gets from the ground to a faucet. Encourage students to look at the illustrations in the lesson. Have them label the parts of the diagram.

Lesson Vocabulary

urbanization	thermal pollution
water pollution	eutrophication
point-source pollution	potable
non-point-source pollution	reservoir

Previewing Vocabulary

👥 whole class
🕐 10 min

Word Origins Explain that understanding where words come from can help with understanding.
- Potable water is water that is safe to drink. The word *potable* comes from the Latin *potare,* which means "to drink."

Reinforcing Vocabulary

👥 individuals
🕐 ongoing

Word Triangles Have students complete each triangle by writing a vocabulary term and its definition in the bottom section. In the middle section, students write a sentence using the term correctly. In the top section, students draw a small picture to help them remember the word.

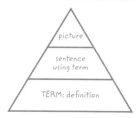

Customize Your Core Lesson

Core Instruction
☐ **Print Path** choices
☐ **Digital Path** choices

Vocabulary
☐ **Previewing Vocabulary** Word Origins
☐ **Reinforcing Vocabulary** Word Triangles

Your Resources

_____

_____

Differentiated Instruction
☐ **Basic** Where Do We Get Water?
☐ **Advanced** Calculating Demand
☐ **ELL** Illustrated Dictionary
☐ **ELL** Diagramming Water Flow

Extend Science Concepts

Reinforce and Review

Activity *Card Responses*

Synthesizing Key Topics whole class | ongoing

1 Have students make answer cards for questions you will ask about the lesson. Cards can be true/false, yes/no/maybe, A/B/C/D, or whatever fits your questions.

2 Ask a question. At your signal, students hold up their cards. To help them answer individually, be very clear about the signal and have everyone give it at the same time, for example, "Ready, one, two, three, cards up!"

3 Every 10 min or so, ask a few recall questions about the lesson. Have students answer by holding up a card. If the class's accuracy rate is less than 90%, it might be time to reteach another way. This technique also helps you pinpoint those who need individual help.

Graphic Organizer

Water Supply and Flow individuals | 20 min

Process Chart After students have studied the lesson, ask them to make a process chart that shows how water travels from a reservoir or lake to their school. When they are finished, encourage volunteers to describe the steps in the process out loud. Write the steps on the board. Have the rest of the students figure out if any steps are missing. If steps are missing, add them as students suggest them.

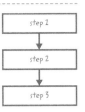

Going Further

Health Connection

Water Pollution whole class | 10 min

Discussion After students have studied the lesson, have them discuss which type of water threat (thermal pollution, chemical pollution, biological pollution, artificial eutrophication) they think is most serious in their community or state. Invite students to share the reasons they think this form of pollution is the most serious problem. Encourage others to share and discuss different thoughts and opinions.

Real World Connection

Water Quality individuals or pairs | ongoing

In-Depth Research Ask students to research and (if possible) visit a water treatment plant nearby. Then have students describe the steps in the treatment of the water they drink and answer the following questions: Does their water have fluoride? What is added to their water to make it safe? How do scientists test the water to know it is safe? What would happen if the water supply were contaminated? Is there a backup water supply?

Customize Your Closing

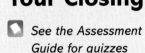 *See the Assessment Guide for quizzes and tests.*

Go Online to edit and create quizzes and tests.

Reinforce and Review

☐ **Activity** Card Responses

☐ **Graphic Organizer** Process Chart

☐ **Print Path** Visual Summary, SE p. 218

☐ **Digital Path** Lesson Closer

Evaluate Student Mastery

Formative Assessment

See the teacher support below the Student Pages for additional Formative Assessment questions.

Have students identify a river, stream, or lake in their area. Make a two-column chart on the board. Ask volunteers to identify possible sources of pollution that affect this water supply in one column and to suggest ways the water could be protected in the other.

Reteach

Formative assessment may show that students need reinforcement for certain topics. The resources below are recommended for reteaching. If students were introduced to a topic through the Print Path, you can also use the Digital Path to reteach, and vice versa.

🎧 *Can be assigned to individual students*

Water as a Resource
Probing Question Water in the Community 🎧
Activity Give Me Water! 🎧

Water Pollution
Quick Lab Ocean Pollution from Land
ELL Illustrated Dictionary 🎧

Water Quality
Activity Cleaning Water
Field Lab Investigating Water Quality
Quick Lab Turbidity and Water Temperature

Water Supply and Flow
Activity Can Water Flow Uphill?

Summative Assessment

Alternative Assessment
Water Pollution

🌐 *Online resources: student worksheet, optional rubrics*

Human Impact on Water

Mix and Match: *Water Pollution*
Mix and match ideas to show what you've learned about how people affect our water supply.

1. Work on your own, with a partner, or with a small group.

2. Choose one source of pollution from Column A, two topics from Column B, and one option from Column C. Check your choices.

3. Have your teacher approve your plan.

4. Submit or present your results.

A. Choose One Pollution Source	B. Choose Six Things to Analyze	C. Choose One Way to Communicate Analysis
___ acid rain	___ drinkability of water	___ diagram or illustration
___ urbanization	___ effect on rivers and lakes	___ model
___ dams	___ effect on aquifers	___ drawings or descriptions
___ chemical spills	___ effect on ground water	___ booklet
___ farm waste/sewage	___ effect on surface water	___ game
___ oil refineries	___ effect on reservoirs	___ story, song, or poem, with supporting details
___ plastics factories	___ effect on oceans	___ skit, chant, or dance, with supporting details
___ fertilizer runoff	___ effect on water temperature	
___ construction work	___ effect on the supply of fresh water	___ multimedia presentation
___ urban runoff		___ mathematical explanation
___ power plants	___ effect on measures of water quality	___ flowchart
___ irrigation		___ timeline
___ human activity _____		

Going Further
☐ Health Connection
☐ Real World Connection
☐ Print Path Why It Matters, SE p. 217

Formative Assessment
☐ Strategies Throughout TE
☐ Lesson Review SE

Summative Assessment
☐ Alternative Assessment Water Pollution
☐ Lesson Quiz
☐ Unit Tests A and B
☐ Unit Review SE End-of-Unit

Your Resources

_____   _____

_____   _____

Answers

Answers for 1–3 should represent students' current thoughts, even if incorrect.

1. Answers may vary. Similarities may include to get food and to drink (or maintain life processes in cells). Differences may include that fish need water to be able to breath and that humans need water for farming, household activities, and industry.

2. water; river

3. Nonrenewable: a resource that cannot be restored

4. *Students' annotations will vary.*

Opening Your Lesson

Discuss students' answers to item 1 to assess their prerequisite knowledge and to estimate what they already know about water pollution, water quality, water flow, and water as a resource.

Prerequisites Students should know what natural resources are and understand the terms *renewable resource* and *nonrenewable resource*.

Probing Questions   GUIDED Inquiry

Generalizing How might life be different for people if water were rationed or difficult to obtain? Sample answers: People probably would not waste so much water. They might collect rainwater to use on lawns or gardens. People might reuse water more often.

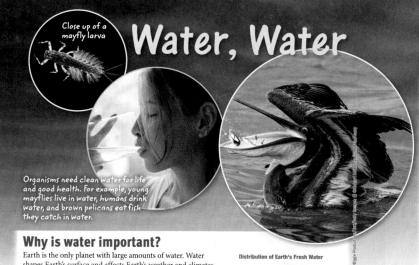

Water, Water Everywhere...

Close up of a mayfly larva

Organisms need clean water for life and good health. For example, young mayflies live in water, humans drink water, and brown pelicans eat fish they catch in water.

Why is water important?

Earth is the only planet with large amounts of water. Water shapes Earth's surface and affects Earth's weather and climates. Most importantly, water is vital for life. Every living thing is made mostly of water. Most life processes use water. Water is an important natural resource. For humans and other organisms, access to clean water is important for good health.

There is lots of water, so what's the problem?

About 97% of Earth's water is salty, which leaves only 3% as fresh water. However, as you can see from the graph, over two-thirds of Earth's fresh water is frozen as ice and snow. But a lot of the liquid water seeps into the ground as groundwater. That leaves much less than 1% of Earth's fresh liquid water on the surface. Water is vital for people, so this small volume of fresh surface and groundwater is a limited resource.

Areas with high densities of people, such as cities, need lots of fresh water. Cities are getting bigger, and so the need for fresh water is increasing. *Urbanization* (ER•buh•ny•zhay•shuhn) is the growth of towns and cities that results from the movement of people from rural areas into the urban areas. The greater demand for fresh water in cities is threatening the availability of water for many people. Fresh water is becoming a natural resource that cannot be replaced at the same rate at which it is used.

208 Unit 4 Human Impact on the Environment

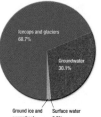
Distribution of Earth's Fresh Water

Icecaps and glaciers 68.7%
Groundwater 30.1%
Ground ice and permafrost 0.86%
Surface water 0.3%

Visualize It!

5 Interpret What percentage of fresh water on Earth is frozen? What percentage of fresh water is liquid?

Where do we get fresh water?

Fresh water may fall directly as precipitation, or may melt from ice and snow. Earth's fresh liquid water is found as surface water and groundwater. *Surface water* is any body of water above the ground. It includes liquid salt or fresh water, or solid water, like snow and ice. Water may seep below the surface to become *groundwater*. Groundwater is found under Earth's surface, in spaces in rocks or in soil, where it can be liquid or frozen.

Aquifers and Groundwater

Aquifers and ground ice are forms of groundwater. An *aquifer* is a body of rock or sediment that can store a lot of water, and that allows water to flow easily through it. Aquifers store water in spaces, called *pores*, between particles of rock or sediment. Wells are dug into aquifers to reach the water. In polar regions, water is often frozen in a layer of soil called *permafrost*.

Rivers, Streams, and Lakes

Rivers, streams, and most lakes are fresh surface waters. A stream or river may flow into a bowl-shaped area, which may fill up to form a lake. Many millions of people around the world depend on fresh water that is taken from rivers and fresh water lakes.

What are water quality and supply?

Water quality is a measure of how clean or polluted water is. Water quality is important because humans and other organisms depend on clean water to survive. It is vital for living things to not only have water, but also to have clean water. Dirty, contaminated water can make us sick or even kill us.

Water supply is the availability of water. Water supply influences where and when farmers grow crops, and where people can build cities. *Water supply systems* carry water from groundwater or surface waters so people can use the water. The systems can be a network of underground pipes, or a bucket for scooping water from a well. A shortage of clean, fresh water reduces quality of life for people. Many people in developing countries do not have access to clean, fresh water.

Active Reading

6 List What are the different sources of fresh water?

Think Outside the Book (Inquiry)

7 Observe Keep a water diary for a day. Record every time you use water at school, at home, or elsewhere. At the end of the day, review your records. How could you reduce your water usage?

Many people do not have a water supply to their homes. Instead, they have to go to a local stream, well, or pump to gather water for cooking, cleaning, and drinking.

209

Answers

5. 69.6% (or 70%) of fresh water on Earth is frozen. 30.4% (or 30%) is fresh liquid water.

6. Surface waters: lakes, rivers, streams
   Groundwater: aquifers

7. Students should keep a record of water use over a 24-hour period and suggest realistic means of reducing his or her water use. For example, not leaving the water on to run from the faucet while brushing teeth, taking quicker showers, or showering instead of taking a bath.

Learning Alert GUIDED Inquiry

Difficult Concepts Some students may not understand how water can be stored in rock. Explain that some rocks are porous like a sponge. Water can get trapped in the holes, but it will flow out when a well is dug. Water can also be stored in sediment, such as sand, and can be accessed by digging a well.

Probing Questions GUIDED Inquiry

Comparing Have students think about where their water comes from (most likely a public water supply). **Ask:** How is our water different from the water in places where people get their water from a stream or public well? Sample answer: Our water comes from a public water supply that is cleaned and tested for safety. Water from a stream or public well may not be as safe, because it is often not cleaned or tested before people use it.

Building Graphing Skills

Have students look at the circle graph on the page. **Ask:** How much of the world's fresh water is available for use? 1% (because most of the fresh water is frozen) **Ask:** Where is the rest of the world's fresh water? It is frozen. **Ask:** Where might people get water if the fresh water is used up? Sample answer: from salt water, which makes up 97% of all water

Under Threat

What threatens fresh water quality?

When waste or other material is added to water so that it is harmful to organisms that use it or live in it, **water pollution** (WAW•ter puh•LOO•shuhn) occurs. It is useful to divide pollution sources into two types. **Point-source pollution** comes from one specific site. For example, a major chemical spill is point-source pollution. Usually this type of pollution can be controlled once its source is found. **Nonpoint-source pollution** comes from many small sources and is more difficult to control. Most nonpoint-source pollution reaches water supplies by runoff or by seeping into groundwater. The main sources of nonpoint-source pollution are city streets, roads and drains, farms, and mines.

Active Reading

8 Identify As you read, underline the sources of water pollution.

Thermal Pollution

Any heating of natural water that results from human activity is called **thermal pollution**. For example, water that is used for cooling some power plants gets warmed up. When that water is returned to the river or lake it is at a higher temperature than the lake or river water. The warm water has less oxygen available for organisms that live in the water.

Chemical Pollution

Chemical pollution occurs when harmful chemicals are added to water supplies. Two major sources of chemical pollution are industry and agriculture. For example, refineries that process oil or metals and factories that make metal or plastic products or electronic items all produce toxic chemical waste. Chemicals used in agriculture include pesticides, herbicides, and fertilizers. These pollutants can reach water supplies by seeping into groundwater. Once in groundwater, the pollution can enter the water cycle and can be carried far from the pollution source. *Acid rain* is another form of chemical pollution. It forms when gases formed by burning fossil fuels mix with water in the air. Acid rain can harm both plants and animals. It can lower the pH of soil and water, and make them too acidic for life.

Biological Pollution

Many organisms naturally live in and around water, but they are not normally polluters. *Biological pollution* occurs when live or dead organisms are added to water supplies. Wastewater may contain disease-causing microbes from human or animal wastes. *Wastewater* is any water that has been used by people for such things as flushing toilets, showering, or washing dishes. Wastewater from feed lots and farms may also contain harmful microbes. These microbes can cause diseases such as dysentery, typhoid, or cholera.

Eutrophication

Fresh water often contains nutrients from decomposing organisms. An increase in the amount of nutrients in water is called **eutrophication** (yoo•TRAWF•ih•kay•shuhn). Eutrophication occurs naturally in water. However, *artificial eutrophication* occurs when human activity increases nutrient levels in water. Wastewater and fertilizer runoff that gets into waterways can add extra nutrients which upset the natural biology of the water. These extra nutrients cause the fast growth of algae over the water surface. An overgrowth of algae and aquatic plants can reduce oxygen levels and kill fish and other organisms in the water.

210 Unit 4 Human Impact on the Environment

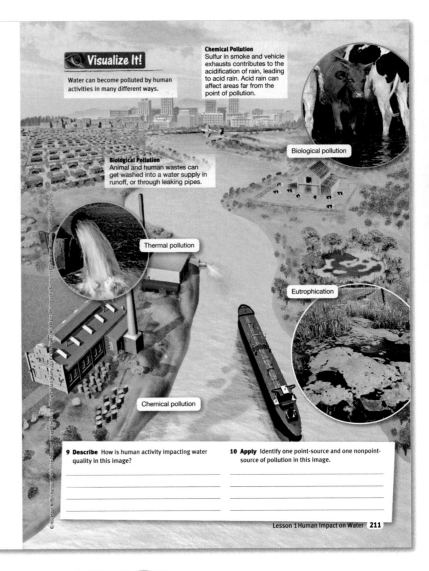

Visualize It!

Water can become polluted by human activities in many different ways.

Chemical Pollution
Sulfur in smoke and vehicle exhausts contributes to the acidification of rain, leading to acid rain. Acid rain can affect areas far from the point of pollution.

Biological pollution

Biological Pollution
Animal and human wastes can get washed into a water supply in runoff, or through leaking pipes.

Thermal pollution

Eutrophication

Chemical pollution

9 Describe How is human activity impacting water quality in this image?

10 Apply Identify one point-source and one nonpoint-source of pollution in this image.

Lesson 1 Human Impact on Water 211

Answers

8. *See students' pages for annotations.*

9. Answers may vary. Sample answer: Thermal pollution is occurring at the factory; the boat is chemically polluting the river; the farm is adding biological pollution, which may also be causing the eutrophication of the pond.

10. Non-point sources: the city, the farm
    Point sources: the factory, the boat

Probing Questions GUIDED Inquiry

Comparing After students read about chemical pollution, biological pollution, and artificial eutrophication, have them think about and discuss how the types of pollution are related. Sample answers: Chemical pollution can involve agricultural chemicals. If these chemicals reach a water supply, they might add extra nutrients to the water, which can cause artificial eutrophication. Artificial eutrophication can also be caused by sewage, which is a type of biological pollution.

Formative Assessment

Ask: What are examples of thermal pollution, chemical pollution, biological pollution, and artificial eutrophication? List student answers on the board. Sample answers: thermal, water that absorbs heat to cool a power plant; chemical, industrial waste and agricultural chemicals; biological, sewage and farm waste; artificial eutrophication, nutrients in fertilizers or waste water **Ask:** Which of the examples on the board are point-source pollution, and which are nonpoint-source pollution? Sample answers: Industrial waste and water that absorbs heat to cool a power plant are point-source pollution. Agricultural chemicals, sewage, and farm waste are probably nonpoint-source pollution.

How is water quality measured?

Before there were scientific methods of testing water, people could only look at water, taste it, and smell it to check its quality. Scientists can now test water with modern equipment, so the results are more reliable. Modern ways of testing water are especially important for finding small quantities of toxic chemicals or harmful organisms in water.

Water is a good solvent. So, water in nature usually contains dissolved solids, such as salt and other substances. Because most dissolved solids cannot be seen, it is important to measure them. Measurements of water quality include testing the levels of dissolved oxygen, pH, temperature, dissolved solids, and the number and types of microbes in the water. Quality standards depend on the intended use for the water. For example, drinking water needs to meet much stricter quality standards than environmental waters such as river or lake waters do.

Water Quality Measurement

Quality measurement	What is it?	How it relates to water quality
Dissolved solids	a measure of the amount of ions or microscopic suspended solids in water	Some dissolved solids could be harmful chemicals. Others such as calcium could cause scaling or build-up in water pipes
pH	a measure of how acidic or alkaline water is	Aquatic organisms need a near neutral pH (approx. pH 7). Acid rain can drop the pH too low (acidic) for aquatic life to live.
Dissolved oxygen (DO)	the amount of oxygen gas that is dissolved in water	Aquatic organisms need oxygen. Animal waste and thermal pollution can decrease the amount of oxygen dissolved in water.
Turbidity	a measure of the cloudiness of water that is caused by suspended solids	High turbidity increases the chance that harmful microbes or chemicals are in the water.
Microbial load	the identification of harmful bacteria, viruses or protists in water	Microbes such as bacteria, viruses, and protists from human and animal wastes can cause diseases.

11 Predict Why might increased turbidity increase the chance of something harmful being in the water? _____

How is water treated for human use?

Active Reading **12 Identify** As you read, number the basic steps in the water treatment process.

Natural water may be unsafe for humans to drink. So, water that is to be used as drinking water is treated to remove harmful chemicals and organisms. Screens take out large debris. Then chemicals are added that make suspended particles stick together. These particles drop out of the water in a process called *flocculation*. Flocculation also removes harmful bacteria and other microbes. Chlorine is often added to kill microbes left in the water. In some cities, fluoride is added to water supplies to help prevent tooth decay. Finally, air is bubbled through the water. Water that is suitable to drink is called **potable** water. Once water is used, it becomes wastewater. It enters the sewage system where pipes carry it to a wastewater treatment plant. There the wastewater is cleaned and filtered before being released back into the environment.

Drinking water is often mixed in large basins to help remove chemicals and harmful organisms. Paddles stir the water in the basins.

Who monitors and protects our water quality?

Active Reading **13 Identify** As you read, underline the government agency that is responsible for enforcing water quality rules.

If a public water supply became contaminated, many people could get very sick. As a result, public water supplies are closely monitored so that any problems can be fixed quickly. The Safe Drinking Water Act is the main federal law that ensures safe drinking water for people in the United States. The act sets strict limits on the amount of heavy metals or certain types of bacteria that can be in drinking water, among other things. The Environmental Protection Agency (EPA) has the job of enforcing this law. It is responsible for setting the standards drinking water must meet before the water can be pumped into public water systems. Water quality tests can be done by trained workers or trained volunteers.

Samples of water are routinely taken to make sure the water quality meets the standards required by law.

Answers

11. The more turbid the water, the more particles in the water, and the greater the chance that some particles might be carrying harmful organisms or chemicals.

12. *See students' pages for annotations.*

13. *See students' pages for annotations.*

Building Reading Skills

Sequence After students read how water is treated for human use, invite volunteers to describe the sequence in which water is treated. Write the sequence on the board. Then encourage other students to check to see that the sequence is correct. Add or rearrange steps as needed until the class agrees that the sequence is correct.

Using Annotations

Main Idea/Details Have students underline the things a water monitor checks for. Then have them explain what each of their underlined words means. Sample answers: turbidity: cloudiness of water; temperature: how warm the water is; dissolved oxygen: how much oxygen is in the water; pH: how acidic or basic the water is; dissolved salt, nitrates, phosphates: measures of how high the levels of dissolved chemicals are; microbial load: levels of bacteria, viruses, or protists in water

Interpreting Visuals

Have students look at the table showing water quality measurements. **Ask:** Are high levels of dissolved oxygen good or bad? Why? Good. Low levels may indicate pollutants. **Ask:** Is a neutral pH good or bad? Why? Good. Acidic water can harm aquatic life.

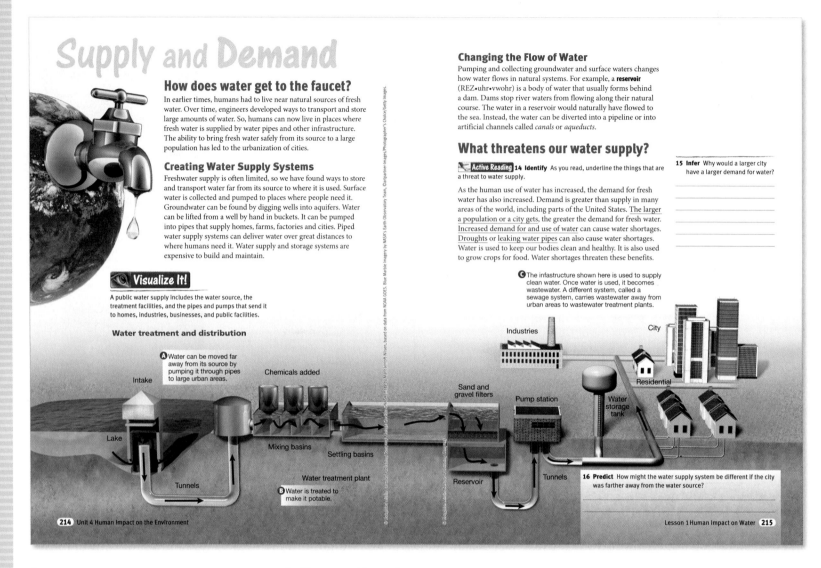

Supply and Demand

How does water get to the faucet?

In earlier times, humans had to live near natural sources of fresh water. Over time, engineers developed ways to transport and store large amounts of water. So, humans can now live in places where fresh water is supplied by water pipes and other infrastructure. The ability to bring fresh water safely from its source to a large population has led to the urbanization of cities.

Creating Water Supply Systems

Freshwater supply is often limited, so we have found ways to store and transport water far from its source to where it is used. Surface water is collected and pumped to places where people need it. Groundwater can be found by digging wells into aquifers. Water can be lifted from a well by hand in buckets. It can be pumped into pipes that supply homes, farms, factories and cities. Piped water supply systems can deliver water over great distances to where humans need it. Water supply and storage systems are expensive to build and maintain.

Visualize It!

A public water supply includes the water source, the treatment facilities, and the pipes and pumps that send it to homes, industries, businesses, and public facilities.

Water treatment and distribution

- **A** Water can be moved far away from its source by pumping it through pipes to large urban areas.
- Intake
- Chemicals added
- Lake
- Tunnels
- Mixing basins
- Settling basins
- **Water treatment plant**
- **B** Water is treated to make it potable.

214 Unit 4 Human Impact on the Environment

Changing the Flow of Water

Pumping and collecting groundwater and surface waters changes how water flows in natural systems. For example, a **reservoir** (REZ•uhr•vwohr) is a body of water that usually forms behind a dam. Dams stop river waters from flowing along their natural course. The water in a reservoir would naturally have flowed to the sea. Instead, the water can be diverted into a pipeline or into artificial channels called *canals* or *aqueducts*.

What threatens our water supply?

Active Reading 14 **Identify** As you read, underline the things that are a threat to water supply.

As the human use of water has increased, the demand for fresh water has also increased. Demand is greater than supply in many areas of the world, including parts of the United States. The larger a population or a city gets, the greater the demand for fresh water. Increased demand for and use of water can cause water shortages. Droughts or leaking water pipes can also cause water shortages. Water is used to keep our bodies clean and healthy. It is also used to grow crops for food. Water shortages threaten these benefits.

C The infrastructure shown here is used to supply clean water. Once water is used, it becomes wastewater. A different system, called a sewage system, carries wastewater away from urban areas to wastewater treatment plants.

- Industries
- City
- Sand and gravel filters
- Pump station
- Water storage tank
- Residential
- Reservoir
- Tunnels

15 Infer Why would a larger city have a larger demand for water?

16 Predict How might the water supply system be different if the city was farther away from the water source?

Lesson 1 Human Impact on Water 215

Answers

14. *See students' pages for annotations.*

15. The greater the number of people in one place, the greater the demand for water because each person needs a certain amount of water every day.

16. Answers may vary. Sample answer: The water supply system would include more piping and more water storage facilities.

Formative Assessment

Have students recall the diagram that shows how water gets from the ground to homes and buildings. **Ask:** What is the first thing that happens? The water is pumped from the source through pipes or tunnels to a treatment plant. **Ask:** Second? At the treatment plant, the water is treated with chemicals to make it potable. **Ask:** Third? The clean water is stored in a reservoir. **Ask:** Fourth? The clean water is pumped through a pumping station to water storage tanks, homes, businesses, and industry.

Probing Questions GUIDED Inquiry

Predicting Ask students to think about what people do if there is not enough water in a region. They pipe it in from far away. **Ask:** What do you think people might do 100 years from now if there is not enough fresh water worldwide? Sample answer: They might remove salt from salt water to make it fresh water. **Ask:** Where else might people get fresh water? Sample answer: They might melt frozen water. **Ask:** What do you think will happen if people use these sources for fresh water? Sample answer: It will change the environment and ecosystems. It might be harmful. **Ask:** What can people do today to conserve water for future generations? Sample answers: They can be careful how they use water. They should not waste water. They can use rainwater to water their yards or gardens. They can limit watering of lawns and the length of showers.

How do efforts to supply water to humans affect the environment?

Growing urban populations place a greater demand on water supplies. Efforts to increase water supply can affect the environment. For example, building dams and irrigation canals changes the natural flow of water. The environment is physically changed by construction work. The local ecology changes too. Organisms that live in or depend on the water may lose their habitat and move away.

Aquifers are often used as freshwater sources for urban areas. When more water is taken from an aquifer than can be replaced by rain or snow, the water table can drop below the reach of existing wells. Rivers and streams may dry up and the soil that once held aquifer waters may collapse, or *subside*. In coastal areas, the overuse of groundwater can cause seawater to seep into the aquifer in a process called *saltwater intrusion*. In this way, water supplies can become contaminated with salt water.

Increasing population in an area can also affect water quality. The more people that use a water supply in one area, the greater the volume of wastewater that is produced in that area. Pollutants such as oil, pesticides, fertilizers, and heavy metals from city runoff, from industry, and from agriculture may seep into surface waters and groundwater. In this way, pollution could enter the water supply. This pollution could also enter the water cycle and be carried far from the initial source of the pollution.

Active Reading

17 Relate How can the increased demand on water affect water quality?

_____

_____

_____

_____

_____

Digging irrigation canals changes the flow of rivers.

Building dams disrupts water flow and affects the ecology of the land and water.

Irrigating arid areas changes the ecology of those areas.

216 Unit 4 Human Impact on the Environment

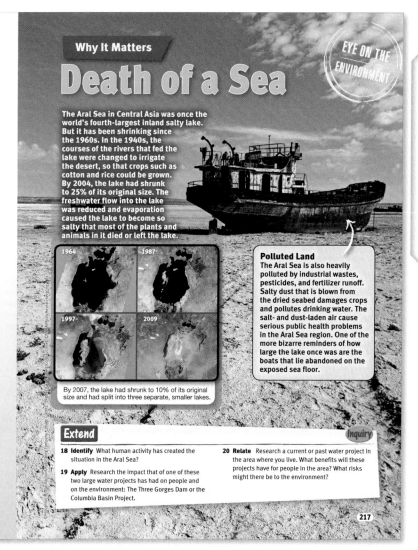

Why It Matters

Death of a Sea

EYE ON THE ENVIRONMENT

The Aral Sea in Central Asia was once the world's fourth-largest inland salty lake. But it has been shrinking since the 1960s. In the 1940s, the courses of the rivers that fed the lake were changed to irrigate the desert, so that crops such as cotton and rice could be grown. By 2004, the lake had shrunk to 25% of its original size. The freshwater flow into the lake was reduced and evaporation caused the lake to become so salty that most of the plants and animals in it died or left the lake.

1964 1987
1997 2009

By 2007, the lake had shrunk to 10% of its original size and had split into three separate, smaller lakes.

Polluted Land
The Aral Sea is also heavily polluted by industrial wastes, pesticides, and fertilizer runoff. Salty dust that is blown from the dried seabed damages crops and pollutes drinking water. The salt- and dust-laden air cause serious public health problems in the Aral Sea region. One of the more bizarre reminders of how large the lake once was are the boats that lie abandoned on the exposed sea floor.

Extend
Inquiry

18 Identify What human activity has created the situation in the Aral Sea?

19 Apply Research the impact that of one of these two large water projects has had on people and on the environment: The Three Gorges Dam or the Columbia Basin Project.

20 Relate Research a current or past water project in the area where you live. What benefits will these projects have for people in the area? What risks might there be to the environment?

217

Answers

17. Sample answer: Increased demand may result in increased use, which would lead to increased volume of waste water. Water quality may decrease if waste and pollution seep into groundwater or surface waters. This is because these water bodies are also used as water sources.

18. diversion of the rivers that fed the sea to irrigate farmland

19. Students' research should show an understanding of how and why such large-scale projects impact both the environment and people.

20. Students' research should show an understanding of some of the inherent risks and benefits that water projects can have.

Why It Matters

Sequence The history of the Aral Sea shows the damage that can occur when waters are mismanaged. Have students help you draw a flow chart on the board that shows the sequence of events that happened to the Aral Sea. 1940, rivers were diverted; 1960s, Aral Sea starts to shrink, and evaporation causes the lake to become so salty that plants and animals die, and fishing is wiped out; 2004, the sea is a quarter of its original size, and salt dust damages crops and pollutes drinking water; 2007, sea is one-tenth of its original size

Interpreting Visuals

Have students describe what they can learn from the satellite images of the Aral Sea. Sample answer: In 1964, the lake was large, with a few islands. By 2002, the lake had shrunk to become three tiny lakes.

Probing Question   GUIDED Inquiry

Evaluating After reading about what happened to the Aral Sea, have students explain the pros and cons of irrigation. Sample answer: Irrigation helps farmers grow crops where there is not enough rain, but it can divert water from lakes and make them shrink. Irrigated runoff is often polluted, which can pollute fresh water.

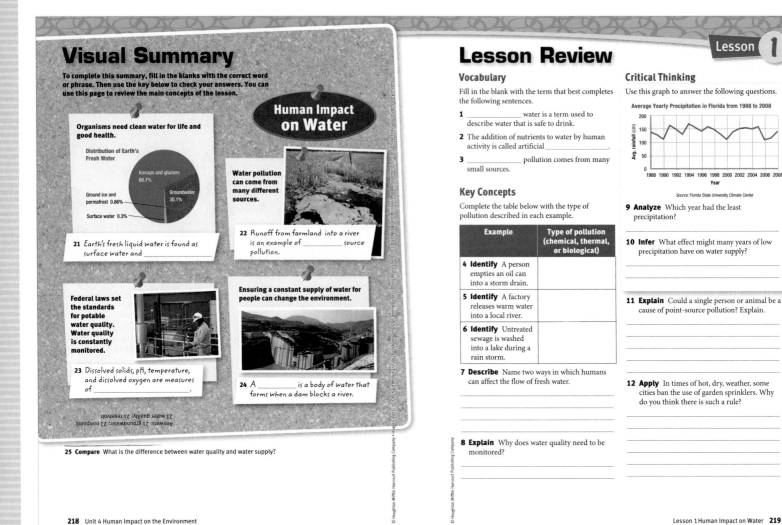

Visual Summary Answers

21. groundwater

22. nonpoint

23. water quality

24. reservoir

25. Water quality is a measure of how clean or dirty water is. Water supply is the availability of water, and the means by which people get water.

Lesson Review Answers

1. Potable

2. eutrophication

3. nonpoint-source

4. chemical

5. thermal

6. biological

7. Building dams and canals affects how water flows. Water can be piped from its source to urban areas that may be far from the water source.

8. To make sure that the water is clean, and will not make people sick.

9. 2006 had the lowest amount of precipitation.

10. The water supply might dry up (or decrease).

11. Sample answer: Yes, a single person or animal could cause point source pollution. Animal or human waste could get into the water, or a person could dump a pollutant in the water or on the ground that could seep into the water.

12. Sample answer: Garden sprinkler systems use a lot of water, and may cause a rapid reduction in available water, especially during a dry spell. Water use is restricted to protect the water supply for more necessary needs such as for drinking and flushing toilets.

People in Science

Angel Montoya

Purpose To learn about Angel Montoya and the work that conservation biologists do

Learning Goals
- Identify the impact that humans have had on Earth.
- Explain ways people can prevent or correct environmental damage.

Informal Vocabulary
conservation biologist, raptors, juveniles

Prerequisite Knowledge
- Natural resources
- How humans use the land
- Land degradation

Activity *Which Job Is Best for Me?*

 individuals   20 min
 GUIDED inquiry

Ranking Ladder Have students draw a ladder on a sheet of paper. Then have them rank the jobs on these pages by putting the job they would most like to do at the top of the ladder and the job they would least like to do at the bottom. Invite students to share their ladders and describe why they ranked the jobs the way they did. As a class, compare and contrast the rankings and identify which jobs were most popular overall and why.

Differentiated Instruction

Basic *Aplomado Falcons*

 pairs   🕐 30 min

Oral Presentations Have pairs of students conduct research to find out more about Aplomado falcons. Direct students to take careful notes on what they learn. Have pairs share their most interesting and important findings with the class.

💿 *Optional Online rubric: Oral Presentations*

Advanced *Identifying Raptors*

👥 individuals or pairs   🕐 30 min

Raptor Poster Have students conduct research and prepare a visual guide that identifies different types of raptors. Encourage them to learn about any raptors that live in their region and discover where raptors might be spotted locally. Then have students share their posters with the class.

💿 *Optional Online rubric: Posters and Displays*

ELL *Falcon Map*

👥 pairs or small groups   🕐 10 min

Have pairs or small groups draw a map that identifies the southwestern region of the United States and shows the locations of El Paso, Texas, and Chihuahua, Mexico. Have students estimate how far apart these two places are. Then have students discuss what it would be like to try to find the Aplomado falcon or another rare animal in such a large area.

Customize Your Feature

- ☐ **Activity** Which Job Is Best for Me?
- ☐ **People in Science** Online
- ☐ **Basic** Aplomado Falcons
- ☐ **Advanced** Identifying Raptors
- ☐ **ELL** Falcon Map
- ☐ **Job Board**
- ☐ **People in Science News**

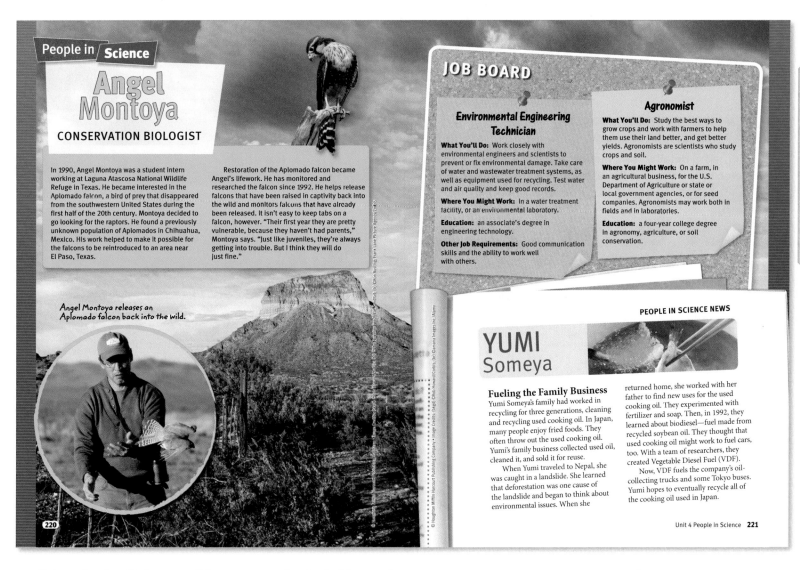

People in Science

Angel Montoya
CONSERVATION BIOLOGIST

In 1990, Angel Montoya was a student intern working at Laguna Atascosa National Wildlife Refuge in Texas. He became interested in the Aplomado falcon, a bird of prey that disappeared from the southwestern United States during the first half of the 20th century. Montoya decided to go looking for the raptors. He found a previously unknown population of Aplomados in Chihuahua, Mexico. His work helped to make it possible for the falcons to be reintroduced to an area near El Paso, Texas.

Restoration of the Aplomado falcon became Angel's lifework. He has monitored and researched the falcon since 1992. He helps release falcons that have been raised in captivity back into the wild and monitors falcons that have already been released. It isn't easy to keep tabs on a falcon, however. "Their first year they are pretty vulnerable, because they haven't had parents," Montoya says. "Just like juveniles, they're always getting into trouble. But I think they will do just fine."

Angel Montoya releases an Aplomado falcon back into the wild.

JOB BOARD

Environmental Engineering Technician

What You'll Do: Work closely with environmental engineers and scientists to prevent or fix environmental damage. Take care of water and wastewater treatment systems, as well as equipment used for recycling. Test water and air quality and keep good records.

Where You Might Work: In a water treatment facility, or an environmental laboratory.

Education: an associate's degree in engineering technology.

Other Job Requirements: Good communication skills and the ability to work well with others.

Agronomist

What You'll Do: Study the best ways to grow crops and work with farmers to help them use their land better, and get better yields. Agronomists are scientists who study crops and soil.

Where You Might Work: On a farm, in an agricultural business, for the U.S. Department of Agriculture or state or local government agencies, or for seed companies. Agronomists may work both in fields and in laboratories.

Education: a four-year college degree in agronomy, agriculture, or soil conservation.

PEOPLE IN SCIENCE NEWS

YUMI Someya

Fueling the Family Business

Yumi Someya's family had worked in recycling for three generations, cleaning and recycling used cooking oil. In Japan, many people enjoy fried foods. They often throw out the used cooking oil. Yumi's family business collected used oil, cleaned it, and sold it for reuse.

When Yumi traveled to Nepal, she was caught in a landslide. She learned that deforestation was one cause of the landslide and began to think about environmental issues. When she returned home, she worked with her father to find new uses for the used cooking oil. They experimented with fertilizer and soap. Then, in 1992, they learned about biodiesel—fuel made from recycled soybean oil. They thought that used cooking oil might work to fuel cars, too. With a team of researchers, they created Vegetable Diesel Fuel (VDF).

Now, VDF fuels the company's oil-collecting trucks and some Tokyo buses. Yumi hopes to eventually recycle all of the cooking oil used in Japan.

Unit 4 People in Science **221**

People in Science News

Design Your Own Investigation

Encourage interested students to collect used cooking oil at home with the help of an adult. Tell students to think about ways to filter this oil to make it reusable. Students may want to try using coffee filters, sand, or other materials as filters. Provide time for students to describe the results of their investigations to the class.

Job Board

Layered Book FoldNote Invite students to use a Layered Book FoldNote to begin compiling a job booklet. In their booklets, have students list and describe any of the professions on this page or professions from earlier lessons that they find interesting. Throughout the year, have them add new professions to their booklets whenever they find one that they might like to do one day.

Optional Online resource: Layered Book FoldNote support

Human Impact on Land

Essential Question What impact can human activities have on land resources?

Professional Development

For more detailed information about the topics in this lesson, refer to the Content Refresher in the Unit Opener pages.

Opening Your Lesson

Begin the lesson by assessing students' prerequisite and prior knowledge.

Prerequisite Knowledge

- Definition of *erosion*
- Identification of the agents of erosion

Accessing Prior Knowledge

Ask: What are some ways that people can negatively affect the land we live on? People can cut down forests, build cities and roads, and fill in wetlands. **Ask:** What are some ways that people can positively affect the land? They can plant trees or plants, reduce chemicals used on lawns, and recycle instead of dumping trash in landfills.

Customize Your Opening

- [ ] **Accessing Prior Knowledge,** above
- [ ] **Print Path** Engage Your Brain, SE p. 223 #1–2
- [ ] **Print Path** Active Reading, SE p. 223 #3–4
- [ ] **Digital Path** Lesson Opener

Key Topics/Learning Goals

How Humans Use Land

1 Describe five ways in which humans use land.
2 Compare and contrast natural, rural, and urban land uses.
3 Define *urbanization* and *urban sprawl*.

Land Degradation

1 Define *land degradation*.
2 Identify three factors that lead to land degradation.
3 Identify the effects of urbanization on land.

Supporting Concepts

- People use land for residential, agricultural, commercial/industrial, transport, and recreational purposes.
- Natural or wild areas have been little changed from their natural state.
- Rural areas have few people and large open spaces.
- Urban areas have many buildings and roads.
- Urbanization is the formation and growth of cities; it involves changing rural or natural land into urban areas.
- Urban sprawl occurs when natural or rural areas near cities are developed.

- Human activity can damage (degrade) land so that it can no longer support the local ecosystem.
- Deforestation, poor farming methods, and urbanization can cause land degradation and may lead to desertification.
- Urbanization removes vegetation, changing erosion, deposition, recharge, and runoff and reducing farmland.

Options for Instruction

Two parallel paths provide coverage of the Essential Questions, with a strong **Inquiry** strand woven into each. Follow the **Print Path,** the **Digital Path,** or your customized combination of print, digital, and inquiry.

 Print Path
Teaching support for the Print Path appears with the Student Pages.

 Inquiry Labs and Activities

 Digital Path
Digital Path shortcut: TS671370

Land of Plenty, SE pp. 224–226	**Activity**	**Land Uses and Types**
Why is land important?	**Collect and Examine Soil**	Interactive Image
What are the different types of land use?	**Activity**	**How Humans Use Land**
• Recreational	**Land Use**	Interactive Graphics
• Transport		
• Agricultural		
• Residential		
• Commercial/Industrial		
Why is soil important?		
• It Is a Habitat for Organisms		
• It Stores Water and Nutrients		

Footprints, SE pp. 228–229	**Quick Lab**	**Land Degradation**
How can human activities affect land and soil?	**Roots and Erosion**	Diagram
• Urban Sprawl	**Quick Lab**	**Causes of Degradation**
• Erosion	**Investigating Human Impact on the Land**	Interactive Images
• Nutrient Depletion and Land Pollution		
• Desertification	**Daily Demo**	**Repairing the Land**
• Deforestation	**Reducing Rainy Runoff**	Interactive Image
	Activity	
	Land Degradation Poster	

Options for Assessment

See the Evaluate page for options, including Formative Assessment, Summative Assessment, and Unit Review.

Engage and Explore

Activities and Discussion

Probing Question *Is Soil a Renewable Resource?*

Engage ▼

How Humans Use Land

 whole class
 10 min
 GUIDED inquiry

Ask: What are three things that you use that could not exist without soil? Sample answers: food, clothes, houses **Ask:** What is a renewable resource? one that replenishes itself faster than it is used **Ask:** Do you think soil is a renewable or nonrenewable resource? Why? Sample answers: Soil is renewable, because our composter can make new organic matter to supplement soil in a matter of months. Soil is not renewable, because it take hundreds or thousands of years to break down rocks to make soil in some areas.

Activity *Collect and Examine Soil*

How Humans Use Land

 individuals or small groups
 20 min
 GUIDED inquiry

Take students outside to examine soil at or near the school. If you have a school garden, examine the soil there. Otherwise, look at moist soil near your school. Have students use a shovel to put some soil in a bucket. Then dump the bucket of soil out on a hard surface and spread it thinly. Give each student a hand lens. Invite students to observe. Have them draw and describe what they see in their journals. **Ask:** Do organisms live in soil? yes **Ask:** What living organisms do you see? Sample answers: worms, grubs, insects If possible, bring some of the soil inside and have students examine it under a microscope. Have them draw any organisms they observe.

Take It Home *Land at Home*

Introducing Key Topics

 adult-student pairs
 10–30 min
 GUIDED inquiry

Have students work with an adult to identify ways land is used near the student's house. They may want to think about yards with gardens, roads, buildings, recreational areas, residential areas, farm areas, and commercial areas. Invite students to share their lists of land uses with the class.

Activity *Land Degradation Posters*

Land Degradation

 individuals or small groups
 ongoing
 GUIDED inquiry

Have pairs of students work together to think about ways land is degraded in their area. Students will want to think about what effects urbanization, erosion, deforestation, pollution, and other factors have had on local land areas. Then students should write a list of ways the soil can be preserved or improved locally. Have students make a poster to share their ideas with the class.

Customize Your Labs

 See the Lab Manual for lab datasheets.

 Go Online for editable lab datasheets.

(l) ©Valerie Giles/Photo Researchers, Inc.; (r) ©Science Source/Photo Researchers, Inc.

Labs and Demos

Daily Demo *Reducing Rainy Runoff*

Engage

Land Degradation

👥 whole class
🕐 10 min
Inquiry **GUIDED** inquiry

PURPOSE **To demonstrate the effect of runoff on soil**

MATERIALS

- large soda bottles (3), each with a large window cut out of one side
- plant material, such as leaves or grass clippings
- potting soil
- beakers or clear cups (3)
- aquarium gravel
- water in a watering can

1 Place each soda bottle on its side. Put a third of the soil in each one. Leave one bare, cover the second with the plant material, and cover the third with the gravel.

2 Invite a student to hold the first soda bottle, with the spout tipped downward over a beaker or cup, while you pour water over the soil. Ask students what comes out of the spout. muddy water Explain that the water carried the unprotected soil away, which is much the same as what happens in areas with disturbed soil that is not protected from rainfall; the runoff carries the soil away.

3 Repeat with another student holding the bottle containing soil and plant material. Discuss the differences students see between the first and second beakers.

4 Repeat with the final bottle. Discuss how effective the gravel was at protecting the soil. Explain that plant materials and gravel can be used to reduce the effect of runoff in an area, thus reducing the amount of soil erosion that occurs.

Quick Lab *Roots and Erosion*

Land Degradation

👥 small groups
🕐 15 min
Inquiry **DIRECTED** inquiry

Using seedling plants with extensive roots, students will compare how quickly soil washes away when it is held in place by roots and how it does so when it is loose.

PURPOSE **To show how plants can prevent soil erosion**

MATERIALS

- plastic bowls (2)
- plastic spoon
- plastic cup
- various potted plants
- potting soil
- water

Quick Lab *Investigating Human Impact on the Land*

Land Degradation

👥 small groups
🕐 30 min
Inquiry **INDEPENDENT** inquiry

Students debate an environmental issue related to local land use.

PURPOSE **To explore the complexity of issues involving land degradation by humans**

MATERIALS

- online news articles related to local land issues

Activities and Discussion

☐ **Probing Question** Is Soil a Renewable Resource?

☐ **Activity** Collect and Examine Soil

☐ **Take It Home** Land at Home

☐ **Activity** Land Degradation Posters

Labs and Demos

☐ **Daily Demo** Reducing Rainy Runoff

☐ **Quick Lab** Roots and Erosion

☐ **Quick Lab** Investigating Human Impact on the Land

Your Resources

_____

_____

_____

Explain Science Concepts

Key Topics	📖 Print Path	💻 Digital Path
How Humans Use Land	☐ **Land of Plenty,** SE pp. 224–226 • Visualize It!, #5 • Active Reading (annotation strategy), #6 • Active Reading, #7 • Active Reading (annotation strategy), #8 • Visualize It!, #9	☐ **Land Uses and Types** Learn about three categories of land use. ☐ **How Humans Use Land** Explore residential, agricultural, commercial, and recreational uses of land.
Land Degradation	☐ **Footprints,** SE pp. 228–229 • Think Outside the Book, #13 • Active Reading (annotation strategy), #14 • Visualize It!, #15	☐ **Land Degradation** See how humans sometimes damage land. ☐ **Causes of Degradation** Explore factors that lead to land degradation. ☐ **Repairing the Land** Learn about ways humans conserve and restore land.

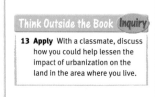

Think Outside the Book Inquiry

13 Apply With a classmate, discuss how you could help lessen the impact of urbanization on the land in the area where you live.

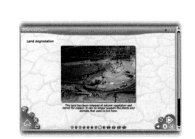

Differentiated Instruction

Basic *Concept Map*

How Humans Use Land

👥 individuals
🕐 10 min

Help students organize the information on land use by using a concept map. Let them write the words *Land Use* in the center oval. In smaller ovals, they should write the uses. Around each small oval, have students add important details, such as how land is used for farming or industry.

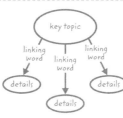

🌐 *Optional Online resource: Concept Map support*

Advanced *Problems and Solutions*

Synthesizing Key Topics

👥 individuals
🕐 ongoing

Have students write about ways to prevent deforestation, urbanization, nutrient depletion, industrial pollution, or desertification. Then have students think about obstacles to their solutions. For example, limited housing may put pressure on local leaders to build housing on open land. Have students make charts listing the advantages and disadvantages of their solutions.

ELL *Vocabulary Cards*

Synthesizing Key Topics

👥 individuals or pairs
🕐 15 min

Have students, individually or in pairs, write the vocabulary words on index cards. Beneath each term, have students write a definition in their own words. On the back of the card, have students draw an illustration that shows what the word means. Encourage students to write other difficult words on cards, too.

Lesson Vocabulary

| urbanization | land degradation |
| desertification | deforestation |

Previewing Vocabulary

👥 whole class
🕐 10 min

Word Parts Remind students that when they encounter long words, they can often figure out the meaning by looking at the word parts. Since *–ation* means "the act or process of," students can make educated guesses about the meaning of each vocabulary word.

- **Urbanization** means "the process of making urban, or citylike."
- **Land degradation** means "the process of degrading land" (that is, making it of poorer quality).
- **Deforestation** means "the process of removing forests."
- **Desertification** means "the process of making desertlike."

Reinforcing Vocabulary

👥 individuals
🕐 ongoing

Word Squares To help students remember the vocabulary terms in the lesson, have them complete a word square graphic organizer for each one.

TERM	symbol or picture
translation	
my meaning	sentence
dictionary definition	

🌐 *Optional Online resource: Word Square support*

Customize Your Core Lesson

Core Instruction

☐ **Print Path** choices

☐ **Digital Path** choices

Vocabulary

☐ **Previewing Vocabulary** Word Parts

☐ **Reinforcing Vocabulary** Word Squares

Your Resources

_____

_____

Differentiated Instruction

☐ **Basic** Concept Map

☐ **Advanced** Problems and Solutions

☐ **ELL** Vocabulary Cards

Extend Science Concepts

Reinforce and Review

Activity *Land Use*

Synthesizing Key Topics   whole class
🕐 20 min

Carousel Review Help students review the material by following these steps:

1 Arrange chart paper in different parts of the room. On each paper, write a question to review content.

2 Divide students into small groups and assign each group a chart. Give each group a different-colored marker.

3 Groups review their question, discuss their answer, and write a response.

4 After 5 min, each group rotates to the next station. Groups put a check by each answer they agree with, comment on answers they don't agree with, and add their own answers. Continue until all groups have reviewed all charts.

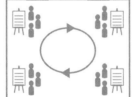

5 Invite each group to share information with the class.

Graphic Organizer

How Humans Use Land   individuals
🕐 15 min

Outline Have students create an outline that explains the five ways humans use land. Their outline should list the five ways people use land. It should also list ways the land can be conserved or degraded in each of the five categories. Remind students that outlines begin with a title. The title of their outline should be "How Humans Use Land." First-level heads are numbered with Roman numerals, second-level heads start with a capital letter, and third-level heads are numbered with Arabic numerals.

⊘ *Optional Online resource: Outline support*

Going Further

Geography Connection

Synthesizing Key Topics   individuals
🕐 20 min

Mapping Land Uses Have students draw a map that shows a bird's-eye view of their school and surrounding land. On the map they should identify each type of land use. Remind them to include a key indicating the types of land use and the meanings of symbols they use to indicate ground cover (grass, concrete), buildings, trees, and so on. Invite students to share their maps with the class.

Social Studies Connection

Synthesizing Key Topics   whole class
🕐 20 min

Role-Play Invite students to role-play a meeting of a community planning board. They have the opportunity to decide how 50 acres of fictional undeveloped land near their school will be used. Choose seven students to be the board; the rest of the class will be concerned citizens attending the meeting. Encourage students to discuss ways of using the land to benefit both the community and the environment.

Customize Your Closing

◧ See the Assessment Guide for quizzes and tests.

⊘ Go Online to edit and create quizzes and tests.

Reinforce and Review

☐ **Activity** Land Use

☐ **Graphic Organizer** Outline

☐ **Print Path** Visual Summary, SE p. 230

☐ **Digital Path** Lesson Closer

Evaluate Student Mastery

Formative Assessment

See the teacher support below the Student Pages for additional Formative Assessment questions.

Show students images of various types of land use and ask them to name the use depicted. **Ask:** What is urbanization? the formation and growth of cities **Ask:** What are the drawbacks of urbanization? Sample answer: Urbanization disrupts or destroys natural or rural areas and changes the ecosystems there; the increased amount of pavement can decrease the rate of groundwater recharge and increase runoff and, possibly, flooding. **Ask:** What other negative affects can human activities have on land? erosion, deforestation, desertification, nutrient depletion, and land pollution

Reteach

Formative assessment may show that students need reinforcement for certain topics. The resources below are recommended for reteaching. If students were introduced to a topic through the Print Path, you can also use the Digital Path to reteach, or vice versa.

🎧 *Can be assigned to individual students*

How Humans Use Land

Take It Home Land at Home

Basic Concept Map 🎧

Land Degradation

Activity Land Degradation Posters 🎧

Daily Demo Reducing Rainy Runoff

Quick Lab Roots and Erosion

Summative Assessment

Alternative Assessment
Discuss a Proposal

🌐 *Online resources: student worksheet, optional rubrics*

Human Impact on Land

Tic-Tac-Toe: *Discuss a Proposal*

Imagine that a coal company has applied for a license to mine an area of land on the outskirts of your town. Local officials have called a town meeting to discuss the proposal. Take on the roles of the people listed below, and explain the advantages and disadvantages of the proposed coal mine.

1. Work on your own, with a partner, or with a small group.
2. Choose three roles to take on. Check one box in each row to complete.
3. Have your teacher approve your plan.
4. Write a paragraph explaining each point of view. Then explain why the mine should or should not be given a license. If you are working in a group, conduct the meeting. Can you find compromises so that the group can reach an agreement?

__ Coal Company Official	__ Wildlife Photographer	__ Parent
You represent the coal company. The proposed mine will improve your company's finances.	You worry the noise and activity of the mine will chase wildlife away from the area and perhaps cause an influx of people to move to the area.	As a parent, you are concerned about any health risks for your children, but hopeful about a promise of new jobs.
__ Environmentalist	__ Government Official	__ Farmer
You are concerned that the proposed mine will degrade the land and perhaps contaminate nearby rivers and lakes.	You are a county official. The proposed mine will create new jobs in your county.	As a farmer on land near the proposed mine, you fear the mine will alter the water table beneath your property, potentially damaging your crops.
__ Landowner	__ Coal Miner	__ Business Owner
As a landowner of property near the mine, you wonder whether the value of your land will increase or decrease after the mine is built.	You think a new mine will pay you a good wage to support your family.	As the owner of a business that uses electricity generated by coal to heat and cool the business, you welcome the additional power that may be available.

Going Further

☐ Geography Connection

☐ Social Studies Connection

☐ **Print Path** Why It Matters, SE p. 227

Formative Assessment

☐ **Strategies** Throughout TE

☐ **Lesson Review** SE

Summative Assessment

☐ **Alternative Assessment** Discuss a Proposal

☐ **Lesson Quiz**

☐ **Unit Tests A and B**

☐ **Unit Review** SE End-of-Unit

Your Resources

_____

_____

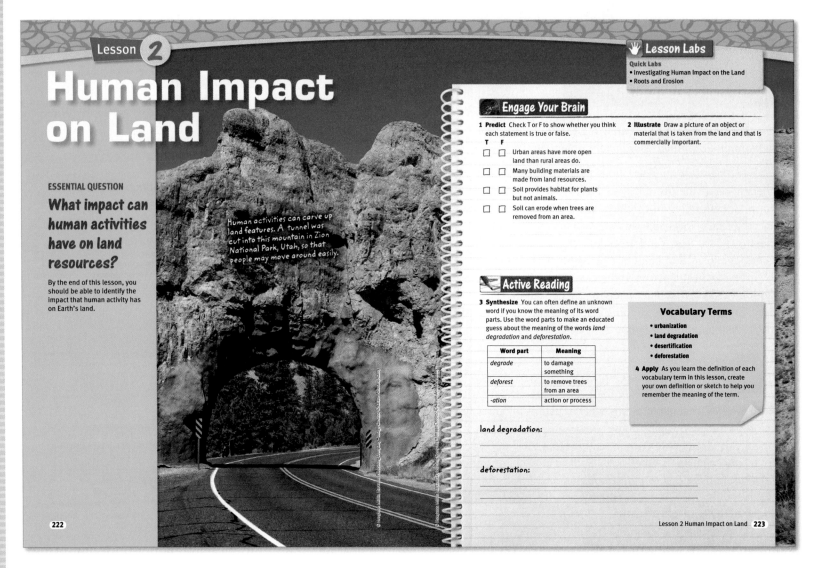

Answers

Answers for 1–3 should represent students' current thoughts, even if incorrect.

1. F; T; F; T

2. Answers may vary. Student will likely draw an object related to construction, such as timber or stone. Other objects or substances students might draw include metals, minerals, or water.

3. Land degradation: The process of damaging land. Deforestation: The process of removing trees and plant cover from land.

4. Students' annotations will vary.

Opening Your Lesson

Discuss students' answers to item 1 to assess their understanding of land as a natural resource, how soil helps people and animals, and how urban and rural areas are different.

Prerequisites Students should know what erosion is and the various factors that contribute to erosion.

Learning Alert

Difficult Concept Students need to learn that there are tradeoffs involved in the choices we make regarding land use. If people didn't change the land by building homes, we would all be living outdoors, but it can just as easily be argued that development can occur without much concern for the land or the ecosystems that it supports. Florida is an excellent example of this balancing act between growth and preservation. Discuss with students how the area they live in has changed in the past 50, 20, and 10 years. As students read the lesson, encourage them to look at both the positive and negative aspects of ways people use land. How does land use affect animals and people locally, regionally, and worldwide?

Land of Plenty

Why is land important?

It is hard to imagine human life without land. Land supplies a solid surface for buildings and roads. The soil in land provides nutrients for plants and hiding places for animals. Minerals below the land's surface can be used for construction materials. Fossil fuels underground can be burned to provide energy. Land and its resources affect every aspect of human life.

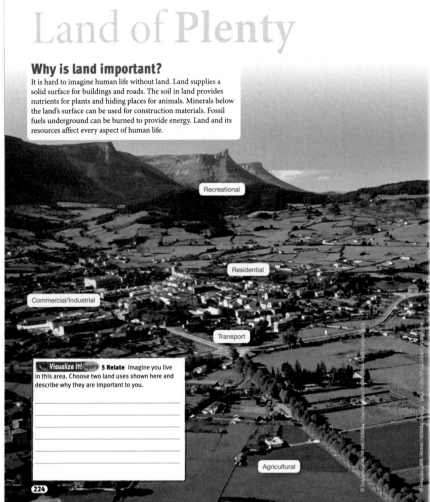

Recreational

Residential

Commercial/Industrial

Transport

Agricultural

Visualize It! Inquiry **5 Relate** Imagine you live in this area. Choose two land uses shown here and describe why they are important to you.

_____
_____
_____
_____

224

What are the different types of land use?

We live on land in urban or rural areas. Cities and towns are urban areas. Rural areas are open lands that may be used for farming. Humans use land in many ways. We use natural areas for *recreation*. We use roads that are built on land for *transport*. We grow crops and raise livestock on *agricultural* land. We live in *residential* areas. We build *commercial* businesses on land and extract resources such as metals and water from the land.

Recreational

Natural areas are places that humans have left alone or restored to a natural state. These wild places include forests, grasslands, and desert areas. People use natural areas for hiking, bird-watching, mountain-biking, hunting, and other fun or recreational activities.

Transport

A large network of roads and train tracks connect urban and rural areas all across the country. Roads in the U.S. highway system cover 4 million miles of land. Trucks carry goods on these highways and smaller vehicles carry passengers. Railroads carrying freight or passengers use over 120,000 miles of land for tracks. Roads and train tracks are often highly concentrated in urban areas.

Agricultural

Much of the open land in rural areas is used for agriculture. Crops such as corn, soybeans, and wheat are grown on large, open areas of land. Land is also needed to raise and feed cattle and other livestock. Agricultural land is open, but very different from the natural areas that it has replaced. Farmland generally contains only one or two types of plants, such as corn or cotton. Natural grasslands, forests, and other natural areas contain many species of plants and animals.

Active Reading **6 Identify** As you read, underline the ways rural areas differ from urban areas.

Residential

Where do you call home? People live in both rural and urban areas. Rural areas have large areas of open land and low densities of people. Urban areas have dense human populations and small areas of open land. This means that more people live in a square km of an urban area than live in a square km of a rural area. **Urbanization** is the growth of urban areas caused by people moving into cities. When cities increase in size, the population of rural areas near the city may decrease. When an area becomes urbanized, its natural land surface is replaced by buildings, parking lots, and roads. City parks, which contain natural surfaces, may also be built in urban areas.

Commercial and Industrial

As cities or towns expand, commercial businesses are built too, and replace rural or natural areas. Industrial businesses also use land resources. For example, paper companies and furniture manufacturers use wood from trees harvested on forest land. Cement companies, fertilizer manufacturers, and steel manufacturers use minerals that are mined from below the land's surface. Commercial and industrial development usually includes development of roads or railways. Transporting goods to market forms the basis of commerce.

Active Reading

7 Identify What effects does urbanization have on land?

_____
_____
_____
_____
_____
_____
_____

Lesson 2 Human Impact on Land **225**

Answers

5. Answers may vary. Sample answer: Recreational use and transport use are important to me because I like to go camping and hiking, and my family needs to drive to the camp sites we visit.

6. *See students' pages for annotations.*

7. Sample answer: Urbanization changes the natural land surface. The land will be covered in asphalt and concrete and will not have a natural surface. Animals that lived in the natural area may move from the developed area.

Building Reading Skills

Main Idea and Details Help students organize the main ideas and supporting details on these pages. **Ask:** What is the main idea on these pages? Sample answer: People use land in different ways. **Ask:** What are ways that people use land? Sample answer: People use land for recreation, for building homes, for roads, for agriculture, and for commercial/industrial purposes.

Probing Questions GUIDED Inquiry

Analyzing **Ask:** If grasslands are turned into farmlands or commercial land, what happens to the plants and animals that live in the grasslands? The plants die out, and the animals move, adapt, or die out. **Ask:** What harm can occur if fewer species of plants and animals thrive when the land use is changed? If there is less biodiversity, then the land will be less healthy. **Ask:** Are there any benefits to changing land from its natural state into a state used by humans? There are benefits to humans, who may need places to live, roads to get places, and resources from the land to use. Some animal and plant species may benefit, but there may be harm to other species as well as harmful effects on people, depending on how the land is used.

Why is soil important?

Soil is a mixture of mineral fragments, organic material, water, and air. Soil forms when rocks break down and dead organisms decay. There are many reasons why soil is important. Soil provides habitat for organisms such as plants, earthworms, fungi, and bacteria. Many plants get the water and nutrients they need from the soil. Because plants form the base of food webs, healthy soil is important for most land ecosystems. Healthy soil is also important for agricultural land, which supplies humans with food.

Active Reading

8 Identify As you read, underline the ways that soil is important to plants.

It Is a Habitat for Organisms

Earthworms, moles, badgers, and other burrowing animals live in soil. These animals also find food underground. *Decomposers* are organisms that break down dead animal and plant material, releasing the nutrients into the soil. Decomposers such as fungi and bacteria live in soil. Soil holds plant roots in place, providing support for the plant. In turn, plants are food for herbivores and are habitats for organisms such as birds and insects. Many animals on Earth depend on soil for shelter or food.

It Stores Water and Nutrients

Falling rain soaks into soil and is stored between soil particles. Different types of soil can store different amounts of water. Wetland soils, for example, store large amounts of water and reduce flooding. Soils are also part of the nutrient cycle. Plants take up nutrients and water stored in soil. Plants and animals that eat them die and are broken down by decomposers such as bacteria and earthworms. Nutrients are released back into the soil and the cycle starts again.

Visualize It!

Nutrients Cycle between Soil and Organisms

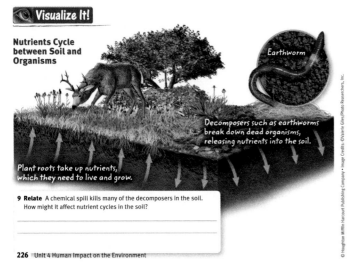

Earthworm

Decomposers such as earthworms break down dead organisms, releasing nutrients into the soil.

Plant roots take up nutrients, which they need to live and grow.

9 Relate A chemical spill kills many of the decomposers in the soil. How might it affect nutrient cycles in the soil?

226 Unit 4 Human Impact on the Environment

Why It Matters

Dust Bowl

EYE ON THE ENVIRONMENT

In the 1930s, huge clouds of dusty soil rolled across the southern Great Plains of the United States. Areas that were once farmlands and homesteads were wiped out. What caused the soil to blow away?

Drought and Overuse
Farmers who settled in the southern Great Plains overplowed and overgrazed their land. When severe drought hit in 1931, topsoil dried out. Winds lifted the soil and carried it across the plains in huge storms that farmers called "black blizzards." The drought and dust storms continued for years.

Modern Day Dust Bowl
Today in northwest China another dust bowl is forming. Large areas of farmland were made there by clearing the natural vegetation and plowing the soil. Herds of sheep and cattle are overgrazing the land, and large dust storms are common.

Extend | Inquiry

10 Identify What type of land use by people contributed to the Dust Bowl? Does it remain a common use of land today?

11 Compare Research another area under threat from overuse that differs from the feature. What type of land use is causing the problem?

12 Illustrate Do one of the following to show how the Dust Bowl or the area you researched affected society: make a poster, write a play, write a song, or draw a cartoon strip. Present your findings to the class.

227

Answers

8. *See students' pages for annotations.*

9. Sample answer: If decomposers are no longer in the soil, dead organic matter is not broken down and nutrients are not put back into the soil for plants to use.

Feature Answers

10. Sample answer: Agricultural land use. Land is still used for agricultural purposes today.

11. Students should research land overuse or land degradation caused by such activities as mining, agriculture, land clearing, or dumping.

12. Answers may vary. Students' work should show how a decrease in land quality can affect many people at once.

Learning Alert 🚧 MISCONCEPTION 🚧

The Soil Is Teeming with Life Students may think that animals live only on top of the soil, but not in the soil itself. Explain that earthworms, insects, moles, and other burrowing animals live in the soil, as do other organisms such as fungi and bacteria.

Interpreting Visuals

Help students interpret the diagram that shows the nutrient cycle among animals, plants, and soil. **Ask:** How are plants part of the nutrient cycle? Plants take up nutrients stored in the soil. **Ask:** How are animals part of the nutrient cycle? They eat plants. When animals die, they are broken down by decomposers. **Ask:** How are decomposers part of the cycle? As they break down dead organisms, they release nutrients into the soil.

Why It Matters

Have students look at the photos of the Dust Bowl. **Ask:** Why is it important to learn about the Dust Bowl? So people will remember what happened and not repeat the same mistakes. **Ask:** What have people learned since the Dust Bowl? They have learned to take better care of the soil by planting crops that hold the soil in place and practicing crop rotation.

Footprints

How can human activities affect land and soil?

Human activities can have positive and negative effects on land and soil. Some activities restore land to its natural state, or increase the amount of fertile soil on land. Other activities can degrade land. **Land degradation** is the process by which human activity and natural processes damage land to the point that it can no longer support the local ecosystem. Urbanization, deforestation, and poor farming practices can all lead to land degradation.

Active Reading

14 Identify As you read, underline the effects that urbanization can have on land.

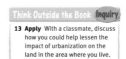

Think Outside the Book Inquiry

13 Apply With a classmate, discuss how you could help lessen the impact of urbanization on the land in the area where you live.

Urban Sprawl

When urbanization occurs at the edge of a city or town, it is called *urban sprawl*. Urban sprawl replaces forests, fields, and grasslands with houses, roads, schools, and shopping areas. Urban sprawl decreases the amount of farmland that is available for growing crops. It decreases the amount of natural areas that surround cities. It increases the amount of asphalt and concrete that covers the land. Rainwater runs off hard surfaces and into storm drains instead of soaking into the ground and filling aquifers. Rainwater runoff from urban areas can increase the erosion of nearby soils.

Erosion

Erosion (ih•ROH•zhuhn) is the process by which wind, water, or gravity transports soil and sediment from one place to another. Some type of erosion occurs on most land. However, erosion can speed up when land is degraded. Roots of trees and plants act as anchors to the soil. When land is cleared for farming, the trees and plants are removed and the soil is no longer protected. This exposes soil to blowing wind and running water that can wash away the soil, as shown in this photo.

228 Unit 4 Human Impact on the Environment

Nutrient Depletion and Land Pollution

Crops use soil nutrients to grow. If the same crops are planted year after year, the same soil nutrients get used up. Plants need the right balance of nutrients to grow. Farmers can plant a different crop each year to reduce nutrient loss. Pollution from industrial activities can damage land. Mining wastes, gas and petroleum leaks, and chemical wastes can kill organisms in the soil. U.S. government programs such as Superfund help to clean up polluted land.

Desertification

When too many livestock are kept in one area, they can overgraze the area. Overgrazing removes the plants and roots that hold topsoil together. Overgrazing and other poor farming methods can cause desertification. **Desertification** (dih•zer•tuh•fih•KAY•shuhn) is the process by which land becomes more desertlike and unable to support life. Without plants, soil becomes dusty and prone to wind erosion. Deforestation and urbanization can also lead to desertification.

Deforestation

The removal of trees and other vegetation from an area is called **deforestation**. Logging for wood can cause deforestation. Surface mining causes deforestation by removing vegetation and soil to get to the minerals below. Deforestation also occurs in rain forests, as shown in the photo, when farmers cut or burn down trees so they can grow crops. Urbanization can cause deforestation when forests are replaced with buildings. Deforestation leads to increased soil erosion.

Visualize It!

15 Relate How has human activity affected the forest in this photo?

_____
_____
_____
_____

229

Answers

13. Students should discuss actions they could take, such as planting native trees or plants in a local area, or by practicing reduce, reuse, recycle in their own homes, or other activities that are specific to the area in which they live.

14. *See students' pages for annotations.*

15. Sample answer: Human activity has caused deforestation (by cutting the trees down), the death of other trees, the destruction of ecosystems, and increased soil erosion.

Formative Assessment

Ask: What are five ways that people use land? People use land for recreation, for building homes, for building roads, for farming, and for commercial uses, such as manufacturing. **Ask:** What do people do that harms the land? People can cause urban sprawl, erosion, deforestation, nutrient depletion, land pollution, and desertification. **Ask:** Why is soil important to the planet? Soil provides a habitat for organisms, and it stores water and nutrients; without soil, most plants couldn't survive.

Interpreting Visuals

Have students look at the photos on these pages. **Ask:** How might urban sprawl affect the land? Rainwater might not soak into the ground, but cause flooding instead. **Ask:** How might slash-and-burn agriculture affect the land? It might cause deforestation, which can contribute to climate change, or lead to desertification. **Ask:** How might overgrazing affect the land? Erosion might increase and lead to desertification.

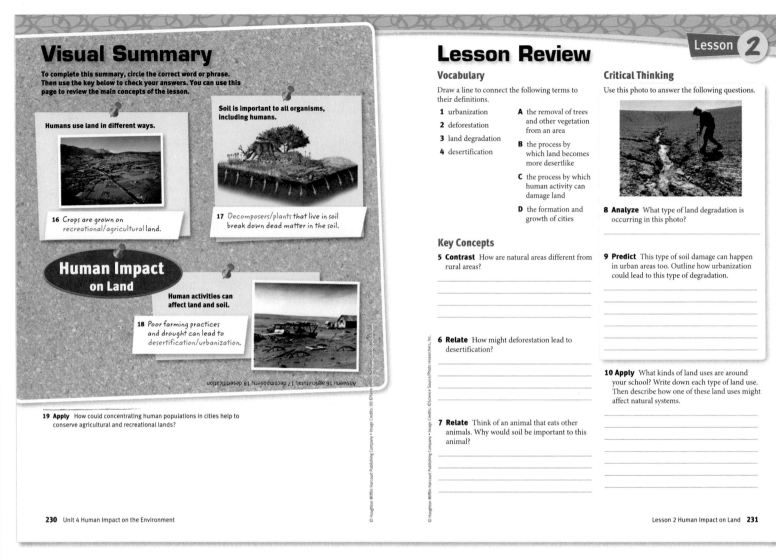

Visual Summary

To complete this summary, circle the correct word or phrase. Then use the key below to check your answers. You can use this page to review the main concepts of the lesson.

Humans use land in different ways.

Soil is important to all organisms, including humans.

16 Crops are grown on recreational/agricultural land.

17 Decomposers/plants that live in soil break down dead matter in the soil.

Human Impact on Land

Human activities can affect land and soil.

18 Poor farming practices and drought can lead to desertification/urbanization.

Answers: 16 agricultural; 17 decomposers; 18 desertification

19 **Apply** How could concentrating human populations in cities help to conserve agricultural and recreational lands?

230 Unit 4 Human Impact on the Environment

Lesson Review

Lesson 2

Vocabulary

Draw a line to connect the following terms to their definitions.

1 urbanization
2 deforestation
3 land degradation
4 desertification

A the removal of trees and other vegetation from an area

B the process by which land becomes more desertlike

C the process by which human activity can damage land

D the formation and growth of cities

Key Concepts

5 **Contrast** How are natural areas different from rural areas?

6 **Relate** How might deforestation lead to desertification?

7 **Relate** Think of an animal that eats other animals. Why would soil be important to this animal?

Critical Thinking

Use this photo to answer the following questions.

8 **Analyze** What type of land degradation is occurring in this photo?

9 **Predict** This type of soil damage can happen in urban areas too. Outline how urbanization could lead to this type of degradation.

10 **Apply** What kinds of land uses are around your school? Write down each type of land use. Then describe how one of these land uses might affect natural systems.

Lesson 2 Human Impact on Land 231

Visual Summary Answers

16. agricultural

17. decomposers

18. desertification

19. Sample answer: If people lived only in cities, then rural lands, which include agricultural and recreational lands, would have fewer people. This would mean that those lands would be affected less by human activity.

Lesson Review Answers

1. D
2. A
3. C
4. B
5. Sample answer: Natural areas are places that humans have left alone or restored to a natural state. Rural areas are areas that have a low density of people and that are not urbanized much.
6. Sample answer: Removing trees and vegetation from an area removes the roots that keep the soil together. This leaves the soil exposed to wind and rain, which can blow or wash the soil away.

7. Sample answer: Such an animal depends on soil because its prey likely eats plants or the prey animal's prey eats plants.

8. erosion

9. Sample answer: The process of urbanization might remove trees and plants, which expose the soil to wind and rain. Covering large amounts of land with asphalt or concrete will cause rain to wash off the surface instead of soaking into the soil. This runoff may cause erosion when it runs onto a natural land surface.

10. Answers may vary. Students should be able to show a comprehension of the content of this lesson.

Human Impact on the Atmosphere

Essential Question How do humans impact Earth's atmosphere?

 Professional Development

For more detailed information about the topics in this lesson, refer to the Content Refresher in the Unit Opener pages.

Opening Your Lesson

Begin the lesson by assessing students' prerequisite and prior knowledge.

Prerequisite Knowledge

- Definitions of *atmosphere, air pollution,* and *natural resources*

Accessing Prior Knowledge

Invite students to discuss what they know about air quality. **Ask:** What affects air quality? Sample answer: what people put into the air, such as smoke or exhaust **Ask:** Is air quality something that humans can affect? Sample answer: yes, because people can choose to pollute or not pollute **Ask:** Is putting things into the air always bad? Sample answers: yes, because it changes air quality; no, because some things are good for the air (Revisit this question after the lesson.)

Customize Your Opening

- ☐ **Accessing Prior Knowledge,** above
- ☐ **Print Path** Engage Your Brain, SE p. 233 #1–2
- ☐ **Print Path** Active Reading, SE p. 233 #3–4
- ☐ **Digital Path** Lesson Opener

Key Topics/Learning Goals

Air and Air Pollution

1. Explain why the atmosphere is important.
2. Define *air pollution,* and identify its sources.
3. Summarize how smog forms.
4. Define *particulates.*

Effects of Human Activities on Atmosphere

1. Summarize vehicle emissions' effects on air.
2. Explain how air pollution can lead to acid precipitation.
3. Describe the effect of acid precipitation.

Air Quality and Health

1. Define *air quality,* and tell how it is measured.
2. Tell how air pollution affects health.

Air Pollution and Earth

1. Describe how air pollution might be affecting our planet.

Supporting Concepts

- Many organisms need air to survive. The atmosphere helps regulate Earth's temperature and protects organisms from harmful radiation.
- Air pollution is atmospheric contamination by natural and human-made pollutants.
- Particulates are tiny particles of solids or liquids in the air.

- Vehicle emissions put particulates and carbon monoxide gas into the air, and contribute to the formation of smog.
- Burning fossil fuels releases gases that mix with water in the air to form acid precipitation.
- Acid precipitation damages plants and soil organisms, increases water acidity, and harms aquatic life.

- Air quality, a measure of how clean or polluted the air is, is assessed by measuring rain pH, ozone, gases, and particulates.
- Prolonged exposure to air pollutants can cause health problems.

- Atmospheric greenhouse gases, including carbon dioxide, have increased since the 1700s.
- Human activities seem to have affected the planet's climate and ozone layer.

Options for Instruction

Two parallel paths provide coverage of the Essential Questions, with a strong **Inquiry** strand woven into each. Follow the **Print Path,** the **Digital Path,** or your customized combination of print, digital, and inquiry.

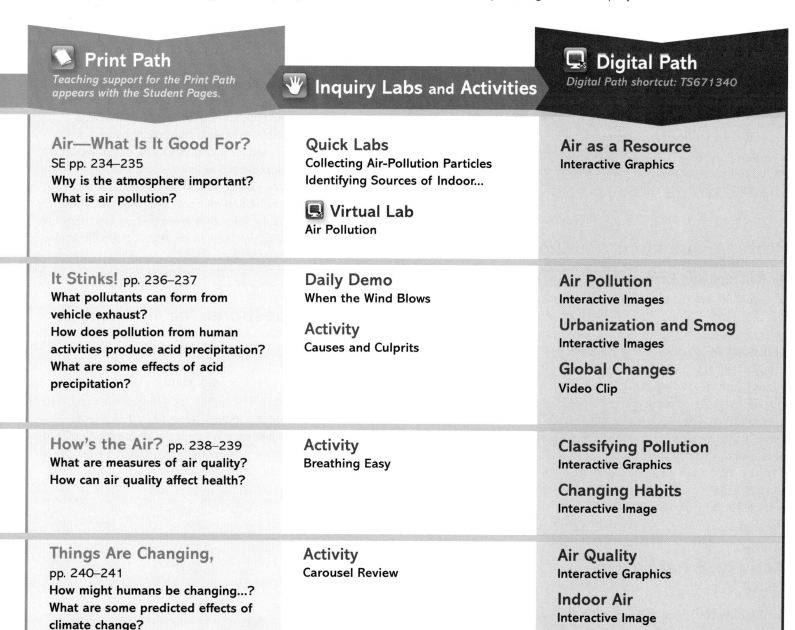

Print Path
Teaching support for the Print Path appears with the Student Pages.

Inquiry Labs and Activities

Digital Path
Digital Path shortcut: TS671340

Air—What Is It Good For?
SE pp. 234–235
Why is the atmosphere important?
What is air pollution?

Quick Labs
Collecting Air-Pollution Particles
Identifying Sources of Indoor...

Virtual Lab
Air Pollution

Air as a Resource
Interactive Graphics

It Stinks! pp. 236–237
What pollutants can form from vehicle exhaust?
How does pollution from human activities produce acid precipitation?
What are some effects of acid precipitation?

Daily Demo
When the Wind Blows

Activity
Causes and Culprits

Air Pollution
Interactive Images

Urbanization and Smog
Interactive Images

Global Changes
Video Clip

How's the Air? pp. 238–239
What are measures of air quality?
How can air quality affect health?

Activity
Breathing Easy

Classifying Pollution
Interactive Graphics

Changing Habits
Interactive Image

Things Are Changing,
pp. 240–241
How might humans be changing...?
What are some predicted effects of climate change?
How is the ozone layer affected by air pollution?

Activity
Carousel Review

Air Quality
Interactive Graphics

Indoor Air
Interactive Image

Options for Assessment

See the Evaluate page for options, including Formative Assessment, Summative Assessment, and Unit Review.

Engage and Explore

Activities and Discussion

Activity *Causes and Culprits*

Engage

Effects of Human Activities

 whole class
 10 min
 GUIDED inquiry

Have students make posters or drawings that show a single cause of air pollution. When students have finished, have them sort the drawings or posters by the causes shown. Then list the causes of air pollution on the board. Add to the list throughout the lesson.

Probing Questions *The Ozone Hole*

Air Pollution and Earth

 whole class
 10 min
 GUIDED inquiry

Evaluating Ask students if they have ever heard of a hole in the ozone layer. **Ask:** What is ozone? It is a gas. **Ask:** Can you have a hole in gas? not really Explain that when people talk about a hole in the ozone layer, they are really talking about a region where there is less ozone gas in the ozone layer. The ozone hole is often shown in images as a region that is a different color. Explain that this color change is there to help people know which region has less ozone. It doesn't mean that there is no ozone at all there. As an extension activity, have students go online and look at UV indexes around the world as they are related to the protection provided by atmospheric ozone.

Activity *Breathing Easy*

Engage

Air Quality and Health

 whole class
 10 min
 GUIDED inquiry

Have students work in small groups to research, write, and record video or audio public service announcements that would help people who have respiratory problems breathe more easily on a day when the air quality is poor.

Discussion *Change in the Air*

Air Pollution and Earth

 pairs or small groups
20 min

Invite students to think about how the air temperature of the planet might be changing. **Ask:** What could make the air temperature change? Pollution can form a layer that acts like a blanket to hold in heat. **Ask:** What might happen if the air temperature increased for a long time? The planet would change. Glaciers might melt. Sea levels might rise. Some living things would become extinct. **Ask:** What can humans do to not pollute the air? Use more fuel-efficient cars, drive less, walk more, regulate polluting industries more, reduce electricity use, avoid using aerosol sprays, and so on. Revisit this topic after students have finished the lesson.

Probing Questions *The Air Around Us*

Introducing Key Topics

 whole class
10 min
GUIDED inquiry

Describing Ask students to think about air in their region. Where is the air the freshest? Where is the air the most polluted? What might cause these differences in air quality? Are people or animals harmed in any way by the air in the region? If so, how?

©PhotoDisc/Getty Images

Customize Your Labs

 See the Lab Manual for lab datasheets.

 Go Online for editable lab datasheets.

Labs and Demos

Daily Demo *When the Wind Blows*

Engage

Effects of Human Activities

whole class
10 min/day
Inquiry DIRECTED inquiry

PURPOSE **To show how plants can reduce pollution**

MATERIALS

- fan
- pot of dry, powdery dirt
- potted plant

Place the plant in front of the turned-off fan. Ask students what they think will happen to the soil when you turn on the fan. nothing Turn on the fan. Explain to students that the plant's roots help to hold soil in place, even when it is windy. Now place the pot of dirt in front of the turned-off fan. Ask students if they want you to turn on the fan. No, because it will create too much dust. Explain that turning on the fan would blow dust all through the classroom. Discuss how plants can prevent pollution.

Quick Lab *Identifying Sources of Indoor Air Pollution*

Air and Air Pollution

small groups
30 min
Inquiry DIRECTED inquiry

Students research causes of indoor air pollution and then document sources of indoor air pollution in the school.

PURPOSE **To identify sources of indoor air pollution and communicate ways to reduce or eliminate this pollution**

MATERIALS

- digital camera
- paper
- pencils
- reference materials

Quick Lab *Collecting Air-Pollution Particles*

Air and Air Pollution

pairs
10 min/day (2 days)
Inquiry DIRECTED inquiry

PURPOSE **To study the types of air pollution around school**

MATERIALS

- index cards, 5-in. X 7-in. (10)
- magnifying lens
- plastic spoon or paintbrush
- tape
- pushpins (10)
- petroleum jelly
- hole punch
- string

Virtual Lab *Air Pollution*

Air and Air Pollution

individuals
flexible
Inquiry GUIDED inquiry

Students test several strategies and compare costs and effects.

PURPOSE To compare several ways to address air pollution

Activities and Discussion

- [ ] **Activity** Causes and Culprits
- [ ] **Probing Questions** Ozone Hole
- [ ] **Discussion** Change in the Air
- [ ] **Probing Questions** The Air Around Us

Labs and Demos

- [ ] **Daily Demo** When the Wind Blows
- [ ] **Quick Lab** Collecting...Particles
- [ ] **Quick Lab** Identifying Sources of Indoor Air Pollution
- [ ] **Virtual Lab** Air Pollution

Your Resources

Explain Science Concepts

Key Topics	📖 Print Path	💻 Digital Path
Air and Air Pollution	☐ **Air, What Is It Good For?** SE pp. 234–235 • Active Reading, #5 • Active Reading (Annotation strategy), #6 • Visualize It!, #7	☐ **Air as a Resource** Explore the different ways the atmosphere supports life.
Effects of Human Activities on Atmosphere	☐ **It Stinks!,** SE pp. 236–237 • Active Reading (Annotation strategy), #8 • Active Reading (Annotation strategy), #9 • Visualize It!, #10 **10 Analyze** Explain how pollution from one location can affect the environment far away from the source of the pollution.	☐ **Air Pollution** Learn about air pollution. ☐ **Urbanization and Smog** Explore the ways pollution leads to smog. ☐ **Global Changes** Learn about greenhouse gases and temperature.
Air Quality and Health	☐ **How's the Air?,** SE pp. 238–239 • Visualize It!, #11 • Visualize It!, #12 • Think Outside the Book, #13 • Identify, #14 **Visualize It!** **11 Recommend** If you were a weather reporter using this map, what would you recommend for people living in areas that are colored orange?	☐ **Classifying Pollution** Learn about clean air. ☐ **Changing Habits** Learn about pollution of indoor air.
Air Pollution and Earth	☐ **Things Are Changing,** SE pp. 240–241 • Visualize It!, #15 • Active Reading (Annotation strategy) #16 • Infer, #17 • Inquiry, #18	☐ **Air Quality** Learn about clean air. ☐ **Indoor Air** Learn about pollution of indoor air.

Basic *What Causes Pollution?*

Air and Air Pollution

 individuals

🕐 20 min

Concept Map Have students use a Concept Map to list ways that air becomes polluted. In a large circle, have them write *Air Pollution.* Surrounding the circle, have them list causes of air pollution. Sample answers: car exhaust, factories, smoke from fires, volcanoes, pollen

⊘ *Optional Online resource: Concept Map support*

Advanced *Monitoring Air Quality*

Synthesizing Key Topics

 individuals

🕐 20 min

Have students use online resources to monitor changes in air quality in your area. Ask them to determine in what month(s) air quality is lowest and when it is highest. Are certain factors, such as ozone and pollen, more of a problem in certain areas? Why do they think this is so?

ELL *Illustrated Dictionary*

Synthesizing Key Topics

 individuals

🕐 20 min

Have students write each of these terms at the top of a separate index card: *particulate, air pollution, smog,* and *acid precipitation.* Under each term, have students draw illustrations that help them remember what each term means.

ELL *Going with the (Air) Flow*

Air and Air Pollution

 individuals

🕐 20 min

Have students draw a diagram that shows how polluted air gets from one region to another. Encourage students to look at the illustrations in the lesson to help them make their diagram. Have them label the parts of the diagram.

air quality	particulate	air pollution
greenhouse effect	smog	acid precipitation

Previewing Vocabulary

 whole class

🕐 10 min

Base Words Explain that looking for smaller words inside longer words can help you figure out what words mean.

• Explain that **particulate** comes from the word *particle.* Particulates are tiny particles in the air.

• **Precipitation** includes the word *precipitate,* which comes from an Old English word that means "fall."

Reinforcing Vocabulary

 individuals

🕐 ongoing

Key Term FoldNote Have students make a Key Term FoldNote to help them learn the lesson vocabulary.

⊘ *Online resource: Key Term FoldNote support*

Customize Your Core Lesson

Core Instruction

☐ **Print Path** choices

☐ **Digital Path** choices

Vocabulary

☐ **Previewing Vocabulary** Base Words

☐ **Reinforcing Vocabulary** Key Term FoldNote

Your Resources

Differentiated Instruction

☐ **Basic** What Causes Pollution?

☐ **Advanced** Monitoring Air Quality

☐ **ELL** Illustrated Dictionary

☐ **ELL** Going with the (Air) Flow

_____

_____

_____

_____

Extend Science Concepts

Reinforce and Review

Activity *Carousel Review*

Synthesizing Key Topics
👥 small groups
🕐 ongoing

1 Arrange chart paper in different parts of the classroom. On each paper, write a question to review lesson content.

2 Divide students into small groups and assign each group a chart. Give each group a different colored marker.

3 Groups review their question, discuss their answer, and write a response.

4 After 5 to 10 min, each group rotates to the next station. Groups put a check by each answer they agree with, comment on answers they don't agree with, and add their own answers. Continue until all groups have reviewed all charts.

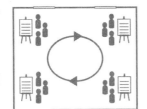

5 Invite each group to share information with the class.

Graphic Organizer

Synthesizing Key Topics
👥 pairs or small groups
🕐 15 min

Two-Panel Flipchart After students have studied the lesson, ask them to work together to make Flipcharts to summarize its content. They should make two two-panel charts. Have them write these words on the outside of each Flipchart panel: *Air and Air Pollution,* on one chart and *Air Quality and Health* and *Air Pollution and Earth* on the other. Under each panel, students should summarize what they learned about each topic.

🔘 *Online resource: Two-Panel Flip Chart support*

Going Further

Real World Connection

Air Quality and Health
👥 whole class
🕐 10 min

Analyze Data Have students look at weather reports in newspapers or on the Internet for information about air quality in their area. Many newspapers give daily updates on air quality. These updates can usually be found under headings such as "UV Factor," "Pollution Standard Index," or "Pollen Index." Have students note the air quality in their area today, and if possible, at different times of the week, month, or year. Have students put their data in a table and use them to make a line graph showing how the air quality has changed over time.

 Optional Online resources: Data Table, Line Graph support

Real World Connection

Synthesizing Key Topics
👥 individuals or pairs
🕐 ongoing

In-Depth Research Ask students to research what the world could be like in 50 or 100 years if global warming increased significantly. Then have students describe the steps they think people should take today to prevent global warming.

Customize Your Closing

🔖 *See the Assessment Guide for quizzes and tests.*

🔘 *Go Online to edit and create quizzes and tests.*

Reinforce and Review

☐ **Activity** Carousel Review

☐ **Graphic Organizer** Two-Panel Flipchart

☐ **Print Path** Visual Summary, SE p. 242

☐ **Digital Path** Lesson Closer

Evaluate Student Mastery

Formative Assessment

See the teacher support below the Student Pages for additional Formative Assessment questions.

Have students name some primary and secondary pollutants. List the examples on the board. Then ask volunteers to identify ways in which these pollutants can harm human health. Last, have students identify ways these pollutants could contribute to global warming. Primary pollutants: dust, salt, volcanic gases, ash, smoke, pollen, heat, exhaust; secondary pollutants: ground-level ozone, smog, acid rain. Many of these pollutants can cause lung damage, coughing, headaches, breathing difficulties, and skin cancer. These pollutants can cause the atmosphere to absorb and trap more heat, causing temperatures to rise.

Reteach

Formative assessment may show that students need reinforcement for certain topics. The resources below are recommended for reteaching. If students were introduced to a topic through the Print Path, you can also use the Digital Path to reteach, or vice versa.
🎧 *Can be assigned to individual students*

Air and Air Pollution
Quick Lab Collecting Air-Pollution Particles 🎧
Virtual Lab Air Pollution 🎧

Effects of Human Activities
Activity Causes and Culprits

Air Quality and Health
Activity Breathing Easy
Graphic Organizer Two-Panel Flipchart 🎧

Summative Assessment

Alternative Assessment
Improve a City

🔘 *Online resources: student worksheet, optional rubrics*

Human Impact on the Atmosphere

Tic-Tac-Toe: *Improve a City*
Imagine you are part of a coalition containing government leaders, business leaders, community leaders, and advisors in health and technology. The people on the coalition want to improve their city and keep it livable. Think about what can be done that has the fewest harmful effects on the air.

1. Work on your own, with a partner, or with a small group.

2. Choose three quick activities from the game. Check the boxes you plan to complete. They must form a straight line in any direction.

3. Have your teacher approve your plan.

4. Complete each activity, and turn in your results.

__ Smog	__ Effects of Urbanization	__ Air Pollution/Acid Rain
Write a plan that explains how you can reduce smog in your city. You may want to include a timeline or flowchart to show the steps in your plan and the time it will take to implement the ideas.	Write a paragraph that describes the effects of urbanization and what the city should do to avoid any more negative effects of urbanization.	Make a multimedia presentation that states your position on air pollution and acid rain. Explain what the city can do to avoid such problems in the future.
__ Maintaining Balance	__ Ozone Layer	__ Secondary Air Pollutants
Describe what can you do to preserve Earth's energy balance (prevent global warming) in your city. Present your finding as a poster or report.	Perform a skit describing how different members of the city can work together to prevent future damage to the ozone layer.	Imagine you are meeting with the mayor. Describe to the mayor what the city should do to prevent secondary air pollutants.
__ Primary Air Pollutants	__ Particulates in the Air	__ Air Quality
Write a memo to government officials describing some steps the city can take to prevent primary pollutants from getting into the air.	Write a public service announcement that tells people how to keep particulates out of the air, and convinces them that this is an important step to take in the city.	Draw or sketch a plan to measure air quality in your city. Describe how the results can be used to track and improve air quality.

Going Further
☐ Real World Connection
☐ Real World Connection

Formative Assessment
☐ Strategies Throughout TE
☐ Lesson Review SE

Summative Assessment
☐ Alternative Assessment Improve a City
☐ Lesson Quiz
☐ Unit Tests A and B
☐ Unit Review SE End-of-Unit

Your Resources

_____   _____

_____   _____

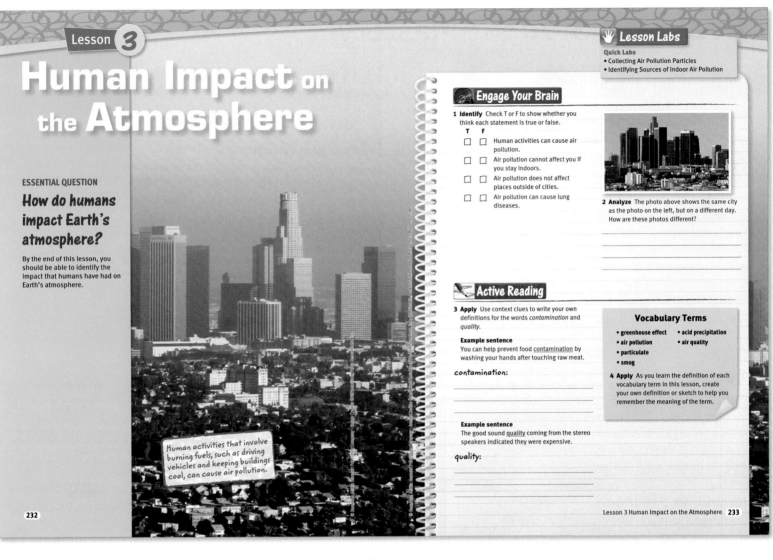

Lesson ③

Human Impact on the Atmosphere

ESSENTIAL QUESTION

How do humans impact Earth's atmosphere?

By the end of this lesson, you should be able to identify the impact that humans have had on Earth's atmosphere.

Human activities that involve burning fuels, such as driving vehicles and keeping buildings cool, can cause air pollution.

232

Lesson Labs

Quick Labs
• Collecting Air Pollution Particles
• Identifying Sources of Indoor Air Pollution

Engage Your Brain

1 Identify Check T or F to show whether you think each statement is true or false.

T | F
☐ ☐ Human activities can cause air pollution.
☐ ☐ Air pollution cannot affect you if you stay indoors.
☐ ☐ Air pollution does not affect places outside of cities.
☐ ☐ Air pollution can cause lung diseases.

2 Analyze The photo above shows the same city as the photo on the left, but on a different day. How are these photos different?

Active Reading

3 Apply Use context clues to write your own definitions for the words *contamination* and *quality*.

Example sentence
You can help prevent food <u>contamination</u> by washing your hands after touching raw meat.

contamination:

Example sentence
The good sound <u>quality</u> coming from the stereo speakers indicated they were expensive.

quality:

Vocabulary Terms
• greenhouse effect   • acid precipitation
• air pollution   • air quality
• particulate
• smog

4 Apply As you learn the definition of each vocabulary term in this lesson, create your own definition or sketch to help you remember the meaning of the term.

Lesson 3 Human Impact on the Atmosphere **233**

Answers

Answers for 1–3 should represent students' current thoughts, even if incorrect.

1. T; F; F; T

2. Sample answer: In the photo on the left page, the city is harder to see because the air is not very clear due to pollution. The photo on the right has clear skies and the city is more visible.

3. Sample answers: contamination: being unclean, unhealthy, or unsuitable for use by humans or other organisms; quality: a measurement of how good a certain property or characteristic of something is

4. Student annotations will vary.

Opening Your Lesson

Discuss students' answers to item 1 to assess students' prerequisite knowledge and to estimate what they already know about air, air pollution, and the human causes of air pollution.

Prerequisites Students should already know what natural resources are and what air pollution is. They should have some general knowledge of the atmosphere.

Interpreting Visuals

Have students examine the images on this page and explain in their own words what is happening. **Ask:** Can you identify what people are doing that affects the air? **Ask:** How are the things people are doing helpful to them and harmful to them? Sample answer: Driving helps people get around faster, but it puts pollutants into the air. Cooling a building makes the people inside cooler and more comfortable, but it heats up the outside air. Adding to the pollution makes it hard for some people to breathe and can make people sick.

AIR
What Is It Good For?

Why is the atmosphere important?

If you were lost in a desert, you could survive a few days without food and water. But you wouldn't last more than a few minutes without air. Air is an important natural resource. The air you breathe forms part of Earth's atmosphere. The *atmosphere* (AT•muh•sfeer) is a mixture of gases that surrounds Earth. Most organisms on Earth have adapted to the natural balance of gases found in the atmosphere.

It Provides Gases That Organisms Need to Survive

Oxygen is one of the gases that make up Earth's atmosphere. It is used by most living cells to get energy from food. Every breath you take brings oxygen into your body. The atmosphere also contains carbon dioxide. Plants need carbon dioxide to make their own food through photosynthesis (foh•toh•SYN•thuh•sys).

It Absorbs Harmful Radiation

High-energy radiation from space would harm life on Earth if it were not blocked by the atmosphere. Fast-moving particles, called *cosmic rays*, enter the atmosphere every second. These particles collide with oxygen, nitrogen, and other gas molecules and are slowed down. A part of the atmosphere called the *stratosphere* contains ozone gas. The ozone layer absorbs most of the high-energy radiation from the sun, called *ultraviolet radiation* (UV), that reaches Earth.

It Keeps Earth Warm

Without the atmosphere, temperatures on Earth would not be stable. It would be too cold for life to exist. The **greenhouse effect** is the way by which certain gases in the atmosphere, such as water vapor and carbon dioxide, absorb and reradiate thermal energy. This slows the loss of energy from Earth into space. The atmosphere acts like a warm blanket that insulates the surface of Earth, preventing the sun's energy from being lost. For this reason, carbon dioxide and water vapor are called *greenhouse gases*.

Active Reading 5 **Explain** How is Earth's atmosphere similar to a warm blanket?

© Houghton Mifflin Harcourt Publishing Company • Image Credits: ©NASA

234 Unit 4 Human Impact on the Environment

What is air pollution?

The contamination of the atmosphere by pollutants from human and natural sources is called **air pollution**. Natural sources of air pollution include volcanic eruptions, wildfires, and dust storms. In cities and suburbs, most air pollution comes from the burning of fossil fuels such as oil, gasoline, and coal. Oil refineries, chemical manufacturing plants, dry-cleaning businesses, and auto repair shops are just some potential sources of air pollution. Scientists classify air pollutants as either gases or particulates.

Active Reading
6 **Identify** As you read, underline sources of air pollution.

Visualize It!
7 **Analyze** Which one of these images could be both a natural or a human source of air pollution? Give reasons for your answer.

Factory emissions

Vehicle exhaust

Forest fires and wildfires

© Houghton Mifflin Harcourt Publishing Company • Image Credits: (l) ©Robert McGouey/Alamy; (r) ©Steve Cole/PhotoDisc/Getty Images; (c) ©Paul Glendell/Alamy;

Gases

Gas pollutants include carbon monoxide, sulfur dioxide, nitrogen oxide, and ground-level ozone. Some of these gases occur naturally in the atmosphere. These gases are considered pollutants only when they are likely to cause harm. For example, ozone is important in the stratosphere, but at ground level it is harmful to breathe. Carbon monoxide, sulfur dioxide, and nitrogen dioxide are released from burning fossil fuels in vehicles, factories, and homes. They are a major source of air pollution.

Particulates

Particle pollutants can be easier to see than gas pollutants. A **particulate** (per•TIK•yuh•lit) is a tiny particle of solid that is suspended in air or water. Smoke contains ash, which is a particulate. The wind can pick up particulates such as dust, ash, pollen, and tiny bits of salt from the ocean and blow them far from their source. Ash, dust, and pollen are common forms of air pollution. Vehicle exhaust also contains particulates. The particulates in vehicle exhaust are a major cause of air pollution in cities.

Lesson 3 Human Impact on the Atmosphere **235**

Answers

5. Sample answer: The atmosphere contains gases that trap the sun's energy, stopping it from radiating back into space. Instead the atmosphere insulates the surface of Earth, much like a blanket would keep a person warm.

6. *See students' pages for annotations*.

7. Forest fires and wildfires could result from natural causes, such as lightning, or be intentionally or accidentally set by humans.

Learning Alert

Ozone: Good Guy or Bad Guy? Students may be confused by the dual aspect of ozone—as a protector against UV rays on one hand, and as a pollutant on the other. Explain that ozone at ground level is considered undesirable, but it's vital as a protective component of Earth's atmosphere.

Probing Questions GUIDED Inquiry

Inferring Explain to students that our oceans absorb carbon dioxide from the air and store it. Cool water absorbs more carbon dioxide than warm water. **Ask:** What might happen to atmospheric levels of carbon dioxide if the oceans got warmer? Carbon dioxide in the atmosphere would increase.

Predicting Explain that increased carbon dioxide in the atmosphere could lead to an increase in global temperatures. **Ask:** If the atmosphere became warmer, how would evaporation of the oceans change? More water would evaporate if the temperatures were warmer.

Synthesizing **Ask:** What would happen if more water evaporated? If more water evaporates into the atmosphere, there will be more rain because there will be more water vapor in the air to condense into rain.

It Stinks!

What pollutants can form from vehicle exhaust?

In urban areas, vehicle exhaust is a common source of air pollution. Gases such as carbon monoxide and particulates such as soot and ash are in exhaust fumes. Vehicle exhaust may also react with other substances in the air. When this happens, new pollutants can form. Ground-level ozone and smog are two types of pollutants that form from vehicle exhaust.

Active Reading

8 Identify As you read, underline how ground-level ozone and smog can form.

Ground-Level Ozone

Ozone in the ozone layer is necessary for life, but ground-level ozone is harmful. It is produced when sunlight reacts with vehicle exhaust and oxygen in the air. You may have heard of "Ozone Action Days" in your community. When such a warning is given, people should limit outdoor activities because ozone can damage their lungs.

Smog

Smog is another type of pollutant formed from vehicle exhaust. **Smog** forms when ground-level ozone and vehicle exhaust react in the presence of sunlight. Smog is a problem in large cities because there are more vehicles on the roads. It can cause lung damage and irritate the eyes and nose. In some cities, there can be enough smog to make a brownish haze over the city.

How does pollution from human activities produce acid precipitation?

Active Reading **9 Identify** As you read, underline how acid precipitation forms.

Precipitation (prih•sip•ih•TAY•shuhn) such as rain, sleet, or snow that contains acids from air pollution is called **acid precipitation**. Burning fossil fuels releases sulfur dioxide and nitrogen oxides into the air. When these gases mix with water in the atmosphere, they form sulfuric acid and nitric acid. Precipitation is naturally slightly acidic. When carbon dioxide in the air and water mix, they form carbonic acid. Carbonic acid is a weak acid. Sulfuric acid and nitric acid are strong acids. They can make precipitation so acidic that it is harmful to the environment.

What are some effects of acid precipitation?

Acid precipitation can cause soil and water to become more acidic than normal. Plants have adapted over long periods of time to the natural acidity of the soils in which they live. When soil acidity rises, some nutrients that plants need are dissolved. These nutrients get washed away by rainwater. Bacteria and fungi that live in the soil are also harmed by acidic conditions.

Acid precipitation may increase the acidity of lakes or streams. It also releases toxic metals from soils. The increased acidity and high levels of metals in water can sicken or kill aquatic organisms. This can disrupt habitats and result in decreased biodiversity in an ecosystem. Acid precipitation can also erode the stonework on buildings and statues.

Visualize It!

Some compounds in smoke and exhaust are harmful by themselves. And some compounds in smoke and exhaust can react in the atmosphere to form other pollutants such as smog and acid precipitation.

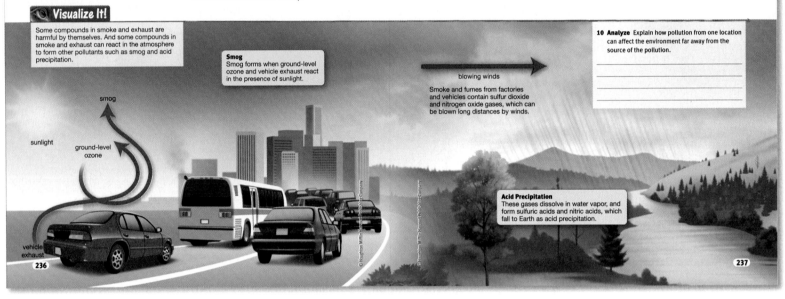

Smog
Smog forms when ground-level ozone and vehicle exhaust react in the presence of sunlight.

blowing winds

Smoke and fumes from factories and vehicles contain sulfur dioxide and nitrogen oxide gases, which can be blown long distances by winds.

10 Analyze Explain how pollution from one location can affect the environment far away from the source of the pollution.

smog

sunlight

ground-level ozone

vehicle exhaust

Acid Precipitation
These gases dissolve in water vapor, and form sulfuric acids and nitric acids, which fall to Earth as acid precipitation.

236

237

Answers

8. *See students' pages for annotations.*

9. *See students' pages for annotations.*

10. Sample answer: Wind blows the pollution over long distances, where the pollutant gases combine with water in the atmosphere, forming acid precipitation.

Interpreting Visuals

Have students look at the visual at the bottom of the spread. **Ask:** What happens first when smog forms? Car exhaust reacts with air and sunlight to form ground-level ozone. **Ask:** What happens next? The ozone reacts with exhaust to form smog.

Learning Alert

Smog Explain that the word *smog* comes from combining **sm**oke and f**og** = smog. It was once caused by smoke from coal fires and fog, but today, smog is usually a combination of vehicle exhaust and ozone. In 2008, Beijing, China, had such terrible smog problems that authorities had to shut down factories and restrict traffic. The smog was so bad, in fact, that the Summer Olympics were nearly canceled because of it.

Interpreting Visuals

Have students look at the visual at the bottom of the spread. **Ask:** What is likely to happen to the soil and river in the diagram? They will become more acidic. **Ask:** What happens if the soil and river become too acidic? The organisms living there may die.

How's the AIR?

What are measures of air quality?

Measuring how clean or polluted the air is tells us about **air quality**. Pollutants reduce air quality. Two major threats to air quality are vehicle exhausts and industrial pollutants. The air quality in cities can be poor. As more people move into cities, the cities get bigger. This leads to increased amounts of human-made pollution. Poor air circulation, such as a lack of wind, allows air pollution to stay in one area where it can build up. As pollution increases, air quality decreases.

Air Quality Index

The Air Quality Index (AQI) is a number used to describe the air quality of a location such as a city. The higher the AQI number, the more people are likely to have health problems that are linked to air pollution. Air quality is measured and given a value based on the level of pollution detected. The AQI values are divided into ranges. Each range is given a color code and a description. The Environmental Protection Agency (EPA) has AQIs for the pollutants that pose the greatest risk to public health, including ozone and particulates. The EPA can then issue advisories to avoid exposure to pollution that may harm health.

🔍 Visualize It!

11 Recommend If you were a weather reporter using this map, what would you recommend for people living in areas that are colored orange?

_____

_____

_____

Indoor Air Pollution

The air inside a building can become more polluted than the air outside. This is because buildings are insulated to prevent outside air from entering the building. Some sources of indoor air pollution include chlorine and ammonia from household cleaners and formaldehyde from furniture. Harmful chemicals can be released from some paints and glues. Radon is a radioactive gas released when uranium decays. Radon can seep into buildings through gaps in their foundations. It can build up inside well-insulated buildings. _Ventilation_, or the mixing of indoor and outside air, can reduce indoor air pollution. Another way to reduce indoor air pollution is to limit the use of items that create the pollution.

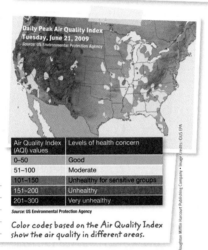

Daily Peak Air Quality Index
Tuesday, June 21, 2009
Source: US Environmental Protection Agency

Air Quality Index (AQI) values	Levels of health concern
0–50	Good
51–100	Moderate
101–150	Unhealthy for sensitive groups
151–200	Unhealthy
201–300	Very unhealthy

Source: US Environmental Protection Agency

Color codes based on the Air Quality Index show the air quality in different areas.

🔍 Visualize It!

12 Apply If this was your house, how might you decrease the sources of indoor air pollution?

_____

_____

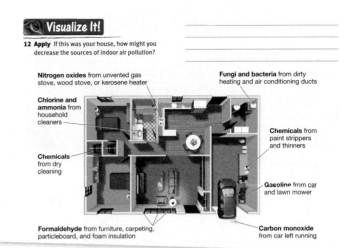

Nitrogen oxides from unvented gas stove, wood stove, or kerosene heater

Chlorine and ammonia from household cleaners

Chemicals from dry cleaning

Fungi and bacteria from dirty heating and air conditioning ducts

Chemicals from paint strippers and thinners

Gasoline from car and lawn mower

Formaldehyde from furniture, carpeting, particleboard, and foam insulation

Carbon monoxide from car left running

How can air quality affect health?

Daily exposure to small amounts of air pollution can cause serious health problems. Children, elderly people, and people with asthma, allergies, lung problems, and heart problems are especially vulnerable to the effects of air pollution. The short-term effects of air pollution include coughing, headaches, and wheezing. Long-term effects, such as lung cancer and emphysema, are dangerous because they can cause death.

Think Outside the Book Inquiry

13 Evaluate Think about the community in which you live. What different things in your community and the surrounding areas might affect the air quality where you live?

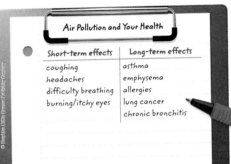

Air Pollution and Your Health

Short-term effects	Long-term effects
coughing	asthma
headaches	emphysema
difficulty breathing	allergies
burning/itchy eyes	lung cancer
	chronic bronchitis

14 Identify Imagine you are walking next to a busy road where there are a lot of exhaust fumes. Circle the effects listed in the table that you are most likely to have while walking.

Answers

11. Sample answer: I'd advise people with lung diseases or the very young or very old to avoid going outside because the air pollution might cause them breathing problems.

12. Answers may vary. Answers may address such things as minimizing the amount of cleaning chemicals used, and keeping the amount of mold and bacteria to a minimum by cleaning AC duct work or filters.

13. Answers may vary. Students should be able to articulate some of the concepts they have learned about air quality and pollution.

14. Answers may vary. Students should circle one or more of the short-term effects.

Formative Assessment

Ask: Why is air quality often poorer in cities than in rural areas? Sample answers: There are more people and cars in cities, so there is more exhaust to cause smog. There may be a lack of wind, which causes pollution to build up. The lack of plants causes heat and carbon dioxide to build up. Chemicals from businesses, such as auto repair shops and dry cleaners, may cause pollution in cities. **Ask:** What forms of air pollution might happen in rural areas? forest fires, pollen, dust storms, decaying organic waste, agricultural wastes, pesticides, herbicides, mining activities

Building Reading Skills

Combination Notes Have students look at the table that shows the diseases that result from air pollution. Have students draw a figure of a person in the right column. In the left column, have them write the diseases from the table. They should then draw a line from each disease to the part of the body that is affected. **Ask:** What part of the body does air pollution seem to affect the most? the lungs

🌐 _**Optional Online resource: Combination Notes support**_

Things Are CHANGING

How might humans be changing Earth's climates?

The burning of fossil fuels releases greenhouse gases, such as carbon dioxide, into the atmosphere. The atmosphere today contains about 37% more carbon dioxide than it did in the mid-1700s, and that level continues to increase. Average global temperatures have also risen in recent decades.

Many people are concerned about how the greenhouse gases from human activities add to the observed trend of increasing global temperatures. Earth's atmosphere and other systems work together in complex ways, so it is hard to know exactly how much the extra greenhouse gases change the temperature. Climate scientists make computer models to understand the effects of climate change. Models predict that average global temperatures are likely to rise another 1.1 to 6.4 °C (2 to 11.5 °F) by the year 2100.

A Sunlight (radiant energy) passes through the windows of the car.

B Energy as heat is trapped inside by the windows.

C The temperature inside the car increases.

Visualize It!

15 Synthesize How is a car with closed windows a good analogy of the atmosphere's greenhouse effect?

How is the ozone layer affected by air pollution?

In the 1980s, scientists reported an alarming discovery about Earth's protective ozone layer. Over the polar regions, the ozone layer was thinning. Chemicals called *chlorofluorocarbons* (klor•oh•flur•oh•kar•buhns) (CFCs) were causing ozone to break down into oxygen, which does not block harmful ultraviolet (UV) rays. The thinning of the ozone layer allows more UV radiation to reach Earth's surface. UV radiation is dangerous to organisms, including humans, as it causes sunburn, damages DNA (which can lead to cancer), and causes eye damage.

CFCs once had many industrial uses, such as coolants in refrigerators and air-conditioning units. CFC use has now been banned, but CFC molecules can stay in the atmosphere for about 100 years. So, CFCs released from a spray can 30 years ago are still harming the ozone layer today. However, recent studies show that breakdown of the ozone layer has slowed.

The dark blue area on this map shows the size of the ozone hole over the South Pole.

17 Infer How might these penguins near the South Pole be affected by the ozone hole?

What are some predicted effects of climate change?

Active Reading 16 Identify As you read, underline some effects of an increasing average global temperature.

Scientists have already noticed many changes linked to warmer temperatures. For example, some glaciers and the Arctic sea ice are melting at the fastest rates ever recorded. A warmer Earth may lead to changes in rainfall patterns, rising sea levels, and more severe storms. These changes will have many negative impacts for life on Earth. Other predicted effects include drought in some regions and increased precipitation in others. Farming practices and the availability of food is also expected to be impacted by increased global temperatures. Such changes will likely have political and economic effects on the world, especially in developing countries.

Melt water pours from an iceberg that broke away from the Jakobshavn Glacier in West Greenland.

Satellite image of Arctic summer sea ice in September 1979.

Satellite image of Arctic summer sea ice in September 2007.

Inquiry

18 Relate What effect might melting sea ice have for people who live in coastal areas?

Answers

15. Sample answer: The glass in the car traps energy in the form of heat from the sun, and the interior of the car gets hotter. In the same way, greenhouse gases trap thermal energy from the sun, which keeps Earth warm.

16. *See student page for annotations.*

17. Sample answer: The penguins may be at risk of developing sunburn, skin cancer, or eye damage.

18. Sample answer: Coastal areas will likely become flooded, which will displace the people living in those areas.

Learning Alert ⚡ MISCONCEPTION ⚡

Ozone Hole Students may think that the ozone hole is similar to a hole in something solid, rather than a region of thinner ozone gas. Look for signs of confusion by asking students to describe in their own words what a hole in the ozone layer is. If students seem to think that there is a physical hole in the ozone layer, remind them that ozone is a gas. There can be fewer ozone particles in a region, but there will always be some ozone there.

Interpreting Visuals

Modeling Trapped Heat Have students look at the illustration of the car. Explain that this illustration is modeling Earth's system. Like the gases in Earth's atmosphere, the car's windows allow sunlight to enter. However, they also prevent the heat from leaving—just as the gases do. As a result, the temperature inside the car rises, as does the temperature on Earth's surface.

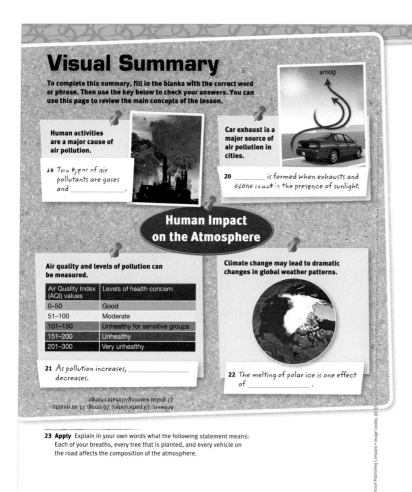

Visual Summary

To complete this summary, fill in the blanks with the correct word or phrase. Then use the key below to check your answers. You can use this page to review the main concepts of the lesson.

smog

Human activities are a major cause of air pollution.

19 Two types of air pollutants are gases and _____.

Car exhaust is a major source of air pollution in cities.

20 _____ is formed when exhausts and ozone react in the presence of sunlight.

Human Impact on the Atmosphere

Air quality and levels of pollution can be measured.

Air Quality Index (AQI) values	Levels of health concern
0–50	Good
51–100	Moderate
101–150	Unhealthy for sensitive groups
151–200	Unhealthy
201–300	Very unhealthy

21 As pollution increases, _____ decreases.

Climate change may lead to dramatic changes in global weather patterns.

22 The melting of polar ice is one effect of _____.

Answers: 19 particulates; 20 smog; 21 air quality; 22 global warming/climate change

23 **Apply** Explain in your own words what the following statement means: Each of your breaths, every tree that is planted, and every vehicle on the road affects the composition of the atmosphere.

242 Unit 4 Human Impact on the Environment

Lesson Review

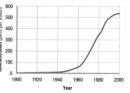

Vocabulary

Draw a line to connect the following terms to their definitions.

1 Air pollution
2 Greenhouse effect
3 Air quality
4 Particulate
5 Smog

A tiny particle of solid that is suspended in air or water

B the contamination of the atmosphere by the introduction of pollutants from human and natural sources

C pollutant that forms when ozone and vehicle exhaust react with sunlight

D a measure of how clean or polluted the air is

E the process by which gases in the atmosphere, such as water vapor and carbon dioxide, absorb and release energy as heat

Key Concepts

6 **Identify** List three effects that an increase in urbanization can have on air quality.

7 **Relate** How are ground-level ozone and smog related?

8 **Explain** How can human health be affected by changes in air quality?

Critical Thinking

Use this graph to answer the following questions.

Concentration of a CFC in the Atmosphere Over Time

9 **Analyze** At what time in the graph did CFCs begin building up in the atmosphere?

10 **Synthesize** Since the late 1970s, the use of CFCs has been reduced, with a total ban in 2010. But CFCs can stay in the atmosphere for up to 100 years. In the space below, draw a graph showing the concentration of CFCs in the atmosphere over the next 100 years.

11 **Apply** Do you think it is important that humans control the amount of human-made pollution? Explain your reasoning.

Lesson 3 Human Impact on the Atmosphere 243

Visual Summary Answers

19. particulates
20. smog
21. air quality
22. climate change
23. Answers may vary. Sample answer: Breathing adds carbon dioxide to the atmosphere. Trees and other plants use carbon dioxide and release oxygen into the atmosphere when they photosynthesize. Vehicles add particulates, nitrogen oxides, and other pollutants into the atmosphere.

Lesson Review Answers

1. B
2. E
3. D
4. A
5. C
6. Sample answer: More vehicles on the road and more industries mean more pollutants in the air that are caused by the burning of fossil fuels.
7. Ground-level ozone and vehicle exhaust react with sunlight to form smog.
8. Decreases in air quality have a negative impact on human health.
9. Accept any answer within the range of the early 1940s to the early 1960s.

10. Students should draw a graph that shows CFC concentration decreasing slowly over time.
11. Answers may vary. Accept answers that articulate the content learned from this lesson, or related, valid content.

Protecting Earth's Water, Land, and Air

Essential Question How can Earth's resources be used wisely?

 Professional Development

For more detailed information about the topics in this lesson, refer to the Content Refresher in the Unit Opener pages.

Opening Your Lesson

Begin the lesson by assessing students' prerequisite and prior knowledge.

Prerequisite Knowledge

- Definitions of *natural resources* and *energy resources*
- The effects that people have on water, land, and air

Accessing Prior Knowledge

KWL Invite students to discuss what they know about wisely using Earth's resources. Invite students to make a KWL chart to organize their thoughts. Have students write what they already know about wise use of Earth's resources in the K column. Have them write what they want to know in the W column. After completing the lesson, have them write what they learned in the L column.

Customize Your Opening

- ☐ **Accessing Prior Knowledge,** above
- ☐ **Print Path** Engage Your Brain, SE p. 245 #1–2
- ☐ **Print Path** Active Reading, SE p. 245 #3–4
- ☐ **Digital Path** Lesson Opener

Key Topics/Learning Goals	Supporting Concepts
Conservation and Stewardship 1 Define *conservation*. 2 Explain the importance of wise stewardship of Earth's resources.	• Conservation is the preservation and wise use of natural resources. • Stewardship is the careful and responsible management of Earth's resources to ensure that these resources will exist in the future and that the environment will be healthy.
Preservation and Conservation of Water 1 Explain the importance of maintaining water quality and sustainable water use. 2 Identify ways to prevent water pollution.	• Water quality is important for maintaining human health and healthy ecosystems and reducing water usage ensures that water is available for future needs. • Water pollution can be reduced by disposing of trash properly, using nontoxic products, and reducing fertilizer use.
Land Management and Conservation 1 Describe benefits of sustainable land management and conservation. 2 Describe ways to prevent or repair land degradation.	• Managing land resources sustainably can prevent reduction in land productivity that results from overuse and pollution. • Ways people can prevent land degradation include reforestation, reclamation, vertical mixed-use development, preservation by recycling and by practicing soil conservation methods such as contour plowing, strip cropping, terracing, no-till farming, and crop rotation.
Reducing Air Pollution 1 Identify four ways people are working to reduce air pollution.	• People are working to reduce air pollution by monitoring air quality and passing protective laws, developing new technologies to reduce pollution, burning fuels more efficiently, and developing alternative energy sources.

Options for Instruction

Two parallel paths provide coverage of the Essential Questions, with a strong **Inquiry** strand woven into each.
Follow the **Print Path,** the **Digital Path,** or your customized combination of print, digital, and inquiry.

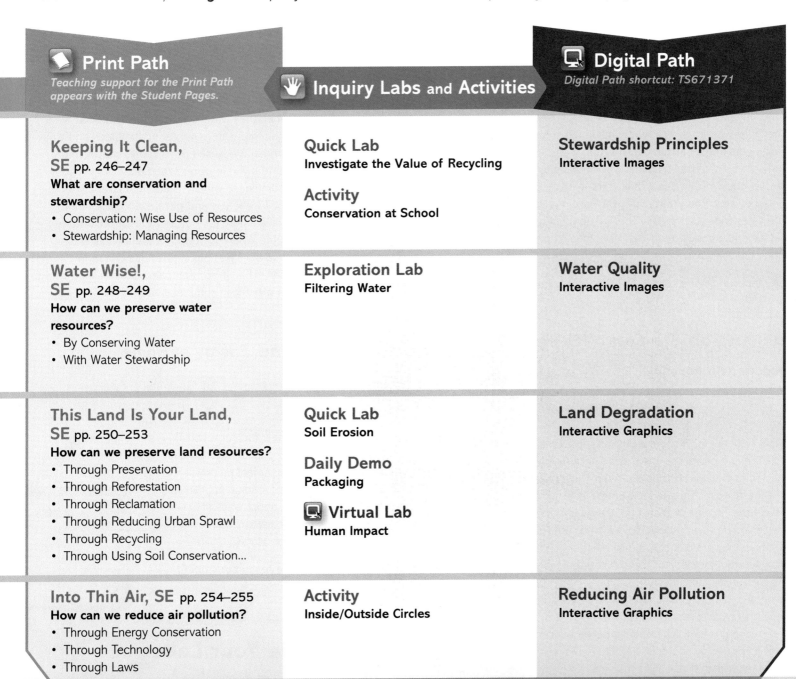

Print Path
Teaching support for the Print Path appears with the Student Pages.

Inquiry Labs and Activities

Digital Path
Digital Path shortcut: TS671371

Keeping It Clean,
SE pp. 246–247
What are conservation and stewardship?
- Conservation: Wise Use of Resources
- Stewardship: Managing Resources

Quick Lab
Investigate the Value of Recycling

Activity
Conservation at School

Stewardship Principles
Interactive Images

Water Wise!,
SE pp. 248–249
How can we preserve water resources?
- By Conserving Water
- With Water Stewardship

Exploration Lab
Filtering Water

Water Quality
Interactive Images

This Land Is Your Land,
SE pp. 250–253
How can we preserve land resources?
- Through Preservation
- Through Reforestation
- Through Reclamation
- Through Reducing Urban Sprawl
- Through Recycling
- Through Using Soil Conservation...

Quick Lab
Soil Erosion

Daily Demo
Packaging

Virtual Lab
Human Impact

Land Degradation
Interactive Graphics

Into Thin Air, SE pp. 254–255
How can we reduce air pollution?
- Through Energy Conservation
- Through Technology
- Through Laws

Activity
Inside/Outside Circles

Reducing Air Pollution
Interactive Graphics

Options for Assessment

See the Evaluate page for options, including Formative Assessment,
Summative Assessment, and Unit Review.

Engage and Explore

Activities and Discussion

Activity *Conservation at School*

Engage

Conservation and Stewardship

 individuals, pairs, whole class
 15 min
 GUIDED inquiry

Think, Pair, Share Have students individually think about and list ways people in their school could better conserve natural resources. They may want to think about lights in the school, recycling paper, food waste in the cafeteria, idling cars at drop-off, a school garden, and so on. Then have students work in pairs to trade ideas and think of new ones. Finally, encourage pairs to share some of their ideas with the class. **For greater depth:** Have students sort their ideas into categories such as "Me" or "Us" to identify who can act to carry out each idea they listed. Then have them choose and take action either as individuals or as a class.

⏱ *Optional Online resource: Think, Pair, Share support*

Discussion *The Cost of Energy*

Reducing Air Pollution

 whole class
 10 min
 **GUIDED** inquiry

Have students think about a business that obtains energy from a coal-burning power plant and a business that generates its own electricity through solar power. **Ask:** Which plant produces electricity at a lesser cost? Sample answer: the coal-burning power plant Students who answer that solar energy is cheaper may hold the misconception that renewable resources are less costly economically because they are plentiful. Explain that from a financial perspective many current methods of using renewable resources such as sunlight are more costly than using fossil fuels. Point out that equipment to generate electricity from sunlight may have a high initial cost but then may have a very low cost over time. Also, new technologies will make solar power a less expensive energy source in the future. Discuss costs other than financial, such as resource suitability to an area and aesthetic issues, to help students identify pros and cons associated with each form of energy.

Probing Questions *Energy Usage*

Introducing Key Topics

 whole class
 10 min
 GUIDED inquiry

Recognizing relationships Ask students to think about the times of the year when they use the most resources. **Ask:** When do you think you use more water—winter or summer—and why? Sample answer: summer, because I drink more, shower more, water the garden, and swim in pools When do you think you use more fossil fuels—summer or winter? Sample answers: winter, because it's cold, so I walk less and get driven places more; summer, because I live where it's hot and the air conditioner is on most of the time When do you think the air quality is worse—summer or winter? Sample answer: It's worse in summer, because car exhaust, sunlight, and ozone cause smog. Because sunlight is greater in summer, smog is worse.

Take It Home *Energy at Home*

Introducing Key Topics

 adult-student pairs
 15–30 min

Appliances have labels to inform consumers of their energy efficiency ratings. The label includes data on the typical operating cost per year. Adult-student pairs will find the typical yearly operating expenses for some appliances in the home and think about ways they can reduce use of each appliance to lower its typical yearly cost of usage.

⏱ *Optional Online resource: student worksheet*

Customize Your Labs

📄 *See the Lab Manual for lab datasheets.*

⏱ *Go Online for editable lab datasheets.*

Levels of  **DIRECTED** inquiry   **GUIDED** inquiry   **INDEPENDENT** inquiry

| introduces inquiry skills within a structured framework. | develops inquiry skills within a supportive environment. | deepens inquiry skills with student-driven questions or procedures. |

Labs and Demos

Exploration Lab *Filtering Water*

Preservation and Conservation of Water

 small groups
🕐 45 min
Inquiry **DIRECTED** or **GUIDED** inquiry

Students design, build, and test a water filtration system to clean muddy water.

PURPOSE **To model groundwater filtration**

MATERIALS

- cotton balls (3)
- graduated cylinder, 100 mL
- muddy water
- gloves
- lab apron
- safety goggles

- pebbles
- plastic bottle, 1 L
- plastic cup
- sand
- small ring and stand
- soil

Quick Lab *Soil Erosion*

PURPOSE **To model different soil-conservation methods and evaluate their effectiveness**

See the Lab Manual or go Online for planning information.

Quick Lab *Investigate the Value of Recycling*

PURPOSE **To investigate how recycling affects the rate at which landfills are filled**

See the Lab Manual or go Online for planning information.

Daily Demo *Packaging*

Engage

Land Management and Conservation

👥 whole class
🕐 10 min
Inquiry **GUIDED** inquiry

PURPOSE **To explore ways product and packaging wastes can be reduced, reused, and recycled**

MATERIALS

- disposable product or one with disposable parts or with a lot of packaging (excess plastic, foam, paper)

Display the product/package. Have students suggest ways its use/packaging materials can be reduced, reused, or recycled. Sample answers: Plastic, paper, and many metals can be recycled; empty container from product can be used to hold/store other items; product can be packaged with less material or with materials that degrade more readily; products packaged with less material can be purchased as an alternative. Have students take into consideration how products are packaged when they shop.

Virtual Lab *Human Impact*

Introducing Key Topics

👥 flexible
🕐 45 min
Inquiry **GUIDED** inquiry

Students use maps, satellite images, and other information to examine the effects of human activities.

PURPOSE **To explore ways human activities affect Earth's resources and ecosystems**

Activities and Discussion

- ☐ **Activity** Conservation at School
- ☐ **Discussion** The Cost of Energy
- ☐ **Probing Questions** Energy Usage
- ☐ **Take It Home** Energy at Home

Labs and Demos

- ☐ **Exploration Lab** Filtering Water
- ☐ **Quick Lab** Soil Erosion
- ☐ **Quick Lab** Investigate Recycling
- ☐ **Daily Demo** Packaging
- ☐ **Virtual Lab** Human Impact

Your Resources

_____

_____

_____

Explain Science Concepts

	📝 Print Path	💻 Digital Path
Key Topics		

Conservation and Stewardship

☐ **Keeping It Clean,** SE pp. 246–247
- Active Reading (Annotation strategy), #5
- Visualize It!, #6
- Compare, #7
- Visualize It!, #8

🌐 *Optional Online resource: Venn Diagram support*

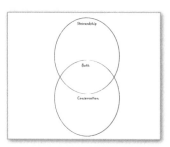

☐ **Stewardship Principles**
Explore "reduce, reuse, and recycle."

Preservation and Conservation of Water

☐ **Water Wise!,** SE pp. 248–249
- Do the Math, #9
- Identify, #10
- Visualize It!, #11

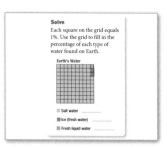

☐ **Water Quality**
Learn about water quality and pollution.

Land Management and Conservation

☐ **This Land Is Your Land,** SE pp. 250–253
- Active Reading (Annotation strategy), #12
- Think Outside the Book, #13
- Visualize It!, #14
- Apply, #15
- Active Reading (Annotation strategy), #16
- Visualize It!, #17–18

☐ **Land Degradation**
Explore ways to manage land and prevent harm.

Reducing Air Pollution

☐ **Into Thin Air,** SE pp. 254–255
- Active Reading (Annotation strategy), #19
- Visualize It!, #20
- Summarize, #21

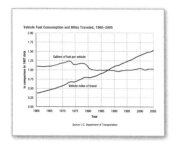

☐ **Reducing Air Pollution**
Explore ways to address air pollution.

(c) ©David R. Frazier/Photo Researchers, Inc.

Differentiated Instruction

Basic *Conserving Resources*

Synthesizing Key Topics

👥 individuals
🕐 20 min

Have students use a concept map to organize information about methods used to conserve resources. In the center circle, have them write, "Ways to Conserve Resources." Then have them add labeled arrows and circles as needed to identify methods used for resource conservation.

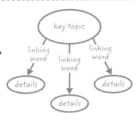

🌐 *Optional Online resource: Concept Map support*

Advanced *Sources of Energy*

Synthesizing Key Topics

👥 individuals
🕐 ongoing

In-Depth Research Have students conduct research to find out about the pros and cons of a source of energy (coal, nuclear, hydropower, propane, bioenergy, geothermal, natural gas, oil, wind, solar). They should consider the environmental impact of the energy source, and the future of the energy source. Students may also want to look into emerging energy technologies, such as hydrogen fuel cells, fusion, or wave energy. Invite students to share their findings with the class.

ELL *Role-Playing to Show Conservation*

Synthesizing Key Topics

👥 pairs
🕐 20 min

Have students work in pairs to perform a skit that shows ways people can conserve water and protect the air and land. For example, students might role-play brushing teeth, showing that you always turn the faucet off before you begin brushing. Pairs will work together to figure out their roles and what they want to show in their skit.

Lesson Vocabulary

conservation   stewardship

Previewing Vocabulary

👥 whole class
🕐 10 min

Suffixes Explain to students that the suffixes *-tion* and *-ship* both refer to a quality, state, or process. Have students use the definition of these suffixes along with what they know about the words *conserve* and *steward* to suggest definitions for the words *conservation* and *stewardship*. Then explain that *conservation* means "the process of conserving, or protecting." A *steward* is someone who carefully manages something for someone else. *Stewardship*, therefore, means "the process of carefully managing something."

Reinforcing Vocabulary

👥 whole class
🕐 ongoing

Four Square Have students make a four square diagram for each vocabulary term. Have students fill out the definition section individually. Then discuss ideas for the other categories as a class.

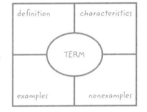

🌐 *Optional Online resource: Four Square support*

Customize Your Core Lesson

Core Instruction

☐ **Print Path** choices
☐ **Digital Path** choices

Vocabulary

☐ **Previewing Vocabulary** Suffixes
☐ **Reinforcing Vocabulary** Four Square

Your Resources

Differentiated Instruction

☐ **Basic** Conserving Resources
☐ **Advanced** Sources of Energy
☐ **ELL** Role-Playing to Show Conservation

Extend Science Concepts

Reinforce and Review

Activity *Inside/Outside Circles*

Synthesizing Key Topics

👥 whole class
🕐 15 min

1 After students have worked through the lesson, give each an index card with a question from the lesson. Have students write their answer on the back of the index card. Check to make sure the answers are correct. Have students adjust incorrect answers.

2 Have students pair up and form two circles. One partner is in an inside circle; the other is in an outside circle. The students in the inside circle face out, and the students in the outside circle face in.

3 Each student in the inside circle asks his or her partner the question on the index card. The partner answers. If the answer is incorrect, the student in the inside circle teaches the other student the correct answer. Repeat this step with the outside-circle students asking the questions.

4 Have each student on the outside circle rotate one person to the right. He or she faces a new partner and repeats the process. Students rotate after each pair of questions. Vary the rotation, if desired, by moving more than one person, moving to the left, and so on, but make sure that partners are always new.

Graphic Organizer

Synthesizing Key Topics

👥 individuals or pairs
🕐 15 min

Venn Diagram After students have studied the lesson, ask them to work alone or in pairs to make a three-circle Venn diagram. Have them label the circles as either *Land, Water,* or *Air*. Have them list ways to conserve or manage each resource in the appropriate circle. Remind students to list ideas that correspond to more than one resource in the correct sections of the overlapping circles.

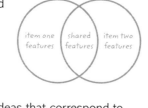

item one features | shared features | item two features

🜹 *Optional Online resource: Venn Diagram support*

Going Further

Math Connection

Synthesizing Key Topics

👥 individuals
🕐 20 min

Analyze Data Have students make line graphs of the data from two utility bills. On the *x*-axis have them list the months. On the *y*-axis have them list the therms or kWh used. Then have students compare the graphs to draw conclusions.

Month	Gas Use (therms)	Electricity Use (kWh)	Month	Gas Use (therms)	Electricity Use (kWh)
Jan	155	150	Jul	5	255
Feb	120	156	Aug	5	340
Mar	70	160	Sep	6	225
Apr	25	165	Oct	25	135
May	10	200	Nov	40	145
Jun	6	210	Dec	125	150

Real World Connection

Synthesizing Key Topics

👥 individuals or pairs
🕐 ongoing

Research Ask students to research what happens when an object, such as a plastic milk container, a steel can, or an old newspaper, undergoes recycling. Have them create a Sequence Diagram that shows the process of recycling their particular item. Invite students to share their findings with the class.

Customize Your Closing

💬 *See the Assessment Guide for quizzes and tests.*

🜹 *Go Online to edit and create quizzes and tests.*

Reinforce and Review

☐ **Activity** Inside/Outside Circles

☐ **Graphic Organizer** Venn Diagram

☐ **Print Path** Visual Summary, SE p. 256

☐ **Digital Path** Lesson Closer

Evaluate Student Mastery

See the teacher support below the Student Pages for additional Formative Assessment questions.

Write *Water, Land,* and *Air* on the board. Have students list ways that each of these resources is threatened. Then have students list ways we can protect each resource. Sample answers: Threats: wasting water or energy; polluting; use of toxic chemicals. We can protect these resources by conserving electricity, water, gas; recycling; wasting less; and so on.

Reteach

Formative assessment may show that students need reinforcement for certain topics. The resources below are recommended for reteaching. If students were introduced to a topic through the Print Path, you can also use the Digital Path to reteach, or vice versa.
🎧 *Can be assigned to individual students*

Conservation and Stewardship
Activity Conservation at School 🎧
Quick Lab Investigate the Value of Recycling

Preservation and Conservation of Water
Exploration Lab Filtering Water

Land Management and Conservation
Daily Demo Packaging

Reducing Air Pollution
Discussion The Cost of Energy
Take It Home Energy at Home 🎧

Alternative Assessment
Water, Land, and Air
🕐 *Online resources: student worksheet, optional rubrics*

> **Protecting Earth's Water, Land, and Air**
>
> **Climb the Ladder:** *Water, Land, and Air*
> Complete the following activities to show what you have learned about protecting Earth's water, land, and air.
>
> 1. Work on your own, with a partner, or with a small group.
> 2. Choose one item from each rung of the ladder. Check your choices.
> 3. Have your teacher approve your plan.
> 4. Submit or present your results.
>
> | ___ **Water Essay** | ___ **Water Poster** |
> |---|---|
> | Write an essay that describes why it is important to maintain water quality. Use facts and details to support your ideas. | Design a poster that describes ways to prevent water pollution. Include drawings or images that make people notice your poster. |
> | ___ **Land Model** | ___ **Land Brochure** |
> | Make a model or sketch a diagram that shows the benefits of sustainable land management and conservation, and explains some actions people can take to prevent or repair land degradation. | Make a brochure that explains the value of recycling, and identifies five methods of soil conservation. |
> | ___ **Air Diagram** | ___ **Air Skit** |
> | Draw a diagram or flowchart that shows what people are doing to reduce air pollution. | Write and perform a skit or podcast that identifies four ways to reduce air pollution. |

Going Further
☐ Math Connection
☐ Real World Connection

Formative Assessment
☐ **Strategies** Throughout TE
☐ **Lesson Review** SE

Summative Assessment
☐ **Alternative Assessment** Water, Land, and Air
☐ **Lesson Quiz**
☐ **Unit Tests A and B**
☐ **Unit Review** SE End-of-Unit

Your Resources

_____

_____

Answers

Answers for 1–3 should represent students' current thoughts, even if incorrect.

1. F; T; T; F

2. Sketches will vary. Check that students' sketches show a recognizable activity, such as picking up trash, recycling materials, or planting a tree.

3. Sample answer: Stewardship is the careful management of a resource.

4. Students should define or sketch each vocabulary term in the lesson.

Opening Your Lesson

Discuss students' answers to item 1 to assess students' prerequisite knowledge and to estimate what they already know about the land, air, and water as resources to be conserved and managed.

Prerequisites Students should already know what natural resources are and what human activities harm the air, water, and land. They should have some general knowledge of protecting the environment.

Learning Alert

Helping and Harming Help students to understand that most human actions toward the planet have both positive and negative effects, although some actions may be much more harmful than helpful, or vice versa. As an example, point out that use of wind turbines can provide clean energy from a renewable resource, but that turbines can harm migrating bats or birds. However, under the right conditions, wind turbines might be more helpful than harmful. Likewise, using biofuels to power vehicles might conserve fossil fuel resources, but these fuels do release some pollutants into the air, and are often made from corn that could otherwise be used to feed people or farm animals.

Keeping It Clean

What are conservation and stewardship?

5 Identify As you read, underline the definitions of *conservation* and *stewardship*.

In the past, some people have used Earth's resources however they wanted, without thinking about the consequences. They thought it didn't matter if they cut down hundreds of thousands of trees or caught millions of fish. They also thought it didn't matter if they dumped trash into bodies of water. Now we know that it does matter how we use resources. Humans greatly affect the land, water, and air. If we wish to keep using our resources in the future, we need to conserve and care for them.

Conservation: Wise Use of Resources

Conservation (kahn•sur•VAY•shuhn) is the wise use of natural resources. By practicing conservation, we can help make sure that resources will still be around for future generations. It is up to everybody to conserve and protect resources. When we use energy or create waste, we can harm the environment. If we conserve whenever we can, we reduce the harm we do to the environment. We can use less energy by turning off lights, computers, and appliances. We can reuse shopping bags, as in the picture below. We can recycle whenever possible, instead of just throwing things away. By doing these things, we take fewer resources from Earth and put less pollution into the water, land, and air.

Visualize It!

6 Identify How are the people in the picture below practicing conservation?

_____

_____

_____

_____

This old tire is being used as a planter instead of being thrown away.

Stewardship: Managing Resources

Stewardship (stoo•urd•SHIP) is the careful and responsible management of a resource. If we are not good stewards, we will use up a resource or pollute it. Stewardship of Earth's resources will ensure that the environment stays clean enough to help keep people and other living things healthy. Stewardship is everybody's job. Governments pass laws that protect water, land, and air. These laws determine how resources can be used and what materials can be released into the environment. Individuals can also act as stewards. For example, you can plant trees or help clean up a habitat in your community. Any action that helps to maintain or improve the environment is an act of stewardship.

7 Compare Fill in the Venn diagram to compare and contrast conservation and stewardship.

Stewardship

Both

Conservation

Turning empty lots into gardens improves the environment and provides people with healthy food.

Visualize It!

8 Identify How is the person in the picture to the right practicing stewardship?

_____

_____

_____

Sea turtles are endangered. Scientists help sea turtles that have just hatched find their way to the sea.

246 Unit 4 Human Impact on the Environment

247

Answers

5. *See students' pages for annotations.*

6. They are using reusable grocery bags, which helps reduce the amount of disposable plastic and paper bags used.

7. (under Stewardship) protects and manages resources; (under Both) preserves resources; (under Conservation) limits the use of resources

8. The person is helping to protect wildlife.

Learning Alert

Clarifying Concepts *Conservation* is defined as the wise use of natural resources. Point out that the "wise use" of resources encompasses two main concepts: sustainability and using resources responsibly. *Sustainability* refers to using resources in a manner that ensures their supply will still be available to future generations while their quality is also preserved. *Responsible use of resources* involves using resources in a manner that is both non-wasteful and non-polluting or otherwise harmful to the environment. Help students recognize that *stewardship* is related to conservation because it involves using resources responsibly.

Probing Questions GUIDED Inquiry

Applying Invite students to think about how conservation and stewardship are related. **Ask:** What are some ways, other than those you read about thus far, that you as an individual can practice conservation? Sample answers: by turning off appliances when not in use; by walking or riding a bike instead of riding in a car; by using less resources when possible; by eating foods that are grown locally instead of those that are shipped long distances **Ask:** What can you do to be a good steward of Earth's resources? Sample answers: dispose of trash properly; compost food wastes; grow vegetables and fruits; avoid use of chemicals that can be harmful to the environment

Water Wise!

How can we preserve water resources?

Most of the Earth's surface is covered by water, so you might think there is lots of water for humans to use. However, there is actually very little fresh water on Earth, so people should use freshwater resources very carefully. People should also be careful to avoid polluting water, because the quality of water is important to the health of both humans and ecosystems. Because water is so important to our health, we need to keep it clean!

By Conserving Water

If we want to make sure there is enough water for future generations, we need to reduce the amount of water we use. In some places, if people aren't careful about using water wisely, there soon won't be enough water for everyone. There are many ways to reduce water usage. We can use low-flow toilets and showerheads. We can take shorter showers. In agriculture and landscaping, we can reduce water use by installing efficient irrigation systems. We can also use plants that don't need much water. Only watering lawns the amount they need and following watering schedules saves water. The photo below shows a simple way to use less water—just turn off the tap while brushing your teeth!

Do the Math

You Try It

9 Calculate How much fresh water is on Earth?

Solve

Each square on the grid equals 1%. Use the grid to fill in the percentage of each type of water found on Earth.

Earth's Water

▢ Salt water _____

◼ Ice (fresh water) _____

▨ Fresh liquid water _____

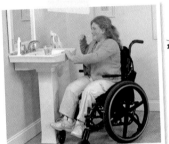

10 Identify What are some ways you can reduce the amount of water you use?

• *Turn off the tap when brushing my teeth.*

• _____

• _____

• _____

248 Unit 4 Human Impact on the Environment

With Water Stewardship

Humans and ecosystems need clean water. The diagram below shows how a community keeps its drinking water clean. The main way to protect drinking water is to keep pollution from entering streams, lakes, and other water sources. Laws like the Clean Water Act and Safe Drinking Water Act were passed to protect water sources. These laws indicate how clean drinking water must be and limit the types of chemicals that businesses and private citizens can release into water. These laws also help finance water treatment facilities. We can help protect water by not throwing chemicals in the trash or dumping them down the drain. We can also use nontoxic chemicals whenever possible. Reducing the amount of fertilizer we use on our gardens also reduces water pollution.

For healthy ecosystems and safe drinking water, communities need to protect water sources. The first step to protecting water sources is keeping them from becoming polluted.

Protecting Water Resources

Water testing makes sure water is safe for people to drink. It also helps us find out if there is a pollution problem that needs to be fixed.

Without clean water to drink, people can get sick. Clean water is also important for agriculture and natural ecosystems.

Water treatment plants remove pollution from wastewater before it is reused or put back into the environment.

Visualize It!

11 Apply What steps should a community take to manage its water resources?

_____

_____

_____

249

Answers

9. Salt water: 97%, Ice (fresh water): 2%, Fresh liquid water: 1%

10. Sample answers: Use low-flow toilets, take short showers, use garden plants that don't need much water

11. Protect the water supply, test the water's quality, and treat wastewater.

Learning Alert

Water Distribution Explain to students that in addition to making up only a small percentage of Earth's total water supply, the distribution of fresh water globally is unequal. For example, deserts receive less than 25 cm of rainfall each year. People who live on an island surrounded by salt water may also have only limited access to fresh water supplies.

Interpreting Visuals

Have students examine the visual that shows how communities work to protect water resources. **Ask:** How can wastewater be prevented from harming the environment? Sample answer: It can be cleaned at water treatment plants before being returned to the environment. **Ask:** Why is it important for bodies of water to be tested regularly? Sample answer: to make sure the water is safe for use

Learning Alert ⚠ MISCONCEPTION ⚠

Conservation of Matter Students may think that cleaning water, as occurs in a water treatment plant, makes the substance of pollutants disappear. Remind students that the law of conservation of matter states that matter cannot be created or destroyed. Thus, removing harmful substances from water (air or soil) does not make the substances disappear. They must still be disposed of in some manner.

This Land Is Your Land

How can we preserve land resources?

12 Identify As you read this page and the next, underline ways that we can protect land resources.

People rely on land resources for recreation, agriculture, transportation, commerce, industry, and housing. If we manage land resources carefully, we can make sure that these resources will be around for generations and continue to provide resources for humans to use. We also need to make sure that there are habitats for wild animals. To do all these things, we must protect land resources from overuse and pollution. Sometimes we need to repair damage that is already done.

Through Preservation

Preservation of land resources is very important. *Preservation* means protecting land from being damaged or changed. Local, state, and national parks protect many natural areas. These parks help ensure that many species survive. Small parks can protect some species. Other species, such as predators, need larger areas. For example, wolves roam over hundreds of miles and would not be protected by small parks. By protecting areas big enough for large predators, we also protect habitats for many other species.

Yosemite National Park is one of the oldest national parks in the country. Like other national, state, and local parks, Yosemite was formed to preserve natural habitats.

Think Outside the Book

13 Apply Plant and animal species depend on land resources. Find out which endangered plant or animal species live in your area. Write a paragraph explaining how your community can help protect those species.

250

Through Reforestation

People use the wood from trees for many things. We use it to make paper and to build houses. We also use wood to heat homes and cook food. In many places, huge areas of forest were cut down to use the wood and nothing was done to replant the forests. Now when we cut trees down, they are often replanted, as in the picture at right. We also plant trees in areas where forests disappeared many years ago in order to help bring the forests back. The process of planting trees to reestablish forestland is called *reforestation*. Reforestation is important, but we can't cut down all forests and replant them. It is important to keep some old forests intact for the animals that need them to survive.

Through Reclamation

In order to use some resources, such as coal, metal, and minerals, the resources first have to be dug out of the ground. In the process, the land is damaged. Sometimes, large areas of land are cleared and pits are dug to reach the resource. Land can also be damaged in other ways, including by development and agriculture. *Reclamation* is the process by which a damaged land area is returned to nearly the condition it was in before people used it. Land reclamation, shown in the lower right photo, is required for mines in many states once the mines are no longer in use. Many national and state laws, such as the Surface Mining and Reclamation Act and the Resource Conservation and Recovery Act, guide land reclamation.

Reforestation

A mine being reclaimed

Visualize It!

14 Compare What are the similarities between reforestation and reclamation?

251

Answers

12. See students' pages for annotations.

13. Answers will vary depending on location. Nature preserves are often the best way to protect endangered species.

14. Both reforestation and reclamation return land close to the condition it was before people changed the land.

Probing Questions GUIDED Inquiry

Analyzing Have students think about the land resources in your local community. **Ask:** How is the land used in our community? Sample answers: Answers will vary, but students might say land is used for farming, for homes and shopping centers, for roads, for parks and playgrounds, and as habitat for organisms. **Ask:** What endangers land in our community? Sample answers: pollution, overuse, urban sprawl, new developments, expanding industry Discuss ways people in your community protect land resources.

Learning Alert

Difficult Concepts Students may not understand why some animals may depend on old-growth forests to survive. Explain that some animals, such as some woodpeckers, eat insects that live in old, decaying trees. Explain that these habitats support thousands of species, including spiders, insects, lichen, fungi, mosses, small mammals, and birds. The high level of biodiversity means that many species depend on the old-growth forest to survive.

One way to reduce urban sprawl is to locate homes and businesses close together.

Through Reducing Urban Sprawl

Urban sprawl is the outward spread of suburban areas around cities. As we build more houses and businesses across a wider area, there is less land for native plants and animals. Reducing urban sprawl helps to protect land resources. One way to reduce sprawl is to locate more people and businesses in a smaller area. A good way to do this is with vertical development—that means constructing taller buildings. Homes, businesses, and even recreational facilities can be placed within high-rise buildings. We also can reduce sprawl using mixed-use development. This development creates communities with businesses and houses very close to one another. Mixed-use communities are also better for the environment, because people can walk to work instead of driving.

Through Recycling

Recycling is one of the most important things we can do to preserve land resources. *Recycling* is the process of recovering valuable materials from waste or scrap. We can recycle many of the materials that we use. By recycling materials like metal, plastic, paper, and glass, we use fewer raw materials. Recycling aluminum cans reduces the amount of bauxite that is mined. We use bauxite in aluminum smelting. Everyone can help protect land resources by recycling. Lots of people throw away materials that can be recycled. Find out what items you can recycle!

Bauxite mine

15 Apply Aluminum is mined from the ground. Recycling aluminum cans decreases the need for mining bauxite. Paper can also be recycled. How does recycling paper preserve trees?

252   Unit 4 Human Impact on the Environment

Through Using Soil Conservation Methods

Soil conservation protects soil from erosion or degradation by overuse or pollution. For example, farmers change the way they plow in order to conserve soil. <u>Contour plowing</u> creates ridges of soil across slopes. The small ridges keep water from eroding soils. In <u>strip cropping</u>, two types of crops are planted in rows next to each other to reduce erosion. <u>Terracing</u> is used on steep hills to prevent erosion. Areas of the hill are flattened to grow crops. This creates steps down the side of the hill. <u>Crop rotation</u> means that crops with different needs are planted in alternating seasons. This reduces the prevalence of plant diseases and makes sure there are nutrients for each crop. It also ensures that plants are growing in the soil almost year-round. In <u>no-till farming</u>, soils are not plowed between crop plantings. Stalks and cover crops keep water in the soils and reduce erosion by stopping soil from being blown away.

Active Reading

16 Identify As you read this page, underline five methods of soil conservation.

Visualize It!

Terracing involves building leveled areas, or steps, to grow crops on.

In contour plowing, crop rows are planted in curved lines along land's natural contours.

Strip cropping prevents erosion by creating natural dams that stop water from rushing over a field.

17 Analyze Which two soil conservation techniques would be best to use on gentle slopes?
- [ ] contour plowing
- [ ] crop terracing
- [ ] strip cropping

18 Analyze Which soil conservation technique would be best to use on very steep slopes?
- [ ] contour plowing
- [ ] crop terracing
- [ ] strip cropping

Lesson 4 Protecting Earth's Water, Land, and Air   253

Answers

15. Sample answer: Reusing paper would decrease the need for raw lumber.

16. *See students' pages for annotations.*

17. contour plowing and strip terracing

18. crop terracing

Building Reading Skills

Combination Notes Five methods of soil conservation are discussed in the text. Encourage students to use Combination Notes to help them identify the main ideas relating to each of these five. Have them title their notes "Some Soil Conservation Methods." On the left side of a sheet of paper, students can list each of the five methods discussed along with a brief description of what that method entails. On the right side, they can make a simple drawing that illustrates the method.

🔘 *Optional Online resource: Combination Notes support*

Formative Assessment

Ask: Why is reducing urban sprawl an example of good stewardship? Sample answer: It is a method of maintaining or improving the environment. **Ask:** What are six ways people can help to protect and preserve land resources? Sample answer: through preservation, by reclamation, with reforestation, by reducing urban sprawl, and by using soil conservation methods.

Into Thin Air

Active Reading

19 Identify Underline the sentences that explain the relationship between burning fossil fuels and air pollution.

How can we reduce air pollution?

Polluted air can make people sick and harm organisms. Air pollution can cause the atmosphere to change in ways that are harmful to the environment and to people. There are many ways that we can reduce air pollution. We can use less energy. Also, we can develop new ways to get energy that produces less pollution. Everybody can help reduce air pollution in many different ways.

Through Energy Conservation

Energy conservation is one of the most important ways to reduce air pollution. Fossil fuels are currently the most commonly used energy resource. When they are burned, they release pollution into the air. If we use less energy, we burn fewer fossil fuels.

There are lots of ways to conserve energy. We can turn off lights when we don't need them. We can use energy-efficient lightbulbs and appliances. We can use air conditioners less in the summer and heaters less in the winter. We can unplug electronics when they are not in use. Instead of driving ourselves to places, we can use public transportation. We can also develop alternative energy sources that create less air pollution. Using wind, solar, and geothermal energy will help us burn less fossil fuel.

Using public transportation, riding a bike, sharing rides, and walking reduce the amount of air pollution produced by cars.

Many cities, such as Los Angeles, California, have air pollution problems.

Energy can be produced with very little pollution. These solar panels help us use energy from the sun and replace the use of fossil fuels.

254

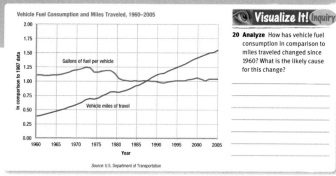

Vehicle Fuel Consumption and Miles Traveled, 1960–2005

(graph: In comparison to 1987 data, y-axis 0.00–2.00; x-axis Year 1960–2005; "Gallons of fuel per vehicle" and "Vehicle miles of travel")

Source: U.S. Department of Transportation

Visualize It! Inquiry

20 Analyze How has vehicle fuel consumption in comparison to miles traveled changed since 1960? What is the likely cause for this change?

Through Technology

There are lots of ways to generate energy without creating much air pollution. By developing these alternative energy sources, we can reduce the amount of pollution created by burning fossil fuels. Wind turbines generate clean power. So do solar panels that use energy from the sun. We also can use power created by water flowing through rivers or moving with the tides. Geothermal energy from heat in Earth's crust can be used to generate electricity. Hybrid cars get energy from their brakes and store it in batteries. They burn less gas and release less pollution. Driving smaller cars that can go farther on a gallon of gas also reduces air pollution.

New technologies, such as this compact fluorescent lightbulb (CFL), help limit air pollution. CFL bulbs use less energy to make the same amount of light.

Through Laws

Governments in many countries work independently and together to reduce air pollution. They monitor air quality and set limits on what can be released into the air. In the United States, the Clean Air Act limits the amount of toxic chemicals and other pollutants that can be released into the atmosphere by factories and vehicles. It is up to the Environmental Protection Agency to make sure that these limits are enforced. Because air isn't contained by borders, some solutions must be international. The Kyoto Protocol is a worldwide effort to limit the release of greenhouse gases—pollution that can warm the atmosphere.

21 Summarize List three ways air pollution can be reduced.

-
-
-

Lesson 4 Protecting Earth's Water, Land, and Air **255**

Answers

19. *See students' pages for annotations.*

20. The number of miles driven by people in cars has increased while the amount of fuel used per vehicle has decreased. This change is likely due to new automobile technologies.

21. Sample answers: use less electricity; develop fuel-efficient technologies; pass laws that limit the amount of pollution factories can produce. Answers should involve reducing consumption and/or developing cleaner energy sources.

Learning Alert

Pros and Cons of Renewable Energy Point out to students that although solar and wind energies are plentiful, their use is often restricted geographically. For example, some areas do not receive adequate amounts of sunlight throughout the year to make solar energy a viable energy resource. Other regions do not receive the sustained winds that are needed to make wind energy viable. In addition, the financial costs involved in purchasing the technology that makes use of some alternative energy resources possible can be high, making it less expensive to continue use of fossil fuels. As new technologies are developed, it is possible that generating electricity through solar or wind power will become less costly, but right now, that is not the case. Encourage students to brainstorm other examples of pros and cons related to using alternative energy resources to generate electricity.

Formative Assessment

Ask: What are some ways that people can reduce air pollution? Sample answer: through energy conservation, through use of technology such as alternative sources of energy, and by establishing and enforcing laws that reduce pollution **Ask:** Besides solar energy and wind power, what are some other technologies that can be used to reduce the use of fossil fuels? geothermal and nuclear energy; hybrid cars; compact fluorescent light bulbs

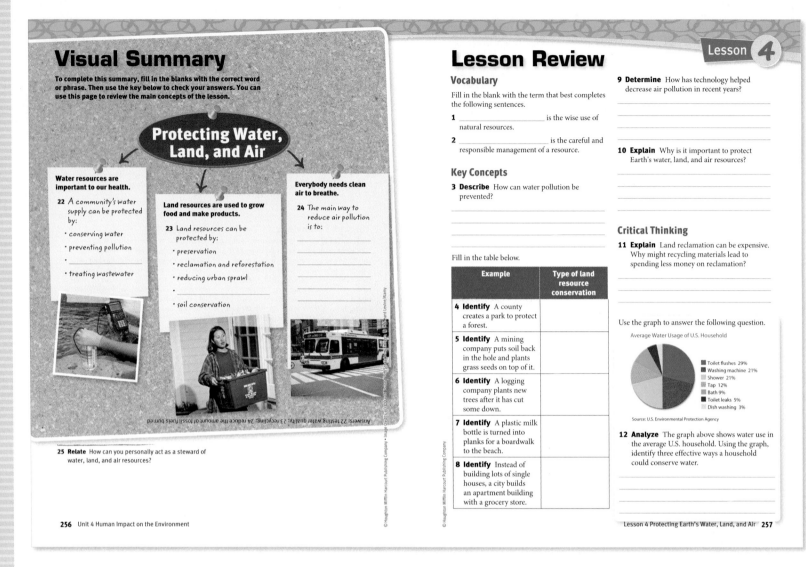

Visual Summary

To complete this summary, fill in the blanks with the correct word or phrase. Then use the key below to check your answers. You can use this page to review the main concepts of the lesson.

Protecting Water, Land, and Air

Water resources are important to our health.

22 A community's water supply can be protected by:
- conserving water
- preventing pollution
- _____
- treating wastewater

Land resources are used to grow food and make products.

23 Land resources can be protected by:
- preservation
- reclamation and reforestation
- reducing urban sprawl
- _____
- soil conservation

Everybody needs clean air to breathe.

24 The main way to reduce air pollution is to:
- _____

Answers: 22 testing water quality; 23 recycling; 24 reduce the amount of fossil fuels burned

25 **Relate** How can you personally act as a steward of water, land, and air resources?

Lesson Review

Vocabulary

Fill in the blank with the term that best completes the following sentences.

1 _____ is the wise use of natural resources.

2 _____ is the careful and responsible management of a resource.

Key Concepts

3 **Describe** How can water pollution be prevented?

Fill in the table below.

Example	Type of land resource conservation
4 **Identify** A county creates a park to protect a forest.	
5 **Identify** A mining company puts soil back in the hole and plants grass seeds on top of it.	
6 **Identify** A logging company plants new trees after it has cut some down.	
7 **Identify** A plastic milk bottle is turned into planks for a boardwalk to the beach.	
8 **Identify** Instead of building lots of single houses, a city builds an apartment building with a grocery store.	

9 **Determine** How has technology helped decrease air pollution in recent years?

10 **Explain** Why is it important to protect Earth's water, land, and air resources?

Critical Thinking

11 **Explain** Land reclamation can be expensive. Why might recycling materials lead to spending less money on reclamation?

Use the graph to answer the following question.

Average Water Usage of U.S. Household

- Toilet flushes 29%
- Washing machine 21%
- Shower 21%
- Tap 12%
- Bath 9%
- Toilet leaks 5%
- Dish washing 3%

Source: U.S. Environmental Protection Agency

12 **Analyze** The graph above shows water use in the average U.S. household. Using the graph, identify three effective ways a household could conserve water.

Visual Summary Answers

22. testing water quality

23. recycling

24. reduce the amount of fossil fuels burned

25. Sample answer: I can use less resources and avoid releasing pollutants into the environment.

Lesson Review Answers

1. Conservation

2. Stewardship

3. People can avoid dumping toxic chemicals. Laws can be passed to limit what types of chemicals businesses can release into bodies of water. Wastewater can be treated before being released back into the environment.

4. Preservation

5. Reclamation

6. Reforestation

7. Recycling

8. Reducing urban sprawl

9. The development of solar technology and other alternative energy technologies have helped decrease the amount of fossil fuels burned. New automobile technology has improved fuel efficiency. Other technologies have improved the efficiency of electrical appliances.

10. Earth's resources are limited. If they are used too quickly or polluted, they won't be available for future generations.

11. Less demand for resources obtained by mining means that fewer mines will need to be dug and eventually reclaimed.

12. Sample answer: People could install low-flow toilets and showerheads. People could take shorter showers. People could repair leaking toilets.

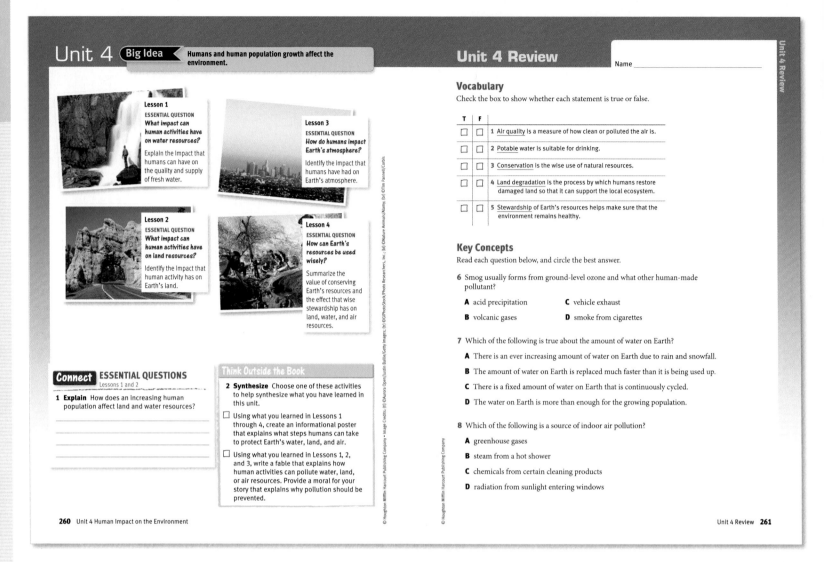

Unit 4 Big Idea ► Humans and human population growth affect the environment.

Lesson 1
ESSENTIAL QUESTION
What impact can human activities have on water resources?
Explain the impact that humans can have on the quality and supply of fresh water.

Lesson 3
ESSENTIAL QUESTION
How do humans impact Earth's atmosphere?
Identify the impact that humans have had on Earth's atmosphere.

Lesson 2
ESSENTIAL QUESTION
What impact can human activities have on land resources?
Identify the impact that human activity has on Earth's land.

Lesson 4
ESSENTIAL QUESTION
How can Earth's resources be used wisely?
Summarize the value of conserving Earth's resources and the effect that wise stewardship has on land, water, and air resources.

Connect ESSENTIAL QUESTIONS
Lessons 1 and 2

1 Explain How does an increasing human population affect land and water resources?

Think Outside the Book

2 Synthesize Choose one of these activities to help synthesize what you have learned in this unit.

☐ Using what you learned in Lessons 1 through 4, create an informational poster that explains what steps humans can take to protect Earth's water, land, and air.

☐ Using what you learned in Lessons 1, 2, and 3, write a fable that explains how human activities can pollute water, land, or air resources. Provide a moral for your story that explains why pollution should be prevented.

260 Unit 4 Human Impact on the Environment

Unit 4 Review

Name _____

Vocabulary
Check the box to show whether each statement is true or false.

T	F	
☐	☐	1 <u>Air quality</u> is a measure of how clean or polluted the air is.
☐	☐	2 <u>Potable</u> water is suitable for drinking.
☐	☐	3 <u>Conservation</u> is the wise use of natural resources.
☐	☐	4 <u>Land degradation</u> is the process by which humans restore damaged land so that it can support the local ecosystem.
☐	☐	5 <u>Stewardship</u> of Earth's resources helps make sure that the environment remains healthy.

Key Concepts
Read each question below, and circle the best answer.

6 Smog usually forms from ground-level ozone and what other human-made pollutant?

A acid precipitation   **C** vehicle exhaust

B volcanic gases   **D** smoke from cigarettes

7 Which of the following is true about the amount of water on Earth?

A There is an ever increasing amount of water on Earth due to rain and snowfall.

B The amount of water on Earth is replaced much faster than it is being used up.

C There is a fixed amount of water on Earth that is continuously cycled.

D The water on Earth is more than enough for the growing population.

8 Which of the following is a source of indoor air pollution?

A greenhouse gases

B steam from a hot shower

C chemicals from certain cleaning products

D radiation from sunlight entering windows

Unit 4 Review 261

Unit Summary Answers

1. An increasing human population results in urban sprawl, which uses up land resources. Another result of a growing human population is an increase in the amount of trash that must be buried in landfills, which also uses up land resources. These activities affect water resources from greater runoff of chemicals into water sources. A larger human population results in greater groundwater usage and an increased need for wastewater treatment.

2. Option 1: Poster presentations should include at least three reasonable steps that people can take to protect water, land, and air resources.

   Option 2: Fables could include a discussion of agricultural or industrial chemical runoff into a river or lake, thermal pollution, or artificial eutrophication for water pollution; accumulation of trash for land pollution; or the burning of fossil fuels for air pollution. Fable morals will vary but should convey the idea that any type of pollution negatively affects human health and ecosystems.

Unit Review ▸ Response to Intervention

A Quick Grading Chart follows the Answers. See the Assessment Guide for more detail about correct and incorrect answer choices. Refer back to the Lesson Planning pages for activities and assignments that can be used as remediation for students who answer questions incorrectly.

Answers

1. True Air that has few contaminants in it is considered to be higher quality. (Lesson 3)

2. True *Potable* is a synonym of *drinkable*, and indicates the water can be consumed. (Lesson 1)

3. True The aim of conservation is to use natural resources wisely and not excessively. (Lesson 4)

4. False Land degradation is the process of damaging land so that it may not be able to sustain the local ecosystem. Land restoration is the correct answer. (Lesson 2)

Unit 4 Review continued

Name _____

9 The graph below shows how the amount of carbon dioxide (CO_2) in our atmosphere has changed since 1960.

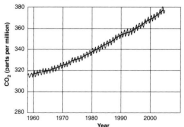

Amount of Atmospheric Carbon Dioxide per Year

Based on the information given in the graph, which of these phenomena has likely increased since 1960?

A land erosion   **C** ozone depletion

B coastal erosion   **D** greenhouse effect

10 A manufacturing plant is built on the bank of the Mississippi River. Water is diverted into the plant for use in the making of a product and is then piped back out into the river. If the water that is released back into the river is contaminated, what is this form of pollution called?

A thermal pollution

B biological pollution

C point-source pollution

D nonpoint-source pollution

11 What is the water from an artificial reservoir most likely to be reserved for?

A for future use by homes and businesses

B for recreational purposes such as swimming

C to provide a habitat for fish

D to cool hot industrial equipment

262   Unit 4 Human Impact on the Environment

12 The picture below shows a common human activity.

What are examples of the effects this kind of pollution may cause?

A acid rain, which may cause diseases such as asthma

B global warming, which may cause diseases such as skin cancer

C respiratory diseases such as emphysema

D artificial eutrophication, harming aquatic animals

13 Humans use land in many ways. How is an area described if it contains few people, has large areas of open space, and is a mix of natural land, farmland, and parks?

A rural area   **C** natural area

B urban area   **D** industrial area

Critical Thinking

Answer the following questions in the space provided.

14 Can the atmosphere be considered a natural resource? Explain.

_____

_____

Give two examples of how the atmosphere is important to life on Earth.

_____

_____

_____

Unit 4 Review   263

Answers *(continued)*

5. **True** This statement is true because stewardship is the careful and responsible management of a resource. (Lesson 4)

6. Answer C is correct because vehicle exhaust is one of the major contributors to smog formation. Exhaust gases react with oxygen in the presence of sunlight to form smog. (Lesson 3)

7. Answer C is correct because water moves through the water cycle, and the total amount does not change. (Lesson 1)

8. Answer C is correct because cleaners can have hazardous chemicals that can become aerosolized when used. (Lesson 3)

9. Answer D is correct because the greenhouse effect occurs when water vapor, CO_2, and other greenhouse gases absorb and reradiate energy back to Earth's surface, acting like a thermal blanket over Earth. An increased concentration of a greenhouse gas would lead to an increase in the greenhouse effect of the atmosphere. (Lesson 3)

10. Answer C is correct because point-source pollution is contamination that comes from a single specific site. (Lesson 1)

11. Answer A is correct because water may be transported over a great distance to serve people in cities and kept in a storage tank or reservoir. (Lesson 1)

12. Answer D is correct because chemicals applied to lawns can wash into streams and creeks through street runoff and cause chemical pollution of water bodies, including artificial eutrophication. (Lesson 1)

13. Answer A is correct because rural areas are used for agriculture and have natural areas for wildlife and recreation. (Lesson 2)

14. Key Elements:

    • The atmosphere provides oxygen, a resource for living things.

    • Students should explain two of these points: Many organisms need oxygen in the atmosphere to breathe; the atmosphere helps regulate Earth's temperature; and the atmosphere helps protect organisms from harmful radiation. (Lesson 3)

Unit 4 Review continued

15 The picture below is of a dam built on a river.

How does a dam affect the surrounding landscape behind and in front of the dam?

How does a dam affect the fish that live and breed in that river?

Connect **ESSENTIAL QUESTIONS**
Lessons 1 and 2

Answer the following question in the space provided.

16 Urbanization has major effects on Earth's land and water. Natural vegetation is removed in order to make room for buildings, roads, and parking lots. How does removing vegetation affect the land?

How do paved parking lots and roads with concrete or asphalt affect water flow on the land?

What are three ways that urban populations can negatively affect water quality?

How can urban populations affect a water supply?

264   Unit 4 Human Impact on the Environment

© Houghton Mifflin Harcourt Publishing Company

Answers *(continued)*

15. Key Elements:
   - In front of the dam, the speed and water flow may change, making a new ecosystem. Water levels may drop, exposing more land that was once aquatic habitat.
   - Behind the dam, water will collect and flood the land. The dam can cause problems for fish, by hindering their ability to reach breeding grounds. (Lesson 1)

16. Key Elements:
   - Removing vegetation causes erosion.
   - Impervious cover prevents the infiltration of water into groundwater aquifers and may lead to flooding and runoff.
   - Growing urban populations negatively affect water quality.
   - Water may be pumped great distances to people that live far from the supply, such as people in cities. Such a demand may cause overuse of aquifer or river water. (Lessons 1, 2)

Quick Grading Chart

Use the chart below for quick test grading. The lesson correlations can help you target reteaching for missed items.

Item	Answer	Cognitive Complexity	Lesson
1.	—	Low	3
2.	—	Low	1
3.	—	Low	4
4.	—	Low	2
5.	—	Low	4
6.	C	Low	3
7.	C	Low	1
8.	C	Low	3
9.	D	High	3
10.	C	Moderate	1
11.	A	Moderate	1
12.	D	High	1
13.	A	Low	2
14.	—	Moderate	3
15.	—	Moderate	1
16.	—	High	1, 2

Cognitive Complexity refers to the demand on thinking associated with an item, and may vary with the answer choices, the number of steps required to arrive at an answer, and other factors, but not the ability level of the student.

Resources

Handbook

References

Mineral Properties

Here are five steps to take in mineral identification:

1 Determine the color of the mineral. Is it light-colored, dark-colored, or a specific color?

2 Determine the luster of the mineral. Is it metallic or non-metallic?

3 Determine the color of any powder left by its streak.

4 Determine the hardness of your mineral. Is it soft, hard, or very hard? Using a glass plate, see if the mineral scratches it.

5 Determine whether your sample has cleavage or any special properties.

TERMS TO KNOW	DEFINITION
adamantine	a non-metallic luster like that of a diamond
cleavage	how a mineral breaks when subject to stress on a particular plane
luster	the state or quality of shining by reflecting light
streak	the color of a mineral when it is powdered
submetallic	between metallic and nonmetallic in luster
vitreous	glass-like type of luster

Silicate Minerals

Mineral	Color	Luster	Streak	Hardness	Cleavage and Special Properties
Beryl	deep green, pink, white, bluish green, or yellow	vitreous	white	7.5–8	1 cleavage direction; some varieties fluoresce in ultraviolet light
Chlorite	green	vitreous to pearly	pale green	2–2.5	1 cleavage direction
Garnet	green, red, brown, black	vitreous	white	6.5–7.5	no cleavage
Hornblende	dark green, brown, or black	vitreous	none	5–6	2 cleavage directions
Muscovite	colorless, silvery white, or brown	vitreous or pearly	white	2–2.5	1 cleavage direction
Olivine	olive green, yellow	vitreous	white or none	6.5–7	no cleavage
Orthoclase	colorless, white, pink, or other colors	vitreous	white or none	6	2 cleavage directions
Plagioclase	colorless, white, yellow, pink, green	vitreous	white	6	2 cleavage directions
Quartz	colorless or white; any color when not pure	vitreous or waxy	white or none	7	no cleavage

Nonsilicate Minerals

Mineral	Color	Luster	Streak	Hardness	Cleavage and Special Properties
Native Elements					
Copper	copper-red	metallic	copper-red	2.5–3	no cleavage
Diamond	pale yellow or colorless	adamantine	none	10	4 cleavage directions
Graphite	black to gray	submetallic	black	1–2	1 cleavage direction
Carbonates					
Aragonite	colorless, white, or pale yellow	vitreous	white	3.5–4	2 cleavage directions; reacts with hydrochloric acid
Calcite	colorless or white to tan	vitreous	white	3	3 cleavage directions; reacts with weak acid; double refraction
Halides					
Fluorite	light green, yellow, purple, bluish green, or other colors	vitreous	none	4	4 cleavage directions; some varieties fluoresce
Halite	white	vitreous	white	2.0–2.5	3 cleavage directions
Oxides					
Hematite	reddish brown to black	metallic to earthy	dark red to red-brown	5.6–6.5	no cleavage; magnetic when heated
Magnetite	iron-black	metallic	black	5.5–6.5	no cleavage; magnetic
Sulfates					
Anhydrite	colorless, bluish, or violet	vitreous to pearly	white	3–3.5	3 cleavage directions
Gypsum	white, pink, gray, or colorless	vitreous, pearly, or silky	white	2.0	3 cleavage directions
Sulfides					
Galena	lead-gray	metallic	lead-gray to black	2.5–2.8	3 cleavage directions
Pyrite	brassy yellow	metallic	greenish, brownish, or black	6–6.5	no cleavage

References

Geologic Time Scale

Geologists developed the geologic time scale to represent the 4.6 billion years of Earth's history that have passed since Earth formed. This scale divides Earth's history into blocks of time. The boundaries between these time intervals (shown in millions of years ago or mya in the table below), represent major changes in Earth's history. Some boundaries are defined by mass extinctions, major changes in Earth's surface, and/or major changes in Earth's climate.

Divisions of Time

The divisions of time shown here represent major changes in Earth's surface and when life developed and changed significantly on Earth. As new evidence is found, the boundaries of these divisions may shift. The Phanerozoic eon is divided into three eras. The beginning of each of these eras represents a change in the types of organisms that dominated Earth. And, each era is commonly characterized by the types of organisms that dominated the era. These eras are divided into periods, and periods are divided into epochs.

The four major divisions that encompass the history of life on Earth are Precambrian time, the Paleozoic era, the Mesozoic era, and the Cenozoic era. The largest divisions are eons. **Precambrian time** is made up of the first three eons, over 4 billion years of Earth's history.

The **Paleozoic era** lasted from 542 mya to 251 mya. All major plant groups, except flowering plants, appeared during this era. By the end of the era, reptiles, winged insects, and fishes had also appeared. The largest known mass extinction occurred at the end of this era.

The **Mesozoic era** lasted from 251 mya to 65.5 mya. During this era, many kinds of dinosaurs dominated land, and giant lizards swam in the ocean. The first birds, mammals, and flowering plants also appeared during this time. About two-thirds of all land species went extinct at the end of this era.

The **Phanerozoic eon** began 542 mya. We live in this eon.

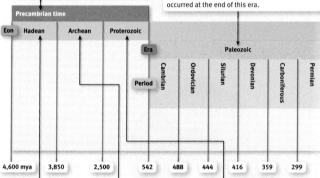

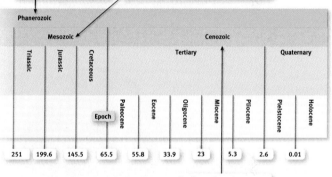

The **Hadean eon** lasted from about 4.6 billion years ago (bya) to 3.85 bya. It is described based on evidence from meteorites and rocks from the moon.

The **Archean eon** lasted from 3.85 bya to 2.5 bya. The earliest rocks from Earth that have been found and dated formed at the start of this eon.

The **Proterozoic eon** lasted from 2.5 bya to 542 mya. The first organisms, which were single-celled organisms, appeared during this eon. These organisms produced so much oxygen that they changed Earth's oceans and Earth's atmosphere.

The **Cenozoic era** began 65.5 mya and continues today. Mammals dominate this era. During the Mesozoic era, mammals were small in size but grew much larger during the Cenozoic era. Primates, including humans, appeared during this era.

References

Star Charts for the Northern Hemisphere

A star chart is a map of the stars in the night sky. It shows the names and positions of constellations and major stars. Star charts can be used to identify constellations and even to orient yourself using Polaris, the North Star.

Because Earth moves through space, different constellations are visible at different times of the year. The star charts on these pages show the constellations visible during each season in the Northern Hemisphere.

Spring

Autumn

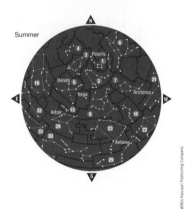

Summer

Winter

Constellations

1 Ursa Minor
2 Draco
3 Cepheus
4 Cassiopeia
5 Auriga
6 Ursa Major
7 Boötes
8 Hercules
9 Cygnus
10 Perseus
11 Gemini
12 Cancer
13 Leo
14 Serpens
15 Sagitta
16 Pegasus
17 Pisces

Constellations

18 Aries
19 Taurus
20 Orion
21 Virgo
22 Libra
23 Ophiuchus
24 Aquila
25 Lepus
26 Canis Major
27 Hydra
28 Corvus
29 Scorpius
30 Sagittarius
31 Capricornus
32 Aquarius
33 Cetus
34 Columba

References

World Map

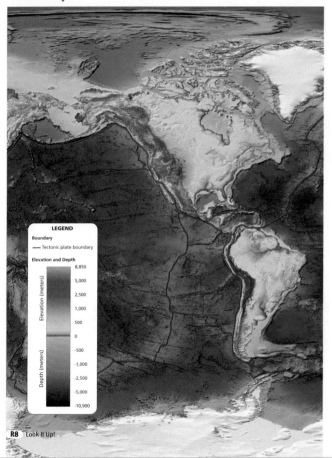

LEGEND

Boundary
— Tectonic plate boundary

Elevation and Depth

Elevation (meters)
- 8,850
- 5,000
- 2,500
- 1,000
- 500
- 0

Depth (meters)
- -500
- -1,000
- -2,500
- -5,000
- -10,900

© Houghton Mifflin Harcourt Publishing Company

© Houghton Mifflin Harcourt Publishing Company

R8   Look It Up!

Look It Up!   **R9**

References

Classification of Living Things

Domains and Kingdoms

All organisms belong to one of three domains: Domain Archaea, Domain Bacteria, or Domain Eukarya. Some of the groups within these domains are shown below. (Remember that genus names are italicized.)

Domain Archaea

The organisms in this domain are single-celled prokaryotes, many of which live in extreme environments.

Archaea		
Group	**Example**	**Characteristics**
Methanogens	*Methanococcus*	produce methane gas; can't live in oxygen
Thermophiles	*Sulpholobus*	require sulphur; can't live in oxygen
Halophiles	*Halococcus*	live in very salty environments; most can live in oxygen

Domain Bacteria

Organisms in this domain are single-celled prokaryotes and are found in almost every environment on Earth.

Bacteria		
Group	**Example**	**Characteristics**
Bacilli	*Escherichia*	rod shaped; some bacilli fix nitrogen; some cause disease
Cocci	*Streptococcus*	spherical shaped; some cause disease; can form spores
Spirilla	*Treponema*	spiral shaped; cause diseases such as syphilis and Lyme disease

Domain Eukarya

Organisms in this domain are single-celled or multicellular eukaryotes.

Kingdom Protista Many protists resemble fungi, plants, or animals, but are smaller and simpler in structure. Most are single celled.

Protists		
Group	**Example**	**Characteristics**
Sarcodines	*Amoeba*	radiolarians; single-celled consumers
Ciliates	*Paramecium*	single-celled consumers
Flagellates	*Trypanosoma*	single-celled parasites
Sporozoans	*Plasmodium*	single-celled parasites
Euglenas	*Euglena*	single celled; photosynthesize
Diatoms	*Pinnularia*	most are single celled; photosynthesize
Dinoflagellates	*Gymnodinium*	single celled; some photosynthesize
Algae	*Volvox*	single celled or multicellular; photosynthesize
Slime molds	*Physarum*	single celled or multicellular; consumers or decomposers
Water molds	powdery mildew	single celled or multicellular; parasites or decomposers

Kingdom Fungi Most fungi are multicellular. Their cells have thick cell walls. Fungi absorb food from their environment.

Fungi		
Group	**Examples**	**Characteristics**
Threadlike fungi	bread mold	spherical; decomposers
Sac fungi	yeast; morels	saclike; parasites and decomposers
Club fungi	mushrooms; rusts; smuts	club shaped; parasites and decomposers
Lichens	British soldier	a partnership between a fungus and an alga

Kingdom Plantae Plants are multicellular and have cell walls made of cellulose. Plants make their own food through photosynthesis. Plants are classified into divisions instead of phyla.

Plants		
Group	**Examples**	**Characteristics**
Bryophytes	mosses; liverworts	no vascular tissue; reproduce by spores
Club mosses	*Lycopodium*; ground pine	grow in wooded areas; reproduce by spores
Horsetails	rushes	grow in wetland areas; reproduce by spores
Ferns	spleenworts; sensitive fern	large leaves called fronds; reproduce by spores
Conifers	pines; spruces; firs	needlelike leaves; reproduce by seeds made in cones
Cycads	*Zamia*	slow growing; reproduce by seeds made in large cones
Gnetophytes	*Welwitschia*	only three living families; reproduce by seeds
Ginkgoes	*Ginkgo*	only one living species; reproduce by seeds
Angiosperms	all flowering plants	reproduce by seeds made in flowers; fruit

Kingdom Animalia Animals are multicellular. Their cells do not have cell walls. Most animals have specialized tissues and complex organ systems. Animals get food by eating other organisms.

Animals		
Group	**Examples**	**Characteristics**
Sponges	glass sponges	no symmetry or specialized tissues; aquatic
Cnidarians	jellyfish; coral	radial symmetry; aquatic
Flatworms	planaria; tapeworms; flukes	bilateral symmetry; organ systems
Roundworms	*Trichina*; hookworms	bilateral symmetry; organ systems
Annelids	earthworms; leeches	bilateral symmetry; organ systems
Mollusks	snails; octopuses	bilateral symmetry; organ systems
Echinoderms	sea stars; sand dollars	radial symmetry; organ systems
Arthropods	insects; spiders; lobsters	bilateral symmetry; organ systems
Chordates	fish; amphibians; reptiles; birds; mammals	bilateral symmetry; complex organ systems

References

Periodic Table of the Elements

13
Al
Aluminum
26.98

- Atomic number
- Chemical symbol
- Element name
- Average atomic mass

The International Union of Pure and Applied Chemistry (IUPAC) has determined that, because of isotopic variance, the average atomic mass is best represented by a range of values for each of the following elements: hydrogen, lithium, boron, carbon, nitrogen, oxygen, silicon, sulfur, chlorine, and thallium. However, the values in this table are appropriate for everyday calculations.

Background
Metals
Metalloids
Nonmetals

Chemical Symbol
Solid **Na**
Liquid **Hg**
Gas

113
Uut
Ununtrium
(284)
Unconfirmed Elements

© Houghton Mifflin Harcourt Publishing Company

© Houghton Mifflin Harcourt Publishing Company

Physical Science Refresher

Atoms and Elements

Every object in the universe is made of matter. **Matter** is anything that takes up space and has mass. All matter is made of atoms. An **atom** is the smallest particle into which an element can be divided and still be the same element. An **element**, in turn, is a substance that cannot be broken down into simpler substances by chemical means. Each element consists of only one kind of atom. An element may be made of many atoms, but they are all the same kind of atom.

Atomic Structure

Atoms are made of smaller particles called **electrons, protons,** and **neutrons.** Electrons have a negative electric charge, protons have a positive charge, and neutrons have no electric charge. Together, protons and neutrons form the **nucleus,** or small dense center, of an atom. Because protons are positively charged and neutrons are neutral, the nucleus has a positive charge. Electrons move within an area around the nucleus called the **electron cloud.** Electrons move so quickly that scientists cannot determine their exact speeds and positions at the same time.

electron cloud

nucleus — proton

neutron

Atomic Number

To help distinguish one element from another, scientists use the atomic numbers of atoms. The **atomic number** is the number of protons in the nucleus of an atom. The atoms of a certain element always have the same number of protons.

When atoms have an equal number of protons and electrons, they are uncharged, or electrically neutral. The atomic number equals the number of electrons in an uncharged atom. The number of neutrons, however, can vary for a given element. Atoms of the same element that have different numbers of neutrons are called **isotopes**.

Periodic Table of the Elements

In the periodic table, each element in the table is in a separate box. And the elements are arranged from left to right in order of increasing atomic number. That is, an uncharged atom of each element has one more electron and one more proton than an uncharged atom of the element to its left. Each horizontal row of the table is called a **period.** Changes in chemical properties of elements across a period correspond to changes in the electron arrangements of their atoms.

Each vertical column of the table is known as a **group.** A group lists elements with similar physical and chemical properties. For this reason, a group is also sometimes called a family. The elements in a group have similar properties because their atoms have the same number of electrons in their outer energy level. For example, the elements helium, neon, argon, krypton, xenon, and radon all have similar properties and are known as the noble gases.

Molecules and Compounds

When two or more elements join chemically, they form a **compound**. A compound is a new substance with properties different from those of the elements that compose it. For example, water, H_2O, is a compound formed when hydrogen (H) and oxygen (O) combine. The smallest complete unit of a compound that has the properties of that compound is called a **molecule**. A chemical formula indicates the elements in a compound. It also indicates the relative number of atoms of each element in the compound. The chemical formula for water is H_2O. So, each water molecule consists of two atoms of hydrogen and one atom of oxygen. The subscript number after the symbol for an element shows how many atoms of that element are in a single molecule of the compound.

Chemical Equations

A chemical reaction occurs when a chemical change takes place. A chemical equation describes a chemical reaction using chemical formulas. The equation indicates the substances that react and the substances that are produced. For example, when carbon and oxygen combine, they can form carbon dioxide, shown in the equation below: $C + O_2 \longrightarrow CO_2$

Acids, Bases, and pH

An **ion** is an atom or group of chemically bonded atoms that has an electric charge because it has lost or gained one or more electrons. When an acid, such as hydrochloric acid, HCl, is mixed with water, it separates into ions. An **acid** is a compound that produces hydrogen ions, H^+, in water. The hydrogen ions then combine with a water molecule to form a hydronium ion, H_3O^+. A **base**, on the other hand, is a substance that produces hydroxide ions, OH^-, in water.

To determine whether a solution is acidic or basic, scientists use pH. The **pH** of a solution is a measure of the hydronium ion concentration in a solution. The pH scale ranges from 0 to 14. Acids have a pH that is less than 7. The lower the number, the more acidic the solution. The middle point, pH = 7, is neutral, neither acidic nor basic. Bases have a pH that is greater than 7. The higher the number is, the more basic the solution.

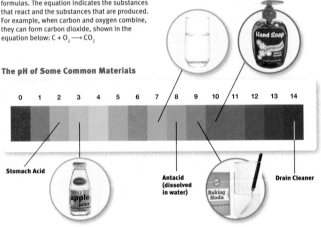

The pH of Some Common Materials

0 1 2 3 4 5 6 7 8 9 10 11 12 13 14

Stomach Acid

Antacid (dissolved in water)

Drain Cleaner

References

Physical Laws and Useful Equations

Law of Conservation of Mass

Mass cannot be created or destroyed during ordinary chemical or physical changes.

The total mass in a closed system is always the same no matter how many physical changes or chemical reactions occur.

Law of Conservation of Energy

Energy can be neither created nor destroyed.

The total amount of energy in a closed system is always the same. Energy can be changed from one form to another, but all of the different forms of energy in a system always add up to the same total amount of energy, no matter how many energy conversions occur.

Law of Universal Gravitation

All objects in the universe attract each other by a force called gravity. The size of the force depends on the masses of the objects and the distance between the objects.

The first part of the law explains why lifting a bowling ball is much harder than lifting a marble. Because the bowling ball has a much larger mass than the marble does, the amount of gravity between Earth and the bowling ball is greater than the amount of gravity between Earth and the marble.

The second part of the law explains why a satellite can remain in orbit around Earth. The satellite is placed at a carefully calculated distance from Earth. This distance is great enough to keep Earth's gravity from pulling the satellite down, yet small enough to keep the satellite from escaping Earth's gravity and wandering off into space.

Newton's Laws of Motion

Newton's first law of motion states that an object at rest remains at rest, and an object in motion remains in motion at constant speed and in a straight line unless acted on by an unbalanced force.

The first part of the law explains why a football will remain on a tee until it is kicked off or until a gust of wind blows it off. The second part of the law explains why a bike rider will continue moving forward after the bike comes to an abrupt stop. Gravity and the friction of the sidewalk will eventually stop the rider.

Newton's second law of motion states that the acceleration of an object depends on the mass of the object and the amount of force applied.

The first part of the law explains why the acceleration of a 4 kg bowling ball will be greater than the acceleration of a 6 kg bowling ball if the same force is applied to both balls. The second part of the law explains why the acceleration of a bowling ball will be greater if a larger force is applied to the bowling ball. The relationship of acceleration (a) to mass (m) and force (F) can be expressed mathematically by the following equation:

$$acceleration = \frac{force}{mass}, \text{ or } a = \frac{F}{m}$$

This equation is often rearranged to read $force = mass \times acceleration$, or $F = m \times a$

Newton's third law of motion states that whenever one object exerts a force on a second object, the second object exerts an equal and opposite force on the first.

This law explains that a runner is able to move forward because the ground exerts an equal and opposite force on the runner's foot after each step.

Average speed

$$average\ speed = \frac{total\ distance}{total\ time}$$

Example:
A bicycle messenger traveled a distance of 136 km in 8 h. What was the messenger's average speed?

$$\frac{136\ km}{8\ h} = 17\ km/h$$

The messenger's average speed was **17 km/h**.

Average acceleration

$$average\ acceleration = \frac{final\ velocity - starting\ velocity}{time\ it\ takes\ to\ change\ velocity}$$

Example:
Calculate the average acceleration of an Olympic 100 m dash sprinter who reached a velocity of 20 m/s south at the finish line. The race was in a straight line and lasted 10 s.

$$\frac{20\ m/s - 0\ m/s}{10\ s} = 2\ m/s/s$$

The sprinter's average acceleration was **2 m/s/s south**.

Pressure

Pressure is the force exerted over a given area. The SI unit for pressure is the pascal. Its symbol is Pa.

$$pressure = \frac{force}{area}$$

Net force

Forces in the Same Direction

When forces are in the same direction, add the forces together to determine the net force.

Example:
Calculate the net force on a stalled car that is being pushed by two people. One person is pushing with a force of 13 N northwest, and the other person is pushing with a force of 8 N in the same direction.

$$13\ N + 8\ N = 21\ N$$

The net force is **21 N northwest**.

Forces in Opposite Directions

When forces are in opposite directions, subtract the smaller force from the larger force to determine the net force. The net force will be in the direction of the larger force.

Example:
Calculate the net force on a rope that is being pulled on each end. One person is pulling on one end of the rope with a force of 12 N south. Another person is pulling on the opposite end of the rope with a force of 7 N north.

$$12\ N - 7\ N = 5\ N$$

The net force is **5 N south**.

Example:
Calculate the pressure of the air in a soccer ball if the air exerts a force of 10 N over an area of 0.5 m².

$$pressure = \frac{10N}{0.5\ m^2} = \frac{20N}{m^2} = 20\ Pa$$

The pressure of the air inside the soccer ball is **20 Pa**.

A How-To Manual for Active Reading

This book belongs to you, and you are invited to write in it. In fact, the book won't be complete until you do. Sometimes you'll answer a question or follow directions to mark up the text. Other times you'll write down your own thoughts. And when you're done reading and writing in the book, the book will be ready to help you review what you learned and prepare for tests.

Active Reading Annotations

Before you read, you'll often come upon an Active Reading prompt that asks you to underline certain words or number the steps in a process. Here's an example.

> **Active Reading**
>
> 12 **Identify** In this paragraph, number the sequence of sentences that describe replication.

Marking the text this way is called **annotating,** and your marks are called **annotations.** Annotating the text can help you identify important concepts while you read.

There are other ways that you can annotate the text. You can draw an asterisk (*) by vocabulary terms, mark unfamiliar or confusing terms and information with a question mark (?), and mark main ideas with a <u>double underline</u>. And you can even invent your own marks to annotate the text!

Other Annotating Opportunities

Keep your pencil, pen, or highlighter nearby as you read, so you can make a note or highlight an important point at any time. Here are a few ideas to get you started.

- Notice the headings in red and blue. The blue headings are questions that point to the main idea of what you're reading. The red headings are answers to the questions in the blue ones. Together these headings outline the content of the lesson. After reading a lesson, you could write your own answers to the questions.

- Notice the bold-faced words that are highlighted in yellow. They are highlighted so that you can easily find them again on the page where they are defined. As you read or as you review, challenge yourself to write your own sentence using the bold-faced term.

- Make a note in the margin at any time. You might
  - Ask a "What if" question
  - Comment on what you read
  - Make a connection to something you read elsewhere
  - Make a logical conclusion from the text

Use your own language and abbreviations. Invent a code, such as using circles and boxes around words to remind you of their importance or relation to each other. Your annotations will help you remember your questions for class discussions, and when you go back to the lesson later, you may be able to fill in what you didn't understand the first time you read it. Like a scientist in the field or in a lab, you will be recording your questions and observations for analysis later.

Active Reading Questions

After you read, you'll often come upon Active Reading questions that ask you to think about what you've just read. You'll write your answer underneath the question. Here's an example.

> **Active Reading**
>
> 8 **Describe** Where are phosphate groups found in a DNA molecule?
> _____
> _____

This type of question helps you sum up what you've just read and pull out the most important ideas from the passage. In this case the question asks you to **describe** the structure of a DNA molecule that you have just read about. Other times you may be asked to do such things as **apply** a concept, **compare** two concepts, **summarize** a process, or **identify a cause-and-effect** relationship. You'll be strengthening those critical thinking skills that you'll use often in learning about science.

Reading and Study Skills

Using Graphic Organizers to Take Notes

Graphic organizers help you remember information as you read it for the first time and as you study it later. There are dozens of graphic organizers to choose from, so the first trick is to choose the one that's best suited to your purpose. Following are some graphic organizers to use for different purposes.

To remember lots of information	To relate a central idea to subordinate details	To describe a process	To make a comparison
• Arrange data in a Content Frame	• Show relationships with a Mind Map or a Main Idea Web	• Use a Process Diagram to explain a procedure	• Compare two or more closely related things in a Venn Diagram
• Use Combination Notes to describe a concept in words and pictures	• Sum up relationships among many things with a Concept Map	• Show a chain of events and results in a Cause-and-Effect Chart	

Content Frame

1 Make a four-column chart.

2 Fill the first column with categories (e.g., snail, ant, earthworm) and the first row with descriptive information (e.g., group, characteristic, appearance).

3 Fill the chart with details that belong in each row and column.

4 When you finish, you'll have a study aid that helps you compare one category to another.

Invertebrates

NAME	GROUP	CHARACTERISTICS	DRAWING
snail	mollusks	mangle	
ant	arthropods	six legs, exoskeleton	
earthworm	segmented worms	segmented body, circulatory and digestive systems	
heartworm	roundworms	digestive system	
sea star	echinoderms	spiny skin, tube feet	
jellyfish	cnidarians	stinging cells	

Combination Notes

1 Make a two-column chart.

2 Write descriptive words and definitions in the first column.

3 Draw a simple sketch that helps you remember the meaning of the term in the second column.

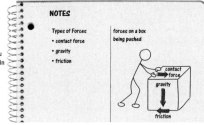

Mind Map

1 Draw an oval, and inside it write a topic to analyze.

2 Draw two or more arms extending from the oval. Each arm represents a main idea about the topic.

3 Draw lines from the arms on which to write details about each of the main ideas.

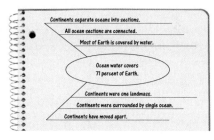

Main Idea Web

1 Make a box and write a concept you want to remember inside it.

2 Draw boxes around the central box, and label each one with a category of information about the concept (e.g., definition, formula, descriptive details).

3 Fill in the boxes with relevant details as you read.

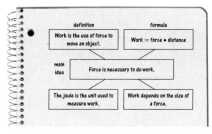

© Houghton Mifflin Harcourt Publishing Company

Reading and Study Skills

Concept Map

1 Draw a large oval, and inside it write a major concept.

2 Draw an arrow from the concept to a smaller oval, in which you write a related concept.

3 On the arrow, write a verb that connects the two concepts.

4 Continue in this way, adding ovals and arrows in a branching structure, until you have explained as much as you can about the main concept.

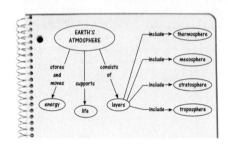

Venn Diagram

1 Draw two overlapping circles or ovals—one for each topic you are comparing—and label each one.

2 In the part of each circle that does not overlap with the other, list the characteristics that are unique to each topic.

3 In the space where the two circles overlap, list the characteristics that the two topics have in common.

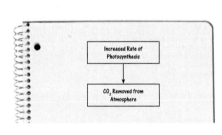

Cause-and-Effect Chart

1 Draw two boxes and connect them with an arrow.

2 In the first box, write the first event in a series (a cause).

3 In the second box, write a result of the cause (the effect).

4 Add more boxes when one event has many effects, or vice versa.

Process Diagram

A process can be a never-ending cycle. As you can see in this technology design process, engineers may backtrack and repeat steps, they may skip steps entirely, or they may repeat the entire process before a useable design is achieved.

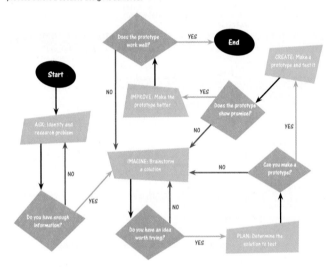

Reading and Study Skills

Using Vocabulary Strategies

Important science terms are highlighted where they are first defined in this book. One way to remember these terms is to take notes and make sketches when you come to them. Use the strategies on this page and the next for this purpose. You will also find a formal definition of each science term in the Glossary at the end of the book.

Description Wheel

1. Draw a small circle.

2. Write a vocabulary term inside the circle.

3. Draw several arms extending from the circle.

4. On the arms, write words and phrases that describe the term.

5. If you choose, add sketches that help you visualize the descriptive details or the concept as a whole.

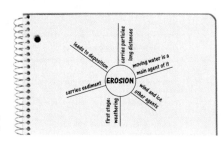

Four Square

1. Draw a small oval and write a vocabulary term inside it.

2. Draw a large rectangle around the oval, and divide the rectangle into four smaller squares.

3. Label the smaller squares with categories of information about the term, such as: definition, characteristics, examples, non-examples, appearance, and root words.

4. Fill the squares with descriptive words and drawings that will help you remember the overall meaning of the term and its essential details.

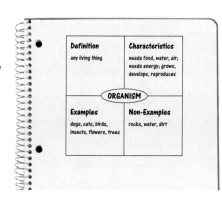

Frame Game

1. Draw a small rectangle, and write a vocabulary term inside it.

2. Draw a larger rectangle around the smaller one. Connect the corners of the larger rectangle to the corners of the smaller one, creating four spaces that frame the word.

3. In each of the four parts of the frame, draw or write details that help define the term. Consider including a definition, essential characteristics, an equation, examples, and a sentence using the term.

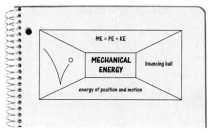

Magnet Word

1. Draw horseshoe magnet, and write a vocabulary term inside it.

2. Add lines that extend from the sides of the magnet.

3. Brainstorm words and phrases that come to mind when you think about the term.

4. On the lines, write the words and phrases that describe something essential about the term.

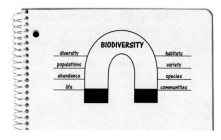

Word Triangle

1. Draw a triangle, and add lines to divide it into three parts.

2. Write a term and its definition in the bottom section of the triangle.

3. In the middle section, write a sentence in which the term is used correctly.

4. In the top section, draw a small picture to illustrate the term.

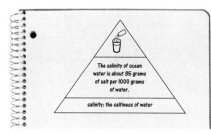

Science Skills

Safety in the Lab

Before you begin work in the laboratory, read these safety rules twice. Before starting a lab activity, read all directions and make sure that you understand them. Do not begin until your teacher has told you to start. If you or another student are injured in any way, tell your teacher immediately.

Dress Code

Eye Protection

Hand Protection

Clothing Protection

- Wear safety goggles at all times in the lab as directed.
- If chemicals get into your eyes, flush your eyes immediately.
- Do not wear contact lenses in the lab.
- Do not look directly at the sun or any intense light source or laser.
- Do not cut an object while holding the object in your hand.
- Wear appropriate protective gloves as directed.
- Wear an apron or lab coat at all times in the lab as directed.
- Tie back long hair, secure loose clothing, and remove loose jewelry.
- Do not wear open-toed shoes, sandals, or canvas shoes in the lab.

Glassware and Sharp Object Safety

Glassware Safety

Sharp Objects Safety

- Do not use chipped or cracked glassware.
- Use heat-resistant glassware for heating or storing hot materials.
- Notify your teacher immediately if a piece of glass breaks.
- Use extreme care when handling all sharp and pointed instruments.
- Cut objects on a suitable surface, always in a direction away from your body.

Chemical Safety

Chemical Safety

- If a chemical gets on your skin, on your clothing, or in your eyes, rinse it immediately (shower, faucet or eyewash fountain) and alert your teacher.
- Do not clean up spilled chemicals unless your teacher directs you to do so.
- Do not inhale any gas or vapor unless directed to do so by your teacher.
- Handle materials that emit vapors or gases in a well-ventilated area.

Electrical Safety

Electrical Safety

- Do not use equipment with frayed electrical cords or loose plugs.
- Do not use electrical equipment near water or when clothing or hands are wet.
- Hold the plug housing when you plug in or unplug equipment.

Heating and Fire Safety

Heating Safety

- Be aware of any source of flames, sparks, or heat (such as flames, heating coils, or hot plates) before working with any flammable substances.
- Know the location of lab fire extinguishers and fire-safety blankets.
- Know your school's fire-evacuation routes.
- If your clothing catches on fire, walk to the lab shower to put out the fire.
- Never leave a hot plate unattended while it is turned on or while it is cooling.
- Use tongs or appropriate insulated holders when handling heated objects.
- Allow all equipment to cool before storing it.

Wafting

Plant and Animal Safety

Plant Safety

Animal Safety

- Do not eat any part of a plant.
- Do not pick any wild plants unless your teacher instructs you to do so.
- Handle animals only as your teacher directs.
- Treat animals carefully and respectfully.
- Wash your hands thoroughly after handling any plant or animal.

Cleanup

Proper Waste Disposal

Hygienic Care

- Clean all work surfaces and protective equipment as directed by your teacher.
- Dispose of hazardous materials or sharp objects only as directed by your teacher.
- Keep your hands away from your face while you are working on any activity.
- Wash your hands thoroughly before you leave the lab or after any activity.

Science Skills

Designing, Conducting, and Reporting an Experiment

An experiment is an organized procedure to study something under specific conditions. Use the following steps of the scientific method when designing or conducting a controlled experiment.

1 Identify a Research Problem

Every day, you make observations by using your senses to gather information. Careful observations lead to good questions, and good questions can lead you to an experiment. Imagine, for example, that you pass a pond every day on your way to school, and you notice green scum beginning to form on top of it. You wonder what it is and why it seems to be growing. You list your questions, and then you do a little research to find out what is already known. A good place to start a research project is at the library. A library catalog lists all of the resources available to you at that library and often those found elsewhere. Begin your search by using:

- keywords or main topics.
- similar words, or synonyms, of your keyword.

The types of resources that will be helpful to you will depend on the kind of information you are interested in. And, some resources are more reliable for a given topic than others. Some different kinds of useful resources are:

- magazines and journals (or periodicals)—articles on a topic.
- encyclopedias—a good overview of a topic.
- books on specific subjects—details about a topic.
- newspapers—useful for current events.

The Internet can also be a great place to find information. Some of your library's reference materials may even be online. When using the Internet, however, it is especially important to make sure you are using appropriate and reliable sources. Websites of universities and government agencies are usually more accurate and reliable than websites created by individuals or businesses. Decide which sources are relevant and reliable for your topic. If in doubt, check with your teacher.

Take notes as you read through the information in these resources. You will probably come up with many questions and ideas for which you can do more research as needed. Once you feel you have enough information, think about the questions you have on the topic. Then, write down the problem that you want to investigate. Your notes might look like these.

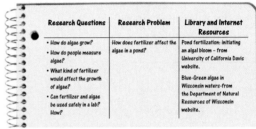

Research Questions	Research Problem	Library and Internet Resources
• How do algae grow? • How do people measure algae? • What kind of fertilizer would affect the growth of algae? • Can fertilizer and algae be used safely in a lab? How?	How does fertilizer affect the algae in a pond?	Pond fertilization: initiating an algal bloom – from University of California Davis website. Blue-Green algae in Wisconsin waters-from the Department of Natural Resources of Wisconsin website.

As you gather information from reliable sources, record details about each source, including author name(s), title, date of publication, and/or web address. Make sure to also note the specific information that you use from each source. Staying organized in this way will be important when you write your report and create a bibliography or works cited list. Recording this information and staying organized will help you credit the appropriate author(s) for the information that you have gathered.

Representing someone else's ideas or work as your own, (without giving the original author credit), is known as plagiarism. Plagiarism can be intentional or unintentional. The best way to make sure that you do not commit plagiarism is to always do your own work and to always give credit to others when you use their words or ideas.

Current scientific research is built on scientific research and discoveries that have happened in the past. This means that scientists are constantly learning from each other and combining ideas to learn more about the natural world through investigation. But, a good scientist always credits the ideas and research that they have gathered from other people to those people. There are more details about crediting sources and creating a bibliography under step 9.

2 Make a Prediction

A prediction is a statement of what you expect will happen in your experiment. Before making a prediction, you need to decide in a general way what you will do in your procedure. You may state your prediction in an if-then format.

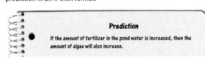

Prediction

If the amount of fertilizer in the pond water is increased, then the amount of algae will also increase.

© Houghton Mifflin Harcourt Publishing Company

3 Form a Hypothesis

Many experiments are designed to test a hypothesis. A hypothesis is a tentative explanation for an expected result. You have predicted that additional fertilizer will cause additional algae growth in pond water; your hypothesis should state the connection between fertilizer and algal growth.

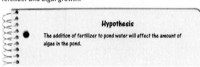

Hypothesis

The addition of fertilizer to pond water will affect the amount of algae in the pond.

4 Identify Variables to Test the Hypothesis

The next step is to design an experiment to test the hypothesis. The experimental results may or may not support the hypothesis. Either way, the information that results from the experiment may be useful for future investigations.

Experimental Group and Control Group

An experiment to determine how two factors are related has a control group and an experimental group. The two groups are the same, except that the investigator changes a single factor in the experimental group and does not change it in the control group.

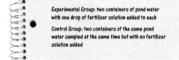

Experimental Group: two containers of pond water with one drop of fertilizer solution added to each

Control Group: two containers of the same pond water sampled at the same time but with no fertilizer solution added

Variables and Constants

In a controlled experiment, a variable is any factor that can change. Constants are all of the variables that are kept the same in both the experimental group and the control group.

The independent variable is the factor that is manipulated or changed in order to test the effect of the change on another variable. The dependent variable is the factor the investigator measures to gather data about the effect.

Independent Variable	Dependent Variable	Constants
Amount of fertilizer in pond water	Growth of algae in the pond water	• Where and when the pond water is obtained • The type of container used • Light and temperature conditions where the water is stored

5 Write a Procedure

Write each step of your procedure. Start each step with a verb, or action word, and keep the steps short. Your procedure should be clear enough for someone else to use as instructions for repeating your experiment.

Procedure

1. Use the masking tape and the marker to label the containers with your initials, the date, and the identifiers "Jar 1 with Fertilizer," "Jar 2 with Fertilizer," "Jar 1 without Fertilizer," and "Jar 2 without Fertilizer."

2. Put on your gloves. Use the large container to obtain a sample of pond water.

3. Divide the water sample equally among the four smaller containers.

4. Use the eyedropper to add one drop of fertilizer solution to the two containers labeled, "Jar 1 with Fertilizer," and "Jar 2 with Fertilizer".

5. Cover the containers with clear plastic wrap. Use the scissors to punch ten holes in each of the covers.

6. Place all four containers on a window ledge. Make sure that they all receive the same amount of light.

7. Observe the containers every day for one week.

8. Use the ruler to measure the diameter of the largest clump of algae in each container, and record your measurements daily.

Science Skills

6 Experiment and Collect Data

Once you have all of your materials and your procedure has been approved, you can begin to experiment and collect data. Record both quantitative data (measurements) and qualitative data (observations), as shown below.

Algal Growth and Fertilizer

Date and Time	Experimental Group		Control Group		Observations
	Jar 1 with Fertilizer (diameter of algal clump in mm)	Jar 2 with Fertilizer (diameter of algal clump in mm)	Jar 1 without Fertilizer (diameter of algal clump in mm)	Jar 2 without Fertilizer (diameter of algal clump in mm)	
5/3 4:00 p.m.	0	0	0	0	condensation in all containers
5/4 4:00 p.m.	0	3	0	0	tiny green blobs in Jar 2 with fertilizer
5/5 4:15 p.m.	4	5	0	3	green blobs in Jars 1 and 2 with fertilizer and Jar 2 without fertilizer
5/6 4:00 p.m.	5	6	0	4	water light green in Jar 2 with fertilizer
5/7 4:00 p.m.	8	10	0	6	water light green in Jars 1 and 2 with fertilizer and Jar 2 without fertilizer
5/8 3:30 p.m.	10	18	0	6	cover off of Jar 2 with fertilizer
5/9 3:30 p.m.	14	23	0	8	drew sketches of each container

Drawings of Samples Viewed Under Microscope on 5/9 at 100x

Jar 1 with fertilizer   Jar 2 with fertilizer   Jar 1 without fertilizer   Jar 2 without fertilizer

7 Analyze Data

After you complete your experiment, you must analyze all of the data you have gathered. Tables, statistics, and graphs are often used in this step to organize and analyze both the qualitative and quantitative data. Sometimes, your qualitative data are best used to help explain the relationships you see in your quantitative data.

Computer graphing software is useful for creating a graph from data that you have collected. Most graphing software can make line graphs, pie charts, or bar graphs from data that has been organized in a spreadsheet. Graphs are useful for understanding relationships in the data and for communicating the results of your experiment.

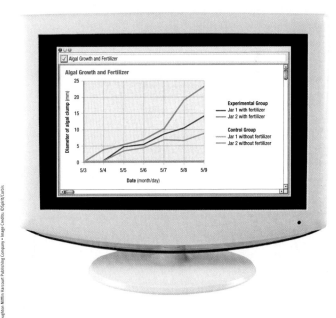

Algal Growth and Fertilizer

Experimental Group
Jar 1 with fertilizer
Jar 2 with fertilizer

Control Group
Jar 1 without fertilizer
Jar 2 without fertilizer

Science Skills

8 Make Conclusions

To draw conclusions from your experiment, first, write your results. Then, compare your results with your hypothesis. Do your results support your hypothesis? What have you learned?

Conclusion

More algae grew in the pond water to which fertilizer had been added than in the pond water to which fertilizer had not been added. My hypothesis was supported. I conclude that it is possible that the growth of algae in ponds can be influenced by the input of fertilizer.

9 Create a Bibliography or Works Cited List

To complete your report, you must also show all of the newspapers, magazines, journals, books, and online sources that you used at every stage of your investigation. Whenever you find useful information about your topic, you should write down the source of that information. Writing down as much information as you can about the subject can help you or someone else find the source again. You should at least record the author's name, the title, the date and where the source was published, and the pages in which the information was found. Then, organize your sources into a list, which you can title Bibliography or Works Cited.

Usually, at least three sources are included in these lists. Sources are listed alphabetically, by the authors' last names. The exact format of a bibliography can vary, depending on the style preferences of your teacher, school, or publisher. Also, books are cited differently than journals or websites. Below is an example of how different kinds of sources may be formatted in a bibliography.

BOOK: Hauschultz, Sara. *Freshwater Algae.* Brainard, Minnesota: Northwoods Publishing, 2011.

ENCYCLOPEDIA: Lasure, Sedona. "Algae is not all just pond scum." *Encyclopedia of Algae.* 2009.

JOURNAL: Johnson, Keagan. "Algae as we know it." *Sci Journal,* vol 64. (September 2010): 201-211.

WEBSITE: Dout, Bill. "Keeping algae scum out of birdbaths." *Help Keep Earth Clean.* News. January 26, 2011. <www. SaveEarth.org>.

Using a Microscope

Scientists use microscopes to see very small objects that cannot easily be seen with the eye alone. A microscope magnifies the image of an object so that small details may be observed. A microscope that you may use can magnify an object 400 times—the object will appear 400 times larger than its actual size.

Body The body separates the lens in the eyepiece from the objective lenses below.

Nosepiece The nosepiece holds the objective lenses above the stage and rotates so that all lenses may be used.

High-Power Objective Lens This is the largest lens on the nosepiece. It magnifies an image approximately 40 times.

Stage The stage supports the object being viewed.

Diaphragm The diaphragm is used to adjust the amount of light passing through the slide and into an objective lens.

Mirror or Light Source Some microscopes use light that is reflected through the stage by a mirror. Other microscopes have their own light sources.

Eyepiece Objects are viewed through the eyepiece. The eyepiece contains a lens that commonly magnifies an image ten times.

Coarse Adjustment This knob is used to focus the image of an object when it is viewed through the low-power lens.

Fine Adjustment This knob is used to focus the image of an object when it is viewed through the high-power lens.

Low-Power Objective Lens This is the smallest lens on the nosepiece. It magnifies images about 10 times.

Arm The arm supports the body above the stage. Always carry a microscope by the arm and base.

Stage Clip The stage clip holds a slide in place on the stage.

Base The base supports the microscope.

Science Skills

Measuring Accurately

Precision and Accuracy

When you do a scientific investigation, it is important that your methods, observations, and data be both precise and accurate.

Low precision: The darts did not land in a consistent place on the dartboard.

Precision, but not accuracy: The darts landed in a consistent place, but did not hit the bull's eye.

Prescision and accuracy: The darts landed consistently on the bull's eye.

Precision

In science, *precision* is the exactness and consistency of measurements. For example, measurements made with a ruler that has both centimeter and millimeter markings would be more precise than measurements made with a ruler that has only centimeter markings. Another indicator of precision is the care taken to make sure that methods and observations are as exact and consistent as possible. Every time a particular experiment is done, the same procedure should be used. Precision is necessary because experiments are repeated several times and if the procedure changes, the results might change.

Example

Suppose you are measuring temperatures over a two-week period. Your precision will be greater if you measure each temperature at the same place, at the same time of day, and with the same thermometer than if you change any of these factors from one day to the next.

Accuracy

In science, it is possible to be precise but not accurate. *Accuracy* depends on the difference between a measurement and an actual value. The smaller the difference, the more accurate the measurement.

Example

Suppose you look at a stream and estimate that it is about 1 meter wide at a particular place. You decide to check your estimate by measuring the stream with a meter stick, and you determine that the stream is 1.32 meters wide. However, because it is difficult to measure the width of a stream with a meter stick, it turns out that your measurement was not very accurate. The stream is actually 1.14 meters wide. Therefore, even though your estimate of about 1 meter was less precise than your measurement, your estimate was actually more accurate.

Graduated Cylinders

How to Measure the Volume of a Liquid with a Graduated Cylinder

- Be sure that the graduated cylinder is on a flat surface so that your measurement will be accurate.

- When reading the scale on a graduated cylinder, be sure to have your eyes at the level of the surface of the liquid.

- The surface of the liquid will be curved in the graduated cylinder. Read the volume of the liquid at the bottom of the curve, or meniscus (muh-NIHS-kuhs).

- You can use a graduated cylinder to find the volume of a solid object by measuring the increase in a liquid's level after you add the object to the cylinder.

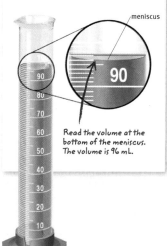
meniscus

Read the volume at the bottom of the meniscus. The volume is 96 mL.

Metric Rulers

How to Measure the Length of a Leaf with a Metric Ruler

1 Lay a ruler flat on top of the leaf so that the 1-centimeter mark lines up with one end. Make sure the ruler and the leaf do not move between the time you line them up and the time you take the measurement.

2 Look straight down on the ruler so that you can see exactly how the marks line up with the other end of the leaf.

3 Estimate the length by which the leaf extends beyond a marking. For example, the leaf below extends about halfway between the 4.2-centimeter and 4.3-centimeter marks, so the apparent measurement is about 4.25 centimeters.

4 Remember to subtract 1 centimeter from your apparent measurement, since you started at the 1-centimeter mark on the ruler and not at the end. The leaf is about 3.25 centimeters long (4.25 cm − 1 cm = 3.25 cm).

© Houghton Mifflin Harcourt Publishing Company

© Houghton Mifflin Harcourt Publishing Company

Triple Beam Balance

This balance has a pan and three beams with sliding masses, called riders. At one end of the beams is a pointer that indicates whether the mass on the pan is equal to the masses shown on the beams.

How to Measure the Mass of an Object

1 Make sure the balance is zeroed before measuring the mass of an object. The balance is zeroed if the pointer is at zero when nothing is on the pan and the riders are at their zero points. Use the adjustment knob at the base of the balance to zero it.

2 Place the object to be measured on the pan.

3 Move the riders one notch at a time away from the pan. Begin with the largest rider. If moving the largest rider one notch brings the pointer below zero, begin measuring the mass of the object with the next smaller rider.

4 Change the positions of the riders until they balance the mass on the pan and the pointer is zero. Then add the readings from the three beams to determine the mass of the object.

300 g	position of largest rider
90 g	position of middle rider
+ 3 g	position of smallest rider
393 g	mass of beaker and water

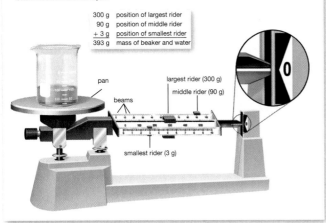

pan
largest rider (300 g)
middle rider (90 g)
beams
smallest rider (3 g)

Using the Metric System and SI Units

Scientists use International System (SI) units for measurements of distance, volume, mass, and temperature. The International System is based on powers of ten and the metric system of measurement.

Basic SI Units		
Quantity	Name	Symbol
length	meter	m
volume	liter	L
mass	gram	g
temperature	kelvin	K

SI Prefixes		
Prefix	Symbol	Power of 10
kilo-	k	1000
hecto-	h	100
deca-	da	10
deci-	d	0.1 or $\frac{1}{10}$
centi-	c	0.01 or $\frac{1}{100}$
milli-	m	0.001 or $\frac{1}{1000}$

Changing Metric Units

You can change from one unit to another in the metric system by multiplying or dividing by a power of 10.

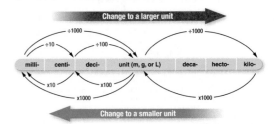

Change to a larger unit

÷1000   ÷1000
÷10   ÷100

milli-   centi-   deci-   unit (m, g, or L)   deca-   hecto-   kilo-

x10   x100
x1000   x1000

Change to a smaller unit

Example

Change 0.64 liters to milliliters.
1 Decide whether to multiply or divide.
2 Select the power of 10.

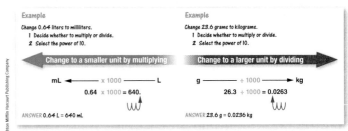

Change to a smaller unit by multiplying

mL ◄——— x 1000 ——— L

0.64 x 1000 = 640.

ANSWER 0.64 L = 640 mL

Example

Change 23.6 grams to kilograms.
1 Decide whether to multiply or divide.
2 Select the power of 10.

Change to a larger unit by dividing

g ——— ÷ 1000 ——► kg

26.3 ÷ 1000 = 0.0263

ANSWER 23.6 g = 0.0236 kg

Science Skills

Converting Between SI and U.S. Customary Units

Use the chart below when you need to convert between SI units and U.S. customary units.

SI Unit	From SI to U.S. Customary			From U.S. Customary to SI		
Length	**When you know**	**multiply by**	**to find**	**When you know**	**multiply by**	**to find**
kilometer (km) = 1000 m	kilometers	0.62	miles	miles	1.61	kilometers
meter (m) = 100 cm	meters	3.28	feet	feet	0.3048	meters
centimeter (cm) = 10 mm	centimeters	0.39	inches	inches	2.54	centimeters
millimeter (mm) = 0.1 cm	millimeters	0.04	inches	inches	25.4	millimeters
Area	**When you know**	**multiply by**	**to find**	**When you know**	**multiply by**	**to find**
square kilometer (km²)	square kilometers	0.39	square miles	square miles	2.59	square kilometers
square meter (m²)	square meters	1.2	square yards	square yards	0.84	square meters
square centimeter (cm²)	square centimeters	0.155	square inches	square inches	6.45	square centimeters
Volume	**When you know**	**multiply by**	**to find**	**When you know**	**multiply by**	**to find**
liter (L) = 1000 mL	liters	1.06	quarts	quarts	0.95	liters
	liters	0.26	gallons	gallons	3.79	liters
	liters	4.23	cups	cups	0.24	liters
	liters	2.12	pints	pints	0.47	liters
milliliter (mL) = 0.001 L	milliliters	0.20	teaspoons	teaspoons	4.93	milliliters
	milliliters	0.07	tablespoons	tablespoons	14.79	milliliters
	milliliters	0.03	fluid ounces	fluid ounces	29.57	milliliters
Mass	**When you know**	**multiply by**	**to find**	**When you know**	**multiply by**	**to find**
kilogram (kg) = 1000 g	kilograms	2.2	pounds	pounds	0.45	kilograms
gram (g) = 1000 mg	grams	0.035	ounces	ounces	28.35	grams

Temperature Conversions

Even though the kelvin is the SI base unit of temperature, the degree Celsius will be the unit you use most often in your science studies. The formulas below show the relationships between temperatures in degrees Fahrenheit (°F), degrees Celsius (°C), and kelvins (K).

$$°C = \frac{5}{9} \ (°F - 32) \qquad °F = \frac{9}{5} \ °C + 32 \qquad K = °C + 273$$

Examples of Temperature Conversions

Condition	Degrees Celsius	Degrees Fahrenheit
Freezing point of water	32	0
Cool day	10	50
Mild day	20	68
Warm day	30	86
Normal body temperature	37	98.6
Very hot day	40	104
Boiling point of water	100	212

Math Refresher

Performing Calculations

Science requires an understanding of many math concepts. The following pages will help you review some important math skills.

Mean

The mean is the sum of all values in a data set divided by the total number of values in the data set. The mean is also called the *average*.

Example

Find the mean of the following set of numbers: 5, 4, 7, and 8.

Step 1 Find the sum.

$$5 + 4 + 7 + 8 = 24$$

Step 2 Divide the sum by the number of numbers in your set. Because there are four numbers in this example, divide the sum by 4.

$$24 ÷ 4 = 6$$

Answer The average, or mean, is 6.

Median

The median of a data set is the middle value when the values are written in numerical order. If a data set has an even number of values, the median is the mean of the two middle values.

Example

To find the median of a set of measurements, arrange the values in order from least to greatest. The median is the middle value.

13 mm   14 mm   16 mm   21 mm   23 mm

Answer The median is 16 mm.

Mode

The mode of a data set is the value that occurs most often.

Example

To find the mode of a set of measurements, arrange the values in order from least to greatest and determine the value that occurs most often.

13 mm, 14 mm, 14 mm, 16 mm, 21 mm, 23 mm, 25 mm

Answer The mode is 14 mm.

A data set can have more than one mode or no mode. For example, the following data set has modes of 2 mm and 4 mm:

2 mm   2 mm   3 mm   4 mm   4 mm

The data set below has no mode, because no value occurs more often than any other.

2 mm   3 mm   4 mm   5 mm

Math Refresher

Ratios

A **ratio** is a comparison between numbers, and it is usually written as a fraction.

Example
Find the ratio of thermometers to students if you have 36 thermometers and 48 students in your class.

Step 1   Write the ratio.
$$\frac{36 \text{ thermometers}}{48 \text{ students}}$$

Step 2   Simplify the fraction to its simplest form.
$$\frac{36}{48} = \frac{36 \div 12}{48 \div 12} = \frac{3}{4}$$
The ratio of thermometers to students is 3 to 4 or 3:4.

Proportions

A **proportion** is an equation that states that two ratios are equal.
$$\frac{3}{1} = \frac{12}{4}$$

To solve a proportion, you can use cross-multiplication. If you know three of the quantities in a proportion, you can use cross-multiplication to find the fourth.

Example
Imagine that you are making a scale model of the solar system for your science project. The diameter of Jupiter is 11.2 times the diameter of the Earth. If you are using a plastic-foam ball that has a diameter of 2 cm to represent the Earth, what must the diameter of the ball representing Jupiter be?
$$\frac{11.2}{1} = \frac{x}{2 \text{ cm}}$$

Step 1   Cross-multiply.
$$\frac{11.2}{1} = \frac{x}{2}$$
$$11.2 \times 2 = x \times 1$$

Step 2   Multiply.
$$22.4 = x \times 1$$
$$x = 22.4 \text{ cm}$$

You will need to use a ball that has a diameter of 22.4 cm to represent Jupiter.

Rates

A **rate** is a ratio of two values expressed in different units. A unit rate is a rate with a denominator of 1 unit.

Example
A plant grew 6 centimeters in 2 days. The plant's rate of growth was $\frac{6 \text{ cm}}{2 \text{ days}}$.
To describe the plant's growth in centimeters per day, write a unit rate.

Divide numerator and denominator by 2:
$$\frac{6 \text{ cm}}{2 \text{ days}} = \frac{6 \text{ cm} \div 2}{2 \text{ days} \div 2}$$
Simplify:
$$= \frac{3 \text{ cm}}{1 \text{ day}}$$

Answer   The plant's rate of growth is 3 centimeters per day.

Percent

A **percent** is a ratio of a given number to 100. For example, 85% = 85/100. You can use percent to find part of a whole.

Example
What is 85% of 40?

Step 1   Rewrite the percent as a decimal by moving the decimal point two places to the left.
$$0.85$$

Step 2   Multiply the decimal by the number that you are calculating the percentage of.
$$0.85 \times 40 = 34$$

85% of 40 is 34.

Decimals

To **add** or **subtract decimals**, line up the digits vertically so that the decimal points line up. Then, add or subtract the columns from right to left. Carry or borrow numbers as necessary.

Example
Add the following numbers: 3.1415 and 2.96.

Step 1   Line up the digits vertically so that the decimal points line up.
$$\begin{array}{r} 3.1415 \\ + 2.96 \\ \hline \end{array}$$

Step 2   Add the columns from right to left, and carry when necessary.
$$\begin{array}{r} 3.1415 \\ + 2.96 \\ \hline 6.1015 \end{array}$$

The sum is 6.1015.

Fractions

A **fraction** is a ratio of two nonzero whole numbers.

Example
Your class has 24 plants. Your teacher instructs you to put 5 plants in a shady spot. What fraction of the plants in your class will you put in a shady spot?

Step 1   In the denominator, write the total number of parts in the whole.
$$\frac{?}{24}$$

Step 2   In the numerator, write the number of parts of the whole that are being considered.
$$\frac{5}{24}$$

So, $\frac{5}{24}$ of the plants will be in the shade.

Math Refresher

Simplifying Fractions

It is usually best to express a fraction in its simplest form. Expressing a fraction in its simplest form is called **simplifying a fraction**.

Example

Simplify the fraction $\frac{30}{45}$ to its simplest form.

Step 1 Find the largest whole number that will divide evenly into both the numerator and denominator. This number is called the greatest common factor (GCF).

Factors of the numerator 30:
1, 2, 3, 5, 6, 10, 15, 30

Factors of the denominator 45:
1, 3, 5, 9, 15, 45

Step 2 Divide both the numerator and the denominator by the GCF, which in this case is 15.

$$\frac{30}{45} = \frac{30 \div 15}{45 \div 15} = \frac{2}{3}$$

Thus, $\frac{30}{45}$ written in its simplest form is $\frac{2}{3}$.

Adding and Subtracting Fractions

To **add** or **subtract fractions** that have the same denominator, simply add or subtract the numerators.

Examples

$\frac{3}{5} + \frac{1}{5} = ?$ and $\frac{3}{4} - \frac{1}{4} = ?$

Step 1 Add or subtract the numerators.

$\frac{3}{5} + \frac{1}{5} = \frac{4}{5}$ and $\frac{3}{4} - \frac{1}{4} = \frac{2}{4}$

Step 2 Write in the common denominator, which remains the same.

$\frac{3}{5} + \frac{1}{5} = \frac{4}{5}$ and $\frac{3}{4} - \frac{1}{4} = \frac{2}{4}$

Step 3 If necessary, write the fraction in its simplest form.

$\frac{4}{5}$ cannot be simplified, and $\frac{2}{4} = \frac{1}{2}$.

To **add** or **subtract** fractions that have **different denominators**, first find the least common denominator (LCD).

Examples

$\frac{1}{2} + \frac{1}{6} = ?$ and $\frac{3}{4} - \frac{2}{3} = ?$

Step 1 Write the equivalent fractions that have a common denominator.

$\frac{3}{6} + \frac{1}{6} = ?$ and $\frac{9}{12} - \frac{8}{12} = ?$

Step 2 Add or subtract the fractions.

$\frac{3}{6} + \frac{1}{6} = \frac{4}{6}$ and $\frac{9}{12} - \frac{8}{12} = \frac{1}{12}$

Step 3 If necessary, write the fraction in its simplest form.

$\frac{4}{6} = \frac{2}{3}$, and $\frac{1}{12}$ cannot be simplified.

Multiplying Fractions

To **multiply fractions**, multiply the numerators and the denominators together, and then simplify the fraction to its simplest form.

Example

$\frac{5}{9} \times \frac{7}{10} = ?$

Step 1 Multiply the numerators and denominators.

$\frac{5}{9} \times \frac{7}{10} = \frac{5 \times 7}{9 \times 10} = \frac{35}{90}$

Step 2 Simplify the fraction.

$\frac{35}{90} = \frac{35 \div 5}{90 \div 5} = \frac{7}{18}$

Dividing Fractions

To **divide fractions**, first rewrite the divisor (the number you divide by) upside down. This number is called the reciprocal of the divisor. Then multiply and simplify if necessary.

Example

$\frac{5}{8} \div \frac{3}{2} = ?$

Step 1 Rewrite the divisor as its reciprocal.

$$\frac{3}{2} \rightarrow \frac{2}{3}$$

Step 2 Multiply the fractions.

$\frac{5}{8} \times \frac{2}{3} = \frac{5 \times 2}{8 \times 3} = \frac{10}{24}$

Step 3 Simplify the fraction.

$\frac{10}{24} = \frac{10 \div 2}{24 \div 2} = \frac{5}{12}$

Using Significant Figures

The **significant figures** in a decimal are the digits that are warranted by the accuracy of a measuring device.

When you perform a calculation with measurements, the number of significant figures to include in the result depends in part on the number of significant figures in the measurements. When you multiply or divide measurements, your answer should have only as many significant figures as the measurement with the fewest significant figures.

Examples

Using a balance and a graduated cylinder filled with water, you determined that a marble has a mass of 8.0 grams and a volume of 3.5 cubic centimeters. To calculate the density of the marble, divide the mass by the volume.

Write the formula for density: $\text{Density} = \frac{mass}{volume}$

Substitute measurements: $= \frac{8.0 \text{ g}}{3.5 \text{ cm}^3}$

Use a calculator to divide: $\approx 2.285714286 \text{ g/cm}^3$

Answer Because the mass and the volume have two significant figures each, give the density to two significant figures. The marble has a density of 2.3 grams per cubic centimeter.

Using Scientific Notation

Scientific notation is a shorthand way to write very large or very small numbers. For example, 73,500,000,000,000,000,000,000 kg is the mass of the moon. In scientific notation, it is 7.35×10^{22} kg. A value written as a number between 1 and 10, times a power of 10, is in scientific notation.

Examples

You can convert from standard form to scientific notation.

Standard Form	Scientific Notation
720,000	7.2×10^5
5 decimal places left	Exponent is 5.
0.000291	2.91×10^{-4}
4 decimal places right	Exponent is −4.

You can convert from scientific notation to standard form.

Scientific Notation	Standard Form
4.63×10^7	46,300,000
Exponent is 7.	7 decimal places right
1.08×10^{-6}	0.00000108
Exponent is −6.	6 decimal places left

Math Refresher

Making and Interpreting Graphs

Circle Graph

A circle graph, or pie chart, shows how each group of data relates to all of the data. Each part of the circle represents a category of the data. The entire circle represents all of the data. For example, a biologist studying a hardwood forest in Wisconsin found that there were five different types of trees. The data table at right summarizes the biologist's findings.

Wisconsin Hardwood Trees	
Type of tree	Number found
Oak	600
Maple	750
Beech	300
Birch	1,200
Hickory	150
Total	3,000

How to Make a Circle Graph

1 To make a circle graph of these data, first find the percentage of each type of tree. Divide the number of trees of each type by the total number of trees, and multiply by 100%.

$$\frac{600 \text{ oak}}{3,000 \text{ trees}} \times 100\% = 20\%$$

$$\frac{750 \text{ maple}}{3,000 \text{ trees}} \times 100\% = 25\%$$

$$\frac{300 \text{ beech}}{3,000 \text{ trees}} \times 100\% = 10\%$$

$$\frac{1,200 \text{ birch}}{3,000 \text{ trees}} \times 100\% = 40\%$$

$$\frac{150 \text{ hickory}}{3,000 \text{ trees}} \times 100\% = 5\%$$

2 Now, determine the size of the wedges that make up the graph. Multiply each percentage by 360°. Remember that a circle contains 360°.

$20\% \times 360° = 72°$ $25\% \times 360° = 90°$

$10\% \times 360° = 36°$ $40\% \times 360° = 144°$

$5\% \times 360° = 18°$

3 Check that the sum of the percentages is 100 and the sum of the degrees is 360.

$20\% + 25\% + 10\% + 40\% + 5\% = 100\%$

$72° + 90° + 36° + 144° + 18° = 360°$

4 Use a compass to draw a circle and mark the center of the circle.

5 Then, use a protractor to draw angles of 72°, 90°, 36°, 144°, and 18° in the circle.

6 Finally, label each part of the graph, and choose an appropriate title.

A Community of Wisconsin Hardwood Trees

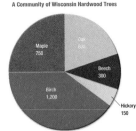

Line Graphs

Line graphs are most often used to demonstrate continuous change. For example, Mr. Smith's students analyzed the population records for their hometown, Appleton, between 1910 and 2010. Examine the data at right.

Because the year and the population change, they are the variables. The population is determined by, or dependent on, the year. Therefore, the population is called the **dependent variable,** and the year is called the **independent variable**. Each year and its population make a **data pair**. To prepare a line graph, you must first organize data pairs into a table like the one at right.

Population of Appleton, 1910–2010	
Year	Population
1910	1,800
1930	2,500
1950	3,200
1970	3,900
1990	4,600
2010	5,300

How to Make a Line Graph

1 Place the independent variable along the horizontal (x) axis. Place the dependent variable along the vertical (y) axis.

2 Label the x-axis "Year" and the y-axis "Population." Look at your greatest and least values for the population. For the y-axis, determine a scale that will provide enough space to show these values. You must use the same scale for the entire length of the axis. Next, find an appropriate scale for the x-axis.

3 Choose reasonable starting points for each axis.

4 Plot the data pairs as accurately as possible.

5 Choose a title that accurately represents the data.

How to Determine Slope

Slope is the ratio of the change in the y-value to the change in the x-value, or "rise over run."

1 Choose two points on the line graph. For example, the population of Appleton in 2010 was 5,300 people. Therefore, you can define point A as (2010, 5,300). In 1910, the population was 1,800 people. You can define point B as (1910, 1,800).

2 Find the change in the y-value.
(y at point A) − (y at point B) =
5,300 people − 1,800 people =
3,500 people

3 Find the change in the x-value.
(x at point A) − (x at point B) =
2010 − 1910 = 100 years

4 Calculate the slope of the graph by dividing the change in y by the change in x.

$$slope = \frac{change \ in \ y}{change \ in \ x}$$

$$slope = \frac{3,500 \text{ people}}{100 \text{ years}}$$

$slope = 35$ people per year

In this example, the population in Appleton increased by a fixed amount each year. The graph of these data is a straight line. Therefore, the relationship is **linear**. When the graph of a set of data is not a straight line, the relationship is **nonlinear**.

Math Refresher

Bar Graphs

Bar graphs can be used to demonstrate change that is not continuous. These graphs can be used to indicate trends when the data cover a long period of time. A meteorologist gathered the precipitation data shown here for Summerville for April 1–15 and used a bar graph to represent the data.

Precipitation in Summerville, April 1–15			
Date	Precipitation (cm)	Date	Precipitation (cm)
April 1	0.5	April 9	0.25
April 2	1.25	April 10	0.0
April 3	0.0	April 11	1.0
April 4	0.0	April 12	0.0
April 5	0.0	April 13	0.25
April 6	0.0	April 14	0.0
April 7	0.0	April 15	6.50
April 8	1.75		

How to Make a Bar Graph

1 Use an appropriate scale and a reasonable starting point for each axis.

2 Label the axes, and plot the data.

3 Choose a title that accurately represents the data.

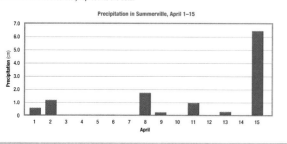

Precipitation in Summerville, April 1–15

Glossary

Pronunciation Key							
Sound	Symbol	Example	Respelling	Sound	Symbol	Example	Respelling
ă	a	pat	PAT	ŏ	ah	bottle	BAHT'l
ā	ay	pay	PAY	ō	oh	toe	TOH
âr	air	care	KAIR	ô	aw	caught	KAWT
ä	ah	father	FAH•ther	ôr	ohr	roar	ROHR
är	ar	argue	AR•gyoo	oi	oy	noisy	NOYZ•ee
ch	ch	chase	CHAYS	ŏŏ	u	book	BUK
ĕ	e	pet	PET	ōō	oo	boot	BOOT
ĕ (at end of a syllable)	eh	settee lessee	seh•TEE leh•SEE	ou	ow	pound	POWND
ĕr	ehr	merry	MEHR•ee	s	s	center	SEN•ter
ē	ee	beach	BEECH	sh	sh	cache	CASH
g	g	gas	GAS	ŭ	uh	flood	FLUHD
ĭ	i	pit	PIT	ûr	er	bird	BERD
ĭ (at end of a syllable)	ih	guitar	gih•TAR	z	z	xylophone	ZY•luh•fohn
				z	z	bags	BAGZ
ī	y eye (only for a complete syllable)	pie island	PY EYE•luhnd	zh	zh	decision	dih•SIZH•uhn
				ə	uh	around broken focus	uh•ROWND BROH•kuhn FOH•kuhs
îr	ir	hear	HIR	ar	er	winner	WIN•er
j	j	germ	JERM	th	th	thin they	THIN THAY
k	k	kick	KIK				
ng	ng	thing	THING	w	w	one	WUHN
ngk	ngk	bank	BANGK	wh	hw	whether	HWETH•er

Glossary

A

abiotic factor (ay·by·AHT·ik FAK·ter) an environmental factor that is not associated with the activities of living organisms (7)
factor abiótico un factor ambiental que no está asociado con las actividades de los seres vivos

acid precipitation (AS·id prih·sip·ih·TAY·shuhn) rain, sleet, or snow that contains a high concentration of acids (237)
precipitación ácida lluvia, aguanieve, o nieve que contiene una alta concentración de ácidos

air pollution (AIR puh·LOO·shuhn) the contamination of the atmosphere by the introduction of pollutants from human and natural sources (235)
contaminación del aire la contaminación de la atmósfera debido a la introducción de contaminantes provenientes de fuentes humanas y naturales

air quality (AIR KWAHL·ih·tee) a measure of the pollutants in the air that is used to express how clean or polluted the air is (238)
calidad de aire una medida de los contaminantes presentes en el aire que se usa para expresar el nivel de pureza o contaminación del aire

atmosphere (AT·muh·sfir) a mixture of gases that surrounds a planet, moon, or other celestial body (142)
atmósfera una mezcla de gases que rodea un planeta, una luna, u otras cuerpos celestes

B

biodiversity (by·oh·dih·VER·sih·tee) the number and variety of organisms in a given area during a specific period of time (106, 117)
biodiversidad el número y la variedad de organismos que se encuentran en un área determinada durante un período específico de tiempo

biomass (BY·oh·mas) plant material, manure, or any other organic matter that is used as an energy source (178)
biomasa materia vegetal, estiércol o cualquier otra materia orgánica que se usa como fuente de energía

biome (BY·ohm) a large region characterized by a specific type of climate and certain types of plant and animal communities (10, 64)
bioma una región extensa caracterizada por un tipo de clima específico y ciertos tipos de comunidades de plantas y animales

biotic factor (by·AHT·ik FAK·ter) an environmental factor that is associated with or results from the activities of living organisms (6)
factor biótico un factor ambiental que está asociado con las actividades de los seres vivos o que resulta de ellas

C

carbon cycle (KAR·buhn SY·kuhl) the movement of carbon from the nonliving environment into living things and back (96)
ciclo del carbono el movimiento del carbono del ambiente sin vida a los seres vivos y de los seres vivos al ambiente

carnivore (KAR·nuh·vohr) an organism that eats animals (21)
carnívoro un organismo que se alimenta de animales

carrying capacity (KAIR·ee·ing kuh·PAS·ih·tee) the largest population that an environment can support at any given time (34)
capacidad de carga la población más grande que un ambiente puede sostener en cualquier momento dado

commensalism (kuh·MEN·suh·liz·uhm) a relationship between two organisms in which one organism benefits and the other is unaffected (46)
comensalismo una relación entre dos organismos en la que uno se beneficia y el otro no es afectado

community (kuh·MYOO·nih·tee) all of the populations of species that live in the same habitat and interact with each other (9)
comunidad todas las poblaciones de especies que viven en el mismo hábitat e interactúan entre sí

competition (kahm·pih·TISH·uhn) ecological relationship in which two or more organisms depend on the same limited resource (38, 48)
competencia la relación ecológica en la que dos o más organismos dependen del mismo recurso limitado

coniferous tree (kuh·NIF·er·uhs TREE) cone-bearing trees that usually keep their leaves or needles during all the seasons of the year (67)
árbol conífero los árboles que producen conos o piñas y que generalmente conservan sus hojas o agujas durante todas las estaciones del año

conservation (kahn·ser·VAY·shuhn) the wise use of and preservation of natural resources (123, 190, 246)
conservación el uso inteligente y la preservación de los recursos naturales

consumer (kuhn·SOO·mer) an organism that eats other organisms or organic matter (21)
consumidor un organismo que se alimenta de otros organismos o de materia orgánica

cooperation (koh·ahp·uh·RAY·shuhn) an interaction between two or more living things in which they are said to work together (39)
cooperación la interacción entre dos o más organismos vivos en la cuales dice que trabajan juntos

D

deciduous tree (dih·SIJ·oo·uhs TREE) trees that lose their leaves at the end of the growing season (70)
árbol caducifolio los árboles que pierden sus hojas al final de una estación de crecimiento

decomposer (dee·kuhm·POH·zer) an organism that gets energy by breaking down the remains of dead organisms or animal wastes and consuming or absorbing the nutrients (20)
descomponedor un organismo que, para obtener energía, desintegra los restos de organismos muertos o los desechos de animales y consume o absorbe los nutrientes

deforestation (dee·fohr·ih·STAY·shuhn) the removal of trees and other vegetation from an area (229)
deforestación la remoción de árboles y demás vegetación de un área

desert (DEZ·ert) a region characterized by a very dry climate and extreme temperatures (68)
desierto una región que se caracteriza por tener un clima muy seco y temperaturas extremas

desertification (dih·zer·tuh·fih·KAY·shuhn) the process by which human activities or climatic changes make arid or semiarid areas more desertlike (229)
desertificación el proceso por medio del cual las actividades humanas o los cambios climáticos hacen que un área árida o semiárida se vuelva más parecida a un desierto

E

ecology (ee·KAHL·uh·jee) the study of the interactions of living organisms with one another and with their environment (6)
ecología el estudio de las interacciones de los seres vivos entre sí mismos y entre sí mismos y su ambiente

ecosystem (EE·koh·sis·tuhm) a community of organisms and their abiotic, or nonliving, environment (9)
ecosistema una comunidad de organismos y su ambiente abiótico o no vivo

energy (EN·er·jee) the ability to cause change (90)
energía la capacidad de producir un cambio

energy pyramid (EN·er·jee PIR·uh·mid) a triangular diagram that shows an ecosystem's loss of energy, which results as energy passes through the ecosystem's food chain; each row in the pyramid represents a trophic (feeding) level in an ecosystem, and the area of a row represents the energy stored in that trophic level (92)
pirámide de energía un diagrama con forma de triángulo que muestra la pérdida de energía que ocurre en un ecosistema a medida que la energía pasa a través de la cadena alimenticia del ecosistema; cada hilera de la pirámide representa un nivel trófico (de alimentación) en el ecosistema, y el área de la hilera representa la energía almacenada en ese nivel trófico

energy resource (EN·er·jee REE·sohrs) a natural resource that humans use to generate energy (152, 160, 172)
recurso energético un recurso natural que utilizan los humanos para generar energía

estuary (ES·choo·ehr·ee) an area where fresh water mixes with salt water from the ocean (80)
estuario un área donde el agua dulce de los ríos se mezcla con el agua salada del océano

eutrophication (yoo·trohf·ih·KAY·shuhn) an increase in the amount of nutrients, such as nitrates, in a marine or aquatic ecosystem (102, 120, 210)
eutrofización un aumento en la cantidad de nutrientes, tales como nitratos, en un ecosistema marino o acuático

F

fission (FISH·uhn) the process by which a nucleus splits into two or more fragments and releases neutrons and energy (165)
fisión el proceso por medio del cual un núcleo se divide en dos o más fragmentos y libera neutrones y energía

food chain (FOOD CHAYN) the pathway of energy transfer through various stages as a result of the feeding patterns of a series of organisms (23)
cadena alimenticia la vía de transferencia de energía a través de varias etapas, que ocurre como resultado de los patrones de alimentación de una serie de organismos

food web (FOOD WEB) a diagram that shows the feeding relationships between organisms in an ecosystem (24)
red alimenticia un diagrama que muestra las relaciones de alimentación entre los organismos de un ecosistema

fossil fuel (FAHS·uhl FYOO·uhl) a nonrenewable energy resource formed from the remains of organisms that lived long ago; examples include oil, coal, and natural gas (149, 160)
combustible fósil un recurso energético no renovable formado a partir de los restos de organismos que vivieron hace mucho tiempo; algunos ejemplos incluyen el petróleo, el carbón, y el gas natural

geothermal energy (jee·oh·THER·muhl EN·er·jee) the energy produced by heat within Earth (179)
energía geotérmica la energía producida por el calor del interior de la Tierra

grassland (GRAS·land) a region that is dominated by grasses, that has few woody shrubs and trees, that has fertile soils, and that receives moderate amounts of seasonal rainfall (69)
pradera una región en la que predomina la hierba, tiene algunos arbustos leñosos y árboles, y suelos fértiles, y recibe cantidades moderadas de precipitaciones estacionales

greenhouse effect (GREEN·hows ih·FEKT) the warming of the surface and lower atmosphere of Earth that occurs when water vapor, carbon dioxide, and other gases absorb and reradiate thermal energy (234)
efecto invernadero el calentamiento de la superficie y de la parte más baja de la atmósfera, el cual se produce cuando el vapor de agua, el dióxido de carbono, y otros gases absorben y vuelven a irradiar la energía térmica

habitat (HAB·ih·tat) the place where an organism usually lives (12)
hábitat el lugar donde generalmente vive un organismo

herbivore (HER·buh·vohr) an organism that eats only plants (21)
herbívoro un organismo que sólo come plantas

hydroelectric energy (hy·droh·ee·LEK·trik EN·er·jee) electrical energy produced by the flow of water (175)
energía hidroeléctrica energía eléctrica producida por el flujo del agua

land degradation (LAND deg·ruh·DAY·shuhn) the process by which human activity and natural processes damage land to the point that it can no longer support the local ecosystem (228)
degradación del suelo el proceso por el cual la actividad humana y los procesos naturales dañan el suelo de modo que el ecosistema local no puede subsistir

law of conservation of energy
(LAW UHV kahn·suhr·VAY·shuhn UHV EN·er·jee) the law that states that energy cannot be created or destroyed but can be changed from one form to another (91)
ley de la conservación de la energía la ley que establece que la energía ni se crea ni se destruye, sólo se transforma de una forma a otra

law of conservation of mass
(LAW UHV kahn·suhr·VAY·shuhn UHV MAS) the law that states that mass cannot be created or destroyed in ordinary chemical and physical changes (91)
ley de la conservación de la masa la ley que establece que la masa no se crea ni se destruye por cambios químicos o físicos comunes

limiting factor (LIM·ih·ting FAK·ter) an environmental factor that prevents an organism or population from reaching its full potential of size or activity (36)
factor limitante un factor ambiental que impide que un organismo o población alcance su máximo potencial de distribución o de actividad

material resource (muh·TIR·ee·uhl REE·sohrs) a natural resource that humans use to make objects or to consume as food and drink (150)
recurso material un recurso natural que utilizan los seres humanos para fabricar objetos o para consumir como alimento o bebida

matter (MAT·er) anything that has mass and takes up space (90)
materia cualquier cosa que tiene masa y ocupa un lugar en el espacio

mutualism (MYOO·choo·uh·liz·uhm) a relationship between two species in which both species benefit (46)
mutualismo una relación entre dos especies en la que ambas se benefician

natural resource (NACH·uh·ruhl REE·sohrs) any natural material that is used by humans, such as water, petroleum, minerals, forests, and animals (148, 188)
recurso natural cualquier material natural que es utilizado por los seres humanos, como agua, petróleo, minerales, bosques, y animales

niche (NICH) the role of a species in its community, including use of its habitat and its relationships with other species (12)
nicho el papel que juega una especie en su comunidad, incluidos el uso de su hábitat y su relación con otras especies

nitrogen cycle (NY·truh·juhn SY·kuhl) the cycling of nitrogen between organisms, soil, water, and the atmosphere (95)
ciclo del nitrógeno el ciclado del nitrógeno entre los organismos, el suelo, el agua y la atmósfera

nonpoint-source pollution
(nahn·POYNT SOHRS puh·LOO·shuhn) pollution that comes from many sources rather than from a single specific site; an example is pollution that reaches a body of water from streets and storm sewers (210)
contaminación no puntual contaminación que proviene de muchas fuentes, en lugar de provenir de un solo sitio específico; un ejemplo es la contaminación que llega a una masa de agua a partir de las calles y los drenajes

nonrenewable resource (nahn·rih·NOO·uh·buhl REE·sohrs) a resource that forms at a rate that is much slower than the rate at which the resource is consumed (149, 188)
recurso no renovable un recurso que se forma a una tasa que es mucho más lenta que la tasa a la que se consume

nuclear energy (NOO·klee·er EN·er·jee) the energy released by a fission or fusion reaction; the binding energy of the atomic nucleus (160)
energía nuclear la energía liberada por una reacción de fisión o fusión; la energía de enlace del núcleo atómico

omnivore (AHM·nuh·vohr) an organism that eats both plants and animals (21)
omnívoro un organismo que come tanto plantas como animales

ozone (OH·zohn) a gas molecule that is made up of three oxygen atoms (143)
ozono una molécula de gas que está formada por tres átomos de oxígeno

parasitism (PAIR·uh·sih·tiz·uhm) a relationship between two species in which one species, the parasite, benefits from the other species, the host, which is harmed (47)
parasitismo una relación entre dos especies en la que una, el parásito, se beneficia de la otra, el huésped, que resulta perjudicada

particulate (par·TIK·yuh·lit) a tiny particle of solid that is suspended in air or water (235)
material particulado una pequeña partícula de material sólido que se encuentra suspendida en el aire o el agua

photosynthesis (foh·toh·SIN·thih·sis) the process by which plants, algae, and some bacteria use sunlight, carbon dioxide, and water to make food (138)
fotosíntesis el proceso por medio del cual las plantas, las algas, y algunas bacterias utilizan la luz solar, el dióxido de carbono, y el agua para producir alimento

pioneer species (py·uh·NIR SPEE·sheez) a species that colonizes an uninhabited area and that starts a process of succession (104)
especie pionera una especie que coloniza un área deshabitada y empieza un proceso de sucesión

point-source pollution (POYNT SOHRS puh·LOO·shuhn) pollution that comes from a specific site (210)
contaminación puntual contaminación que proviene de un lugar específico

population (pahp·yuh·LAY·shuhn) a group of organisms of the same species that live in a specific geographical area (8)
población un grupo de organismos de la misma especie que viven en un área geográfica específica

potable (POH·tuh·buhl) suitable for drinking (213)
potable que puede beberse

predator (PRED·uh·ter) an organism that kills and eats all or part of another organism (44)
depredador un organismo que mata y se alimenta de otro organismo o de parte de él

prey (PRAY) an organism that is killed and eaten by another organism (44)
presa un organismo al que otro organismo mata para alimentarse de él

producer (pruh·DOO·ser) an organism that can make its own food by using energy from its surroundings (20)
productor un organismo que puede elaborar sus propios alimentos utilizando la energía de su entorno

renewable resource (rih·NOO·uh·buhl REE·sohrs) a natural resource that can be replaced at the same rate at which the resource is consumed (149, 188)
recurso renovable un recurso natural que puede reemplazarse a la misma tasa a la que se consume

reservoir (REZ·er·vwar) an artificial body of water that usually forms behind a dam (215)
represa una masa artificial de agua que normalmente se forma detrás de una presa

S

smog (SMAHG) air pollution that forms when ozone and vehicle exhaust react with sunlight (236)
esmog contaminación del aire que se produce cuando el ozono y sustancias químicas como los gases de los escapes de los vehículos reaccionan con la luz solar

solar energy (SOH·ler EN·er·jee) the energy received by Earth from the sun in the form of radiation (176)
energía solar la energía que la Tierra recibe del Sol en forma de radiación

species (SPEE·sheez) a group of organisms that are closely related and can mate to produce fertile offspring (8)
especie un grupo de organismos que tienen un parentesco cercano y que pueden aparearse para producir descendencia fértil

stewardship (STOO·erd·ship) the careful and responsible management of a resource (122, 190, 247)
gestión ambiental responsable el manejo cuidadoso y responsable de un recurso

succession (suhk·SESH·uhn) the replacement of one type of community by another at a single location over a period of time (104)
sucesión el reemplazo de un tipo de comunidad por otro en un mismo lugar a lo largo de un período de tiempo

symbiosis (sim·by·OH·sis) a relationship in which two different organisms live in close association with each other (46)
simbiosis una relación en la que dos organismos diferentes viven estrechamente asociados uno con el otro

T

taiga (TY·guh) a region of evergreen, coniferous forest below the arctic and subarctic tundra regions (67)
taiga una región de bosques siempreverdes de coníferas, ubicado debajo de las regiones árticas y subárticas de tundra

thermal pollution (THER·muhl puh·LOO·shuhn) a temperature increase in a body of water that is caused by human activity and that has a harmful effect on water quality and on the ability of that body of water to support life (210)
contaminación térmica un aumento en la temperatura de una masa de agua, producido por las actividades humanas y que tiene un efecto dañino en la calidad del agua y en la capacidad de esa masa de agua para permitir que se desarrolle la vida

tundra (TUHN·druh) a region found at far northern and far southern latitudes characterized by low-lying plants, a lack of trees, and long winters with very low temperatures (67)
tundra una región que se encuentra en latitudes muy al norte o muy al sur y que se caracteriza por las plantas bajas, la ausencia de árboles, y los inviernos prolongados con temperaturas muy bajas

U–V

ultraviolet radiation (uhl·truh·VY·uh·lit ray·dee·AY·shuhn) electromagnetic wave frequencies immediately above the visible range (143)
radiación ultravioleta longitudes de onda electromagnéticas inmediatamente adyacentes al color violeta en el espectro visible

urbanization (er·buh·nih·ZAY·shuhn) an increase in the proportion of a population living in urban areas rather than in rural areas (117, 225)
urbanización un aumento de la proporción de población en las áreas urbanas en lugar de en las áreas rurales

W–Z

water cycle (WAW·ter SY·kuhl) the continuous movement of water between the atmosphere, the land, the oceans, and living things (94)
ciclo del agua el movimiento continuo del agua entre la atmósfera, la tierra, los océanos, y los seres vivos

water pollution (WAW·ter puh·LOO·shuhn) waste matter or other material that is introduced into water and that is harmful to organisms that live in, drink, or are exposed to the water (210)
contaminación del agua material de desecho u otro material que se introduce en el agua y que daña a los organismos que viven en el agua, la beben o están expuestos a ella

wetland (WET·land) an area of land that is periodically underwater or whose soil contains a great deal of moisture (78)
pantano un área de tierra que está periódicamente bajo el agua o cuyo suelo contiene una gran cantidad de humedad

wind energy (WIND EN·er·jee) the use of the force of moving air to drive an electric generator (174)
energía eólica el uso de la fuerza del aire en movimiento para hacer funcionar un generador eléctrico

State STANDARDS FOR ENGLISH LANGUAGE ARTS
Correlations

This table shows correlations to the *Reading Standards for Literacy in Science and Technical Subjects* for grades 6–8.

Go online at **thinkcentral.com** for correlations of all *ScienceFusion* Modules to Common Core State Standards for Mathematics and to the rest of the *Common Core State Standards for English Language Arts*.

Grade 6–8 Standard Code	Citations for Module K "Introduction to Science and Technology"
READING STANDARDS FOR LITERACY IN SCIENCE AND TECHNICAL SUBJECTS	
Key Ideas and Details	
RST.6–8.1 Cite specific textual evidence to support analysis of science and technical texts.	*Student Edition* pp. 25, 75, 113 *Teacher Edition* pp. 98, 117
RST.6–8.2 Determine the central ideas or conclusions of a text; provide an accurate summary of the text distinct from prior knowledge or opinions.	*Student Edition* pp. 25, 32, 60, 75, 113, 132, 137, 149, 157, 163, 171, 189 *Teacher Edition* pp. 17, 21, 22, 35, 51, 61, 62, 98, 106, 117, 128, 130, 161, 178, 179, 206, 213, 237, 240. Also use "Synthesizing Key Topics" items in the Extend Science Concepts sections of the Teacher Edition.
RST.6–8.3 Follow precisely a multistep procedure when carrying out experiments, taking measurements, or performing technical tasks.	*Student Edition* pp. 83, 90–91 *Teacher Edition* p. 94 *Other* Use the Lab Manual, Project-Based Assessments, Video-Based Projects, and the Virtual Labs.
Craft and Structure	
RST.6–8.4 Determine the meaning of symbols, key terms, and other domain-specific words and phrases as they are used in a specific scientific or technical context relevant to *grades 6–8 texts and topics.*	*Student Edition* pp. 5, 17, 31, 43, 63, 64, 77, 93, 115, 131, 141, 153, 169, 181 *Teacher Edition* p. 111. Also use "Previewing Vocabulary" and "Reinforcing Vocabulary" items in the Explain Science Concepts sections of the Teacher Edition.

Grade 6–8 Standard Code (continued)	Citations for Module K "Introduction to Science and Technology"
RST.6–8.5 Analyze the structure an author uses to organize a text, including how the major sections contribute to the whole and to an understanding of the topic.	*Student Edition* p. 75 *Teacher Edition* pp. 51, 128, 213, 237, 240
RST.6–8.6 Analyze the author's purpose in providing an explanation, describing a procedure, or discussing an experiment in a text.	*Student Edition* pp. 25, 75 *Teacher Edition* pp. 14, 47, 98

Integration of Knowledge and Ideas

RST.6–8.7 Integrate quantitative or technical information expressed in words in a text with a version of that information expressed visually (e.g., in a flowchart, diagram, model, graph, or table).	*Student Edition* pp. 3, 35, 54, 66–67, 81, 122–123, 144, 147, 158, 159 *Teacher Edition* pp. 21, 40, 53, 54, 123, 194, 201, 206, 208, 224, 237, 240. Also use the "Graphic Organizer" items in the Teacher Edition. *Other* Use the lessons in the Digital Path.
RST.6–8.8 Distinguish among facts, reasoned judgment based on research findings, and speculation in a text.	*Student Edition* pp. 13, 25, 74–75, 113 *Teacher Edition* pp. 14, 17, 98
RST.6–8.9 Compare and contrast the information gained from experiments, simulations, video, or multimedia sources with that gained from reading a text on the same topic.	*Student Edition* pp. 113, 137, 163 *Teacher Edition* pp. 40, 79, 117 *Other* Use the Lab Manual, Project-Based Assessments, Video-Based Projects, and the lessons in the Digital Path.

Range of Reading and Level of Text Complexity

RST.6–8.10 By the end of grade 8, read and comprehend science/technical texts in the grades 6–8 text complexity band independently and proficiently.	*Student Edition* pp. 3, 22, 75, 90, 113, 132, 137, 149, 157, 163, 171, 189. Also use all lessons in the Student Edition. *Teacher Edition* pp. 47, 48, 61, 62, 117

Bibliography

This bibliography is a compilation of trade books that can supplement the materials covered in *ScienceFusion* Grades 6–8. Many of the books are recommendations of the National Science Teachers Association (NSTA) and the Children's Book Council (CBC) as outstanding science trade books for children. These books were selected because they meet the following rigorous criteria: they are of literary quality and contain substantial science content; the theories and facts are clearly distinguished; they are free of gender, ethnic, and socioeconomic bias; and they contain clear, accurate, up-to-date information. Several selections are award-winning titles, or their authors have received awards.

As with all materials you share with your class, we suggest you review the books first to ensure their appropriateness. While titles are current at time of publication, they may go out of print without notice.

Grades 6–8

Acids and Bases (Material Matters/ Express Edition) by Carol Baldwin (Heinemann-Raintree, 2005) focuses on the properties of acids and bases with photographs and facts.

Acids and Bases by Eurona Earl Tilley (Chelsea House, 2008) provides a thorough, basic understanding of acid and base chemistry, including such topics as naming compounds, writing formulas, and physical and chemical properties.

Across the Wide Ocean: The Why, How, and Where of Navigation for Humans and Animals at Sea by Karen Romano Young (Greenwillow, 2007) focuses on navigational tools, maps, and charts that researchers and explorers use to learn more about oceanography. AWARD-WINNING AUTHOR

Adventures in Sound with Max Axiom, Super Scientist (Graphic Science Series) by Emily Sohn (Capstone, 2007) provides information about sound through a fun graphic novel.

Air: A Resource Our World Depends on (Managing Our Resources) by Ian Graham (Heinemann-Raintree, 2005) examines this valuable natural resource and answers questions such as "How much does Earth's air weigh?" and "Why do plants need wind?"

The Alkaline Earth Metals: Beryllium, Magnesium, Calcium, Strontium, Barium, Radium (Understanding the Elements of the Periodic Table) by Bridget Heos (Rosen Central, 2009) describes the characteristics of these metals, including their similar physical and molecular properties.

All About Light and Sound (Mission: Science) by Connie Jankowski (Compass Point, 2010) focuses on the importance of light and sound and how without them we could not survive.

Alternative Energy: Beyond Fossil Fuels by Dana Meachen Rau (Compass Point, 2010) discusses the ways that water, wind, and sun provide a promising solution to our energy crisis and encourages readers to help the planet by conserving energy. AWARD-WINNING AUTHOR

Amazing Biome Projects You Can Build Yourself (Build it Yourself Series) by Donna Latham (Nomad, 2009) provides an overview of eight terrestrial biomes, including characteristics about climate, soil, animals, and plants.

Archaea: Salt-Lovers, Methane-Makers, Thermophiles, and Other Archaeans (A Class of Their Own) by David M. Barker (Crabtree, 2010) provides interesting facts about different types of archaeans.

The Art of Construction: Projects and Principles for Beginning Engineers and Architects by Mario Salvadori (Chicago Review, 2000) explains how tents, houses, stadiums, and bridges are built, and how to build models of such structures using materials found around the house. AWARD-WINNING AUTHOR

Astronomy: Out of This World! by Simon Basher and Dan Green (Kingfisher, 2009) takes readers on a journey of the universe and provides information about the planets, stars, galaxies, telescopes, space missions, and discoveries.

At the Sea Floor Café: Odd Ocean Critter Poems by Leslie Bulion (Peachtree, 2011) provides poetry to educate students about how ocean creatures search for food, capture prey, protect their young, and trick their predators.

Battery Science: Make Widgets That Work and Gadgets That Go by Doug Stillinger (Klutz, 2003) offers an array of activities and gadgets to get students excited about electricity.

The Biggest Explosions in the Universe by Sara Howard (BookSurge, 2009) tells the story of stars in our universe through fun text and captivating photographs.

Biology: Life as We Know It! by Simon Basher and Dan Green (Kingfisher, 2008) offers information about all aspects of life from the animals and plants to the minuscule cells, proteins, and DNA that bring them to life.

Birds of a Feather by Jane Yolen (Boyds Mills Press, 2011) offers facts and information about birds through fun poetry and beautiful photographs. AWARD-WINNING AUTHOR

Blackout!: Electricity and Circuits (Fusion) by Anna Claybourne (Heinemann-Raintree, 2005) provides an array of facts about electricity and how we rely on it for so many things in everyday life. AWARD-WINNING AUTHOR

Cell Division and Genetics by Robert Snedden (Heinemann, 2007) explains various aspects of cells and the living world, including what happens when cells divide and how characteristics are passed on from one generation to another. AWARD-WINNING AUTHOR

Chemistry: Getting a Big Reaction by Dan Green and Simon Basher (Kingfisher, 2010) acts as a guide about the chemical "characters" that fizz, react, and combine to make up everything around us.

Cool Stuff Exploded by Chris Woodford (Dorling Kindersley, 2008) focuses on today's technological marvels and tomorrow's jaw-dropping devices. OUTSTANDING SCIENCE TRADE BOOK

Disaster Deferred: How New Science Is Changing Our View of Earthquake Hazards in the Midwest by Seth Stein (Columbia University, 2010) discusses technological innovations that make earthquake prediction possible.

The Diversity of Species (Timeline: Life on Earth) by Michael Bright (Heinemann, 2008) explains how and why things on Earth have genetic and physical differences and how they have had and continue to have an impact on Earth.

Drip! Drop!: How Water Gets to Your Tap by Barbara Seuling (Holiday House, 2000) introduces students to JoJo and her dog, Willy, who explain the water cycle and introduce fun experiments about filtration, evaporation, and condensation. AWARD-WINNING AUTHOR

Eat Fresh Food: Awesome Recipes for Teen Chefs by Rozanne Gold (Bloomsbury, 2009) includes more than 80 recipes and places a strong emphasis on fresh foods throughout the book.

Eco-Tracking: On the Trail of Habitat Change (Worlds of Wonder) by Daniel Shaw (University of New Mexico, 2010) recounts success stories of young people involved in citizen science efforts and encourages others to join in to preserve nature's ecosystems.

Electric Mischief: Battery-Powered Gadgets Kids Can Build by Alan Bartholomew (Kids Can Press, 2002) offers a variety of fun projects that include making battery connections and switches and building gadgets such as electric dice and a bumper car.

Electricity (Why It Works) by Anna Claybourne (QED Publishing, 2008) provides information about electricity in an easy-to-follow manner. AWARD-WINNING AUTHOR

Electricity and Magnetism (Usborne Understand Science) by Peter Adamczyk (Usborne, 2008) explains the basics about electricity and magnetism, including information about static electricity, electric circuits, and electromagnetism.

Energy Transfers (Energy Essentials) by Nigel Saunders and Steven Chapman (Raintree, 2005) explains the different types of energy, how they can change, and how different forms of energy help us in our everyday lives.

The Everything Machine by Matt Novak (Roaring Brook, 2009) tells the silly story of a machine that does everything for a group of people until they wake up one day and discover that the machine has stopped working. AWARD-WINNING AUTHOR

Experiments with Plants and Other Living Things by Trevor Cook (PowerKids, 2009) provides fun, hands-on experiments to teach students about flowers, plants, and biology.

Exploring the Oceans: Seafloor by John Woodward (Heinemann, 2004) takes readers on a virtual tour through the bottom part of the ocean, highlighting the plants and animals that thrive in this environment.

Extreme Structures: Mega Constructions of the 21st Century (Science Frontiers) by David Jefferis (Crabtree, 2006) takes a look at how some of the coolest buildings in the world were built and what other kinds of structures are being planned for the future. AWARD-WINNING AUTHOR

Fascinating Science Projects: Electricity and Magnetism by Bobbi Searle (Aladdin, 2002) teaches the concepts of electricity and magnetism through dozens of projects and experiments and color illustrations.

Fizz, Bubble and Flash!: Element Explorations and Atom Adventures for Hands-on Science Fun! by Anita Brandolini, Ph.D. (Williamson, 2003) introduces chemistry to students in a nonintimidating way and focuses on the elements and the periodic table. PARENTS' CHOICE

Floods: Hazards of Surface and Groundwater Systems (The Hazardous Earth) by Timothy M. Kusky (Facts on File, 2008) explores the processes that control the development and flow in river and stream systems and when these processes become dangerous.

Fossils (Geology Rocks!) by Rebecca Faulkner (Raintree, 2008) educates students about rock formation and the processes and characteristics of rocks and fossils.

Friends: True Stories of Extraordinary Animal Friendships by Catherine Thimmesh (Houghton Mifflin Harcourt, 2011) depicts true stories of unlikely animal friendships, including a wild polar bear and a sled dog as well as a camel and a Vietnamese pig. AWARD-WINNING AUTHOR

The Frog Scientist (Scientists in the Field) by Pamela S. Turner (Houghton Mifflin Harcourt, 2009) follows a scientist and his protégés as they research the effects of atrazine-contaminated water on vulnerable amphibians. BOOKLIST EDITORS' CHOICE

From Steam Engines to Nuclear Fusion: Discovering Energy (Chain Reactions) by Carol Ballard (Heinemann-Raintree, 2007) tells the fascinating story of energy, from the heat produced by a simple fire to the extraordinary power contained in an atom.

Fully Charged (Everyday Science) by Steve Parker (Heinemann-Raintree, 2005) explains how electricity is generated, harnessed, and used and also the difference between electricity, including static electricity, and electronics. AWARD-WINNING AUTHOR

Galileo for Kids: His Life and Ideas by Richard Panchyk (Chicago Review, 2005) includes experiments that demonstrate scientific principles developed by the astronomer Galileo.

Genes and DNA by Richard Walker (Kingfisher, 2003) offers an abundance of information about characteristics of genes, gene function, DNA technology, and genetic engineering, as well as other fascinating topics. NSTA TRADE BOOK; OUTSTANDING SCIENCE TRADE BOOK

Hands-on Science Series: Simple Machines by Steven Souza and Joseph Shortell (Walch, 2001) investigates the concepts of work, force, power, efficiency, and mechanical advantage.

How Animals Work by David Burnie (Dorling Kindersley, 2010) provides vivid photographs and intriguing text to describe various animals and their characteristics, diets, and families. AWARD-WINNING AUTHOR

How Does an Earthquake Become a Tsunami? (How Does it Happen?) by Linda Tagliaferro (Heinemann-Raintree, 2009) describes the changes in water, waves, and tides that occur between an earthquake and a tsunami. AWARD-WINNING AUTHOR

How the Future Began: Machines by Clive Gifford (Kingfisher, 1999) acts as a guide to historical and current developments in the field of machinery, including mass production, computers, robots, microengineering, and communications technology. AWARD-WINNING AUTHOR

How Scientists Work (Simply Science) by Natalie M. Rosinsky (Compass Point, 2003) discusses the scientific method, equipment, and procedures and also describes how scientists compile information and answer questions.

How to Clean a Hippopotamus: A Look at Unusual Animal Partnerships by Steve Jenkins and Robin Page (Houghton Mifflin Harcourt, 2010) explores animal symbiosis with fun illustrations and a close-up, step-by-step view of some of nature's most fascinating animal partnerships. ALA NOTABLE BOOK

Human Spaceflight (Frontiers in Space) by Joseph A. Angelo (Facts on File, 2007) examines the history of space exploration and the evolution of space technology from the dawn of the space age to the present time.

The Hydrosphere: Agent of Change by Gregory L. Vogt, Ed.D. (Twenty-First Century, 2006) discusses the impact this 20-mile-thick sphere has had on the surface of the planet and the processes that go on there, including the ability of Earth to sustain life. AWARD-WINNING AUTHOR

In Rivers, Lakes, and Ponds (Under the Microscope) by Sabrina Crewe (Chelsea Clubhouse, 2010) educates readers about the microscopic critters that live in these various bodies of water.

A Kid's Guide to Climate Change and Global Warming: How to Take Action! by Cathryn Berger Kaye, M.A. (Free Spirit, 2009) encourages students to learn about the climate changes happening around the world and to get involved to help save our planet.

Lasers (Lucent Library of Science and Technology) by Don Nardo (Lucent, 2003) discusses the scientific discovery and development of lasers—high-intensity light—and their use in our daily lives. AWARD-WINNING AUTHOR

Leonardo's Horse by Jean Fritz (Putnam, 2001) tells the story of Leonardo da Vinci—the curious and inquisitive artist, engineer, and astronomer—who created a detailed horse sculpture for the city of Milan. ALA NOTABLE BOOK; NOTABLE SOCIAL STUDIES TRADE BOOK; NOTABLE CHILDREN'S BOOK IN THE LANGUAGE ARTS

Light: From Sun to Bulbs by Christopher Cooper (Heinemann, 2003) invites students to investigate the dazzling world of physical science and light through fun experiments. AWARD-WINNING AUTHOR

Magnetism and Electromagnets (Sci-Hi: Physical Science) by Eve Hartman (Raintree, 2008) offers colorful illustrations, photographs, quizzes, charts, graphs, and text to teach students about magnetism.

Making Good Choices About Nonrenewable Resources (Green Matters) by Paula Johanson (Rosen Central, 2009) focuses on the different types of nonrenewable natural resources, alternative resources, conservation, and making positive consumer choices.

Making Waves: Sound (Everyday Science) by Steve Parker (Heinemann-Raintree, 2005) describes what sound is, how it is formed and used, and properties associated with sound, such as pitch, speed, and volume. AWARD-WINNING AUTHOR

The Manatee Scientists: Saving Vulnerable Species (Scientists in the Field Series) by Peter Lourie (Houghton Mifflin Harcourt, 2011) discusses three species of manatees and the importance of preserving these mammals. AWARD-WINNING AUTHOR

The Man Who Named the Clouds by Julie Hannah and Joan Holub (Albert Whitman, 2006) tells the story of 18th-century English meteorologist Luke Howard and also discusses the ten classifications of clouds.

Medicine in the News (Science News Flash) by Brian R. Shmaefsky, Ph.D. (Chelsea House, 2007) focuses on medical advancements that are in the news today and the innovative tools that are used for diagnosis and treatment.

Metals and Metalloids (Periodic Table of the Elements) by Monica Halka, Ph.D., and Brian Nordstrom, Ed.D. (Facts on File, 2010), offers information about the physics, chemistry, geology, and biology of metals and metalloids.

Meteorology: Ferguson's Careers in Focus by Ferguson (Ferguson, 2011) profiles 18 different careers pertaining to the science of the atmosphere and its phenomena.

The Microscope (Great Medical Discoveries) by Adam Woog (Lucent, 2003) recounts how the microscope has had an impact on the history of medicine.

Microscopes and Telescopes: Great Inventions by Rebecca Stefoff (Marshall Cavendish Benchmark, 2007) describes the origin, history, development, and societal impact of the telescope and microscope. OUTSTANDING SCIENCE TRADE BOOK

Mighty Animal Cells by Rebecca L. Johnson (Millbrook, 2007) takes readers on a journey to discover how people and animals grow from just one single cell. AWARD-WINNING AUTHOR

Moon (Eyewitness Books) by Jacqueline Mitton (Dorling Kindersley, 2009) offers information about our planet's mysterious nearest neighbor, from the moon's waterless seas and massive craters to its effect on Earth's ocean tides and its role in solar eclipses. AWARD-WINNING AUTHOR

MP3 Players (Let's Explore Technology Communications) by Jeanne Sturm (Rourke, 2010) discusses the technological advances in music in our society.

Nanotechnologist (Cool Science Careers) by Ann Heinrichs (Cherry Lake, 2009) provides information about nanotechnologists—scientists who work with materials on a subatomic or atomic level.

Ocean: An Illustrated Atlas by Sylvia A. Earle (National Geographic, 2008) provides an overview on the ocean as a whole, each of the major ocean basins, and the future of the oceans. AWARD-WINNING AUTHOR

Oceans (Insiders) by Beverly McMillan and John A. Musick (Simon & Schuster, 2007) takes readers on a 3-D journey of the aquatic universe—exploring the formation of waves and tsunamis as well as the plant and animal species that live beneath the ocean's surface.

Organic Chemistry and Biochemistry (Facts at Your Fingertips) by Graham Bateman (Brown Bear, 2011) provides diagrams, experiments, and testing aids to teach students the basics about organic chemistry and biochemistry.

An Overcrowded World?: Our Impact on the Planet (21st Century Debates) by Rob Bowden (Heinemann, 2002) investigates how and why the world's population is growing so fast, the effects of this growth on wildlife and habitats, and the pressure on resources, and suggests ways of controlling growth.

The Pebble in My Pocket: A History of Our Earth by Meredith Hooper (Viking, 1996) follows the course of a pebble, beginning 480 million years ago, through a fiery volcano and primordial forest and along the icy bottom of a glacier and how it looks today as the result of its journey. AWARD-WINNING AUTHOR

The Periodic Table: Elements with Style! by Simon Basher and Adrian Dingle (Kingfisher, 2007) offers information about the different elements that make up the periodic table and their features and characteristics.

Phenomena: Secrets of the Senses by Donna M. Jackson (Little, Brown, 2008) focuses on the senses and how to interpret them and discusses ways that technology is changing how we experience the world around us. AWARD-WINNING AUTHOR

Pioneers of Light and Sound (Mission: Science) by Connie Jankowski (Compass Point, 2010) focuses on various scientists and their accomplishments and achievements.

Planet Animal: Saving Earth's Disappearing Animals by B. Taylor (Barron's, 2009) focuses on the planet's most endangered animals, their relationships to the environment, and steps that are being taken to try to save these animals from extinction.

Plant and Animal Science Fair Projects (Biology Science Projects Using the Scientific Method) by Yael Calhoun (Enslow, 2010) provides an array of experiments about plants and animals and describes the importance of the scientific method, forming a hypothesis, and recording data for any given project.

Plant Secrets: Plant Life Processes by Anna Claybourne (Heinemann-Raintree, 2005) includes informative text, vivid photographs, and detailed charts about characteristics of various plants. AWARD-WINNING AUTHOR

Polar Regions: Human Impacts (Our Fragile Planet) by Dana Desonie (Chelsea House, 2008) focuses on pollutants and global warming in the Arctic and Antarctic and future dangers that will occur if our planet continues on its current path.

Potato Clocks and Solar Cars: Renewable and Non-renewable Energy by Elizabeth Raum (Raintree, 2007) explores various topics, including alternative energy sources, fossil fuels, and sustainable energy.

The Power of Pressure (How Things Work) by Andrew Dunn (Thomson Learning, 1993) explains how water pressure and air work and how they are used in machines.

Protists and Fungi (Discovery Channel School Science) by Katie King and Jacqueline A. Ball (Gareth Stevens, 2003) focuses on the appearance, behavior, and characteristics of various protists and fungi, using examples of algae, mold, and mushrooms.

Protozoans, Algae and Other Protists by Steve Parker (Compass Point, 2010) introduces readers to the parts, life cycles, and reproduction of various types of protists, from microscopic protozoans to seaweedlike algae, and some of the harmful effects protists have on humans. AWARD-WINNING AUTHOR

Sally Ride: The First American Woman in Space by Tom Riddolls (Crabtree, 2010) focuses on the growth and impact of Sally Ride Science—an educational program founded by the astronaut to encourage girls to pursue hobbies and careers in science.

Science and Technology in 20th Century American Life by Christopher Cumo (Greenwood, 2008) takes readers on a history of technology from agricultural implements through modern computers, telecommunications, and skateboards.

Sedimentary Rock (Geology Rocks!) by Rebecca Faulkner (Raintree, 2008) educates students about rock formation and the processes and characteristics of sedimentary rock.

Shaping the Earth by Dorothy Hinshaw Patent (Clarion/Houghton Mifflin, 2000) combines vivid photographs with informative text to explain the forces that have created the geological features on Earth's surface. AWARD-WINNING AUTHOR

Silent Spring by Rachel Carson (Houghton Mifflin, 2002) celebrates marine biologist and environmental activist Rachel Carson's contribution to Earth through an array of essays.

Skywalkers: Mohawk Ironworkers Build the City by David Weitzman (Flash Point, 2010) focuses on the ironworkers who constructed bridges and skyscrapers in New York and Canada. AWARD-WINNING AUTHOR

Sustaining Earth's Energy Resources (Environment at Risk) by Ann Heinrichs (Marshall Cavendish, 2010) offers information on Earth's sources of nonrenewable and renewable energy, how they are used, and their disadvantages and benefits.

Team Moon: How 400,000 People Landed Apollo 11 on the Moon by Catherine Thimmesh (Houghton Mifflin, 2006) tells the story of the first moon landing and celebrates the dedication, ingenuity, and perseverance of the people who made this event happen. ALA NOTABLE BOOK; ORBIS PICTUS HONOR; NOTABLE CHILDREN'S BOOK IN THE LANGUAGE ARTS; ALA BEST BOOK FOR YOUNG ADULTS; GOLDEN KITE HONOR

The Top of the World: Climbing Mount Everest by Steve Jenkins (Houghton Mifflin, 1999) describes the conditions and terrain of Mount Everest, attempts that have been made to scale this peak, and information about the equipment and techniques of mountain climbing. ALA NOTABLE BOOK; SLJ BEST BOOK; BOSTON GLOBE–HORN BOOK AWARD; ORBIS PICTUS HONOR

Transmission of Power by Fluid Pressure: Air and Water by William Donaldson (Nabu, 2010) describes the transmission of fluid pressure as it pertains to the elements of air and water in the world of motion, forces, and energy.

Tsunami: The True Story of an April Fools' Day Disaster by Gail Langer Karwoski (Darby Creek, 2006) offers a variety of viewpoints about the wave that struck Hawaii in 1946. NOTABLE SOCIAL STUDIES TRADE BOOK

Vapor, Rain, and Snow: The Science of Clouds and Precipitation (Weatherwise) by Paul Fleisher (Lerner, 2010) answers an array of questions about water, such as "How does a cloud form?" and "Why do ice cubes shrink in the freezer?" AWARD-WINNING AUTHOR

Water Supplies in Crisis (Planet in Crisis) by Russ Parker (Rosen Central, 2009) describes a world where safe drinking water is not readily available, polluted water brings disease, and lakes are disappearing.

Weird Meat-Eating Plants (Bizarre Science) by Nathan Aaseng (Enslow, 2011) provides information about a variety of carnivorous plants, reversing the food chain's usual order. AWARD-WINNING AUTHOR

What Are Igneous Rocks? (Let's Rock!) by Molly Aloian (Crabtree, 2010) explains how granite, basalt, lava, silica, and quartz are formed after hot molten rock cools.

What's Living Inside Your Body? by Andrew Solway (Heinemann, 2004) offers information about an array of viruses, germs, and parasites that thrive inside the human body.

Why Should I Bother to Keep Fit? (What's Happening?) by Kate Knighton and Susan Meredith (Usborne, 2009) motivates students to get fit and stay fit.

The World of Microbes: Bacteria, Viruses, and Other Microorganisms (Understanding Genetics) by Janey Levy (Rosen Classroom, 2010) describes the world of microbes, a history of microbiology, and the characteristics of both harmful and beneficial bacteria.

Written in Bone: Buried Lives of Jamestown and Colonial Maryland by Sally M. Walker (Carolrhoda, 2009) describes the way that scientists used forensic anthropology to investigate colonial-era graves near Jamestown, Virginia. ALA NOTABLE BOOK; OUTSTANDING SCIENCE TRADE BOOK; NOTABLE SOCIAL STUDIES TRADE BOOK

You Blink Twelve Times a Minute and Other Freaky Facts About the Human Body by Barbara Seuling (Picture Window, 2009) provides fun and unusual facts about various ailments, medical marvels, and body parts and their functions. AWARD-WINNING AUTHOR

Correlation to
ScienceSaurus

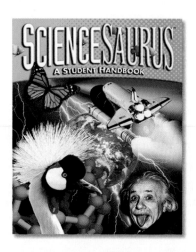

ScienceSaurus, **A Student Handbook,** is a "mini-encyclopedia" that students can use to find out more about unit topics. It contains numerous resources including concise content summaries, an almanac, many tables, charts, and graphs, history of science, and a glossary. *ScienceSaurus* is available from Houghton Mifflin Harcourt..

ScienceFusion **Page References**	Topics	*ScienceFusion* **Grades 6-8**
Scientific Investigation, pp. 1–19		
	Scientific Inquiry	Mod K, Unit 1, Lessons 1-3
		Mod K, Unit 2, Lessons 1, 3
	Designing Your Own Investigations	Mod K, Unit 1, Lessons 2, 4
Working in the Lab, pp. 20–72		
	Laboratory Safety	Mod K, Unit 2, Lesson 2
	Glassware and Microscopes	Mod K, Unit 2, Lesson 2
	Measurement	Mod K, Unit 2, Lesson 2
Life Science, pp. 73–164		
	Structure of Life	Mod A, Unit 1, Lessons 1-3
		Mod A, Unit 2, Lessons 1, 3
	Human Biology	Mod C, Unit 1, Lessons 1-6
		Mod C, Unit 2, Lesson 1
	Physiology and Behavior	Mod A, Unit 1, Lesson 5
		Mod B, Unit 2, Lessons 3-6
	Genes and Heredity	Mod A, Unit 2, Lessons 2-6
	Change and Diversity of Life	Mod B, Unit 1, Lessons 2-4

ScienceFusion Page References	Topics	*ScienceFusion* Grades 6-8
Life Science, pp. 73–164 (continued)		
	Ecosystems	Mod D, Unit 1, Lessons 1-4
		Mod D, Unit 2, Lessons 1-4
		Mod D, Unit 2, Lesson 5
	Classification	Mod B, Unit 1, Lesson 5
		Mod B, Unit 2, Lessons 3, 5
Earth Science, pp. 165–248		
	Geology	Mod E, Unit 4, Lesson 1
		Mod E, Unit 3, Lessons 1-3
		Mod E, Unit 4, Lessons 2-5
		Mod E, Unit 1, Lessons 2-4
		Mod E, Unit 2, Lessons 1-4
		Mod E, Unit 1, Lessons 3, 5
	Oceanography	Mod F, Unit 1, Lesson 1
		Mod F, Unit 2, Lessons 1, 3
	Meteorology	Mod F, Unit 3, Lesson 1
		Mod F, Unit 1, Lesson 2
		Mod F, Unit 4, Lesson 1, 2, 3, 6
	Astronomy	Mod G, Unit 3, Lessons 1-3
		Mod G, Unit 2, Lessons 2-6
		Mod G, Unit 1, Lessons 1-3
Physical Science, pp. 249–321		
	Matter	Mod H, Unit 1, Lessons 1-6
		Mod H, Unit 3, Lessons 1-4
		Mod H Unit 4, Lessons 1-3
		Mod H, Unit 5, Lessons 1-3

ScienceFusion **Page References**	**Topics**	*ScienceFusion* **Grades 6-8**
Physical Science, pp. 249–321 (continued)		
	Forces and Motion	Mod I, Unit 1, Lessons 1-5
		Mod I, Unit 2, Lessons 1-3
	Energy	Mod H, Unit 2, Lessons 1-4
		Mod I, Unit 3, Lessons 1-5
		Mod J, Unit 1, Lessons 1, 2
		Mod J, Unit 2, Lessons 1, 2
		Mod J, Unit 3, Lessons 1-4
Natural Resources and the Environment, pp. 322–353		
	Earth's Natural Resources	Mod D, Unit 3, Lessons 2-5
	Resource Conservation	Mod D, Unit 3, Lesson 5
	Solid Waste and Pollution	Mod D, Unit 4, Lessons 1-4 Mod F, Unit 4, Lesson 7
Science, Technology, and Society, pp. 354–373		
	Science and Technology	Mod A, Unit 2, Lesson 7
		Mod G, Unit 4, Lesson 2
		Mod I, Unit 3, Lesson 6
		Mod J, Unit 2, Lesson 3
		Mod J, Unit 3, Lesson 5
	Science and Society	Mod K, Unit 1, Lesson 4
		Mod K, Unit 3, Lesson 6

ScienceFusion **Page References**	**Topics**	*ScienceFusion* **Grades 6-8**
Almanac, pp. 374–438		
	Scientific Numbers	May be used with all units.
	Using Data Tables and Graphs	Mod K, Unit 2, Lesson 1
	Solving Math Problems in Science	May be used with all units.
	Classroom and Research Skills	May be used with all units.
	Test-Taking Skills	May be used with all units.
	References	May be used with all units.
Yellow Pages, pp. 439–524		
	History of Science Timeline	See People in Science features.
	Famous Scientists	See People in Science features.
	Greek and Latin Word Roots	Glossary
	Glossary of Scientific Terms	Glossary

Index

P

S

T